GOD, JUSTICE, AND SOCIETY

GOD, JUSTICE, AND SOCIETY

ASPECTS OF LAW AND LEGALITY IN THE BIBLE

JONATHAN BURNSIDE

OXFORD
UNIVERSITY PRESS
2011

OXFORD
UNIVERSITY PRESS

Oxford University Press, Inc., publishes works that further Oxford University's objective of excellence in research, scholarship, and education.

Oxford   New York
Auckland   Cape Town   Dar es Salaam   Hong Kong   Karachi   Kuala Lumpur   Madrid   Melbourne
Mexico City   Nairobi   New Delhi   Shanghai   Taipei   Toronto

With offices in
Argentina   Austria   Brazil   Chile   Czech Republic   France   Greece   Guatemala   Hungary   Italy
Japan   Poland   Portugal   Singapore   South Korea   Switzerland   Thailand
Turkey   Ukraine   Vietnam

Copyright © 2011 by Oxford University Press, Inc.

Published by Oxford University Press, Inc.
198 Madison Avenue, New York, New York 10016

Oxford is a registered trademark of Oxford University Press
Oxford University Press is a registered trademark of Oxford University Press, Inc.

All rights reserved. No part of this publication may be reproduced, stored in a retrieval system, or transmitted, in any form or by any means, electronic, mechanical, photocopying, recording, or otherwise, without the prior permission of Oxford University Press, Inc.

Library of Congress Cataloging-in-Publication Data

Burnside, Jonathan P. (Jonathan Patrick)
   God, justice, and society: aspects of law and legality in the Bible / Jonathan Burnside.
       p. cm.
   Includes bibliographical references and index.
   ISBN 978-0-19-975921-7 (hardback : alk. paper)
1. Bible and law. 2. Law (Theology)—Biblical teaching. I. Title.
BS680.L33B87 2010
220.8'34—dc22
                                                                                            2010016530

Note to Readers
This publication is designed to provide accurate and authoritative information in regard to the subject matter covered. It is based upon sources believed to be accurate and reliable and is intended to be current as of the time it was written. It is sold with the understanding that the publisher is not engaged in rendering legal, accounting, or other professional services. If legal advice or other expert assistance is required, the services of a competent professional person should be sought. Also, to confirm that the information has not been affected or changed by recent developments, traditional legal research techniques should be used, including checking primary sources where appropriate.

(Based on the Declaration of Principles jointly adopted by a Committee of the American Bar Association and a Committee of Publishers and Associations)

> You may order this or any other Oxford University Press publication by visiting the Oxford University Press website at www.oup.com

I dedicate this volume to Bernard S. Jackson in recognition of his outstanding contribution to scholarship and his immense kindness in my own studies.

CONTENTS

Acknowledgments xi
How to use this book xiii
Glossary xix
Abbreviations xxi
Time line xxiii
Introduction: The Horizon of Biblical Law xxv

Chapter 1: The Character of Biblical Law 1
    I. Top Ten Texts in Biblical Law 1
    II. Conclusion 29

Chapter 2: A Deal With God 31
    I. Deal or No Deal 31
    II. The Divine Concordat 35
    III. Close Encounters of the Divine Kind 40
    IV. The Sinai Event 45
    V. Mercy Etched in Stone 50
    VI. Spiritual Counterfeit 54
    VII. The Newness of the New? 56
    VIII. Conclusion 64

Chapter 3: Beyond Sinai 67
    I. Biblical Law and Natural Law 67
    II. Continuity Between the Divine and Creation 69
    III. Continuity Between the Created World and Human Behavior 73
    IV. Universal Knowledge of Certain Norms 76
    V. Continuity Between Different Forms of Revelation 81
    VI. Continuity Between Divine and Human Acts of Judgment 84
    VII. Rethinking Natural Law 92
    VIII. Conclusion 100

Chapter 4: Justice as a Calling 103
    I. Top Ten Ways of Pursuing Justice 103
    II. Grassroots Justice 116
    III. Divine and Human Justice 119
    IV. Falls the Shadow 133
    V. Judging in a Spiral 137
    VI. Thinking Relationally about Justice 139
    VII. Conclusion 144

viii CONTENTS

Chapter 5: Humanity and the Environment 145
       I. Earth Under Threat 145
      II. Earthing the Earthling 150
     III. The Chosen Species 152
     IV. Mother Earth 157
      V. Judgments in Genesis 162
     VI. New Laws for a New Earth 167
    VII. Eco-Law 171
   VIII. Conclusion 176

Chapter 6: People and Land 179
       I. Divine Ownership 179
      II. Chosen People, Promised Land 182
     III. People, Land, and Narrative 185
     IV. Favored Sons, Rebellious Sons 190
      V. "Restonomics" 197
     VI. "Sabbath-Plus" 198
    VII. Squaring the Sabbath 201
   VIII. Developing Property 212
     IX. Conclusion 218

Chapter 7: Social Welfare 219
       I. Freedom from Demands 219
      II. A Welfare System or a Welfare Society? 222
     III. The Debt Penalty 232
     IV. Laws of Abundance 234
      V. Social Welfare or Social Justice? 240
     VI. The Sabbath Spectrum 242
    VII. The Original "Third Way"? 247
   VIII. Conclusion 252

Chapter 8: Homicide and Vengeance 253
       I. The Interpretation of Murder 253
      II. How to Save a Life 265
     III. First Blood 271
     IV. "V" for Vendetta? 275
      V. Conclusion 283

Chapter 9: Theft and Burglary 285
       I. Who's the Thief? 286
      II. To Catch a Thief 288
     III. A Thief in the Night 299
     IV. Payback 303
      V. The Law of Theft in the Parable of Nathan 308
     VI. Conclusion 316

Chapter 10: Marriage and Divorce 317
　　　　I. Family Circles 317
　　　　II. Scenes from a Marriage 319
　　　　III. Anything for Love? 324
　　　　IV. Wedding Lists 326
　　　　V. Dangerous Liaisons 329
　　　　VI. Breaking Up 336
　　　　VII. Deconstructing Marriage 340
　　　　VIII. Conclusion 345

Chapter 11: Sexual Offenses 347
　　　　I. The Good Sex Guide 348
　　　　II. The Decalogue Pattern in Leviticus 20 349
　　　　III. Who Punishes Whom? 356
　　　　IV. Sex, Harm, and Society 358
　　　　V. From Foreplay to Horseplay 361
　　　　VI. Sleep with Me 367
　　　　VII. Secrets and Lies 368
　　　　VIII. Sex in the City 373
　　　　IX. Consent *versus* Community 375
　　　　X. Conclusion 386

Chapter 12: New Laws for a New Age 389
　　　　I. In the Shadow of the Temple 389
　　　　II. Secrets from the Desert 390
　　　　III. Sleeping with the Enemy 395
　　　　IV. Another Brick in the Wall 397
　　　　V. Biblical Law at Qumran 403
　　　　VI. Law in the Hands Of Jesus 404
　　　　VII. Adultery—But Not As We Know It 411
　　　　VIII. Adulterers Cannot Benefit 416
　　　　IX. Conclusion 424

Chapter 13: The Trials of Jesus 427
　　　　I. Gospel Truth? 427
　　　　II. Dodging Bullets 430
　　　　III. The Stigmata of Jesus 431
　　　　IV. Moral Panics 438
　　　　V. Before the Sanhedrin 439
　　　　VI. Framing the Charges 441
　　　　VII. "Crucified Under Pontius Pilate" 447
　　　　VIII. "What Charges Do You Bring Against This Man?" 453
　　　　IX. Miscarriages of Justice Then and Now 456

X. The Silence of the Lamb 458
XI. Conclusion 463

Conclusion: Law in the Purpose of God 465

Bibliography 479

Index of Biblical Sources 505

General Index 527

ACKNOWLEDGMENTS

In writing a book that draws on various academic disciplines, including ancient Near Eastern and biblical studies, not to mention law and social policy, I am grateful for the interest and support of a number of colleagues. My primary debt is to the core members of a reading group who read—and in some cases reread—draft chapters of the book and who each made significant comments for its improvement. These were Professors Bernard Jackson, Kenneth Kitchen, Julian Rivers, and Gordon Wenham, as well as Dr. Michael Schluter and Chris Willmore. I am grateful to each for sharing their wisdom so generously. I am equally grateful to a group of colleagues in the School of Law, University of Bristol, who made pertinent contributions to specific chapters, including Drs. Pat Capps and Michael Naughton, as well as to John Ashcroft and Rose Cregan (Relationships Foundation, Cambridge) and Jason Fletcher (Jubilee Centre, Cambridge). The usual disclaimers are even more pertinent than usual, given that biblical law presents itself as a journey into wisdom and hence is something we know only in part. Most of this book was completed in draft while on a year's research leave from the School of Law, and so I am deeply grateful to the school and to the University of Bristol for providing this opportunity. Biblical quotations are derived from the Revised Standard Version translation of the Holy Bible, unless otherwise noted. Jewish Publication Society translations are reprinted from *Tanakh: The Holy Scriptures: The New JPS Translation to the Traditional Hebrew Text,* © 1985 by The Jewish Publication Society, with the permission of the publisher. I also wish to thank the estate of Marc Chagall for its generosity in authorizing the reproduction of the artist's work, *Moses* (1956), copyright © 2010 by DACS, London/ADAGP, Paris. Above all, I am grateful to the team at Oxford University Press USA and most especially to Christopher Collins, who oversaw the entire project with enthusiasm. I could not have asked for a more supportive editor.

HOW TO USE THIS BOOK

The goal of this book is to explore aspects of law and legality in the Bible and to do so from the perspective of a modern lawyer. As such, it takes a legal, as opposed to, say, a purely "biblical studies" approach to the materials under discussion. This means that instead of using conventional means of exegesis (such as source criticism and form criticism), this book draws on the types of categories and analyses that would be used within almost any legal system, whether secular or religious. It tries to show the application of law and legal theory to biblical literature by looking at the subject of biblical law in relation to legal thought. It thus aims to take the idea of law seriously by applying jurisprudential thinking to the analysis of biblical texts and, in so doing, to unpack the nature and intellectual significance of biblical law. This should not, of course, be taken to imply that the biblical texts can be reduced to a purely legal approach; after all, part of the value of studying biblical law is precisely that it requires us to consider how law functions in a theological context.

The phrase "biblical law" commonly refers, first and foremost, to what we normally think of as "law" in the Bible, namely, the legal collections that are found in the books of Exodus, Leviticus, Numbers, and Deuteronomy. However, it also ranges beyond these to include other types of texts, genres, and materials. Hence, there is a great deal of elasticity in the term biblical law and, as we shall see in the introductory chapter, this is reflected in the Hebrew word Torah (usually translated "law" in most Bible translations) which also has a wide breadth of meaning. We will see that Torah has the basic meaning of "instruction" and "teaching" (something which characterizes other biblical genres as well) and that biblical law itself is an expression of wisdom. However, lawyers are frequently lost without a definition of some sort and so, with this in mind—and subject to what follows in the rest of the book—I would characterize "biblical law" as *an integration of different instructional genres of the Bible which together express a vision of society ultimately answerable to God.*

In this book, "the Bible" refers both to the Hebrew Bible and the New Testament. This gives the book a broad remit, potentially. Needless to say, the book does not aim to cover every aspect of law and legality found in the Bible. It does not claim to offer a complete, comprehensive encyclopedia of the overall subject. Indeed, a comprehensive treatment of even a single topic in this book would take an extensive volume or two in itself.

The criterion of selection and ordering of the material derives from the book's primary orientation toward teaching in law schools (hence the inclusion of chapters on natural law and adjudication, for example). I have also tried to strike a balance between what we today call "civil" and "criminal" law. This results in the inclusion of chapters on property, social welfare, and marriage and divorce to complement those on homicide, theft, and sexual offenses. These subjects are staple ingredients in nearly all law courses. I have also included substantive legal topics from later sources which I hope will add to the value of the book for many readers. This consists of material from the Dead Sea Scrolls and the New Testament relating to marriage and divorce, which shows how ideas in the Hebrew Bible are presented in later Jewish traditions. I have also included a chapter on the trial of Jesus, since the question of the legality of Jesus's trial is a perennial topic of debate.

There are, of course, many other areas that are of potential interest to law students which are not included in this book, including aspects of the law of tort, legal procedure, judicial ethics, government ethics, the "law of war," and so on. But perhaps this is for another time; after all, for a single text to cover every subject within biblical law and to do so in any depth would require at least a dozen volumes. For the same reason, it is beyond the scope of this book to summarize or address the extensive scholarship relating to the development of biblical law[1] in the material and cultural context of the ancient Near East (though interested readers are referred to several recent works)[2] nor to interact with trends in Jewish jurisprudential tradition over the past two thousand years, since the alternative is a book that reaches to the mountain tops!

The orientation toward teaching in a law school also means that the book does not address the large corpus of material (more than half of biblical law, in fact) which regulates the proper worship of God through the priestly cult and its sacrifices, the festival calendar, dietary laws, and ritual purity practices. It is not that this material is any less a part of biblical law than the biblical laws in Deuteronomy relating to the environment. Nor does it imply that this material has nothing to say about ethical issues. Indeed, as a number of scholars have shown, ritual law is something of a gold mine for cultural anthropologists and, in fact, the ritual purity laws have much to say of an ethical and normative nature regarding the sanctity of life.[3] My goal, however, is to present aspects of law in the Bible in a

---

1. Useful starting points might include JEAN-LOUIS SKA, INTRODUCTION TO READING THE PENTATEUCH (Winona Lake, In.: Eisenbrauns, 2006) and BERNARD M. LEVINSON, LEGAL REVISION AND RELIGIOUS RENEWAL IN ANCIENT ISRAEL (Cambridge: Cambridge University Press, 2008), ch. 6, which provides an overview of research inquiries.

2. *See, for example,* RAYMOND WESTBROOK ED., A HISTORY OF ANCIENT NEAR EASTERN LAW (Leiden: Brill, 2003, 2 vols.) and RAYMOND WESTBROOK & BRUCE WELLS, EVERYDAY LAW IN BIBLICAL ISRAEL: AN INTRODUCTION (Westminster John Knox Press, 2009).

3. *E.g.,* MARY DOUGLAS, PURITY AND DANGER: AN ANALYSIS OF CONCEPTS OF POLLUTION AND TABOO (London: Routledge, 2005); Jacob Milgrom, *Leviticus,* Anchor Bible Commentary (New York: Doubleday, 1991–2001, 3 vols.); JONATHAN KLAWANS, PURITY, SACRIFICE, AND THE TEMPLE: SYMBOLISM AND SUPERSESSIONISM IN THE STUDY OF ANCIENT JUDAISM (Oxford: Oxford University Press, 2006).

way that enables modern law students to deal with them in a meaningful way; this means choosing areas that are already familiar to them.

Accordingly, the book spends its initial chapters setting out the basic theoretical legal propositions on which biblical law rests: it then turns to a number of substantive subject areas and goes into each of these in some significant depth. In this way, it seeks to introduce readers to a multiplicity of subtopics, thereby leading them gradually into a deeper consideration of the general theme—biblical law. For this reason, it is probably best if readers did not view the book as something to "dip in and out" of. The structure of the book relies on readers reading at least the introductory chapters so as to gain a sense of the appropriate context and methodology for the topic chapters that follow.

My hope is that the depth and coverage offered is sufficient to give the reader a good understanding of biblical law both as a system and as applied, while at the same time leaving room for meaningful thought and discussion. With this in mind, contemporary cases are included to engage the reader in thinking about the issues (such as what exactly counts as murder or theft, for example) so that the biblical laws can be seen as a means of thinking legally "outside the box." It is hoped that this approach will provoke thought and further inquiry, as well as stimulate a variety of intriguing discussions in the classroom.

By looking at biblical law in ways that are meaningful in terms of today's legal system, at least today's Anglo-American legal system, the book tries to locate the subject of biblical law within a contemporary cultural landscape. In this way, it explores the question of how modern-day issues can be evaluated in the light of contemporary scholarship on biblical law. Studying biblical law in its original setting does not mean we always have to stay there! There are plenty of areas where the horizon of the text might speak to the horizon of today's reader. It is our modern problems relating to social justice, building social capital, caring for the environment, and so on that provide the contemporary intellectual context into which the biblical material is relevant. Of course, I do not necessarily expect readers to agree with potential areas of application; however, I hope that it will stimulate discussion. The aim is to show how biblical law contributes insights into legal dilemmas in today's world and to illustrate its continuing value for modern legal and ethical theory and practice.

The book also recognizes that law and religion are inextricably linked in the biblical world. Biblical law has to be understood in its theological context; and as a result, the book integrates material that we would today think of as "law" with material which is clearly theological. The book combines both legal and theological insights and presents particular theological points of view at various times throughout the book. Sometimes the theological context is that of the Hebrew Bible itself while at other points, the theological context is that of the New Testament. This reflects the fact that biblical law has been historically of interest to Christians as well as to Jews.

The book seeks to introduce this material to readers who may have no previous familiarity with the subject. My own experience of teaching the subject in a law school has shown me that the task of familiarizing students with the biblical materials is made overly complex by introducing them, at the same time, to a wide range of hypothetical reconstructions regarding the provenance and composition of the biblical texts. As a result, as we shall see in the introductory chapter, this book adopts a canonical, or "final form" approach to the biblical texts.

Indeed, there is a parallel between a canonical reading and the traditional doctrinal lawyer's handling of a modern legal system's sources (although the practical and justificatory reasons for reading law doctrinally are not necessarily the same as the reasons for reading Scripture canonically). As a result, a canonical approach is compatible with the overall goal of this book, which is to explore aspects of law and legality from the perspective of a modern lawyer. Although not all lawyers approach law canonically (for example, sociologists and anthropologists of law) there is an affinity between "doctrinal law" and a canonical approach. Both work with the finished product and seek to make sense of it as a body of normative materials (that is, as materials claiming authority). Indeed, belief in the consistent and hierarchical normative character of legal doctrine can be said to be the central, or natural, mindset of the lawyer. As a result, approaching biblical law as a consistent and normative body of materials is compatible with the scope of this book (which does not seek to engage with source criticism and sociological reconstructions), as well as its general mode of presentation and choice of materials.

The introductory nature of the book means that I have kept transliterations as simple as possible, while still providing a reasonable approximation of the phonetics of the language.[4]

Finally, the book is supported by a holistic teaching Web site that will be regularly updated at http://www.seekjustice.co.uk. From here, teachers and students will be able to download podcasts and study materials designed to be used in conjunction with this book. The combination of this textbook and Web site will mean that anyone, anywhere who wants to initiate studies in this subject at an advanced level will have the means to do so. A workbook, with questions on the primary texts, is downloadable from this site and is intended as an aid to the first-time student. The workbook is based largely on chapters in this book

---

4. I use the letter *h* to indicate aspiration but only for those consonants for which the presence or absence of aspiration makes an actual difference in pronunciation. I have not always chosen to represent the Hebrew letters *aleph* or *ayin* unless they occur in the middle of a word and make a difference for pronunciation.

but also includes additional primary texts. The goal is to give students greater confidence in handling the primary sources for themselves as opposed to relying simply on the approach taken in this book.

Jonathan Burnside
Bristol
October 2010

GLOSSARY

This glossary merely provides initial, nontechnical observations to help the reader of this book; some terms may have a significantly different meaning elsewhere.

Ancient Near East	Term given to early civilization within a region roughly covering the modern Middle East, including ancient Egypt, ancient Iran, the Levant, and Mesopotamia.
Covenant Code	Term given to the biblical legal collection found in Exodus 20:22(MT 20:19)–23:33.
Masoretic Text	Name given to the traditional Hebrew text of the Jewish Bible (derived from the Hebrew word *masoret*, meaning "tradition").
Mishpatim	Term given to the biblical text found in Exodus 21:1–24:18.
"Self-executing" rule	A rule formulated in such a way as to reduce the need for third-party adjudication.
Semiotics	Term given to the study of how meaning is constructed and conveyed, especially to the study of sign structures and sign processes.
Speech act	An action that we perform, or try to perform, by means of speech.
Succession narrative	Term given to the biblical account of the succession to the throne of King David described in 1 Kings 1–2.
Thematic repetition	A literary technique in which words, images, or ideas are repeated to create associations between different texts.

ABBREVIATIONS

ANE	Ancient Near East
JPS	New Jewish Publication Society translation of the Hebrew Bible
KJV	King James Version translation of the Holy Bible
LH	Laws of Hammurabi
MAL A	Middle Assyrian Laws (Tablet A)
MT	Masoretic Text
NIV	New International Version translation of the Holy Bible
RSV	Revised Standard Version translation of the Holy Bible

TIME LINE

This chronology is not comprehensive but identifies dates for some events, historical sources, and figures referred to in this book.

circa 2100 BC	Laws of King Ur-Nammu (of Ur)
circa 2000–1700 BC	Period of the patriarchs (Abraham, Isaac, and Jacob)
circa 1930 BC	Laws of King Lipit-Ishtar (of Isin)
circa 1770 BC	Laws of the kingdom of Eshnunna
circa 1750 BC	Laws of King Hammurabi
circa 1750–1640 BC	Joseph
circa 1650–1500 BC	Laws of the Hittites
circa 1350–1230	Moses (based on c. 1270 Exodus; 1527–1407 BC based on 1447 Exodus)
circa 1250–1270 BC	Later placement for the Exodus from Egypt (1447/6 BC–earlier placement)
circa 1200–1050 BC	Period of Judges (based on c. 1230 conquest; 1380–1050 based on 1407 conquest)
circa 1076 BC	Middle Assyrian Laws (originating earlier)
1050–1010 BC	Reign of King Saul (United Israelite Monarchy)
1010–970 BC	Reign of King David (United Israelite Monarchy from 1003)
970–930	Reign of King Solomon (United Israelite Monarchy)
967–960 BC	Establishment of First Temple in Jerusalem
930 BC	Division of Israel into kingdoms of Israel (930–722 BC) and Judah (930–586 BC)
875/874–853 BC	Reign of King Ahab of Israel
871/870–849/848 BC	Reign of King Jehoshaphat of Judah
722 BC	Fall of Samaria; kingdom of Israel conquered by Shalmaneser V (727–722 BC) and Sargon II (722–705 BC) of Assyria
609/08	End of Assyrian empire
597 BC	Jerusalem capitulates to Nebuchadnezzar II of Babylon (605–562 BC); first wave of deportations from Jerusalem to Babylon

586 BC	Destruction of First Temple and Jerusalem by Nebuchadnezzar II; second wave of deportations from Jerusalem to Babylon
539–331 BC	Period of Persian rule
537 BC	First wave of Israelite repatriation to Jerusalem (Sheshbazzar and others)
520 BC	Rebuilding of Second Temple in Jerusalem (completed 516 BC)
332 BC	Alexander the Great conquers Judea; period of Macedonian rule (331–320 BC)
320–198 BC	Period of Ptolemaic rule
285–246 BC	Translation of Torah into Greek (the LXX, or Septuagint) during reign of Ptolemy II Philadelphus
198–67 BC	Period of Seleucid rule
166 BC	Maccabeean uprising
150 BC–AD 70	General period of the Dead Sea Scrolls
142–37 BC	Founding of Maccabean or Hasmonean dynasty
63 BC	Pompey conquers Judea; Roman rule begins
circa 7 BC–AD 30	Jesus of Nazareth
66–74	Jewish uprising against Rome (the "Great Revolt"); Destruction of Second Temple and sack of Jerusalem by Titus (AD 70)
132–135	Second Jewish war of independence (Bar Kokhba/Ben Koseva) against Rome
circa 220	Mishnah compiled
circa 415	Jerusalem Talmud compiled
589	Babylonian Talmud compiled
1040–1105	Rashi
1138–1204	Maimonides
circa 1275	Zohar compiled

Early chronologies draw on JAMES K. HOFFMEIER, THE ARCHAEOLOGY OF THE BIBLE (Oxford: Lion, 2008), pp. 8–9.

INTRODUCTION: THE HORIZON OF BIBLICAL LAW

Biblical law is a truly remarkable body of law. This is partly because of the sheer length of its continuous history of transmission and interpretation. Although other legal materials are older than biblical law, such as the ancient Laws of King Ur-Nammu of Ur (*circa* 2100 BC), these have not had a continuous history of transmission and interpretation to the present day: on the contrary, they were forgotten until their chance rediscovery last century. By contrast, biblical law has a history of engagement that can be traced back more than two thousand years to the fall of the Temple in Jerusalem in the first century AD and even beyond. According to estimates by some conservative scholars, biblical law can be followed back another thousand years to the time of Israel's first kings and even to the late second millennium BC, which is the period traditionally associated with the giving of Torah to Moses.[1] Even this does not exhaust the potential history of biblical law because we should also take into account the customary law practiced by Israel's patriarchs (Abraham, Isaac, and Jacob) and their descendants. These practices are consistent with what we know of life in Egypt and the Levant in the early second millennium BC, regardless of when the materials in the form we have them now were actually written. This further extends the history of tradition of biblical law. Of course, there are scholarly debates about the age and historicity of these materials,[2] the interaction between oral tradition and written records,[3] and the relationship between the various written sources and the final form of the biblical texts.[4] Nevertheless, the fact remains that biblical law is unique among ancient legal systems for the length of its continuous history as an object of study.

A. Why study biblical law?

This continuity has, at the same time, given biblical law a claim to historical influence unmatched by any other legal system of antiquity. As far as the West is concerned, this influence is due largely to the spread of Christianity. Lord Denning averred that "the common law of England has been moulded for centuries by

---

1. *See* Time line (above).
2. E.g., Kenneth A. Kitchen, On The Reliability of the Old Testament (Grand Rapids: Eerdmans, 2003).
3. E.g., Susan Niditch, Oral World and Written Word: Orality and Literacy in Ancient Israel (London: SPCK, 1997).
4. E.g., Jean-Louis Ska, Introduction to Reading the Pentateuch (Winona Lake, In.: Eisenbrauns, 2006).

judges who have been brought up in the Christian faith."[5] English canon law drew substantially upon biblical law. Indeed, the application of biblical law to inheritance law prompted the nineteenth-century jurist Sir Frederick Pollock to call Numbers 27:1–11 "the earliest recorded case which is still of authority."[6] Some of the application of biblical law in English legal history is surprisingly specific. If we travelled back in time to AD 1540, we would discover King Henry VIII establishing seven cities of refuge based on the biblical model (e.g., Numbers 35:9–29), and if we travelled even further back to the ninth century AD and to the period of King Alfred the Great, we would find that codified English law starts off with the Ten Commandments. Likewise, the early Puritan settlers of New England self-consciously styled their new commonwealth after the pattern of biblical law (witness the *Order of the General Court of Massachusetts* 1636 and the *General Lawes of Plymouth Colony* 1658). This means that to study biblical law is to explore materials that have been of profound significance in giving shape and color, not only to English law and legal history, but also to Western civilization as a whole.[7]

Nor is the influence of biblical law limited to the past. Biblical law has a continuing and living influence in the world today (as distinct from some of the more universally shared moral sentiments such as prohibitions of murder and theft). This influence is felt to some degree not only in the lives of modern Jews around the world, and in the laws of the State of Israel, but even by many in the West who see themselves as "secular." Biblical law continues to exert a hold over popular culture at a basic level, including the structure of the working week and the idea of a day of rest, the constraints placed upon political authority, the use of everyday language (such as references to a "scapegoat"), the idea of mercy, employee rights, and the special significance historically attached to marriage and the monogamous family unit. The word "covenant", which is prominent in biblical law, used to be the standard word for a contract in English law and is still used in the law of property today. This is not to say that such language entered our culture exclusively through the Bible; nevertheless, there are deeply rooted biblical concepts that are well understood and used today. Justice Scalia, giving the dissenting judgement in a U.S. Supreme Court decision regarding the public display of the Ten Commandments, observed that the depiction of Moses with

---

5. LORD DENNING, THE INFLUENCE OF RELIGION ON LAW (Newport: Starling Press, 1989), 19. *See also* S. J. Bailey, *Hebrew Law and its influence on the Law of England*, LAW Q. REV. 47, 533–35 (1931); and D. S. DAVIES, THE BIBLE IN ENGLISH LAW (London: Jewish Historical Society of England, 1954).

6. HENRY SUMNER MAINE, ANCIENT LAW, with introduction and notes by Sir Frederick Pollock (London: John Murray, 1930), p. 23.

7. *See generally* HAROLD J. BERMAN, LAW AND REVOLUTION: THE FORMATION OF THE WESTERN LEGAL TRADITION (Cambridge, Mass.: Harvard University Press, 1983); HAROLD J. BERMAN, LAW AND REVOLUTION II: THE IMPACT OF THE PROTESTANT REFORMATIONS ON THE WESTERN LEGAL TRADITION (Cambridge, Mass.: Harvard University Press, 2003), and GABRIEL SIVAN, THE BIBLE AND CIVILIZATION (Jerusalem: Keter, 1973).

the Ten Commandments in the U.S. Supreme Court building, and throughout Washington D.C., "testifies to the popular understanding that the Ten Commandments are a foundation of the rule of law, and a symbol of the role that religion played, and continues to play, in our system of government."[8] Biblical ideals also form the basis of grassroots movements; witness the recent Jubilee 2000 campaign (which, post-2000 is known as the Drop the Debt campaign). These instinctive cultural references show how much biblical law still anchors people today.

Finally, as these modern campaigns show, biblical law is also remarkable for its revolutionary breadth and depth of vision. It has the imaginative power to disturb the world. The language of biblical law, like that of the Hebrew Bible itself, is forged from "letters of fire... beaten out upon an anvil."[9] It "pour[s] out floods of anger, and utter[s] cries of rage against the abuses of the world, calling the four winds of heaven to the assault of the citadels of evil."[10] As the social commentator Will Hutton noted in a leading United Kingdom broadsheet in the context of the international Drop the Debt campaign: "Leviticus Chapter 25 [which is partly concerned with abolishing debt and reuniting people with the means of production] is a passage that makes *Das Kapital* look tame... it is no longer Morris, Keynes and Beveridge who inspire and change the world—it's *Leviticus*"[11] (see further, Chapter 7).

B. Biblical law in the twenty-first century

In addition to these remarkable qualities—of staying power, relevance, and challenge—there are other good reasons for studying biblical law in the twenty-first century. As a result of its historical influence, biblical law is part of our cultural DNA. Tertiary-level students who study biblical law with no previous schooling in the subject find to their surprise that they are familiar with its texts, even though they may not remember reading them before. Biblical law bleeds into popular culture, like *Big Brother* and Michael Jackson. It is part of our background ambience, thanks to the Bible's iconic status in Western civilization. At the same time, however, although biblical law is part of our cultural and legal identity, it is not always recognized as such. A great deal of modern law is an indirect engagement with biblical law (for example, the abolition of the English laws of blasphemy in 2008), but often it is so implicit that we are not aware of it. We have taken our understanding of biblical law for granted for so long that it

---

8. McCreary County v. American Civil Liberties Union of Ky., 545 U.S. 844 (2005); http://supreme.justia.com/us/545/03-1693/case.html, accessed September 24, 2009.

9. Renan, *cited in* ABRAHAM I. KATSH, THE BIBLICAL HERITAGE OF AMERICAN DEMOCRACY (Ktav Publications, 1977), p. 49.

10. Ibid.

11. *The Jubilee line that works*, THE OBSERVER, October 3, 1999.

has become unfamiliar.[12] This is the immanence of biblical law: it is part of our culture—but it is alien. We do not understand how it is supposed to work. Biblical law is unfamiliar to us—yet it is also in our midst. This means that now is a good time to be studying biblical law. It is time to uncover the immanence of biblical law.

Studying biblical law also enables us to appreciate law from a theological point of view. This is important because law and theology "share common goals and face common problems... if, indeed, one may not view the two as ultimately the same endeavour."[13] Both are concerned with the mystery of our sense of obligation (why should I behave in such and such a way?), the need for a sense of purpose in the law, as well as questions of guilt, innocence, and judgment. Biblical law is an example—perhaps it is the supreme example—of how, as Philip Allott writes in a different context: "law is inevitably connected with our ideas about the ultimate things—our ultimate ideas about the natural world, and our ultimate ideas about humanity's relationship to the supernatural and the spiritual."[14] Law is a "backstage pass" to theology. Indeed, to the extent that law always reflects ultimate concerns, "much of jurisprudence collapses into theology."[15] Biblical law shows how theological categories can be applied to law and legal phenomena, to the benefit of both. It is high time, therefore, to overcome the "intellectual provincialism"[16] under which both law and theology have struggled.[17]

In particular, there is always a danger that the study of law becomes parochial and self-referential, partly because of the dominance of legal positivism in the

---

12. As Levinson remarks, in relation to the 2005 decisions of the U.S. Supreme Court regarding the display of the Ten Commandments in public places: "The back and forth [between the parties]... generated significant debate over the role of religion in contemporary society, but it produced very little intelligent dialogue about the legal texts in [t]he Bible itself." (Bernard M. Levinson, *The first constitution: Rethinking the origins of rule of law and separation of powers in light of Deuteronomy*, CARDOZO L. REV. 27, 1853–1888 (2006), italics omitted).

13. Troy Harris-Abbott, *On law and theology*, AM. J. JURIS. 35, 105–27, 127 (1990).

14. Philip Allott, *The true function of law in the international community*, IND. J. GLOBAL LEG. STUDS. 5, 391–413, 398 (1998).

15. Harris-Abbott, *Law and theology*, p. 126.

16. Ibid., 127. For a good example of this division in relation to the Hebrew Bible (Ezekiel) and philosophy (Kant), see BERNARD M. LEVINSON, LEGAL REVISION AND RELIGIOUS RENEWAL IN ANCIENT ISRAEL (Cambridge: Cambridge University Press, 2008), pp. 67–71.

17. In *The first constitution*, Levinson pleads for an "interdisciplinary dialogue" that would "provide an overdue corrective to the ideological and polarizing use of [t]he Bible in contemporary political debate and jurisprudence: a use that does justice neither to [t]he Bible nor to the history of law" (p. 1888; italics omitted).

twentieth century.[18] Legal philosophy can become limited to its own narrow purview, isolated from everything that makes it interesting. As part of an attempt to counter this insularity, it is necessary to engage in what we could call "spiritual jurisprudence." "Spiritual jurisprudence" can be defined in a preliminary way as the recognition that belief in God, in one form or another, is among the influences upon law and legal practice. (In the context of English law, an example might include the practice of "swearing upon the Bible" before giving testimony in an English court). Spiritual jurisprudence reflects the belief that the task of bringing order to society is ultimately a humble one because political and legal authorities are accountable to God for their decisions.

The language of spiritual jurisprudence can make us nervous because it juxtaposes "God" and "law." However, this is because we have wrongly tended to assume that the only options for modern society are either secularism on the one hand (where God is purely a matter for consenting adults) or a "theo-tyranny" on the other (where religious authorities tell us what to do). The reality, however, is different. We have a legal system that is what it is because it is the product of a large number of influences, including biblical law.[19] In this respect, biblical law does not function in relation to English law or U.S. law as an external or parallel body of law (cf. Islamic religious law or *sharia*). This is because, unlike *sharia* law, biblical law is nascent in the history of English law and so continues to be an influence on many citizens. It is simply unrealistic to suggest that we live in a wholly secular legal system. It follows, then, that understanding one of the traditions that has historically shaped modern law is a productive thing to do, regardless of whether we are personally committed to the biblical texts.

The study of biblical law is all the more important at a time when we are becoming increasingly aware that we cannot shut religion out of the public square. As a result, radical postmodern thinkers such as William Connolly have concluded that "the time of the secular *modus vivendi* is drawing to a close."[20] An article in *The Economist* concludes with reference to the revelation of God to Moses, that "the twigs of the burning bush are still aflame with the fire of God."[21] Nor have politicians been successful in finding a dominant alternative discourse to the ethical language of the Bible, with the result that religious rhetoric has

---

18. Ronald Dworkin, *Thirty years on: Review of Jules Coleman* The Practice of Principle, HARV. L. REV. 115, 1655–87 (2002). Legal positivism is rooted in the belief that "law" in any given society is essentially a question of social fact or convention, and further, that there is no necessary connection between law and morality.
19. *See*, for example, Bernard M. Levinson, *The first constitution*.
20. WILLIAM E. CONNOLLY, WHY I AM NOT A SECULARIST (Minneapolis: University of Minnesota Press, 1999), p. 4.
21. *The battle of the books*, THE ECONOMIST, December 22, 2007, p. 79.

been an increasing feature of political discourse.[22] Again, this means that the study of biblical law is relevant. Regardless of how we try to address the issues raised by religion and politics, we need to understand the nature of the material we are dealing with.

Our discussion of biblical law can be set within the broader context of legal pluralism, which acknowledges that there are competing accounts of the purposes of law and the derivations of these purposes. In understanding the nature of this pluralism and engaging with it, it is particularly important that those individuals and groups who are part of the biblical tradition understand how they should conceive of biblical law, including its purposes and functions. This is because churches and Christians, for example, have unfortunately misconstrued and misapplied biblical law. Mistakes have been made historically and continue to be made today. This means that among Christians, for example, there is a need for a better understanding and better adherence to this tradition in order to draw appropriately from it in the future. There is also a need for learning on the part of those in other religious traditions so they have an appreciation of what biblical law is seeking to achieve and how to engage with it. Effective pluralism requires that each group understands the other and the more this happens, the better the accommodation that society is likely to achieve. To this extent, the study of biblical law may help us to resolve some of the issues surrounding the place of faith in the public square.

C. The horizon of Torah

Another reason for studying biblical law is because it contributes to our understanding of law in general. Biblical law can be read as a case study that helps us to understand the nature of law and the different forms law can take within a tradition of legal pluralism.[23] One of the ways biblical law does this is by presenting us with an understanding of law that is wider than State law (see (1)–(7) below). We can see this by looking at the Hebrew word that has become synonymous with biblical law–Torah. If we look at this single word, we find that Torah can be seen as an expanding horizon, as follows:

(1) Torah can be seen as the handing down of an individual legal precept or body of laws (e.g., Leviticus 26:46, where it appears in the plural form *torot*). On this narrow reading, the word Torah is almost interchangeable with the words "commandment" (*mitswah*) or "commandments" (*mitswot*). Sometimes the words are used in parallel (e.g., Exodus 24:12).

---

22. *The church may be struggling, but in politics its rhetoric is on the rise*, THE GUARDIAN, July 2, 2007.

23. E.g.,WILLIAM L. TWINING, GLOBALISATION AND LEGAL THEORY (London: Butterworths, 2000).

Jewish tradition holds that the Torah consists of 613 commandments and prohibitions.

(2) Torah can be seen more broadly, not simply as legal precepts that are applied in the course of legal disputes but also as the *outcome* of judicial decisions. These are the "instructions" (*hattorah*) given by the judges to the parties in a hard case (e.g., Deuteronomy 17:11).

(3) Torah can be said to go beyond legal precepts and judicial decisions to be identified with a major literary work. For example, Torah is used in references to "this book of Teaching" (*hattorah hazzot*; e.g., Deuteronomy 28:61; JPS), which is usually taken to refer to the book of Deuteronomy.

(4) Torah expands beyond this to encompass *all* of Moses's teachings and instructions. For example, at the start of the book of Joshua, God instructs Joshua to "observe faithfully all the Teaching (*hattorah*) that My servant Moses enjoined upon you" (Joshua 1:7; JPS).

(5) Torah goes beyond even this to become synonymous with the first five books of the Hebrew Bible (also known as the Pentateuch, from the Greek word *pentateuchos*, meaning "five volume" work). Here, Torah refers not just to law but to a whole host of other literary genres, including narrative, poetry, genealogical record, and so on. Jewish tradition formally divides the *Tanakh*, or Hebrew Bible, into *Torah* (commonly designated "The five books of Moses"), *Nevi'im* (the Prophets) and *Kethuvim* (the Writings).

(6) Torah expands beyond even the Pentateuch to be equated with "the word of the LORD." The most famous biblical laws are of course described as "the ten commandments (*haddebharim*)" (Exodus 34:28), which is more accurately translated "the ten words" or "the ten utterances."[24] There are synonymous parallels between the Hebrew words *Torah* and *dabhar*. For example, the prophet Isaiah pleads: "Hear the word of the LORD (*debhar-Adonai*). . ., Give ear to the teaching of our God (*torat Eloheynu*)" (Isaiah 1:10). Numbers 12:1–8 indicates that there is no tension between law and prophecy: indeed, Torah is seen to be "the highest form of prophecy."[25] The interdependency of Torah and prophecy is captured in references to "the Teaching (*hattorah*) that I [God] commanded your fathers and that I transmitted to you through My servants the prophets (*hannebhi'im*)" (2 Kings 17:13; JPS). Torah needs prophets to deliver God's message, but equally the prophetic message is based upon Torah. For this reason,

---

24. *See also* Exodus 20:2–17 and Deuteronomy 5:6–21, and generally, Chapter 2.

25. S. David Sperling, *The Law and the Prophet*, in JEWS, CHRISTIANS AND THE THEOLOGY OF THE HEBREW SCRIPTURES (Alice Ogden Bellis & Joel S. Kaminsky eds.; Atlanta: Society of Biblical Literature, 2000), pp 123–36, 131.

the phrase "the law and the prophets" (e.g., Matthew 5:17) is used by Jesus as a form of shorthand for the Hebrew Scriptures as a whole.

(7) The most expansive horizon of all sees Torah as something that goes beyond prophecy and "the word of the LORD" to link up with "all divine revelation as the guide to life."[26] This is the sense in which Torah is used in the Psalms. In Psalm 119, particularly (the longest in the Psalter), "the meaning of Torah is all-embracing; it refers to God's entire revelation."[27] Elsewhere, too, Torah is associated with God's "paths" (Isaiah 2:3). Here, Torah becomes indistinguishable from "wisdom" (*hokhmah*) because both are ultimately concerned with "how to live life well" (e.g., "The teaching of the wise (*torat hakham*) is a fountain of life. . ."; Proverbs 13:14). Both Torah and wisdom are written into the structure of the physical universe and the reality of all that is (Psalm 19; Proverbs 8:22ff).

Seeing Torah as an expanding horizon has several implications for our study of biblical law. It shows us that Torah is capable of a range of different meanings in the Bible. Nor do we have to choose one over the other: they are all necessarily present in everything that Torah is. Torah *is* legal precept. Torah *is* judicial decision. Torah *is* instruction. Torah *is* the fusion of law and narrative. Torah *is* prophecy. And so on. Torah is an accumulated phenomenon.[28] In fact, it would be fair to describe Torah, essentially, as an integration of all these things.

D. What is biblical law?

One of the implications of this is that if the word Torah—which is usually translated "law" in most Bible translations—is such a complex entity, then it follows that there can be no simple answer to the question: what is biblical law? Biblical law, like Torah, can be found at all sorts of different levels, including: individual legal precepts, legal collections, judicial decisions, wisdom, and so on. To keep things simple, though, we should remind ourselves that Torah has the basic meaning of instruction and teaching. This is something which characterizes other biblical genres as well, including biblical narratives and the wisdom literature, as well as the legal collections themselves. Accordingly—and because lawyers are frequently lost without a definition of some sort and subject to what follows in the rest of the book—we could characterize biblical law as *an integration of different instructional genres of the Bible which together express a vision of society ultimately answerable to God*. This is a broad and flexible definition which reflects the expansive meaning that is given to Torah in the Bible as well as its

---

26. García López, *Tôrâ*, in THEOLOGICAL DICTIONARY OF THE OLD TESTAMENT (G. Johannes Botterweck, Helmer Ringgren & Heinz-Josef Fabry eds.; David E. Green trans.; Grand Rapids, Mich.: Eerdmans, 2007), vol. XV, pp. 609– 44, 628.
27. López, *Tôrâ*, p. 631.
28. *Cf.* Allott, *True function of law*, on the nature of law.

multiple literary genres. To speak of biblical law in relation to the many different facets of Torah is to begin to acknowledge something of its power and complexity as a legal phenomenon.

It is precisely because Torah and biblical law is an integration of many different kinds of legal phenomena and literary genres that handling biblical law is rather like grappling with a Rubik's cube. Biblical law has various interconnected sides, all of which have to be tackled simultaneously and held together. This means that our study of biblical law cannot be neatly restricted to what are sometimes termed the "biblical legal collections," such as the Covenant Code (Exodus 20:22/MT 20:19–23:33). Even a distinct literary unit such as this is fully integrated with its surrounding narrative. The fact that biblical law can be said to operate on a number of different levels means that we have to engage with a broad range of texts, genres and materials to get a rounded sense of what biblical law is and how it works. This means that, in addition to individual legal precepts and bodies of law, this book will also draw upon customary social practices (e.g. rules about inheritance; Numbers 27:3–4) and ad hoc judicial decisions (e.g., the case of the blasphemer; Leviticus 24:10–23), as well as juridical parables (e.g., Nathan's parable; 2 Samuel 12:1–14). We will also draw, where appropriate, on biblical narratives (e.g. the primeval history, Genesis 1-11), prophetic oracles (e.g., Amos 1-2), including the prophetic use of legal metaphors (e.g., Hosea 2:16 [MT 2:18]) and Wisdom texts (especially *Proverbs*).

This means that when we encounter the phrase "biblical law" in this book, we should not think simply of the Pentateuchal regulations that cover the A to Z of biblical Israel, from the high priest Aaron's vestments (Exodus 28:3–39) to the daughters of Zelophehad (Numbers 27:1–11). We should also be thinking of individual judicial decisions such as Moses's judgement in the case of the Sabbath breaker (Numbers 15:32–36)[29] and David's ruling in the case of the widow of Tekoa (2 Samuel 14:1–24). Likewise, we should keep in mind the general hortatory teaching found in Deuteronomy as well as the incubation of wisdom, in a domestic setting, between parents and children (e.g., Deuteronomy 6:6–7 and Proverbs 1:8–9). Nor should we forget the epic stories that speak of God's just interventions in history (such as the story of the Exodus[30]) as well as many, smaller, narratives that speak of the application of particular norms to individuals and society (e.g., the Naboth story in 1 Kings 21 and the book of Ruth). These are all different ways in which the biblical materials reflect upon the order and regulation of society, and so they are necessarily part of what it means to study biblical law.

---

29. See Jonathan Burnside, *What shall we do with the Sabbath-gatherer? A narrative approach to a "hard case" in biblical law (Numbers 15:32–36)*, Vetus Testamentum 60, 45–62 (2010).

30. See Jonathan Burnside. *Exodus and Asylum: Uncovering the Relationship between Biblical Law and Narrative*, J. Stud. Old Testament 34, 243–266 (2010).

The study of biblical law thus potentially covers a great deal of biblical material although, for reasons set out elsewhere, this book will only concentrate on particular subject areas (see "How to use this book"). It also means we should not try to make any sharp distinctions between what counts as "law" on the one hand and "ethical judgments" on the other. Nor should we try to detach biblical law from narrative or from theological considerations. Indeed, there has been a healthy tendency in recent years *not* to isolate the pentateuchal laws from the rest of biblical literature (including narrative and wisdom).[31]

The study of biblical law should also be careful to include the administration of law in biblical Israel (what we would today call a legal system). This is obviously an important aspect of the internal order and regulation of biblical society and includes such matters as the appointment of judges (see generally Chapter 4) as well as the role of quasi-judicial persons (such as the "avenger of blood") and social institutions (such as the "cities of refuge"; see generally Chapter 8). This raises the general question of whether there were ever contradictions between what the biblical authors believed the law should be and what the law actually was in Israelite society. While it is reasonable to presume that the biblical texts provide evidence of the social reality of biblical Israel it is, at the same time, plausible to suggest that there is some disjuncture between social reality and biblical ideology. This is all the more likely, given that the biblical texts themselves describe biblical Israel as a society that was, right from the start, pluralistic in its attitudes and beliefs (e.g., the story of the golden calf in Exodus 32). Indeed, the prophets frequently denounce Israel for her failure to abide in God's covenant, presupposing a lack of compliance on a national scale. For this reason, it is fair to draw a distinction between "biblical law" (understood as a general ideology) and the "law of biblical society" (understood as what was actually practiced).[32]

A further question is whether biblical law, understood as a general ideology, was ever *meant* to be applied in practice. To put it another way, was "best practice" ever intended to be "common practice"? Some scholars take the view that the biblical laws were in some way utopian, or idealized, retrojections from a later era. Our position in this book is that although biblical law provides only a partial view of the norms of biblical Israel, they are nevertheless a primary source for reconstructing the ideals and practices of that society. The texts are literary constructions that connect, to a greater or lesser extent, to the law as actually practiced.[33] So, in my view, it goes too far to claim that the biblical laws were

---

31. *See*, for example, Gordon Wenham, Story As Torah: Reading the Old Testament Ethically (Edinburgh: T & T Clark, 2000).

32. Bernard Jackson, *The ceremonial and the judicial: Biblical law as sign and symbol*, J. Stud. Old Testament 30, 25–50, 29 (1984).

33. Bernard Jackson, *Reflections on Biblical Criminal Law*, J. of Jewish Studs. 24, 29–37, 29 (1973).

purely literary creations. For example, some have argued that the Jubilee provisions in Leviticus 25 were merely stated ideals that were never intended to be put into practice,[34] although, as we will see in Chapter 8, this view is discounted by other scholars.[35] Yet, although debates about the historicity of the particular laws and legal procedures are important, as are the competing theories regarding the provenance and interrelationships of the biblical legal collections, such issues are beyond the scope of this book. It aims to present the biblical material from the standpoint of the completed canon, without consideration of its history or theories as to its composition or historical development. This is because the world of biblical law is one that we access today by means of the finished canon, and so the literary choices that have been made in the final editing of the text are an important aspect of how we make sense of biblical law. Moreover, as noted above (see "How to use this book"), there is a parallel between a canonical reading and the traditional doctrinal lawyer's handling of a modern legal system's sources (although the practical and justificatory reasons for reading law doctrinally are not necessarily the same as the reasons for reading Scripture canonically). As a result, a canonical approach is compatible with the overall goal of this book, which is to explore aspects of law and legality from the perspective of a modern lawyer. Although not all lawyers approach law canonically (for example, sociologists and anthropologists of law), there is an affinity between doctrinal law and a canonical approach. Both work with the finished product and seek to make sense of it as a body of normative materials (that is, as materials claiming authority). Indeed, belief in the consistent and hierarchical normative character of legal doctrine can be said to be the central, or natural, mindset of the lawyer. This is not necessarily to presuppose harmony between all the materials in all respects; however, it does presuppose that biblical law constitutes a coherent body of jurisprudence that makes sense from the standpoint of the final editors at the end of the redaction process. Moreover, it is this finished product which has been authoritative in both Judaism and Christianity—and has had the influence on Western culture and English law that we noted earlier in this chapter.

E. Law and order

The horizon of Torah outlined above, and the correspondingly broad definition that has been given to biblical law might seem rather expansive, especially when compared to the ways in which we normally tend to think about law. Indeed, to some, it might only heighten the difference between ideas of law found in the Bible and popular "modern" ideas of law which see law, in simple terms, as a coercive instrument of the State. However, if we reflect for a moment on the

---

34. *E.g.*, Karl Elliger, *Leviticus*, HANDBUCH ZUM ALTEN TESTAMENT 4 (Tübingen: Mohr, 1966).

35. *E.g.*, Jacob Milgrom, *Leviticus 23-27*, Anchor Bible Commentary (New York: Doubleday, 2001), p. 2251.

nature of law as it has been understood in Western legal philosophy, we do in fact find that law has been understood in similarly broad terms. Even a very brief survey of Western legal philosophy shows that law, like Torah, can be seen as an expanding mental horizon.[36] Of course, the transitions from a narrow view of law toward a more expansive view of law do not map exactly onto the expanding horizon of Torah presented above, and so, as we look at each of these ideas of law, the steps will be different. The point, however, is that even in Western legal thought, there are different ideas about law that require us to see it as an accumulated phenomenon of great complexity, and as something that encompasses, but which also goes beyond, national laws. This means that although a biblical understanding of law is very different from a Western philosophical understanding, there is also a sense in which biblical law is familiar because the understanding of law in the Bible has a similar complexity in treatment to modern ideas about the meaning of law, as follows.

On a narrow reading of law, law can be seen as a closed system, isolated from social and moral considerations. This is the "law as law" view,[37] classically expressed by Austin.[38] Law is a form of command whose validity is derived from social facts—chiefly, the fact of sovereign power and the fact of habitual obedience on the part of most of the citizens.

A broader view sees law not simply as a self-contained mechanical exercise but instead as a particular subsystem within society that is connected to other social systems (such as politics and economics). Law is seen as "a value-processing system"[39] which processes the values of society into various forms, depending on what society seeks to become. This means that "[l]aw is a purposive social phenomenon like any other."[40] Here, the meaning of law is bound up with the character and goals of society itself. For a legal theorist such as Dworkin,[41] the purpose of law is to enable society to become a "genuine" community, in accordance with a deep conception of equality.

Broadening the horizon still further, law can be seen not just as one social system among others but as something that takes in society as a whole. This is the "law as society" view. "Law and society are coterminous,"[42] viz., the meaning of law is found in the social conditions that produce law and legal ideas.

---

36. PHILIP ALLOTT, THE HEALTH OF NATIONS (Cambridge: Cambridge University Press, 2002), pp. 45–56.
37. Ibid., 56.
38. JOHN AUSTIN, THE PROVINCE OF JURISPRUDENCE DETERMINED, CAMBRIDGE TEXTS IN THE HISTORY OF POLITICAL THOUGHT (Cambridge: Cambridge University Press, 1832/1995).
39. Allott, True function of law, p. 396.
40. ALLOTT, HEALTH OF NATIONS, p. 49.
41. RONALD DWORKIN, LAW'S EMPIRE (Oxford: Hart, 1986), p. 96.
42. Allott, True function of law, p. 397.

For Marx,[43] law is part of the superstructure of material reality and is ultimately determined by material forces of production.

A yet wider view sees law as something that transcends the laws of a given society to encompass the order of all societies in all times and all places. This is the "law beyond society"[44] view. It is the traditional haunt of natural lawyers who see the role of law as being to reconcile, by means of reason, certain widely held assumptions about human existence, with some conception of what constitutes a "good" and worthwhile life for human beings. Classic expressions of this can be found in Roman,[45] medieval,[46] and modern times.[47]

Finally, the most expansive horizon of all extends the meaning of law to the ultimate degree by seeing law as part of the hidden order of the universe. This is the "law as universal order" view.[48] The unity and order of everything is interconnected, and what is seen as real is simply the shadow of a higher reality. This hidden reality is part of a universal order which goes all the way up to meet with God (whether understood in philosophical or theological terms), who is the ultimate unity of everything. This is classically expressed by Plato,[49] who seems to have believed that what we call "justice" and the "good" are manifestations of Justice and the Good which are the universal forms, or ideas, of "justice" and the "good." From this perspective, law and society—along with everything else—is on the march back to God.

The point of this brief overview is to show that there is a great breadth of ideas, even in Western philosophy, regarding the nature of law. This ranges from the particularity of legal positivism to the universality of Platonism and all stops in between. Law (like Torah) is an accumulated phenomenon. And all of these different ideas are necessarily present in all we think and do and in all that the law is, just as the different facets of Torah are necessarily present in everything that Torah is.

So although the breadth of biblical law might seem strange to us, ultimately it is not unfamiliar because modern debates about the nature of law are similar to the different ways we can think about Torah. The difference is that nowadays

---

43. KARL MARX, PREFACE AND INTRODUCTION TO A CONTRIBUTION TO THE CRITIQUE OF POLITICAL ECONOMY (Peking: Foreign Languages Press, 1859/1976).

44. ALLOTT, HEALTH OF NATIONS, p. 56.

45. E.g., MARCUS TULLIUS CICERO, DE RE PUBLICA: SELECTIONS, CAMBRIDGE GREEK & LATIN CLASSICS (Cambridge: Cambridge University Press, 1995).

46. E.g., SAINT THOMAS AQUINAS, SUMMA THEOLOGIAE: A CONCISE TRANSLATION, (Timothy McDermott ed.; London:Eyre and Spottiswoode, 1989).

47. E.g., JOHN FINNIS, NATURAL LAW AND NATURAL RIGHTS (Oxford: Clarendon Press, 2001).

48. Ibid.

49. PLATO, THE REPUBLIC, edited by G.R.F. Ferrari, translated by Tom Griffith, Cambridge Texts in the History of Political Thought (Cambridge: Cambridge University Press, 2000).

we tend to shunt ideas about law being anything other than, say, a system of rules, or a basis for punishment into a general sociology of law, or else we put such ideas at the back of our minds and fail to acknowledge how complex law is.

To sum up, we find that law is capable of a broad meaning, both in the biblical materials and in Western legal philosophy. Consequently, it is not surprising that this book takes a broad approach both to the meaning of biblical law and to understanding law in general.

F. Biblical law—and modern lawyers

Finally, biblical law is an important field of study, especially for modern lawyers and law students. We live in a neophiliac culture, which means that we value what is new and automatically assume—correctly—that the latest iPod is better than the previous version. In the same vein, we naturally assume that subjects such as medicine and the natural sciences are far more sophisticated than they were three or four thousand years ago. Unfortunately, the same reasoning does not apply when carried over to other fields of human endeavor, such as law. We cannot assume that "new law" is always "best," that antiquity is a disqualification when it comes to legal reasoning, and that the past has nothing to do with today. The reverse, in fact, is as likely to be true. We find in biblical rules and judgments a level of insight that has rarely, if ever, been surpassed. Nor do we find in any other legal system a more positive vision for humanity and the world than that found in the biblical legal collections. Neither should we underestimate the intellectual or the literary powers of people in biblical society. The student of biblical law who explores the texts in detail finds that they are sound, wise, and practical. Just as in Dworkin's theory of liberal jurisprudence, we find *Law's Empire*[50]; so in biblical jurisprudence, we encounter what we can call "Law's Splendor."

The study of biblical law is also a chance to study the law of a society with very different values and assumptions. This forces the reader to question the "naturalness" and the "normality" of what appears to be the social consensus in our own society. We should not assume that what *is*, is inevitable—especially when what *is*, is wrong. Biblical law reminds us that the world can be other than it is—and that the actual is merely the possible.[51] It is a way of stirring the imagination—and the indignation—of law students. For this reason, biblical law should be at the heart of legal study because "legal education must inculcate an understanding of the ideals, social role and importance of lawyers as well as the ethical rules they observe."[52]

---

50. Ronald Dworkin, Law's Empire (Oxford: Hart, 1986).

51. *Cf.* Philip Allott, *Kant or won't: theory and moral responsibility* (The British International Studies Association Lecture, December 1995), *Review of International Studies* 23 (1997), 339–57, on the society-making capacities of law.

52. Andrew Boon, *Good lawyers, good people?*, Westminster Law 4, 3 (2002).

In addition, there is a tendency for most lawyers to study aspects of a given country's legal system, such as its criminal law and land law, as discrete subjects. They are all isolated from each other, and so the opportunities to make connections between them are rare. The study of biblical law is thus important because it enables us to see how different aspects of the legal order and regulation of society connect. We will see how, for example, biblical land law fits with a concern for the environment, which also coheres with our understanding of sexual offenses and the administration of justice. Studying biblical law also provides an opportunity to see how law develops over a long period of time and to reflect on aspects of its narrative and literary presentation. These are all things that rarely (if ever) happen in other legal subjects.

Furthermore, most law students who go into legal practice find that some of what they study in law will not be relevant. By contrast—and perhaps contrary to expectations—the study of biblical law will always be relevant, no matter what branch of the law students enter and even if they do not go into the law at all. This is because biblical law consciously presents itself as a journey into wisdom (see Chapter 1). The study of law should not be valued simply for its contribution to students' economic well-being. Law is far too important for that. Biblical law aims to teach all who encounter it the essentials of justice. If you allow it to do so, biblical law will make its mark upon you and leave you with a set of attitudes that will profoundly determine how you view life and the world.

Ultimately, the study of biblical law helps lawyers to become better barristers and solicitors. To excel in legal practice, you must possess, inter alia, the ability to find new creative possibilities for legal problems. Biblical law helps in this regard because it encourages us to think broadly about how law works. It opens the mind to new approaches and helps us to come up with new solutions. Lawyers, especially, need to study the things that stimulate the imagination and which open the door to a change of perceptions. Otherwise, the danger is that we end up with a very narrow view of what law is—law as a body of rules or commands that are enforced by punishment, and so on. The former Lord Chief Justice of England and Wales, Lord Woolf, rightly observed that the lawyer's task is to make complex value judgements between competing rights and values. "The facts of a dispute have to be carefully assessed against the conflicting social and human values before the law can be ascertained. This is a task which is fundamentally different to that involved in seeking to make sense of badly drafted contracts or legislation."[53] The study of biblical law helps in this regard because it encourages us to look beyond the traditional context of legal analysis and to consciously reflect on social and human values. It links the study of law up with

---

53. "The education the justice system requires today," 29th Lord Upjohn Lecture, Inns of Court School of Law, June 14, 2000.

the humanities at large. And it enables us to develop larger perspectives on law, legal institutions, and the vocation of lawyers themselves.

G. Conclusion

To summarize, there is a wide range of reasons for studying biblical law in the modern world. Any one of them would be enough to justify a new spirit of inquiry into biblical law. Nor is this effort in vain because if its track record is anything to go by, biblical law will continue to be a source of inspiration and debate when modern legal empires have long been forgotten.

*

We begin our journey by exploring the general outlines of biblical law, starting with: its character, the theme of covenant, whether there is such a thing as "natural law" in the Bible, and humanity's vocation to pursue justice. We will then look at a range of specific issues, including: the relationship between humanity and the environment, people and land, social welfare, homicide and vengeance, theft and burglary, marriage and divorce, and sexual offenses, before closing with an exploration of how different interpretive communities understood biblical law during the late Second Temple period.

Welcome to the study of biblical law.

Selected reading

Roger P. Booth, "Early Jewish law and university education," *Denning Law Journal* 11 (1986), 29–39.

Bernard S. Jackson, "The teaching of Jewish Law in British universities," The Second Jewish Law Fellowship Lecture (Yarnton Manor, Oxford: Oxford Centre for Hebrew and Jewish Studies, 1990).

Raymond Westbrook, "Biblical law," in *An Introduction to the History and Sources of Jewish Law* N. S. Hecht, B. S. Jackson, S. M. Passamaneck, D. Piattelli, A. M. Rabello eds. (Oxford: Oxford University Press, 1996), pp. 1–17.

1. THE CHARACTER OF BIBLICAL LAW

Imagine that you are walking through a neighborhood, and you see the following graffiti, spray painted on a wall:

Insects Bite!
Squashed Insects
Don't Bite
Mad Mentals Rule

What would you make of it? Not a lot. But if you knew that the "Insects" were an urban gang and that the "Mad Mentals" were their rivals, then you would know what it meant.[1] The enmity between the two gangs is part of your "presupposition pool": in other words, all the things you take for granted and which other people might not know.

Not surprisingly, there are many things which belong to the presupposition pool of biblical Israel that the author or compiler could assume made sense to his readers but which might not make sense to us. Biblical Israel is a world where a brother may be required to have intercourse with his dead brother's wife, where slaves have their ears pierced with a screwdriver on someone's doorpost, and where people gather a mysterious substance called "manna" and go into battle carrying the "Ark of the Covenant." It all sounds weird to us, but it was everyday to them and did not need explaining by an author or editor. If we are to understand biblical law, then we need to immerse ourselves in its world. It is tempting to read biblical law as if it is like modern law, but this is a mistake because it does not take into account the presupposition pool of biblical Israel.

This chapter presents my "Top Ten" texts in biblical law, each of which looks at a different aspect of the presupposition pool of biblical law. These texts are in my Top Ten, not necessarily because they are the best known but because they illustrate ten important things about the character of biblical law, which we need to understand before we go any further. They give us ideas of how to read it well: because to read biblical law well, we have to read in sympathy with its character.

I. TOP TEN TEXTS IN BIBLICAL LAW

Reconstructing the social world of biblical Israel—the world in which biblical law made sense—is a tricky task. Our job is like that of a palaeontologist "struggling

---

1. GILLIAN BROWN & GEORGE YULE, DISCOURSE ANALYSIS (Cambridge: Cambridge University Press, 1983), 42–44.

to piece together a set of bones which a dinosaur had used all its life without even thinking about it."[2] The rest of this chapter aims to set out the "bare bones" of biblical law and, without wishing to push the "skeleton" argument too far, identify its main points of articulation. Each text is chosen to reflect a particular characteristic of biblical law. We will see that biblical law is similar to—but also different from—ancient Near Eastern (ANE) law. It is also different from modern law. It is bound up with the story of God, Israel, and humanity, as well as being an integral part of the vocation of Israel. For these reasons, biblical law is didactic and incomplete and relies on rhetoric and literary art to convey its meaning. Biblical law also receives new expressions as God performs new acts of generosity for Israel. Finally, biblical law is an expression of something called "wisdom" and is relational in character. We shall look at each of these characteristics in turn, although, given the importance of the ancient Near Eastern context and the need to make comparisons between biblical and ANE law, we will have more to say about these initial subjects than some of the other texts.

A. Biblical law is similar to ancient Near Eastern law

When one man's ox hurts another's, so that it dies, then they shall sell the live ox and divide the price of it; and the dead beast also they shall divide.
—(Exodus 21:35; God speaking)

We are distanced from biblical law not only by time (several millennia, at least) but also by space (the Middle East rather than Mid-America). This creates an initial presumption that biblical law has more in common with ancient Near Eastern law than it does with modern law. This claim to the greater comparability of the ANE is, of course, only a relative one since there are important respects in which biblical law differs from the rest of the ANE (see below). The deep significance of the ANE means that it is vital to acknowledge—right at the start of our studies—some of the ways in which biblical law is similar to ANE law. This is important if we are to avoid projecting our own modern assumptions about how law works onto biblical law.

We cannot step into the TARDIS (Time and Relative Dimension in Space), or some other time machine, and travel back to Bronze Age Mesopotamia, where many of these legal collections originated. But each new archaeological discovery opens up a sort of "time corridor" by which we can travel back to the ancient world and allow the past to come to us. Over the past hundred years or so, archaeologists have made amazing discoveries of ANE legal collections. Some of the most important finds are summarized in Table 1.

---

2. N. T. Wright, The New Testament and the People of God (London: SPCK, 1993), 101.

TABLE 1 SUMMARY OF MAIN ANE LEGAL COLLECTIONS IN APPROXIMATE ORDER OF ANTIQUITY.[3] THE REFERENCE TO "+ x" IN THE FINAL COLUMN INDICATES THAT THE KNOWN TEXTS OF THESE COLLECTIONS ARE INCOMPLETE AND THAT x PARAGRAPHS ARE LOST.

Name of legal collection	Estimated date of composition	Place of origin	Date and place of discovery	Language	No. of provisions
Laws of King Ur-Nammu (of Ur) (LU)	circa 2100 BC	Ur, southern Mesopotamia (= modern Tell el-Muqayyar, about 360 km southeast of Baghdad, Iraq)	Site of ancient city of Ur (= details adjacent)	Sumerian	37 + x (+ prologue and possibly epilogue)
Laws of King Lipit-Ishtar (of Isin) (LL)	circa 1930 BC	Isin, southern Mesopotamia (= modern Ishan Bakhriyyat, south of Baghdad, Iraq)	Site of ancient city of Nippur (= modern Tell Nuffar, southern Iraq)	Sumerian	38 + x (+ prologue and epilogue)
Laws of the kingdom of Eshnunna (LE)	1770 BC	Eshnunna, Mesopotamia (= modern Tell Asmar, 50 km northeast of Baghdad, Iraq)	1945–47; Tell Harmal, (= 10 km east of Baghdad, Iraq)	Sumerian	60 (+ superscription)
Laws of King Hammurabi (LH)	circa 1750 BC	Babylon (= modern Al Hilla, about 80 km south of Baghdad, Iraq)	1901; Louvre stela found at site of ancient city of Susa (= modern plain of Susiana, Khuzestan, eastern Iran)	Akkadian	282 (+ prologue and epilogue)
Hittite Laws (HL)	circa 1650–1500 BC	Hattusha, Anatolia (= modern Boğazköy, about 170 km east of Ankara, Turkey)	1906; royal archives, site of ancient city of Hattusha (= details adjacent)	Hittite	200
Middle Assyrian Laws (MAL)	circa 1076 BC	Assur, Assyria (= near Qalat Sharqat, about 280 km north of Baghdad, Iraq)	1903–1913; site of ancient city of Assur (= details adjacent)	Akkadian	123

3. See generally Martha T. Roth, Law Collections from Mesopotamia & Asia Minor (Atlanta: Scholars Press, 2nd ed. 1997).

We will draw on some of these comparative texts at certain points in this book.

In addition to these public legal documents, archaeologists have also uncovered a host of private legal arrangements. Private records cover every aspect of social life, from tax receipts to marriage contracts and property disputes, and so on. The scale of some of these finds is immense. For example, the discovery in 1933 of the ancient city of Mari (located in modern Syria, close to the border with Iraq) has revealed, to date, a vast archive of around 25,000 cuneiform tablets from around 1810–1750 BC. (Cuneiform tablets are tablets of clay which were impressed with a cuneiform script while they were damp and allowed to dry in the sun, forming a permanent record). There are so many private documents from the ANE in existence that a large number have yet to be translated and documented. Much more still remains to be discovered, even at Mari itself, which is still only partially excavated. Of course, our knowledge of the ANE is as hit and miss as the vagaries of time (in terms of what has survived) and the archaeologist's spade (in terms of what we have recovered). We don't know what it is we don't know. Unlike modern law, there are no new cases to be decided in the ancient Near East. However, there are potentially many new cases and legal texts to be discovered and translated.

Exodus 21:35, quoted above, is included in the Top Ten because it is an example of how biblical law is similar to ANE law and, in particular, to the Laws of Eshnunna (LE) §53, which states: "If an ox gores another ox and thus causes its death, the two ox-owners shall divide the value of the living ox and the carcass of the dead ox."[4] It is said that the similarities between the two cases provide us with what seems to be, based on the available sources, "the closest textual parallel between provisions in the Bible and an early near eastern rule."[5]

Not all the similarities between biblical and ANE law are as close as this, however. Nevertheless, there are sufficient parallels to make this an important aspect of our understanding of biblical law, especially when viewed from a modern perspective. Biblical law does not exist in a cultural vacuum. It is one of the laws of the ancient Near East and needs to be understood in that context. "Generic conventions cross cultural boundaries in antiquity as well as today"[6]; consequently, we have to study biblical genres in the light of their ANE equivalents. Indeed, Deuteronomy 4:8, in which Moses rhetorically inquires of the

---

4. Ibid., 67.

5. Reuven Yaron, *Biblical law: Prolegomena*, in THE JEWISH LAW ANNUAL (SUPPLEMENT TWO): JEWISH LAW IN LEGAL HISTORY AND THE MODERN WORLD (Bernard S. Jackson ed., Leiden: E.J. Brill, 1980), 27–44, 34.

6. Tremper Longman III, *Israelite genres in their Ancient Near Eastern Context*, in THE CHANGING FACE OF FORM CRITICISM FOR THE TWENTY-FIRST CENTURY (Marvin A. Sweeney & Ehud Ben Zvi eds., Grand Rapids: Eerdmans, 2003), 177–95, 177.

Israelites: "What great nation is there, that has statutes and ordinances [or "laws and rules"; JPS] so righteous as all this law [or "Teaching"; JPS] which I set before you this day?" might suggest that the author is aware of and responding to comparable claims made elsewhere: for example, in the Laws of Hammurabi.

Some of the principal similarities between biblical and ANE law can be summarized as follows:

(1) Both have shared social norms that govern cases involving miscarriage (e.g., MAL Tablet A §50 and cf. Exodus 21:22–25; see Chapter 8); battery (e.g., HL §§1–4 and cf. Exodus 21:22–25; see Chapter 8); and the rape of a betrothed girl (e.g., HL §197 and cf. Deuteronomy 22:23–27; see Chapter 11). Westbrook[7] claims that three-quarters of Covenant Code of Exodus 20:22/MT 20:19–23:33 can be traced back to standard legal problems found in the cuneiform texts.

(2) Both draw on common social customs. For example, in both ANE and biblical law, the use of an unusual execution site reflects the nature of the offense (e.g., HL §§21, 25, 256; HL §166; and cf. Deuteronomy 22:13–21; see Chapter 11); likewise, both ANE and biblical law are familiar with the operation of "talion" or "vengeance" (e.g., LH §§196, 200, 201 and cf. Exodus 21:24–25; see Chapter 8).

(3) Both use common legal forms, such as the "casuistic" form (if . . . [+ consequence]). Examples can be found throughout all the legal collections listed in Table 1 as well as in, for example, the Covenant Code. Both ANE and biblical law also make use of prologues at the head of legal collections (e.g., LU, LL, and LH and cf. Exodus 19:3–6 and Deuteronomy 1–4).

(4) Both are characterized by a lack of abstract conceptions or legal definitions and instead by the use of case examples. Again, examples can be found throughout all the legal collections listed in Table 1 as well as in, for example, the Covenant Code.

(5) Neither ANE nor biblical law is comprehensive in scope. Even the Laws of Hammurabi, with its 280-odd provisions, is not a comprehensive legal collection, nor does biblical law present itself as complete (see further below).

(6) Both have a religious and theological aspect, including the belief that the deity has ultimate authority for law. The Hammurabi stela depicts Hammurabi, king of Babylon, standing before the sun god Shamash, who is also the Babylonian god of justice. This can be compared with the

---

7. Raymond Westbrook, *Biblical Law*, in AN INTRODUCTION TO THE HISTORY AND SOURCES OF JEWISH LAW (N.S. Hecht, B.S. Jackson, S.M. Passamaneck, D. Piattelli & A.M. Rabello eds., Oxford University Press 1996), 1–17, 7.

biblical presentation of Moses receiving Torah from the God of Israel at Mount Sinai in Exodus 20:18ff (see Chapter 2).

(7) Both have examples of civil leaders who are responsible for propagating and administering the law (e.g., the role of Mesopotamian kings in proclaiming "freedom" and "liberation" and cf. the role of Moses in making similar proclamations in the context of the septennial and Jubilee years; see Chapter 7).

What are the implications of these parallels for the study of biblical law?

First, the similarities remind us that biblical law is part of a long-standing ANE legal tradition that developed throughout the second millennium BC (see Table 1, above). Until the re-emergence of this tradition, various claims were made to the uniqueness of biblical law, which went unchallenged due to the lack of any other information. Certain rules that previously were regarded as unique to biblical law have now turned out to represent more widespread Near Eastern practice. One example is the individualization of criminal liability, which appears in Deuteronomy 24:16 and which we now know is also found in an earlier Hittite text.[8] The discovery of other ANE legal collections has finally provided a context in which we are better able to see biblical law as it really is. This is not to say that there are no respects in which biblical law is different from the ANE (see below); however, it does mean we are better able to evaluate any claims to difference and uniqueness.

Second, the parallels raise the question of the relationship between biblical and ANE law. The possibilities can be ranged along a continuum of literary dependence, ranging from complete dependence to no dependence at all. Some scholars claim direct literary dependence, viz., the biblical writers had a copy of certain ANE laws before them, in one form or another, when the biblical materials were written.[9] David Wright goes so far as to claim that the Laws of Hammurabi were the "primary source"[10] for the *Mishpatim* and specifically influenced the sequence of 14 laws in the Covenant Code. The argument in favor of direct literary dependence is at its strongest when dealing with texts such as Exodus 21:35 and LE §53. This is often regarded as the best case for literary dependence, given the similarity of language and grammatical structure. Yet claims to direct dependence are not straightforward, as its proponents recognize. For example, we have no evidence that LE was widely disseminated, and while an intermediate literary source could have provided the "missing link" between LH and the *Mishpatim*,

---

8. Reuven Yaron, *The Evolution of Biblical Law*, LA FORMAZIONE DEL DRITTO NEL VICINO ORIENTE ANTICO (1988), 76–108, 83.

9. Raymond Westbrook, *Biblical and Cuneiform Law Codes*, in REVUE BIBLIQUE 92 (1985), 247–64, 257.

10. David P. Wright, *The Laws of Hammurabi as a source for the covenant collection* (Exodus 20:23–23:19); MAARAV 10, (2003), 11–87.

we have no evidence of this to date. Even if there is direct dependence between LE and the *Mishpatim*, the adoption of LE is itself highly selective. We need to explain why the *Mishpatim* might copy one part of LE but not others. Other scholars claim an indirect literary relationship based on oral tradition, while others caution against any form of literary dependence.

There are several reasons why we might hesitate to place too much emphasis on direct or indirect literary influence. For one thing, all the ANE legal collections that have so far been recovered were found in parts of Mesopotamia and Anatolia (see Table 1, above). Each location is hundreds of miles from Canaan (that is, the region occupied by biblical Israel). Had they been found closer to Canaan and its environs, there would be a stronger claim to literary influence. Eichler[11] points to structural similarities between LE §§27–30 and LH §§128–136. This is understandable inasmuch as LE and LH both hailed from the same geographical area and were probably quite close in time (see Table 1). We should not have the same expectations of similarities when legal collections are more widely separated in time and space, as is the case with the *Mishpatim* and the Laws of Eshnunna.

In addition, it is likely that the wide circulation of "cuneiform culture" as a result of war, conquest, and diplomacy left the ANE with a broad cultural experience, including common legal customs that were applicable to similar circumstances in many regions. It may be that this is reflected in the different settings of surviving texts, making equivalent language on specific topics almost unavoidable, rather than "proof" copying of a text. This does not, however, exclude the possibility of a distinction between common customary origins and literary influence at the redactional stage: that is, the points at which the biblical texts were assembled and edited.

Third, the similarities between biblical and ANE law means that the latter can be used to generate hypotheses regarding the meaning of the former, especially when this is unclear. Such hypotheses need to be tested in the light of other data. A good example of the way in which ANE law can be used to fill in the background to biblical law is seen in the following juxtaposition between Exodus 21:2 and LH §117:

> When you buy [or "acquire"] a Hebrew slave, he shall serve six years, and in the seventh he shall go out free, for nothing. (Exodus 21:2; *God speaking*)
>
> If an obligation is outstanding against a man and he sells or gives into debt service his wife, his son, or his daughter, they shall perform service in the

---

11. B. L. Eichler, *Literary structure in the Laws of Eshnunna*, in LANGUAGE, LITERATURE & HISTORY: PHILOLOGICAL AND HISTORICAL STUDIES PRESENTED TO ERICA REINER (Francesca Rochberg-Halton ed., New Haven: American Oriental Society, 1987) 71–84, 82–84.

house of their buyer or of the one who holds them in debt service for three years; their release shall be secured in the fourth year. (LH §117)[12]

There are two main kinds of slavery in the ANE: (1) capture in war; and (2) debt slavery, where a person sold its services for a specific period of time in order to pay off a debt. "War captive" slaves would normally be foreigners, whereas "debt slaves" would normally be impoverished fellow countrymen. Although we do not know for certain the circumstances in which the slave was acquired in Exodus 21:2, LH §117 suggests that it was as a result of debt. This hypothesis is confirmed by Exodus 21:2 itself, which refers to "a Hebrew slave," indicating that the subject is an indebted countryman.[13] We know from other ANE sources that debt slavery itself could arise either at the time of the loan or later, as a result of agreement or unilateral action on the part of the creditor, known as "distraint." This, in turn, might be part of the background to how the master "acquires" his slave in Exodus 21:2.[14] Consequently, ANE law can be used to generate hypotheses and explain aspects of biblical law that cannot be explained from the law itself. Further examples will be discussed throughout this book.

B. Biblical law is different from ancient Near Eastern law

Keep [the laws] and do them; for that will be your wisdom and your understanding in the sight of the peoples, who, when they hear all these statutes, will say, "Surely this great nation is a wise and understanding people." For what great nation is there that has a god so near to it as the LORD our God is to us, whenever we call upon him? And what great nation is there, that has statutes and ordinances [or "laws and rules"; JPS] so righteous as all this law [or "Teaching"; JPS] which I set before you this day?
—(Deuteronomy 4:6–8; *Moses speaking*)

We have seen that the similarities between ANE and biblical law can illuminate our understanding of biblical law. This is preferable to making presuppositions based on our own cultural context because of the increased distance of modern law from biblical law, when compared to ANE law. However, there are limits to the comparability of ANE and biblical law. This is why Deuteronomy 4:6–8, quoted above, is included in the Top Ten because it illustrates that biblical law saw itself as different from other ANE laws. Not surprisingly, there are a

---

12. Roth, Law Collections, p. 103.
13. Bernard S. Jackson, Wisdom-Laws: A Study of the Mishpatim of Exodus 21:1–22:16 (Oxford: Oxford University Press, 2006), pp. 80-85.
14. Ibid.

number of important differences between biblical and ANE law, including the following:

(1) Biblical law is presented as divine revelation. As Crüsemann notes, "the basic notion that Israelite law is direct divine utterance is not at all common in the ancient world."[15] This contrasts with, say, the Laws of Hammurabi in which the king, Hammurabi, presents his laws *to* the deity for approval, as opposed to receiving them *from* the deity, as in biblical law (see Chapter 2).

(2) Following from (1), biblical law presents Moses as the mediator of Torah (see Chapter 2). This contrasts with the practice of Mesopotamian kings who simply commend themselves to deities and subjects alike (witness the prologues of Ur-Nammu, Lipit-Ishtar, and Hammurabi).

(3) Biblical law differs from ANE law in its ideology and function. Biblical law envisages practical application: the priests are expected to teach Torah (e.g., Leviticus 10:10–11), judges are expected to follow them (Deuteronomy 16:18–20), kings are accountable for their enforcement (Deuteronomy 17:18–20; 2 Kings 23), and the prophets exhort their observance (Amos 8:4–8; Micah 2:1–2; Hosea 4:6). No comparable statements of ideology and function are found in other ANE legal collections. Indeed, Hammurabi's practice of erecting a stela of his laws in public places seems to have had a predominantly monumental function.

(4) Following on from (3) above, biblical law contains explicit endorsements of a didactic model (e.g., "The teaching of the LORD (*Torat Adonai*) is perfect, renewing life; the decrees of the LORD are enduring, making the simple wise (*mahkhimat*)" Psalm 19:8; JPS). This is not found in the extant ANE legal sources.

(5) Biblical law omits a number of issues that are seen as important in ANE law (e.g., adoption and the problem of the "missing" or "absent" husband).[16]

(6) Biblical law differs from ANE law in form as well as content. The laws of both the *Mishpatim* and Deuteronomy frequently use the second person masculine singular form of address (e.g., Exodus 21:2 and Deuteronomy 15:3), which emphasizes the individual's responsibility to keep Torah. This is without parallel in ANE law, although it does occur in the ANE treaty tradition.[17] In addition, biblical law is also different because of

---

15. Frank Crüsemann, The Torah: Theology and Social History of Old Testament Law (Edinburgh: T & T Clark, 1996), 15.
16. Yaron, *Evolution of Biblical Law*, p. 82.
17. J. Gordon McConville, *Singular Address in the Deuteronomic Law & the Politics of Legal Administration*, J. Stud. Old Testament 97, 19–36 (2002).

its extensive use of the "motivation clause," which supplies reasons for obeying Torah (e.g., Deuteronomy 5:15). The explanatory function of these clauses underlines the didactic character of biblical law (see further below). Moreover, biblical law differs from ANE law by having a large proportion of what are technically called "apodictic" laws. These include unconditional commands (e.g., "You shall/ shall not [do such and such] . . ."; see, for example, Exodus 20:4) and curses ("Cursed be anyone/be he who [does such and such] . . ."; see, for example, Deuteronomy 27:15–16). By contrast, there are few apodictic laws in the ANE (although see, for example, MAL A §40).

(7) Biblical law differs from ANE law because of its literary context. The *Mishpatim* and Deuteronomy "are in a literary context too different from that of their Mesopotamian counterparts to allow any meaningful comparison."[18] Biblical law is part of a treaty between God and Israel, whilst the Laws of Hammurabi, for example, are representative of a different literary genre, namely the royal *apologia*. Hammurabi's prologue and epilogue set the laws in the context of a "grand auto-panegyric" designed to bring the attention of the Babylonian god Shamash "to bear upon the deeds and accomplishments of the king."[19] This differs from the position of Moses, who makes no such claims for himself.

Consequently, although ANE law can generate hypotheses that may enhance our understanding of biblical law, we must beware of "parallelomania."[20] There is value in comparative study, but it needs to be handled carefully. Responsible comparative work means understanding the relevant laws as best we can in their original cultural context—and this means taking account of differences as well as similarities.[21] Ultimately, comparisons between biblical and ANE law can never be an exact science because there will always be gaps in our knowledge about literature and genres in the ANE. This is typical of the problems of trying to correlate the biblical materials with the findings of archaeology generally.[22]

---

18. Westbrook, *Law codes*, p. 250.
19. Shalom Paul, Studies in the Book of the Covenant in the Light of Cuneiform and Biblical Law, Supplements to Vetus Testamentum 17 (Leiden: Brill, 1970), 23.
20. Longman, *Israelite genre*, p. 194.
21. Cf. Longman, *Israelite genres*.
22. E.g., Alan R. Millard, *The Bible B.C.: What can archaeology prove?*, in Archaeology In The Biblical World 1 (1991), 18–38.

C. Biblical law is not like modern law

If the thief is seized while tunnelling [through or under a wall for housebreaking] and he is beaten to death [by the householder], there is no bloodguilt in his case [that is, on the part of the householder]. If the sun has risen on him, there is bloodguilt in that case [on the part of the householder].
—(Exodus 22:2–3/MT 22:1–2; God speaking; JPS)

Biblical law is not only different from ANE law; it is also different, as we would expect, from modern law. The increased cultural, temporal, and geographical distance of modern law means that biblical law is removed even further from modern law than it is from ANE law. This distance does not undercut the contemporary relevance of biblical law noted in the Introduction. On the contrary, it is precisely because of the potential application of biblical law that we have to "mind the gap" as we step between the biblical and the modern world.

One of the obvious ways in which biblical law differs from modern law is its application to individual attitudes (e.g., Exodus 20:17/MT 20:14) and thoughts (e.g., Deuteronomy 29:18–19); areas which are regarded as beyond the purview of modern law.

Another, less obvious, way in which biblical law differs from modern law is in its form of legal interpretation. The cognitive structures that go into reading the text of biblical law are narrative, not semantic.[23] Modern scholarly assumptions on how to read biblical law are often based on the values of modern liberalism, particularly the "rule of law" (the belief that adjudication should be governed by laws and not by people). The dominant paradigm of "conventional meaning" today is "literal meaning," which is closely tied, as its name suggests, to writing.[24] A literal or semantic reading sees the rule as covering all cases which may be subsumed under the meaning of its words. This often amounts to paraphrasing the legal rule and substituting one set of words with another.

However, there is another way of thinking about language and about legal rules, and this is to take a "narrative" approach. Narrative meaning consists of typical stories or images that are evoked by the use of words. Whereas a semantic interpretation asks: "What is the literal meaning of the words?," a narrative approach asks: "What typical situations do the words of this rule evoke?," or more straightforwardly, "What does it make you think of?" It is a picture-oriented or "imagistic" approach, rather than a literal one. Narrative meaning arises in the context of a group which shares the social knowledge necessary to

---

23. JACKSON, WISDOM-LAWS, pp. 24–25.
24. BERNARD S. JACKSON, STUDIES IN THE SEMIOTICS OF BIBLICAL LAW, JOURNAL FOR THE STUDY OF THE OLD TESTAMENT SUPPLEMENT SERIES 314 (Sheffield: Sheffield Academic Press, 2000), 14.

evoke those images without needing to "spell them out."²⁵ (Social knowledge refers to our knowledge of social situations which is informed by our social and historical contexts and which we normally take for granted).

This distinction between literal and imagistic approaches is an important one in practice. Rules that are read literally cover all cases that may be included under its language. By contrast, rules that are understood as pictures apply only to the typical cases it makes you think of. We can take a simple example, such as the "eye for eye, tooth for tooth" formula in Exodus 21:24–25. One of the classical arguments against this rule (posed by Plato and others) was, "what happens if a one-eyed man puts out one of the eyes of a two-eyed man?" This objection assumes a literal reading; viz., it assumes that the rule applies whatever the circumstances of the parties. A literal application of the "eye for an eye" rule would mean that the offender's eye must be taken, even though this means that he will be completely blind, whereas his victim was made only half-sighted.²⁶ An alternative approach, preferred by Bernard Jackson,²⁷ is to read Exodus 21.24–25 narratively. The typical offender is pictured as a two-eyed man, which means that the case of the one-eyed offender is far removed from the typical case. Under this picture-oriented approach, the further the real-life case is from the typical case, the less likely it is that the rule applies, and the more room there is for negotiation between the parties.²⁸ The question is no longer whether the dispute is "covered" by the literal meaning of the words of the rule but whether the dispute is sufficiently similar to the picture evoked by the rule to justify its use in order to resolve the problem. If it is sufficiently similar, it applies, even though it is not the literal meaning of the words.

Significantly, questions of relative similarity evoke intuitive judgements of justice to a greater degree than literal interpretations. "How similar . . ." questions are evaluative questions ("how justified is it to treat these cases as similar?"). This in itself suggests a more popular form of dispute resolution than is nowadays the case.²⁹ It also means that biblical law demanded a great deal of private and creative reflection (cf. Deuteronomy 6:6–9).

Exodus 22:2–3/MT 22:1–2—the case of the nocturnal thief—quoted above, is included in the Top Ten because it is a good example of the difference between semantic and narrative approaches to biblical law. If we take a modern semantic approach to this case, then the drafting of verses 2 and 3 seems odd and contradictory. The first part of the rule apparently gives carte blanche to the householder who kills an intruder at any time of day or night, while the second part of the rule

---

25. Bernard S. Jackson, *Law, wisdom and narrative*, in NARRATIVITY IN BIBLICAL AND RELATED TEXTS (G. J. Brooke & J. D. Kaestli eds., Leuven: Leuven University Press, 2000), 31–51, 45.
26. JACKSON, STUDIES, p. 285.
27. Ibid., 286.
28. Ibid., 75–82.
29. Ibid., 82ff.

denies self-help if the break-in occurs during the day. However, the text makes perfect sense if we take a narrative approach and ask "what is the typical situation evoked by the words "tunnelling thief?" We know from elsewhere in the Bible that thieves typically tunnelled into other people's houses at night: "The murderer rises in the dark, that he may kill the poor and needy; and in the night he is as a thief . . . In the dark they dig through houses . . ." (Job 24:14–16). In other words, it is clear from Job 24 that the typical situation evoked by the words in Exodus 22:2/ MT 22:1 is one in which the thief tunnels at night. There is therefore no tension with the subsequent part of the rule which contrasts the legitimate action of the householder at night with the illegitimate action of the householder by day.[30]

As we have seen, one of the implications of this approach is that the narrative image represents the core of the message. The further one departs from the typical case, the less sure we can be that the message is intended to apply or would be regarded as applicable by the audience[31] (e.g., killing a thief who was breaking in at dusk would probably have been regarded as questionable and would have led to negotiations for compensation between the householder and the deceased thief's family).

To sum up, the distinction between semantic and narrative readings of the law is all part of the presupposition pool of biblical law, and we will see a number of examples of narrative readings of biblical law throughout this book. B.L. Eichler argues that the Laws of Eshnunna and the Laws of Hammurabi make use of "polar cases with maximal variation,"[32] viz. contrasting cases with extreme variations in circumstances. Such cases make sense because they, too, rely on narrative stereotypes, indicating that the process of reading the Bible narratively has comparative support from the ANE.

As the narrative reading of biblical law suggests, norms are frequently told as stories in the Bible. This has a number of knock-on effects which further distances biblical law from modern law. If we take, for the sake of argument, the law of primogeniture in Deuteronomy 21:15–17, we find that it is not expressed in general terms, as we would expect in modern law (e.g., "The first born shall have a double portion"[33]). Instead, it is framed in narrative terms (i.e., "If a man has two wives, the one loved and the other disliked, . . . and if the first-born son is hers that is disliked"; Deuteronomy 21:15). This presentation informs our understanding of the law itself: you should not discriminate against a firstborn just because you prefer another son's mother. The formulation of Deuteronomy 21:15–17 recalls the patriarchal narratives in which Joseph—son of Jacob's

---

30. Ibid., 75–81.
31. Bernard S. Jackson, Modelling biblical law: The covenant code, CHI.-KENT L REV. 70, 1745–1827, 1767–68 (1995).
32. B. L. Eichler, Literary structure in the Laws of Eshnunna, in LANGUAGE, LITERATURE & HISTORY: PHILOLOGICAL & HISTORICAL STUDIES PRESENTED TO ERICA REINER (Francesca Rochberg-Halton ed., New Haven: American Oriental Society 1987), 71–84, 72.
33. Jackson, Law, wisdom and narrative, p. 47.

preferred wife Rachel—receives the birthright over Reuben—the eldest but also the son of Jacob's unloved wife Leah. This is despite the fact that Jacob does not act for the reason specified in Deuteronomy 21:15–17 (partiality) but because Jacob wanted to punish Reuben for sleeping with Jacob's concubine (1 Chronicles 5:1).[34]

This is consistent with the general approach in biblical law (and also ANE law) which does not present us with "a systematic ethic but, rather, conveys its teaching through the particular and the specific."[35] Biblical law talks about concrete things—going oxen instead of "tort" or "liability for damage caused by animals." As in modern Africa, abstract nouns are expressed in concrete terms; thus, instead of a concern for society, we have a concern for land (see Chapter 6), and when biblical law speaks of power, it refers to the hand (see Chapter 7).

To conclude, biblical law is different from modern law, and this is due in large measure to the way in which it is shaped by narrative. This is the focus of the next subsection.

D. Biblical law is bound up with the story of God's involvement with humanity

You shall not oppress a stranger; you know the heart of a stranger,
for you were strangers in the land of Egypt.
—(Exodus 23:9; *God speaking*)

One of the most striking aspects of how law is presented in the Hebrew Bible is its integration with narrative, by which we mean the specific biblical story of God's involvement with humanity. It is crucial to recognize that biblical law is not presented as "codified law" but is integrated "at every stage" into the wider story of God's purposes for Israel and, beyond that, for the world. For example, the Sinai narrative (see Chapter 2) switches between story (e.g., Exodus 19:1–25); law (Exodus 20:1–17); story (Exodus 20:18–21), law (Exodus 20:22–23:33), and back to story again (Exodus 24:1–18). What is true of the Sinai narrative (Exodus 19–24) is true of the Pentateuch as a whole. All of the Pentateuch's legal collections are firmly embedded in their own narrative contexts. This means that to be good readers of biblical law, we should not split what authors and compilers have joined together. Nor should we imagine we have arrived at the "true" meaning of biblical law when we have "boiled off" the narrative to a set of rules or underlying principles. There is increasing recognition of the importance of narrative in human sense construction; indeed "the brains of human beings seem built to process stories better than other forms of input."[36] This contrasts with modern

---

34. Ibid., 47–48; cf. Calum Carmichael, Women, Law & The Genesis Traditions (Edinburgh: Edinburgh University Press, 1979), 31–32.

35. P. J. Harland, *Review of John Barton Ethics and the Old Testament*, Vetus Testamentum 49 (1999), 135–36.

36. Thomas B. Newman, *The power of stories over statistics*, Brit. Medical J. 327, 1424–27, 1426 (2003).

law which, although it makes use of narrative, principally in the form of case law,[37] it does not rely on narrative to structure legal thought to anything near the same degree as biblical law.

One of the key turning points in the story of God and Israel is the Exodus, in which God rescues Israel from the condition of being enslaved to Pharaoh in Egypt (Exodus 12–13). Israel's experience of the Exodus becomes the motivation for obeying the law in Exodus 23:9, quoted above. It is included in the Top Ten because it is a good example of the way in which biblical law is bound up with the story of God's involvement with humanity and, particularly, Israel.

In fact, there are many narrative allusions to the Exodus in biblical law. First, there is an explicit narrative reference to the Exodus in the opening words of the Decalogue:

> I the LORD am your God who brought you out of the land of Egypt, the house of bondage. (Exodus 20:2; *God speaking*)

Second, we find that there is an explicit narrative allusion to the Exodus at the head of individual sections within biblical law, such as Exodus 23:9, noted above. Third, we find that there is an implicit narrative allusion at the head of the entire *Mishpatim* itself. This takes the form of a reference to slavery which alludes to the Exodus from Egypt:

> These are the rules (*hammishpatim*) that you shall set before them: When you acquire a Hebrew slave.... (Exodus 21:1–2; *God speaking*)

Fourth, there is evidence that slavery—and liberation from slavery—is the main organizing theme of Exodus 21:2–27, which is the first section of laws in the *Mishpatim*. This section is structured according to a literary pattern known as a chiasmus. This is "a pattern in which a series of elements is repeated in reverse order, with the first and last elements also often forming the centrepiece of the group,"[38] as follows:

```
A  (Exodus 21:2–11)                  Liberation of male and female slaves
 B  (Exodus 21:12–17)                Capital provisions
  C  (Exodus 21:18–19)               Injuries from a brawl
   D  (Exodus 21:20–21)              Fatal assault on one's own slave
  C` (Exodus 21:22–23)               Brawl affecting pregnant woman
 B` (Exodus 21:24–25)                Talionic provisions
A` (Exodus 21:26–27)                 Liberation of male and female slaves
```

FIGURE 1. CHIASTIC STRUCTURE OF EXODUS 21:2–27 (JACKSON 2006:447)

---

37. *See generally* BERNARD S. JACKSON, LAW, FACT & NARRATIVE COHERENCE (Liverpool: Deborah Charles Publications, 1991).

38. Bernard S. Jackson, *On the nature of analogical argument in early Jewish law*, JEWISH L. ANN. 11, 137–68, 144 (1993).

Explicit and implicit allusions to the Exodus have several functions in biblical law. They are reminders that Torah is given to those whom God freed from slavery in Egypt. For this reason, the laws sometimes allude to the Exodus in order to act as a check on oppressive behavior, lest the formerly oppressed become the new oppressors. They also emphasize that Torah is an expression of the character of God who liberates and gives life to Israel. For this reason, the Exodus allusions are a spur to generous and selfless behavior (e.g., Deuteronomy 15:12–15; see Chapter 7). "Narrative gives moral truth an existential force which cannot be done by law."[39] The use of narrative allusions reminds us once again that we are not dealing with law in a modern sense. Unlike modern law, biblical law harnesses narrative to shape national identity and to promote personal compliance.

E. Biblical law is an integral part of the vocation of Israel
You shall be to me a kingdom of priests and a holy nation
—*(Exodus 19:6; God speaking)*

Biblical law is an integral part of the vocation of Israel. This is not surprising because the story of God's involvement with humanity, which we saw was relevant to biblical law in the previous section, is, in part, the story of Israel's vocation. This vocation is expressed in Exodus 19:6, quoted above, which is why it is part of the Top Ten. At Mount Sinai, and prior to the giving of Torah, Israel is called to be "a priestly kingdom and a holy nation." In other words, Israel's declared role within the purpose of God is to serve the nations by standing in the same relationship to them as a priest stands in relation to the people at the Tabernacle, or Temple, of Israel's God. Among other things, it signifies the way in which Israel is intended to be a conduit of blessing to the world, in the same way that a priest is a conduit of God's blessing to the people (e.g., Numbers 6:22–27). This contrasts with a modern "systems theory" of law (also known as "autopoesis"), which sees law as simply one subsystem among many others, including politics, that characterize the modern state.[40]

This vocation is in keeping with the story arc that develops throughout the Pentateuch. It starts off with Genesis 1–11 (the "primeval history") which establishes the origins of the cosmos and humanity and introduces what is, perhaps, the dominant theme of the Bible—namely, the divine-human relationship. Genesis 1 begins with a picture of the earth "unformed and void" (1:2), from which an ordered universe is brought into being by God. Genesis 3 narrates the subversion of that order, as the serpent challenges the humans who in turn disobey God. The result is a situation of disorder where the man and woman accuse

---

39. Harland, *Review of Barton*, p. 135.
40. E.g., P. Capps & H. Olsen, *Legal autonomy & reflexive rationality in complex societies*, Soc. L. Studs. 11, 547–67 (2002).

each other and God and are in conflict with the rest of creation. The rest of the primeval history expresses this disorder in various ways, including murder (4:1–16), vengeance (4:23–24), and strange sexual offenses (6:1–4). The physical disorder of Genesis 1 is resolved, but the moral and relational disorder of Genesis 3 remains unresolved. A major theme of Genesis 1–11 is thus the movement from disorder to order and then back to disorder.

The primeval history (Genesis 1–11) then gives way to the Abraham story (Genesis 12:1–25:18), which is followed by that of Abraham's descendants, including Jacob (Genesis 25:26–37:1) and Jacob's family, including the "Joseph cycle" (Genesis 37:2–50:26). The rest of the Pentateuch, and indeed the Hebrew Bible, takes up the story of Jacob's descendants: that is, the people of Israel. But although there is a major contrast between the universalism of the primeval history and the particularism of Genesis 12 onwards, there is a connection between the two. The link is Genesis 12:1–3, which is the call of Abram (later Abraham). These verses introduce the theme of the Pentateuch, namely, God's choice of Abraham from among all the people of the earth for a special relationship and the establishment of Abraham's descendants as "a great nation" (12:2), which will be the means of blessing "all the families of the earth" (Genesis 12:3). The universal is related to the particular and vice versa. Nehemiah 9:6–8 presents God's call of Abraham as God's first act after creation. Rendtorff claims that if we take our cue from this, "we can even say that this divine act is seen on almost the same level as creation itself."[41] The juxtaposition of the primeval history with the Abraham story indicates that somehow resolving the outstanding problems of Genesis 1–11 will have something to do with Abraham and his family, although this story is not resolved within the Pentateuch itself.[42]

This, then, is the background to the vocation of Israel in Exodus 19:6. Being "a kingdom of priests and a holy nation" is how Israel will be a "blessing to the nations." Like a priest officiating in the Temple, Israel holds out the knowledge of God to the rest of the world. Biblical law is given in the context of a theophany (that is, the visual and auditory manifestation of God), which signifies that Torah is associated first and foremost with the person and character of God (Exodus 19–20). And because Israel's God has a certain character, Israel is to reflect that character "in the sight of the peoples" (Deuteronomy 4:6) by following Torah.

The vocation of Israel is how we can understand laws such as, "You shall not hate your brother in your heart" (Leviticus 19:17; *God speaking*). From a modern perspective, such a law seems strange because it commands an attitude. No modern Western law would be framed in those terms. We would ask what is the point of having a law that everyone is going to break—and who is going to

---

41. Rolf Rendtorff, *The Covenant Formula: An Exegetical & Theological Investigation*, in OLD TESTAMENT STUDIES (Margaret Kohl trans., Edinburgh: T&T Clark, 1998), 1.

42. David J. A. Clines, *The Theme of the Pentateuch*, in JOURNAL FOR THE STUDY OF THE OLD TESTAMENT SUPPLEMENT SERIES 10 (Sheffield: Sheffield Academic Press, 1978).

enforce it when it is broken? However, Leviticus 19:17 makes sense within the presupposition pool of biblical Israel because biblical law is part of God's call that Israel should "be" a certain quality of people and reflect the character of God to the nations. At one level, Israel's obedience to Torah is presented as being in her own best interests as a community (e.g., Deuteronomy 32:46–47), but ultimately, biblical law is fulfilled when Israel carries out her mission to the nations—a mission framed not so much in terms of *going* somewhere but of *being* something.

F. Biblical law is didactic—and incomplete

Take to heart these instructions with which I charge you this day. Impress them upon your children. Recite them when you stay at home and when you are away, when you lie down and when you get up. Bind them as a sign on your hand and let them serve as a symbol on your forehead; inscribe them on the doorposts of your house and on your gates.
—(Deuteronomy 6:6–9; Moses speaking)

Deuteronomy 6:6–9 is included in the Top Ten because another important aspect of biblical law is its didacticism. Biblical law is meant to be taught. This teaching is not limited merely to "legal knowledge" but is, instead, presented as a guide to "life, the universe and everything." As Jethro advises Moses: "Teach them the statutes and the decisions, and make them know *the way in which they must walk* . . ." (Exodus 18:20). The priests' job is "to teach the people of Israel all the statutes which the LORD has spoken to them by Moses" (Leviticus 10:11), while Deuteronomy 1:5 describes how Moses "undertook to explain this law (Torah) [or "Teaching"; JPS]." Torah is something that needs to be understood and fully internalized.

This is all the more necessary given that biblical law, in common with ANE law, was not comprehensive. Biblical law never aimed to be an ancient equivalent of *Enquire Within About Everything*, a nineteenth-century handbook of the necessities of domestic life in Victorian Britain. Many problems are simply not covered in biblical law—including some which were common to other ANE legal collections (see above). This contrasts with modern assumptions that law is a complete system, even when the law itself is silent on a given issue.

Of course, our sense that law in biblical Israel was fragmentary and incomplete may be more apparent than real. Simply because a rule is not mentioned in biblical law does not mean that it did not exist. Absence of evidence is not evidence of absence. Nor can we assume, as Yaron rightly points out, that the Pentateuchal texts are "a comprehensive collection of at least all that there ever was in writing."[43] The Bible itself refers to books and materials which it assumes

---

43. Yaron, *Evolution of Biblical Law*, p. 98.

are common knowledge but to which we do not have access (e.g., "the Book of the Wars of the LORD"; Numbers 21:14). Biblical law may also seem incomplete to us because the Israelites were relying on customary law, which again is unknown to us.

At the same time, however, we know there were still serious gaps in biblical law because these gaps were acknowledged by biblical society itself. Examples include the ad hoc legal situations presented by, variously, the daughters of Zelophehad (Numbers 27:1–11); the impure celebrants (Numbers 9:6–14); the wood gatherer (Numbers 15:32–36); and the blasphemer (Leviticus 24:10–23). In all four cases, the legal norms operating at the time of the event were insufficient and needed an ad hoc oracular supplement.[44] There was always a need to "mind the gap" in biblical law; and this is true of any legal system.

Every legal system has to deal with the fact that "in many contexts, our knowledge of what constitutes appropriate behaviour depends upon a background of understandings that we could not fully articulate in advance of the situations that call them into play."[45] Practical reasoning depends upon "a never fully articulable" background consensus.[46] Biblical law addresses this by offering rules that are limited in number but which are designed to promote wisdom (see further below). There is a cultural expectation which finds its classic expression in the Book of Proverbs—that the study of biblical law in a domestic context, both privately and in groups, results in the formation of a person's character and leads to the acquisition of wisdom. "Minding the gap" in biblical law meant applying wisdom. When faced with a problem that is not explicitly covered by biblical law, the Israelite is expected to apply the wisdom that comes from practicing and meditating upon Torah, although in "hard cases," he may have recourse to those who are regarded as having superior wisdom (see Chapter 4). This means that while biblical law is incomplete, its purpose is to teach wisdom, which is complete.

If biblical law is not a complete representation of the issues facing biblical society, the question is raised, "what criterion is used for selecting those that are included?" It is commonly claimed that ANE legal collections included either controversial or common cases, the former being those that changed customary law. A number of the Hittite Laws state that while formerly such and such was the rule, it has now been replaced by something else (e.g., §§166–167, although it is not known whether the Hittite Laws themselves *make* the change or merely record it). On the other hand, scholars generally regard the Covenant Code in Exodus as a statement of common, rather than controversial, cases. It is hard to generalize, of course, and we should not assume that the laws of any ancient

---

44. JACKSON, WISDOM-LAWS, pp. 425–30.
45. N. E. SIMMONDS, CENTRAL ISSUES IN JURISPRUDENCE (London: Sweet & Maxwell, 2002), 148.
46. SIMMONDS, CENTRAL ISSUES, p. 149.

legal collection are cast all from the same mold. But if the stated purpose of biblical law is to impart wisdom by means of teaching, practice, and meditation, it is reasonable to conclude that cases were included which were thought to promote wisdom.

G. Biblical law relies upon rhetoric and literary art to convey meaning

If there is among you a poor man, one of your brethren, in any of your towns within your land which the LORD your God gives you, you shall not harden your heart or shut your hand against your poor brother, but you shall open your hand to him, and lend him sufficient for his need, whatever it may be.
—(Deuteronomy 15:7–8; *Moses speaking*)

Biblical law is also characterized by the use of rhetoric and sophisticated literary structure. First, biblical law is rhetorical in the strict sense of the term because it is "persuasive speech." Biblical law is presented as having originally been delivered in oral form. The "giving of the law" by God to Moses (Exodus 20:19ff) and by Moses to the people (Exodus 24:7; Deuteronomy 5:1ff) is delivered orally, with the latter giving rise to a tradition of septennial public law readings (Deuteronomy 31:10–13). This means that in our overall understanding of biblical law, some account has to be taken of its rhetorical features. Deuteronomy 15:7–8, quoted above, is part of the Top Ten because it is a good example of a text that is designed to "influenc[e] the audience's thoughts and persuad[e] them to alter their behaviour."[47] Appeal is made on behalf of the "poor man" who is identified as a "brother" (verse 7), while an unfavorable contrast is drawn between the "shut hand" and the "open hand" (verses 7–8). Moses's rhetoric switches between corporate Israel (verse 7a) and the individual Israelite (verses 7b–8). The audience is "addressed both as individuals and as a whole, reinforcing both these identities . . . [Moses'] appeal to the solidarity of the group reinforces his appeal to each individual."[48]

Deuteronomy is the most rhetorical of all the biblical legal collections, emphasizing as it does, "the ultimate consequences of urgent choices."[49] This is not surprising because Deuteronomy is presented as a series of four farewell speeches by Moses to Israel, immediately prior to his death. Rhetoric is thus another way in which biblical law differs from modern law. Although there are rhetorical features in modern law, particularly in oral and written legal judgments,[50] it is less significant than in biblical law. Oral delivery need not

---

47. James W. Watts, *Rhetorical strategy in the composition of the Pentateuch*, J. STUD. OLD TESTAMENT 68, 3–22, 3 (1995).
48. T. A. LENCHAK, CHOOSE LIFE!: A RHETORICAL-CRITICAL INVESTIGATION OF DEUTERONOMY 28:69–30:20 (Rome: Pontifical Biblical Institute, 1993), 106.
49. Watts, *Rhetorical strategy*, p. 20.
50. E.g., Lord Denning in *Miller v. Jackson* [1977] Queen's Bench Division 966.

necessarily imply a lack of consistency in the use of biblical legal language. For example, the offense of having sexual relations with a wife and her mother is described as "depravity" (*zimmah*; JPS) both in Leviticus 18:17 and 20:14. But this offense is also described, along with other kinds of prohibited sexual relations, in Leviticus 18:26, as "abominations" (*to'ebhot*). Here, language is used more broadly for rhetorical purposes and to influence behavior.

Biblical law is also characterized by sophisticated literary structure. "Holy writ" is brilliantly "writ". This contrasts with modern law, which does not regard literary presentation as key to the construction of meaning. To give a random example, necrophilia is prohibited under section 70 of the Sexual Offences Act 2003, but there is no reason why it has to appear at that particular point in the statute, and its meaning would not be affected if it appeared somewhere else. It is frequently the case that the way in which biblical law is structured and organized internally determines the meaning of its content. The biblical texts are craftily assembled: both at the level of metanarrative and the detail of individual pericopes. This is the art of biblical law. It is practical and functional; but it is also esthetic. This is one of the many things biblical law has in common with wisdom. The perfect arrangement of words is a thing of wonder:

Like golden apples in silver showpieces
Is a phrase well turned. (Proverbs 25:11)

Biblical law is an expression of wisdom (see further below). One of the features of wisdom in the Bible is that it provides insight into the structure of things (e.g., Proverbs 8:22–31, which describe the role of wisdom in constructing the world). Since one of the functions, then, of biblical law is to provide insight into how things fit together, it is appropriate that biblical law should itself be characterized by a high degree of internal structure. The form is the message.

Some of these literary units are simply structured, such as Exodus 21:28–35, where four cases involving a goring ox are structured according to the declining social status of the victim:

TABLE 2 LITERARY ARRANGEMENT OF EXODUS 21:28–35[51]

A	Exodus 21:28	When an ox gores *a [free] man or a woman to death*...	
B	Exodus 21:31	... if it [the ox] gores *a [free] man's son or daughter*...	DECLINING SOCIAL STATUS OF VICTIM
C	Exodus 21:32	If the ox gores *a slave*, male or female...	
D	Exodus 21:35	When one man's ox hurts *another's [ox]*...	

---

51. Jackson, Wisdom-Laws, p. 286.

Other literary arrangements can be more complex. An example of this is the chiastic structure of Exodus 21:2–27, noted in Figure 1, above, which is centered upon slavery. A highly complex chiasmus can be found in Leviticus 24:13–23. It is too large to reproduce here but spans a total of eleven verses.[52] We also find examples of detailed literary structure in Leviticus 20 (see Chapter 11). However, while literary arrangements in biblical law may seem complex to us—indeed, so complex they frequently remain hidden from our eyes—they might not have seemed that way to the original audience. A model of oral popular rhetoric does not exclude the possibility that a biblical audience, or at least certain parts of it such as a scribal elite or priests, might have been able to take complex literary arrangements in its stride. We might compare the ability of modern television audiences to follow complex dramas with only the minimum of plot, dialogue, and characterization—and even to absorb multiple storylines juxtaposed on a split screen.

Doing justice to biblical law thus means paying attention to the way in which it is presented. Throughout this book, we will find examples of how the interpretation of biblical law is guided by its literary presentation.

H. Biblical law receives new expressions as God does more for Israel

If a fellow Hebrew, man or woman, is sold to you, he shall serve you six years, and in the seventh year you shall set him free. When you set him free, do not let him go empty-handed. Furnish him out of the flock, threshing floor, and vat, with which the LORD your God has blessed you. Bear in mind that you were slaves in the land of Egypt and the LORD your God redeemed you; therefore I enjoin this commandment upon you today.
—(Deuteronomy 15:12–15; *Moses speaking*)

Biblical law is dynamic. As we study it, we will see how Torah adapts itself to new circumstances. This is partly because, as we have seen, it is integrated into the story of God's involvement with Israel and the world—and this story keeps on developing. Because biblical law is embedded in a story arc, we must keep a constant eye on such things as plot, character, and setting. We need to know where we are "in the story" to be able to interpret biblical law. This contrasts with modern law, which is less inclined to indicate in its sources the processes that have led to its development.

A good example of the dynamism of biblical law is the story line that unfolds after the Exodus events. This results in changes to the characters and the setting. It is important for our understanding of biblical law because it helps to explain the differences between the *Mishpatim* in Exodus and the Deuteronomic laws. We discover that the people who came out of Egypt and who received Torah at

---

52. Ibid., 448.

Mount Sinai rebelled (with a few exceptions) against God in the wilderness and died without entering the promised land (Deuteronomy 1:19–45). This means that the promised land is inherited by the next generation, which was born in the wilderness. Because of this, Moses repeats the covenant that was given at Sinai to the new generation on the plains of Moab at the entrance to the promised land. But although the Moab covenant corresponds to the one at Sinai (Deuteronomy 5:2–5), it is not identical.

A classic example of the differences—and hence the dynamism of biblical law—is Deuteronomy 15:12–15, quoted above. This is the reason why this text is included in the Top Ten. This slavery law differs from the previous law on the release of slaves in Exodus 21:2–6 because Deuteronomy 15:12–15 enjoins generosity, while Exodus 21:2–6 does not.[53] The change in setting—a series of military victories that have led the Israelites to the entrance to the promised land—means that the Israelites have experienced much more of God's bounty than the previous generation (Deuteronomy 2:24–3:22). Moreover, they are going to experience much more of God's generosity when they enter the land. As a result, more is expected of them than the previous generation. This is why Deuteronomy makes frequent references to "the land which the LORD . . . gives you" (e.g., Deuteronomy 4:1).

Consequently, Moses's teaching in Deuteronomy 15:12–15, and Deuteronomy as a whole, reinterprets Sinai for a new generation. Biblical law is reexpressed to bring it up to date with changes in the biblical narrative which speaks of God's new acts of generosity toward Israel. This in turn results in a higher standard that is expected of Israel. Israel is now expected to behave even more generously toward God and others, including debt slaves, in response to God's new acts. Deuteronomy is not, of course, the only example of a reexpression of biblical law, which calls forth a higher standard of ethical behavior. Christians would see in the teaching of Jesus in the New Testament a reexpression of biblical law which calls for an even higher standard of ethical behavior (including, for example, the areas of divorce and remarriage; see Chapter 12). This response, Christians believe, is in keeping with changes in the biblical narrative which see in Jesus the ultimate demonstration of God's love and generosity toward Israel and the world.

The second main reason why biblical law is dynamic is because it is not complete, as we saw above. Because it is incomplete, it keeps being added to. A good example of this is the case of the daughters of Zelophehad (Numbers 27:1–11). In biblical law, there is a presumption that property devolved onto sons, not daughters (see Chapter 6). Zelophehad died without leaving a male heir, and his daughters petitioned Moses with a request to inherit his property (Numbers 27:4), on the occasion of entry to and division of the promised land. Although

---

53. For further differences, SEE JACKSON, WISDOM-LAWS, pp. 79–102.

this arrangement had not been provided for under existing biblical law, the daughters' appeal is emphatically vindicated by God:

> The daughters of Zelophehad are right; you shall give them possession of an inheritance among their father's brethren . . . .. (Numbers 27:7)

Nor is that the end of the matter. In Numbers 36, the Josephites (family heads of the clan to which Zelophehad belonged; Numbers 36:1) express concern that if the daughters receive the inheritance but marry outside the tribe, the land will be absorbed into their husband's family and thus into another tribe (see Chapter 6). This concern is also legitimated by God in somewhat similar terms to the daughters (Numbers 36:5–6). This example indicates that there is scope for innovation when biblical law is applied to unspecified cases. Biblical law is, in this sense, "up for grabs"—both by the daughters of Zelophehad and by the Josephites. God is portrayed as having new words to speak in view of life's ongoing twists and turns.

The case of the daughters of Zelophehad provides an unusual insight into the process by which legal innovations are received into the prevailing corpus.[54] Divine legal revelation is supplemented by fresh divine legal revelation, a process about which we are normally unaware. We know that biblical law is dynamic because we can see there is an interactive relationship between law and social process, as a result of which law is reinterpreted and transformed. The gaps in biblical law are opportunities for fresh revelation, and this makes biblical law dynamic. God is presented as being open to human questioning, and God's interaction with the questioning human party—whether the daughters of Zelophehad or the Josephites—leads to a fuller knowledge of the divine will.

I. Biblical law is an expression of wisdom

> *The teaching of the LORD* (Torat Adonai) *is perfect, renewing life; the decrees of the LORD are enduring, making the simple wise* (mahkhimat).
> —(Psalm 19:7/MT 19:8; *David speaking*; JPS)

Biblical law is an expression of wisdom *(hokhmah)*. It "covers a wide range of attributes that constitute wisdom in particular contexts,"[55] and so one-sentence summaries of biblical wisdom usually fail to capture its diversity. *Hokhmah* includes "the skill needed to win a war or complete a technical enterprise; the cleverness and shrewdness required in government or administration; the hidden secrets and knowledge of prophets or magicians; the prudence required to deal with difficult situations; the ability to make ethical . . . decisions, and ultimately the ability to discern God as the one who created the world through

---

54. Ibid., 426–27.
55. KATHARINE DELL, GET WISDOM, GET INSIGHT: AN INTRODUCTION TO ISRAEL'S WISDOM LITERATURE (London: Darton, Longman & Todd, 2000), 1.

wisdom and who is the fount of all knowledge and understanding."[56] The idea that biblical law is an expression of wisdom contrasts with modern law, which is usually seen as concentrating on minimum standards of obligatory behavior, viz., what citizens need to do to "stay on the right side of the law."

Wisdom needs to be distinguished from what is termed the biblical "wisdom literature" (including Proverbs and Job). This refers to those biblical materials that are specifically identified with the theme of wisdom; however, scholars recognize the influence of wisdom on other material in the Hebrew Bible, including biblical law. A further distinction is sometimes made between literary wisdom, which is the product of scribal activity and popular wisdom, which need not necessarily have existed in literary form and could have been generated orally by means of either a formal or an informal controlled oral tradition.[57]

There are a number of connections between biblical law and wisdom. First, there are numerous "sapiential counterpart[s]"[58] to biblical law in the Book of Proverbs, for example. Just as it is impossible to separate law from narrative, so it is impossible to separate law from other genres in the Bible, including, as here, proverbs. To take just one area of concern—the proper administration of justice— we find equivalents to the biblical prohibitions regarding partiality (Deuteronomy 16:18–19) and bribes (Exodus 23:8 and Deuteronomy 16:19) in the book of Proverbs (Proverbs 24:23; 28:21, respectively). Indeed, Exodus 23:8 and Deuteronomy 16:19 could be said to be "more proverbial than *Proverbs*" inasmuch as the legal texts use "a striking metaphor (blindness) to convey their message."[59] Many of the values of biblical law are also expressed in Proverbs (e.g., adultery is subject to the death penalty in biblical law and is also presented as "leading to death" in Proverbs 7:24–27). The point is that biblical law can be taught as wisdom rather than laws to be applied in a modern sense. We noted above that biblical law is incomplete and that its purpose is to teach wisdom, which is complete (see further Chapter 4).

Second, one of the functions of wisdom—which is evident from even the most cursory reading of Proverbs—is to provide practical guidance for daily living. One of the core competencies of the wise person in the Bible is the ability to resolve interpersonal disputes, which is part of the reason why wise people were appointed as Israel's judges (see Chapter 4). Likewise, one of the aims of biblical law is to provide an understanding of what to do in specific circumstances. One of the ways in which it does this is by formulating a number of

---

56. Ibid.
57. JACKSON, WISDOM-LAWS, p. 30 n. 137.
58. William P. Brown, *The law and the sages: A re-examination of Torah in Proverbs*, in CONSTITUTING THE COMMUNITY: STUDIES ON THE POLITY OF ANCIENT ISRAEL IN HONOUR OF S. DEAN MCBRIDE JR. (John T. Strong & Steven S. Tuell eds., Eisenbrauns: Winona Lake, 2005), 251–80, 255.
59. Jackson, *Law, wisdom and narrative*, pp. 34–35.

what Jackson[60] calls "self-executing rules," in other words, "rules of thumb" that enable a "rough and ready" resolution of the dispute in hand. An example of this is Exodus 21:35, quoted above, involving the bovicidal ox. The owner of the dead ox will only be compensated for his loss if the value of the live ox is equal to or greater in value to that of the dead ox. However, any "rough justice" is outweighed by the fact that the parties can resolve the matter quickly between themselves without the need to have recourse to arbitration by third parties or formal institutions.[61] Indeed, avoiding the shame of involving third parties in interpersonal disputes is itself a hallmark of wisdom (Proverbs 25:7–10). This leads into the final text in this Top Ten, which emphasises the importance of relationships in biblical law.

J. Biblical law is relational

Hear, O Israel: The LORD our God is one LORD; and you shall love the LORD your God with all your heart, and with all your soul, and with all your might.
—(Deuteronomy 6:4–5; *Moses speaking*)

Biblical law is relational because it is given in the context of God's desire for a relationship with Israel. God's command to Pharaoh, through Moses, is, "Let my people go, that they may hold a feast to me in the wilderness" (Exodus 5:1). This is a demand that Israel should be free to enter into a relationship with the ancestral deity. Pharaoh's response is telling: "Who is the LORD, that I should heed his voice and let Israel go? I do not know the LORD, and moreover I will not let Israel go" (Exodus 5:2). Pharaoh does not know the LORD; therefore, he is not able to obey him. Knowledge of God is a prerequisite for following Torah. Indeed, the giving of the law is preceded by a revelation of God's character, in the context of Israel's own experience: "I am the LORD your God, who brought you out of the land of Egypt, out of the house of bondage" (Exodus 20:2). These circumstances suggest that biblical law is intended to preserve Israel's newly won freedom and her relationship with God. The laws provide further opportunities for Israel to practice her faith in God, as she had done in the journey from Egypt. "Living by the law" is thus pictured as a dynamic relationship rather than as a duty. This is classically summed up in Deuteronomy 6:4–5, which is commonly known in Jewish tradition as the *Shema*. It is the most famous biblical text in modern Judaism, and it is the final case in our Top Ten.

Biblical law is relational because God "addresses Himself not, or not primarily, to individuals but to a people."[62] Israel is called not merely to a covenant relationship with God (see Chapter 2) but also, and as a consequence to, right

---

60. JACKSON, WISDOM-LAWS, pp. 29–30.
61. Jackson, *Law, wisdom and narrative*, p. 31.
62. Bernard Harrison, *The strangeness of* Leviticus, JUDAISM 48, 208–28, 216 (1999).

relationships within the body of the people—hence the law of Leviticus 19:17–18, which includes the command to "love your neighbour as yourself" (19:18). The "skull beneath the skin" of biblical law is concerned with promoting the quality of relationships in biblical society.

This concern for right relationships is reflected in the Hebrew term *tsedaqah* ("righteousness," although the word itself is not restricted to a concern for right relationships). "When people fulfil the conditions imposed on them by relationships, they are righteous."[63] *Tsedaqah* is the goal of *mishpat* (justice), and both "justice and righteousness" (*mishpat utsedaqah*) are major concerns of the prophets (e.g., Isaiah 56:1; see Chapter 4). Israel's righteousness is to be seen in her relationship with God, the nations, and at the level of relationships between individual Israelites. This is reflected in Jesus's response, in the New Testament, to the challenge of identifying relative priority within biblical law:

> One of them [the Pharisees], a lawyer, asked him [Jesus] a question, to test him. "Teacher, which is the great commandment in the law?" And he said to him, "You shall love the Lord your God with all your heart, and with all your soul, and with all your mind" [quoting Deuteronomy 6:5]. This is the great and first commandment. And a second is like it, "You shall love your neighbour as yourself" [quoting Leviticus 19:18]. On these two commandments depend all the law and the prophets. (Matthew 22:35–40; *narrator speaking*)

The relational values of biblical law are also seen in the following summary of Torah by Hillel (a Pharisaic teacher from the first century BC):

> Whatever you yourself hate, that do not do to your neighbour: in this is the whole Torah. The rest is but comment upon it. Go and take it as your guide! (Shabbat 31a).

The relational character of biblical law broadly contrasts with modern law, which has a predominantly individualistic approach.

There are a number of different aspects to "the relationships factor" and biblical law. First, it means individuals have to put "the interests of other parties to the relationship on a par with their own."[64] This is signified by Leviticus 19:17–18, quoted above. The Israelite's attitude toward others should not be, "what is the minimum I can get away with?," but "what is important is the quality of the continuation of the relationship between us." A practical example of this is Exodus 22:5/MT 22:4 where, in a case involving agricultural damage, the person responsible "shall make restitution (*yeshallem*) *from the best* in his own field (*meytabh sadehu*) and in his own vineyard". Jackson[65] has argued that the phrase *meytabh sadehu* may mean simply "the produce of his field" although even here,

---

63. Ibid., 16.
64. Harrison, *Strangeness of* Leviticus, p. 218.
65. Jackson, Wisdom-Laws, p. 325.

the semantic field of *yeshallem*, derived from a form of the verb *shalam*, which here means "to make good," points toward the restoration of social relationships between the parties. This is one way in which biblical law promoted social solidarity and relational well being.

Second, it means that individuals have to exercise positive concern and restraint in order to keep social relationships healthy. This involves something that is over and above "[the] terms of any legally enforceable contract."[66] We will see examples of this in Deuteronomy's concern for the "poor brother" (see 15:7–8, below). Here, a sense of obligation arises from the fact that the wealthy Israelite has been the recipient of God's generosity. Likewise, biblical law restrains the extent to which an Israelite can allow himself "to profit from the distress of another."[67] For example, we will see that the economic provisions of the Jubilee limit the degree to which one can profit from another person's hardship and indebtedness (Leviticus 25:39–41; see Chapter 7).

Third, Israel's vocation to be "the people of God" is something that "comes into being as the precipitate of innumerable well-conducted relationships between individual and individual,"[68] as well as between each individual and God. The sense of "belonging to a people" is thus "relationship led," as opposed to being, say, "project led" in which the people are asked to give their allegiance to "an overarching social project of some sort" (such as Communism or Fascism[69]).

Finally, biblical law is relational because relationships are at the heart of practical reasoning about law in the Bible. "Eliciting the further requirements of a basic moral stance is not to be understood [*per* the Enlightenment] . . . by analogy with the deductive unpacking of theorems from a set of axioms, but in terms of the extension of relationships."[70] The application of biblical law is relational, not propositional. A good example of this is found in Leviticus 19:34:

> The stranger (*ger*) who sojourns with you shall be to you as the native among you, and you shall love him as yourself; for you were strangers (*gerim*) in the land of Egypt: I am the LORD your God.

Behavior toward the *ger* is conceived as an extension of several relationships: the Israelite's relationship with their fellow citizens, their own experience of having been *gerim*, and their relationship with God.

It is because biblical law "hinges upon the lived character of relationships" that the first requirement for understanding biblical law is "wisdom" rather

---

66. Harrison, *Strangeness of* Leviticus, p. 218.
67. Ibid., 219.
68. Ibid., 218.
69. Ibid.
70. Ibid., 220.

than, say, reason or logic.[71] An important aspect of wisdom is the ability to grasp the significance and nature of relationships and so to be capable of making shrewd, clever, and prudent decisions in different areas of life (see Chapter 4). This is not to say that biblical law does not also require reason and logic, but it is to say that wisdom is the cornerstone of biblical law, and this is reflected in a concern for the quality of relationships.

On this reading, the purpose of biblical law is to enable us to love God and to love our neighbor. Biblical law is a guide on how to love appropriately. However, this is not merely an agenda for improved interpersonal contact; it is also an agenda for institutions. In biblical law, love for God, and love for neighbor influences the design of our financial and lending relationships, our political relationships, our conditions of employment, our impact upon the environment, and so on. Love is institutionalized. The challenge is to see how biblical law advances being about something more than just an interpersonal agenda, important though that is. It is to recognize that biblical law goes far beyond this to inform the whole of politics and public administration. This means that from the perspective of biblical law, "spiritual jurisprudence" goes far beyond the mere recognition that belief in God, in one form or another, is among the influences upon law and legal practice. Instead, it sees the law as having a transcendent reference point in the God of Israel and that its primary concern is with promoting love for God and neighbor. Its goal is to develop a worldview that is shaped at every point by an understanding of what it means to live a life of love as persons made in the image of God and which, in turn, feeds into our understanding and aspirations regarding the sort of world we want to live in.

II. CONCLUSION

Making sense of biblical law from the distance of our modern twenty-first century means being aware of those things that were part of the presupposition pool of biblical society at the time, especially in relation to law and its social practice. This presupposition pool includes the things that biblical Israel took for granted and that we might not know. We have seen that biblical law is similar to ancient Near Eastern (ANE) law in certain respects and to this extent, ANE law can be used to generate hypotheses and explain aspects of biblical law that cannot be explained from the Bible itself. This is preferable to making presuppositions based on our own cultural context because of the increased distance of modern law from biblical law, when compared to ANE law. At the same time, though, biblical law is also different from ANE law in a number of key respects, and this sets limits to the comparability of ANE and biblical law. Modern law is even

---

71. Ibid.

further removed from biblical law, and so we have to be careful not to project things from our own modern presupposition pool onto biblical law. This includes not imposing a semantic reading on biblical law when a narrative reading is appropriate.

Biblical law is not presented as codified law but is integrated, at every stage, into the wider story of God's purposes for Israel and, beyond that, for the world. It is also bound up with the vocation of Israel and the call that she should "be" a certain quality of people and reflect the character of God to the nations. Unlike modern law, biblical law offers a limited number of rules that are primarily designed to have a teaching function. To this end, biblical law is also characterized by rhetoric and sophisticated literary presentation, while also being relational, dynamic, and an expression of wisdom. As we progress through the remainder of this book, we will try to pay attention to all these features. This is part of what it means to take biblical law seriously.

Selected reading

Samuel Greengus, "Biblical and ANE Law." In *Anchor Bible Dictionary*, edited by David Noel Freedman, 6 vols. (London: Doubleday, 1992), vol. IV, pp. 242–252.

Bernard Harrison, "The strangeness of *Leviticus*," *Judaism* 48 (1999), 208–228.

Bernard S. Jackson, "The ceremonial and the judicial: Biblical law as sign and symbol," *Journal for the Study of the Old Testament* 30 (1984), 25–50.

Joe M. Sprinkle, "Law and narrative in Exodus 19–24," *Journal of the Evangelical Theological Society* 47 (2004), 235–252.

Raymond Westbrook, "Biblical and cuneiform law codes," *Revue Biblique* 92 (1985), 247–264.

2. A DEAL WITH GOD

There are two things that almost everyone knows about biblical law—that Abraham's descendants are a "chosen people" and that God gave Moses "the Ten Commandments." What few realize is that these fragments of popular knowledge are connected by one "big idea" which is often overlooked, not least in relation to the Ten Commandments themselves. Thus, a campaign to find an "Eleventh Commandment," which was launched on beer mats throughout the United Kingdom, produced a range of responses that reflect the popular view of the Ten Commandments as a sort of ethical "shopping list." Notable entries included "Thou shalt not change allegiance if thy football team is relegated," and "Thou shalt not dump thy lover by text."[1] The "big idea" that gets submerged in all this is the idea of a "covenant." Indeed, covenant is much bigger even than the idea of a particular "chosen people" because covenant is the key way in which God relates to human beings generally. It is precisely because covenant is a distinctive mode of God's operation with humanity that it is a good place from which to begin our subject-specific analysis of biblical law.

The word covenant can mean many different things in both the Bible and the ancient Near East (ANE). Basically, it consists of an obligation or an agreement between two parties. Covenants were an everyday fact of ancient life, like writing a check, making a promise, or doing a deal. This chapter will begin by looking at how covenants are used in the Bible and the ANE before taking an overview of the basic "covenant formula" which recurs throughout the biblical texts. We will then take a synoptic view of the main turning points in the history of covenantal relations between God and humanity. This includes the covenant between God and Abraham and between God and Israel at Mount Sinai. The Sinai covenant itself includes the story of Moses delivering the Ten Commandments, and this will also be explored. Finally, we will reflect on the place of "new covenant" language in both the Hebrew Bible and the Christian New Testament. This approach has the advantage of reminding us of the story arc that sweeps its way through the Bible, while at the same time, bringing into greater focus the way in which biblical law operates.

I. DEAL OR NO DEAL

We begin by looking at how covenants were used in the Bible and the ANE. The purpose of this chapter is to provide a synoptic overview of covenant and so

---

1. *The Times*, April 6, 2004.

throughout this chapter (as explained in the Introduction), we will be taking a synchronic "final form" reading of the text. A covenant (*berit*) refers to "the binding commitment taken on by one or both of the parties to an agreement, or even a unilateral decision."[2] The obligatory nature of the agreement is reflected in the fact that one or both parties swear an oath, although this is not always explicit.[3]

The word *berit* is used hundreds of times in the Bible, in a variety of settings. There are many different kinds of covenant in the ANE and the Bible, including: (1) a treaty between independent nations (e.g., 1 Kings 5:12/MT 5:26); (2) a constitutional agreement between a king and his subjects (e.g., 2 Samuel 5:3); (3) the marriage relationship (e.g., Malachi 2:14); (4) a pledge between friends (e.g., 1 Samuel 20:8); (5) a treaty between an empire and a vassal state (e.g., Ezekiel 17:11–21[4]); and (6) settlement of a dispute between parties (e.g., Genesis 21:27).

The precise nature of the agreement in any given case is determined by the context. For example, both the covenant at Mount Sinai—at least insofar as we can reconstruct it (see further below)—and the covenant at Moab (Deuteronomy) have characteristics in common with Hittite vassal treaties[5] and the Laws of Hammurabi. (A vassal treaty is an agreement between a conquering overlord and a compliant people who become his "vassal" or dependent). However, it is not the case that the vassal treaty form is inherent to the meaning of the word *berit*. Rather, the nature of the covenant is derived from the context. In the case of the covenants at Sinai and Moab, the claim that they are "vassal treaties" is derived, for example, from the "victorious conqueror" language found in the opening words of the Ten Commandments (and cf. also Exodus 19:4):

> I am the LORD your God, who brought you out of the land of Egypt, out of the house of bondage. (Exodus 20:2)

Traces of the victorious conqueror form are also found in other biblical covenants (e.g., Genesis 9:12–17, 15:7; Deuteronomy 3:1–11; Joshua 23:2, 9–10; 24:5–12).

The vassal treaty is a common form of covenant in the ANE. Indeed, we can compare the biblical covenants with about eighty to ninety ANE treaties, law collections, and covenants; the latter covering a period from around 2500–650 BC.[6]

---

2. Jan Joosten, *Covenant theology in the holiness code*, ZEITSCHRIFT FÜR ALTORIENTALISCHE UND BIBLISCHE RECTSGESCHICHTE 4, 145–164, 148 (1998).

3. PAUL R. WILLIAMSON, SEALED WITH AN OATH: COVENANT IN GOD'S UNFOLDING PURPOSE, NEW STUDIES IN BIBLICAL THEOLOGY (Downers-Grove: Apollos/InterVarsity Press, 2007).

4. Joosten, *Covenant theology*.

5. *See* MOSHE WEINFELD, DEUTERONOMY AND THE DEUTERONOMIC SCHOOL (Oxford: Clarendon Press, 1972), 59–72.

6. D. J. MCCARTHY, TREATY AND COVENANT (Rome: Biblical Institute Press, 1978), and more recently, KENNETH A. KITCHEN, ON THE RELIABILITY OF THE OLD TESTAMENT (Grand Rapids: Eerdmans, 2003).

In particular, Kitchen[7] finds close structural similarities between the covenant at Sinai and the Hittite treaty corpus (which includes 30 Hittite-inspired documents and versions). Covenants were thus a part of the social world of the Bible and the ANE (including Egypt, Ugarit, and Qatna[8]). So too were stories of divine involvement in lawmaking, such as the famous Hammurabi stela, dated to around 1750 BC, which portrays the Babylonian King Hammurabi standing before the sun god Shamash, the god of justice. Even so, there are important differences between the biblical and ANE materials (see further below).

Turning from ancient to modern law, we note that "covenant" in English law means something different from biblical law. For medieval English lawyers, the word "covenant" (*conventio*) meant what we nowadays understand by a contract, that is, a legally binding agreement (and cf. the use of the word "convention" to describe a treaty in modern international law). However, as a result of historical changes in the English common law, the word "contract" assumed the meaning formerly carried by the word "covenant."[9] The result is that, in modern English law, the word "covenant" now has a narrow meaning within the law of property. The modern covenant is "an undertaking contained in a deed by which one party ("the covenantor") promises another party ('the covenantee') that he will or will not engage in some specified activity in relation to a defined area of land"[10] (for example, the use of a restrictive covenant to prevent building on land).

More broadly, it should be noted that while modern lawyers are familiar with the law of gift and the law of contract, the biblical covenant does not fit either of these models because it has elements of both and neither.

The biblical covenant has elements of the law of gift inasmuch as God is presented as taking the initiative and bestowing unconditional favors upon Abraham and his descendants (e.g., Genesis 15). It also has elements of the law of contract: first, because there is a voluntary "offer and acceptance" (e.g., Exodus 19:5–6; though cf. Shabbat 88a, in the Babylonian Talmud, which presents the Israelites accepting under duress). Second, it contains terms that are, in a sense, "finite and reducible to writing."[11] Indeed, some versions of the Bible translate *diberey habbhrit* ("the words of the covenant"; Deuteronomy 29:1/ MT 28:69) as "the *terms* of the covenant" (JPS). Third, and related to this, the biblical covenant

---

7. KITCHEN, RELIABILITY OF THE OLD TESTAMENT; Kenneth A. Kitchen, *The patriarchal age: myth or history?* BIBLICAL ARCHAEOLOGY REV. 21, 48–57, 88–95, 106 (1995).

8. Kenneth A. Kitchen, *Egypt, Ugarit, Qatna & covenant, in* UGARIT-FORSCHUNGEN (Kurt Bergerhof, Manfried Dietrich & Oswald Loretz eds., Neukirchen Vluyn: Neukirchener Verlag 1979), 453–64.

9. J. H. BAKER, AN INTRODUCTION TO ENGLISH LEGAL HISTORY (Bath: Butterworths, 4th ed. 2002), 317–18.

10. KEVIN GRAY & SUSAN FRANCIS GRAY, ELEMENTS OF LAND LAW (Oxford: Oxford University Press, 4th ed. 2005), 1349.

11. Louis E. Newman, *Covenant and contract: A framework for the analysis of Jewish ethics*, J. LAW & RELIGION 9, 89–112, 98 (1991).

contains terms that make it clear what would constitute a breach, akin to a modern contract (e.g., Deuteronomy 28:15–68). Fourth, like a modern contract, it is possible to terminate a biblical covenant (e.g., the golden calf episode in Exodus 32, see below), although whether God ever actually does so is open to question (cf. Hosea 1:9).[12] Fifth, modern contractual analyses are also helpful in terms of identifying who takes the initiative and what God gives in order for the Israelites to accept him as their sovereign. Finally, the modern contractual paradigm sees contracts as conferring personal and property rights that are durable because they bind future persons who take the benefit and so, to this extent, we might say that the biblical covenant evokes the durability associated with a property right.

At the same time, however, there are major differences between the biblical covenant and the modern contract. First, the biblical covenants concern a relationship between God and humanity. The "radically unequal power" of the partners to this relationship consequently distinguishes it from any legal relationship between human persons.[13] Second, and related to this, although the terms of the covenant are in one sense finite, they are, in another sense, "potentially infinite [because] they arise not from the text of *Torah*, or even from the interpretations of that text, but from living in relationship with God."[14] Finally, the biblical covenant has a unique durability: "God, being eternal, has the ability to enter into a relationship which transcends the time limits of individual human lives, or even of whole generations."[15] God is understood to make a covenant not only with the present generation of Israelites but with succeeding generations as well (e.g., Deuteronomy 5:2–4; see further below). In these respects, the biblical covenant is radically different to modern legal contracts (although it still has some affinity with international treaties that bind "states" in perpetuity).

This brief comparison of biblical covenants and modern contracts raises the interesting question whether the biblical covenant is truly voluntary. Certainly the covenant appears to be voluntary in the case of the Exodus generation (see above). But is this equally true for subsequent generations? For example, how should we understand the significance, for later generations, of the Torah readings described in Deuteronomy 31:10–13? Are such readings merely reminders of covenantal obligations that the Israelites were born into? Is their choice merely whether to break it or not? The notion that a person "[can] truly be born into

---

12. Ibid., 92–101.
13. Ibid., 91.
14. Ibid., 98.
15. Ibid., 92.

specific obligations and responsibilities without their consent"[16] is, of course, one that is familiar to many modern Jews.[17]

Finally, we need to recognize—at the outset—that the subject of "covenant" is at the heart of theological differences between Jews and Christians. To speak of continuity between the covenants of the Hebrew Bible and that of the New Testament is to devalue, from a Jewish perspective, the covenant(s) of the Hebrew Bible. Likewise, to stress *discontinuity* between the covenants is to devalue, from a Christian perspective, the New Testament (which itself means "new covenant"). There is always a cost to the one or other group. This chapter aims to present the material in such a way that the covenants of the Hebrew Bible can be read on their own terms, but not exclusively, on their own terms. It thus takes seriously the possibility that covenantal texts in the Hebrew Bible and New Testament can be read in more than one direction, that is, from the Hebrew Bible to the New Testament and vice versa.[18]

II. THE DIVINE CONCORDAT

Covenant is a mode of interaction between God and human beings. It is a universal form of divine relating, which is partly why there are so many covenants in the Bible. Covenant is the key way in which God relates to human beings, and as we look at covenants in the Bible, we will see how this form of interaction grows and develops.

The first reference to covenant in the Hebrew Bible is found in Genesis 6:17–18, where it refers to God's covenant with Noah and his family. This ensures that they survive the catastrophic flood that God is described as bringing upon the earth (Genesis 7). Although this covenant seems quite specific, it is clear from the narrative that the covenant with Noah is intended to provide for the survival of creation as a whole. This is explicit in the so-called "universal covenant" in Genesis 9:1–17, which is said to be between Noah, his descendants, and all creation (see further Chapter 5). It is impossible to imagine a more inclusive covenant than this.

It is important to emphasize that covenant in the Bible can have a universal character. For the remainder of this chapter, we will concentrate on the primary way in which covenant is worked through in the Bible, namely, in the context of the specific relationship between God and Israel. However, as we do this,

---

16. Jonathan Sacks, Radical Then, Radical Now: On Being Jewish (London: Continuum, 2000), 28.

17. Sacks, Radical Then.

18. Brooks Schramm, *Exodus 19 & its Christian appropriation, in* Jews, Christians and the Theology of the Hebrew Scriptures (Alice Ogden Bellis & Joel S. Kaminsky eds., Atlanta: Society of Biblical Literature, 2000), 326–51.

we need to keep in mind that early on in the biblical canon, covenant has been established as a universal mode of divine-human interaction.

As we turn to the specific relationship between God and Israel, we find that although there are many different forms of covenant in the Bible, the covenant between God and Israel is presented in terms of a basic "covenant formula." This can be expressed in the form, "I . . . will be your God, and you shall be my people" (e.g., Leviticus 26:12). This runs through the Bible like lettering through a stick of rock (see Table 3, below).

As Rolf Rendtorff notes, "The linguistic formulations [of the covenant between God and Israel] are firmly fixed."[19] The recurrence of the covenant formula, together with the fact that the Hebrew Bible only ever refers to the word *berit* in the singular, makes it difficult to speak of different covenants—plural—between God and Israel.[20] This suggests that it is more accurate to speak of a single covenant than a multiplicity of covenants. The idea of a single covenant is deeply rooted in Israel's traditions. First, from the divine perspective, there is only

TABLE 3 OVERVIEW OF COVENANT FORMULA

Text	Formula
Exodus 6:7 [*God speaking*]	"I will *take* you for my people, and I will be your God"
Exodus 19:5 [*God speaking*]	"[I]f you will obey my voice and keep my covenant, you shall be my own possession among all peoples"
Exodus 29:45 [*God speaking*]	"I will *dwell among* the people of Israel, and will be their God"
Leviticus 26:12 [*God speaking*]	"I will *walk among you*, and will be your God, and you shall be my people"
Deuteronomy 26:17-18 [*Moses speaking*]	"You have declared this day concerning the LORD that he is your God. . .; and the LORD has declared this day concerning you that you are a people for his own possession. . ."
Jeremiah 31:33 [*God speaking*]	"I will be their God, and they shall be my people"
Jeremiah 32:38 [*God speaking*]	"[T]hey shall be my people, and I will be their God"
Ezekiel 34:30 [*God speaking*]	"[T]hey shall know that I, the LORD their God, am with them, and that they, the house of Israel, are my people. . ."

---

19. Rolf Rendtorff, The Covenant Formula: an Exegetical and Theological Investigation, translated by Margaret Kohl, Old Testament Studies (Edinburgh: T&T Clark 1998), 79.

20. Rendtorff, Covenant Formula.

one covenant. This is because although Israel breaks the covenant many times (cf., Leviticus 26:15), God promises to keep the covenant (Leviticus 26:44). Second, God's initial covenant with Abraham is referred to in "once-for-all" terms as an "everlasting covenant" (Genesis 17:7, 19), although of course it is true that different facets of it receive different emphases at different times. Third, as we will see, events such as Israel's encounter with God at Mount Sinai are *not* seen as supplying a separate, additional covenant. Instead, an event such as the deal with God at Mount Sinai is "regarded rather as a constituent element *within* the one covenant."[21] Finally, it is striking that Nehemiah's corporate declaration of repentance and confession (Nehemiah 9), which is presented as taking place on return from exile, recounts Israel's history in terms of a *single* covenant, that is, the covenant with Abraham (Nehemiah 9:8).

The heart of the "everlasting covenant" is God's commitment to being God for Israel: ". . . to be God to you and to your descendants to come" (Genesis 17:7). What God's "being God for Israel" means exactly depends on the particular context. As a result, the covenant formula is frequently linked with "other formula-like elements or expressions which touch on the relationships between God and Israel."[22] These elements include God dwelling among the people of Israel (Exodus 29:42b–46), calling Israel to share in God's holiness (Leviticus 11:45), giving Israel the land (Leviticus 25:38), and demonstrating God's power before the nations (Leviticus 26:45[23]).

Variations in the covenant formula also arise because the everlasting covenant is inevitably colored, to some degree, by the nature of the issues facing the human parties. This is illustrated by an overview of the key covenantal texts (see Table 4 below). (It should be noted that the distinction between "unilateral" and "bilateral" in the final column distinguishes between those cases when God does not tell the other party how they are to respond (unilateral cases) from other covenants where a given response is expected (bilateral cases). Of course, in both unilateral and bilateral cases, the covenant itself is nonnegotiable, and hence, the latter are not bilateral in a modern sense).

This shows how God binds himself to the party's problems so that they, in turn, can be bonded to God's promises.[24] Thus, the covenant with Abram reflects his anxiety about being childless, the covenants with Isaac and Jacob relate to their fears about famine and vengeance, and so on. The varying expressions of God's covenant with Israel thus reflect changes in the relationship between God and Israel. They mark key points in the story of God and his people. As a result,

---

21. Schramm, Exodus 19, p. 342, italics original.
22. RENDTORFF, COVENANT FORMULA, p. 39.
23. RENDTORFF, COVENANT FORMULA.
24. Adapting WALTER BRUEGGEMANN, THE COVENANTED SELF: EXPLORATIONS IN LAW AND COVENANT (Minneapolis: Fortress, 1999), 7.

TABLE 4 KEY TURNING POINTS IN COVENANTAL RELATIONS BETWEEN GOD AND ABRAHAM, AND HIS DESCENDANTS

#	Text	Party to divine covenant	Party's problems	Divine promises [God speaking]	Unilateral/bilateral
1	Genesis 15	Abram	Childlessness (15:2-3)	(1) Descendants as numerous as the stars (15:5); (2) Promise of land (15:18-21)	Unilateral (God)
2	Genesis 17:2-14	Abraham	Lack of descendants	(1) 'I will make you exceedingly fruitful, and I will make nations of you; (2) and kings shall come forth from you' (17:6); (3) 'I will give to you, and to your descendants after you, the land of your sojournings, all the land of Canaan, for an everlasting possession' (17:8)	Bilateral (17:9)
3	Genesis 26	Isaac	Famine (26:1)	(1) 'I will multiply your descendants as the stars of heaven' (26:4a); (2) '[I] will give to your descendants all these lands; and by your descendants all the nations of the earth shall bless themselves' (26:4b)	Bilateral (26:2-3)
4	Genesis 28:13-15	Jacob	Threat to life (27:41-45); quest for wife (27:46-28:2)	(1) 'the land on which you lie I will give to you and to your descendants' (28:13); (2) 'your descendants shall be like the dust of the earth' (28:14)	N/A
5	Exodus 6:2-8	Israel	Slavery (6:5)	'I will bring you out from under the burdens of the Egyptians, and I will deliver you from their bondage... and I will take you for my people, and I will be your God' (6:6-7)	Unilateral (God)
6	Exodus 19:3-6	Israel	Slavery	'You have seen what I did to the Egyptians, and how I bore you on eagles' wings and brought you to myself. Now therefore, if you will obey my voice and keep my covenant, you shall be my own possession among all peoples... a kingdom of priests and a holy nation' (19:4-6)	Bilateral (19:5)

#	Reference	Party	Problem	Quote	Type
7	Exodus 24	Israel	Slavery	Moses came and told the people all the words of the LORD and all the ordinances; and all the people answered with one voice, and said, 'All the words which the LORD has spoken we will do' (24:3)	Bilateral (24:3)
8	Exodus 34:10-27	Israel	Need to resolve breach of covenant following golden calf episode (Exodus 32)	'Behold, I make a covenant. Before all your [Moses'] people I will do marvels, such as have not been wrought in all the earth or in any nation...' (34:10)	Bilateral (34:11-27)
9	Deuteronomy 5ff	Israel	Wandering/Landlessness	'For the LORD your God is bringing you into a good land, a land of brooks of water, of fountains and springs, flowing forth in valleys and hills.... And you shall eat and be full, and you shall bless the LORD your God for the good land he has given you' (e.g. 8:7, 10)	Bilateral (e.g. 5:1-3)
10	Jeremiah 31:31-34	Israel	Unfaithfulness	'... I will make a new covenant... not like the covenant which I made with their fathers.... But this is the covenant which I will make.... I will put my law ['Teaching'; JPS] within them, and I will write it upon their hearts...' (31:31-33)	Unilateral (God)
11	Ezekiel 37	Israel	Physical and spiritual exile	'I will make a covenant of peace with them.... I will bless them and multiply them, and will set my sanctuary in the midst of them for evermore' (37:26)	Unilateral (God)
12	Luke 22:19-20	Jesus' followers	Spiritual exile	And [Jesus] took bread, and when he had given thanks he broke it and gave it to them, saying, 'This is my body which is given for you. Do this in remembrance of me.' And likewise the cup after supper, saying, 'This cup which is poured out for you is the new covenant in my blood' (22:19-20)	Unilateral (Jesus)

covenant is a particularly good example of the way in which biblical law embodies narrative.

There are several reasons why there are multiple expressions of the covenant formula in the Hebrew Bible, as well as in the New Testament. Bernard Jackson[25] identifies three main types of covenant ceremonies: (1) *confirmation and incorporation*, that is, ceremonies that clarify or confirm who belongs to the covenant, or incorporate new groups of people; (2) *reaffirmation*, that is, ceremonies where there is "reason to doubt the strength of the previous commitment"[26]; and (3) *revision*, that is, where the content of the covenant is "revised . . . or supplemented by reference to a new text."[27] Revision differs from the previous two types of covenant ceremonies where the content of the covenant is not altered. Jackson[28] objects to the use of "renewal" to describe certain covenant ceremonies, on the ground that there is no phrase in the Bible for "to renew a covenant." However, this does not mean that we cannot use the word "renewal." There is a sense in which the word "renewal" can be used of covenants of confirmation and incorporation because it is a continuation of an existing agreement (e.g., "renewing" a subscription), whether that agreement is modified in format or content, or not. It can also be used of covenants of "reaffirmation" (e.g., the reaffirmation or renewal of wedding vows). Renewal simply means reaffirmation of the existing relationship, albeit in varying formats. Although it is not always appreciated that "to renew" is not the same as "new," this chapter eschews the use of the word "renewal" to avoid any confusion on the part of those who might think that renewal means entirely new.

III. CLOSE ENCOUNTERS OF THE DIVINE KIND

We are now in a position to identify some of the key turning points in the history of covenantal relations between God and Abraham (and his descendants). As noted earlier, we will adopt a synchronic, "final form" approach to the subject, in the interests of providing a clear overview. This chapter is not a comprehensive tour of every covenant mentioned in the Bible[29] but rather a synopsis of key transitional moments (see Table 4 above). As mentioned, the covenant with Noah and creation is considered in Chapter 5, and so we will begin here with Genesis

---

25. BERNARD S. JACKSON, STUDIES IN THE SEMIOTICS OF BIBLICAL LAW, JOURNAL FOR THE STUDY OF THE OLD TESTAMENT SUPPLEMENT SERIES 314 (Sheffield: Sheffield Academic Press, 2000).
26. Ibid., 233.
27. Ibid.
28. Ibid., 232.
29. For which, *see* WILLIAMSON, SEALED WITH AN OATH.

15 and the covenant with Abram. Some brief comments on each turning point listed in Table 4 are in order.

We begin by considering the first covenant event in Table 4, God's covenant with Abram (later "Abraham") in Genesis 15. God's covenant with Abram follows on from God's call of Abram in Genesis 12:1–3, which as we saw in Chapter 1, is pivotal to the structure of Genesis as a whole because it links Chapters 1–11 with Chapters 12–50. Indeed we can see God's covenant with Abraham in Genesis 15 (and Genesis 17) as being an expansion of the call of Abraham. God promises Abram a hereditary blessing (Genesis 15:13–16), while verse 18 states, "To your descendants I give this land . . .". Because the blessing is hereditary, it is hard to see why God's dealings with subsequent generations should be characterized as covenant renewals. There is no need for renewal because the qualifying descendants are explicitly included in the covenant with Abram (including Isaac, for example). However, since not all of Abraham's descendants qualified, there is a need for some covenant of confirmation or incorporation with subsequent generations to show which of Abraham's descendants are the intended beneficiaries (thus Isaac and not Ishmael, for example, though Ishmael is not entirely left out; Genesis 17:23, 26; 21:18). This is a different question from covenant renewal.[30]

We turn next to the second covenant event in Table 4, which is the "covenant of circumcision" in Genesis 17:2–14. Here, God restates his covenant with Abraham (as he is now called). This time the hereditary promise/blessing is accompanied by a reciprocal obligation, namely male circumcision, which, in turn, is hereditary (Genesis 17:9–14[31]). Jackson[32] argues that this does not undercut the unilateral nature of the covenant: it is a self-interested sign of being a beneficiary. It is a ceremony of confirmation because it confirms who belongs to the covenant. There are close similarities between the covenant pericopes in Genesis 15 and 17, but equally, there are significant discontinuities, chief among which is the international dimension, emphasizing that Abraham will become "the father of a multitude of nations."[33] This idea of becoming "father," that is, a "spiritual benefactor"[34] to the nations picks up the promise of Genesis 12:3, according to which God promises Abraham that "all the families of the earth shall bless themselves because of you" (JPS). It is this international dimension that is alluded to in subsequent covenantal developments (e.g., Exodus 19:6; Ezekiel 37:28).

---

30. JACKSON, STUDIES, pp. 239–40.
31. Ibid., 239.
32. Ibid., 243.
33. PAUL R. WILLIAMSON, ABRAHAM, ISRAEL & THE NATIONS: THE PATRIARCHAL PROMISE AND ITS COVENANTAL DEVELOPMENT IN GENESIS, JOURNAL FOR THE STUDY OF THE OLD TESTAMENT SUPPLEMENT SERIES 315 (Sheffield: Sheffield Academic Press, 2000).
34. Ibid., 216.

A. The mark of Israel

The covenant of circumcision raises the question of why the sign of the covenant is applied to the penis "rather than upon some other, sexually-neutral, body part."[35] Unlike other "signs" in the Bible, no explanation is given in the text itself (cf. Exodus 13:9; 31:13). One traditional explanation is that because the promise to Abraham involved descendants, the symbol of the covenant is applied to the penis as the organ of generativity.[36]

However, there is, in my view, a further way of understanding circumcision which takes account of the uniqueness of the relationship between God, Abraham, and his descendants. Writing from an anthropological perspective, Meir Malul notes that "the [circumcised] penis, by virtue of being 'peeled' of its covering membrane and made visible . . . belongs to the sphere of knownness."[37] The exposure of "the hitherto covered male member, was understood as tantamount to *uncovering* the whole man, making him *known*, and thus transferring him from the status of 'unknown' to that of 'known'. . .."[38] Malul's anthropological reasoning can be applied quite specifically to the covenant with Abraham. Circumcision is an apt sign of the covenant because the people of the covenant are defined as those who both "know" God and who are known by him in a special way (e.g., Amos 3:2). Both knowledge and circumcision are the distinguishing marks of Israel.

The third covenant event in Table 4 is the covenant with Isaac in Genesis 26:24. This is the first occasion where the promise to Abraham is repeated and confirmed to the second generation ("The Lord appeared to [Isaac] and said . . ."; Genesis 26:2a). This resolves any doubt which there may have been about the status of Isaac: he is going to be the next direct recipient of the hereditary blessing. Something similar happens in the covenant with Jacob in Genesis 28:13–15. God communicates the hereditary blessing directly to one of Isaac's sons, Jacob. This confirms and incorporates Jacob and his descendants into the Abrahamic covenant. Jackson claims there seems to be "an assumption that the hereditary blessing does not descend *automatically*."[39] There has to be some form of explicit incorporation, such as a speech act[40] of succession or a restatement of the promise by God himself.[41]

---

35. Meir Malul, Knowledge, Control & Sex: Studies in biblical thought, culture and worldview (Tel Aviv-Jaffa: Archaeological Centre Publication, 2002), 396.

36. An overview of some of the different interpretations of circumcision can be found in Gordon Wenham, *Genesis 16-50*, Word Biblical Commentary (Dallas: Waco, 1994), 23–24.

37. Malul, Knowledge, Control & Sex, p. 395.

38. Ibid., 403–04, italics original.

39. Jackson, Studies, p. 243, italics original.

40. A speech act is an action that we perform, or that we try to perform, by means of speech.

41. Ibid.

The covenant between God and Israel in Exodus 6:2–8 (see Table 4) refers back to the covenants with "Abraham, Isaac and Jacob" (6:2). Clearly, the covenant with Israel is seen as a constituent element within the covenant with Abraham. There are close thematic links between Genesis and Exodus. At the start of Exodus, Pharaoh is presented as a threat to Israel's existence, and hence to the fulfillment of the Abrahamic promise (Exodus 1:8–22). The covenant formula in Exodus 6:7 is of great significance because we find that, for the first time, Israel is large enough to be called a "people" (*'am*). Consequently, the formula signals the partial fulfillment of the Abrahamic covenant.

B. Fused horizons

The covenant with Israel at Mount Sinai in Exodus 19:3–6 (see Table 4) confirms and incorporates the Exodus generation into the Abrahamic covenant. The requirement to "keep My covenant"—once restricted to Abraham (Genesis 17:9)—is now extended to Israel as a whole (Exodus 19:5). However, the meaning of "keeping the covenant" is no longer focused on circumcision (cf. Genesis 17:10–14): rather, it is now extended to "obeying God's voice" ("if you will obey my voice and keep my covenant"; Exodus 19:5). Exodus 19:6 marks the point at which Israel first becomes a nation and thus can be seen as partial fulfillment of Genesis 12:2 when God promises Abraham, "I will make of you a great nation (*goy*)." This reminds us that one of the functions of thematic repetition in biblical law is to provide formal recognition that what has been promised by God has actually happened, in one sense or another.[42] It provides official recognition of the fact that the God of the biblical covenants is a promise-making *and* a promise-keeping God.

The covenant at Sinai is really a calling and a vocation: "you shall be to me a kingdom of priests and a holy nation (*goy*)" (Exodus 19:6). This is not surprising: the covenant with Israel's ancestor, Abraham, was also the product of a calling (Genesis 12:1-3). Israel is a nation "set apart" to serve the nations in the same way as a priest is a person "set apart" to serve other people (see Chapter 1). Exodus 19 thus holds together the particular (priestly Israel) and the universal (the nations). This parallels the covenant with Abraham in Genesis 17, according to which Abraham is said to be a spiritual benefactor to the nations. This too holds together the particular (Abraham, the spiritual father) with the universal (the nations). Consequently, Sinai is rightly characterized as a "vocational" covenant (in the sense of a "calling") within the context of the Abrahamic covenant.

Part of Israel's covenant at Sinai involves a blood ceremony (Exodus 24:3–8; see Table 4). What distinguishes this covenant from the others is the combination of a ritual reading with a covenantal affirmation of the law and a sacrificial ritual. The public reading and oral acceptance of the "book of the covenant"

---

42. Ibid., 234–35.

(Exodus 24:7) is sandwiched between two parts of a blood ritual (Exodus 24:4b–6; 24:8). The blood itself is designated "the blood of the covenant which the LORD has made with you in accordance with all these words" (Exodus 24:8). It is a covenant of incorporation which—even more graphically than the covenant of Exodus 19—incorporates the Exodus generation into the Abrahamic covenant and symbolizes the union of God and Israel.

The eighth covenant event in Table 4 is that between God and Israel in Exodus 34. This follows Israel's breach of the covenant at Sinai by worshipping the golden calf (Exodus 32)—a violation symbolized by the destruction of the covenant documents (Exodus 32:19). This covenant in Exodus 34 is not a new or renewed covenant because there is no reference to an earlier covenant that is being renewed or replaced. Instead, Jackson[43] sees this covenant as the formal resolution of a breach between God and Israel, occasioned by the golden calf incident. We know from elsewhere that covenants are used as a way of resolving disputes (e.g., Abraham and Abimelech in Genesis 21:27; Isaac and Abimelech in Genesis 26:28; and Jacob and Laban in Genesis 31:44). Even the covenant between God and Noah can be seen as a form of "dispute resolution" after the trauma of the Flood (Genesis 9:9–17). It would not be surprising, then, if the formal resolution of the dispute explicitly referred to the conflict itself. This is in fact what we do find. The first provision of the so-called "ritual Decalogue" (Exodus 34:17–26) states, "You shall not make molten gods for yourselves" (34:17; JPS). This was exactly the offense that caused the breach (Exodus 32:4, 8). We will return to consider the Sinai narrative more fully in the next section.

Finally, we turn to the covenant between God and Israel at the borders of the promised land (Deuteronomy 5ff). This was not the Exodus/Sinai generation, the one which rebelled against God in the wilderness and perished there (Numbers 14) but, rather, their children who were born during the "wilderness wanderings" (Numbers 14:20–35). This covenant was made on the plains of Moab at the entrance to the promised land (Deuteronomy 1:1, 5) and essentially repeats the Sinaitic covenant. It confirms and incorporates the post-Exodus generation into the covenant at Sinai:

> The LORD our God made a covenant *with us* in Horeb. *Not* with our fathers did the LORD make this covenant, but *with us*, who are all of us here alive this day. The LORD spoke *with you* face to face at the mountain, out of the midst of the fire. (Deuteronomy 5:2–4; *Moses speaking*)

The horizons between Sinai and Moab are fused. This confirms the sense that the Bible speaks of a *single* covenant, rather than a variety of different covenants. The covenant at Sinai does not belong to the past but to their present. Moses's rhetoric "induce[s] Israel to step into the position of the generation of

---

43. Ibid., 254–55.

Sinai . . . life in covenant is . . . something won anew, rekindled and reconsecrated in the heart of each Israelite in every generation."[44] The Sinaitic covenant is dynamic and continuing, with successive generations being incorporated into it.

IV. THE SINAI EVENT

Mount Sinai dominates the landscape of biblical law. Its shadow looms so large—and stretches so far—that there are times when it seems to eclipse the subject as a whole. In both religious and popular imagination, Mount Sinai is a form of shorthand for biblical law itself. This is true in both literary as well as visual terms. For once, this common perception of the centrality of Sinai is well founded in the biblical texts themselves. The stopover at Sinai accounts for a massive one-third of the Pentateuch (from Exodus 19:1 through Numbers 10:10). This is all the more remarkable when one considers the huge time span which the Pentateuch claims to cover, from the creation of the universe to the death of Moses. Regardless of what one thinks about the tradition which ascribes to this period, a history of 2706 years, the fact remains that the visit to Mount Sinai is presented as lasting a mere 11 months and 19 days (according to Exodus 19:1 and Numbers 1:1; 10:11). Time warps around Mount Sinai. For this reason, we need to look more closely at what Jewish tradition calls "the Sinai event" (*Ma'amad Har Sinai*).

Despite—or perhaps because of—its importance, the Sinai event has the most complicated narrative structure of any aspect of biblical law. There is not just one account of the "giving of the Law" but several: Moses ascends and descends the mountain three times, and even the Ten Commandments are issued twice. This section considers how best to make sense of the literary presentation of the Sinai story. But whatever conclusion we come to, we can at least say this: the poly-vocal nature of the story contradicts the popular myth of God "handing down" a monolithic set of laws to a passive Israel. Whatever else is said about the literary arrangement of the "giving of the law," we have to acknowledge that it is presented as a dynamic and relational process. It involves creativity and innovation from all the parties if it is to stay on track; and there are many twists and turns along the way. In that regard, the Sinai event is characteristic of biblical law and can be said to be symbolic of the whole.

The ANE materials leading to the establishment of covenantal relations typically consist of treaty, law, and covenant. The same triptych is apparent in the Sinai account. Treaties and covenants are closely related; however, they are also distinct. The difference between a treaty and a covenant is that a treaty governs

---

44. Jon D. Levenson, *Creation and covenant*, in OLD TESTAMENT THEOLOGY: FLOWERING AND FUTURE (Ben C. Ollenburger ed., Winona Lake: Eisenbrauns, 2004), 409–23, 420.

relations between two or more distinct communities, whereas covenant can cover not only group relationships but also dealings between individuals, or between humans and deity/ies. In the case of the Sinai and Moab covenants, what we have does not correspond precisely with either a treaty or a formal legal collection (such as the Laws of Hammurabi, for example). The Sinai and Moab covenants represent a confluence of law and treaty and combine the basics of both.[45] This is perhaps because of the importance of the relationship between God and his people and the need to explore this from several angles. The overall framework of the Sinai/Moab covenants is derived from the well-established treaty tradition in the ANE. Prologues (historical and otherwise) are common to early law collections and to treaties (*circa* fourteenth and thirteenth centuries BC): so too is the use of titles, preambles, epilogues, blessings, and curses.

Biblical covenants are integrated with narrative; thus the Sinai covenant is a narrative presentation of the establishing of an agreement between God and Israel. Exodus (and Deuteronomy) thus contain accounts of covenant making rather than the covenant itself. In neither case do we have the formal, "final" text of the covenant as deposited in the Ark of the Covenant (2 Chronicles 5:10). We can only speculate on what this document may have looked like since it is long lost, along with the Ark of the Covenant itself, following the destruction of Solomon's Temple. However, it is likely that it consisted of the following:

Title line
+ Prologue (perhaps longer than Exodus 19 and shorter than the prologue in Deuteronomy)
+ Stipulations (as per the stipulations of Exodus 20-23 and Deuteronomy)
+ Witnesses ("heaven and earth" (cf. Deuteronomy 4:26); the "book of Teaching" (cf. Deuteronomy 31:26); stones (Exodus 24:4; cf. Genesis 31:44–52); the people splashed with blood (Exodus 24:6–8; cf. Joshua 24:22))
+ Blessings (perhaps fewer in number compared with the curses, consistent with Leviticus and Deuteronomy)
+ Curses (perhaps larger in number compared with the blessings, consistent with Leviticus and Deuteronomy)
+ Colophon (which may have said something such as, "These are the words of the covenant which the LORD commanded Moses to make with the people of Israel at Mount Sinai"; cf. Deuteronomy 29:1)

In the ANE, copies of covenants were kept in places where they could be consulted by the parties. What is interesting about the covenant between God and Israel is that the chosen place for locating God's copy (as the sovereign) and Israel's copy (as the vassal) coincided in the Ark of the Covenant. This is because

---

45. Kitchen, Reliability of the Old Testament, p. 289.

the Ark was both the place where the deity resided and the center of Israel's cultic worship.

As is the case in other ANE examples, the narrative shows the enactment of a treaty or covenant on which a formal document was subsequently based and deposited in a given location. We have examples from the ANE of the process of negotiation between the parties describing the drafting, finalizing, and agreement between the parties. These show that the order of proceedings in the physical enactment is not necessarily that of the final format of the deposited document. An example of this is Mari 372 [A.107 + A.110], which was found in the archives of the ancient city of Mari[46] (see Chapter 1). This takes the form of a letter from Yarim-Addu to Zimri-Lim, detailing a military alliance between Hammurabi of Babylon and Eshnunna, with envoys as go-betweens. This parallels the biblical description of the process leading to agreement between God and Israel with Moses as a go-between. (The Mari document, of course, differs from the biblical materials in that the former is a negotiation between equals, whereas the biblical account is the agreement between overlord and vassal).

A. Law's glory

The various proceedings at Mount Sinai (Exodus 19:1–24:2) can be read as "one set of interlinked events."[47] The proceedings are structured around the theophany, which begins in Exodus 19:16 and Moses's repeated mediations between God and the people. (Theophany refers to the visual and auditory manifestation of the Presence of God.[48]) We will consider each structural element, as follows.

First is the role of theophany. The centrality of theophany to the Sinai event is clearly signalled at the start of the account. Exodus 19:9–23 has a chiastic structure (see Chapter 1) which is centered upon Exodus 19:18 and, in particular, the descent of the LORD upon Mount Sinai "in fire." This is "the pivot of the entire [Sinaitic] account"[49]: the God of Abraham appears to his descendants in visual

---

46. DOMINIQUE CHARPIN, FRANCIS JOANNES, SYLVIE LACKENBACHER & BERTRAND LAFONT, ARCHIVES ÉPISTOLAIRES DE MARI I/2, ARCHIVES ROYALES DE MARI XXVI/2 (Paris: Editions Recherche sur les Civilisations, 1988), 179–82.

47. MARTIN RAVNDAL HAUGE, THE DESCENT FROM THE MOUNTAIN: NARRATIVE PATTERNS IN EXODUS 19-40, JOURNAL FOR THE STUDY OF THE OLD TESTAMENT SUPPLEMENT SERIES 323 (Sheffield: Sheffield Academic Press, 2001), 49.

48. *See generally* JEFFREY J. NIEHAUS, GOD AT SINAI: COVENANT AND THEOPHANY IN THE BIBLE AND ANCIENT NEAR EAST, STUDIES IN OLD TESTAMENT BIBLICAL THEOLOGY (Carlisle: Paternoster Press, 1995).

49. Yitzhak Avishur, The narrative of the revelation at Sinai (Ex. 19–24), *in* STUDIES IN HISTORICAL GEOGRAPHY AND BIBLICAL HISTORIOGRAPHY (Gershon Galil & Moshe Weinfeld eds., Leiden: Brill, 2000), 197–214, 200.

and auditory form. The Sinai story (Exodus 19–24) repeatedly emphasizes the manifestation of God in the "cloud" upon the "mountain":

> When Moses had ascended the *mountain*, the *cloud* covered the *mountain*. The Presence of the LORD abode on Mount Sinai, and the *cloud* hid it for six days. On the seventh day He called to Moses from the midst of the *cloud*. Now the Presence of the LORD appeared in the sight of the Israelites as a consuming fire on the top of the *mountain*. Moses went inside the *cloud* and ascended the *mountain* forty days and forty nights. (Exodus 24:15–18; *narrator speaking*)

The repetition highlights the importance of the divine manifestation. This sort of presentation is highly unusual when compared with documents from the ANE. A fourteenth/thirteenth century BC hymn to El from Ugarit refers to that deity as "*Eli-beriti, Eli-dini,*" that is, "El of Covenant, El of Judgement" (cf. the reference to "El-berith" in Judges 9:46 and "Baal-berith" in Judges 9:4).[50] This implies that the idea of a deity making a covenant with human beings is not unique to ancient Israel.[51] However, Noth's claim that "the basic substance of ... [the Sinai tradition] is quite unique and unrelated to any other phenomenon in the history of religion"[52] has so far gone unchallenged. If Noth is correct, it is not surprising that the Sinai story is structured around this extraordinary event (e.g., Deuteronomy 4:32–33). The central role of theophany to the Sinai story means that ultimately, theophany is at the heart of biblical law—so much so that "the theophany *itself* takes the form of law."[53] The story of God's activity within the world and with Israel, which includes the gift of the law, is a demonstration of his character. While it is the case that "all biblical law is interwoven with narrative history ... perhaps nowhere do the two come together more markedly than in the theophany at Sinai, where they are presented in the biblical text as one and the same."[54]

B. Running up that hill

Second, we consider the role of mediation in the Sinai story. Avishur notes that the whole Sinai story is structured around "the mediation of Moses between God

---

50. Kenneth A. Kitchen, *A preliminary look at Hurrian poetics*, in STUDI SUL VICINO ORIENTE ANTICO (Simonetta Graziani ed., Naples: Istitute Universitario Orientale, 2000), 555–61, 557.

51. Kenneth A. Kitchen, *Egypt, Ugarit, Qatna and covenant*, in UGARIT-FORSCHUNGEN (Kurt Bergerhof, Manfried Dietrich & Oswald Loretz eds., Neukirchen-Vluyn: Neukirchener Verlag, 1979), 453–64.

52. MARTIN NOTH, THE HISTORY OF ISRAEL (New York: Harper & Row, 3th ed. 1960), 128.

53. NANETTE STAHL, LAW AND LIMINALITY IN THE BIBLE, JOURNAL FOR THE STUDY OF THE OLD TESTAMENT SUPPLEMENT SERIES 202 (Sheffield: Sheffield Academic Press, 1995), 55; italics original.

54. Ibid.

and the people."[55] The structural elements of mediation and theophany are related to each other. It is because God appears at Mount Sinai that Moses's mediation is necessary: the people cannot approach the mountain because of God's holiness (Exodus 19:21), nor can they bear to hear God's voice (Exodus 20:18–19). The story of God coming down upon Mount Sinai "in fire" (Exodus 19:18) establishes a "spatial duality"[56] between "above the mountain" and "below the mountain." Right from the start, Sinai unfolds "as a series of contacts between the[se] spatial levels."[57] The ascent of humanity, as represented by Moses, corresponds to God's "descent from above."[58] Since God himself is presented as "coming down," Mount Sinai becomes the "middle ground" where the divine and human meet.[59]

The existence of these different spatial levels means that the Sinai story is ultimately "dedicated to a theme of 'who may ascend.' "[60] It thus shares a similar formal structure to Psalm 24,[61] which asks:

Who shall ascend the hill of the LORD?
And who shall stand in his holy place? (Psalm 24:3; *David speaking*)

The answer to this question, as given in the psalm, is:

He who has clean hands and a pure heart,
who does not lift up his soul to what is false,
and does not swear deceitfully. (Psalm 24:4; *David speaking*)

This echoes the purity requirements of the Sinai narrative (e.g., Exodus 19:6, 10, 14–15) and the Decalogue (Exodus 20:3–5, 7). As it happens, the only person who can ascend to the top of Mount Sinai and into the Presence of God is Moses (evoking the singular access of the high priest to the Holy of Holies in the Temple[62]). His status as mediator is visualized by his constant going up and down the mountain.[63] As a result, Moses's vertical movement becomes the primary way of structuring the story.[64] Indeed, the "imagery is so basic for the

---

55. Yitzhak Avishur, *The narrative of the revelation at Sinai (Ex. 19–24)*, in STUDIES IN HISTORICAL GEOGRAPHY AND BIBLICAL HISTORIOGRAPHY (Gershon Galil & Moshe Weinfeld eds., Leiden: Brill, 2000), 197–214, 205.
56. HAUGE, DESCENT FROM THE MOUNTAIN, p. 31.
57. Ibid., 30.
58. Ibid., 31.
59. Ibid.
60. Ibid., 49.
61. Ibid., 104–10.
62. Angel Manuel Rodríguez, *Sanctuary theology in the Book of Exodus*, ANDREWS UNIV. SEMINARY STUDS. 24, 127–45 (1986).
63. HAUGE, DESCENT FROM THE MOUNTAIN, p. 31.
64. Thomas B. Dozeman, *Spatial form in Exodus 19:1–8a and in the larger Sinai narrative*, in NARRATIVE RESEARCH ON THE HEBREW BIBLE (Miri Amihai, George W. Coats & Anne M. Solomon eds., Semeia 46 Atlanta: Scholars Press, 1989), 87–101.

presentation of the materials that it is easily disregarded."[65] The Sinai story is thus made up of four episodes, each of which begins and ends with "the four ascents of Moses to God to hear his words and [Moses'] four descents to the people bringing with him the word of God."[66] (The four ascents are found at Exodus 19:3; 19:20–21; 24:1–2, 9, 12, and 34:2; while the four descents are found at Exodus 19:7,14; 19:25; 32:7, 15; and 34:29). The cyclical trips between God and Israel, in which Moses tells the people what God has said and tells God about the state of play among the people, is a form of thematic repetition.[67] Indeed, Jackson has argued that the repetition *at Sinai itself*—of Moses going up and down and getting acceptance "from the people"—recognizes and emphasizes "the validity of God's promise to make Israel a special people."[68]

Like theophany, the role of mediation in the structure of the Sinai story is crucial for our understanding of biblical law. Mediation reflects the tension throughout the Sinai story between motifs of "intimacy and alienation."[69] It quickly becomes apparent that law is "the crucial mediating factor in the interaction between God and Israel. It provides a means of communication but preserves the proper distance . . . ."[70] Mediation is also of great importance from the point of view of how law is communicated: from whom, to whom, and by whom. From a semiotic perspective, it is impossible to overstate the significance of Moses's role as mediator. He is the person through whom the vast majority of biblical law is communicated and—dare one say it—filtered. The study of biblical law must therefore give due weight to Moses's oral delivery and rhetorical style.[71] It is Moses himself and his personality who is the means by which divine speech becomes accessible to human beings.[72] In addition, Moses also issues laws on his own account without saying that God has told him (e.g., Deuteronomy 27:2–8; 31:10–13).[73]

V. MERCY ETCHED IN STONE

There is no question that the most famous aspect of the Sinai event—and indeed of all biblical law—is the Ten Commandments (Exodus 34:28); also commonly

---

65. Hauge, Descent from the Mountain, p. 32.
66. Avishur, *Revelation at Sinai*, p. 205.
67. Jackson, Studies.
68. Ibid., 250.
69. Stahl, Law and Liminality, p. 51.
70. Ibid., 54.
71. *E.g.*, James W. Watts, Reading Law: The Rhetorical Shaping of the Pentateuch, The Biblical Seminar 59 (Sheffield: Sheffield Academic Press, 1999).
72. Stahl, Law and Liminality, p. 72.
73. Jackson, Studies, pp. 260, 264.

referred to as the Decalogue. The picture of Moses coming down the mountain carrying "the two tablets of the Pact [or "covenant']" (Exodus 31:18; JPS) is the most iconic image of the Torah, if not the whole of the Hebrew Bible. It is also one of the most misunderstood.

For a start, we should not imagine Moses staggering down the mountainside carrying stones the size of paving slabs. It is much more likely that he carried stone flakes which, in the case of the second set of tablets, were scratched upon with sharp stones. Writings inscribed on stone flakes or rocks have been found in the ANE, including at Sinai itself.[74] More importantly, the translation of the Hebrew word *debharim* as "commandments" is misleading. The noun *dabhar* simply means "speech," or a "word" or a "thing," and so the Ten Commandments are better translated the Ten Proclamations or the Ten Utterances or the Ten Words. The trouble with translating *debharim* as "the Ten Commandments" is that it tends to flatten God's words to Israel into a set of rules. There is, however, much more to the ten *debharim*—and to biblical law. Translating the ten *debharim* as the Ten Proclamations immediately brings to mind God's "utterances" and "words" at creation. "The voice that speaks at Sinai in giving the words of the Decalogue also spoke the words that created the world . . . just as there are ten pronouncements at creation," for example, "And God said, 'Let there be light,' so there are ten words at Sinai [Genesis 1:3, 6, 9, 11, 14, 20, 24, 26, 28 and 29]"[75] (cf. Mishnah Avot 5:1). Deuteronomy 4:32–33 provides further internal evidence that links the creation of the world with the giving of the Decalogue[76]:

> For ask now of the days that are past, which were before you, since the day that God created man upon the earth, and ask from one end of heaven to the other, whether such a great thing as this has ever happened or was ever heard of. Did any people ever hear the voice of a god speaking out of the midst of the fire, as you have heard, and still live? (Deuteronomy 4:32-33; *Moses speaking*)

This relationship between the Decalogue and creation suggests that there is a relationship between the particular and the universal, viz., between that which is given specifically to Israel and that which is common to the world. We will explore this relationship in greater detail in Chapter 3. For now, we note that the idea of a parallel between the Decalogue and creation is fully consistent with what we have already argued: namely, that God at Sinai is engaged in a new act of creation which takes the form of "liberated Israel"[77] (cf. the reference to "the

---

74. ALAN R. MILLARD, *Recreating the tablets of the law*, BIBLE REV. 49–53 (1994).
75. CALUM M. CARMICHAEL, LAW & NARRATIVE IN THE BIBLE (London: Cornell University Press, 1985), 337.
76. Ibid.
77. JEFFREY J. NIEHAUS, GOD AT SINAI: COVENANT AND THEOPHANY IN THE BIBLE AND ANCIENT NEAR EAST, STUDIES IN OLD TESTAMENT BIBLICAL THEOLOGY (Carlisle: Paternoster Press, 1995), 199.

Creator of Israel" in Isaiah 43:15). From this perspective, the ten proclamations of the Decalogue are the words that bring this new creation into being. The Decalogue is not primarily about social restraint or social control but "possibilities for life."[78]

This being so, the utterances themselves are *not* to be understood, first and foremost, as a set of rules or commands but as a *vocation*. This is not to deny that the Decalogue consists of rules, but it is to deny that it *only* consists of rules. The rules themselves are best understood as part of an overall calling. They are "a summons to, and authorisation for, membership in a quite alternative society"[79] where God is king. Because of this, the Decalogue is constitutive of Israel's identity.[80] "In this new relation of covenant, the command is ... manifestation of true self ... [and] disobedience becomes a violation of one's own self."[81]

This argument is fully in keeping with the idea, above, that the Sinai covenant is a vocational covenant, as indicated by Exodus 19:5–6:

> ... you shall be my own possession among all peoples; for all the earth is mine, and you shall be to me a kingdom of priests and a holy nation. These are the words (*debharim*) which you [Moses] shall speak to the children of Israel. (*God speaking*)

Israel was to be God's showcase to the world. In this sense, the Decalogue is not a list of demands or requirements. Rather, it is an invitation to know, respond, and demonstrate the character of God—a character that is reflected in the proclamations. The character of this God is, above all, full of goodness, mercy, and compassion (Exodus 33:19). This is seen in the opening words of the Decalogue:

> I am the LORD your God, who brought you out of the land of Egypt, out of the house of bondage. (Exodus 20:2; *God speaking*)

What follows, that is, the rest of the Decalogue (20:3–14), is an opportunity for Israel to respond to what God has already done in setting Israel free. In that sense, "the commands, rightly understood, are not restraints as much as they are empowerments."[82] They are opportunities for Israel to live out the freedom won for her at the Exodus. The Decalogue is mercy etched in stone.

---

78. BRUEGGEMANN, COVENANTED SELF, p. 42.
79. Ibid., 26.
80. *See generally* FRANZ VOLKER GREIFENHAGEN, EGYPT ON THE PENTATEUCH'S IDEOLOGICAL MAP, JOURNAL FOR THE STUDY OF THE OLD TESTAMENT SUPPLEMENT SERIES (London: Continuum, 2002).
81. BRUEGGEMANN, COVENANTED SELF, p. 32.
82. BRUEGGEMANN, COVENANTED SELF, p. 32.

A. The moving finger

The Decalogue symbolizes "the importance of law in the relationship between God and Israel."[83] It is unique in biblical law because it records the only words that are said to be spoken directly by God to Israel (Exodus 20:2–17). Their distinctiveness is underlined in the biblical legal texts where Moses is presented as distinguishing between the Decalogue and other forms of legal expression. This occurs in Exodus 24:3 where Moses refers to "all the commands (*hammishpatim*) of the LORD and all the rules (*haddebharim*)"(JPS).

A further sign of the uniqueness of the Decalogue is the remarkable claim that the words upon the tablets were "inscribed with the finger of God" (Exodus 31:18; JPS). This relates only to the first set of tablets which were subsequently broken by Moses as a sign that the covenant itself had been breached (Exodus 32:19; see further below). Interestingly, when it comes to preparing substitute tablets, God promises:

> I will write upon the tables the words that were on the first tables . . .
> (Exodus 34:1; *God speaking*)

In this event, however, it is ambiguous who actually does the writing. The phrase, "and he wrote upon the tables the words of the covenant, the ten commandments" could refer either to God or Moses, although the context favors Moses. Some ambiguity is understandable. After all, if God writes like Moses, "on stone, on both sides, carving tablets," this might in turn suggest that Moses's writing "takes on a divine connotation."[84]

What, then, is meant by "the finger of God"? As the ambiguity in Exodus 34 suggests, it is not a simple question of handwriting. The phrase appears earlier on in Exodus (at 8:19/ MT 8:15) in the context of the power struggle between God and Pharaoh, which resulted in the plagues on Egypt. The words are an acknowledgment by Pharaoh's magicians that "they have truly encountered the presence of a divine being."[85] More than that, they have come to acknowledge the power of a deity who is in fact the Creator God whose "fingers," we learn elsewhere, created the moon and the stars (Psalm 8:3/ MT 8:4). The phrase "the finger of God" thus signifies "the presence of God, his creative power and his involvement in human affairs."[86] Each of these elements are present in the vocational covenant at Sinai and summed up in the Decalogue.

---

83. STAHL, LAW AND LIMINALITY, p. 54.

84. Massimo Leone, *Divine dictation: Voice and writing in the giving of the law*, INT'L. J. SEMIOTICS LAW 14, 161–77 (2001), although Leone's original reference is to the writing of humankind.

85. Gerald A. Klingbeil, *The finger of God in the Old Testament*, ZEITSCHRIFT FÜR DIE ALTTESTAMENTLICHE WISSENSCHAFT 112, 409–15, 415 (2000).

86. Ibid.

VI. SPIRITUAL COUNTERFEIT

The famous story of the "giving of the law" (Exodus 20–31) is immediately followed by the infamous tale of the golden calf and its consequences (Exodus 32–34). There is a harsh contrast between these two stories. The divine manifestation of God at the top of the mountain, which culminates in the divine crafting of the stone tablets (Exodus 31:18), is negatively paralleled by the false materialization at the bottom of the mountain, in which the high priest crafts a golden calf (Exodus 32:2–4). The idol is both a "Moses-substitute" (Exodus 32:1) and a "God-substitute" (Exodus 32:4), being identified as the god who delivered the Israelites from Egypt (Exodus 32:4). Making the golden calf was the worst imaginable breach of the Sinaitic covenant (cf. Exodus 20:3–5)—and "tantamount to an act of adultery committed on a honeymoon."[87]

As a result, God was legally entitled to regard the Sinaitic covenant as abrogated (Exodus 32:7–10). With Moses's subsequent destruction of the tablets (Exodus 32:19), "law becomes literally the embodiment of the failed communication between God and Israel."[88] It continues the theme of distance and withdrawal on the part of the people (cf. Exodus 20:19). "The first tablets, fashioned and written by God himself (32:16), were the embodied literal manifestation of the unmediated divine communication which the Israelites proved incapable of receiving."[89]

Again, there are a number of parallels between the Sinai story and the primeval history. First, God's charge that "[the] people . . . have corrupted themselves (*shichet*); they have turned aside quickly out of the way (*derek*) which I commanded them" (Exodus 32:7–8) recalls the divine indictment in Genesis 6:12 that the earth "was corrupt (*nishchatah*); for all flesh had corrupted (*hishchit*) their way (*darko*) upon the earth." Second, in Genesis 6:7–8, God's judgment meant destroying humanity and starting again with Noah; likewise, God's judgement in Exodus 32 begins with a proposal to destroy Israel and make a new start with Moses (32:10). Third, the disobedience in both cases is said to be firmly entrenched. Both humanity and Israel are described in identical terms before and after their punishment. Humanity is described as "evil" (Genesis 6:5; 8:21) before and after the Flood (Genesis 7), while Israel is described as "stiff-necked" (Exodus 32:9; 33:3) before and after the Levitical massacre (Exodus 32:26–27). Finally, in both cases, "[what] assures the future existence of sinful humanity and of sinful, hard-necked Israel is the establishment or the reestablishment of a covenant."[90]

---

87. Schramm, *Exodus* 19, p. 338.
88. Stahl, Law and Liminality, p. 63.
89. Ibid., 72.
90. Schramm, *Exodus* 19, p. 340.

The key difference between Genesis 6 and Exodus 32 is that "unlike Noah, Moses refuses to become the new father of the nation."[91] Instead, Moses acts as mediator on behalf of the people and succeeds in "averting for Israel the fate of the flood generation,"[92] although there is still a partial destruction (Exodus 32:27–28). It is very striking that the basis of Moses's appeal to God is to:

> Remember Abraham, Isaac, and Israel [i.e. Jacob], thy servants, to whom thou didst swear by thine own self, and didst say to them, "I will multiply your descendants as the stars of heaven, and all this land that I have promised I will give to your descendants, and they shall inherit it for ever." (Exodus 32:13; *Moses speaking*)

Moses apparently understands that any basis for resolving the breach between God and Israel must lie beyond the Sinaitic covenant. "A primary function, therefore, of the golden calf episode is to emphasize that the covenant of Exodus 19 does not and cannot stand on its own: were it not for Moses' invocation of God's prior promise to Abraham, Israel would have been destroyed then and there."[93] The story underlines the point made above that the Sinai covenant is a constituent element within the one everlasting covenant between God and Abraham.[94]

A. Tanned by glory

The main Sinai story—which was interrupted at 32:1 by the golden calf episode—gets back on track in Exodus 34. Moses cuts new stone tablets "like the first" (Exodus 34:1) and heads back up the mountain (34:4) for a further theophanic manifestation and new laws (34:5ff). However, we have not merely pressed the reset button in the story of God and Israel. For although Moses does receive the Decalogue a second time, it is not verbally repeated, and God does not speak directly to the people (Exodus 34:27; cf. Exodus 20:2–17). Nor do we have a "scene of popular commitment"[95] when the commands are mediated a second time (Exodus 34:32; cf. Exodus 24:7).

A further sign of distance, or withdrawal, between God and the people is signified by the account of Moses's veil. This is worn because the people were not willing to tolerate the divine radiance on Moses's face after his encounters with God (Exodus 34:29–35). As Nanette Stahl writes, "even Moses can no longer maintain entirely unmediated communication with the Israelites; the mediator himself thus becomes a degree further removed from the people."[96] The veil thematically "repeats . . . the terror caused by the theophany at the time of the

---

91. Ibid., 339.
92. Ibid.
93. Schramm, *Exodus* 19, p. 340.
94. Ibid., 342.
95. Hauge, Descent from the Mountain, p. 149.
96. Ibid., 70.

Decalogue"[97] (Exodus 20:18–19), which had a distancing effect upon the people. From a semiotic point of view, the veil may be a sign that the divine commands mediated by Moses have the same status as the Decalogue. The veil communicates that the words spoken by Moses to the people have the same status as those spoken by God to the people.

VII. THE NEWNESS OF THE NEW?

Finally, we turn from the covenant at Sinai to another defining moment in the development of covenant in the Bible. This is the introduction of "new covenant" language in the Hebrew Bible. The phrase "a new covenant" (*berit chadashah*) is used only once in the entire Hebrew Bible, in Jeremiah 31:31. This section of the Bible is doubly interesting because Jeremiah 30–32 contains the greatest concentration of references to the covenant formula in the whole of the Hebrew Bible (four times in all).[98] Why? The reason is because the book of Jeremiah describes the fall of Jerusalem and the exile to Babylon. Exile was the ultimate sign that the Sinai covenant had failed and that Israel was not the people God wanted them to be. We can thus see why Jeremiah would have been preoccupied with the covenant formula and why he would have found the idea of a new covenant desirable. Holladay suggests that the setting for the declaration of Jeremiah 31:31 ("Behold, the days are coming, says the LORD...") was the septennial reading of Deuteronomy which, it is argued, fell on the same year that the Temple was destroyed (587 BC). "The radical implication of Jeremiah's announcement, that the covenant mediated by Moses was now a dead letter, would almost demand such a setting."[99]

The new covenant therefore has a negative and a positive task. Negatively, it has to address the cause of the exile, which Jeremiah identifies as the corruption of the human will (Jeremiah 13:23; 17:9–10). Jeremiah uses the language of the "heart" because, in biblical thought, the heart is the seat of choice and volition. Positively, the new covenant needs to put the relationship between God and his people on a new footing. To be consistent with Jeremiah's preceding analysis, this will require "*unilateral* action on YHWH's part on the heart [or will] of the individual."[100] This is exactly what we find in Jeremiah 31:31–34:

> ... I will put My Teaching into their inmost being and inscribe it upon their hearts. Then I will be their God, and they shall be My people. (Jeremiah 31:33)

---

97. JACKSON, STUDIES, p. 66 n. 51.
98. RENDTORFF, COVENANT FORMULA, p. 33.
99. William L. Holladay, *The structure and possible setting of the new covenant passage, Jer. 31:31-34, in PALABRA, PRODIGIO, POESIA* (Vicente Collado Bertomeu ed., Analecta Biblica 151, Roma: Editrice Pontificio Istituto Biblico, 2003), 185–89, 189.
100. Bernard P. Robinson, *Jeremiah's new covenant: Jer. 31:31-34*, SCANDINAVIAN J. OF OLD TESTAMENT 15, 181-204, 203 (2001), italics original.

Unlike the other forms of covenant we have been considering so far, this is not a work of confirmation or incorporation. Indeed, we are expressly told that this covenant "will *not* be like the covenant I made with their fathers, when I took them by the hand to lead them out of the land of Egypt" (Jeremiah 31:32). It is something "new."

A. Flesh and Stone

How, precisely, does the "new covenant" prophecied by Jeremiah differ from previous arrangements? What is new about the newness of the new? Jeremiah 31:31–34 describes three main differences: Torah is interiorized, there is no need for teaching, and wrongdoing is forgiven.

First, the new covenant differs because its symbols are interior rather than exterior. The gift of Torah is said to be placed *in* the people themselves, rather than something external to the people, such as the Ark of the Covenant (Deuteronomy 10:2). It also contrasts with the Deuteronomic covenant where the Israelite is supposed to "impress" God's words "upon your very heart" (Deuteronomy 11:18; *God speaking*, JPS). In the new covenant, God does for the people what they clearly cannot do for themselves.

This contrast between interior and exterior is reflected in the locus of the divine writing; on the hearts of the people in the case of the new covenant, as opposed to the tablets of stone at Sinai. Again, this also contrasts with the idea, found in the Wisdom literature, that the Israelite is supposed to "write [Torah] on the tablet of your heart" (Proverbs 3:3; *Solomon speaking*). Once again, under the new covenant, God does for the people what they are not able to do for themselves.

It is important to recognize that there is no difference in terms of *what* is written on the heart. What is written on stone tablets and human hearts—*plural*, signifying the collective will of the community—is the same in both cases, that is, Torah. What is different is the object of the divine writing. The fact that God now chooses to write on human hearts, rather than on stone tablets, is significant from a semiotic perspective (who is communicating what to whom, and how); even today, our choice of stationery sends different "messages"— handmade paper or Basildon Bond? Human hearts are a very different sort of divine notepaper from stone tablets. What does the new form of divine stationery signify?

At one level, the contrast between writing on the heart rather than on stone is a way of saying that the new covenant "will overcome all the problems of exteriorised materiality and will make good whatever defects may be imagined to have inhered in the original covenant."[101] But we can be more precise than this.

---

101. R. P. Carroll, *Inscribing the covenant: Writing and the written in Jeremiah*, in UNDERSTANDING POETS AND PROPHETS (A. Graeme Auld ed., Journal for the Study of the Old Testament Supplement Series 152 (Sheffield: Sheffield Academic Press, 1993), 61–75, 66.

The "writing on the heart" alludes to "the finger of God" at Sinai. There, we saw that the moving finger signifies "the presence of God, his creative power and his involvement in human affairs."[102] The picture of writing on the heart thus signifies that *under the new covenant, the direct object of God's Presence, creativity, power, and involvement is the human will.* This is what makes the new covenant new.

What it does not signify is any sentimental idea that the heart is somehow more receptive to the divine inscription than stone. Jeremiah has closed off that option with his previous statements about the human heart:

> The sin of Judah is written
> with a pen of iron;
> with a point of diamond it is engraved
> on the tablet of their heart,
> and on the horns of their altars. (Jeremiah 17:1)

Guilt is "'written into' the people's character."[103] Indeed, sin is "so deep-seated . . . that it had become engraved on the very horns of the altar where the blood of the sin offering, which was supposed to wipe away sin, was smeared."[104] The contrast between the finger of God and the pen of iron makes Jeremiah 31:31–34 a sort of reversal of 17:1. Another aspect, then, of what the new stationery signifies is that the new covenant is, in some sense, a greater divine achievement because the sin written on the heart must first be erased before it can be replaced with Torah (see further below).

The second major difference between the old and the new covenant is that there is no need for teaching. The divine inscription is effective because it brings knowledge of God. Gerhard Von Rad describes it as a "creative grafting of the will of God on the hearts of men."[105] This is a radical departure because it means that instruction and exhortation, viz., "the entire legal tradition on which *Deuteronomy* is so insistent, will no longer be necessary."[106] As H. D. Potter writes, "the whole point of these verses is that they are a deliberate contrast to *Deuteronomy*, not a complement to it, or a restatement of it."[107] We should not forget that Jeremiah attributed the fall of Judah, in large measure, to corrupt leaders who peddled false teaching to the masses (e.g., Jeremiah 8:8–12). Against

---

102. Klingbeil, *Finger of God*, p. 415.

103. H. D. Potter, *The new covenant in Jeremiah 31:31-34*, VETUS TESTAMENTUM 33 (1983), 347–57, 351.

104. Potter, *New covenant*, p. 352.

105. GERHARD VON RAD, OLD TESTAMENT THEOLOGY VOLUME II: THE THEOLOGY OF ISRAEL'S PROPHETIC TRADITIONS (D. M. G. Stalker trans., Edinburgh: Oliver & Boyd, 1970), 215.

106. Joseph Blenkinsopp, *Structure and meaning in the Sinai-Horeb narrative (Exodus 19-34)*, in A BIBLICAL ITINERARY (Eugene E. Carpenter ed., Journal for the Study of the Old Testament Supplement Series 240, Sheffield: Sheffield Academic Press, 1997), 109–25, 123.

107. Potter, *New covenant*, p. 350.

this background, it is understandable that the new covenant dispenses with the need for teaching and elitism. "[God] will himself write [Torah] upon men's hearts, and no longer will others be able to falsify it."[108] Torah will be understood by all, "from the least of them to the greatest" (Jeremiah 31:34).

Some scholars see Jeremiah's prophecy at this point as "a counsel of despair."[109] It is claimed that the new covenant amounts to a lack of hope in several respects: first and most obviously because it acknowledges that "all hope in the capability of Israel in its present state to live up to its ideal purpose has been lost."[110] The people are being punished, and there is no possibility of breaking out of the cycle because they are human beings. The only way, therefore, to fulfill God's purposes is "to change human nature."[111] Second, it is a counsel of despair because it shows "the poverty of imagination which cannot conceive of anything better (or more radical) than yet another version of a failed system."[112] To put it bluntly, "the new covenant is more of the same but with the cracks papered over."[113] Finally, it is despairing because it amounts to an admission that "there will be no need for . . . moral change *by* the people because Yahweh will change them automatically."[114] This is seen as problematic because it means that the prophets effectively "throw in the towel" and give up trying to persuade the people to change. "If people will not change, then to hope for God to change them is to move from the moral sphere [in which the prophets persuade the people] to piety and transcendentalism."[115]

Such interpretations of the new covenant, which refer to "changing human nature" and "changing people automatically," raise the question of the nature of the compliance under the new covenant. Some have argued that since Israel's experience was proof that "human beings could not voluntarily rise to the standards required,"[116] God would have to "hardwire" Torah into Israel's consciousness so that she is "genetically programmed" to fulfill the covenant.[117] On this reading, Israel's obedience under the new covenant is a matter of automatic

---

108. Ibid., 353.
109. ROBERT P. CARROLL, FROM CHAOS TO COVENANT: USES OF PROPHECY IN THE BOOK OF JEREMIAH (London: SCM Press, 1981), 219; also Moshe Greenberg, *Three Conceptions of the Torah in Hebrew Scriptures, in* STUDIES IN THE BIBLE AND JEWISH THOUGHT (Philadelphia: Jewish Publication Society, 1995), 11–24, 19.
110. Greenberg, *Three Conceptions,* p. 20.
111. Ibid., 19.
112. Carroll, *Chaos to Covenant.*
113. Ibid.
114. Ibid., 220, italics original.
115. Ibid.
116. BERNARD S. JACKSON, ESSAYS ON HALAKHAH IN THE NEW TESTAMENT (Leiden: Brill, 2008), 7.
117. JACKSON, ESSAYS ON HALAKHAH, p. 8. Cf. BERNARD M. LEVINSON, LEGAL REVISION AND RELIGIOUS RENEWAL IN ANCIENT ISRAEL (Cambridge: Cambridge University Press, 2008), 47–48.

compliance. "[God] will alter their hearts . . . and make it impossible for them to be anything but obedient to his rules and his commandments."[118] Moshe Greenberg[119] finds further support for this approach in a related prophecy of Ezekiel, where God says, "I will put my spirit within you, and *cause you* to walk in my statutes and be careful to observe my ordinances" (Ezekiel 36:27). On this reading, Israel's obedience cannot be said to be voluntary.

In my view, the new covenant is more than simply a "counsel of despair." Despair is present; indeed, Israel's desperate circumstances are what demonstrate the need for direct and radical intervention by God himself. As I have argued above, the picture of God writing on the heart alludes to the finger of God at Sinai and hence signifies that under the new covenant, the direct object of God's Presence, creativity, power, and involvement is the human will. Accordingly, in my view, the compliance that is described in the new covenant is that of intuitive compliance rather than automatic compliance. The divine inscription is effective because it brings knowledge of God. Torah "on the heart" is understood intuitively—as opposed to what we might call Torah on "the tablet of stone," which is not so understood (cf. 2 Corinthians 3:3).

Finally, as indicated above, the third difference between the old and the new covenant is that wrongdoing is finally forgiven. This is placed at the end of the promise (Jeremiah 31:34). This emphasizes both "the need for the forgiveness of sins as the basis for the new covenant, and . . . God's readiness to forgive, in order that this covenant may be maintained."[120]

To sum up, the essence of the new covenant is that Torah is placed in the Israelites' hearts. But it is still the same Torah, and it still expresses a relationship with God. God has not changed. In that sense, it is "not a new covenant at all; it is the same, unaltered covenant which the forefathers broke (31:32). What is new are the presuppositions for its acceptance and realisation."[121] The content is the same, but the method of communication and practice is different. The new covenant of Jeremiah 31:31–34 is followed by reference to a "covenant of friendship" (*berit shalom*; JPS) in Ezekiel 37:26–28. This has the effect of extending the benefits of God's Presence to "the nations" (37:28), instead of just to Israel (Exodus 29:46). The increased depth of the new covenant (being applied to the will) is matched by increased breadth (being applied to the nations).

What Jeremiah 31:31–34 does not make clear is "how the new covenantal relationship is to be socially embodied."[122] This brings us to the heart of the interfaith difference between Jews and Christians regarding the meaning of the new covenant.

---

118. Greenberg, *Three Conceptions*, p. 20.
119. Ibid., 19–20.
120. RENDTORFF, COVENANT FORMULA, p. 86.
121. Ibid., 73.
122. Blenkinsopp, *Structure and meaning*, p. 123.

The Christian understanding of the fulfillment of the new covenant (outlined in the next section) can be contrasted with a rabbinical understanding, although it should be said at once that a rabbinical understanding of the "new covenant" of Jeremiah 31 is often couched in terms of a much broader rabbinical debate, namely, the future role of Torah. This, in turn, receives different emphases, depending on whether that future is conceived in terms of a new "Messianic age" or the "age to come."[123]

Midrash Ecclesiastes 2:1 confirms the idea that Jeremiah's new covenant refers to the Mosaic Torah and implies that the chief distinction of the new covenant is that the subjects of the Mosaic Torah "will learn and not forget"[124]:

> Rabbi Hezekiah [*circa* AD 300] said in the name of Rabbi Simon bar Zabdai: All the *Torah* which you learn in this world is "vanity" in comparison with *Torah* [which will be learnt] in the World to Come; because in this world a man learns *Torah* and forgets it but with reference to the World to Come what is written there? *I will put My law in their inward parts* (Jeremiah 31:33).[125]

According to this reading, it is not Torah that will change but humanity's relation to it: "*Torah* will then be differently and more satisfactorily studied."[126] In the Babylonian Talmud, Rabbi Simeon ben Eleazar (AD 165–200) describes the Messianic era as one in which "there is neither merit nor guilt" (Shabbath 151b[127]). Seen from this perspective, Jeremiah's new covenant is part of a future in which "the *Torah* will be so fully obeyed that there will be no guilt, and so spontaneously or easily fulfilled that there will be no merit."[128] The bottom line, as far as Rabbinic perspectives are concerned, "was that the messianic age had not yet arrived, and thus the promise of Jeremiah, whatever it meant, was deferred."[129]

B. New Covenant, New Testament

According to the New Testament, the "new covenant" is inaugurated by Jesus at his final Passover meal with his disciples (traditionally referred to as the Last Supper):

> This cup which is poured out for you is the new covenant in my blood. (Luke 22:20; *Jesus speaking*)

---

123. *See generally* W. D. DAVIES, TORAH IN THE MESSIANIC AGE AND/OR THE AGE TO COME, JOURNAL OF BIBLICAL LITERATURE MONOGRAPH SERIES, VOLUME VII (Philadelphia: Society of Biblical Literature, 1952), 50–83.
124. DAVIES, MESSIANIC AGE, p. 72.
125. *Midrash Rabbah Eccelesiastes* (A. Cohen trans., London: Soncino Press, 1939), 51.
126. DAVIES, MESSIANIC AGE, p. 73.
127. *Babylonian Talmud, Tractate Shabbath*, translated into English with notes, glossary, and indices by R. Freedman under the editorship of I. Epstein, Hebrew-English edition (London: Soncino Press, 1976), vol. II.
128. DAVIES, MESSIANIC AGE, p. 65.
129. JACKSON, ESSAYS ON HALAKHAH, p. 9.

It is not surprising that Jesus's reference to the new covenant takes place in the context of remembering the Exodus. We noted, above, how the deliverance of the Israelites from Egypt led into the use of the covenant formula (e.g., Exodus 6:6–7); likewise, deliverance from Babylon leads into the (new) covenant formula of Jeremiah 32:37–39:

> Behold, I will gather them from all the countries to which I drove them in my anger and my wrath and in great indignation; I will bring them back to this place, and I will make them dwell in safety. And they shall be my people, and I will be their God. I will give them one heart and one way [or "nature"; JPS], that they may fear me for ever . . . (*God speaking*)

Observing Passover means recalling a whole sequence of events that includes the substitutionary death of a lamb and which leads, via the Exodus, up to the Sinaitic covenant. In the Gospels, the Last Supper is presented as inseparable from the crucifixion and death of Jesus, who is seen as a sacrificial Passover lamb. This is said to lead onto a "new Exodus" and to a "new covenant." Jesus's words anticipate deliverance from exile, like Jeremiah 32, although this time the exile is claimed to be spiritual and not merely physical (see further Chapter 13). The New Testament claims that with the death and resurrection of Jesus the Messiah, the full expression of the covenant formula—"I will be their God, and they shall be my people"—has finally opened up. Jesus's new covenant is not only a *revision* of the Abrahamic covenant but also an *incorporation* of a new body of people. This new covenant is said to be for all who believe in Jesus – not only believing Jews but also believing Gentiles. Once again, we see how the idea of a biblical covenant is presented as holding together the particular (Jesus) and the universal (blessing to the nations; cf. Genesis 12:2–3). In this way, the New Testament presents the new covenant of Jesus as the ultimate expansion of the Abrahamic covenant.

C. Access all areas

This chapter has provided evidence of thematic repetition in terms of how the Hebrew Bible presents different covenants. Some accounts of covenant making repeat aspects of earlier divine covenant making. Interestingly, the New Testament also displays evidence of thematic repetition and, in particular, re-presents aspects of the Sinai narrative in the context of its understanding of the "new covenant."

First, as we have already seen, the New Testament re-presents Jesus's death as an essential precursor to a "new Exodus" and hence to a "new covenant." This thinking is explicit in the New Testament book of Hebrews where references to "a new covenant (*diatheke*)" (e.g., 9:15) use the same Greek word as that used for a legal will (*diatheke*; e.g., 9:16). Like a will, the new covenant requires the death of a relevant person in order to come into effect—in this case, the death of Jesus (9:15–17). It is for this reason that the New Testament evokes the Sinaitic blood ritual of Exodus 24:5–8 in connection with Jesus's crucifixion (9:18–20). By emphasizing how everything under the Sinaitic covenant was sprinkled with blood, the writer is able to stress the necessity of Jesus's blood to inaugurate the new covenant. From the perspective of the writer of Hebrews, Moses's activity points forward to Jesus's crucifixion, and the crucifixion is understood in the light of Moses's prior actions.

Second, the New Testament develops and applies the interiority of the new covenant described in Jeremiah 31:31–34. It does this by relating it to the differing degree of spatial penetration allowed to the high priest under the Sinaitic and the Jesus covenants. Thus, the Sinaitic high priest is described as being able to access the holiest part of the Tabernacle/Temple where the Presence of God is found. This is the innermost room of the Tabernacle/Temple, which is called the Holy of Holies. However, he is only authorized to do this once a year (Leviticus 16:2ff). By contrast, the high priest of Jesus's covenant, who is said to be Jesus himself (e.g., Hebrews 4:14), is presented as having *continuous* access. Moreover, Jesus is said to have constant access, not merely to the man-made "Holy of Holies" but to the divine sanctuary itself:

> But when Christ appeared as a high priest of the good things that have come, then through the greater and more perfect tent (not made with hands, that is, not of this creation) he entered once for all into the Holy Place, taking not the blood of goats and calves but his own blood, thus securing an eternal redemption . . . For Christ has entered, not into a sanctuary made with hands, a copy of the true one, but into heaven itself, now to appear in the presence of God on our behalf. (Hebrews 9:11–12, 24)

The point that the writer of Hebrews seems to be making is that there is a correlation between the degree of spatial penetration by the different high priests, under the Sinaitic and the Jesus covenants, and the degree of penetration of Torah. That is, the greater the degree of spatial penetration for the different high priests, the greater is the degree of penetration for Torah. This point is developed by means of a simple series of binary oppositions. Thus, under the Sinai covenant, the high priest is allowed a fairly limited degree of spatial penetration (to a man-made "Holy of Holies," once a year). This is reflected in the fact that Torah is written in the exterior form of "stones." By contrast, under the Jesus covenant, the high priest is said to be permitted the ultimate form of spatial penetration, that is, to a divinely made "Holy of Holies," all the time. This is reflected in the fact that Torah is written in the interior form of hearts. The New Testament thus seems to re-present the interior/exterior motif of Jeremiah 31 in terms of the degree of spatial penetration permitted by the high priest in the Sinaitic cultic laws (Hebrews 9).

Finally, we may consider Paul's re-presentation of the Sinai narrative in the Second Letter to the Corinthians. Paul reminds his readers how the Sinaitic covenant was attended by what he describes as "the dispensation of death"

(2 Corinthians 3:7), a reference to the fact that the opening words of the Decalogue which prohibit idolatry, condemned the golden-calf-worshipping Israelites to death (Exodus 20:1–5; 32:10, 28). Yet despite all this, when Moses descends again, after a revelation of God's mercy (Exodus 34:6–7), his face is radiant. Paul's argument is that:

> if the dispensation of death, carved in letters on stone, came with such splendour that the Israelites could not look at Moses' face because of its brightness, fading as this was, will not the dispensation of the Spirit be attended with greater splendour? For if there was splendour in the dispensation of condemnation, the dispensation of righteousness must far exceed it in splendour. (2 Corinthians 3:7–9)

The contrast between the dispensation of death and the dispensation of the Spirit is a reference to the prophetic belief that the inauguration of the new covenant involves God putting his spirit into the new community (e.g., Ezekiel 36:26–27). The Sinai story is thus re-presented by Paul to advance an argument from the lesser to the greater. Paul's claim is that even the revelation of God's mercy witnessed by Moses is nothing compared with the revelation of God's mercy in the Gospels. By the same token, Paul implies that when God is active by his Spirit among the Corinthians, even Moses would need to put his sunglasses on (2 Corinthians 3:18).

VIII. CONCLUSION

Covenant is part of the DNA of biblical law. For this reason, the way in which we think about covenant powerfully shapes our understanding of the entire subject. Many of the things that we can say are characteristic of covenant in the Bible are equally true of biblical law as a whole. For example, although the covenant with Abraham is presented in unitary terms, covenant in the Bible is not monolithic. Like biblical law, covenant has many different facets, some of which come into particular focus for later generations. Covenant, like biblical law, reflects changes in the relationship between God and Israel. Creativity on God's part is required if this relationship is to overcome various external and internal threats. This means that covenant, like biblical law, is dynamic and new for each generation to whom it applies. It is not a system but a story—and an ongoing one at that. Covenant thus shows the dependence of biblical law on narrative history and, in turn, upon vocation. Covenant involves calling; and so does biblical law. Finally, the central place of theophany to the biblical covenant illustrates God's Presence, creative power, and engagement in human affairs. Biblical law is an equally powerful illustration of these aspects of God's activity. All these things will become more apparent as we develop our understanding of biblical law in subsequent chapters.

Selected reading

Walter Brueggemann, *The Covenanted Self: Explorations in Law and Covenant* (Minneapolis: Fortress, 1999), Chapter 2.

Bernard S. Jackson, *Studies in the Semiotics of Biblical Law*, Journal for the Study of the Old Testament Supplement Series 314 (Sheffield: Sheffield Academic Press, 2000), Chapter 9.

Kenneth A. Kitchen, *On The Reliability of the Old Testament* (Grand Rapids: Eerdmans, 2003), excerpt from Chapter 6, pp. 283–307.

Jeffrey J. Niehaus, *God At Sinai: Covenant and Theophany in the Bible and Ancient Near East, Studies in Old Testament Biblical Theology* (Carlisle: Paternoster Press, 1995), Chapter 6.

Rolf Rendtorff, *The Covenant Formula: An Exegetical and Theological Investigation.* Translated by Margaret Kohl, Old Testament Studies (Edinburgh: T&T Clark, 1998), Chapter 4.

3. BEYOND SINAI

We saw in Chapter 2 how Mount Sinai dominates the landscape of biblical law. This is reflected in the lively Jewish belief that all of Israel was present at the mountain to receive the law, including those who are yet unborn (Deuteronomy 5:2ff; see Chapter 2). According to this tradition, all Jews were "present at Sinai."[1] At the same time, however, a survey of the biblical legal material quickly shows that there was law *apart* from Israel and that there was law *before* Mount Sinai. For these reasons, the student of biblical law is obliged to consider not only those who were present at Sinai but also those who were *not* present at Sinai. Just as the tradition of being present at Sinai has shaped our understanding of biblical law, so too must the notion of being *absent* from Sinai.

It should be said at once that as soon as we tackle this question, we are beginning to think about the ways in which biblical law might potentially be known or accessible by other peoples than Israel. This subject is the traditional preserve of what has become known as natural law, and it raises the question of whether there is any such thing as a natural law theory in the biblical materials. In this chapter, we will see that there are a number of different ways in which natural law could be said to exist in the Bible. This includes texts that are addressed squarely at those outside God's covenant with Israel, as well as texts that are addressed to Israel herself. This is because the understanding of natural law in the Bible is broad and complex enough to encompass a number of different strands.

I. BIBLICAL LAW AND NATURAL LAW

Before we address this question, we must start by explaining what is meant by natural law. Natural law asserts a continuity between acts of human lawmaking and ethical requirements that we experience as imposed on us. The study of natural law—like the study of law in general—addresses one of the mysteries of human consciousness, namely the origin of our sense of obligation. Why do human beings feel that they ought to behave in such and such a way?

This means that natural law is not a purely philosophical exercise. It raises important questions that impinge on everyday choices and behavior. In particular, natural law raises major ontological questions about the status of moral

---

1. *E.g.*, S. Y. AGNON, PRESENT AT SINAI: THE GIVING OF THE LAW (Michael Swirsky trans., Philadelphia: The Jewish Publication Society, 1999); Judith Plaskow, STANDING AGAIN AT SINAI: JUDAISM FROM A FEMINIST PERSPECTIVE (San Francisco: Harper, 1991).

judgments. In other words, when human beings make moral judgments, do they access anything other than their individual subjective preferences and choices? If the answer is no and the source of our moral judgements is not objective, can we legitimately claim to control other people's behavior by an appeal to ethical or moral standards?

Natural lawyers have given different answers to the question of the source of human obligation. They have included responses from theologians as well as legal philosophers. They suggest, variously, that our sense of obligation might be rooted in the world around us; or in our minds, as constituting us as human beings; or that it may come from God. Such views were held, for example, by Ulpian, Kant and Blackstone respectively. This sense of obligation may in turn be mediated in various ways by express command (per Ambrosiaster and Gratian) or through nature (per Ulpian).

In modern jurisprudence, natural law is usually seen as contrasting with another approach within legal theory called "legal positivism." Legal positivism holds that there is no necessary connection between law and morality and that the question of what is and is not law can be identified by reference to social facts and need not involve moral assumptions. Legal positivism, which sets moral issues to one side, may be seen as the quintessential liberal legal theory. By contrast, natural law theory holds that law can only be understood as a moral phenomenon and that there is some necessary connection between law and morality. In straightforward terms, one of the classic differences between these two broad approaches is the general claim that, from a natural law position, an unjust law is not a law, whereas, from a legal positivist perspective, a law can be valid even if it violates morality.[2]

Of course, we must be careful not to caricature complex philosophical positions. In particular, we should recognize that natural law is a broad tradition that can refer to a multiplicity of theses (see Table 5, p. 93, below). It is plausible to suggest that the same might also be true of natural law in the Bible. This means that in our preinterpretative stage of asking whether there is natural law in the Bible, we cannot assume that the entire tradition of natural law can be reduced to a single idea such as "law according to nature" or "universal law" and ask whether this is present in the biblical materials. If we want to explore natural law in the Bible, we must start by recognizing that we could be looking for a number of different things.

We could begin by noting that *natural law asserts continuity between, on the one hand, acts of human lawmaking and legal judgment and, on the other, that which is required of human beings (either by virtue of their nature, or the world in which they exist, or "things as they are," including God)*. This suggests that in relation to the

---

2. *See generally* N. E. SIMMONDS, CENTRAL ISSUES IN JURISPRUDENCE (London: Sweet & Maxwell, 2008).

biblical materials, what we are looking for is *a connection between divine activity and human activity in the realm of normativity (that is, why we feel we ought to do things)*. This opens up a range of possibilities for exploring the possible relationship between natural law and the Bible.

Consequently, the discovery of natural law in the Bible could mean asserting one or more of the following theses:

(1) Continuity between the divine and creation
(2) Continuity between the created world and human behavior
(3) Universal knowledge of certain norms
(4) Continuity between different forms of revelation
(5) Continuity between divine and human acts of judgment

One of the implications of discovering natural law in the Bible, as expressed in the above theses, is that the early chapters of Genesis are far more foundational to our understanding of biblical law than is often recognized. Certain moral norms seem to be implicit in the Creation narratives which, later materials show, God expects all human beings to know and respect. In this sense, there is nothing new about the Decalogue. Its commands and prohibitions do not appear "out of the blue." On the contrary, there is a sense in which they have always been commands and prohibitions. Something can be commended, not because God has explicitly said so but because it recognizes what God has already done in creating the universe. By the same token, something can be forbidden, not because God has given a specific commandment, but because it is not consistent with what God has done in creation.

This chapter does not examine the long history of interpretation of various biblical texts from within the Western philosophical tradition of natural law.[3] This is consistent with the focus of this book, which is on the biblical texts themselves and not, as in this case, on how they have been received in Western philosophy.

II. CONTINUITY BETWEEN THE DIVINE AND CREATION

One of the ways in which we might find a connection between divine activity and human activity in the realm of normativity is the existence of continuity between the divine and creation, which includes humanity. This is one way in which we can speak meaningfully about the existence of natural law in the Bible.

---

3. For which see, for example, JEAN PORTER, NATURAL AND DIVINE LAW: RECLAIMING THE TRADITION FOR CHRISTIAN ETHICS (Grand Rapids: Eerdmans, 1999).

A. The primordial Torah

Continuity between the divine and creation is asserted most notably in the story of universal creation (Genesis 1:1–2:3; although debates within science and religion about whether and how God created the universe are not central to the argument). This continuity has considerable implications for the discovery of natural law in the Bible. The so-called "nature psalms (e.g., Psalms 19, 119, and 147) confirm that Torah is intimately connected with God's activity in creation. Torah, too, is closely identified with Wisdom (e.g., Psalm 119:130) and Wisdom herself is presented as being God's "confidant" (Proverbs 8:30; JPS) in creation:

> I was there when He set the heavens into place;
> When He fixed the horizon upon the deep.
> (Proverbs 8:27; *Wisdom speaking;* JPS)

These convictions are expressed in certain rabbinic traditions which claim that Torah existed before the creation of the world (Leviticus Rabbah 19:1) and that God used Torah in creation:

> The *Torah* declares: "I was the working tool of the Holy One, blessed be He." In human practice, when a mortal king builds a palace, he builds it not with his own skill but with the skill of an architect. The architect moreover does not build it out of his head, but employs plans and diagrams to know how to arrange the chambers and the wicket doors. Thus God consulted the *Torah* and created the world, while the *Torah* declares, "In the beginning God created" (Genesis 1:1), "beginning" referring to the *Torah*, as in the verse, "The Lord made me as the beginning of His way" (Proverbs 8:22).
> (Rabbi Oshaya, Genesis Rabbah 1:1)[4]

As a result, biblical law reflects nature in that it is "the most perfect expression of law that is in accordance with creation rightly understood."[5] There is a correspondence between law and nature because both proceed from the same God, and both demand loyalty. As the psalms attest, "nature is by no means inanimate or dumb . . . it speaks with a voice which makes powerful claims of allegiance."[6] The commandments practiced by the psalmist "constitute a kind of revealed natural law,"[7] reflecting the belief that biblical law is intrinsic to the natural order. A similar idea is expressed in Genesis 8:21–22 where the rhythms

---

4. *Midrash Rabbah Genesis*, (H. Freedman & Maurice Simon trans., London: Soncino Press, 1939), vol. I, p. 1.
5. MARKUS BOCKMUEHL, JEWISH LAW IN GENTILE CHURCHES (Grand Rapids: Baker Academic, 2000) 97.
6. BOCKMUEHL, JEWISH LAW, p. 89.
7. JAMES K. BRUCKNER, IMPLIED LAW IN THE ABRAHAM NARRATIVE: A LITERARY AND THEOLOGICAL ANALYSIS, JOURNAL FOR THE STUDY OF THE OLD TESTAMENT SUPPLEMENT SERIES 335 (Sheffield: Sheffield Academic Press, 2001), 45.

of creation are said to reflect the steadfastness of God. The juxtaposition of nature and Torah—the glory of God in the heavens and the glory of God in Torah—"emphasises the universality of both."[8] Like the sun, biblical law has "universal scope and accessibility."[9]

One specific aspect of the continuity between the divine and creation is God's "rest" on the seventh day of creation. This rest is presented as the climax of the story of universal creation (Genesis 2:2–3) where God is shown to triumph over the forces of chaos (Genesis 1:2ff and cf. Psalm 29). "Victory in battle" followed by "rest" is a common motif in ancient Near Eastern (ANE) stories. Canaanite mythology describes the defeat of the sea god Yamm by the storm god Baal, who thereupon constructs a "temple" in which to rest.[10] As a result, the commandments to keep *Shabbat* (Sabbath) invite and permit Israel to imitate God's activity in creation. This continuity between divine and human activity is explicit in Exodus 20:8–11:

> Remember the sabbath day, to keep it holy. Six days you shall labor, and do all your work; but the seventh day is a sabbath to the LORD your God; in it you shall not do any work, you, or your son, or your daughter, your manservant, or your maidservant, or your cattle, or the sojourner who is within your gates; for in six days the LORD made heaven and earth, the sea, and all that is in them, and rested the seventh day; therefore the LORD blessed the sabbath day and hallowed it. (*God speaking*)

This continuity between divine and human activity is thus a sense in which we can speak of natural law in the Bible. It is also an example of the way in which the Decalogue is not, in a sense, declaring anything new. From a canonical perspective, the obligation to observe *Shabbat* pre-dates Mount Sinai. It is true that Genesis 2:2–4 does not contain an explicit reference to the Hebrew noun *shabbat*, which does not appear until Exodus 16:23. However, it is generally recognized that "the seventh day" in Genesis 2:2 refers to the Sabbath because it is the day on which God rested (*wayyishbot*), and there is a similarity between the verb *shabhat* ("to rest") and the noun *shabbat*.

In this respect, the Sabbath commandments are a good example of the relationship between the particular and the universal in biblical law: on the one

---

8. James Barr, *Biblical law and the question of natural theology*, in THE LAW IN THE BIBLE AND IN ITS ENVIRONMENT, (Timo Veijola ed., Publications of the Finnish Exegetical Society 51, Helsinki: Finnish Exegetical Society, 1990), 1–22, 16.

9. Ibid.

10. H. L. Ginsberg, *Ugaritic myth, epics, and legends* in ANCIENT NEAR EASTERN TEXTS RELATING TO THE OLD TESTAMENT (James B. Pritchard ed., Princeton: Princeton University Press, 1950), 129–55, 129–42; JEFFREY J. NIEHAUS, GOD AT SINAI: COVENANT AND THEOPHANY IN THE BIBLE AND ANCIENT NEAR EAST, STUDIES IN OLD TESTAMENT BIBLICAL THEOLOGY (Carlisle: Paternoster Press, 1995), 181–85.

hand, the commandments are specifically given to Israel at Sinai, but on the other hand, the Sabbath is also held out as God's gift to humanity as a whole. Indeed, historians have suggested that one of the reasons for the growth in Judaism in the first centuries BC and AD was the attraction to the Gentiles of the biblical laws relating to the Sabbath. "The very stability of the Jewish way of life . . . often impressed sensitive pagans [who were] [d]isturbed by the anarchical diversity of modes of living and worship . . . ."[11]

Another example of continuity between divine and human activity is humanity's mandate to "be fruitful and multiply" (Genesis 1:28). Regardless of whether this proclamation is best characterized as a blessing or as a command, it certainly involves the expectation that humanity should behave in ways that will reflect God's activity in creation. This includes being creative and productive, exercising benign dominion, and maintaining the optimum conditions under which life can prosper (see further Chapter 5). This proclamation is similar to the Sabbath laws inasmuch as it enjoins the imitation of God's activity in creation.

If it is the case that one of the ways in which natural law could be said to exist in the Bible is through continuity between the divine and creation, then this has several implications for traditional natural law theory.

First, it challenges the way in which much natural law thinking has become caught up in an assumed dualism between nature and revelation. Clearly, this is a dualism that the Bible does not accept. Second, the biblical materials challenge the tendency among legal philosophers to distinguish physical laws of nature (such as the law of gravity)—which are really predictive statements based on observation—from "ought" norms (such as "you should not kill"). Thus, Kant, for example, claims that norms are in a separate universe to cause and effect (creation) (e.g., "In nature, everything *is*: the question of *ought* does not arise there"[12]). Again, the Bible rejects the duality of secular modernism. According to Genesis, the word of God has physical *and* moral effects. Something happens *physically* (e.g., God creates humanity), and it follows from this that something *morally* ought to happen (e.g., human beings should uphold the value of human life). It is because God says, "Let there be . . ." (e.g., Genesis 1:3) that existence itself is a good. Natural law in the Bible breaks down the philosophical distinction between "fact" and "value"—a distinction that, of course, only arises because nature is assumed to be nonnormative. This is a key respect in which biblical jurisprudence differs from modern jurisprudence.

---

11. Salo Wittmayer Baron, A social and religious history of the Jews: Ancient Times: Volume I, (New York: Columbia University Press, 2nd ed. 1952), 174.

12. Immanuel Kant, The Conflict of the Faculties, translation and Introduction by Mary J. Gregor (Lincoln and London: University of Nebraska Press, 1798/1979), 129; emphasis original.

We conclude that the story of universal creation, which moves from the earth being "without form and void" (Genesis 1:2) to full completion and Sabbath rest (Genesis 2:4) is everywhere infused by Torah. It is a story of the triumph of God, the triumph of Wisdom, and the triumph of Torah. Continuity between divine and human activity is one aspect of what it means to speak of natural law in the Bible.

III. CONTINUITY BETWEEN THE CREATED WORLD AND HUMAN BEHAVIOR

Another way in which we could find a connection between divine and human activity is by means of a connection between the created world and human behavior. This is another sense in which natural law could exist in the Bible. It is closely tied to the previous thesis. The biblical assertion of continuity between the divine and creation is consistent with the claim that there might also be a connection between the created world and human behavior.

The biblical materials seem to make room for "moral principles that correspond to 'the way things are.'"[13] It asserts that there are ways of acting which breach a kind of natural order in things. Certain forms of behavior have certain inevitable physical consequences. There is a cosmological relationship between the moral and physical orders of creation: what Bruckner calls a "moral-physical cosmology."[14] This is slightly different to the claim in the Book of Proverbs, that bad behavior ultimately has ruinous consequences for the individual (e.g., Proverbs 26:27).[15] In this section, we are concerned more broadly with the interactions between human behavior and the created order as a whole. It explores the various interconnections between the natural world as we now conceive it: the created world, the world of plants and animals and things, and human behavior.

A. Fire from heaven

A dramatic example of the connection between the created world and human behavior can be found in the overthrow of the cities of Sodom and Gomorrah (Genesis 19:23–27), which is presented as a "pre-Sinaitic" text. The behavior of the men of Sodom—attempted homosexual gang rape—can also be read in its ancient Near Eastern context as an extreme violation of customary ANE rules of

---

13. BOCKMUEHL, JEWISH LAW, p. 90.
14. BRUCKNER, IMPLIED LAW, p. 163.
15. *See generally* R. E. Clements, *The concept of abomination in the Book of Proverbs*, in TEXTS, TEMPLES AND TRADITIONS (Michael V. Fox, Victor Avigdor Hurowitz, Avi Hurvitz, Michael L. Klein, Baruch J. Schwartz & Nili Shupak eds., Winona Lake: Eisenbrauns, 1996), 211–25.

hospitality toward strangers.[16] In the literary context of Genesis 18 and 19, the lack of hospitality shown by the Sodomites contrasts with the hospitality shown by Abraham toward the same strangers in Genesis 18:2–8. Inhospitality has severe environmental consequences:

> [T]he LORD rained on Sodom and Gomorrah brimstone and fire from the LORD out of heaven; and he overthrew those cities, and all the valley, and all the inhabitants of the cities, and what grew on the ground.
> (Genesis 19:24–25)

Genesis 19 is an extreme example of the impact of human behavior on the created world. The "well-watered" plain "like the garden of the LORD" (Genesis 13:10) becomes a smoky "furnace" (Genesis 19:28). The violence and inhospitality of the Plain's inhabitants are magnified by the violent convulsion of the Plain, "making it inhospitable to all life."[17] Unethical behavior and environmental disaster are intertwined; the result is poetic justice. There is an implied opposition between the "fire" that comes from heaven and the rain that normally falls. "The hospitality of the earth depends on rainfall. The lack of that falling rain and its fiery substitut[e] graphically demonstrates the realm of Sodom's failure and violation."[18]

This should not be taken to mean that the judgment upon Sodom is an automatic consequence of the Sodomites' behavior; after all, the point about the wider narrative and Abraham's prior intercession is that judgment is contingent on God's decision (Genesis 18:16–33; see Chapter 4). Instead, the story shows the close connection between the human behavior (inhospitality) and the created world (fire from heaven). It is an example of natural law because the consequences of human behavior are expressed through, and have an effect upon, the natural world.

B. Earthdeath

A further example of unethical behavior that has consequences for creation is found in Hosea 4, which is presented as a "post-Sinaitic" text:

> Hear the word of the LORD,
> O people of Israel;
> for the LORD has a controversy
> with the inhabitants of the land.
> There is no faithfulness or kindness,

---

16. Weston W. Fields, Sodom and Gomorrah: History and Motif in Biblical Narrative, Journal for the Study of the Old Testament Supplement Series 231 (Sheffield: Sheffield Academic Press, 1997), 54–85.
17. Bruckner, Implied Law, p. 202.
18. Ibid., 168.

and no knowledge of God in the land;
there is [false] swearing, lying, killing,
stealing, and committing adultery;
they break all bounds and murder follows murder.
Therefore the land mourns,
and all who dwell in it languish,
and also the beasts of the field,
and the birds of the air;
and even the fish of the sea are taken away. (Hosea 4:1–3)

Bockmuehl characterizes this as "a kind of reverse natural law argument [which] explicitly links the sins of Israel with the ecological disasters that have befallen the land."[19] Verses 2 and 3 recall the Decalogue, although it is notable that the prophet does not explicitly make this the ground of his appeal, preferring instead to rely upon a more general ethical standard ("faithfulness and kindness"). As in Genesis 19, the text posits a link between human ethical behavior and the well-being of the physical environment. As such, it can be seen as a further example of natural law in the Bible.

On the face of things, however, there seems to be a difference in emphasis between Genesis 19, where the consequences are very clearly the result of direct divine intervention, and Hosea 4, where we do not find the same degree of direct personal intervention on the part of God. Seen in isolation from the wider canon, Hosea might support the view that when things go wrong environmentally, as a result of human behavior, this is simply a matter of "cause and effect." It is a mechanistic consequence because it is "how the world works." From this perspective, natural law could be said to be natural because unethical behavior does not fit our human existence as creatures made in the image of God.

However, it would be unwise to stress the distinction between natural causation and divine intervention because it is not clear that the Bible accepts this distinction. The processes are not opposed to each other because the Bible sees God as working through both (cf. Hosea 4:1). What happens through natural causes also happens through divine causes. Although it is clear from Genesis 19 that God acts through natural phenomena, it is not clear from the Hosea oracle that the phenomenon itself operates as "part of an independent system."[20] Whatever the difference in presentation, the Bible's view of causation remains, as McAfee notes in another context, "radically theistic."[21]

---

19. BOCKMUEHL, JEWISH LAW, p. 93.
20. Gene McAfee, *Chosen people in a chosen land: Theology and ecology in the story of Israel's origins*, in THE EARTH STORY IN GENESIS, (Norman C. Habel & Shirley Wurst eds., Earth Bible Series, 5 vols., Sheffield: Sheffield Academic Press, 2000), vol. II, 158–74, 165.
21. Ibid.

Viewed from a wider canonical perspective, it is likely that Hosea presumes knowledge of the covenant between God and Israel, which includes curses for disregard of its laws. The covenant curses are set out in Leviticus 26:14–45 and in Deuteronomy 28:15–68. A number of these curses have specifically environmental effects. However, although these consequences are the result of human behavior, they are also presented as being the direct action of God:

> I will make your heavens like iron and your earth like brass; . . . your land shall not yield its increase, and the trees of the land shall not yield their fruit. (Leviticus 26:19–20; *God speaking*)

Specific groups of curses in Deuteronomy 28 appear to be arranged in a natural sequence of cause and effect. For example, verses 49–57 are concerned with the following sequence: invasion → agricultural pillage → siege → warfare → starvation → cannibalism, while verses 58–68 deal with disease → decimation → deportation → dispersion → conditions of exile.[22] But although these disasters can be seen as a natural consequence of breaching the covenant, they are simultaneously presented as being at God's initiative (e.g., "The LORD will bring a nation against you from afar . . ."; Deuteronomy 28:49).

To conclude, continuity between the created world and human behavior is another aspect of what it means to talk about natural law in the Bible. The idea that in Genesis 19, we find "a dynamic cosmological connection between the physical creation and the human moral order under judgement by God"[23] applies also to Hosea 4, when seen through the lens of Leviticus 26 and Deuteronomy 28.

IV. UNIVERSAL KNOWLEDGE OF CERTAIN NORMS

A third way in which natural law could exist in the Bible is through universal knowledge of certain norms. The Bible finds a connection between divine activity and universal knowledge of certain norms; this is closely tied to the previous thesis. The biblical assertion of a connection between the created world and human behavior is consistent with a claim to universality. If behavior toward the physical world has certain universal consequences, this sort of knowledge can be universal and entail universal knowledge of certain norms. We know that something is wrong because it has harmful consequences; this is another aspect of what natural law could mean in the Bible. This starting point produces a range of epistemological questions. Who knows of God's requirements? What is known? How is it known? We will bear these questions in mind as we explore the relevant texts.

---

22. JEFFREY H. TIGAY, DEUTERONOMY: THE JPS TORAH COMMENTARY (Philadelphia: The Jewish Publication Society, 1996), 489–92.
23. BRUCKNER, IMPLIED LAW, p. 200.

The first indication that the Bible finds a connection between divine revelation and universal knowledge of certain norms is the story of universal creation (see above). As Barton summarizes, "... the primary horizon of the Old Testament is not God's choice of Israel and the giving to them of the law, but the creation of the world and the moral order that derives from its created character. This implies that morality is first and foremost a matter of human beings recognizing their finite created status and seeking a way of life which embodies their sense of belonging in the hierarchical universe whose head and origin is God."[24] As we have already noted, something can be commended, not because God has explicitly said so, but because it recognizes what God has already done in creating the universe. By the same token, something can be forbidden, not because God has given a specific commandment, but because it is not consistent with what God has done in creation. Biblical law operates "beyond the confines of a historical past or a single culture."[25] Instead, it is established "in the bone and flesh of created humanity."[26]

We will explore the connection between divine activity and universal knowledge of certain norms by reference to the following materials: (1) the primeval history (Genesis 1–11), (2) the Noahide laws (Genesis 9:1–7), and (3) the oracles of Amos (Amos 1–2).

A. Primal screams

First, we begin by considering how this approach to natural law plays out in the primeval history. We will do this in regard to three key texts: (1) Cain (Genesis 4), (2) the sexual activities of the "sons of God" (Genesis 6), and (3) the spread of violence (Genesis 6). These texts are chosen because each concerns persons who are judged in the absence of particular revelation. As such, they help us to address the epistemological questions noted above: namely, the basis on which people are supposed to know that their behavior is wrong.

Our starting point is the story of Cain, which raises the question of the basis on which Cain is judged. Here we find the rhetorical question: "Am I my brother's keeper (*hashomer*)?" (Genesis 4:9). David Daube[27] argues that *hashomer* refers to the special relationship which exists between a person and a thing that is entrusted to his care. The verb *shamar* is used of a bailee who looks after someone else's valuables (Exodus 22:7/ MT 22:6) and who holds them, as we would say, in safe*keeping*. It is also used of the shepherd who looks after someone else's sheep; thus Jacob promises Laban that he will "feed your flock and keep (*eshmor*) it" (Genesis 30:31). We cannot be certain if Cain owed a duty to Abel that was

---

24. JOHN BARTON, ETHICS AND THE OLD TESTAMENT (London: SCM, 1998), 67.
25. BRUCKNER, IMPLIED LAW, p. 209.
26. Ibid.
27. DAVID DAUBE, STUDIES IN BIBLICAL LAW (Cambridge: Cambridge University Press, 1947), 13–15.

analogous to that of a shepherd and his sheep; however, the use of *shomer* in Genesis 4:9 suggests that some special responsibility was owed by the elder to the younger brother. Cain's question is thus an outright rejection of his fraternal duty.

Novak[28] suggests that Cain's response should be taken as a plea of ignorance. Cain is not denying that he had an obligation toward his brother, simply that he did not know about it. Yet even Cain's claim of ignorance, on this reading, seems implausible. Just as the heavens pour forth speech (Psalm 19:1–4), so too does the earth. Abel's blood "cries out" to God "from the ground," which implies that even the ground knows murder is wrong (Genesis 4:10). At any rate, Cain's response does not function as a defence to the charge. Cain had a duty to look out for his brother, and he ought not to have committed murder. His behavior is wrong—not because God has expressly forbidden it—but because it misunderstands humanity's mandate to replicate the image of God by creating human life, not destroying it (Genesis 1:28).

Several chapters later, we find an account of sexual relations between "the sons of God" and the "daughters of men" (Genesis 6:2). There is some ambiguity about the identity of the male sexual partners: some suggest angelic beings of some description, while others propose more mundane earthly potentates.[29] Either way, they are engaged in illicit sexual activity. The punishment—a restriction on humanity's life span (Genesis 6:3—once again begs the epistemological question: how did the parties know it was wrong? Their behavior is wrong, not because God has specifically forbidden it, but because it misunderstands the limits that are set to sexual expression in Genesis 1–2, that is, heterosexual monogamy between one man and one woman.

The incident is said to precede God's decision to destroy humanity and animal life by the Flood (Genesis 6:5–7). Novak thinks it significant that "when Noah and his family and the representative animals are saved in the Ark from the flood, they enter the Ark as married couples."[30] This is based on the description of the animals entering the ark, "two of each [kind], male and female" (Genesis 7:9; JPS). Novak's view is supported by one of the Dead Sea Scrolls which sees Genesis 7:9 as a proof text for monogamy (Damascus Document 4:20–5:2[31]; see Chapter 12). If this reading is correct, it confirms the connection between the sexual offenses described in Genesis 6:1–4 and God's decision to send the Flood in Genesis 6:5–7.

Subsequent verses narrate God's decision to destroy "all flesh" on account of the way in which the earth had been "filled with 'violence' (*chamas*)" (Genesis 6:11;

---

28. David Novak, Natural Law in Judaism (Cambridge: Cambridge University Press, 1998), 33–34.
29. Novak, Natural Law, p. 36.
30. Ibid., 38.
31. Geza Vermes, *Sectarian matrimonial halakah in the Damascus Rule*, J. Jewish Studies 25, 197–202 (1974).

see further Chapter 5). Yet again, there is no indication that *chamas* had been specifically prohibited by God. It is, however, a reversal of the divine commandment to humankind to "fill the earth" with the image of God (Genesis 1:26–27). *Chamas* is wrong because, once again, it is inconsistent with God's behavior in the story of universal creation.

For all these reasons, the Bible seems to presume universal knowledge of certain norms, and this is another way in which we may say there is natural law in the Bible.

B. Paint the whole world with a rainbow

A further example of universal knowledge of certain norms may be found in the so-called Noahide laws. These are the commands given by God to Noah and his descendants when they came out of the Ark, after the Flood (Genesis 9:1–7). They should not be confused with the adjacent Noahide covenant in Genesis 9:8–11.

The biblical Noahide laws are not very extensive. In fact, apart from the warning about shedding blood, the laws really only contain one prohibition, which is against eating meat with its lifeblood (Genesis 9:4). However, because Genesis 9:1–7 is addressed to all humanity, it is another example of a text which makes explicit universal knowledge of certain norms. In this sense, the Noahide laws are an example of natural law in the Bible. They are also a good example of how direct commands can be an example of natural law.

Subsequent Jewish tradition added further commandments, including (1) observing righteousness, (2) covering "the shame of their flesh", (3) blessing the Creator, (4) honoring father and mother, (5) loving one's neighbor, and (6) "guard[ing] their souls from fornication and uncleanness and all iniquity" (Jubilees 7:20–21). These commandments are all *additional* to those referred to in Genesis 9:1–7 and make no reference to the dietary law of Genesis 9:4. This extended tradition became a way of enabling Jewish law to express certain beliefs about what laws were universal to all humankind. Over time, they also became an important way of regulating relationships between Jews and Gentiles. As a logical consequence, postbiblical Judaism ends up making Adam subject to the Noahide tradition (as with the twelfth-century Rabbi Maimonides in his commentary on Avodah Zarah 9:4) even though in canonical terms, Adam pre-dates the Noahide tradition. This seems anachronistic: the first *pre*-diluvian human is subject to the laws of the first *post*-diluvian human. However, it reflects rabbinic beliefs that since the laws were truly universal they must have applied to Adam as much as they did to Noah.

C. International law in the first millennium BC

Our final example of universal knowledge of certain norms is found in Amos's oracles against the nations. Here we find that the non-Israelite nations are charged with a number of "war crimes." There is no indication that the non-Israelite nations had received any special revelation from God that their behavior was wrong. This raises the question, yet again, of the basis upon which God judges, apart from the covenant at Sinai. The specifics of the offenses may be debated at certain points but seem to be as follows: Aram is charged with "threshing Gilead," which may refer generally to callous treatment during war or else to an actual form of physical torture (Amos 1:3); Philistia is indicted for selling enemies into slavery (Amos 1:6); Tyre and Edom are denounced for breaching interstate treaties, in different ways (Amos 1:9, 11)[32]; Ammon is charged with ripping open pregnant women to gain land (Amos 1:13); and Moab is arraigned for burning the king of Edom's bones "to lime," which was a gross form of corpse defilement (Amos 2:1). Remarkably, the non-Israelite nations are as eligible for judgment for their behavior toward each other as Judah and Israel (Amos 2:4–16).[33] Amos "simply assumes that other nations have a moral conscience, and that atrocities are wrong and are known to be wrong by whomever and against whomever they are committed."[34]

Amos's rhetoric builds to a climax, where he then turns the tables on his hearers in Israel. Having joined the prophet in condemning non-Israelite nations and Judah, the Israelites now find themselves on trial (Amos 2:6–16). In a remarkable and shocking twist, Amos goes straight on to denounce Judah for rejecting "the law of the LORD" (Amos 2:4) and Israel for a variety of offenses, including social injustice and sexual immorality (Amos 2:6–12). The accusers become the accused. But Amos's rhetorical strategy only makes sense if we assume that his audience shared the following assumptions: (1) that the nations' behavior was wrong, (2) that the peoples in question knew it was wrong, and (3) that God was active in judging the affairs of non-Israelite nations.[35] These popular assumptions are crucial from the point of view of natural law in the Bible. Again, the Bible asserts that human beings, universally, have knowledge of certain norms which are the basis of divine judgment.

Amos does not, however, indicate the source of this knowledge. Barton suggests that the nations are condemned on the basis of "international customary law."[36] Yet the fact that Amos's hearers expect God to avenge breaches in international conduct suggests that the source is not simply a matter of human moral consensus. Behind Amos's oracles stands the belief that God is a certain sort of God who judges on the basis of knowledge of universal norms. The surprising thing about Amos's oracles is that universal norms have been made concrete in international consensus. This means that there are different modes of

---

32. JOHN BARTON, AMOS' ORACLES AGAINST THE NATIONS: A STUDY OF AMOS 1:3–2:5 (Cambridge: Cambridge University Press, 1980), 20–21.
33. John Barton, *Natural law and poetic justice in the Old Testament*, J. THEOLOGICAL STUDS 30, 1–14, 3 (1979).
34. BARTON, ETHICS AND THE OLD TESTAMENT, p. 62.
35. BARTON, AMOS' ORACLES, p. 4.
36. Ibid., 44.

expression through which normative judgments come to be made, including, in this case, international consensus. It also means that behind the oracles is the belief that human beings are created to be moral reasoners, both morally creative and connected to a God who has moral character. This development is an example of a particular creative moment in the expression of natural law in the Bible.

To sum up, the Bible finds a connection between divine activity and universal knowledge of certain norms. Examples can be found in a range of texts, including the primeval history, the Noahide laws, and Amos's oracles against the nations.

V. CONTINUITY BETWEEN DIFFERENT FORMS OF REVELATION

A fourth way in which natural law could exist in the Bible is through continuity between different forms of revelation: universal knowledge—which comes from being made in the image of God—and particular revelation. There is evidence in the Bible that innate knowledge and particular revelation go hand in hand, such that the latter is never surprising or tends to be confirmatory, rendering explicit that which is implicit. Here is another example of the interconnection between human and divine activity. It is closely tied to the previous thesis which asserted the universal knowledge of certain norms.

This raises the question of the relationship between universal knowledge and the revelation at, say, Mount Sinai. Certainly there seems to be some relationship between universal knowledge and particular revelation. Even random examples show that the two are not very different. The story of creation in Genesis 1 points toward the ban on idols in Exodus 20:2–6; the dietary laws of Genesis 2–3 and the distinction between clean and unclean animals (Genesis 7:2-9) anticipate the ritual food laws and taxonomies of Leviticus 11 and Deuteronomy 14:3–21; the story of Cain points toward the various Sinaitic homicide laws (see further Chapter 8) while the various stories of sexual misdemeanors in Genesis (including, inter alia, the "sons of God" episode and Sodom and Gomorrah) anticipate various Sinaitic sexual offenses (see further Chapters 10 and 11). It is fair to say that at Mount Sinai, "the formula is revelatory, the mode of expression and the context are revelatory, but the basic legal content has nothing tremendously original about it."[37]

What, then, is the point of revelation such as Sinai? According to Spohn, "Scripture *reminds us* what it means to be human and calls us to live an integrated human life that our egotism would ignore."[38] The purpose of revelation,

---

37. Barr, Natural Theology, p. 18.
38. William Spohn, What Are They Saying About Scripture and Ethics? (Paulist Press, 1996), p. 38, italics added.

including Sinai, is to be a moral reminder.[39] On this view, there is not a stark contrast between innate knowledge and particular revelation.

The continuity between general and specific revelation can also be seen as an expression of the continuity between the primeval (Genesis 1–11) and the ancestral histories (Genesis 12–50) which we noted in the Introduction. The giving of the law at Mount Sinai is presented as partial fulfillment of the promise to Abraham, which itself is for the benefit of all the peoples of the world. Law is central to God's creative activity, both in creating the world and creating Israel at Mount Sinai.

Yet at the same time, it equally remains the case that the Decalogue is uniquely addressed to a particular people in a particular time and place who have experienced a particular event.

On this basis, we could not necessarily assume that this particular concrete expression of God's requirements for this particular people at this particular time applies to all peoples in all times and in all places. The Ten Commandments are addressed to a group of people who have experienced a particular historical event in the form of the Exodus:

> He declares his word to Jacob,
> his statutes and ordinances to Israel.
> He has not dealt thus with any other nation;
> they do not know his ordinances. (Psalm 147:19–20)

What the other nations do not know is the particularity of the revelation at Mount Sinai and their reception as part of a specific experience of deliverance in the form of the Exodus. Indeed, Israel's experience of the Exodus gives her "some new *motivations* for keeping the law (Exodus 22:21/MT 22:20; 23:9), indeed empowers Israel to that end."[40] At the same time, however, other peoples have also experienced manifestations of divine activity and so, once again, we are back to noting continuity between innate knowledge and particular revelation:

> "Are you not like the Ethiopians
> to me, O people of Israel?" says the LORD.
> "Did I not bring up Israel from the land of Egypt,
> and the Philistines from Caphtor
> and the Syrians from Kir?" (Amos 9:7; *God speaking*)

This continuity between general and specific revelation is captured in Israel's vocation to be "a kingdom of priests" (Exodus 19:6). Israel has a universal calling and is normative for the rest of the world but, at the same time, she remains a concrete expression of true wisdom. She is morally attractive—paradigmatic even—but she is not in any straightforward sense universalisible. Her vocation is at once general and specific. The specificity of her calling means that the

---

39. Spohn, What Are They Saying?, p. 39.
40. Ibid.

Sinaitic laws cannot be carried over automatically to a relational context other than that between God and Israel because outsiders are not part of the story. As Novak observes, the uniqueness of the covenant with Israel lies not so much in the content—much of which has analogues and antecedents elsewhere—but "in its overall Gestalt, which constitutes a full and abiding relationship between God and a people on earth."[41] The priestly function of Israel is to invite non-Israelite nations to come and join in the national story; come and join us in our Exodus! This is, of course, the vision of the later prophets:

> It shall come to pass in the latter days
> that the mountain of the house of the LORD
> shall be established as the highest of the mountains,
> and shall be raised above the hills;
> and all the nations shall flow to it,
> and many peoples shall come, and say:
> "Come,
> let us go up to the mountain of the LORD,
> to the house of the God of Jacob;
> that he may teach us his ways
> and that we may walk in his paths." (Isaiah 2:2-3)

As Novak concludes, ". . . the normative content of the Sinai covenant need not be regarded as originally instituted at the event of the Sinai revelation."[42] But Sinai does say it with greater clarity, precision, and detail. Random examples might include repaying the theft of a sheep fourfold (Exodus 22:1/MT 21:37), not withholding offerings from one's granaries (Exodus 22:29/MT 22:28), and not boiling a kid in its own mother's milk (Exodus 23:19). In Deuteronomy, Moses commands obedience to the Sinaitic laws because

> . . . that will be [proof of] your wisdom and your understanding in the sight of the peoples, who, when they hear all these statutes, will say, "Surely this great nation is a wise and understanding people." For what great nation is there . . . that has statutes and ordinances so righteous as all this law [or "Teaching"; JPS] which I set before you this day? (Deuteronomy 4:6–8; *Moses speaking*)

It has been argued that "[t]his implies some standard by which YHWH's laws can be measured, which must logically be prior to those laws."[43] (The personal name 'YHWH' is the most widespread designation for God in the Pentateuch, and is composed of the Hebrew consonants *yhwh*, also known as the 'Tetragrammaton'). But is not the standard that which is already known? Do they not commend themselves because they are consistent with what we already know? To adapt John Barton's observation on the relationship between Scripture and natural

---

41. Novak, Natural Law, p. 60.
42. Ibid.
43. Barton, Ethics and the Old Testament, p. 73.

law, Sinai does not legislate; it illustrates.[44] Sinai is profoundly affirming of the emerging human sense of that which is right. Yet it is more than a mere reminder of what we already know. It deepens our understanding and fills it out. We go further up and further in.

Increasing specificity is characteristic of Jesus's application of Torah in the New Testament (see Chapter 12). Here, Jesus's teaching of the law is presented as a fuller, greater, and more complete account of that which was already emerging or that which was implicit. Indeed, the New Testament goes so far as to present Torah in the most specific way imaginable: Jesus as the Word-made-flesh is the ultimate embodiment of Torah (1 John 1:1). And just as the Exodus gives Israel new motives for obedience, so too the "new Exodus" of Jesus's crucifixion and resurrection is said to provide the followers of Jesus with new motivations for living as the people of God. This "new Exodus" is presented in terms of the deliverance from sin that is achieved by Christ's substitutionary death on the Cross. An example of this new motivation is expressed by the apostle Paul who writes, "the life I now live in the flesh I live by faith in the Son of God, who loved me and gave himself for me" (Galatians 2:20).

To sum up, the Bible asserts a continuity between innate knowledge and particular revelation such that the latter tends to be confirmatory of universal norms, even as that body of revelation becomes more detailed, and the people of God find fresh motivation to live obedient lives.

VI. CONTINUITY BETWEEN DIVINE AND HUMAN ACTS OF JUDGMENT

A fifth and final way in which natural law could be said to exist in the Bible is in the form of continuity between divine and human acts of judgment. This is another example of the interconnection between human and divine activity in the realm of normativity.

Certainly, the Bible never sees adjudication as a pure act of human convention. This is reflected in a few general examples. For example, in Exodus 18, which is centrally concerned with the organization of adjudication in biblical Israel (see further Chapter 4), there is a clear divine/human juxtaposition. There is a parallelism between "all that (*kol-asher*) God had done for Moses and for Israel" (Exodus 18:1) and "all that (*kol-asher*) he [Moses] was doing for the people" (Exodus 18:14). As we would expect in a theocratic legal system, the sacral and the judicial are intimately bound together. Similarly, we find that Jehoshaphat's judicial reforms take place in the context of a wider "teaching mission"[45] designed to bring the people back to God (2 Chronicles 17:1–9).

---

44. Ibid., 60.
45. KEITH W. WHITELAM, THE JUST KING: MONARCHICAL JUDICIAL AUTHORITY IN ANCIENT ISRAEL, JOURNAL FOR THE SOCIETY OF THE OLD TESTAMENT SUPPLEMENT SERIES 12 (Sheffield: Journal for the Society of the Old Testament Press, 1979), 191.

In this section, we will consider some specific examples of continuity between divine and human acts of judgment, although these examples do not, of course, exhaust the theme of continuity. They are (1) the delegation of judgment from God to humanity in the primeval history (Genesis 1–9); (2) the involvement of God and humanity in the "reckoning for human life" (Genesis 9:5–6); (3) God's personal tutoring of Abraham in "the way" of "righteousness and justice" (Genesis 18); (4) the expansion of human reality in the Sinai story (especially Exodus 19–40), which is the context for allocating sacral judicial roles to ordinary people in local settings; and (5) Solomon's famous judgment concerning the disputed son (1 Kings 3:16–28).

A. New world order

The first example is God's progressive delegation of judgment to humanity in the primeval history. Devorah Steinmetz[46] finds a structural parallel between three key stories in the primeval history: namely, Adam and Eve (Genesis 3:9–24), Cain and Abel (Genesis 4:9–16), and Noah and Ham (Genesis 9:18–27). Each begins with mankind inhabiting a "new world." The first world is the Garden of Eden, the second is the world outside of Eden (later destroyed by the Flood), and the third is the postdiluvian world (that is, the world after the Flood). In each story, the "new beginning" of humankind is characterized by human failure (eating from the tree, murder, and Ham's strange violation of his father, Noah). Even more interesting, there are structural parallels in regard to adjudication. In Genesis 3:9–24, God administers direct divine justice by appearing in person, questioning, accusing, pronouncing punishment, and then carrying it out. Exactly the same sequence occurs in Genesis 4:9–16. However, in Genesis 9:18–27, there is no direct intervention by God regarding Ham's offense. Instead, for the first time, adjudication and punishment are presented as being carried out by a human being (Genesis 9:24–25). Noah curses Ham, which is significant, because until now, the power to curse has been a divine prerogative (Genesis 3:14, 17; 4:11).

It seems to be the case that as we move from the antediluvian world to the postdiluvian one, God devolves an increased responsibility to secure justice upon human beings. This may even be a consequence of Noah's cooperation with God in building the Ark. Certainly, Noah and his descendants are given greater mastery over the world that he and his family helped to re-create (Genesis 9:3). Among these new rights and responsibilities is adjudication. It is a sign that in the postdiluvian world, divine justice is to be carried out, so far as practicable, by humanity. Adjudication is part of humanity's divinely devolved responsibility to order the postdiluvian world. It is part of our vocation.

---

46. Devora Steinmetz, *Vineyard, farm and garden: The drunkenness of Noah in the context of primeval history*, J. BIBLICAL LITERATURE 113, 193–207 (1994).

The structural parallels between the three stories in the primeval history thus indicate that there is continuity between divine and human acts of judgment, and this is a sense in which we can speak of natural law in the Bible.

B. The homicide squad

The idea that adjudication is part of humanity's divinely devolved responsibility to order the postdiluvian world is confirmed in the homicide laws of Genesis 9:6. They address the question of who is authorized to respond to homicide in biblical law. The classic statement of accountability is found in Genesis 9:5–6, which declares:

> For your lifeblood I will surely require a reckoning; of every beast I will require it and of man; of every man's brother I will require the life of man.
> Whoever sheds the blood of man,
> by man (*ba'adam*) shall his blood be shed;
> for God made man in his own image. (*God speaking to Noah and his sons*)

It is a rather ambiguous declaration. Verse 5 states that *God* will hold animals and humanity accountable for human bloodshed ("I will surely require a reckoning") while verse 6 apparently states that *humankind* will hold killers to account ("By man shall his blood be shed"). On this reading, both God and humanity are involved in the "reckoning" for human life (9:5).

Alternatively, we could put an end to the ambiguity by noting that the word *ba'adam* in verse 6—which is usually translated "by man"—can mean "in exchange for that man." On this view, verse 6 does not explicitly require any human involvement. The ambiguity is resolved because *both* verses 5 *and* 6 can be taken to refer to divine punishment.

Yet even this restrictive reading of Genesis 9:5–6 does not exclude the possibility that human beings may be involved in the divine reckoning for human blood. This is because the motive clause in verse 6 (". . . for God made man in his own image") operates on several levels. On one level, it means that God has an interest in punishing the killer because humanity is made in God's image. But on another level, it means that humanity *also* has a stake in punishing homicide. This is because part of what it means for humanity to be made "in the image of God" (Genesis 1:27) is to judge as God judges,[47] which, according to verse 5, includes holding killers to account. The result is that regardless of whether we recognize an ambiguity in Genesis 9:5–6 or not, humanity is supposed to be involved in the divine "reckoning" of human life.

The involvement of humanity in this aspect of divine justice is consistent with the argument elsewhere in this section: namely, that there is some continuity between divine and human judicial activity. Examples of this continuity in

---

47. See the discussion of Genesis 1:27 in Chapter 5.

relation to homicide can be found in the biblical narratives. For instance, King Solomon commands his "strong arm" man Benaiah to strike down Joab, the former commander of King David's army, on account of Joab's "bloody deeds" (1 Kings 2:32). Solomon's command and divine judgment are presented as one and the same:

> strike him [Joab] down and bury him . . . The LORD will bring back his bloody deeds upon his own head . . . . (1 Kings 2:31–32; *Solomon speaking to Benaiah*)

Of course, this continuity may simply reflect the king's privileged position as a recipient of divine wisdom (e.g., Proverbs 10:10). But at the same time, it is compatible with a dual reading of Genesis 9:5–6, in which both God and humanity are involved in responding to homicide. If this understanding of Genesis 9:5–6 was widespread, there may well have been a popular belief that a system of private vengeance was compatible with divine justice. Thus, the victim's family may have seen *themselves* as the agents of divine justice. Only if they failed to slay the killer could they expect God to intervene and punish the killer directly.

To sum up, Genesis 9:5–6 does not support a straightforward "either/or" in terms of who is involved in the divine "reckoning" for human life. As far as the text is concerned, it is neither "all down to God" nor "all down to humanity." Exactly the same duality is found in the biblical legal materials which affirm *both* the role of human institutions in judging homicide (e.g., the go'el haddam or "avenger of blood") *and* direct divine involvement (see further Chapter 8). There is continuity between divine and human acts of judgment, and consequently, it is a further sense in which we can speak of natural law in the Bible.

C. Higher education

Third, the divine delegation of adjudication upon humankind which is presented in Genesis 1–9 suggests something about the relative priority of judgment in divine-human relations. This theme is developed further in our third example, God's decision to involve Abraham in his judgment of Sodom:

> . . . Shall I hide from Abraham what I am about to do . . .? No, for I have chosen him, that he may charge his children and his household after him to keep the way of the LORD by doing righteousness and justice . . . .
> (Genesis 18:17–19; *God speaking*)

God's stated interest is to train Abraham to be an adjudicator. God does this by reference to a real-life case—a sort of divine Judicial Studies Board. Abraham receives his training in the context of his relationship with God. The context thus has overtones of the "tutoring in wisdom" that is supposed to occur in a domestic context between fathers and sons (e.g., Proverbs 3:1ff). As we will see in Chapter 4, the family is at the cutting edge of day-to-day justice because it is in this setting that wisdom is internalized, with wisdom being essential to doing justice. This idea is explicitly present in the divine speech: Abraham is to instruct his own children with the adjudicatory skills that he himself has learned from God. This connection clearly indicates that there is continuity between divine and human acts of judgment.

The word *derek* ("way") usually refers to "behavior" in the wisdom literature (e.g., Proverbs 1:15) and when combined—uniquely—with the words "righteousness (*tsedaqah*) and justice (*mishpat*)," it means "to proceed in conformity with the law."[48] If *derek* does have "a legal procedural meaning then Abraham is receiving valuable adjudicatory experience."[49] Adjudication is not only central to legal systems; it is also central to "the way of the LORD." This is confirmed in the subsequent Sinaitic legislation. Bruckner claims that approximately one-third of the 613 commandments traditionally numbered in the Torah are concerned with judicial process.[50]

Abraham's subsequent didactic exchange with God (Genesis 18:23–32) concerns the need to administer proper legal procedure. Abraham's famous rhetorical question, "Shall not the Judge of all the earth do right?" (Genesis 18:25) can be translated: "shall not the judge . . . make a just decision?"[51] Certainly, the dialogue revolves around the need for judicial integrity in reaching a decision. Abraham expresses concern for the following:[52]

(1) That the innocent should not be punished for the actions of the guilty (e.g., Genesis 18:23)
(2) Detailed discovery of the facts, combined with a thorough procedure (e.g., Genesis 18:32)
(3) A reprieve for the guilty majority (e.g., Genesis 18:32)

Each point focuses on "the authoritative act of discerning, separating and deciding between what/when is just and what/when is unjust, between the innocent and the guilty."[53] All are part of what it means to "keep the way of the LORD by doing righteousness and justice. . ." (Genesis 18:19). Item (3) is striking: Abraham moves from seeking a pardon for the innocent of Sodom to a reprieve for Sodom itself, Abraham himself having shown mercy to Sodom on a previous occasion (Genesis 14). "The righteousness and justice of Abraham . . . [are] a passion for the well-being of the very ones who have violated God."[54]

---

48. Pietro Bovati, Re-Establishing Justice: Legal terms, concepts and procedures in the Hebrew Bible, translated by Michael J. Smith, Journal for the Study of the Old Testament Supplement Series 105 (Sheffield: Sheffield Academic Press, 1994), p. 192 note 52.
49. Ibid.
50. Bruckner, Implied Law, p. 142.
51. Ibid., 140.
52. Ibid., 132–34.
53. Bovati, Re-Establishing Justice, p. 185.
54. Walter Brueggemann, Genesis, Interpretation Bible Commentary (Louisville: John Knox Press, 1982), 169.

To conclude, Abraham participates in an act of divine adjudication as he stands in the divine Presence (Genesis 18:22). The scene anticipates Moses and Jehoshaphat's judicial appointees (Exodus 18:21–22, 24–26; 2 Chronicles 19:5–11). These judges are Abraham's "posterity"—and they are the ones who are said to discover God "with" them in giving judgment (see Chapter 4, Table 6). Once again, there is continuity between divine and human adjudication, which can be seen as a further example of natural law in the Bible.

D. Seized by justice

Fourth, the divine delegation of adjudication upon humankind in general, and on Abraham's descendants in particular, is developed further in the Sinai story (especially Exodus 19–40). Exodus 18 describes the judicial reforms implemented by Moses on the advice of his father-in-law, Jethro. These have the effect of drawing a large body of persons into the administration of divine justice. But more than this, the judicial reform of Exodus 18 is seen to parallel the radical redefinition of divine-human relations in Exodus 19–40 itself.

Although Exodus 19–40 starts by emphasizing the great distance between God and the people—symbolized by the "devouring fire" (Exodus 24:17) atop Mount Sinai and the terrified people at its foot—it goes on to describe the divine movement from the top of the mountain to "the tent of meeting ... outside the camp" (Exodus 33:7–11) and, ultimately, to the Tabernacle, God's "dwelling" in the midst of the people (Exodus 40:33–38; see Chapter 2). It is a radical transition. It means that ordinary life, at the foot of Mount Sinai, is now "the locus of divine manifestation."[55] This movement from "high" to "low" parallels the transfer of some of Moses's functions to the people's representatives. It signifies that the "profoundly sacred" character of divine adjudication has been "transferred to the baseness of human reality."[56] The baseness is reflected in Moses's complaint: "How can I bear alone the weight and burden of you and your strife?" (Deuteronomy 1:12). Exodus 18 is significant in the light of Exodus 19–40 because that which has been "emphatically defined as burdensome and rather sordid, is profoundly sanctified."[57]

Exodus 18 anticipates the larger story of Exodus 19–40. It points forward to a new stage in the ongoing story arc of the Bible in which ordinary human reality becomes the place of "sacred action performed by human subjects."[58] One point where the separation between divine and human seems particularly blurred is in the story of Moses's shining skin (Exodus 34:29). The choice of *qaran* for the verb

---

55. Martin Ravndal Hauge, The Descent from the Mountain: Narrative Patterns in Exodus 19–40, Journal for the Study of the Old Testament Supplement Series 323 (Sheffield: Sheffield Academic Press, 2001), 254.
56. Hauge, Descent from the Mountain, p. 312.
57. Ibid., 275.
58. Ibid., 258.

(which can mean, in certain contexts, to be horned) "can hardly be understood as anything but a deliberate allusion to the other horned being of the context, namely the Golden Calf."[59] Horns were a symbol of strength and hence of divine power in the ANE. A number of ANE deities are depicted wearing bovine horns or "horned headgear"[60]; consequently, such attire was also favored by human kings (see, for example, the victory stele of Naram-Sin, king of Akkad, *circa* 2270 BC). Indeed, it was for exactly this reason that the Israelites hailed their golden calf as the deity who delivered them from Egypt (Exodus 32:4). The description of Moses's skin should thus be understood as "an indication of the divine character of Moses' presence."[61]

In the New Testament, the divine character of human judgement, in all its physicality, is extended to the furthest degree possible. This is seen in its claim that Jesus of Nazareth is the incarnation of God's justice and specifically in the belief that God "has given all judgment to the Son" (John 5:22, Jesus speaking) as the world's judge (e.g., Revelation 19:15). For all their strangeness, such beliefs can be seen to have their roots in traditions found in the Hebrew Bible.

To conclude, the biblical materials present the subject of judicial reform in the context of a close redefinition of divine-human relations. This also underlines the continuity between the divine and the human in relation to adjudication, which can thus be seen as a further example of natural law in the Bible.

E. Ruling in justice

Our last example is perhaps the most famous legal case in the whole of the Hebrew Bible; the judgment of King Solomon (1 Kings 3:16–28). Solomon's adjudication is presented as the immediate outworking of a dream revelation in which Solomon asks God for:

> an understanding mind to govern thy people, that I may discern between good and evil.... (1 Kings 3:9)

The revelation takes place while the king is at Gibeah, Israel's premier "high place" (1 Kings 3:4) which thus has strong cultic associations. For these reasons, then, there is strong continuity between divine and human acts of judgment.

The disputants in the case are two prostitutes. The fact that Solomon was willing to adjudicate in a case involving two streetwalkers does not indicate that the king was approachable by anyone with an axe to grind[62] but rather that these petitioners lacked any male family members who could sue for justice on their

---

59. Ibid., 168.
60. B. Kedar-Kopfstein, *Qeren*, in THEOLOGICAL DICTIONARY OF THE OLD TESTAMENT (G. Johannes Botterweck, Helmer Ringgren & Heinz-Josef Fabry eds.; David E. Green trans., Grand Rapids, Mich.: Eerdmans, 2004), vol. XIII, 167–74, 169.
61. HAUGE, DESCENT FROM THE MOUNTAIN, p. 168.
62. PER WHITELAM, JUST KING, p. 162.

behalf (1 Kings 3:17–18). Care for the outcast was one of the main tasks of the just and righteous king in both the Bible and the ANE.[63]

Infanticide was not the issue. The death of a human being in biblical Israel was largely regulated by blood feud (see Chapter 8), but since neither woman had any male family members to progress the matter, no one had an interest in identifying the person responsible for the death. Instead, the issue was identifying the mother of the live son; this is what Solomon is interested in. It is a hard case "on the facts" because in the absence of witnesses (1 Kings 3:18), it could not be solved by conventional legal means. It is a doubly hard case because the stereotypical view of the prostitute in the Bible is that of a habitual liar (e.g., Proverbs 7:21). Getting the truth from not one but two such persons would have been seen as the ultimate judicial challenge.[64]

In the end, Solomon does not judge the two women: they judge themselves. He resorts to a "psychological ordeal"[65] which reveals the underlying attitudes of the parties. Each woman "gives herself away" by her spontaneous response. This enables Solomon to look upon their hearts.[66] He sees past the stereotypical prostitute to the mother underneath.[67] It is wisdom in action because he sees to the heart of things which is, of course, God's prerogative. His adjudication is seen as proof that God has given him what he asked for. His proposal to "Divide the living child in two . . ." (1 Kings 3:25) is evidence of an "understanding mind" because it does succeed in judging between the two women, and it does distinguish between good and evil (1 Kings 3:9).

The claim to continuity between divine and human acts of judgment is not merely of interest from the point of view of natural law in the Bible: it is an extremely powerful part of the claim to be a legitimate king. The preceding chapters of 1 Kings uncovered the machinations and bloody intrigues that put Solomon on the throne. It would not have been surprising if there were those who doubted that Solomon's authority was valid. The story of his adjudication is clearly intended to justify and legitimize Solomon's claim to being a divinely appointed king.[68]

To conclude this section, there are a number of ways in which we can identify continuity between divine and human acts of judgment in the biblical materials.

---

63. MOSHE WEINFELD, SOCIAL JUSTICE IN ANCIENT ISRAEL (Jerusalem: Magnes Press, 1995), 25–44.

64. Phyllis Bird, *The harlot as heroine, in* WOMEN IN THE HEBREW BIBLE, (Alice Bach ed., New York: Routledge, 1999), 99–117, 110.

65. Bernard S. Jackson, *Literal meaning: Semantics and narratives in biblical law and modern jurisprudence*, INT'L. J. SEMIOTICS OF LAW 13, 433–57, 449 (2000).

66. Moshe A. Zipor, *The cannibal women and their judgment before the helpless king (2 Kings 6:24ff,)* ABR-NAHRAIN 35, 84–94, 89 n. 16 (1998).

67. Bird, *Harlot as heroine.*

68. WHITELAM, JUST KING, pp. 155–66.

Consequently, it is a further sense in which we can speak of natural law in the Bible, in addition to the other strands outlined in this chapter.

VII. RETHINKING NATURAL LAW

So far we have seen that there are a number of ways in which natural law could exist in the Bible. How does this resonate with the identification of natural law in the Western philosophical tradition? There is much within the Bible that is consistent with the different theses held by classical and modern natural lawyers. At the same time, however, there is also a tension between natural law in the Bible and the Western philosophical tradition. This is because the Western natural law tradition has developed in ways that are not consistent with natural law in the Bible. One of the side effects of this is that not only is there a tendency to see the Bible as different from natural law and therefore irrelevant, but there is *also* a tendency to misread certain passages of the Bible as if they were examples of natural law when, in fact, they are not. In this final section, we caution against an overly natural law reading of the biblical texts and consider how the biblical materials might encourage us to modify the Western natural law position.

A. Diversity and tensions within natural law

To do this, we must first say something about the development and reception of natural law within the Western philosophical tradition. We noted at the start of this chapter the danger of cariacturing complex philosophical positions. Certainly, the history of ideas shows that the tradition of natural law is complex. However, we can make two basic points: (1) natural law is a broad tradition which can refer to a multiplicity of theses, and (2) natural law has different emphases within the Western legal philosophical tradition.

First, *natural law is a broad tradition which can refer to a multiplicity of theses*. Some of the different theses that are part of the natural law tradition are listed in Table 5 below, along with examples of their exponents. This list is not of course intended to be comprehensive; it is merely intended to illustrate diversity within the natural law tradition.[69]

In addition, there is considerable diversity even among those scholars who find a relationship between the Bible and the natural law tradition.[70] Of course, some will disagree with the broad-brush identification of positions and

---

69. For an overview of some of the different positions within the natural law tradition see Jes Bjarup, Continental perspectives on natural law theory and legal positivism', in THE BLACKWELL GUIDE TO THE PHILOSOPHY OF LAW AND LEGAL THEORY (Martin P. Golding & William A. Edmundson eds., Oxford: Blackwell, 2005), 287–99; M. D. A. FREEMAN, LLOYD'S INTRODUCTION TO JURISPRUDENCE (London: Sweet and Maxwell, 8th ed. 2008).

70. *See generally* PORTER, NATURAL AND DIVINE LAW.

TABLE 5 EXAMPLES OF DIVERSE THESES WITHIN THE NATURAL LAW TRADITION

	Examples of some theses within the natural law tradition	Examples of leading exponents
1	Morality is rooted in objective reality, independent of human knowledge of that reality	e.g., Marcus Tullius Cicero
2	Morality takes the form of law, that is, rules—and later rights	e.g., Immanuel Kant
3	Everybody everywhere shares a basic moral code	e.g., Hugo Grotius
4	Law is never independent of social consensus	e.g., Jean-Jacques Rousseau
5	Human law always incorporates a minimum of justice	e.g., Thomas Aquinas
6	Law should be obeyed simply because it is law	e.g., Sir William Blackstone
7	If human laws become sufficiently unjust, they cease to be laws and ought not to be obeyed	e.g., Augustine of Hippo
8	Complex social phenomena (including law) can only be identified using moral criteria	e.g., John Finnis
9	Some political authority (that is, the power to create obligations) is natural	e.g., Aristotle

exponents in Table 5. Nevertheless, it has several implications for our understanding of the relationship between natural law and the Bible. For one thing, it illustrates that the natural law tradition is broad and complex enough to encompass these different strands. We have already seen in this chapter that the same is true of natural law in the Bible. The understanding of natural law in the Bible is broad enough to include the following strands: (1) continuity between the divine and creation, (2) continuity between the created world and human behavior, (3) universal knowledge of certain norms, (4) continuity between different forms of revelation, and (5) continuity between divine and human acts of judgment.

The second main point about the reception and development of natural law is that not only does it receive different expressions at different times, but *natural law has different emphases within the Western legal philosophical tradition.*

A good example of this can be seen in the different approaches taken to natural law by William of Ockham (1285–1347) and Thomas Aquinas (*circa* 1225–1274), which spilled over into fourteenth-century debates about the nature of divine law. The question was whether divine law is a matter of pure command and an expression of the will of God or whether divine law is something that is written into the structure of the universe and the nature of things, including

God's nature. The former is the Ockhamist "will theory" approach, and the latter can be identified as the Thomist rationalist position. The distinction between the voluntarist "will theory" tradition and the rationalist approach is important if one is using natural categories to understand the Bible. The issue is, can one know divine law from natural categories, that is, the structure of the universe? Or are natural categories insufficient, in which case we need pure command to know divine law? At root, what the scholastics are really arguing about is a set of assumptions about the relationship of God to the world, the way that God is supposed to work, and the character of God himself. In terms of how that debate played out over the centuries, it was the Thomist position that tended to win, while the Ockhamist "will theory" approach either tended to lose or gradually became transmuted into a traditional legal positivist approach—that law is the command of a legislator. But while this is a significant debate from a twenty-first century perspective, both Ockhamists and Thomists can still be seen as part of a single natural law tradition. This is because they all believe in a natural order or a divine order of some description.

The fact that natural law has received different emphases which have emerged at certain historical periods also has implications for our understanding of the relationship between natural law and the Bible. Again, it is reasonable to hypothesize that something similar might also be true of the biblical materials. For example, we have seen in this chapter that there are differences in emphasis between those texts that present continuity between the created world and human behavior as being a matter of direct divine intervention and those that present it as being less direct.

To sum up, this chapter has shown that natural law in the Bible is broad and complex enough to encompass a number of different strands, some of which receive different emphases at different times.

By framing the issue in these terms, it may be possible to move us on from some of the ways in which natural law in the Bible has been addressed in the past. I believe this is necessary because previous debates have been overinformed by medieval concerns about the sources of knowledge of morality and ethics. This legacy has not been helpful for either our understanding of natural law or the biblical materials.

To give merely one example, there is a distinction in Aquinas between "divine law" which is revealed by God in Scripture and "natural law" which is accessible to human beings by virtue of their nature as creatures made in the image of God. While this distinction may have had its uses at one time, it is not ultimately helpful. It is, in fact, misconceived not least because it creates an epistemological problem, namely, the relationship between divine law and natural law. Aquinas creates a pair of corresponding epistemological categories, that is, divine laws that can only be known because they are revealed in the Bible (e.g., not having sexual relations with an uncle's wife, impliedly after the uncle is dead or has divorced his wife; cf. Leviticus 20:20) and natural laws that can be known simply by virtue of being human (such as, "you must keep your promises"). In the end, it leads to the misleading expectation that the Bible is to be seen only as a repository of divine law and not as illuminating our understanding of natural law.

Unfortunately, this medieval baggage still frequently sets the terms of the debate. Karl Barth writes against the background assumption that the Bible cannot have a natural law theory.[71] For too long, we have allowed ourselves to be dominated by the concerns of a particular period in history which was interested in the question of "how do we know truth in the field of morality?" and which answered it in terms of a binary opposition between nature and the Bible. It turns the Bible into an answer to an epistemological problem (how can we know divine law?) which the Bible itself has not created. It is the wrong way of addressing the question of the relationship between natural law and the Bible. It also makes the Bible into a book that seems to have nothing to say about natural law. Therefore, we need to get away from the idea that the Bible is an example of a certain answer to the problem of natural law. We also need to recast the issue of natural law in the Bible. I have argued throughout this chapter that one way in which we can do this is by looking for a connection between divine activity and human activity in the realm of normativity (that is, why we feel we ought to do things). This yields a number of different themes which can all be seen as different manifestations of natural law in the Bible, some of which receive different emphases at different times.

B. What shall we do with the Gentile Christians?

Another way in which a traditional natural law reading of the Bible can be misleading is found in the New Testament. The book of Acts recounts a decision of the Apostolic Council of Jerusalem, which is normally seen to apply a minimum standard of Jewish law to Gentiles. This is often read as a manifestation of the Noahide laws and hence of natural law, although there are good grounds for thinking that this is not the case.

Acts 15 describes the decision of the Apostolic Council in relation to what behavior is expected of local Gentile believers who accept Jesus of Nazareth as Israel's messiah. The apostle James, the leader of the mainly Jewish church in Jerusalem, appears to accept the apostle Peter's argument that Gentile believers are accepted by God as Gentiles and not as Jews (Acts 15:7–11). This leads James to the following conclusion:

> Therefore my judgment is that we should not trouble those of the Gentiles who turn to God, but should write to them to abstain from the pollutions of idols and from unchastity and from what is strangled and from blood. (Acts 15:19–20)

---

71. EMIL BRUNNER & KARL BARTH, NATURAL THEOLOGY (Peter Fraenkel trans., London: Geoffrey Bles, 1946).

A subsequent letter, written by the Apostolic Council, presents the decision in slightly reordered form. It begins by identifying the authors and the addressees of the letter which, as we shall see, is very significant in terms of the natural law argument:

> [Opening salutation] The brethren, both the apostles and the elders: To the brethren who are of the Gentiles in Antioch and Syria and Cilicia. Greeting . . . it has seemed good to the Holy Spirit and to us to lay upon you no greater burden than these necessary things: that you abstain from what has been sacrificed to idols and from blood and from what is strangled and from unchastity. If you keep yourselves from these, you will do well . . . (Acts 15:28–29)

The letter is thus written by a group of *Jewish* believers in Jesus to a group of *Gentile* believers in Jesus. It is not hard to find some connections between the prohibitions of Acts 15 and the Noahide laws. It is clear, particularly from Acts 15:28–29, that we are dealing with a prohibition of fornication and three different dietary laws: (1) food (typically meat) sacrificed to idols, (2) meat with blood still in it, and (3) meat from strangled animals who have thus not been ritually slaughtered. The prohibition on blood (Acts 15:29) recalls the dietary restrictions of Genesis 9:4, while the general prohibition of bloodshed recalls Genesis 9:5–6. On the face of things, there is clearly some overlap with the biblical Noahide laws in Genesis 9.

At the same time, however, there are important differences. Most obviously, Acts 15:29 refers to "unchastity," which typically means prostitution and fornication. This is not mentioned in the biblical Noahide laws. As a result, some scholars see Acts 15:29 as anticipating the rabbinic expansion of the Noahide laws, which does prohibit sexual offenses (see above). However, this difference between Acts 15:29 and the biblical Noahide laws can equally be taken as evidence that Acts 15 is about something *other* than the Noahide laws.

The solution may lie in paying closer attention to the text. The letter does not formally address itself to "all Gentile believers in Jesus" but only to those living in a specific geographical area, namely "Antioch and Syria and Cilicia" (verse 23). For first-century Jews, these territories were of great symbolic significance because they were adjacent to the borders of Israel or were actually imagined as part of Israel itself, at least in an ideal sense.[72] We might call them "liminal lands" or "in-between places." They are not obviously part of the land of Israel, but they are not exactly separate from it either—like other parts of the Roman Empire. This may help to explain why these believers were the subject of a special ruling by the Jerusalem church, whereas other Gentile Christians were not.[73]

---

72. Bockmuehl, Jewish Law, pp. 61–70.
73. Ibid., 75–83.

Further support for this reading comes from some notable parallels between Acts 15 and Leviticus 17–18. This sets out a range of obligations for resident aliens living in the land of Israel. The parallels are found in the blood taboos of Leviticus 17:10–14, the dietary laws of Leviticus 17:15ff, and the list of forbidden sexual relationships in Leviticus 18:6–30. It mirrors the concerns of Acts 15.[74] There are good reasons, then, for thinking that Acts 15 is really a creative New Testament application of Leviticus 17–18, in much the same way as, for example, the prophet Ezekiel appears to draw on Leviticus 17–18 in his insistence that there are certain preconditions to living in the land of Israel (Ezekiel 33:24–26). Acts 15 applies the paradigm case of resident aliens in the land of Israel to a situation that is slightly removed from the paradigm, namely Gentile believers in Jesus living in border lands. At any rate, it is a different matter to the Noahide laws. Acts 15 does not impose a universal minimum standard, and so it is not an example of natural law.

C. Ethics and calling

In this closing subsection, we consider some of the ways in which our study of the biblical materials might encourage us to modify the Western natural law position. One of the problems with the Western natural law tradition is its tendency to reduce ethics into things which are universal to all. For example, John Finnis's modern natural law theory lays claim to a number of "basic goods," all of which are universal and none of which can be regarded as more important than the other.[75] Against this background, the misreading of Acts 15 is perfectly understandable. It simply reflects the tendency, when looking for natural law in the Bible, to find uniform norms that apply to everyone. However, the biblical claim to universality is more complex than this.

First, although there are grounds for thinking that knowledge of certain norms is universal in the Bible, they are not "flattened out" into an *equal* claim to universal significance. By contrast, there appears to be some sense of hierarchy within the Bible. The identification and repetition of certain offenses such as idolatry, violence, eating blood, and sexual immorality suggest that these things were regarded more seriously than other natural law offenses. We find a similar selection and priority in rabbinic lists of the sins that a Jew may not commit under any circumstances, even at the cost of losing one's life, namely idolatry, the shedding of blood, and incest (Sanhedrin 74a). These have been related by some scholars to rabbinic traditions regarding the Noahide laws (Tosefta Avodah

---

74. RICHARD BAUCKHAM, THE BOOK OF ACTS IN ITS PALESTINIAN SETTING, THE BOOK OF ACTS IN ITS FIRST CENTURY SETTING (Grand Rapids: Eerdmans, 1995), vol. IV, 459–62.

75. JOHN FINNIS, NATURAL LAW & NATURAL RIGHTS (Oxford: Clarendon Press, 2001), 85–99.

Zarah 8:4; Sanhedrin 56a). Whatever the reasons for it, some breaches of natural law are seen as worse than others.

Second, any straightforward claim to universalism in the Bible is complicated by the fact that moral truth is presented as a matter of personal relationship with God. In the Hebrew Bible, Wisdom declares:

> . . . he who listens to me will dwell in safety. (Proverbs 1:33)

while in the New Testament, Jesus asserts:

> Every one who is of the truth hears my voice. (John 18:37)

Such proclamations should make us think twice before reading in mechanical notions of natural law which claim that if something is morally true, it must be true for everybody, everywhere. We must be careful not to confuse ideas of universality with ideas of uniformity. God may command a person to go and do something that is slightly different from what he commands another person.

Third, there is evidence in the early chapters of Romans of a tension between universal norms and personal circumstances. In Romans 1:18–32, Paul stresses the universality of certain norms on the basis of knowledge, while Romans 2 claims that persons are judged on the basis of what they themselves claim to adhere to (see especially verses 12–16). The standard of judgment is specific to the person being judged. The charge is effectively one of moral inconsistency. There is universal knowledge of certain norms, but it is a "common-sense *knowledge* of the one law of God, subjectively mediated by the individual's moral consciousness."[76] Once again, there is a personal dimension. Divine judgment does not appear to involve the application of an abstract system of norms. Judgment is not on the basis of universal norms; instead, *it is on the basis of norms known by those to whom they are applied.*

Finally, we must reckon with the way in which the New Testament relativizes universal norms. "Endorsements of the perceived order of creation stand side by side with cases of profound subversion or subordination of that same order."[77] Jesus's teaching on marriage and the family, for example, is on the one hand, firmly supportive of creational norms, and on the other hand, highly revolutionary because biological family ties are relativized in the face of primary allegiance to Jesus (cf. the teachings recorded in Matthew 19:4–8 with Matthew 12:48–50; Luke 14:26). As far as the New Testament is concerned, there is clearly room for a pluralism which says, for example, that not marrying and not having children for the sake of the "kingdom of God" is more important than marriage and procreation (e.g., Matthew 19:12, and see further Chapter 12).

---

76. BOCKMUEHL, JEWISH LAW, p. 131, italics original.
77. Ibid., 125.

Nor do we find any sweeping universalism in Jesus's cousin and forerunner, John the Baptist. It is very striking that John issues different ethical imperatives for different social groups, whether they be crowds, tax collectors, or soldiers. The general ethical requirement might well be to "produce fruit in keeping with repentance" (Luke 3:8 NIV), but there is considerable allowance and variation as to what that might be. John's command to the soldiers is to:

> Rob no one by violence or by false accusation, and be content with your wages. (Luke 3:14)

Some might think that this does not amount to very much, especially when compared with the command to the "multitudes":

> He who has two coats, let him share with him who has none; and he who has food, let him do likewise. (Luke 3:11)

Of course, John's command to the soldiers might have been as radical in their context as his commands to Joe and Jean Public, but there is no denying the difference.

One way of making sense of this is to recognize that there are different moral strengths, virtues, and capacities which are not all expressible by one person, and that the expression of particular strengths creates in themselves the tendency to devalue other virtues. As an individual takes on certain beliefs and sets certain goals; some of these will be incommensurable in the sense that they cannot be traded off against each other.[78] The classic medieval example is that if one wishes to display the virtues of a mother, one has to be slightly dismissive of the virtues of a nun. The mother possesses knowledge of the virtues of a nun, but as an *experiential* matter, she knows that being a successful mother means caring about certain things and living in a certain way. This incommensurability of being both a mother and a nun leads the mother to say not only, "I could not be a nun," but also, "There are aspects of a nun's life that I cannot but see as not fulfilling." In this context, for the mother to say that being a nun is "not fulfilling" does not simply mean "not fulfilling for me"; it also means "not fulfilling for me as a human being," full stop.

This recognizes that there is a tension between on the one hand, what we feel ethically, which is bound up with our sense of calling, and on the other hand, our ethical judgments, which are bound up with what we rationally know to be true. The mother can, as a rational human being, affirm the different lifestyle of the nun and value the qualities of celibacy. But as a living person who experiences the call to motherhood, she surely wants to say more than simply "motherhood is right for me." Even though the mother may recognize, in humility, the equal value of another person's calling, even if its merits are not part of her experience,

---

78. JOSEPH RAZ, THE MORALITY OF FREEDOM (Oxford: Clarendon Press, 1990), 321–66.

there is an inevitable tendency for the mother to end up feeling that her particular calling vis-à-vis the nun is better, at least to some degree, simply because she is committed to motherhood and not to being a nun. This is what happens when there is a combination of call and corresponding commitment.

The continuity toward calling and ethics tends toward a version of moral pluralism which depends upon the *experiential* reality of displaying particular moral virtues in one's own life and committing to them. It is plausible to suggest that the expression of moral virtues consistent with a particular call and commitment varies from one person to the next. Hence, the commands given by John the Baptist vary from group to group, and Jesus upholds different obligations in relation to marriage and family. If this is the case then we are, once again, a long way from the assumption that natural law in the Bible involves a straightforward commitment to universalism. It also challenges any assumption that "what is not universal is not ethical." Instead, it is possible that the New Testament suggests a way of thinking about ethics that is not necessarily universal.

VIII. CONCLUSION

The tradition of natural law refers to a multiplicity of different theses and emphases. Discovering natural law in the Bible means looking for a connection between divine activity and human activity in the realm of normativity (why we feel we ought to do things). In this chapter we have seen this interconnectivity in five main ways: (1) continuity between the divine and creation, (2) continuity between the created world and human behavior, (3) universal knowledge of certain norms, (4) continuity between general and specific revelation, and (5) continuity between divine and human acts of judgment. Most modern natural lawyers would be willing to accept the idea that human beings are morally creative and that they develop different expressions of natural law over time, such as international consensus. However, they might struggle with a number of aspects of natural law in the Bible, including the idea that there is a correspondence between law and nature because both proceed from the same God; that everyone shares a basic moral code based on the imitation of God and his relationship with creation; that God works through nature to bring about certain ends; and that adjudication is more than a pure act of human convention, and is, in fact, a sphere in which God is actively involved. The Bible also has a more nuanced approach to universalism than the Western natural law tradition, which disjoins ethics and calling. As a result, there are a number of ways in which natural law in the Bible differs from the natural law tradition in both its classical and modern forms and presents it with a challenge. In that sense, the Bible has a multifaceted approach to questions of natural law—as multifaceted indeed—as the tradition of natural law itself.

Selected reading

Gary A. Anderson, *The status of the Torah before Sinai*, Dead Sea Discoveries 1 (1994), 1–29.

James Barr, "Biblical law and the question of natural theology," in *The Law in the Bible and in its Environment*, edited by Timo Veijola, *Publications of the Finnish Exegetical Society* 51 (Helsinki: Finnish Exegetical Society, 1990), 1–22.

John Barton, *Ethics and the Old Testament* (London: SCM, 1998), Chapter 4.

Markus Bockmuehl, *Jewish Law in Gentile Churches* (Grand Rapids: Baker Academic, 2000), Chapter 5.

Terence E. Fretheim, "The reclamation of creation," in *Interpretation* 45 (1991), 354–365.

4. JUSTICE AS A CALLING

The pursuit of justice is central to any legal system. Accordingly, there are few more important subjects for any society than the organization of its judicial processes. This includes such issues as the extent to which victims can gain access to justice, the involvement of local communities in making judicial decisions, and the criteria for making judicial appointments. Other important questions include what constitutes a just decision in a legal case, and how should judges decide hard cases? All these questions are fundamental to societies everywhere, including our own. However, they are especially important in the context of biblical Israel. We saw in Chapter 3 that Abraham receives a lesson in divine adjudication so that he can teach his descendants (Genesis 18:19). They, in turn, are meant to pass this teaching on and so be a source of blessing for "all the nations of the earth" (Genesis 18:18). Justice is a calling for the descendants of Abraham and the world, but the pursuit of justice is especially important for Israel.

This chapter explores how Israel was supposed to work out her vocation and do justice. The call of justice has both an ideological and a practical aspect, and we shall consider each in turn. Regarding the former, we will see that Israel's ideology of adjudication is founded on the central and overwhelming belief that God is the sole source of justice. All justice is therefore divine. Regarding the latter practical aspect, we will see that human judges are thought to be capable of mediating actual divine decisions. However, this depends on the appointment of judges who have the moral capacity to exercise wisdom. This did not always happen, and so this chapter will explore what happens when judges failed. Finally, since the desire for justice is common to all societies, we will consider the points of contact that exist between biblical Israel and our own modern society, where justice is frequently perceived to be in short supply.

I. TOP TEN WAYS OF PURSUING JUSTICE

The heart of law lies in the judicial decision. This means that we can understand much about biblical law by exploring adjudication, although for reasons of space, this chapter will focus on the premonarchic and preexilic periods. We begin with an exploration of the ideology of adjudication and its practice, starting with the ideological aspect of the call to justice. We can identify a number of key elements in a biblical ideology of adjudication, as follows. Participants in Israel's judicial process should (1) believe that God is the ultimate source of justice; (2) believe that judges have the potential to mediate actual divine decisions; (3) fight to overthrow the oppressor and liberate the oppressed; (4) put things right—from God's perspective; (5) put justice in the hands of the many, not the few; (6) respect the position of provincial courts; (7) involve a range of authorities in adjudication; (8) sort out their own legal disputes; (9) apply practical wisdom; and (10) be inspired by a divine sense of justice. We will explore each of these in turn.

A. Believe that God is the ultimate source of justice

First, *the cornerstone of biblical adjudication is the belief that God is the ultimate source of justice* (e.g., Deuteronomy 32:4). This lies at the very heart of the biblical ideology of sacred adjudication. It ensures that ideas about justice in the Bible always have a transcendental reference point. Strange as it might seem, the idea that God is the source of justice is established at the start of Genesis. Here, God is portrayed as having the power to make distinctions which bring the universe into being (Genesis 1:1–2:3). Throughout the Bible, acts of divine justice involve making distinctions, such as those between order and chaos and between good and evil. There is thus a close relationship between the way in which God establishes order in the universe and his concern for justice in society.[1] Viewed from this angle, it is the link between "macrocosm and microcosm—right order in society parallels order in the cosmos."[2]

The belief that divine justice involves making distinctions is confirmed in the Exodus, which is the paradigmatic act of justice in the Hebrew Bible. Distinctions are here made between the power of God and the power of Pharaoh, between a life of freedom and a life of oppression. We see here also that divine justice distinguishes between those who are bound to God's covenant purposes (that is, the people of Israel) and those who are not (the people of Egypt). As with God's acts of creation, this distinction is drawn in a very physical way: some of the plagues affect Pharaoh and his people but not Moses or the Israelites (Exodus 8:22–23; 9:4, 26, 10:22–23; 11:7). This means ultimately that the Israelite belief in God as the ultimate source of justice is not simply a proposition but something that is rooted in God's intervention in history on behalf of the oppressed (see further C, below).

B. Judges have the potential to mediate actual divine decisions

Second, because God is the only source of justice, it follows that *judges who reach decisions based on their knowledge of the character of God have the potential to mediate actual divine decisions*. This belief in sacred adjudication is reflected in the promises made by a number of key legal reformers that God would be "with" the human adjudicators in the act of giving judgment. Such promises are made by

---

1. ADRIAN CURTIS, GOD AS JUDGE, IN UGARITIC AND HEBREW THOUGHT, IN LAW AND RELIGION: ESSAYS ON THE PLACE OF THE LAW IN ISRAEL & EARLY CHRISTIANITY (Barnabas Lindars ed., Cambridge: James Clarke, 1988), 3–12, 12.
2. Ibid.

TABLE 6 THE ROLE OF DIVINE JUSTICE IN HUMAN ADJUDICATION

Source	Legal reformer	Promise of divine delegation to human mediators
Exodus 18:19	Jethro (addressing Moses)	"... God be <u>with</u> you."
Deuteronomy 1:16–17	Moses (addressing Israel)	"And I charged your judges ... you shall not be afraid of the face of man, *for the judgment is God's.*"
2 Chronicles 19:6	King Jehoshaphat (addressing his judges in the fortified cities)	"Consider what you do, for you judge not for man but for the LORD; *he is <u>with</u> you in giving judgment.*"
2 Chronicles 19:11	King Jehoshaphat (addressing his judges in Jerusalem)	"... may the LORD be <u>with</u> the upright!"

Jethro (Moses's father-in-law and Israel's first legal reformer), Moses and King Jehoshaphat, and are summarized in Table 6, above.

These promises should not be downplayed as mere theological "window dressing" or even as simply making the claim that God holds the judges accountable for their decisions. Instead, the belief seems to be that the human judge "[participates] with God in the act of judging"[3] so that their adjudication mediates actual divine decisions.[4] It is divine inspiration rather than divine authorization.[5] Adjudication in the Bible goes beyond the claim that there is a creative moment in all legal activity which distinguishes it from morality; instead, it seems to assert that *the creative moment in the act of judgment takes the form of divine inspiration.* This might explain the strange way in which human beings are sometimes said to be related to the divine by virtue of their judicial office.[6]

---

3. Hanina Ben-Menahem, *Postscript: The judicial process and the nature of Jewish law*, in AN INTRODUCTION TO THE HISTORY AND SOURCES OF JEWISH LAW, (N. S. Hecht, B. S. Jackson, S. M. Passamaneck, D. Piattelli & A. M. Rabello eds., Oxford: Oxford University Press, 1996), 421–37, 423.

4. Bernard S. Jackson, *Law and Justice in the Bible*, J. JEWISH STUDS. 49 (1998), 218–29, 226.

5. Ben-Menahem, *Postscript*, p. 424.

6. Judges are referred to as *elohim* in Exodus 21:6, 22:8–9/MT 22:7–8 and Psalm 82:6, which is one of the names of God. The name *Elohim* takes the form of a plural noun. However, although it takes a plural form, we should not see it as indicating polytheism. This is because when it is used of God, it always uses a singular verb (*e.g.*, Genesis 1:1).

C. Fight to overthrow the oppressor and liberate the oppressed

Third, as the Exodus from Egypt shows, God's justice and righteousness is seen most clearly in rescuing the weak and oppressed. This means that *adjudication in the Bible should recall the Exodus by fighting to overthrow the oppressor and liberate the oppressed.*[7] For this reason, the verb to judge (*shaphat*) has overtones of vindication and rescue (e.g., Psalms 72:4 and 82:3). There are strong links between justice and salvation, as seen in the following picture of monarchical adjudication:

> Behold, a king will reign in righteousness,
> and princes will rule in justice.
> Each will be
> like a hiding place from the wind,
> a covert from the tempest,
> like streams of water in a dry place,
> like the shade of a great rock
> in a weary land. (Isaiah 32:1-2)

The idea that justice in the Bible involves overthrowing oppression and liberating the oppressed means that there are two sides to justice. On the one hand, justice brings down the oppressor and, on the other, it liberates the oppressed. For example, Psalm 146:7–9 is a song of praise to:

> [The LORD] who executes justice for the oppressed;
> who gives food to the hungry.
> The LORD sets the prisoners free;
> the LORD opens the eyes of the blind.
> The LORD lifts up those who are bowed down;
> the LORD loves the righteous.
> The LORD watches over the sojourners,
> he upholds the widow and the fatherless;
> but the way of the wicked he brings to ruin.

The same act of justice that brings oppressors "to ruin" also "lifts up those who are bowed down." This means that the recipients of justice can experience it very differently (either as retribution or restoration), depending on whether they happen to be the persecutor or the victim.

The Exodus is seen as the ultimate act of divine justice in the Hebrew Bible. This is because it is an act of God that overthrows the totalitarian rule of Pharaoh (in respect of the Israelites) and liberates them from slavery. God is seen as the ultimate king and judge who hears his people's cry and saves them in giving

---

7. At the same time, however, God is not partial and does not therefore automatically favor a poor person in a dispute just because they are poor (Deuteronomy 1:16–17). At times, the poor person may be the oppressor.

judgment (e.g., Psalm 5:2; Isaiah 33:22). This is the same divine justice that human judges—especially kings—are supposed to mediate. Kings and judges are supposed to model themselves on God's behavior (contrast 2 Kings 6:26–27).[8] Like God, they are expected to battle against oppressors and the forces of chaos because the pursuit of justice involves a fight. This is explicit in the following juxtaposition:

> Justice, justice shall you pursue [*tirdof*], that you may thrive and occupy the land that the LORD your God is giving you.
> (Deuteronomy 16:20; *Moses speaking*)

Just as the Israelites were not going to acquire the Promised Land without a battle, neither were they going to secure justice without a fight. Moses's judges were appointed as "officials over thousands, hundreds, fifties and tens" (Exodus 18:25; JPS, and see also Deuteronomy 1:15), that is, as heads of military units. They could equally be described as "generals, colonels, captains and sergeants."[9] Even the verb "to pursue" (*radaph*; Deuteronomy 16:20) has a military connotation: it is used of Pharaoh's pursuit of the Israelites across the Red Sea (Exodus 14:8).

For all these reasons, it is thought that the verb "to judge" in the Bible (*shaphat*) means "to save the oppressed from the hands of the oppressor, or the enslaved from his enslaver."[10] This salvation could be achieved by means of "a judicial decision, through active intervention, by proclamation of an edict from on high, or through battle and struggle . . . ."[11] It would also explain why the word "judges" (*shophtim*) is used for Israel's charismatic deliverers who waged war to deliver the Israelites from oppression in the premonarchical period.

D. Put things right—from God's perspective

Fourth, since human justice is supposed to be modeled on divine activity, it follows that justice in the Bible is ultimately about putting everything to right in the way God intends it to be. This means that *the purpose of adjudication is to restore the parties, so far as possible, to a divinely mandated social order.* It is understood in terms of "a social order in which the free Israelite was conceived as the occupant

---

8. *See generally* Moshe A. Zipor, *The cannibal women and their judgment before the helpless king* (2 Kings 6:24ff), ABR-NAHRAIN 35, 84–94 (1998).

9. Martin Ravndal Hauge, The Descent from the Mountain: Narrative Patterns in Exodus 19–40, Journal for the Study of the Old Testament Supplement Series 323 (Sheffield: Sheffield Academic Press, 2001), 253.

10. Moshe Weinfeld, Social Justice in Ancient Israel (Jerusalem: Magnes Press, 1995), 40.

11. Ibid.

of his due allocation of the promised land . . . [It is] more a matter of individual place (with all the personal ties associated therewith) than individual rights."[12]

For example, the restoration of alienated persons to land is rooted in the divine claim that the land belongs to God and that he has the right to parcel it out according to a predetermined pattern (Leviticus 25:23; see Chapter 6). It is also consistent with the way in which ancient Near Eastern (ANE) kings made regular proclamations of liberty.[13] This too was intended to restore "an original divinely-mandated social order."[14] Some scholars change the emphasis slightly and see the purpose of adjudication, not in terms of restoration between the parties concerned, but the restoration of Eden (or what Eden represents).[15] However, even the idea of restoring Eden can itself be understood in terms of the restoration of relationships within a divinely mandated social order.[16]

E. Put justice in the hands of the many, not the few

Fifth, because all Israel has experienced divine justice firsthand in the form of the Exodus (see C, above), it follows that biblical justice is characteristically "grass roots." It means that *the quest for justice is in the hands of the many, not the few.* This too is a key aspect of the biblical ideology of adjudication and is reflected in the covenant ratification ceremony at Sinai. All Israel is required to approve the laws and judgments presented to them (Exodus 21:1). Likewise the whole people are taught the law (Exodus 24:12; Deuteronomy 17:10–11) and "all the statutes" (Leviticus 10:11). The people receive the same general instructions to avoid partiality and bribes as do the appointed judges (Exodus 23:1–8). In these and other ways, justice is seen as a communal responsibility (Zechariah 7:9–10). This, in turn, is consistent with the theme of Genesis 18, namely, that justice is the vocation of all of Abraham's descendants (see Chapter 3).

F. Respect the position of provincial courts

Sixth, *the high degree of lay involvement, coupled with an absence of bureaucracy in the legal system, at least in the preexilic period, means that provincial courts are not subordinated within any clear legal hierarchy.* This too is an important aspect of biblical adjudication. Deuteronomy 17:8–13 describes how referrals can be made

---

12. Bernard S. Jackson, *Justice and righteousness in the Bible: Rule of law or royal paternalism?*, ZEITSCHRIFT FÜR ALTORIENTALISCHE UND BIBLISCHE RECTSGESCHICHTE 4, 218–62, 227 (1998).

13. WEINFELD, SOCIAL JUSTICE, pp. 75–96.

14. Jackson, *Justice and righteousness*, p. 227.

15. Such as JACOB NEUSNER, THE HALAKHAH. AN ENCYCLOPAEDIA OF THE LAW OF JUDAISM. VOLUME I: BETWEEN ISRAEL AND GOD. PART A, Brill Reference Library of Judaism (Leiden: Brill, 2000), 19.

16. As Neusner writes, "'Eden' stands for Man and God dwelling together," JACOB NEUSNER, THE THEOLOGY OF THE HALAKHAH (Leiden: Brill, 2001), xxix.

from provincial courts to the judges at "the place which the LORD your God will choose" (verse 8). The precise referent of this location is hotly contested, but the key issue for present purposes is the basis of the referral, which is made on the ground that the case is "too difficult." This implies that the central court is not being used as a "court of appeal."[17] Examples of the sort of areas that might give rise to "hard cases" include homicide, civil law, or assault (Deuteronomy 17:8). According to Deuteronomy 17:11, the judgment is supposed to result both in "instructions" (*hattorah*) and a "decision" (*hammishpat*). The same combination of "judicial decision" plus "further teaching" is found in the accounts of Moses's desert adjudications (e.g., Numbers 27:5–11), where the teaching element extends further than the case in hand (e.g., Numbers 27:8–11). The central court is thus "acting like Moses."[18]

The particular relationship between central and provincial courts may be comparable to the two-tier system attributed to the time of Jehoshaphat (869–845 BC). This consisted of (1) local royally appointed judges in all the fortified cities (2 Chronicles 19:5) and (2) a central Jerusalem court run by royally appointed Levites, priests, and family heads (2 Chronicles 19:8). The parallels between the institutional structures described in Deuteronomy 17 and 2 Chronicles 19 are close (and indeed some scholars assume that the dating of the Deuteronomic text can be aligned with that of 2 Chronicles).[19] The key point, once again, is that the organization of the courts is not hierarchical in the sense that there was no "right of appeal" from the provincial courts to the central one. Instead, the Jerusalem court seems to have been a "court of reference" for the provincial courts.[20] Cases were referred to the Jerusalem court by the local judges and not by the complainants. This suggests that the basis of referral was legal rather than factual difficulty.[21] The relationship between these courts seems closer to the way in which national courts in the modern European Union (EU) make references to the European Court of Justice in order to seek clarification upon the meaning or validity of an aspect of EU law.[22] The idea that a court, such as the one in Jerusalem, could exercise both first instance *and* referral jurisdictions is

---

17. Bernard S. Jackson, "Law in the ninth century: Jehoshaphat's 'judicial reform'", Proceedings of the British Academy 143, 357–85, 384 (2007).

18. Jackson, *Law in the ninth century*, p. 391.

19. *E.g.*, MOSHE WEINFELD, DEUTERONOMY & THE DEUTERONOMIC SCHOOL (Oxford: Clarendon Press, 1972), 235–36.

20. KEITH W. WHITELAM, THE JUST KING: MONARCHICAL JUDICIAL AUTHORITY IN ANCIENT ISRAEL, JOURNAL FOR THE SOCIETY OF THE OLD TESTAMENT SUPPLEMENT SERIES 12 (Sheffield: Journal for the Society of the Old Testament Press, 1979), 200.

21. Bernard S. Jackson, *The practice of justice in Jewish law*, DAIMON 4, 31-48, 46 (2004).

22. Ibid.

just one of the ways in which biblical and modern institutions differ (cf. also Exodus 18:13–15).[23]

G. Involve a range of authorities in adjudication

A seventh feature of the biblical ideology of adjudication is *the absence of a formal "separation of powers."* Monarchs (e.g. Deuteronomy 17:18–20; Psalm 72), Levites, priests, and non-priests are all involved in adjudication (Deuteronomy 17:8–13). This reflects the fusion of law and religion in biblical Israel. Nor is there any distinction, at least in the early period, between administration and adjudication[24] or between executive and judiciary in early Israel. "It is difficult to believe that the local courts were ever completely separate from the jurisdiction of the king."[25] A good example of this can be found in the Naboth story (1 Kings 21:1–16), which describes how the monarchy (strictly speaking, Queen Jezebel, writing letters in King Ahab's name) interfered with Naboth's local court to frame him of a capital charge (1 Kings 21:8–10).

H. Sort out your own legal disputes

Eighth, a key aspect of the biblical ideology of adjudication is *the strong presumption, at least in early times, that Israelites should not engage in disputes with their neighbor or rely on third parties to settle their problems for them.* Ironically, the ideology of adjudication in the Bible includes the value of avoiding adjudication. This stems partly from the belief that justice was in the hands of the many, not the few (see E, above) and partly from the way in which biblical law promotes an attitude of forbearance toward enemies that makes litigation unlikely in the first place (cf. Exodus 34:6–7). Exodus 23:4–5 (the so-called "litigation pericope" enjoins proactive behavior on behalf of one's enemy:

> If you meet your enemy's ox or his ass going astray, you shall bring it back to him. If you see the ass of one who hates you lying under its burden, you shall refrain from leaving him with it, you shall help him to lift it up.
> (Exodus 23:4-5; *God speaking*)

This occurs in the context of a series of prohibitions relating to *judicial* proceedings (Exodus 23:1–8), including false rumors, false charges, and bribery. Why? This is because there is a thematic connection between "enmity" and litigation, with litigation itself being the result of enmity.[26] If enmity leads to adjudication, generosity avoids it.

---

23. See Jackson, *Law in the ninth century*, p. 384.
24. Jackson, "*Law*" & "*Justice*," p. 223.
25. WHITELAM, THE JUST KING, p. 194.
26. Bernard S. Jackson, WISDOM-LAWS: A STUDY OF THE MISHPATIM OF EXODUS 21:1-22:16 (Oxford: Oxford University Press, 2006), 403–05.

Even if people should find themselves in conflict, there is a strong preference for private settlement and for avoiding third-party intervention. Such resolution may be achieved through the use of self-executing narrative rules such as those governing the bovicidal ox (Exodus 21:35) and burglary (Exodus 22:1–4/MT 21: 37–22:3; see Chapter 1). Adjudication could be a shaming experience (Proverbs 25:9–10). This might have been because it shows the parties lack the relational skills with which to resolve their own disputes.

Interestingly, this stance is mirrored by Jesus in the New Testament. The Sermon on the Mount urges the avoidance of judicial proceedings in favor of out-of-court settlement (Matthew 5:25–26). Jesus refuses to act as an arbitrator when requested and instead criticizes the complainant's desire for adjudication (Luke 12:13–15).

I. Apply practical wisdom

Ninth, *in order for Israelites to resolve their disputes successfully among themselves, they needed to apply practical wisdom.* Wisdom is thus central to a biblical ideology of sacred adjudication. This is seen in Proverbs 2:6–8:

> For the LORD gives wisdom; from his mouth come knowledge and understanding; he stores up sound wisdom for the upright; . . . guarding the paths of justice . . . .

Wisdom (*hokhmah*) denotes "a general innate mental capacity . . . common sense [and] ability."[27] This is often applied in a particular way, including political astuteness (1 Kings 2:9) and judicial discernment (1 Kings 3:12), as well as cleverness and perception (2 Samuel 14:20).[28] But although wisdom can take many forms, it is essentially practical (e.g., Exodus 28:3). Since there is no greater display of practical ability than creating an entire universe out of nothing, the Bible sees God as the ultimate source of wisdom (Job 12:13), as well as justice. This means that he is able to dispense wisdom to others (e.g., Isaiah 11:2), including the Israelites as they apply self-executing rules (see above) to resolve their disputes.

J. Be inspired by a divine sense of justice

A final feature of biblical adjudication is that *"doing justice" means drawing on "divinely-inspired intuition as to the appropriate solution on the facts of the*

---

27. Norman Whybray, *Slippery words IV: Wisdom, in* WISDOM: THE COLLECTED ARTICLES OF NORMAN WHYBRAY, (Katharine J. Dell & Margaret Barker eds., Aldershot: Ashgate, 2005), 6–9, 6.

28. MARC ZVI BRETTLER, GOD IS KING: UNDERSTANDING AN ISRAELITE METAPHOR, JOURNAL FOR THE STUDY OF THE OLD TESTAMENT SUPPLEMENT SERIES 76 (Sheffield: Sheffield Academic Press, 1989), 53.

*particular case."*²⁹ In biblical law, judicial decisions are considered of great significance because they reflect the interests and mind of God himself. But on what basis did judges make their decisions?

Although reference is made to a written "book of the law" in the hands of the king (Deuteronomy 17:18) and to the fact that Jehoshaphat's judges carried "the Book of the Law of the LORD" wherever they went (2 Chronicles 17:9), there is no reference, at least in the preexilic sources, to any duty to apply these written laws in a modern positivistic sense. It is true that Jehoshaphat's instructions to the Jerusalem judges refer to "commands, decrees, or ordinances" (2 Chronicles 19:10; JPS), but the immediate context refers to the wide variety of cases that the judges will encounter ("whether bloodshed or other concerns of the law"; JPS). Consequently, the "commands, decrees, or ordinances" are identifiable because of their subject matter and not because they form the basis of "black-letter" rules that are applied in the case of adjudication.³⁰ On the contrary, the king prepares a copy of the "book of the law" in order to educate himself (Deuteronomy 17:19–20). Similarly, Jehoshaphat's judges carry copies of the same book to teach the people (2 Chronicles 17:9).

We saw in Chapter 1 that while biblical law is incomplete, its purpose is to lead to wisdom, which is complete. For this reason, we do not have to assume that the written law necessarily formed the basis of adjudication in every case. Nor do we have to assume that in those cases where it did form the basis of adjudication, the law was applied in a modern positivistic sense. The didactic function of the law is to impart wisdom and thus shape the character of the judges with the goal of ensuring that the decisions they reach conform to the just character of God.

Support for this general position can be found in David Carr's³¹ analysis of orality, cultural memory, and literacy. This highlights the role of memory and recitation in the production, revision, and reception of ancient texts. Carr argues that the goal of ANE scribal education was the internalization and memorization of key classic texts, which were performed periodically at banquets and public festivals. Jehoshaphat's "teaching mission" is in some respects similar to the reciting of national epics throughout antiquity (and cf. Israel's practice of priestly readings on public occasions; e.g., Deuteronomy 31:10–13). It can be seen as an example of the dissemination of "long-duration" texts that have been cognitively mastered for socialization and ongoing enculturation, as was common in the ANE. If Carr's model can be extrapolated to ancient Israel,³² it is likely that

---

29. Jackson, *Justice & righteousness*, p. 219.
30. Bernard S. Jackson, *Ideas of law and legal administration: A semiotic approach*, in THE WORLD OF ANCIENT ISRAEL: SOCIOLOGICAL, ANTHROPOLOGICAL AND POLITICAL PERSPECTIVES, (R. E. Clements ed., Cambridge: Cambridge University Press, 1989), 185–202, 188.
31. DAVID M. CARR, WRITING ON THE TABLET OF THE HEART: ORIGINS OF SCRIPTURE AND LITERATURE (Oxford: Oxford University Press, 2005).
32. *See* CARR, TABLET OF THE HEART, pp. 111–73.

the texts disseminated by Jehoshaphat's judges had already been committed to memory. If so, the text of "the book of the law" might only have been used for reference purposes, in the same way that a musical score functions for "a musician who already knows the piece."[33] This is consistent with the impression given in the Hebrew Bible itself that complete written versions of Torah were few and far between. The description of the king's special copy of the "book of the law" (Deuteronomy 17:18–20) is the exception which proves the rule. This approach also suggests that there was no room for improvization with regard to content: audiences expected an exact repetition.

If the book of the law is a memorized text, then this is consistent with the biblical emphasis on the need for Torah to be internalized so that it can shape the character of the person who has memorized and reflected upon it (e.g, Psalm 19:7–8/MT 19:8–9). In this way, the book of the law shapes and constrains judges' decisions, even though they do not need to quote from it in a modern positivistic sense. They are supposed to follow an internalized sense of wisdom that has been shaped by the book of the law, rather than apply rules in a modern sense. This would explain why, when judges are commissioned in the Bible, there is no need to give them any detailed advice other than "judge righteously" (Deuteronomy 1:16; Moses speaking), uphold "righteous judgment (*mishpat tsedeq*)" (Deuteronomy 16:18; Moses speaking), "justice, justice shall you pursue (*tsedeq tsedeq tirdoph*; Deuteronomy 16:20; Moses speaking; JPS) and "let the fear of the LORD be upon you" (2 Chronicles 19:7; Jehoshaphat speaking). Finally, Carr's account of how texts were circulated in antiquity may also help to explain why Jehoshaphat based his legal reforms around fortified cities (2 Chronicles 19:5). As centers of population, the cities would have drawn in crowds from surrounding areas, making the teaching mission more efficient and increasing the level of exposure.

There are parallels between the nonpositivistic basis of adjudication in biblical law and examples of adjudication elsewhere in the ANE. Old Babylonian judges were those "who knew what the community considered just and whose attitudes were respected by it and by the litigants."[34] Such judges "were not guided by written codes but by their own socially constructed ideas of fairness and right."[35] Weinfeld[36] suggests that the general instructions in the Bible recall the ancient Near Eastern tradition of social justice, especially the Mesopotamian

---

33. Ibid., 4.
34. RIVKAH HARRIS, ANCIENT SIPPAR: A DEMOGRAPHIC STUDY OF AN OLD-BABYLONIAN CITY (1894-1595 B.C.) (Belgium: Nederlands Historisch-Archaeologisch Instituut Te Instanbul, 1975), 116.
35. Lisbeth S. Fried, *"You shall appoint judges": Ezra's mission and the rescript of Artaxerxes, in* PERSIA & TORAH: THE THEORY OF IMPERIAL AUTHORISATION OF THE PENTATEUCH (James W. Watts ed., Atlanta: Society of Biblical Literature, 2001), 63–89, 79.
36. WEINFELD, SOCIAL JUSTICE, pp. 75ff.

practice of *kittum u misharum*. This refers to the "sense" of "truth and justice,"[37] which establishes social equity.

To sum up, judges make decisions based on biblically inspired wisdom that is shaped and constrained by the book of the law. This is consistent with the belief that God is the ultimate source of wisdom and justice in the Bible. It is also consistent with various hints that biblical justice and adjudication have "nonpositivist biblical connotation[s]."[38] For example, the phrase "justice and righteousness (*mishpat utsedaqah*)," which recurs frequently in the Bible (e.g., 1 Kings 10:9) uses the feminine form of the noun *tsedeq* (*tsedaqah*), which means more specifically "charity."[39] Another broad hint is found in Exodus 19:5, where "keeping the covenant" is framed, not simply in terms of "following a specific set of rules," but in terms of "obeying God's voice," a point later picked up by Jeremiah:

> But this command I gave them, "Obey my voice . . . ."
> (Jeremiah 7:23; *God speaking*)

The juxtaposition of the words "command" (which has positivist connotations) and "voice" (which includes commands but also other normative forms of speech) is striking. According to Exodus and Jeremiah, what Israel agreed to was simply to "listen to God's voice." Of course, "obeying the voice" included rule-orientated behavior in one form or another—including, of course, all the law at Mount Sinai that was spoken by God to Moses. But "listening to the voice" also meant living up to the vocation of Exodus 19:6—that of being "a kingdom of priests and a holy nation." It is not surprising then that *the primary obligation of judges under the covenant is not simply to apply rules but to "listen to God's voice."*

K. Summary

We have seen that there are a number of key beliefs that were to guide Israel in her quest for justice. Participants in Israel's judicial process were supposed to (1) believe that God is the ultimate source of justice, (2) believe that judges have the potential to mediate actual divine decisions, (3) fight to overthrow the oppressor and liberate the oppressed, (4) put things right, from God's perspective, (5) put justice in the hands of the many, not the few, (6) respect the role of provincial courts, (7) involve a range of authorities in adjudication, (8) sort out their own legal disputes, (9) apply practical wisdom, and (10) be inspired by a divine sense of justice. In this sense, Israel's system of justice can be considered effective

---

37. Ibid., 75.
38. Bernard S. Jackson, *Historical observations on the relationship between letter and spirit*, in LAW AND RELIGION: CURRENT LEGAL ISSUES (Richard O'Dair & Andrew Lewis eds., Oxford: Oxford University Press, 2001), 101–10, p. 103, n. 10.
39. Ibid.

inasmuch as it enables the judge to make the right decision, understood in terms of "listening to God's voice."

These elements can usefully be compared with key elements of a modern Western ideology of adjudication, which is summarized in Table 7, below.

TABLE 7 CONTRASTS BETWEEN BIBLICAL AND MODERN IDEOLOGIES OF ADJUDICATION[40]

	Biblical ideology of adjudication	Modern Western ideology of adjudication
1	God is the ultimate source of justice	"Justice" is closely tied to "law," which in turn derives its legitimacy from human sources and institutions
2	Judges make their decisions based on their knowledge of the character of God, with the result that judges have the potential to mediate actual divine decisions	Adjudication is largely separate from religion
3	Justice is deliverance from oppression and restoration to God's creative intent	Justice is achieved by the application of rules
4	Justice is rooted in a divinely mandated social order	Justice is rooted in some conception of individual human rights
5	Judges are mostly nonprofessional, and the quest for justice is a communal responsibility	Being a judge is a professional occupation, and justice is the responsibility of the few
6	No positivistic "sources of law"; higher courts used as "court of reference" for provincial courts	Operation of the legal "sources of law," within a positivistically conceived secular system of law, depends on a clear hierarchy of courts which set precedents for lower courts
7	Unclear separation of powers	Clear separation of powers
8	Strong preference for private settlement	The legal system is the privileged medium for resolving disputes
9	Law has the character of "practical wisdom" rather than "rules"	Law is seen as a system of general rules, applicable equally to all individuals
10	Judges are not under any duty to "apply" general legal rules	Judges are under an obligation to "apply" these general rules

---

40. *See* Bernard S. Jackson, *The practice of justice in Jewish law*, DAIMON 4, 31–48 (2004); BERNARD S. JACKSON, STUDIES IN THE SEMIOTICS OF BIBLICAL LAW, JOURNAL FOR THE STUDY OF THE OLD TESTAMENT SUPPLEMENT SERIES 314 (Sheffield: Sheffield Academic Press, 2000); Jackson, *Justice and righteousness*.

Space prohibits a full comparative analysis, and so the features of contemporary adjudication are listed for illustration only. They are simply premises that help to clarify the main ways in which biblical adjudication can be distinguished from modern conceptions of adjudication.[41]

II. GRASSROOTS JUSTICE

What did the day-to-day administration of justice look like in biblical Israel? As modern Western readers, it is all too easy to assume that Israel had the trappings of a modern judicial process, including civil tribunals, police, and a Crown Prosecution Service. This is a mistake. We should beware of projecting modern institutional assumptions onto the biblical texts. Once again, we need to pay attention to the presupposition pool of biblical Israel—the things they took for granted but which might not be familiar to us. Aspects of the presupposition pool include: a system of private prosecution with extensive victim participation, the centrality of local justice, a high level of responsibility on the part of witnesses, community participation, and a relative lack of professionals. An overall picture of grassroots justice can be briefly sketched, as follows, though of course we have no way of telling to what extent the practices described in the biblical materials represented common practice or best practice.

First, biblical Israel was characterized by a system of private prosecution. Justice was pursued, for the most part, by the injured party or the victim's nearest male relative. Deuteronomy 25:5–10, where a widow takes the initiative in bringing her case, is the exception that proves the rule. The ethos is one of self-help within permissible limits. Examples of regulated self-help include the *lex talionis* ("eye for an eye") formula, which is best understood as setting limits to retaliation ("no more than an eye"), in contrast to the disproportionate ("seventy-sevenfold") response typified by Lamech (Genesis 4:23–24; see further Chapter 8). Compensation was made directly by the offender to the victim (e.g., restitution cases, Exodus 22:1–5/MT 21:37–22:4; Numbers 5:6–7).

Second is the centrality of local justice. If the dispute could not be resolved by the parties concerned, it became a matter for arbitration by the elders in the town gate. This location was typically an open area, just inside the city, against the back wall of the gates (cf. excavations at Dan).[42] When privacy was required, arbitration may also have taken place in a complex of rooms built into the city gate

---

41. For more detailed discussion of contemporary forms of adjudication *see* William Lucy, *Adjudication, in* THE OXFORD HANDBOOK OF JURISPRUDENCE AND PHILOSOPHY OF LAW (Jules Coleman & Scott Shapiro eds. Oxford: Oxford University Press, 2002), 206–67.

42. A. Biran, *Dan, in* THE NEW ENCYCLOPAEDIA OF THE HOLY LAND, (Ephraim Stern et al., eds., London: Simon and Schuster, 1993), 323–32, 325.

(cf. recesses found during excavations at Gezer).[43] Either way, the town gate is the seat of local government and the place where justice is delivered.[44] Executions took place there, as well as the resolution of what we would nowadays term civil disputes (e.g., Boaz's challenge to the "kinsman-redeemer"; Ruth 4:1–12). The elders were typically the heads of families, and they functioned as "judges in the gate." The modern comparison is with magistrates, who serve from a sense of public duty, rather than paid judges. Job paints a picture of the esteem in which the local judge could be held:

> When the ear heard, it called me blessed,
> and when the eye saw, it approved;
> because I delivered the poor who cried,
> and the fatherless who had none to help him.
> The blessing of him who was about to perish came upon me,
> and I caused the widow's heart to sing for joy.
> I put on righteousness, and it clothed me;
> my justice was like a robe and a turban.
> . . .
> Men listened to me, and waited,
> and kept silence for my counsel.
> After I spoke they did not speak again
> . . .
> I chose their way, and sat as chief,
> and I dwelt like a king among his troops . . . . (Job 29:11–14, 21–22, 25)

Access to justice was local, except for certain categories of cases which were dealt with centrally (e.g., Exodus 18:26; Deuteronomy 17:8–9; 2 Chronicles 19:10–11). Legally significant sites in ancient Israel (as in the ANE generally) included everyday locations such as the city gate (e.g., Deuteronomy 21:19), the threshing floor (e.g., 1 Kings 22:10), or the threshold of a relevant parties' house (e.g., Exodus 21:6; Deuteronomy 22:21; Judges 19:27).[45] The number of people subject to local jurisdictions would have been relatively small. Even fortified Israelite towns such as Dan, the remains of which survive today as a large archaeological site, cover an area of under one square mile (50 acres).[46] This is not large by today's standards: a modern city such as Bristol, in England, covers an area

---

43. W. G. Dever, *Gezer*, in THE NEW ENCYCLOPAEDIA OF THE HOLY LAND, (Ephraim Stern et al., eds., London: Simon and Schuster, 1993), 496–506.

44. *See generally* LUDWIG KÖHLER, HEBREW MAN (London: SCM Press, 1956), 149–75; Donald A. McKenzie, *Judicial procedure at the town gate*, VETUS TESTAMENTUM 14, 100–04 (1964).

45. Victor H. Matthews, *Entrance ways and threshing floors: Legally significant sites in the Ancient Near East*, FIDES ET HISTORIA 19, 25–40 (1987).

46. Biran, *Dan*, p. 323.

of 42.5 square miles. The relatively small size of Israelite towns also meant the contrast between urban and rural living is not as great as it is today: even urban society was rural and intimate.

Third, witnesses had an important role to play in the town gate and took on a high degree of responsibility. Unlike modern law, where witnesses are seen as suppliers of neutral information, biblical witnesses took sides. The Hebrew word "witness" could refer both to a witness on *behalf* of the accused (e.g., Job 16:19) and *against* the accused (e.g., Numbers 5:13).[47] This is why witnesses took personal responsibility for their testimony, cast the first stone, and were eligible for the same penalty as the accused if their testimony proved false (Deuteronomy 19:16–19).

Fourth, biblical justice was supposed to operate against a background of regard for due process. Ensuring that sentencers were of sound moral character was one aspect of this (noted above); rules of evidence were another. According to Numbers 35:30, a single witness was inadequate. Deuteronomy 17:6 (= Deuteronomy 19:15) states that someone should only be put to death "on the testimony of two or more [literally, 'three'] witnesses" (JPS). The formula is an intensifying rhetorical device that emphasizes the need for as many witnesses as possible. The greater the number, the safer the conviction (cf. the similar formula of "a day or two" of Exodus 21:21, which could mean two days, a week, or several years). The requirement to "inquire diligently" and ensure that "the thing [is] certain" (Deuteronomy 17:4) means that the "two or three witnesses" formula could never be reduced to a numbers game—especially if the witnesses themselves were of doubtful character. We should not, therefore, regard 1 Kings 21:1–15 (the Naboth incident) as demonstrating the weakness of biblical rules of evidence. Accepting the testimony of "two scoundrels" (verses 10–13; JPS) was itself an outrage and at odds with the purpose of Deuteronomy 19:15. The author makes it clear that not only Jezebel and the false witnesses were guilty of the death of Naboth but also "the elders and the nobles" for accepting such testimony.

Fifth, all the people were supposed to be involved in securing justice. The Israelite was not to turn a deaf ear or a blind eye if he was a witness to an offense. Leviticus 5:1 suggests that a curse be pronounced against the witness who withheld testimony. The whole community, or representatives thereof, take direct and personal responsibility for punishing the offender. Punishment is carried out in their sight and in their midst. Proactive witnesses and communities were necessary, given the relative lack of "professionals." The judges appointed in Deuteronomy 16:18–20 may have been intended to be relatively specialist, although subordinate to the judge at the central sanctuary (Deuteronomy 17:8–9). Apart from these, the only professionals apparently involved in ancient Israel were "semiprofessionals" whose role in the judicial process derived from some

---

47. McKenzie, *Judicial procedure*, p. 102.

other social status, e.g., the King (1 Kings 3:16–28), the high ranking "civil servant," or high priest (2 Chronicles 19:11) and the Levitical priesthood (Deuteronomy 17:8–9). Even the social role of the avenger of blood (*go'el haddam*), who punishes the manslayer, appears to be carried out by a close relative rather than someone who is specially appointed to the task (see Chapter 8).

The communal aspect of grassroots justice is reinforced by the distribution of land. We noted above that Moses appointed judges over military units as small as "tens" (Exodus 18:25). This meant that judges would have been appointed over extended families. We will see in Chapter 6 that, in contrast to the Egyptian approach to land ownership, each Israelite family was to "cleave" to a particular parcel of land in perpetuity (Numbers 36:7, 9). It helped to integrate the family and also made a grassroots approach to justice practicable. This is because it is possible to have a widespread network of community courts when there is a broadly based system of land ownership. It also prevents the local justice process from falling into the hands of a ruling elite. If every family owns some land, each will have their own independent economic base. Systems of land ownership thus impact on the delivery of local justice. This is particularly appropriate in Israel's case because Israel herself is presented as receiving the land as a result of an act of justice, in other words, God's judgment upon the previous inhabitants of the promised land (e.g., Numbers 33:51–54). The conflict between King Ahab and Naboth described in 1 Kings 21:1–16 is a good example of the way in which attempts to subvert the traditional Israelite system of land tenure have the effect of perverting local justice. The monarchy's determination to acquire Naboth's family land by foul means leads to judicial corruption. This was, no doubt, the result of Ahab or Queen Jezebel "granting favours or lands to those who cooperated"[48] in bringing false charges against Naboth.

Our brief overview of local justice in biblical Israel forms the background to a discussion of the following practical issues.

III. DIVINE AND HUMAN JUSTICE

From a modern perspective, biblical Israel's ideology of sacred adjudication seems problematic from a practical point of view. How does one go about operationalizing a system of divine justice? Does this not imply a "counsel of perfection"? What sort of people could possibly be capable of delivering divine justice successfully? Is there such a thing as a hard case in a system of divine justice and, if so, on what basis are such cases resolved? And so on.

---

48. ELLEN F. DAVIS, SCRIPTURE, CULTURE & AGRICULTURE: AN AGRARIAN READING (Cambridge: Cambridge University Press, 2008).

This section addresses some of the practical problems that might be thought to arise from a system of divine justice. They include the following subjects: (1) the compatibility of human adjudicatory agencies with the goal of divine justice, (2) the requirements for appointing a judge who could carry out God's will, (3) the *modus operandi* for reaching actual divine decisions, (4) the use of wisdom to decide hard cases, (5) the freedom to experiment within a system of divine justice, and (6) the establishment of a "mixed economy" of adjudication, which involves a broad range of different institutional groups.

A. Human nature

First, we saw in I. A above, that Israel's ideology of adjudication involves the belief that God is the ultimate source of justice. This seems to give rise to a practical problem, namely, if God is the source of justice, then does that not tend to exclude the operation of human adjudicatory agencies? This practical problem is addressed in the texts. Here we see that the Israelite belief that God is the source of justice does *not* exclude the use of human adjudicatory agencies.

This is apparent from the immediate aftermath of the Exodus, where we find that Moses is the mediator of actual divine decisions (Exodus 18:13, 15–16). It is an extraordinary turnaround from Exodus 2, where Moses's attempt to adjudicate in the case of a victimized Israelite is rejected by a fellow Israelite with the words, "Who made you a prince and a judge over us?" (2:14). After that, Moses goes on the run from Pharaoh for killing an Egyptian and finds refuge in the land of Midian, where he meets his future father-in-law, Jethro (Exodus 2–4; and see Chapter 8). Indeed, it is Jethro's return in the "adjudication" chapter of Exodus 18 which shows the contrast between Exodus 2 and 18. Moses's role as judge over the Israelites in Chapter 18 is in complete contrast to his earlier rejection as a judge. The answer to the question of Chapter 2—"who made you a judge?"—is clearly "God."[49] This is consistent with a divine ideology because it indicates that the human power to adjudicate comes from God. Leviticus 24:13–23 (the case of the blasphemer) and Numbers 27:5–11 (the case of the daughters of Zelophehad) are examples of Moses's importance in mediating divine decisions.

In Exodus 18:13–16, Moses is the only mediator of divine decisions, which amounts to a "Rolls-Royce" legal system. After all, if justice is from God, and Moses is the one with whom God speaks "face to face" (Exodus 33:11), getting justice from Moses is the best way of getting access to divine justice (see Figure 2, below).

---

49. Eugene Carpenter, *Exodus 18: Its structure, style, motifs and function in the Book of Exodus*, in A BIBLICAL ITINERARY, (Eugene E. Carpenter, ed., Journal for the Study of the Old Testament Supplement Series 240, Sheffield: Sheffield Academic Press, 1997), 91–109, 101.

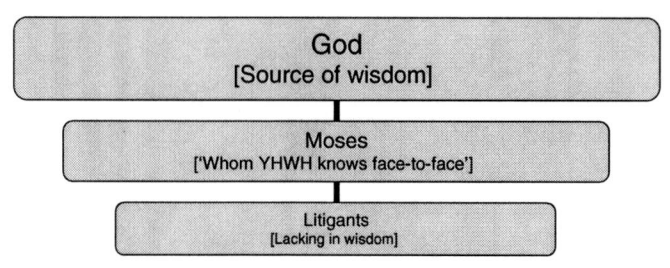

```
┌─────────────────────────────────────┐
│              God                    │
│      [Source of wisdom]             │
└─────────────────────────────────────┘
                │
┌─────────────────────────────────────┐
│             Moses                   │
│  ['Whom YHWH knows face-to-face']   │
└─────────────────────────────────────┘
                │
     ┌──────────────────────────┐
     │        Litigants         │
     │   [Lacking in wisdom]    │
     └──────────────────────────┘
```

FIGURE 2. THE 'ROLLS-ROYCE' SYSTEM OF ADJUDICATION IN THE BIBLE (EXODUS 18:13-16)

Of course, the trouble with running a "Rolls-Royce" legal system is that it is prohibitively costly. Here it exacts a huge burden upon Moses and the people (Exodus 18:18). Moses's difficulties in "[dealing] with the burdensome aspects of human reality"[50] emphasize the thrust of Exodus 18, which is that the wisdom to judge well only comes from God. Even Moses needs wisdom. Moses's problems also show that the ideology of avoiding third-party adjudication (see I. H, above) had not caught on. This in turn suggests that the advice of Proverbs 25:7-9 indicated best practice, rather than common practice. The solution—devised by Moses's father-in-law, Jethro—is a delegated system according to which Moses only handles the hard cases (Exodus 18:22; see Figure 3, overleaf). These are dealt with by means of an oracle, as suggested by the language of Moses "bring[ing] their cases to God" (Exodus 18:19). The people sort out the rest of their problems by themselves, assisted by judges arranged in a military hierarchy (Exodus 18:25; see I. C, above). The implication is that cases that could not be solved at the lowest level could be referred further up the chain of command.

The expression "God be with you" (Exodus 18:19) is an assurance that the desire for divinely inspired decisions will not be thwarted by dispersing Moses's judicial functions. It is a better structure for "the dissemination of *mishpat* [justice] and the knowledge of Yahweh in Israel."[51] Notably, Exodus 18:13–27 uses the word *dabhar* ("word," "thing") ten times (nine times in the singular and once in the plural). This foreshadows the ten *debharim* ("words") of the Decalogue[52] (see Chapter 2), which in turn implies that God's spoken utterances are themselves part of the adjudicatory process. The word *dabhar* is used in connection both with the judicial process and its substantive content. The implication is that Jethro's advice on how to mediate divine justice is itself divinely inspired. Perhaps this is why Moses himself is confident that God will be "with" him when he implements Jethro's system (Exodus 18:19).

---

50. Hauge, Descent from the Mountain, p. 256.
51. Carpenter, *Exodus 18*, p. 97.
52. Ibid.

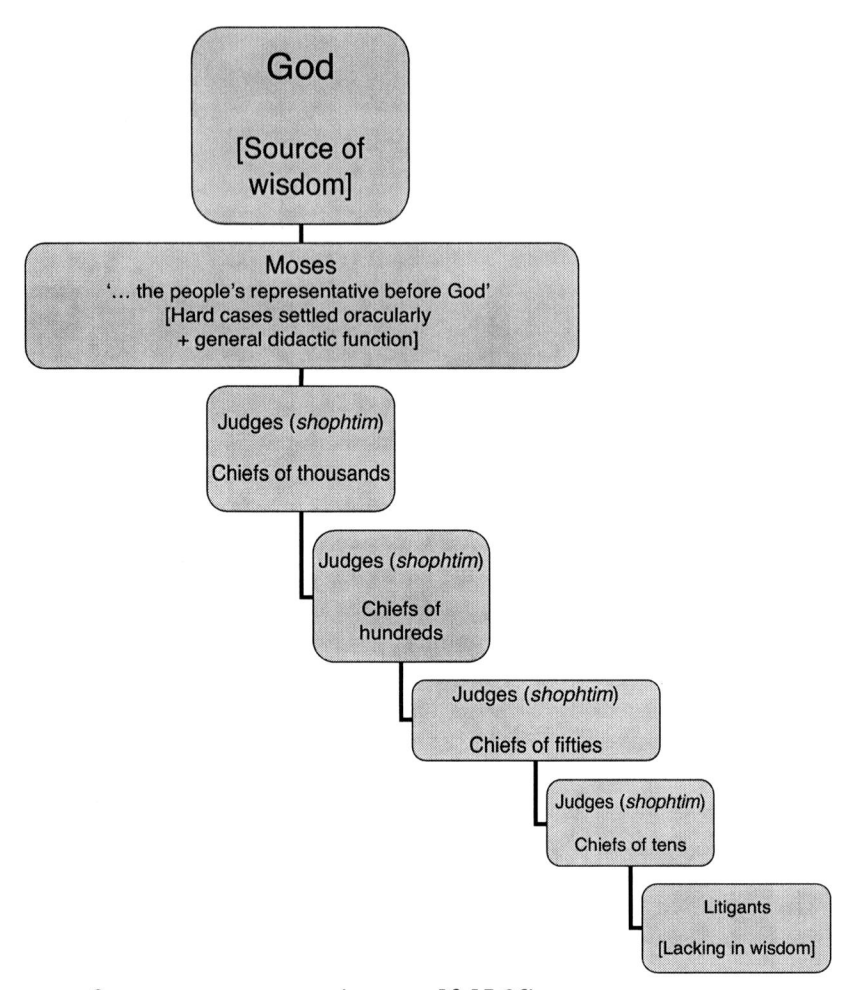

```
                    ┌──────────────┐
                    │    God       │
                    │ [Source of   │
                    │  wisdom]     │
                    └──────┬───────┘
                           │
              ┌────────────┴─────────────────┐
              │          Moses               │
              │ '... the people's representative before God' │
              │ [Hard cases settled oracularly │
              │  + general didactic function] │
              └────────┬─────────────────────┘
                       │
                  ┌────┴──────────────┐
                  │ Judges (shophtim) │
                  │ Chiefs of thousands│
                  └─────┬─────────────┘
                        │
                    ┌───┴───────────────┐
                    │ Judges (shophtim) │
                    │ Chiefs of hundreds │
                    └────┬──────────────┘
                         │
                     ┌───┴───────────────┐
                     │ Judges (shophtim) │
                     │ Chiefs of fifties │
                     └────┬──────────────┘
                          │
                      ┌───┴───────────────┐
                      │ Judges (shophtim) │
                      │ Chiefs of tens    │
                      └────┬──────────────┘
                           │
                       ┌───┴──────────────┐
                       │   Litigants      │
                       │ [Lacking in wisdom]│
                       └──────────────────┘
```

FIGURE 3. THE JETHRO SYSTEM (EXODUS 18:17-26)

That Jethro himself is capable of being divinely inspired may seem surprising, bearing in mind that he is presented in no uncertain terms as a Midianite and hence as a pagan priest (Exodus 18:1). However, Jethro's response to the story of the Exodus is effectively that of a convert (Exodus 18:10–12a), while the food he subsequently shares with Israel's elders can be seen as a covenant meal that marks his incorporation into the people of God (Exodus 18:12b[53]).

---

53. Allen Guenther, *A typology of Israelite marriage: Kinship, socio-economic, and religious factors*, J. STUD. OLD TESTAMENT 29, 387–407 (2005).

Israel's administrative system is set up, not on the word of a Gentile, but by Israel's latest convert.

There is a thematic parallel between Exodus 18:13–27, where Moses's adjudicatory function is shared more widely, and Numbers 11:16–30, where Moses's prophetic role is distributed among 70 of Israel's elders. The parallel is between what we might call the "democratization of adjudication" in Exodus 18 and the "democratization of prophecy" in Numbers 11.[54] The parallel makes perfect sense when we consider the structure of the Sinai story as a whole within the Pentateuch. Exodus 18 is "the last episode of the pre-Sinai journey," while Numbers 11 is "the first concrete episode of the post-Sinai journey."[55] This means that we can juxtapose the "oracular soldiers" of Exodus 18 (who receive the power to judge) and the "ecstatic scribes" of Numbers 11 (who receive the power to prophecy[56]). The parallel between these two groups suggests that the newly appointed judges of Exodus 18 had a similar ecstatic experience to that of the scribes in Numbers 11:26–28. If so, it underlines the idea that human judges could deliver divine charismatic judgments. To push the parallel a little further, we could even suppose that Moses's attitude toward his newly installed judges paralleled his recorded feelings toward the newly installed prophets. In addition to saying, "Would that all the LORD's people were prophets, that the LORD would put his spirit upon them!" (Numbers 11:29), we should perhaps imagine Moses saying, "Would that all the Lord's people were *judges*, that the Lord would put his spirit upon them!" Such an arrangement would be in keeping with the ideology of divine adjudication, even though it seems to reflect the reality that not all "the LORD's people" were judges.

Several practical features of the Jethro model are worth noting. First, we have already seen that these judges are organized along military lines (Exodus 18:21–22). This may mean that the judges had recourse to some form of law enforcement, though we should not conceive of this in formal terms.

Second, it is likely that the "rulers . . . of tens" (Exodus 18:21) correspond to the heads of families. They are the true "judges at first instance." It is entirely appropriate that the family should be at the cutting edge of day-to-day justice. After all, it is in this very setting that wisdom is internalized (see generally the Book of Proverbs). This is the practical outworking of the belief that wisdom is essential to doing justice (see I. I, above). The Jethro model makes wisdom and the family the bedrock of the legal system. The domestic setting also highlights the fact that biblical Israel's adjudicatory institutions were somewhat informal.

---

54. Marc Zvi Brettler, *The many faces of God in Exodus 19*, in JEWS, CHRISTIANS & THE THEOLOGY OF THE HEBREW SCRIPTURES, (Alice Ogden Bellis & Joel S. Kaminsky eds., Atlanta: Society of Biblical Literature, 2000), 353–67, 363.
55. HAUGE, DESCENT FROM THE MOUNTAIN, p. 248.
56. Ibid., 266, 268.

Third, the most important practical outcome of Exodus 18 is that it frees Moses "for the higher aspects of mediation."[57] In the very next chapter, he is liberated to ascend Mount Sinai. Jethro's legal reforms result in the people becoming "upwardly mobile" in a spiritual sense: the judges are elevated to the status of "Moses-substitutes,"[58] and Moses himself goes higher still.

Finally, the biblical presentation shows that there is a trend toward involving human beings increasingly in matters of divine judgement. It is as though God thinks it important that human beings should be involved in the task of passing divine judgment on other human beings—a responsibility that fell particularly on kings, priests, and prophets. This is cognate with the New Testament's claim that God has committed the delivery of divine justice to a human being who is uniquely qualified to judge precisely *because* of his humanity (e.g., Acts 10:42). Here, human nature is not opposed to divine judgement on human beings; instead, it is a valuable precondition.

To sum up, human adjudicatory agents were not incompatible with a belief in divine justice, and the Israelites were given wide discretion on how to organize their divine mediators.

B. The right stuff

Second, we saw above that Israel's ideology of sacred adjudication involves the belief that human judges have the potential to mediate actual divine decisions (see I. B, above). This raises the practical problem of how should such persons be selected, and on what basis? This issue is also addressed in the texts.

It is clear from Exodus 18 that the Jethro system depended on choosing the right people to serve as judges (*shophtim*). Whereas modern liberal democracies are based on the ideology of "governance by rules, not by men," biblical Israel is based on "governance by men, not by rules."[59] However, Israel was not to be governed by *any* men, only those who are divinely inspired.[60] Appointments were made on the basis of their character. Having "the right stuff" was the crucial link between the Israelite belief in divine justice and the reality that, in the majority of cases, this would be mediated through people who, although not of the same unique status as Moses, were nevertheless men of integrity. To maintain confidence in a system of divine justice, then, biblical Israel had to be very careful whom it appointed as judge.

Some of the most heated constitutional debates in modern states concern the basis of judicial selection, appointment, and retention.[61] Such criteria make a

---

57. Ibid., 250.
58. Ibid., 254.
59. Ben-Menahem, *Postscript*, p. 422.
60. Ibid.
61. Lee Epstein & Jack Knight, Courts and judges, in THE BLACKWELL COMPANION TO LAW & SOCIETY, (Austin Sarat ed., Oxford: Blackwell, 2005), 170–94, 175–79.

great difference to the type of persons who serve as judges and the choices they make. Modern U.S. presidents, for example, face potential conflicts of interest in making judicial appointments. Like them, Moses could have made judicial appointments on the basis of: (1) personal factors (nominating friends and family), (2) partisan reasons (shoring up popular support), (3) policy (promoting a specific policy agenda), or (4) some combination of the above. Which did he choose?

Moses adopted the selection procedure recommended by Jethro. If we look at Jethro's criteria more closely we find that it is steeped in the language of proverbial wisdom. Judges are to be "able men . . . [who] fear God" (Exodus 18:21), "the fear of the LORD" being, of course, the beginning of wisdom (e.g., Proverbs 1:7). They are also to be people who avoid partiality (Exodus 18:21; Deuteronomy 16:19) and bribery (Deuteronomy 1:17; 16:19). Partiality and bribery are similar, except that in the case of partiality or favoritism, "the relationship is established by prior association, or by the presumed status of one of the litigants, rather than by a cash payment."[62] In practical terms, this requirement of integrity was one way of eradicating "the inherent weaknesses in the local administration of justice, which was open to abuse and manipulation from the influence of powerful local families."[63] But once again, the language recalls the wisdom literature (Proverbs 17:23) which presents justice and bribery as binary opposites (e.g., Proverbs 29:4). Judges who eschew bribery and partiality are like God (Deuteronomy 10:17) who is, of course, the wise and perfect judge. In all these ways, the biblical judge fits the profile of the "wise man" who walks closely with God and does his will (Exodus 18:21; Deuteronomy 1:13, 15–17; 16:19). This is explicitly confirmed by Moses's statement that he appointed "wise (*chakamim*), discerning and experienced" persons (Deuteronomy 1:13; JPS). It is not sufficient that the judge merely avoids negative practices. Instead, he is supposed to actively pursue and embrace wisdom (Proverbs 3:13,18). In modern terms, Moses's judges were political activists who had some measure of popular support and who could be relied upon to promote a particular policy agenda.

To sum up, human adjudicatory agents had the potential to mediate actual divine decisions, provided the right judicial appointments were made in the first place, with the basis of selection being the ability to exercise wisdom, which is seen as a moral capacity.

C. Discerning justice

The third issue follows logically from the previous two: human beings can indeed be part of a system of divine justice, but even if care is taken to make the right

---

62. Lawrence H. Schiffman, *The prohibition of judicial corruption in the Dead Sea Scrolls, Philo, Josephus and Talmudic Law*, in HESED VE-EMET (Jodi Magness & Seymour Gitin eds., Atlanta: Scholars Press, 1998), 155–78, 174.

63. WHITELAM, THE JUST KING, p. 196.

appointments, how do human beings actually go about delivering actual divine decisions? This is an important question because in any jurisdiction, the effective legal system is the one which enables the judge to make the right decision. In biblical Israel, the "right decision" is one that is accordance with God's will. But how is this supposed to happen?

To answer this, we need to understand what is meant by the assurance, "He [God] is with you in giving judgment" (2 Chronicles 19:6). Does the judge go into some sort of trance and deliver the verdict while under some mesmeric influence? The problem with this interpretation is that it turns the human judge into a passive conveyer of the divine will. This is inconsistent with the picture developed from the biblical materials in this chapter (and in Chapter 3) which emphasize partnership and continuity between divine and human acts of judgment.

Another view might be that the phrase "God is with you..." is simply a way of recognizing that the judges have been "invested" with the appropriate authority to make human decisions. These decisions are made entirely independently of divine influence. However, the notion that the words are just a way of designating "delegated" human, authority sells them short. In a theocratic society like biblical Israel, it is reasonable to assume that the words did imply some active divine engagement with human adjudication. But how did this take place?

In my view, the best starting point is to recognize that the process of deciding what God's will is in a legal dispute is not, in principle, different from the question of identifying God's will in any other sort of situation. Or to put it another way, the question of how God acts through human judges is not, in principle, any different from the question of how God acts through *any* human agent, such as a prophet. It can be argued that knowing what God wants someone to do in a given situation involves the human agent lining up behind what God is *already* doing in the situation. Recognizing what God is doing involves "a process of discernment [that is] guided by key biblical symbols and perspectives."[64] For a judge delivering a divine verdict, it is reasonable to suppose that these symbols and perspectives include the stories of God's just acts and the paradigm cases contained in "the book of the law." The point about discernment is that it is not a mechanical exercise. Instead, discernment "employs imaginative and affective criteria to discover what the appropriate response should be to God's action."[65]

In this sense, the application by the judge of paradigm cases to the legal dispute is no different, in principle, from the application of biblical paradigms in general, including biblical narratives. Biblical paradigms "provide motivation in definite directions: they generate *dispositions*, that is, dynamic attitudes that are

---

64. William Spohn, What Are They Saying About Scripture and Ethics? (Paulist Press, 1996), 105.
65. Ibid.

"disposed" or lean toward acting in certain ways."[66] This is a fruitful way to think of divine-human adjudication: biblical law, like Scripture in general, "primarily exerts its normative function by setting a pattern of dispositions rather than dictating directly the content of action."[67]

William Spohn argues that the moral authority of Scripture functions "on a different level of experience than the rational application of principles"; instead, it operates at the level of "virtue and character ethics."[68] It relies "more on mature character and virtuous habits to recognise what is going on, to appreciate the values involved, the interactions with others, and discern an appropriate response."[69] Although Spohn does not make this connection, his analysis is very close to the "job criteria" of the Israelite judge which, as we have seen, emphasizes moral maturity. Biblical adjudication can thus be seen as an example of "virtue ethics." In turn, the "book of the law" can be understood, in Spohn's terms, as something that "guide[s] the moral agent to recognise action which is consonant with the biblical exemplar."[70] At the same time, because the paradigm cases contain an affective component (making the judge *feel* in a certain way), "[t]hose same dispositions provide the motivation to carry the discernment into action."[71] On this basis, the goal of the right judgment is the same as the purpose of moral reflection, namely, the virtuous and appropriate response.[72] The virtuous response is one that is "good and right, [but] it should also be appropriate because it is done in the right way to the right person in the right manner and at the right time. Appropriateness indicates that the action is affectively correct, considerate, sensitive and fitting . . . [to] both underlying scenarios and the situation of action."[73]

Consequently, there is no particular reason why we should see the process of delivering divine judgment as being either mystical on the one hand or secular on the other. Instead, the process of reaching a judgment is, in principle, the same as reaching any other decision about God's will: it is a process of discernment, guided by the symbols and perspectives of Israel's writings and history.

D. Hard cases—and good law

Fourth, Israel's ideology of sacred adjudication involves the belief that the purpose of adjudication is to put things right, from God's perspective (see I. D, above).

---

66. Ibid., 106, italics original.
67. Ibid., 108.
68. Ibid., 107.
69. Ibid.
70. Ibid.
71. Ibid.
72. Ibid., 108.
73. Ibid.

This raises the question of how do judges handle hard cases, and what counts as a hard case in a system of divine justice?

We have seen that the Jethro model is structured around the assumption that Moses would deal with "every great matter" (Exodus 18:22). The fact that Moses needed oracular assistance suggests that these cases were characterized by legal or factual difficulty. Other references to hard cases include problems which are "too difficult for you" (Deuteronomy 17:8). But can we be any more precise as to what characterizes the hard case?

We know from Exodus 18 that even easy cases, including those dealt with by judges on the lowest rung of the judicial ladder, require wisdom. If so, it follows that a hard case must be at the limits of the human capacity to exercise wisdom. To define this more closely, we must consider how wisdom is applied in legal cases. We can explore this by reference to the story of the woman of Tekoa who brings a made-up case for adjudication before King David (2 Samuel 14:1–20). This woman invents a plot about a family feud which supposedly involves her son. She claims that her two sons fought one another and that one of them was killed. Her family clan seeks to avenge the dead son by demanding that she hand over her sole surviving son for execution. This would leave her without a son to inherit her land and so continue the family name. (For the close relationship between a person's family, land, and name, see Deuteronomy 25:5–10.[74]) Thus presented, her story has certain parallels with the position of King David's exiled son, Absalom, who killed his brother, Amnon, in a family feud (2 Samuel 13:28–29). This is no coincidence: her goal is to get David to reflect on his family situation and reestablish Absalom at court.

The text is a classic example of the role of wisdom in adjudication because the woman hired for the task of challenging David is chosen on the basis of her wisdom (2 Samuel 14:2). Her mission is to construct a story that is, on the one hand, a genuine parallel to David's circumstances but is, at the same time, "[not] conspicuously so, in order that the 'unsuspecting hearer' may not easily suspect the relationship between both cases."[75] She has to strike a delicate balance of "closeness and remoteness" toward the object of her application.[76]

If we combine this account with a paradigmatic approach to biblical legal reasoning (see Chapter 1), it is immediately apparent why wisdom is necessary even to handle easy cases. In any given dispute, a relative judgment has to be made about how close the problem is to the relevant paradigm case in biblical

---

74. Jonathan P. Burnside, The Signs of Sin: Seriousness of Offence in Biblical Law. Journal for the Study of the Old Testament Supplement Series 364 (London: Continuum International, 2003), 85–90.

75. J. Hoftijzer, *David & the Tekoite woman*, Vetus Testamentum 20, 419–44, 421 (1970).

76. Uriel Simon, *The poor man's ewe lamb: An example of a juridical parable*, Biblica 48, 207–42, 223 (1967).

law. Wisdom is needed because *wisdom, in an adjudicatory setting, concerns the art of knowing where to position a case in relation to a given paradigm.* If so, the hard case is one where human wisdom runs out, and it is not possible to determine the relationship between a case and its closest paradigm.

How does this compare with the identification of hard cases in modern law? There are different models of hard cases in modern liberal jurisprudence. For Ronald Dworkin, a leading Anglo-American legal theorist, a classic example of a hard case is found in the American case of *Riggs v Palmer* (1889), in which a murderer claimed that he was entitled to inherit under the will of his victim. In his early work, Dworkin[77] presented the hard case as one where the legal rules conflict with our intuitive understanding of the requirements of justice. In his later work, Dworkin[78] redefines the hard case as one where there is a tension between two fundamental principles, each of which point in different directions. Judges faced with hard cases struggle to integrate several different levels of legal reasoning: (1) the intuitive search for justice (or "what is the right answer in this particular case?"), (2) the need to be consistent with authoritative legal principles that seem to point in a different direction, and (3) the problem of whether—and how—the law should be extended to cover the new situation presented by the hard case.

We saw in I. A, above, that the biblical ideology of adjudication means drawing on "divinely-inspired intuition as to the appropriate solution on the facts of the particular case."[79] We also saw that while this intuition was informed and shaped by "the book of the law," the written law did not necessarily form the basis of adjudication. It thus seems as though the hard case in biblical law only touches the first of these levels, viz., the question of the right decision in a given case. It follows from this that judges in biblical Israel did not have to deal with the sort of hard case that modern judges have to deal with because there is no well-invoked system of rules such that tensions between (1) and (2) could arise.

If this is correct, then the difference between hard cases in biblical and modern law also reflects the difference in attitudes toward judicial discretion in biblical and modern law. The biblical approach affords great discretion to judges in whom the community is prepared to invest considerable trust because of the judges' moral character. By contrast, under the modern "rule of law," we require like cases to be treated alike and expect judicial discretion to be carefully bounded and structured. This does not mean that similar cases in biblical law did not have similar outcomes, simply that this was not the formal expectation in a system which set high value upon parties sorting out their own legal disputes (see I. H, above) and which would have involved negotiation in individual cases.

---

77. RONALD DWORKIN, TAKING RIGHTS SERIOUSLY (London: Duckworth, 1977), 81–130.
78. RONALD DWORKIN, LAW'S EMPIRE (Oxford: Hart, 1986), 255–56.
79. Jackson, *Justice and righteounsess*, p. 219.

E. Trial and error

Fifth, Israel's ideology of divine justice also raises the practical problem of to what extent institutions under a system of divine and human justice are free to change and develop. This is addressed in the texts which show how adjudicatory institutions changed and developed from the start.

We have already discussed how right from the beginning, Moses's adjudicatory functions came to be shared more widely among the people (Exodus 18). This sets the tone for what follows, as Israel's judicial process continued to develop. For example, the tribally chosen judges (Deuteronomy 1:13) are supplemented by priests and Levites upon entry to the promised land (Deuteronomy 17:9). From a canonical perspective, further innovations include Jehoshaphat making the "chief priest" the ultimate judge in cultic matters and "the governor of the house of Israel" the final judge in royal matters (2 Chronicles 19:11), although both are under monarchical authority. (It should be noted that critical scholars align the dating of Jehoshaphat's reforms with those of Exodus 18 and Deuteronomy 1,[80] while others have argued that even if Jehoshaphat is postexilic, its elements might date to the period of the early monarchy and hence pre-date Exodus 18 and Deuteronomy 1).

A synchronic, or final form, reading of the development of Israel's system of adjudication makes it clear that the single biggest change in the organization of human and divine justice was the introduction of monarchical adjudication. The demand for a king (1 Samuel 8:5) and the introduction of a royal judicial system was in part a reaction against a history of institutional failures in the judicial process. Neither the high priestly family (1 Samuel 3–4) nor the family of Israel's foremost prophet, Samuel, were fit for purpose (1 Samuel 7:15–8:3). Jethro's system ultimately depended on "the existence of a hierarchical social structure with ultimate judicial authority in the hands of a single authority or group."[81] It was a workable system when someone of the caliber of Moses or Joshua was in charge, but not every generation had such leaders nor sufficient "wise men" to fill all the necessary positions. The general contours of the early monarchical judiciary under Israel's first king, Saul, "seems to have been an uneasy mixture of an incipient royal judiciary and traditional lineage judicial procedures" (e.g., 1 Samuel 14:24–26).[82] This suggests a gradual transition from tribal organization to monarchy.

The introduction of monarchy shows that there was room under a system of divine justice for "trial and error" and for trying out different forms of judicial authority. It was even possible to experiment when the motive was to copy the

---

80. WEINFELD, DEUTERONOMIC SCHOOL, pp. 163–64.
81. Robert R. Wilson, *Israel's judicial system in the preexilic period,* JEWISH QUARTERLY REV. 74, 229–48, 240 (1983).
82. Ibid., 241.

styles of other ANE nations (1 Samuel 8:5).[83] Monarchy itself evolved within Israel and apparently became institutionalized between the time of King Saul (*circa* 1020–1000 BC) and that of King Ahab (*circa* 873–853 BC). When Queen Jezebel reminds King Ahab that he is king, "she refers not merely to the person but to the office, *melukah*, the same nominal form used in 1 Samuel 10:25, at the institution of the monarchy" (1 Kings 21:7).[84] Jackson suggests that "*melukah* reflects a further stage of institutionalisation, and thereby legitimation, of the position of the king, compared with the simpler *mishpat hamelekh* ['monarchical rule']"[85] used in 1 Samuel 8 (e.g., verses 5–6).

To sum up, a system of divine justice does not seem to stifle innovation but rather appears to be dynamic and open to change, like biblical law itself (see Chapter 1).

F. Knowing God, knowing justice

Sixth, we saw in I. G, above, that a range of authorities such as Levites, priests, prophets, and kings were involved in adjudication, as well as elected judges. This raises the practical question of how this plural system was organized.

Figure 4 (below) indicates that there is great diversity in the forms of adjudication. This reflects the fact that the problem of "how can judges know God's will in a given case" is not, in practice, much different from the general problem of "how does God reveal anything to anyone?" To put it another way, the question, "how do *judges* know that they are implementing divine justice?" is related to the question, "how do *individuals* know that they are doing God's will?" There is pluralism in "divine epistemology,"[86] that is, in ways of knowing the divine will. This means that we should expect variety in forms of divine-human adjudication also.

Figure 4 suggests a range of possible ways in which both judges and individuals can know the divine will, including divination, intuition, prophecy, and reason (see Figure 4). (Figure 4 does not exclude the possibility of there being connections between the different modalities of divine knowledge. Thus, a connection could be made between "divination" and the "intuition of an individual," for example, through dreams).

To the extent that each of these modes of communication has the potential to be institutionalized to varying degrees, there is potential for competition between different forms of adjudication. If all justice is from God, it follows that the agency which claims better access to divine justice—for example, because of the impartiality and "holiness" of its personnel—is in a position to make a bid for increased social power. From an ideological perspective, there is no inherent

---

83. See generally MOSHE WEINFELD, SOCIAL JUSTICE, pp. 45–56.
84. Bernard S. Jackson, Speaker's Lectures, University of Oxford (1984–1986), unpublished lectures.
85. Ibid.
86. Jackson, *Practice of justice*, p. 34.

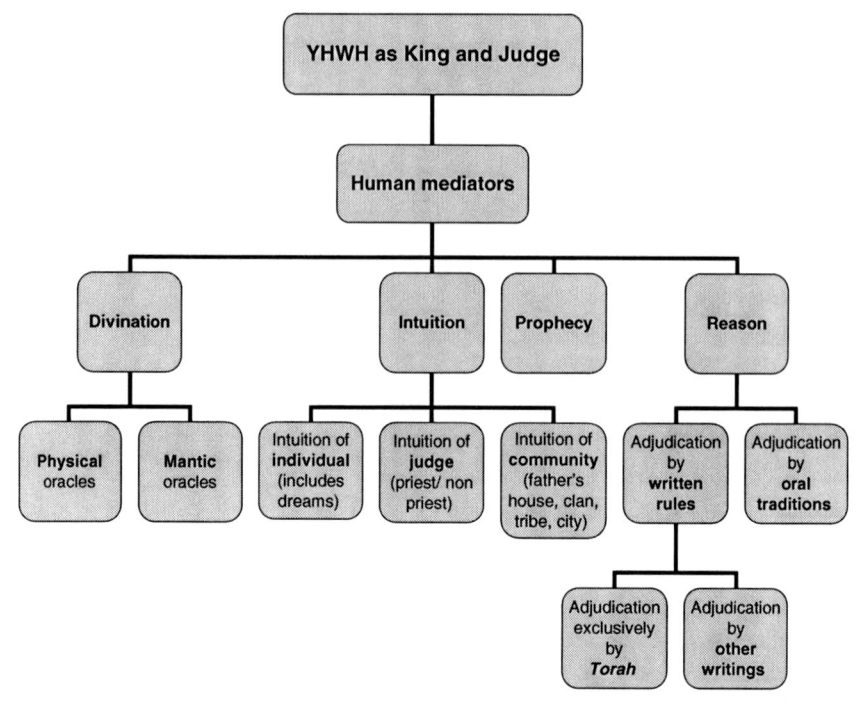

FIGURE 4. DIFFERENT MODALITIES OF DIVINE KNOWLEDGE

reason why intuition, for example, should be preferred over oracular or rule-based methods, but that does not, of course, exclude the possibility that such claims were made. Fashion, too, may have played a part. A mantic oracle—one in which the human mediator of the oracle speaks (e.g., Leviticus 24:13, 23; Numbers 15:35–36; 27:8–11)—from someone like King Solomon, might have been preferable to receiving a physical oracle from the high priest because Solomon was an international celebrity. Keith Whitelam goes so far as to claim that "the internalization of judicial wisdom within the king . . . ended the dominance of the priesthood in the sacro-judicial sphere."[87] The potential for conflict between priests, prophets, and king is also understandable because each group had "different legitimation patterns,"[88] that is, different ways of "legitimating new laws, exegetical innovations, or older customs and rules."[89] Over time, it seems that "exegetical rationality [emerged] as a dominant type."[90]

---

87. WHITELAM, JUST KING, p. 165.
88. MICHAEL FISHBANE, BIBLICAL INTERPRETATION IN ANCIENT ISRAEL (Oxford: Clarendon Press, 1985), 263.
89. Ibid., 262.
90. Ibid., 263.

This being so, it seems likely that some of these different forms of divine epistemology—and hence adjudication—might have been more prominent at certain times than others, depending on the relative strength of the king, priests, and prophets. An example of a significant change in adjudication can be seen with regard to the Urim and the Thummim (e.g.,1 Samuel 14:41–42). No one knows exactly what this was, but we do know that it was a physical sacral device kept by the high priest and used when the Israelites needed divine guidance.[91] Ezra 2:63 (= Nehemiah 7:65) suggests that the Urim and Thummim fell out of use after the exile. The deportation to Babylon seems to have resulted either in the loss of the objects themselves or the knowledge of how to operate them.[92] The loss of the Urim and Thummim would have cut down on the role of physical oracles in adjudication and increased reliance on the other forms of adjudication identified in Figure 4.

To sum up, Israel's ideology of adjudication raises a number of potential problems. Although it envisaged a practical system of divine-human justice, it is clear that Israel's system was not monolithic. There was wide discretion about how to structure Israel's mediating agencies, and these were not incompatible with cultural adaptation. Nor did it exclude the conventions of rival nations, including kingship. Innovations caused divine justice to take different forms, although the multiplicity of institutions could be a source of potential competition and conflict.

IV. FALLS THE SHADOW

Whatever the relationship between Israel's ideology of adjudication and its practice, it is clear that the administration of justice in biblical Israel did not always live up to the ideal of divine justice. As T. S. Eliot wrote in *The Hollow Men*, "Between the idea/ And the reality. . ./Falls the Shadow."[93] Thus, we find that the biblical texts bear witness, on the one hand, to the hope of divine justice and, on the other, to the reality of human failure.

The biblical sources are only too aware of the difficulties human beings have in mediating divine justice. The legal reforms of Exodus 18—in which Moses's oracular functions were shared more widely—were all the more remarkable given the general inability of the people to cope with the divine presence. The people could not bear to hear the voice of God (Exodus 20:18–19) and, not long

---

91. *See generally* CORNELIS VAN DAM, THE URIM & THUMMIM: A MEANS OF REVELATION IN ANCIENT ISRAEL (Winona Lake: Eisenbrauns, 1997).

92. *See generally* Victor Avigdor Hurowitz, *True light on the Urim and Thummim*, JEWISH Q. REV. 88, 263–74 (1998).

93. T. S. ELIOT, THE COMPLETE POEMS AND PLAYS OF T. S. ELIOT (London: Faber and Faber, 1969), 85.

after that, made a golden calf (Exodus 32:1–6). Moses's newly appointed judges were not immune from these temptations either; nor is there any indication that they abstained from these mass follies. On the contrary, we know that most of the judges participated in the popular revolt against the spies' report on the promised land; an uprising that led to the death of the entire Exodus generation in the wilderness (Numbers 14; see Chapter 1).

Discontinuity between divine and human acts of judgment is a recurring issue in the Bible. We have already seen how institutional failures to deliver divine justice led to Israel's demand for a king. But even the kings themselves frequently failed to deliver justice, according to the accounts of *1 & 2 Kings*. And to judge from the later prophets, even Jehoshaphat's legal reforms were a failure. The prophetic calls to avoid bribery testified to the corruption that remained endemic in the judicial system (Isaiah 1:23; 5:23; Micah 3:11, 7:3).[94]

A. Who judges the judges?

So what happens in a system of human and divine justice when judges fail? Who judges the judges? Several answers can be given from the period of the early monarchy; popular revolt and prophetic intervention.

First, there are several popular revolts against capital sentences issued by King Saul. The leaders of Saul's army revolt against the death penalty passed on his son Jonathan (1 Samuel 14:45), while the only person who is willing to execute the priests of Nob for their supposed offense of helping David is a foreigner (Doeg the Edomite; 1 Samuel 22:16–18).[95]

Saul's successor, King David, provides a more spectacular example of a popular uprising. David's perceived failures in adjudication resulted in his having to flee from Jerusalem to the Transjordan (2 Samuel 15:13ff). His son Absalom waged a secret propaganda war against David's government by waylaying complainants before they reached the royal court and turning them away with tales of maladministration (2 Samuel 15:2–4). The petitioners' cases were probably concerned with royal matters (such as taxation) as well as the hard cases that exceeded the competence of other established courts.[96] We have of course no way of telling whether there was any truth in Absalom's propaganda. Perhaps there was tribal resistance to moving from a lineage system of adjudication to a monarchical one. Or perhaps David, the man of war, struggled to build a peacetime administration that would keep up with his expanding kingdom. On the other hand, had Absalom's claims been true, it would have been more to his advantage to "buttonhole" the disputants *after* they had unsuccessfully sought David's

---

94. Schiffman, *Prohibition of judicial corruption*, pp. 156–57.
95. Wilson, *Israel's judicial system*, p. 242.
96. WHITELAM, JUST KING, p. 139.

judgment.[97] Either way, the episode illustrates the possible consequences for judges who are perceived to fail in their judicial role.

Second comes prophetic intervention. This is consistent with the ideology that "all justice comes from God." If God is the ultimate guarantor of the system of human and divine justice, then it follows that prophets—who speak in God's name—should intervene when judges fail. God promises to step in when there are cases of abuse, such as where "the rich litigant takes advantage of his poor opponent's inability to present his case":[98]

> Do not rob the poor, because he is poor,
> or crush the afflicted at the gate;
> for the LORD will plead their cause
> and despoil of life those who despoil them. (Proverbs 22:22–23)

As the true king of Israel, God steps in and does justice, especially for the poor and oppressed who should have been protected by human kings (Psalms 103:6; 146:7–9). There are several examples of how this was thought to operate in practice, with God's judicial intervention being communicated by the prophets. The prophet Elijah delivers God's word of judgment to King Ahab (1 Kings 21:17–21) when Ahab acquiesces with the judicial murder of Naboth. Likewise, God "sends" the prophet Nathan to speak divine judgment upon David (2 Samuel 12:1) because of the murder of Uriah the Hittite (2 Samuel 12:1–2; see further Chapter 9). God's personal interest in this case is explicit in verse 9, as Nathan asks David: "why have you despised the word of the LORD, to do what is evil in his sight?" God's interest may be said to stem partly from the fact that Uriah was "a resident foreigner, a *ger*, someone who was generally assumed to be under God's especial protection" (e.g. Deuteronomy 10:18)[99] and partly because David has orchestrated a "cover-up" at the highest judicial level. Divine intervention is needed because the victim concerns a vulnerable outsider who cannot get justice because of corruption on the part of the king. As a result, "[God] takes over the judging job from David."[100]

B. Confessions of a cannibal mother

Perhaps the most unusual form of prophetic intervention concerns the case of the cannibal mothers in 2 Kings 6:24–7:2. Under conditions of extreme starvation during a siege, two women agreed to cook and eat their sons. However, while

---

97. Elizabeth Bellefontaine, *Customary law and chieftainship: Judicial aspects of 2 Samuel 14:4-21*, J. STUD. OLD TESTAMENT 38, 47–72, 59 (1987).

98. RAYMOND WESTBROOK, STUDIES IN BIBLICAL AND CUNEIFORM LAW (Paris: Gabalda, 1988), p. 26, n. 19.

99. J. W. Wesselius, *Joab's death and the central theme of the succession narrative (2 Samuel 9–1 Kings 2)*, VETUS TESTAMENTUM 40, 336–51, 344 (1990).

100. Ellen Van Wolde, *In words and pictures: The sun in 2 Samuel 12:7-12*, BIBLICAL INTERPRETATION 11, 259–78, 260 (2003).

one mother sacrificed her son and shared it with the other, the second mother reneged on the deal. The first mother protested to the king. If Solomon's judgment in 1 Kings 3:17–28 is the apotheosis of monarchical adjudication, then this is its nadir. There are a number of similarities between the two cases, as follows: (1) there is a dispute between two women who are neighbors; (2) neither appears to have a husband or a male family member who can plead for justice; (3) the case concerns two sons, at least one of whom is dead; (4) one woman is said to have behaved deceitfully in order to gain an unfair advantage; and finally (5) there is a desire on the part of one woman to rob another woman of her child.[101]

The similarities between the two cases merely serve to highlight the contrast: that whereas Solomon resolves the case with a dazzling display of legal legerdemain, the anonymous king of 2 Kings 6 is simply useless:

If the Lord will not help you, whence shall I help you?" (2 Kings 6:27)

In other words, "I have not the wherewithal to give you salvation."[102]

This fundamental contrast between the two kings is supported by further differences between the two cases, as follows: (1) the women before Solomon disagree about the facts; whereas here they are agreed, which ought to make the case a little easier; (2) Solomon is engaged with the dispute, whereas the anonymous king does not want to be involved; and (3) Solomon talks about wielding a sword to good effect, whereas the anonymous king threatens to decapitate Elisha, the prophet whose word actually brings about the end of the siege.

Small wonder then, that whereas Solomon's reputation became great (1 Kings 3:28), the name of this king is not identified (although from other evidence, he was probably Jehoram, son of Ahab).[103] He is king "in name only" because he cannot perform one of the basic tasks of a king, that is, to bring justice to his people. His comprehensive lack of ability reflects the depths to which Israel has succumbed - cannibalism. Whereas the prostitute in 1 Kings 3:26 wanted to save her child, there is a suspicion that the woman in 2 Kings 6:29 only wants to save her child so she can eat it all by herself (cf. Deuteronomy 28:53–57).[104]

Once again, when kings fail, we find that the prophets step in, this time in the form of Elisha. The siege is lifted, and deliverance comes "not by adjudication but miraculously" (2 Kings 7). In contrast to the failure of the king, Elisha "provides salvation for everybody."[105]

---

101. Zipor, *Cannibal women*, p. 87.
102. Ibid., 91.
103. Ibid., 86 n. 9.
104. Ibid., 87 n.12.
105. Ibid., 94.

C. All fall down

What happens when kings *and* priests *and* prophets all fail? Such situations were not unknown and were interpreted as being a sign that the nation as a whole was under God's judgment:

> [T]hey judge not with justice the cause of the fatherless, to make it prosper, and they do not defend the rights of the needy.
> Shall I not punish them for these things? says the LORD,
> . . .
> An appalling and horrible thing
> has happened in the land:
> the prophets prophesy falsely,
> and the priests rule at their direction;
> my people love to have it so,
> but what will you do when the end comes? (Jeremiah 5:28–31)

Ironically, even the absence of divine adjudication is interpreted as a sign of God's judgment—there is no escape. God's judgment is present even when divine adjudication by human mediators is absent.

Finally, when human processes fail to produce justice, the Hebrew Bible sees the final appeal as being to God in prayer. The extent of this problem is shown by the numerous lament psalms which cry out for divine intervention. These constitute about one-third of the Psalter. In particular, the imprecatory psalms (such as Psalms 10 and 82) reflect the belief that God was the all-knowing, just Judge who would ultimately render the wicked their deserts, even though divine justice had so far failed to be manifest on earth.[106]

V. JUDGING IN A SPIRAL

Perhaps the most surprising thing about the interrelationship between divine ideology and its outworking is the way in which a belief in divine justice is not a counsel of perfection. There is room for trial and error. This, in turn, is consistent with the way in which the texts present Israel's leading judges as being on a "learning curve" (see further, below). It raises the question of what theoretical model makes best sense of the interplay between the divine and the human in the area of adjudication.

Perhaps the best way of understanding the dynamics is to see the tension worked out in the form of a spiral. Judges who are committed to pursuing wisdom and justice travel in a "virtuous spiral," getting closer and closer to divine justice. Judges who do not share this commitment slip further down the spiral.

---

106. *See generally* ERICH ZENGER, A GOD OF VENGEANCE? UNDERSTANDING THE PSALMS OF DIVINE WRATH (Westminster: John Knox Press, 1996).

Divine justice stands over them as they seek to bring their understanding of justice closer to God's justice. They can grasp it more truly, even if not exhaustively. The judges do not have to claim perfection, but nor do they have to say their task is futile, either. Their knowledge of God can be sufficient to produce divine justice.

"Judging in a spiral" is the adjudicatory equivalent of the "hermeneutic spiral." We are justified in making this connection because the Bible itself specifically locates the ability to judge in the context of a didactic relationship with God (e.g., Genesis 18:19, see above). The tension between divine and human justice takes the form of an ongoing process of "knowing" God, receiving wisdom, and allowing that to form character and develop insight.

"Judging in a spiral" takes seriously the biblical idea that adjudication is a progressive experience. People can be at different points along the spiral. What matters is their commitment to the process. The Bible presents the leading judges as being on a "learning curve" (e.g., Moses in Exodus 18). This is not surprising: Abraham and his descendants are explicitly said to be "on a journey" in learning about adjudication (Genesis 18:19). Impressive as Abraham's debate with God is, the text carries a sense that even Abraham had much to learn. Abraham "engage[s] in a bartering exercise" with God and seems oblivious to the fact that "[God] refuses to participate in this game."[107] He stops at the number 10, which is only significant because it is "a number of Abraham's choosing."[108] Why did he not go further? Whereas God speaks of his desire that Abraham's descendants should "keep the way of the LORD by doing righteousness and justice" (Genesis 18:19), Abraham asks only: "shall not the Judge . . . do right?" (Genesis 18:25). Perhaps "the omission of righteousness from Abraham's question" is significant.[109] Abraham is on a learning curve; he has yet to learn what Moses, Amos, and the other prophets discover, namely, that "YHWH . . . [is] far more merciful than Abraham imagines" (cf. Jeremiah 5:1 and Ezekiel 22:30).[110]

There are a number of advantages to this theoretical model. First, it avoids a "split-level" worldview in which divine and human decision making are inherently separate from each another and can never be merged. This is foreign to biblical thought. At the same time, however, it allows for the fact that judicial decisions are sometimes far distant from the ideal. Second, it is consistent with biblical texts which make it clear that adjudication is a vocation. Third, it fits the idea that the pursuit of wisdom is central to divine adjudication. The spiral ensures there is a link between virtue and judgment. There are judicial virtues, which are explicitly identified as such, by modern theorists, including

---

107. Nathan Macdonald, *Listening to Abraham—Listening to YHWH: Divine justice and mercy in Genesis 18:16-33*, CATHOLIC BIBLICAL Q. 66, 25–43, 35 (2004).
108. Ibid.
109. Ibid., 37.
110. Ibid., 40.

"impartiality . . . fairness, justice, rationality, and legitimacy."[111] Equally, there are judicial vices which we could identify in broad terms as including partiality, susceptibility to bribes, naivety, and gullibility. These will affect progress along the spiral and the quality of the judgment.

Fourth, it preserves the emphasis in the sources that adjudication is a dynamic process. Thus, for example, the word for "doing right" (*tsedaqah*) is not primarily concerned with ethics in the abstract but with relationships between persons. Biblical Israel "did not . . . measure a line of conduct or an act by an ideal norm, but by the specific relationship in which the partner had at the time to prove himself true."[112] Likewise, "the just [person] is called upon . . . not only to deal correctly with the other, but to *re-establish justice*, so as to promote a right relationship between all the members of the society."[113]

Fifth, the idea of a spiral enables judges to hold together wisdom and humility so that the choice is never simply between judicial experts (who think they know it all) and novices (who believe they will never be able to execute divine justice). Sixth, it means that the incentive for exercising wisdom is greater wisdom and that the rewards for judging well are further opportunities to judge. These rewards are inherent to the activity, which is itself characteristic of divine justice. Above all, the idea of a spiral enables us to reconcile the suspicion of injustice with our belief in justice—and the need to make a decision in imperfect circumstances.

To sum up, it is possible to understand adjudication in the Bible in a way that takes seriously both the claim to divine involvement and the reality of human failure. Seeking justice means journeying with God.

VI. THINKING RELATIONALLY ABOUT JUSTICE

A biblical vision of justice might inspire a range of policies in the modern world. The danger lies in isolating one element of an inseparable whole to the exclusion of others. The temptation is to stress, for example, restoration without retribution (e.g., the belief that retribution is morally unacceptable) or retribution without any thought of restoration (e.g., the claim that "prison works"). Either approach, on its own, quickly leads to injustice. Moreover, the implications of a

---

111. Lucy, *Adjudication*, p. 206.

112. GERHARD VON RAD, OLD TESTAMENT THEOLOGY VOLUME I: THE THEOLOGY OF ISRAEL'S HISTORICAL TRADITIONS, (D.M.G. Stalker trans., Edinburgh: Oliver & Boyd, 1962), 71.

113. PIETRO BOVATI, RE-ESTABLISHING JUSTICE: LEGAL TERMS, CONCEPTS & PROCEDURES IN THE HEBREW BIBLE, translated by Michael J. Smith, Journal for the Study of the Old Testament Supplement Series 105 (Sheffield: Sheffield Academic Press, 1994), p. 191, italics original.

biblical approach for a given judicial process at a given point in time will depend on current practices and previous penal history. However, several general points can be made.[114]

The first and most important point is the biblical belief that seeking justice is part of the vocation of humanity as a whole (see Chapter 3). From a biblical perspective, therefore, people are reduced from their full humanity when their involvement in the call to justice is taken away from them. The same is true of communities. No institution can survive without a function, chief among which is the function of doing justice (and providing welfare). Communities, too, are diminished when they have no role to play in adjudication.

The biblical emphasis on the value of grassroots justice, particularly when it acts as a check on the abuse of centralized power, is relevant in England and Wales. Here, the justice system has become increasingly centralized and susceptible to political control. This is indicated by the fact that although only six criminal justice Acts were passed by Parliament between 1925 and 1985, Conservative governments since 1979 passed one Act every 18 months, while the Labour government under Tony Blair passed three a year.[115] The introduction during the 1980s and 1990s of the Crown Prosecution Service, the Courts Services Agency, and the Legal Aid Board, combined with the transfer of all responsibility for magistrates from localities to the Lord Chancellor's department (now part of the Ministry of Justice) means that "what had been a pluralist, localised and part-privatised judicial system was now a national industry."[116] There is now a need for greater local accessibility and accountability of the justice process, including courts, affiliated services, and local prisons.

Second, the biblical ideal of popular knowledge of the law, combined with a widespread capacity to adjudicate, contrasts with the modern acceptance of law as a highly technical and professionalized enterprise that is focused upon the courts. Devolving responsibility to citizens and communities is a major challenge, given the huge presence that is nowadays assumed for the state in criminal justice and which grows continually. Government needs to recognize its inadequacy and the need to draw on the strengths of local communities. There needs to be a formal recognition that the criminal justice process can have, by itself, only a limited effect on the general level of crime. Action is needed by

---

114. For a fuller treatment, *see* Jonathan Burnside, *Criminal justice, in* JUBILEE MANIFESTO, (Michael Schluter & John Ashcroft eds. Leicester: InterVarsity Press, 2005), 234–54.

115. SIMON JENKINS, THATCHER & SONS: A REVOLUTION IN THREE ACTS (London: Penguin, 2007), 186.

116. Ibid., 188.

communities, and between individuals as citizens, and that is beyond the scope and capacity of formal criminal justice agencies.[117]

This approach also means that communities need to have more realistic expectations of the justice system and must be prepared to take more responsibility. In some democratic countries, expectations of the ability of the state to deal with every social problem needs to be scaled down—with agencies working with rather than "at" troublesome communities.[118] Crime prevention, for example, should flow from engaging people and communities in finding solutions to problems of alienation and dysfunction. In Western urban settings, community reparation schemes involve local communities in the rehabilitation of young offenders.[119] In Rwanda, community-style *Gacaca* (or lawn) courts show the value of widespread community involvement even in the extreme circumstances of genocide.[120]

Third, and related to this, biblical adjudication sees social order as founded on the family. This is the context for developing wisdom, informal social controls, and self-restraint. The biblical approach is consistent with the notion that the purpose of government is self-government, in every area of life. By contrast, modern approaches to justice, and especially criminal justice, "offer an approach to social order that is, for the most part, amoral and technological."[121] Social order is seen to emerge, not from "moral discipline and obedience to authority . . . [but] smart arrangements that minimise the opportunities to disruption and deviance."[122] We have lost sight of the need for more relational strategies.[123] There is value in seeing crime, as Emile Durkheim suggested, not just as a crisis but as an opportunity to rebuild relationships and informal social controls.[124] Everyone affected by crime has an interest in the outcome, and so we are required to take account of the needs of the wider community in which the offense occurred. This wider community may include the school, workplace, housing

---

117. David Faulkner, *Turning prisons inside-out*, RELATIONAL JUST. BULL. 16, 1–3, 1 (2002).

118. *E.g.*, David Bowes, *The real Kindergarten Cop*, RELATIONAL JUST. BULL. 16, 4–5 (2002).

119. Leroy White, *Turning reparation into reality*, RELATIONAL JUST. BULL. 20, 6–8 (2004).

120. Riddell, Jennifer, 2005. *Addressing Crimes Against International Law: Rwanda's Gacaca in Practice*. Unpublished thesis presented for the degree of LL.M at the University of Aberdeen.

121. DAVID GARLAND, THE CULTURE OF CONTROL (Oxford: Oxford University Press, 2001), 183.

122. Ibid.

123. Jonathan Burnside, Nicola Baker eds., RELATIONAL JUSTICE: REPAIRING THE BREACH (Winchester: Waterside Press, 1994).

124. EMILE DURKHEIM, SELECTED WRITINGS, edited, translated, and with an introduction by Anthony Giddens (Cambridge: Cambridge University Press, 1972), 127–28.

estate, faith group, ethnic group, or whatever other context(s) the victim or the defendant operates. However, some of these communities may be in conflict with others.

Fourth, biblical law emphasizes the need to "seek justice" and to make it a national priority. However, in many parts of the world, social, economic, and political forces push the quest for divine justice down the national agenda. Garland argues that the social organization of Western societies (notably the United States and United Kingdom) has moved away from a more inclusionary "solidaristic" culture to a more exclusionary and controlling one.[125] This is reflected in institutions of crime control and criminal justice, and the result has been a shift away from what has been termed "penal welfarism" (the prevention of crime, individual correction, and social reform) and toward a "culture of control." The latter approach identifies an underclass as the source of the problem and suggests progressively punitive ways of excluding and controlling it. Garland argues that this change is not entirely due to rising crime, linking it to a civic culture that has become increasingly less tolerant, less inclusive, and less capable of trust. "The risky, insecure character of today's social and economic relations is the social surface that gives rise to our ... concern with control and to the urgency with which we segregate, fortify and exclude."[126] The result is that issues such as "crime control and criminal justice have come to be disconnected from the broader themes of social justice and social reconstruction."[127] The need to reconnect them is illustrated by criminological studies which have shown how, for example, police interventions can be counterproductive when criminal justice is not interleaved with social justice.[128]

Fifth, the proactive role of the victim in biblical Israel is different to the place of victims in the modern criminal justice process. There has been a "victimological turn" in criminal justice polices in many jurisdictions since about 1960, as seen in such initiatives as victim impact statements, victim support, and so on.[129] This means that victims have a greater public profile than has previously been the case. However, this does not necessarily mean that increased value is being placed on victims themselves, for several reasons. "[A]s the offender's perceived worth tends towards zero, victim's interests expand to fill the gap."[130] Victims may also serve a useful function in a pluralistic moral order where we do not agree on right

---

125. Garland, *Culture of Control*, pp. 193–205.
126. Ibid., 194.
127. Ibid., 199.
128. *See generally* Lawrence W. Sherman, Policing Domestic Violence: Experiments and Dilemmas (The Free Press, 1992).
129. Anthony E. Bottoms, *Some sociological reflections on restorative justice*, in Restorative Justice & Criminal Justice: Competing or Reconcilable Paradigms?, (Andrew von Hirsch et al., eds., Oxford: Hart, 2003), 79–113, 103–04.
130. Garland, *Culture of Control*, p. 181.

and wrong. "Collective moral outrage more easily proceeds from an individualised basis than from a public one."[131] In addition, emphasizing the suffering of victims reflects the values of mass media news coverage. It also helps to drive punitive policies, and to sustain the "war on crime." Seeking justice for the oppressed means ensuring that the criminal justice process and, as far as possible, its outcomes, take sufficient account of the needs and interests of victims of crime, although this may not always be reflected in victim-related policies. There is still scope for increased contact or negotiations between victims and offenders (e.g., family group conferences and community group conferences) where this is both possible and desirable.[132] It may also involve giving a much greater role for (imaginative) forms of reparation and (multiple) restitution.

Finally, punishment in the Bible is carried out by the community, in their sight and in their midst. Modern-day communities need to be better informed about criminal justice (e.g., levels of actual crime and the effectiveness of different kinds of penalties). They also need to know what sentencing options are currently available and what they mean (e.g., mistaken assumptions that modern "community penalties" means "planting flowers"). Nor should prisons be "invisible institutions." What is done in them is done in our name. "The central principle should be that prisons are part of society and not set apart from it; that they exist for the benefit of society as a whole and should contribute actively to its health and well-being; that prisoners deserve its compassion and staff should receive its respect."[133] Citizens need to feel "some sense of ownership for their prisons, and some responsibility for their prisoners, as they often do for their schools and hospitals . . . [rather than] a means by which that responsibility can be avoided."[134] Policy makers and sentencers should recognize the built-in hunger of the incarceration industry, especially where new prison places are provided by private enterprise. This is particularly urgent where, as in England and Wales, it appears that people are being sent to prison for crimes that would not have attracted a prison sentence 10 years ago and where there are large disparities in the ratio of custodial to community penalties. Individual sentencers should know the consequences of their sentences, for example, in the form of court digests[135] and, as the former Lord Chief Justice Lord Woolf suggested, judges should occasionally visit those whom they sentence to custody.

---

131. Ibid., 200.
132. *See generally* J. PENNELL & G. BURFORD, FAMILY GROUP DECISION MAKING: AFTER THE CONFERENCE; PROGRESS IN RESOLVING VIOLENCE AND PROMOTING WELL-BEING; OUTCOME REPORT, 2 vols. (St. Johns, Newfoundland: Memorial University of Newfoundland, School of Social Work, 1998).
133. Faulkner, *Turning prisons inside-out*, p. 2.
134. Ibid., 3.
135. Sarah Curtis, *Lepers or learners*, RELATIONAL J BULL. 16, 4–5 (2002).

VII. CONCLUSION

The ideology of adjudication in the Bible has many facets, but is essentially grounded in the belief that all justice is divine. This means that law and justice in the Bible always has a transcendental reference point. The claim that human beings could be involved in mediating actual divine decisions seems rather extreme, but it is more comprehensible when viewed in the wider context of the Pentateuch. Here, it appears that adjudication is an important aspect of divine-human relations. It is part of the vocation of humanity as a whole—and it is a key part of the calling of Abraham and his descendants, who are expected to teach the rest of the world how to judge rightly. Sacred adjudication is in keeping with the vocation of Israel to know the presence of God in the burdensome conflicts of ordinary life. The ability to mediate divine justice—in all its facets—is presented as a progressive experience. Israel's most famous judges—including Abraham, Moses, and David—are all presented as being on a learning curve. Judicial training is received in the context of a relationship with God because doing justice means growing in wisdom and in sympathy with the divine character. At their best, such mediators blur the separation between the divine and the human. Despite this, Israel's system of divine justice was not monolithic: there was room for creativity, diversity, and experimentation. Legal thought and legal structures were pluriform. Nor did the reality of human failure obliterate the possibility of divine justice on earth.

Selected reading

Pietro Bovati, *Re-Establishing Justice: Legal terms, concepts and procedures in the Hebrew Bible*. Translated by Michael J. Smith, Journal for the Study of the Old Testament Supplement Series 105. (Sheffield: Sheffield Academic Press, 1994), Chapter 5.

Jonathan Burnside, "Criminal justice," in *Jubilee Manifesto*, Michael Schluter and John Ashcroft eds. (Leicester: InterVarsity Press, 2005), 234–254.

Michael Fishbane, *Biblical Interpretation in Ancient Israel* (Oxford: Clarendon Press, 1985), Chapter 9.

Bernard S. Jackson, "Human law and divine justice in the methodological maze of the Mishpatim," in *Jewish Law Association Studies XVI: The Boston 2004 Conference Volume*, E. Dorff ed. (Binghampton: Global Academic Publishing, 2007), 101–122.

Bernard S. Jackson, "Justice and righteousness in the Bible: Rule of law or royal paternalism?," *Zeitschrift für Altorientalische und Biblische Rectsgeschichte* 4 (1998), 218-262.

Moshe Weinfeld, *Social Justice in Ancient Israel* (Jerusalem: Magnes Press, 1995), Chapters 1 and 2.

5. HUMANITY AND THE ENVIRONMENT

We considered in previous chapters some of the "big picture" questions central to our understanding of biblical law. These include its overall character, as well as such issues as covenant, natural law, and what it means to "do justice." It is now time to turn from some of these general questions to specific subject areas—beginning with the broadest of them all—humanity and the environment. We begin with this topic because its very scope allows us to hold onto the metanarrative of God's involvement with his creation, which spans the whole of the Hebrew Bible and the New Testament. At the same time, the subject of humanity and the environment enables us to explore in more detail how biblical law actually works.

This chapter acknowledges from the outset that the question of humanity and the environment is one of the most pressing of our age and that the biblical materials are relevant to meeting this challenge. They show that the relationship between humanity and the environment is complex, and indeed there are four main ways in which this relationship is structured. The first is the creation narrative (Genesis 1:1–2:25) which consists of the story of universal creation (Genesis 1:1–2:4) and the story of humanity's creation (Genesis 2:5–25). The story of universal creation shows how God's sovereign activity in relation to the whole of creation is the paradigm for humanity's exercise of its sovereignty. It also contains divine speech acts that give humanity a vocation in regard to the environment (Genesis 1:26, 1:28); and these are developed further in the story of humanity's creation. The second main way in which the relationship between humanity and the environment is regulated is by means of divine judgements in the primeval history, including the judgment in Eden (Genesis 3:14–24) and the judgment of the Flood (Genesis 6:11–13). The third main way is seen in the "postdiluvian" blessing conferred by God upon humanity (Genesis 9:1–7), the blessing given after the Flood. Finally, we will see that the relationship between humanity and the environment is structured by means of the various "eco-laws" that are found in biblical law.

I. EARTH UNDER THREAT

Before turning to each of these areas, we begin by acknowledging the contemporary relevance of the biblical materials. This will come as a surprise to those who think the Bible is as eco-friendly as an oil slick. Although there is no doubt that certain misreadings of the Bible have, in the past, favored an exploitative approach to the environment, there is equally no doubt that an attentive reading of the biblical texts is relevant to current ecological crises. Apart from anything else, the Bible advocates "a modest materialism"[1] at a time when we are "desperately overdrawn at the environmental bank."[2] For this reason, Davis is right to warn that some aspects of the biblical texts may address us more sharply than any previous generation of readers.[3]

First, we will see that the story of universal creation includes the refrain, "And God saw that it was good" (e.g., Genesis 1:12) in regard to different aspects of the created order. There can be no doubt that how we "see" creation determines how we respond to it. If we see creation as something that has integral worth, we will treat it differently than if we only see it as something that has value in relation to humanity. Davis draws upon the work of Erazim Kohák in arguing that the root of the ecological crisis is less a failure in thinking than in perceiving.[4] It is ironic that, for example, the Millennium Ecosystem Assessment, which is commonly recognized as one of the most comprehensive scientific studies of its kind, expressed its concerns about planetary degradation in terms of a "service delivery" model, focusing on "ecosystem services and human well-being."[5] By contrast, the biblical worldview is that creation is "very good" (Genesis 1:31). It has an independent worth, irrespective of its instrumental value. Creation is not to be understood primarily in terms of a "provider of goods and services." This is merely one modern example of how "The painful flaws in our conception of value . . . call less for a new conception of the good than for a new way of *seeing* the good."[6]

Second, we will see that the creation narrative establishes a vertical hierarchy (God → humanity → fish/birds/cattle/all the earth/creeping things). This, in turn, enables humanity to orientate itself on a horizontal level and so act in ways that fit our station. We will also see that what counts as fitting behavior for humanity is defined in terms of a vocation. Humanity's calling is to "mediate God's creation blessing to Earth and stand in creative, not exploitative, relationship with

---

1. ELLEN F. DAVIS, SCRIPTURE, CULTURE AND AGRICULTURE: AN AGRARIAN READING (Cambridge: Cambridge University Press, 2008), 36.

2. Barbara Kingsolver, Foreword, in THE ESSENTIAL AGRARIAN READER: THE FUTURE OF CULTURE, COMMUNITY, AND THE LAND, (Norman Wirzba & Barbara Kingsolver eds., USA: Counterpoint, 2003), ix–xvii, xiii.

3. DAVIS, SCRIPTURE, CULTURE AND AGRICULTURE, p. 45.

4. Ibid., 46.

5. MILLENNIUM ECOSYSTEM ASSESSMENT, ECOSYSTEMS & HUMAN WELL-BEING: SYNTHESIS (Island Press: Washington, DC, 2005), 10, also available online at http://www.millenniumassessment.org/documents/document.356.aspx.pdf, accessed September 29, 2009.

6. Erazim Kohák, *Perceiving the good*, in THE WILDERNESS CONDITION: ESSAYS ON ENVIRONMENT & CIVILIZATION (Max Oelschlaeger ed., San Francisco: Sierra Club Books, 1992), 173–87, 173, italics original.

[Earth] and the rest of creation."[7] This contrasts with destructive practices in relation to the world's oceans, for example, which are being pushed beyond the point of "no return" as a result of overfishing, pollution, and climate change.[8] The Stern Review on the economics of climate change forecasts that 40 percent of the world's species will be gone in the next fifty years if, as current models predict, global average temperatures rise by two degrees centigrade.[9] More than 5000 animal species are threatened with extinction, and nearly 6500 plants species are endangered or vulnerable.[10] Tropical rain forests, home to more than half of the world's species, are disappearing at the rate of 54 acres per minute.[11] Instead of fruitfulness, there is biocide and ecocide (the destruction of natural resources), and instead of preserving prospective generations, we are eliminating future life on Earth.

Third, we will discover that humanity's dependence on and "grounding" in "Mother earth" is prominent in both the story of universal creation and the story of humanity's creation. This awareness is reflected in modern concerns about humanity and the environment and is at the heart of sustainable development. "We are and always will be part of Nature, embedded in the natural world and totally dependent...."[12] We will see that the biblical story is of particular value because it creates an ethic of care by creating a sense of attachment to the environment. It is difficult for humanity to care about that to which it feels no attachment.

Fourth, we will see that humanity's vocation to rule the earth in Genesis 1:26 is a discretion that is supposed to be exercised in the interests of the earth community as a whole. This vocation is especially relevant at a time when modern Western practice eschews "single-planet living." Earth's supply cannot meet the rapid growth in human demand, especially in those countries where "consumption has become the collective national identity."[13] It is estimated that worldwide, there exists 1.8 biologically productive global hectares per person. Ecological

---

7. Laurie J. Braaten, *Earth community in Hosea 2*, in THE EARTH STORY IN THE PSALMS & THE PROPHETS (Norman C. Habel ed., Sheffield: Sheffield Academic Press, 2001), 185–203, 197 n. 14.

8. UNITED NATIONS ENVIRONMENT PROGRAMME, ECOSYSTEMS AND BIODIVERSITY IN DEEP WATERS AND HIGH SEAS: REGIONAL SEAS REPORT AND STUDIES NO. *178* (New York: United Nations Environment Programme, 2006).

9. HM TREASURY, THE STERN REVIEW ON THE ECONOMICS OF CLIMATE CHANGE (Cambridge: Cambridge University Press, 2006).

10. United Nations Environment Programme, http://www.unep.org/geo/yearbook/yb2007/, accessed September 29, 2009.

11. GHILLEAN T. PRANCE, THE EARTH UNDER THREAT (Leicester: Inter-Varsity Press, 1996), 45.

12. SUSTAINABLE DEVELOPMENT COMMISSION, PROGRESS: SUSTAINABLE DEVELOPMENT COMMISSION CRITIQUE (London: Sustainable Development Commission, 2004), 4.

13. SUSTAINABLE DEVELOPMENT COMMISSION, PROGRESS, p. 21.

footprints are a means of measuring individual and national demand in relation to biological capacity.[14] It is estimated that the United Kingdom has an average national footprint of 5.6 global hectares per person,[15] compared with a global average of 2.2 global hectares.[16] "Ecological Debt Day," the point at which the earth is no longer capable of replenishing itself and the planet's resources go into deficit, is reached earlier every year, falling on September 25 in 2009.[17]

Fifth, we will see that humanity is also given the vocation of nurturing the earth. Nurture seeks development in the interests of Earth as a whole, and so it sets limits to profligate consumption. It challenges the daily transportation of billions of ton of food around the world, so Westerners can eat "whatever they want whenever they want it."[18] It is estimated that the range of products stocked by a leading United Kingdom supermarket chain increased from 5000 products in 1983 to 40,000 in 2004.[19] "Nurture" also contrasts with the instincts of economic capitalism, which sees all physical resources as potential assets that must be commodified in order to function within a market environment. This has serious implications for water, which instead of being seen as a gift belonging to a collective communal whole, finds itself a commodity that is subject to private ownership.[20] The vocation to nurture, however, is reflected in sustainable development policies,[21] which are commonly based on the "carrying capacity of the receiving environment" and the "polluter pays" principle. Here, the costs of pollution and inefficient resource use are mirrored in the prices paid for goods and services. This is a "nurture" issue because it asks, "how much can be taken from [the environment] without diminishing it?"[22]

Sixth, we will also see that the creation narrative tells a story in which human beings imitate God's relationship with creation. This leads naturally into

---

14. *See generally* http://www.ecologicalfootprint.org, accessed September 29, 2009.

15. HOUSE OF COMMONS INTERNATIONAL DEVELOPMENT COMMITTEE, DEPARTMENT FOR INTERNATIONAL DEVELOPMENT ANNUAL REPORT 2007. FIRST REPORT OF SESSION 2007–08 (London: The Stationery Office Limited, 2007), volume II, p. 126, also available at http://www.publications.parliament.uk/pa/cm200708/cmselect/cmintdev/64/64ii.pdf, accessed September 29, 2009).

16. WORLD WILDLIFE FUND, LIVING PLANET REPORT 2006 (2006), 3, http://assets.panda.org/downloads/living_planet_report.pdf, September 29, 2009.

17. www.footprintnetwork.org, accessed September 29, 2009.

18. SUSTAINABLE DEVELOPMENT COMMISSION, PROGRESS, p. 20.

19. Ibid.

20. *See generally* François Du Bois, *Water rights and the limits of environmental law*, J. ENVT'L L. 6, 73–84 (1994).

21. Sustainable development can be broadly defined as "meeting the needs of our generation without compromising the ability of future generations to meet their needs."

22. WENDELL BERRY, THE UNSETTLING OF AMERICA: CULTURE AND AGRICULTURE, (San Francisco: Sierra Club, 3rd ed. 1996), 7.

concern for animal welfare. Modern animal rights theorists offer different justifications for animal rights (at least for those theories that treat the animal as an animal, rather than as if it was human). These include the *social contract* approach, which means we care about animals because this is what rational agents would agree on in certain ideal circumstances; *utilitarianism*, because animals' preferences to avoid pain should be treated equally to that of a human being's; *direct and indirect instrumentalism*, which means we look after animals because they are useful or potentially useful to us, perhaps as a future genetic resource; and *anthropomorphism*, because we attribute to animals human emotions and characteristics. This is not the place for a detailed exploration of animal rights, which is as difficult as talk of human rights.[23] The point is that biblical law does not need "rights language" to make animals the object of moral concern. Instead, it assumes that if humanity tells the right story about creation and so imitates God, animals will be honored and protected. The constraints on killing animals in Genesis 9 is relevant in light of the massive increase in the scale and intensity of "factory farming." As Davis writes, the West has "the most death-dealing meat market the world has ever known."[24] In the United States alone, it is estimated that 27 million animals—typically cows, pigs, and chickens—are slaughtered per day, which equates to more than a million per hour.[25]

Sixth, we will see that judgments from the primeval history reflect a belief that "if humans do not work with God in preserving life on Earth according to God's ecosystems, human survival is itself in jeopardy."[26] Experience shows that lack of care for the environment harms humanity. Nowhere is this more relevant than in relation to global warming. The Stern Review on the economics of climate change forecasts that if no action is taken, the concentration of greenhouse gases in the atmosphere could reach double its preindustrial level as early as 2055. This virtually commits the planet to a global average rise in temperature of over two degrees centigrade. This would place 200 million people at risk of losing their homes through drought or flooding. In the longer term, there is more than a 50 percent chance of a temperature rise in excess of five degrees.[27]

Seventh, the biblical story may give current environmental debates a moral energy they currently lack. This is important because debates about the relationship between humanity and the environment are increasingly seen as

---

23. *See generally* ROBERT GARNER, ANIMAL ETHICS (Cambridge: Polity Press, 2005).
24. DAVIS, SCRIPTURE, CULTURE AND AGRICULTURE, p. 97.
25. TOM REGAN, EMPTY CAGES: FACING THE CHALLENGE OF ANIMAL RIGHTS (Lanham: Rowman & Littlefield, 2004).
26. Abotchie Ntreh, *The survival of Earth: An African reading of Psalm 104, in* THE EARTH STORY IN THE PSALMS AND THE PROPHETS, (Norman C. Habel ed., Sheffield: Sheffield Academic Press, 2001), 98–108, 104.
27. HM TREASURY, STERN REVIEW, p. 57.

moral issues. The Stern Review on climate change points out that "the poorest developing countries will be hit earliest and hardest by climate change, even though they have contributed little to causing the problem."[28] The present environmental crisis is "principally moral and theological rather than technological."[29] For this reason, it needs to be informed by moral and theological resources.

Finally, biblical law is relevant because we will see that the relationship between humanity and the environment is ultimately a question of narrative. What we do about our environment depends on what we think about ourselves in relation to what is around us. Even our public discussions about climate change show that we have difficulties telling the right story about humanity and the environment. For example, there have been calls to put the United Kingdom on a "war footing" in relation to the environment, as if support can only be mobilized in proportion to anxiety and fear. One study found that discourse about climate change is commonly conducted through an "alarmist repertoire." This tends to evoke fictional and sensationalist Hollywood movies and has the effect of distancing people from the issue.[30] "The planet is no longer a network of interdependent Earth relationships, but a space for apocalyptic productions eagerly consumed at the news-stand."[31] The same study pointed to the need for other kinds of discourse (e.g., nonrational metaphor) to enable people to "engage emotionally and make desired behaviours [regarding climate change] appear attractive."[32] For these reasons, it is said by a leading secular environmentalist that *"There are no solutions for the systemic causes of ecocrisis, at least in democratic societies, apart from religious narrative."*[33]

II. EARTHING THE EARTHLING

With this in mind, we turn to one of the most well-known religious narratives in the West, namely, the creation narrative of Genesis 1:1–2:25. We will see that the relationship between God and creation, as described in the creation narrative, is paradigmatic of the relationship that ought to exist between humanity and the

---

28. Executive Summary, HM Treasury, Stern Review, p. 26.
29. Davis, Scripture, Culture and Agriculture, p. 9.
30. Gill Ereant & Nat Segnit, Warm Words: How Are We Telling the Climate Story and Can We Tell it Better? (London: Institute for Public Policy Research, 2006), 7.
31. Harry O. Maier, *There's a new world coming! Reading the apocalypse in the shadow of the Canadian Rockies, in* The Earth Story in the New Testament, (Norman C. Habel & Vicky Balabanski eds., Earth Bible Series, 5 vols., Sheffield: Sheffield Academic Press, 2002), vol. V, 166–79, 174.
32. Ereant & Segnit, Warm Words, p. 9.
33. Max Oelschlaeger, Caring for Creation: An Ecumenical Approach to the Environmental Crisis (New Haven: Yale University Press, 1994) 5, italics original.

environment. From a synchronic or "final form" perspective, the creation narrative consists of two aspects: (1) the story of *universal* creation (Genesis 1:1–2:4) and (2) the story of *humanity's* creation (Genesis 2:5–25). We will consider both stories in more detail, below. For now, we need to note that each has a different emphasis: the first culminates with the completion of creation and the institution of the Sabbath (Genesis 2:2–3), while the second climaxes with the completion of humanity as male and female and with the institution of marriage (Genesis 2:23–25).

At the same time, however, the difference in emphasis between Genesis 1:1–2:4 and Genesis 2:5–25 should not be exaggerated. Genesis 1:1–2:4 also reflects anthropocentric concerns, although these are not as obvious as they are in Genesis 2:5–25. In Genesis 1:1–2:4, humanity's creation is introduced by the fanfare, "Let us make man in our image, after our likeness" (Genesis 1:26). In addition, the previous days of creation (days one to five) describe what matters most for human existence—the creation of the sun and the moon, the emergence of dry land, the growth of plants, and so on. This anthropocentric bias also explains why on the sixth day, twice as much is described as happening as on any of the other days, because this is the day on which humanity is also created (cf. Genesis 1:24–31 with 1:1–23). Consequently, there is an anthropocentric, or "special species," perspective in Genesis 1:1–2:4, though this is not as overt as it is in Genesis 2:5–25.

The fact that the creation narrative contains similar but different stories about humanity and the environment tells us something about what we should expect in other biblical materials, including biblical law. First, we should expect changes of emphasis in different biblical texts. This is, in fact, what we find. Some texts seem to reflect the story of universal creation. Here, humanity is celebrated but also subsumed within the whole of creation (e.g., Psalm 104; Job 38–39). On the other hand, some texts appear to reflect the story of humanity's creation. Here, animals fit around a human-oriented world (e.g., Proverbs 14:4). Second, the creation narrative illustrates the interdependence of humanity and the environment. The story of *universal* creation, even though its scope is universal, nevertheless highlights the unique status of *humanity* (Genesis 1:26–29); while the story of *humanity's* creation, even though its focus is on humanity, has much to say about *Eden* and its vicinity (Genesis 2:5–6, 9–14). The creation narrative shows from the outset that it is impossible to separate biocentric from anthropocentric values, and this is reflected in biblical law. The bird law of Deuteronomy 22:6–7 expresses concern for mother birds, but the motive clause stresses the self-interest of humanity. Biocentric and anthropocentric values are held together. Finally, although the creation narrative leads us to expect a mixture of biocentric and anthropocentric values, there is nevertheless a bias towards the latter. This too is reflected in biblical law. We will see that the eco-law of Deuteronomy 20:19–20 is concerned both with preserving arboreal *and* human life, although the didactic force of the passage is concerned with the preservation of human life (see further below). Exodus 23:12, which places animals ahead of humans in a list of beneficiaries of Sabbath rest, is the exception that proves the rule.

III. THE CHOSEN SPECIES

We noted that the creation narrative consists of two stories (universal creation and humanity's creation). We now need to consider how each story provides normative guidance (that is, what does it tell us about how humanity ought to behave in relation to the environment?). We begin with the story of universal creation (Genesis 1:1–2:4). This shows how God's sovereign activity in relation to the whole of creation is the paradigm for humanity's sovereignty over the environment.

God's sovereignty over creation is seen in the movement from chaos to an ordered universe. God structures and maintains the created order by means of a series of distinctions and binary oppositions (day/night; water above/water below; seas/land; vegetation/animals; male/female; Genesis 1:3–28; and cf. the importance of binary oppositions as a means of sense construction in biblical law in Chapter 1). The story of universal creation contains a number of divine speech acts, in other words, actions that are performed by God by means of divine speech. The successful performance of the divine *fiats* "Let there be light" (Genesis 1:3), and so on, show that God is extremely powerful, creative, abundant and life-giving. Speech acts are often thought to carry "metamessages," a message about the message. There is a subtle difference between the metamessage of this speech act ("Let there be . . .") and some other form of divine command (e.g., "I command there to be . . ."). "Let there be" connotes freedom and permission. The metamessage conveys the sense of creating a space for life; for being and becoming. To be is to be creative and to create that which is good (cf. God's verdict upon his creative activity in Genesis 1:31).

God's sovereign acts in Genesis 1:1–25 are important because they are the backdrop to the divine speech act of Genesis 1:26. This gives humanity a vocation in relation to the environment.

A. Kingship, image, and rule

The creation narrative defines humanity's relationship to the environment in terms of a vocation:

> And God said, "Let us make man in our image (*tselem*), after our likeness (*demut*). They shall rule (*weyirdu*) the fish of the sea, the birds of the sky, the cattle, the whole earth, and all the creeping things that creep on earth." (Genesis 1:26; JPS)

Once again, we see that questions of justice—in this context, "right relationships" between humanity and the environment, or "ecojustice"—are understood primarily in terms of a vocation. This coheres with Chapter 4 which presented the pursuit of justice in biblical Israel in terms of a "calling." Genesis 1:26 uses different phraseology for the creation of humanity, compared to the creation of other species (e.g., "Let us make" for humanity instead of "Let there be" for other species and "in our image" instead of "every kind"). This implies that there is a unique relationship between God and this part of his creation (although this inference comes from a final form reading of Genesis 1:1–2:4). In my view, there is a parallel between God's speech in Genesis 1:26—which creates a chosen species—and God's speech in Genesis 15, the covenant with Abraham—which creates a chosen people. The parallel is apt because both the chosen species, and the chosen people have a vocation: they are designed to represent God to others. Humanity as a whole uniquely represents God to the rest of creation while the descendants of Abraham uniquely represent God to the rest of humanity. But what exactly is meant by being made in the "image and likeness" of God?

Material representations of deities and human rulers were common throughout the ancient Near East (ANE). They reminded people that someone ruled them, even though the ruler was not physically present. Sometimes human rulers claimed to be made in the "image of God", for example, claims by some Roman emperors of being a "Son of God." Genesis 1:26 is remarkable because it vests the image of God in the entire human race as opposed to a certain individual. Humanity is the representative on earth of "the absent God who is nevertheless present by his image."[34] In linguistic terms, there is a close affinity between the words "image" and "likeness" (note their usage in Ezekiel 23:14–15). Both express the idea that God and humanity have something in common, and although this has given rise to much discussion,[35] Genesis 1:28 implies that it lies in "a co-operative sharing in dominion."[36] This idea is present in Genesis 1:26; it is because humanity is made in the "image and likeness" of God that its vocation is to "rule" (Genesis 1:26). The phrase "they shall rule" (*weyirdu*) creates a hierarchy that did not previously exist (God → humanity → fish/birds/cattle/ all the earth/creeping things). As Wirzba notes, "there is an integrity to creation that depends on humans seeing themselves as properly placed within a network of creation and God."[37] To put it another way, Genesis 1 establishes a "vertical

---

34. David Clines, *The Image of God in Man*, TYNDALE BULL. 19, 53–103, 88 (1967).

35. Summarized in CLAUS WESTERMANN, GENESIS I-II, (John J. Scullion trans., Continental Commentary, Minneapolis: Fortress Press, 1994), 147–58.

36. H. D. Preuss, *Damah*, in THEOLOGICAL DICTIONARY OF THE OLD TESTAMENT (Johannes Botterweck & Helmer Ringgren eds., Grand Rapids: Eerdmans, 1978), vol. 3, pp. 250–60, 259.

37. NORMAN WIRZBA, THE PARADISE OF GOD: RENEWING RELIGION IN AN ECOLOGICAL AGE (New York: Oxford University Press, 2003), 34.

orientation" that enables humanity to get its bearings on "the horizontal plane; we can see where we are in the world and act in ways that fit our place."[38]

The word translated "rule," and in other translations as "dominion" (e.g., RSV), is derived from the verb *radah* (to rule). This is fully consistent with the royal ideology we noted, governing the use of images and likenesses in the ANE. Humanity, being made in the image and likeness of God, rules over the rest of the created order in such a way as to remind the creation of its true King. But in what does humanity's rule consist?

Some have equated the meaning of rule or dominion with subjugation.[39] From this perspective, the biblical text can be criticized for appearing to endorse environmental abuse. Certainly, there is a sense in which human domination has had a negative effect upon the planet. Scientists report that the term "human-dominated ecosystems" now "applies with greater or lesser force to all of Earth," often to detrimental effect.[40] Human dominance is such that even "maintaining the diversity of 'wild' species and the functioning of 'wild' ecosystems will require increasing human involvement."[41] It might therefore seem as though human rule automatically makes it impossible for ecosystems to flourish.

However, the meaning of rule or dominion in Genesis 1:26 and Genesis 1:28 need not be simply reduced to subjugation. There is, of course, no doubt that rule or dominion involves some degree of power and authority. But how this power is exercised depends on the type of rule one has in mind. It does not follow that all rule is abusive: it can equally be benign. As far as Genesis 1:26 is concerned, humanity is supposed to exercise its rule in a way that reflects the character of God, as set out in Genesis 1:1–25 and indeed the whole of the creation narrative. This provides the narrative typification of the meaning of "rule" in Genesis 1:26. Rule thus has a number of elements. First, humanity's rule is exercised by subduing any forces of chaos that might challenge the creation. Second, humanity rules by upholding the binary oppositions that God has created. Third, humanity exercises rule by maintaining the optimum conditions in which life can flourish. Dominion "discerns and abets goodness wherever it may be found."[42] Humanity's calling is thus to imagine "the endlessly diverse and

---

38. DAVIS, SCRIPTURE, CULTURE AND AGRICULTURE, p. 58.

39. *E.g.*, Norman C. Habel, *Geophany: The Earth story in Genesis 1, in* THE EARTH STORY IN GENESIS (Norman C. Habel & Shirley Wurst eds., Sheffield: Sheffield Academic Press, 2000), 34–48, 47.

40. Peter M.Vitousek, Harold A. Mooney, Jane Lubchencho & Jerry M. Melillo, *Human domination of Earth's ecosystems*, SCIENCE 277, 494–99, 494 (1997).

41. Ibid., 499.

42. Applying the language of DIANE KELSEY MCCOLLEY, A GUST FOR PARADISE: MILTON'S EDEN AND THE VISUAL ARTS (Chicago: University of Illinois Press, 1993), p. 5 on a different topic.

expansible" forms of goodness.⁴³ Fourth, it follows from this that rule involves wisdom. This is because, as Proverbs 3:19 puts it, "The LORD by wisdom founded the earth." Consequently, it is *wisdom* which "shows knowledge and respect for the material world as God's own well-crafted work."⁴⁴

Finally, we have already noted that the climax of the story of universal creation is not the creation of humanity but a day of rest and appreciation of creation (Genesis 2:2–3). This means that a vital part of God's rule over creation involves recognizing creation's true value as "the work of [God's] hands" (Psalm 28:5). The seventh day represents the "paradigmatic exercise"⁴⁵ of God's dominion, and this determines the form of our own. "Appreciation and enjoyment of the creatures are the hallmark of God's dominion and therefore the standard by which our own attempts to exercise dominion must be judged."⁴⁶ This involves seeing creation as God sees it. The refrain "God saw" (Genesis 1:4) and "God saw that this was good" (Genesis 1:10) recurs throughout Genesis 1, culminating with the creation of humanity and the words, "God saw all that He had made, and found it very good" (Genesis 1:31). Humanity's rule therefore involves seeing creation properly. Creation has an independent value ("very good") because it is "the work of [God's] hands" (Psalm 28:5) and not simply because it has an instrumental value.

To sum up, humanity's vocation is "to imitate God's enabling and sustaining care for the world."⁴⁷ Its role is to "mediate God's creation blessing to Earth and stand in creative, not exploitative, relationship with [Earth] and the rest of creation."⁴⁸ Humanity reigns through service.

B. The Genesis mandate

Humanity's vocation, as set out in the divine speech act of Genesis 1:26, is expanded further in the divine speech act of Genesis 1:28:

> God blessed them [humanity] and said to them: "Be fertile and increase, fill the earth and master it; and rule the fish of the sea, the birds of the sky, and all the living things that creep on earth." (Genesis 1:28; JPS)

Although the context is that of a blessing, there is also an element of command, which is why Genesis 1:28 is often referred to as the "Genesis mandate." This mandate has four elements: (1) "Be fertile and increase," (2) "fill the earth," (3) "master [the earth]," and (4) "rule." It is probably best to see the divine speech

---

43. McColley, Gust for Paradise, xvi.
44. Davis, Scripture, Culture and Agriculture, p. 142, italics original.
45. Ibid., 64.
46. Ibid., 64–65.
47. Ibid., 145.
48. Braaten, *Earth community*, p. 197 n. 14.

of Genesis 1:28 as a mixture of command and blessing: the first element is a blessing; the second and third can be regarded as either a blessing or a command, while the fourth can be seen as empowering because it confers competence.

We will consider each element in turn. The first confers fecundity upon humanity ("Be fertile and increase"), while the refrain ("And it was so") confirms successful performance (Genesis 1:30). It differs from the procreation formula of Genesis 1:22 by adding the command to rule (*uredu*), using the same verb used in Genesis 1:26 (*radah*). This links the divine speech of Genesis 1:28 with that of Genesis 1:26. The second element confers the task of replenishing the earth, which has the positive sense of filling that which was formerly empty. The third element gives humanity authority to "master" (*wekhibhshuhah*) the earth or, in other translations, to "conquer" it. The second and third elements are related to each other: humanity subdues the earth as it multiplies and occupies more of it.[49] It is not clear why humanity needs to master that which God has declared good (Genesis 1:10), although the serpent story suggests a continuing need to see off potential challenges to God's authority (Genesis 3).

As with the meaning of the word "rule" in Genesis 1:26 (see above), some have equated the meaning of the verb "to master" (*kabhash*) with harsh control and hence, once again, with environmental abuse.[50] Support for this is said to be derived from the fact that *kabhash* refers, in a specialist context, to an assault upon a woman (Esther 7:8).[51] However, it by no means follows that Genesis 1:28 refers to the "rape" of the earth. This is because the verb in Genesis 1:28 does not refer to a specific person but to a more general object; in this case, the earth. Of course, there can be no doubt that the verb "to master" presupposes a relationship between stronger and weaker parties.[52] Like the verb "to rule," it involves the exercise of some degree of power and authority. But once again, how this mastery is exercised depends on the type of rule one has in mind. It does not follow that all mastery is abusive: it can equally be benevolent. In Genesis 1, the image is a royal one of a sovereign who exercises "mastery" over weaker parties. As far as Genesis 1:28 is concerned, humanity is supposed to "master" the earth in such a way as to reflect the character of God, as set out in Genesis 1:1–25. Davis[53] finds a parallel between humanity's mission to "master" the earth (*ha'aretz*) in Genesis 1:28 and Israel's mission to "master" the promised land (*eretz Kenaan*; e.g., Joshua 21:2). The similarities include the fact that God is the

---

49. Michael A. Bullmore, *The four most important biblical passages for a Christian environmentalism*, TRINITY J. 19, 139–62, 154 (1998).

50. Habel, *Geophany*, pp. 46–47.

51. S. Wagner, *Kabash*, in THEOLOGICAL DICTIONARY OF THE OLD TESTAMENT (G. Johannes Botterweck, Helmer Ringgren & Heinz-Josef Fabry eds.; David E. Green trans., Grand Rapids: Eerdmans, 1995), vol. VII, pp. 52–57, 54–55.

52. Ibid.

53. DAVIS, SCRIPTURE, CULTURE & AGRICULTURE, pp. 59–61.

owner of both the created order in Genesis 1 and the promised land (Leviticus 25:23) and the fact that both creation in Genesis 1 and the promised land are abundantly fruitful (e.g., Numbers 13:23). From this perspective, Israel's activity in Canaan is "the paradigm of proper management of the earth...."[54] "Mastering" the earth means seeing that it is "claimed for God's purposes and rendered hospitable to the whole created order."[55]

The final element empowers humanity, once again, to "rule." This is the same verb used in Genesis 1:26 and considered above. It reinforces a connection between the divine speech of Genesis 1:26 and that of Genesis 1:28.

These four elements provide an integrated picture of humanity's vocation in regard to the environment ("be fertile, fill, master and rule"). As in Genesis 1:26, this picture is based on the paradigm of God's sovereignty in relation to creation. God's activity is characterized by (1) fecundity, (2) replication "according to its kind," (3) overcoming chaos, and (4) providing the optimum conditions in which life can flourish. This picture of royal rule is not limited to Genesis 1:26 and Genesis 1:28 but is also found in the Psalms. Psalm 72 combines what it means to "be fertile, master and rule" in its image of the ideal king.[56] The ideal human king is one who champions the poor and defends the weak and afflicted (72:4). Wherever he rules, "from the river to the ends of the earth" (72:8), there is fecundity and abundance. The picture is close to the royal vocation of humanity as expressed in Genesis 1:28.[57]

To sum up, Genesis 1:1–25, and indeed the whole of the creation narrative, provides the narrative typification for the meaning of the Genesis mandate in Genesis 1:28. God's sovereign activity in relation to creation is the relevant paradigm for understanding humanity's vocation to "be fertile/fill/master and rule" the earth. This vocation is similar to humanity's calling to rule the earth in Genesis 1:26.

IV. MOTHER EARTH

We turn from the story of *universal* creation to the story of *humanity's* creation (Genesis 2:4–25). This story builds on what we have already seen by

---

54. Ibid., 60.
55. Hava Tirosh-Samuelson, *Nature in the sources of Judaism*, DAEDALUS: J. OF THE AMER. ACAD. ARTS & SCIENCES 130, 99–124, 104–05 (2001).
56. The prayer for Solomon is understood as a prayer for the perfect king who is yet to come. This is because although this psalm is attributed to Solomon, its present setting in the Psalter is messianic.
57. Mark G. Brett, *Earthing the human in Genesis 1–3, in* THE EARTH STORY IN GENESIS (Norman C. Habel & Shirley Wurst eds., Sheffield: Sheffield Academic Press, 2000), 73–86, 78.

highlighting: (1) the mutuality between humanity and the environment, (2) intimacy between the divine and creation, (3) humanity's vocation to "till and tend" the earth, and (4) Adam's successful "naming" of the animals in Genesis 2:19.

First, Genesis 2:7–8 stresses mutuality between humanity and the environment:

... the LORD God formed man (*adam*) of dust from the ground (*adamah*) ....
And the LORD God *planted* a garden in Eden, in the east; and there he *put* [or "placed"; JPS] the man whom he had formed.

There is a parallel between God "planting" the "forest"[58] of Eden and "placing" humanity in it. The wordplay between *adam* (the man) and *adamah* (the earth) reinforces the fact that humanity is "grounded" in the environment. The human being is "Earthenware"[59]; the "Earthling" from "Planet Earth." Humanity and the environment share "common ground . . . because we *are* common ground."[60] Although humanity's "breath of life" comes from God (Genesis 2:7), it is *through* earth that life is embodied, and it is *on* earth that life is lived. "Without Land or Earth there is no locus for life [and] blessing"[61] (and see further Chapter 6). Humanity depends on Mother Earth: "dominion and dependency go hand in hand."[62] At the same time, the environment needs human activity to care for it and to enable it to be fruitful. Genesis 2:5 states that "no herb of the field had yet sprung up—*for . . . there was no man to till the ground*". "Humans serve the ground so the ground can serve humans . . . neither party . . . [is] able to reach its potential and live fully, without the other."[63] The picture is one of "mutual custodianship: when we take care of Earth it takes care of us."[64]

Second, Genesis 2:4–25 highlights intimacy between the divine and creation. The breath of life is given to humanity, face-to-face:

[The LORD God] breathed into [man's] nostrils the breath of life, and man became a living being. (Genesis 2:7)

---

58. Carol A. Newsom, *Common ground: An ecological reading of Genesis 2–3*, in THE EARTH STORY IN GENESIS, (Norman C. Habel & Shirley Wurst eds., Sheffield: Sheffield Academic Press, 2000), 60–72, 64.

59. D. SUZUKI & A. MCCONNELL, THE SACRED BALANCE: REDISCOVERING OUR PLACE IN NATURE (St. Leonards: Allen & Unwin, 1997), 77.

60. Newsom, *Common ground*, p. 63, emphasis mine.

61. Braaten, *Earth community*, p. 202.

62. Ellen Van Wolde, *The earth story as presented by the Tower of Babel narrative*, in THE EARTH STORY IN GENESIS (Norman C. Habel & Shirley Wurst eds., Sheffield: Sheffield Academic Press, 2000), 147–57, 153.

63. Shirley Wurst, *Beloved, come back to me: Ground's theme song in Genesis 3?*, in THE EARTH STORY IN GENESIS (Norman C. Habel & Shirley Wurst eds., Sheffield: Sheffield Academic Press, 2000), 87–104, 91.

64. Ntreh, *Survival of Earth*, p. 108.

It is the "kiss of life." This picture adds to the paradigm of God's sovereign activity by making intimate care part of what it means for humanity to share God's rule.

Third, as with the story of universal creation, the story of humanity's creation includes a divine speech act (Genesis 2:15) which further develops humanity's vocation in relation to the environment (cf. Genesis 1:26 and 1:28):

> The LORD God took the man and placed him in the garden of Eden, to till it (*le'obhdah*) and tend it (*le'shomrah*). (Genesis 2:15; JPS)

The vocation "to till . . . and tend" in Genesis 2:15 expands on the call to "till the soil" in Genesis 2:5. This extension is similar to the way in which the vocation to "master . . . and rule" in Genesis 1:28 develops the call to rule in Genesis 1:26. "Tilling and tending" go together, like "master and rule." Within the space of a few verses, humanity's vocation has developed into a more complex vision of the good.

The verb translated "to till" (*abhad*) means "to work on" or "develop" where the object is inanimate.[65] The verb translated to "tend" (*shamar*) and in other translations as to "guard or protect" means "careful and close observation."[66] It conveys the sense of "attentive and protective tending."[67] We should remind ourselves that this "green belt development" is not particularly intensive. The word translated "garden" (*gan*) is somewhat misleading: it is really a forest of trees and fruits.[68] Looking after a forest is less intensive than managing a classic English country garden. A bit of "light pruning and raking"[69] may have been all that was required.

The vocation to "master . . . and rule" is not opposed to the vocation "to till . . . and tend" in Genesis 2:15. They are not two different things. This is because the meaning of "master . . . and rule" is also based on the paradigm of God's sovereignty in Genesis 1:1-25; to maintain the optimum conditions that enable life to flourish. As Trible writes, "[T]o till the garden is to serve the garden; to exercise power over it is to reverence it."[70]

---

65. Helmer Ringgren, *Abad*, in THEOLOGICAL DICTIONARY OF THE OLD TESTAMENT (G. Johannes Botterweck & Helmer Ringgren eds., Grand Rapids: Eerdmans, 1999), vol. X, pp. 376–90, 382.
66. Wurst, *Beloved*, p. 91.
67. Ibid.
68. Newsom, *Common ground*, p. 64.
69. J. B. Callicott, *Genesis and John Muir*, in COVENANT FOR A NEW CREATION: ETHICS, RELIGION & PUBLIC POLICY (C. S. Robb & C. J. Casebolt eds., Maryknoll: Orbis, 1991), 107–40, 125.
70. P. Trible, GOD AND THE RHETORIC OF SEXUALITY (Philadelphia: Fortress Press, 1978), 85.

A. The first judgment

Fourth, the story of humanity's creation highlights Adam's successful naming of the animals in Genesis 2:19:

> ... out of the ground the LORD God formed every beast of the field and every bird of the air, and brought them to the man to see what he would call them; and whatever the man called every living creature, that was its name.

This builds on the picture of what it means for humanity to share God's rule because it imitates God's successful naming of day, night, sky, and so on in the story of universal creation (Genesis 1:5–10). Once again, humanity's relationship with the environment is based on the paradigm of God's relationship with creation. Here, humanity reflects the image of God because, like God's speech acts, humanity's speech acts establish the status and identity of created things. Naming in the Bible is not simply a matter of conferring nomenclature ("I name this cat "Stripey""). Instead, it is a mode of discernment in which the speaker identifies the true nature and characteristic of the thing being named. In this sense, naming is a form of judgment.

Naming also involves the exercise of wisdom. This is because wisdom involves an ability to "see to the heart of things," as in Solomon's classic display of wisdom in 1 Kings 3:16–28 (see Chapter 4). Genesis 2:19 is thus consistent with the argument, above, that humanity's rule over creation in the image of God involves the exercise of wisdom (cf. Proverbs 3:19). Here, the man is able to look beneath the surface of each beast and give it its name. We can perhaps see the naming of the animals as a test of discernment. If so, it suggests that humanity's relationship with the environment presents unique opportunities both to demonstrate wisdom and to grow in wisdom (cf. the image of "judging in a spiral" in Chapter 4). The man passes the test because he rightly recognizes that none of the animals is a suitable "corresponding other."[71] As Genesis 2:20 puts it, "for the man there was not found a helper fit for him." Here we note that humanity's exercise of wisdom in Genesis 2:19 is "law creating" in the sense that it prohibits sexual relationships with animals. They can be "close companions, [but] their relationship will never result in 'one flesh.'"[72] The man's exercise of wisdom is thus similar to God's law giving in Leviticus 20:15, which prohibits sexual relations between humanity and animals (see further Chapter 11). It is another example of the connection between law and wisdom. Finally, Genesis 2:19 shows how humanity's rule over creation involves upholding the binary oppositions established by God in creation, in this case, the distinction between humanity and the animals.

Humanity is able to name the animals because it is made "in the image of God" with powers of language and speech. But humanity's exercise of judgment may also reflect the fact that the man belongs to the same descent group as the

---

71. Wurst, *Beloved*, p. 92.
72. Ibid.

animals. As Genesis 1:24–27 sees, all were formed from the land on the sixth day. There may be an important issue of identification here. Perhaps humanity is uniquely equipped to name the animals because they are his relatives. If so, it raises, in my view, the intriguing possibility of a parallel between the first act of human judgment in the Hebrew Bible and the last act of human judgment anticipated in the New Testament. In the Hebrew Bible, the animals are brought by God before humanity for naming, while in the New Testament, humanity is brought by God before Jesus for judgment (John 5:22; Acts 10:42; 17:31). Jesus is explicitly presented as the "New Adam" (1 Corinthians 15:45–49) and "the image of the invisible God" (Colossians 1:15). As "the-Word-made-flesh," he is "[a new] *species* of creaturely flesh. . ."[73] who judges by divine appointment, while at the same time sharing the same "descent group" as those who are judged. Lest this sound far-fetched, we should remind ourselves that Genesis 2:19 is not too far removed from New Testament images of divine judgment. After all, Jesus himself describes a scene of divine judgment over which he presides, precisely in terms of distinguishing "sheep" from "goats" (Matthew 25:31–33).

Finally, we turn from humanity's speech in naming the animals to humanity's speech in naming the woman (Genesis 2:23):

Then the man said,
"This at last is bone of my bones
and flesh of my flesh;
she shall be called Woman,
because she was taken out of Man."

This is yet another significant development in a narrative already bursting with precedents. Whereas the man's speech acts of naming the animals went unrecorded, Genesis 2:23 records the man's speech act of naming the woman. Naming in the Bible has different social functions, and although we cannot tell exactly what the social function is in Genesis 2:23, the context—"no fitting helper"—suggests that the naming of the woman is best seen as "a celebration of intimacy."[74] As in Genesis 2:19, the man exercises discernment by recognizing similarity ("bone of my bones") and difference ("she shall be called Woman"). Unlike the animals, the man's sexual partner comes directly from his body and not from the earth (Genesis 2:23). Sexual compatibility is achieved through difference but not too much of it, which was the reason why the animals were not compatible (Genesis 2:20). Again, we note that the man's exercise of wisdom in Genesis 2:23 is law creating because it prohibits same-sex behavior. Once again, humanity's exercise of wisdom is similar to God's law giving, in this case, Leviticus 20:13, which prohibits male homosexual behavior (see further Chapter 11).

---

73. Oliver O'Donovan, *Where were you . . .?, in* THE CARE OF CREATION, (R. J. Berry ed., Leicester: InterVarsity Press, 2000), 90–93, 92, italics original.
74. Brett, *Earthing the human*, p. 81.

Yet again, Genesis 2:23 shows how humanity's rule over creation involves upholding binary oppositions established by God in creation, in this case, the distinction between male and female. We saw in Genesis 1:1–2:3 that God's speech acts create a series of binary oppositions: humanity/animals; ground/flesh; male/female. Here in Genesis 2:23, the man's first recorded speech involves the creation of categories (man/woman). Again, humanity's relationship with the environment draws on the paradigm of the relationship between God and creation.

To summarize, the creation narrative consists of two stories, both of which show how humanity's relationship with creation takes the form of a vocation. In the story of universal creation, this is expressed in the form of divine speech in Genesis 1:26 and Genesis 1:28 (the Genesis mandate). This is developed further in the story of humanity's creation, most notably in the call to "till and tend." Consequently, the vocation laid out in the creation narrative is the first major way in which the relationship between humanity and the environment is structured.

V. JUDGMENTS IN GENESIS

The second major way in which humanity and the environment is structured is by means of divine judgments. This means turning from the creation narrative to the primeval history (Genesis 1–11), which contains a number of such judgments (including Genesis 4 and 11). However, for reasons of space, we will concentrate on two: namely, the judgment in the forest of Eden (Genesis 3:14–24) and the judgment of the Flood (Genesis 6:11–13).

A. In the forest of good and evil

We begin with the judgment in the forest of Eden. The offense which attracts God's judgement in Genesis 3:14–24 is Adam and Eve's decision to eat from "the tree of the knowledge of good and evil" (Genesis 2:17; 3:1–13). This is an offense within the context of Genesis 1–3 because humanity has failed to play its proper role within the hierarchy established in the story of universal creation (God → humanity → fish/birds/cattle/all the earth/creeping things; see above). Humanity has disobeyed God (Genesis 3:11) and has also failed to "master . . . and rule" the serpent (Genesis 3:13). However, the offense is more than simply a failure to follow the paradigm of God's sovereign activity in relation to creation. The only other reference to Eden in the Hebrew Bible is found in Ezekiel 28:12–19, which is a prophecy against the king of Tyre (a major seaport on the Phoenician, now Lebanese, coast). The prophecy contains a list of kingly abuses, including pride, unjust trade, and tyranny (Ezekiel 26:16–18).[75] This suggests

---

75. Ibid., 83–84.

that humanity's offense in Genesis 3:6 is more than simply a failure to exercise proper kingship, but is an abuse of monarchical privilege.

Humanity's abuse of its position within the overall "chain of command" changes relationships within the earth community. This is what we would expect because of the mutuality between humanity and the environment (see above). God's judgment upon humanity has environmental consequences. These include: (1) a curse upon Earth, (2) a change in relationships within the earth community, (3) animal death, and (4) humanity's expulsion from Eden, which means living in a hostile ecosystem.

First, humanity's abuse of its monarchical privileges leads to a change in the relationship between the *adam* and the *adamah* and to a curse upon the earth (Genesis 3:1). One of the outworkings of the curse is the loss of former fecundity:

> [T]horns and thistles it shall bring forth to you;
> and you shall eat the plants of the field.
> In the sweat of your face
> you shall eat bread
> till you return to the ground,
> for out of it you were taken;
> you are dust, and to dust you shall return. (Genesis 3:18-19; *God speaking*)

"Thorns and thistles" (Genesis 3:18) are associated (though not exclusively) with "exhausted soil"[76]: weeds become much more hard work. Humanity will also revert to the earth upon death (Genesis 3:19). From a structural perspective, this is actually a collapse of the binary opposition between "ground" and "flesh." There is an element of poetic justice here. Humanity's role was to uphold the binary oppositions established by divine activity. The failure to do so, not least by failing to "master" the serpent, results in the collapse of these distinctions. It reverses the original act of creation ("dust to dust"). Humans *from* dust now become humans *to* dust.

A second environmental consequence is the changed relationship between the serpent and the earth community (Genesis 3:15). This too is a form of poetic justice because the serpent's behavior changed the relationship between humanity and the rest of creation. The serpent led humanity to an awareness of its nakedness and hence to self-consciousness (Genesis 3:7–13).[77] This has an impact upon the environment because humanity's self-consciousness leads to self-centeredness. "For once aware of themselves, [the man and woman] may treat themselves as an axiological point of reference . . . to which other creatures and the creation as a whole may be referred for appraisal."[78] It is a further step

---

76. Callicott, *Genesis and John Muir*, p. 139 n. 83.
77. Newsom, *Common ground*, pp. 68–69.
78. Callicott, *Genesis and John Muir*, pp. 123–24.

away from imitating God's pattern of care for creation and toward an exploitative relationship with the creation. Humanity's interests are now seen as the primary reference point for its behavior, rather than God's sovereign activity or the interests of creation as a whole.

A third environmental consequence, as presented in the narrative, is animal death. This is not named as such but is presented as part of the overall judgment. Humanity sought to deal with its nakedness by clothing itself with vegetation (Genesis 3:7). God deals with humanity's nakedness by clothing it with animal skins (Genesis 3:21). "Where formerly we had talked with the animals, henceforth we wear them."[79] The final environmental consequence is humanity's expulsion from the garden with no way back (Genesis 3:23–24). Losing Eden means an irrevocable shift from one ecological location to another—to the more hostile ecosystem east of Eden (Genesis 3:24), characterized by a cursed earth, conflict with creation, and toil (Genesis 3:15, 17–19).

Elements of the judgment in the forest of Eden are developed in the prophetic literature and the New Testament. These texts anticipate the restoration of humanity and the environment. The restoration of the one entails the restoration of the other, in keeping with the theme of mutuality. "The healing of Earth comes with the healing of humanity."[80] One of the best-known examples of this is the vision of the prophet Isaiah who paints a picture of normally predatory animals living at peace with vulnerable creatures (Isaiah 11:6–7). The motif of "playing children" harks back to the harmlessness of humanity in Genesis 1 and 2, while the infant's safety by the cobra hole (Isaiah 11:8) signifies the end of enmity between humanity and the serpent (cf. Genesis 3:15).[81] "Harmful" and "destructive" animals are not banished but rather "share in the transformation with humans."[82] All are included in the "knowledge of the LORD" on the "holy mountain" (Isaiah 11:9). This is the new Eden and the place of God's Presence. "Animals and humans are tied together in this world and in the world to come."[83]

Moving onto the New Testament, the restoration of humanity and the environment is seen as operating through "the-Word-become-flesh": "the Word which gave rise to the universe has become the partner of our threatened

---

79. Newsom, *Common ground*, p. 71.

80. Adrian M. Leske, *Matthew 6:25–34: Human anxiety and the natural world*, in THE EARTH STORY IN THE NEW TESTAMENT, (Norman C. Habel & Vicky Balabanski eds., Earth Bible Series, 5 vols., Sheffield: Sheffield Academic Press, 2002), vol. V, pp. 15–27, 26.

81. John. W. Olley, *The wolf, the lamb, and a little child*, in THE EARTH STORY IN THE PSALMS AND THE PROPHETS (Norman C. Habel ed., Sheffield: Sheffield Academic Press, 2001) 219–29, 223–27.

82. Ibid., 227.

83. S. H. Webb, *Ecology vs. the peaceable kingdom*, SOUNDINGS 79, 239–52, 240 (1996).

humanity."[84] Jesus's disciples are called "the salt of the Earth" and "the light of the world" (Matthew 5:13–16). As with the prophetic literature, the images are those of human and environmental transformation. In John's Gospel, Jesus's resurrection is described as taking place in a garden, and the resurrected Jesus is mistaken for its gardener (John 19:41–20:17). The picture is of a garden inhabited by a new humanity. The book of Revelation speaks of a restored humanity *and* a renewed earth (Revelation 22). Upgraded humanity needs an upgraded environment. Human v.2 needs Earth v.2 and *vice versa*. The book of Revelation itself is not so much about the end of the world as it is about the end of Roman domination and everything opposed to God's creation.[85] Its vision of "New Earth" is, among other things, "a new way of *relating* with Earth."[86] Humanity and the environment are dependent on each other to the very last page of the New Testament.

B. Water world

The second divine judgment from the primeval history that structures the relationship between humanity is that of the Flood (Genesis 6:11–13). This time, humanity's offense is that it has "filled" the earth with "lawlessness" or "violence" (*chamas*; Genesis 6:11), instead of "filling" the earth in beneficial ways as *per* humanity's vocation in Genesis 1:28. As part of this negation of the Genesis mandate, it is possible that humanity has violated its vocation to follow a herbivorous diet (Genesis 1:28). "Lawlessness" or "violence" could therefore include humanity's taste for flesh, whether that of animals or even other people.

The wisdom literature parallels *chamas* with "the wrong way" (Proverbs 16:29; JPS). Humanity has done a U-turn on God's original creative intent and taken the planet with it. *Chamas* is not restricted to humanity: the text repeatedly refers to "all flesh" (*kol-basar*; Genesis 6:12, 13, and see also Genesis 7:15, 16). *Kol-basar* is elsewhere equated with creatures that have "the breath of life" (Genesis 7:21–22), suggesting they too have not followed the relevant divine dispensations. Perhaps they have also been carnivorous or unrestrained in their consumption of vegetation.[87] Genesis 6:12 confirms the reversal of the Genesis mandate. God "sees"

---

84. O'Donovan, *Where were you . . . ?*, p. 92.

85. Barbara R. Rossing, *Alas for Earth! Lament and Resistance in Revelation 12*, in THE EARTH STORY IN THE NEW TESTAMENT, (Norman C. Habel & Vicky Balabanski eds., Earth Bible Series, Sheffield: Sheffield Academic Press, 2002), vol. V, pp. 180–92, 184ff.

86. Norman C. Habel, *Editorial preface*, in THE EARTH STORY IN THE NEW TESTAMENT, Norman C. Habel & Vicky Balabanski eds., Earth Bible Series, 5 vols., Sheffield: Sheffield Academic Press, 2002), vol. V, pp. ix–xii, x, my italics.

87. Anne Gardner, *Ecojustice: A study of Genesis 6:11-13*, in THE EARTH STORY IN GENESIS (Norman C. Habel & Shirley Wurst eds., Sheffield: Sheffield Academic Press, 2000), 117–29, 122.

the earth and judges it "corrupt," in complete contrast to Genesis 1:31 where God "sees" the earth and judges it "very good." It is a negative image of what Earth should be.

The result is the judgment of the Flood (Genesis 6:17). As in Genesis 3:14–21, this is a form of poetic justice. Just as *chamas* reversed the divine speech of Genesis 1:28–29, so the Flood reverses the divine speech of Genesis 1:1–28. Like humanity's return to the earth in Genesis 3:19, the Flood shows what happens when the binary oppositions that create the necessary preconditions for life are dissolved. As Genesis 3:19 collapses the distinction between "ground" and "flesh," so Genesis 6 collapses the distinction between the "dry land" and the "seas" (Genesis 1:10), as well as the distinction between "the waters below" and "the waters above" (Genesis 1:6–7). Humanity returns to earth, and the earth returns to water. The result is planetary death. The "geophany," or "appearance of the earth," as described in Genesis 1:9, is thrown into terrifying reverse.

The Flood narrative is thus "a 'decreation' story in which God reverses the processes that he himself had set in motion."[88] There is even a similarity between the list of created life-forms in Genesis 1:20, 24, and the list of exterminated creatures in Genesis 7:19–21.[89] Decreation recurs as a motif in the prophetic literature (Zephaniah 1:3; Jeremiah 4:23; Isaiah 24:6). Perhaps the most striking example from the prophets is Hosea 4:1–3:

> There is no faithfulness or kindness,
> and no knowledge of God in the land;
> there is [false] swearing, lying, killing,
> stealing, and committing adultery;
> they break all bounds and murder follows murder.
> Therefore the land mourns,
> and all who dwell in it languish,
> and also the beasts of the field, and the birds of the air;
> and even the fish of the sea are taken away. (*Hosea speaking*)

This evokes a similar three-stage process to Genesis 6, viz., (1) absence of faithfulness, loyalty, and the "knowledge of God" essential to life (4:1–2); followed by (2) lawlessness and violence (4:2); and (3) the death of creation (4:3). Where there is no "knowledge of God," humanity loses the pattern by which it is supposed to relate to Earth. The result is environmental destruction.

To sum up, the divine judgments in the primeval history spell out the consequences of failing to follow the paradigm of God's sovereign activity in relation to creation. At the same time, however, some of the biblical texts look forward to the

---

88. Nanette Stahl, Law and Liminality in the Bible, Journal for the Study of the Old Testament Supplement Series 202 (Sheffield: Sheffield Academic Press, 1995), 37.

89. Ibid., 38.

restoration of a proper relationship between God, humanity, and the environment. Until that restoration, further guidance is given in the form of specific legal provisions, and it is to these we now turn.

VI. NEW LAWS FOR A NEW EARTH

The third major way in which the relationship between humanity and the environment is structured is seen in God's postdiluvian blessing upon humanity (the blessing that takes place in Genesis 9:1–7). After the Flood, there is a new deal for a new earth—and this means new divine speech. Just as the creation narrative contained speech addressed to humanity and the animals about dietary provisions (Genesis 1:28–30), so there is further divine speech in the story of *re*-creation (Genesis 8:1ff). The ebbing of the Flood and the dove's return to the Ark with a "plucked-off olive leaf" (Genesis 8:11) represents the "new creation" because it evokes the separation of dry land and water and the appearance of plants, which were part of the story of universal creation (Genesis 1:1–2:4). This divine speech, which contains a mixture of blessings and legal provisions, is found in Genesis 9:1–7.

The parallels between the story of universal creation and the story of re-creation, following the Flood, are the basis on which we are justified in finding parallels between God's speech to humanity in Genesis 1:28–30 and God's speech to humanity (now reduced to Noah and his family) in Genesis 9:1–7. In both cases, humanity receives a blessing from God, and in particular, Genesis 9:1 reaffirms humanity's original vocation to "be fruitful and multiply, and fill the earth." Moreover, in both cases, God provides dietary laws for humanity and the animals.

A. The tree and the blood

Some of the parallels between Genesis 1:28–30 and Genesis 9:1–7 have wider implications for our understanding of biblical law. First, there is a parallel between the command to "be fruitful and multiply" in the Genesis mandate (Genesis 1:28) and the same command in Genesis 9:1, 7. However, unlike the Genesis mandate, there is a tension between this command and the prohibition of murder in Genesis 9:5–6. The postdiluvian blessing of Genesis 9:1–7 consists of a legal frame, which is concerned with the blessing of procreation, and a narrative center, whose subject is the prohibition of murder. As Stahl writes, the repetition of elements from the Genesis mandate in the postdiluvian blessing highlights "the dissonance between the legal frame [the blessing of procreation] and its narrative centre [the prohibition of murder]."[90] The result is a contrast

---

90. Stahl, Law and Liminality, p. 46.

between procreation and murder in Genesis 9:1–7. In my view, it is interesting that this juxtaposition between procreation and murder is also found in the sixth and seventh commandments of the Decalogue (Exodus 20:12–13; Deuteronomy 5:16–17). This suggests that there may be thematic repetition between the divine speech of Genesis 9:1–7, which precedes the global covenant of Genesis 9:8-17, and the subsequent covenants of Sinai (Exodus 19ff) and Moab (Deuteronomy 1ff), which incorporate the Ten Commandments.

Second, there is a parallel between the dietary laws of Genesis 2:16–17 and those of Genesis 9:3–4:

You may freely eat of every tree of the garden; *but* . . ..
(Genesis 2:16-17; *God speaking*)

Every moving thing that lives shall be food for you; and as I gave you the green plants, I give you everything. *Only you shall not* . . ..
(Genesis 9:3-4; *God speaking*)

In both cases, there is tension between permission and restraint ("able to eat of all the trees, except one" and "able to eat from all creatures, except the blood"). Both laws also contain references to death: human in Genesis 2:17 and animal in Genesis 9:3–5.[91]

However, there is in my view a third parallel between the two cases which Stahl overlooks. This is the parallel between the food taboos of Genesis 2:16–17 and Genesis 9:3–4, namely, "the tree of the knowledge of good and evil" (Genesis 2:17) and animal lifeblood (Genesis 9:3–4). The significance of this parallel is as follows. In the ritual laws of *Leviticus*, there is a connection between life and blood and also between blood and atonement:

For the life of every creature is the blood of it . . .. (Leviticus 17:14; *God speaking*)

[Aaron, the high priest] shall then slaughter the people's goat of sin offering, bring its blood behind the curtain [of the Tabernacle], and do with its blood as he has done with the blood of the bull: he shall sprinkle it over the cover and in front of the cover [on top of the Ark of the Covenant]. Thus he shall purge the Shrine [or the Holy Place] of the uncleanness and transgression of the Israelites, whatever their sins . . . . (Leviticus 16:15-16; *God speaking;* JPS)

The building of the Tabernacle is the means by which the Israelites are able to enjoy the Presence of God within their midst. The Tabernacle is, in fact, a sort of "flat-pack Mount Sinai." The book of Exodus reaches its climax with the completion of the Tabernacle, which is then indwelt by the visual Presence of God (known in later Jewish tradition as the *Shekhinah*; Exodus 40:33–38). The ritual laws of Leviticus signify that the function of the Tabernacle is to deal, in an ongoing manner, with the sins of the Israelites and so enable a holy God to dwell in

---

91. Ibid., 15.

the midst of a sinful people. The proper manipulation of blood in the Tabernacle has the effect of purging the Israelites of their sins. It provides a partial way back to the Edenic experience of being able to stand in God's Presence (cf. Genesis 3:8a). The reason why it is only a partial experience is because it is limited to the high priest on the Day of Atonement (Leviticus 16:2ff). There is a deep and abiding connection between the Tabernacle, and later the Temple, and the forest in Eden. Like Eden, the Tabernacle/Temple is associated with God's Presence, and both are orientated toward the east (Genesis 3:24; Numbers 3:38), while the Temple is decorated with symbols of fecundity (e.g., 1 Kings 6:18, 32).[92] This ritual worldview is consistent with the parallel between the food taboos of Genesis 2:16–17 and Genesis 9:3–4. Obedience in *not eating* the blood (in Genesis 9:3-4) and handling it according to the proper rituals appears to partially undo the effects of *eating* the fruit from the tree of the knowledge of good and evil (in Genesis 2:16–17).

There is also a parallel in the penalty for these food taboos. The penalty for eating from the tree of knowledge of good and evil in Genesis 2:16–17 is death. We see part of the outworking of this in Genesis 3:17–24 where the penalty means a curtailed life, expulsion from the forest of Eden and, ultimately, physical death. There is no stated penalty for eating lifeblood in Genesis 9:3–4, although Leviticus 17:14 describes it as being "cut off" (from the verb *karat*). Although there is debate about the meaning of *karat*, it is thought to include a number of different aspects, including a shortened life; being cut off from the promised land; and sudden, premature death. There is therefore a parallel not only between the food taboos of Genesis and Leviticus but also between their penalties. There may even be an association, at a visual level, between the *kerubhim* with the revolving sword (Genesis 3:24) and the verb "cut off" itself.

B. Licence revoked

In addition to these parallels between what God says in the story of universal creation and the story of re-creation, there are also important differences: (1) animals are formally accountable for killing humanity, (2) humanity is allowed to eat the animals, (3) humanity's vocation to master the earth is *not* reaffirmed, and (4) the animals now fear and dread humanity. These differences show the changes that have occurred in the relationship between humanity and the environment. They are further examples of how law and a sense of vocation regulate the relationship between humanity and the environment. We will consider each of these differences in turn.

First, we find that for the first time, animals are formally accountable for killing humanity (Genesis 9:5). This is an extraordinary development, given their

---

92. *See generally* Gordon Wenham, *Sanctuary symbolism in the Garden of Eden story*, in Proceedings of the World Council of Jewish Studies 9 (1986), 19–25.

herbivorous character in Genesis 1:30. It is also unusual in the light of modern animal welfare theories, many of which explicitly deny any form of moral accountability for animals.[93] It is possible that Genesis 9:5 is a response to the charge against the animals in Genesis 6:12, which may have included violence against humans. At any rate, animals have the same level of responsibility for homicide as human beings (9:5), which implies that animals and humans are put on the same footing. This is reflected in biblical law (e.g., the law of the homicidal ox in Exodus 21:28–29, 32).

Second, we find that for the first time, humanity is formally allowed to eat animals, albeit without their blood (9:3, cf. 1:30). This is the basis of kosher slaughtering laws (*shechitah*). The development may have been understood as an attempt to limit the pre-Flood practice of eating animals *and* their blood.[94] Medieval and modern commentators[95] claim that Noah is allowed to eat the animals because of his role in saving them from destruction, by looking after them in the Ark. This interpretation implies that the new permission is a positive development. However, the context suggests otherwise. Killing animals (9:3–4) is juxtaposed with killing human beings (9:5–6). The implication is that "meat is murder." Humanity has permission, all right—to eat its relatives. The reference to lifeblood (9:4) confirms the unease. The fact that biblical law gives permission to do something does not necessarily mean that the practice is welcomed or encouraged (see, for example, the laws of vengeance in Chapter 8 and divorce in Chapter 12).

A third departure is that while Genesis 9:1 and 9:7 repeat the procreation formula, they do *not* repeat the call to "rule" (Genesis 1:28). Has it been revoked? Either way, the new laws assume that humanity no longer has the capacity to exercise kingship in the form originally envisaged. This implicit but extreme claim finds some support in the Wisdom literature. God's questions to Job regarding the wild ass (Job 39:5–8) and the wild ox (Job 39:9–12) query not merely whether humanity is currently capable of exercising *dominion* over creation but whether it can even manage *domestication*:

> Is the wild ox willing to serve you?
> Will he spend the night at your crib?
> Can you bind him in the furrow with ropes,
> or will he harrow the valleys after you? (Job 39:9-10; *God speaking*)

---

93. E.g,. ALISON HILLS, DO ANIMALS HAVE RIGHTS? (Cambridge: Icon Books, 2005), 98ff.

94. Tikva Frymer-Kensky, *The Atrahasis Epic and its significance for our understanding of Genesis 1–9*, BIBLICAL ARCHAEOLOGIST 40, 147–55, 152 (1977).

95. Including the famous Jewish interpreter Nahmanides, or Ramban, as well as Devora Steinmetz, *Vineyard, farm and garden: The drunkenness of Noah in the context of primeval history*, J. BIBLICAL LITERATURE 113, 193–207, 195–96 (1994).

It is a far cry from the authority and insight which humanity exercised in Genesis 2:19–20. "Behind the parody [of Job 39:9–12] . . . lies an implied rejection of the tradition that humans are commissioned, as part of their basic role under God, to rule over all living creatures."[96] It is not, however, clear to what extent Genesis 9:1–7 and Job 39 simply describe humanity's position (as they see it) or regard humanity's reduced role as normative. Other biblical texts do not see it as normative, viz., humanity should still be able to rule in a postdiluvian world. As we have seen, traditions such as Psalm 72 affirm the ideal of humanity's vocation in Genesis 1 and 2, even in the light of its failure from Genesis 3 onwards.

Whatever the reason, the absence of rule in Genesis 9:1–7 is consistent with a fourth change: the animals "fear and dread" humanity ("The fear of you and the dread of you (*umora'akhem wehittekhem*) shall be upon . . . everything that creeps on the ground . . . into your hand they are delivered"; Genesis 9:2). Fear and dread have military connotations and imply that the animals are under the heel of an oppressive ruler.[97] Whereas before the Flood the animals "went with" Noah (Genesis 7:9), now they run away. Some commentators present fear and dread as a blessing because it occurs in the immediate context of God's provision for humanity (Genesis 9:2–3). However, it is hard to see this as a positive development. The contrast between benevolent rule in Genesis 1:28 and militarized tyranny in Genesis 9:2 simply emphasizes how far relationships have deteriorated in the postdiluvian world.

Key elements of the divine speech in Genesis 9:1–7 are developed further in the prophetic literature and in the New Testament. Isaiah's picture of restored creation sees the transformation of carnivores to herbivores (Isaiah 11:7; 65:25) while the book of Revelation envisages a transformed humanity with access to "the tree of life . . . in the paradise of God" (Revelation 2:7; 22:1–2).

Consequently, there are some important differences between divine speech in the story of universal creation and divine speech in the story of re-creation. Changes in law and humanity's vocation reflect the changes that have taken place in the relationship between humanity and the environment. This is thus a third way in which the relationship between humanity and the environment is structured.

VII. ECO-LAW

Finally, we turn to the fourth major way in which the biblical materials regulate humanity and the environment, namely, the environmental laws found in

---

96. Norman C. Habel, *Is the wild ox willing to serve you?*, in THE EARTH STORY IN WISDOM TRADITIONS (Norman C. Habel & Shirley Wurst eds., Cleveland: Sheffield Academic Press, 2001), 179–89, 188.

97. Olley, *The wolf, the lamb*, p. 139.

the Torah. In doing so, we should say at once that although a great deal of biblical law is concerned with the land and with agrarianism (see Chapters 6 and 7), we do not find in Torah much of what we would nowadays call "environment law," such as water regulation, species protection, and so on (although we do find in Genesis 29:1-8 customary social practices regarding the use of wells and so on that have environmental implications). This is not altogether surprising. As we have seen, the creation story provides a narrative typification of how humanity should relate to the environment, based on the paradigm of God's relationship with creation. At one level, this was all the guidance biblical Israel needed. Even in English law, there was not much environmental law until comparatively recently. It was not until the emergence of the Industrial Revolution in England in the late eighteenth century, with the side effects of environmental pollution, urbanization, poor sanitation, and disease that English law began to regulate the environment in a modern sense.[98] Today, we have extensive environmental protection laws, but this is because we live in a high-urban, high-impact society which has the means and the technology to destroy the environment. Biblical Israel did not have this technological capacity, and so we should not project modern assumptions about the extent of environmental law onto biblical law. Nevertheless, there are a number of examples of "eco-law" in Torah.

Space precludes a comprehensive survey of environmentally related texts in Torah. Suffice it to say that these laws develop the paradigm of God's relationship with creation into specific guidance for human beings. First, the story of universal creation ends with the institution of Sabbath (Genesis 2:2–3) which in turn forms the basis of care for animals on the Sabbath:

> Six days you shall do your work, but on the seventh day you shall rest; that your ox and your ass may have rest, and the son of your bondmaid, and the alien, may be refreshed. (Exodus 23:12; *God speaking*)

> Six days you shall work, but on the seventh day you shall rest; [even] in plowing time and in harvest you shall rest. (Exodus 34:21; *God speaking*)

Exodus 23:12 shows particular care and concern for animals by putting the ox and the donkey ahead of the slave and alien. Limiting animal labor is also an aspect of Exodus 34:21. Second, Deuteronomy 22:6-7 provides a further limit: human beings are not allowed to eat wild mother birds. The motive clause is interesting: "that your days may be prolonged, and that it may go well with you" (cf. the similar formulation of Deuteronomy 5:16, which is also concerned with "parents" and which suggests thematic repetition between these texts). Humanity will prosper if it limits its exploitation of the environment. This is consistent

---

98. *See* Sean Coyle & Karen Morrow, The Philosophical Foundations of Environmental Law: Property, Rights and Nature (Oxford and Portland, Oregon: Hart, 2004), 107ff.

with the picture of mutuality between humanity and the environment in the story of humanity's creation, above. As humanity takes care of the environment, so the environment takes care of humanity.

A third form of eco-law is found in the covenant blessings and curses of Deuteronomy 28, which are expressed in terms of their environmental impact. The blessings of obedience recall the fecundity of Eden (Deuteronomy 28:4-5, 8, 11–12); likewise, the curses of disobedience include death, disease, and a ravaged land (Deuteronomy 28:16–68, *passim*). We saw in Chapter 3 that specific groups of curses in Deuteronomy 28 appear to be arranged in a natural sequence of "cause and effect." This is not surprising: environmental destruction has "knock-on" effects. Cutting down a section of rain forest leads to soil erosion, which makes the land harder to replant, which in turn reduces the number of plants available to convert carbon dioxide in the atmosphere, which contributes to global warming. Deuteronomy 11:29 provides that the blessings and curses be proclaimed from specific geographical locations; the blessing at Mount Gerizim and the curse at Mount Ebal. The two mountains overshadow the modern town of Nablus, which is not far from the ancient site of biblical Shechem. There is a visual contrast between the two slopes: Mount Gerizim is lush and symbolizes blessing while Mount Ebal is barren and symbolizes cursing.[99] The medium is the message.

A. The fruits of war

The final eco-law we will consider in the Torah is the most important from the perspective of contemporary Jewish environmental ethics, namely Deuteronomy 20:19–20, which prohibits cutting down fruit trees. It is strange that this text should bear this weight because it is one of the most difficult environmental laws in Torah. The text is as follows, using the King James Version (1611) because it provides a more literal translation than others:

> When thou shalt besiege a city a long time, in making war against it to take it, thou shalt not destroy the trees thereof by forcing an axe against them: for thou mayest eat of them, and thou shalt not cut them down (for the tree of the field *is* man's *life*) to employ *them* in the siege. Only the trees which thou knowest that they *be* not trees for meat, thou shalt destroy and cut them down; and thou shalt build bulwarks against the city that maketh war with thee, until it be subdued. (Deuteronomy 20:19–20)

The standard reading of this text is that some trees could be used as wood for siege works while others could not. Commentators have tried to rationalize the choice of certain trees over others in various ways, with one of the strongest

---

99. Daniel Hillel, The Natural History of the Bible: An Environmental Exploration of the Hebrew Scriptures (New York: Columbia University Press, 2006), 149–50.

justifications being the argument from self-interest, viz., the army will want to eat the fruit after the siege.[100] However, this reading is problematic because it does not address the central difficulty of the text. This is the strange phrase in verse 19 which, in the Masoretic Text (MT) of the Hebrew Bible, can only be translated:

... man is the tree of the field ... (*ha'adam etz hassadeh*).
(Deuteronomy 20:19)[101]

On its own, this is a hard phrase to understand because it does not seem to make much sense. Accordingly, translators and commentators have added supplements of their own: for example, "man *consists of* the tree of the field" (added words in italics), viz., "man lives off the tree."[102] This is reflected in some Bible translations such as the King James Version (above) which states, "for the tree of the field *is* man's *life*" (added words in italics). It is because of these difficulties with the MT that most modern translations of the Bible follow the LXX version of Deuteronomy 20:19 instead. This phrase turns *ha'adam etz hassadeh* into a rhetorical question: "Surely the tree of the field is not a human . . .?"[103] This implies, rather whimsically, that one should not cut down the trees because they, unlike the city, do not have a choice whether to surrender or withdraw. The famous medieval Rabbi Solomon ben Isaac (Rashi) describes the trees as "innocent bystanders."[104] The problem with Rashi's reading is that it sees *all* trees as "innocent bystanders," yet the text explicitly allows *some* trees to be cut down. Rashi's approach does not explain why some trees can be cut down while others cannot.

In my view, there is a better way of making sense of the text. This means starting with the *lectio difficilior* (the harder reading) and taking seriously the MT version of Deuteronomy 20:19. In doing so, we need to recognize two things: (1) the MT says "man" and although the assumption is made by commentators that this means "human being," it can of course refer to the male gender; and (2) there is a binary opposition in the text between "trees of the field" and "trees for fruit" (verse 19–20). If we put these two elements together, we have—in my view—the key to unlocking the passage.

---

100. James Barr, A puzzle in Deuteronomy, in READING FROM RIGHT TO LEFT (J. Cheryl Exum & H. G. M. Williamson eds., Journal for the Study of the Old Testament Supplement Series 373, Sheffield: Sheffield Academic Press 2003), 13–24, 21.

101. *Per* S. R. DRIVER, A CRITICAL AND EXEGETICAL COMMENTARY ON DEUTERONOMY (Edinburgh: T&T Clark, 3rd ed. 1906), 240.

102. Ibid.

103. Translation by Barr, *Puzzle in Deuteronomy*, p. 15.

104. RASHI, COMMENTARY ON THE TORAH, DEVARIM/DEUTERONOMY, translated, annotated, and elucidated by Yisrael Isser Zvi Herczeg (New York: Mesorah Publications, 1998), vol. V, p. 218.

Deuteronomy 20:10–20 is concerned with regulating the Israelites' behavior when conquering non-Israelite cities. If the city refuses to surrender then, following a successful siege, all males are "put ... to the sword" (verse 13). However, the women and children are preserved and "enjoyed" as part of "the spoil of your enemy" (verse 14). This exactly mirrors the treatment meted out to various trees. On the other hand, "trees of the field" which do not bear fruit can be cut down, in the same way that males in a besieged city are put to the sword. There is also a visual parallel: men who are put to the sword ooze blood, and trees that are cut down bleed sap. This bark exudant can sometimes be abundant and sticky, like blood. On the other hand, trees which bear fruit are not to be cut down, just as women and children in a besieged city are spared. There is thus an exact parallel between (1) "trees of the field" and "men" and (2) "trees for fruit" and women and children. "Trees for fruit" can naturally be compared with women and children because women have the capacity to "bear fruit," that is, children while the children themselves can be compared to the "fruit" of the tree. This explains why Deuteronomy 20:19–20 allows some trees to be cut down while others are spared. They reflect the fate of those inside the besieged city.

If this reading is correct, it has a number of implications for our understanding of biblical law. First, it confirms the educational function of biblical law. The army's treatment of trees during wartime teaches it how to treat human beings. What they do with the trees prepares them for how they are going to treat men, women, children, and cattle in the besieged city. The trees are, as it were, a biblical PowerPoint presentation on military ethics. They teach the army that they are to preserve future generations, especially in the midst of war. This emphasis on fecundity, even in wartime conditions, evokes the "Genesis mandate" of Genesis 1:28. Naturally, the longer the siege goes on, the keener the troops will be to kill, but by the same token, the longer they will have had to decide what to do about the trees and to internalize the need for restraint.

Some may object that this anthropocentric reading has the effect of diminishing the value of the trees themselves. But the text's educative function cuts both ways. If there is a parallelism between trees and human beings, then not only does it teach the army to value human beings, it teaches the army (and everyone else) to value trees as well. And if the trees are identified with human beings, then arguably they will be treated better than if they are seen as merely trees. The educative purpose of the text helps to explain why fruit trees are singled out for protection. This is not a form of species protectionism in which humanity arbitrarily cares about one species more than another ("hug a fruit tree"). It is chosen because it is an excellent symbol of mothers and children. Fruit trees or food trees such as the olive tree are the product of long-term commitment. They take generations to grow, and so they symbolize future generations.

Second, the treatment of trees may also have educative value for the people within the besieged city. It demonstrates to the men of the city what will happen to them if they do not surrender. If so, it is also a form of psychological warfare.

This is not unknown in the conquest narratives (cf. the tactics used by Joshua and Gideon's armies in Joshua 6 and Judges 7, respectively).

Finally, Deuteronomy 20:19–20 shows that there is a parallel between what human beings ought to do to one another and what we ought to do the environment. Likewise, what we ought to do the environment mirrors what we ought to do to each other. This normative connection between humanity and the environment is also valid in a descriptive sense. Sadly, it is all too true that how we treat one another reflects how we treat the environment and vice versa.

VIII. CONCLUSION

The relationship between humanity and the environment is complex. The biblical materials reflect this by drawing on a wide range of registers to reflect its concerns, including blessings, commands, and curses, as well as human and divine speech acts. However, it is possible to identify four main ways in which the relationship between humanity and the environment is structured. The first is by means of the creation narrative which presents humanity as a species made in the image of God. Its vocation is to exercise a particular kind of royal rule over creation, one that involves developing and watching over the earth. This is the heart of the relationship between humanity and the environment. The specific nature of the image of God requires that humanity relates to the environment in a similar manner to God and creation, as seen in the creation narrative. God creates life and the conditions under which life can flourish. This is the model for early human law giving and human judgment, which requires wisdom. When humanity departs from this paradigm, the result is environmental destruction. Accordingly, the second main way in which the relationship between humanity and the environment is regulated is by means of divine judgments in the primeval history, while the third main way is seen in the postdiluvian blessing conferred by God upon humanity. This underlines the mutual dependence between humanity and the earth. Finally, the relationship between humanity and the environment is regulated by means of the various eco-laws that are found in biblical law. These identify clear rules for planetary protection that are designed to turn the pattern of God's relationship with creation into specific guidance for humanity.

Select reading
Mark G. Brett, "Earthing the human in Genesis 1–3." In Norman C. Habel and Shirley Wurst eds., *The Earth Story in Genesis*. (Sheffield: Sheffield Academic Press, 2000), 373–386.

Ellen F. Davis, *Scripture, Culture and Agriculture: An Agrarian Reading*. (Cambridge: Cambridge University Press, 2008), Chapter 2.

Anne Gardner, "Ecojustice: A study of Genesis 6:11-13." In Norman C. Habel and Shirley Wurst eds., *The Earth Story in Genesis*. (Sheffield: Sheffield Academic Press, 2000), 117–129.

Carol A. Newsom, "Common ground: an ecological reading of Genesis 2–3." In Norman C. Habel and Shirley Wurst eds., *The Earth Story in Genesis*. (Sheffield: Sheffield Academic Press, 2000), 60–72.

Nanette Stahl, *Law and Liminality in the Bible*. Journal for the Study of the Old Testament Supplement Series 202. (Sheffield: Sheffield Academic Press, 1995), Chapters 2 and 3.

6. PEOPLE AND LAND

People and land are inexorably linked in biblical law. One of the key turning points in the Bible is Genesis 15, in which God promises to Abraham that his descendants will receive the promised land. Not surprisingly, land law is of great significance in biblical law. The land is far more than just the "playing board" of biblical Israel. It is at the heart of her identity because the land embodies, perhaps more than anything else, the story of her journey with God. For this reason, we will find that narrative and law together regulate the relationship between people and land. We saw that this was also true for the relationship between humanity and the environment, and so this chapter follows naturally from the previous study.

We begin by looking at how the biblical ideology of divine ownership affects the practice of land tenure and land use although this chapter, like biblical law itself, focuses on rural land rather than urban property. We will then explore the nature of the relationship between people, land, and narrative. Biblical law sees the land as a network of memories and relationships. It is an expression of God's covenant with Israel. It is not a commodity that can be bought and sold like a freehold. We will then consider different aspects of the biblical law of property, including inheritance and disinheritance. This raises important questions about the different sources of law in the Bible, including customary law, divine revelation, and the relationship between them. A key part of biblical land law is the way in which the people are regularly required to suspend their claims over land. This means looking at the various sabbatical laws. These form what we can call a "Sabbath spectrum" which consists of the weekly Sabbath, the sabbatical year, and the jubilee year. These point to an underlying contrast between Egyptian and Israelite ideologies of land tenure. Finally, we will see that the biblical texts are aware of a conflict between those who treat land as a commodity and those who see it as a unique form of property. This tension is also found in the modern English law of property.

I. DIVINE OWNERSHIP

Like "planetary management" (see Chapter 5), biblical ideas about land management are ultimately derived from the biblical creation narrative (Genesis 1:1–2:25). This tells the story of a Creator God who has ultimate title in property. He made everything, so he owns it. This is the ideology of divine ownership. Rather obviously from a legal point of view, divine ownership means that God has the power to make land grants to individuals and their descendants. This is seen in God's covenant with Abram (later "Abraham") in Genesis 15 in which God promises land for Abraham's descendants: "To your descendants I give this land . . ." (Genesis 15:18). This is restated in Genesis 17:8 ("I will give to you, and to your descendants after you, the land of your sojournings, all the land of Canaan, for an everlasting possession"; see Chapter 2). This story is of course central to the relationship between Israel and the promised land, and we will consider the relationship between people, land, and narrative, further below.

For now, we need to acknowledge, right at the outset, that the ideology of divine ownership has four major implications for biblical land law. It means that: (1) no human person ultimately owns anything; (2) all property is ultimately received as a gift; (3) agricultural land is only worth what can be grown on it (with urban land being valued on a different basis; see Leviticus 25:29–30); and (4) certain uses of land and its produce are prohibited. We will look at each of these in turn.

A. The divine landlord

First, *divine ownership means that no one ultimately owns anything, including agricultural land.* In biblical law, no one can buy or sell a freehold in land:

> The land shall not be sold in perpetuity, for the land is mine . . . And in all the country you possess, you shall grant a redemption of the land.
> (Leviticus 25:23–24; *God speaking*)

Because the Israelites had no absolute title in agricultural land, they could never sell it in perpetuity. It could only be leased for a limited period (see further, below). This is a major limit: "one cannot buy or sell what one does not own; therefore, literal transfers of [agricultural] land are impossible, thus the accumulation of large estates is impossible."[1] Urban property such as houses in walled cities were subject to different rules (Leviticus 25:29–30). Divine ownership meant that the only things that could be sold were the *produce* of the agricultural land (that is, crops) and the *produce* of an individual (that is, their labor; Leviticus 25:16, 40)—not the land or the people themselves (see also Exodus 21:2–4; Deuteronomy 15:12–18). Second, *divine ownership means that all property is ultimately received as a gift.* Abraham receives the promised land from God as a gift (Genesis 17:8), and the biblical texts are full of reminders of this (e.g., Exodus 3:7–8; Deuteronomy 8:7–10, 18).

Third, *divine ownership means that land is only worth what can be grown on it.* Israelites who got into financial difficulties could rent their rural land. But because this land could not be sold in perpetuity—and had no value in and of itself—its worth was determined by what could be grown upon it. This is partly

---

1. Jeffrey A. Fager, Land Tenure and the Biblical Jubilee: Uncovering Hebrew Ethics through the Sociology of Knowledge, Journal for the Study of the Old Testament Supplement Series 155 (Sheffield: Sheffield Academic Press, 1993), 117.

the reason why biblical legal texts such as Leviticus 25:19 refer to the land yielding its "fruit." In addition, calculations of worth are supposed to take into account the number of years until the next jubilee year (Leviticus 25:15–16). This event reunited people and land that had been alienated and was supposed to take place every 50 years (see further, below). It follows that the maximum value that could be placed on land is 49 harvests:

> According to the number of years after the jubilee, you shall buy [agricultural land] from your neighbour, and according to the number of years for crops he shall sell to you. If the years are many you shall increase the price, and if the years are few you shall diminish the price, for it is the number of the crops that he is selling to you. You shall not wrong one another, but you shall fear your God; for I am the LORD your God. (Leviticus 25:15–17; *God speaking*)

This means that if there are 40 years until the next jubilee, then the land is worth the estimated value of 40 years' crops. Similarly, if there is only one year until the jubilee, then the land is worth the estimated value of one year's crops. Of course, the value attached to rural land in this sense depends on there being people to work the land; if there is no one, the land is worth far less. This system did not entirely avoid the problems of a speculative property market. Under a system of divine ownership, there is no increase in the *capital* value of the land because the market is rental only. However, this does not exclude the possibility of speculation in the *rental* market. Since it was possible to rent for up to 49 years' maximum, one could still have "overheated" rental values. No advantage was to be taken of the fact that these figures were only estimates, which is the meaning of the injunction not to "wrong one another." (Leviticus 25:17).

Leviticus 25:15–17 can be seen as another example of a "self-executing rule," that is, something that can be applied between buyer and seller. There is no need to involve third parties or experts, in this case, the ancient equivalent of estate agents. The parties themselves can agree the rental value of the land on the basis of a "rule of thumb," the typical value of crops. The problem with a rule of thumb is that it can involve "rough justice": you may pay more for the rent or not depending on the yield. In that sense, God fixes the rental value of the land. This makes sense in a system of divine ownership because God is the one who makes "the land . . . yield its fruit" (25:19). Such language rightly evokes the original creation (Genesis 1:11–12). As the divine landlord, God fixes the price—the rental value for the Israelites, who are merely tenants.

Fourth, *divine ownership prohibits certain uses of property*. We saw in Chapter 5 that God's sovereignty over creation is characterized by fecundity, replication "according to its kind," overcoming chaos, and providing the optimum conditions in which life can flourish (Genesis 1:1–2:4). It follows that the promised land—land that is uniquely associated with God's Presence (Numbers 35:34)—will be characterized by these elements. Indeed, the promised land is described as "a land flowing with milk and honey" (Exodus 3:8). Like the original creation, the promised land is "the gift that keeps on giving."² Abundance means that certain uses of the land are prohibited. This includes selling "food for profit" to the needy Israelite (Leviticus 25:37; and Chapter 7). As Davis writes, "food is, more than anything else, an expression of God's sovereignty over creation and generosity toward humankind."³ Accordingly, there is something wrong with using food to gain advantage over another.

To sum up, the ideology of divine ownership has a number of practical implications. It means there is a rental market in agricultural land but no purchase market. In one sense the Israelites own the land because they can trade in it to a limited extent, but in a more important sense, they do not own the land at all. "The paradoxical experience of both owning and not owning one's own property precisely signifies the moment at which the divine depth of meaning and power breaks into the structure of acquiring, using, and exchanging property."⁴

II. CHOSEN PEOPLE, PROMISED LAND

God's gift of the land to Abraham and his descendants in Genesis 15:18 ensures that, in the Hebrew Bible at least, people and land are ideologically inseparable. This section explores the various ways in which they are conjoined. We will also see that this has parallels with the relationship between humanity and the environment (see Chapter 5).

A. A place and a name

There are numerous connections between people and land. First and most obvious, the declaration of Israel as a "people" is everywhere accompanied by the promise of land. As Braaten writes, "the grace of God declaring them God's people does not and cannot reach them in a placeless void."⁵ As Hosea puts it, "*in the place where* it was said to them, 'You are not my people,' it shall be said to them, 'Sons of the living God'" (1:10/ MT 2:1). Israel becomes a people in a place.

---

2. WALTER BRUEGGEMANN, THE COVENANTED SELF: EXPLORATIONS IN LAW AND COVENANT (Minneapolis: Fortress, 1999), 87.

3. ELLEN F. DAVIS, SCRIPTURE, CULTURE AND AGRICULTURE: AN AGRARIAN READING (Cambridge: Cambridge University Press, 2008), 73.

4. David E. Klemm, *Material grace: The paradox of property and possession, in* HAVING: PROPERTY AND POSSESSION IN RELIGIOUS AND SOCIAL LIFE (William Schweiker & Charles Mathewes eds., Grand Rapids: Eerdmans, 2004), 222.

5. Laurie J. Braaten, *Earth community in Hosea 2, in* THE EARTH STORY IN THE PSALMS AND THE PROPHETS, (Norman C. Habel ed., Sheffield: Sheffield Academic Press, 2001), 185–203, 201.

Second, according to the divine land grant of Numbers 33, God's gift of the land to Abraham's descendants is parcelled out "according to your families . . . according to the tribes of your fathers you shall inherit" (33:54).[6] The allocation of land under Joshua has the effect of identifying a specific family and its descendants with a particular plot of land, promoting rootedness and affinity. The division of land is by lot, although care was taken to ensure a degree of equity (Numbers 33:54; Joshua 17:14–18). This means that although everyone in Israel has access to land, there is no attempt to create absolute equality with regard to land because this is impossible to achieve. One plot of land might contain gold while another might benefit from a trade route that allows a farmer to sell his vegetables. Every piece of land has advantages and disadvantages, and each family has to make the best of what they have been given.

One of the effects of demarcating land into tribal groups and extended families is that a geographical area can be referred to either by its place name or by the name of the clan or subclan that lives there. Bethlehem is the name of a town, but it is also a place where a clan lives. The identification of family and land is so close that under the jubilee legislation of Leviticus 25 (see further, below), land that has been alienated from the original family as a result of hardship will revert to them every 50 years. The jubilee legislation equates "family" with "property": in the year of jubilee, "each of you shall return to his *property* and each of you shall return to his *family*" (Leviticus 25:10). Family and land are often described in parallel (e.g., "they oppress a man and his house [i.e., his family], a man and his inheritance'; Micah 2:2). Legal challenges regarding property are made with explicit reference to the family. Thus, the legal demand of the daughters of Zelophehad for their father's inheritance is prefaced by a genealogical statement (Numbers 27:1). In biblical Israel, "a [family] name exists as long as it is attached to land" (see also Deuteronomy 25:5–10).[7] The identification of particular families with particular plots of land means that the appropriate person for buying back land that has been rented out to someone else is the next of kin (Leviticus 25:25). This is known as redemption of land, and it keeps property within the family that would otherwise have been alienated.

Finally, we learn that each Israelite (Numbers 36:7) and tribe (Numbers 36:9) is to "cleave" (*yidhbequ*) to his or her inheritance. This is the same verb (*dabhaq*) used in Genesis 2:24 to describe the husband who "cleaves" (*wedhabhaq*) to his wife. It suggests that the people's relationship with the land is comparable to "one-flesh" intimacy between man and wife. This has, of course, profound implications for

---

6. This command is said to be given to the Exodus generation that left Egypt, prior to the conquest of Canaan, although the actual allocation of the land itself is not described as taking place until after the conquest, in respect of the subsequent generation (Joshua 14–19).

7. JACOB MILGROM, NUMBERS (Philadelphia: The Jewish Publication Society, 1990), 231.

land management: people deal with land appropriately when they have deep knowledge of it. The reverse is also true, and so in the biblical materials, misbehavior on the part of the people affects the land. Just as adultery threatens a marital relationship, so violence, idolatry, and sexual misconduct on the part of the Israelites causes the land to "vomit" them out (Leviticus 20:22). When the people are separated from the land in the form of exile, the experience will be like a divorce or the death of a spouse (cf. Lamentations 1:1).

B. Mirror, mirror

The relationship between the Israelites and the promised land is similar to that between humanity and the environment. This is not surprising since the Bible grounds both in divine ownership and the creation narrative. In addition, I argued in Chapter 5 that there is a parallel between God's speech in Genesis 1:26 which creates a chosen species, that is, humanity, and God's speech in Genesis 15 which creates a chosen people: Abraham and his descendants. The parallel exists because both humanity and Israel have a vocation that involves representing God to others. Humanity uniquely represents God to the rest of creation, and the descendants of Abraham uniquely represent God to the rest of humanity.

First, the close relationship between the Israelites and the promised land mirrors the close connection between humanity (*adam*) and the earth (*adamah*; Genesis 2:7; see Chapter 5). Second, the allocation to the families of Israel of specific parcels of land parallels the "planting" of humanity in the forest in Eden (Genesis 2:8; see Chapter 5). Both are established by God in a personalized place. Third, we noted above that the rental value of rural land depends on there being people to work the land. This parallels the position in Genesis 2:5 which states that "no herb of the field had yet sprung up—for . . . there was no man to till the ground." Agricultural land *needs* humanity in order to develop. Just as humanity and the environment shape one another in a relationship of mutual nurture, so do the people of Israel and the promised land. Finally, there is a parallel between humanity's mission to master the earth (*ha'aretz*) in Genesis 1:28 and Israel's mission to master the promised land (*eretz Kenaan*; e.g., Joshua 21:2). From this perspective, Israel's activity in Canaan is a microcosm of "the whole human project on the earth"[8] (see Chapter 5). These parallels are important because they remind us of the wider story within which the biblical land laws made sense. It also reminds us that the biblical laws which regulate the relationship between the Israelites and the promised land are relevant, in some respects, to the relationship between humanity and the environment.

To summarize, Israelites and promised land go together in biblical law. Both people and land have similar characteristics: both are personally identified with God, both belong to God, and accordingly, both have holy status. Biblical Israel

---

8. Davis, Scripture, Culture and Agriculture, p. 60.

is, of course, unique, but a close identification between people and land is not unknown in English legal history. Bell notes that the "basic and original meaning [of property] had been in reference to a *characteristic of* a person, so that when first applied to land during the 1700s, it was understood that property in land was indicative of the social position of the individual who owned it."[9]

III. PEOPLE, LAND, AND NARRATIVE

Narrative holds together the chosen people and the promised land. The divine allocation of land to Israel in Numbers 34 and Joshua 14–19 means that it is impossible to think about the relationship between people and land apart from the story of how that land was acquired. Israel's possession of the promised land made sense in the light of three things: (1) God's original creation, (2) the call of Abraham, and (3) Israel's vocation to bless the rest of humanity. As a result, land has a crucial role to play in biblical law because uniquely among all forms of property, land embodies the story of Israel.

A. Land as a network of memories

A classic example of how narrative binds together people and land is seen in Deuteronomy 26:1–15. This describes the ritual offering of the first fruits of the land by the Israelite worshipper, who also makes the following ritual declaration:

> And you shall make response before the LORD your God, "A wandering Aramean was my father; and he went down into Egypt and sojourned there, few in number; and there he became a nation, great, mighty, and populous ... and the LORD brought us out of Egypt with a mighty hand and an outstretched arm, with great terror, with signs and wonders; and he brought us into this place and gave us this land, a land flowing with milk and honey." (Deuteronomy 26:5, 8–9; *Moses speaking*)

Although the ritual context of this declaration may seem strange to us, English legal historians and even modern lawyers can recognize what is going on. First, we see that establishing title to land—like establishing title to anything—means telling a story. This is familiar to modern property lawyers. Attwood argues that "a good deal of story-telling ... concerns the origins of things, among the most important of which are property."[10] Even a contemporary institution such as the Land Registry, which registers title to land in England and Wales, relies in the

---

9. Duran Bell, *The structure of rights in the context of private property*, J. Socio-Economics 24, 608–21, 608 (1995).

10. Bain Attwood, *The Law of the Land or the law of the land? History, law and narrative in a settler society*, History Compass 2, 1–30, 2 (2004).

first instance on memory and narrative to create an administrative archive. Registration codifies and reconstitutes narrative.[11] Second, the ritual declaration can be understood by modern land lawyers as a "narrative construction of title,"[12] an account of how ownership came to be vested in a particular person. Title to land in biblical Israel—as in English legal history—is shown to depend on "networks of organic or practical memory."[13] Deuteronomy 26:5–10 keeps these pathways alive and roots "the place of land in local memory."[14] Third, the ritual declaration can also be seen as a kind of "juridical history" which reads the past in such a way as to construct an approved legal present.[15] The recital does not simply state a claim; it also legitimizes it. The story of divine initiative establishes title as against other inhabitants of the land. Fourth, the collective memory of Deuteronomy 26:5–10 juxtaposes the dramatic and highly visual events of the Exodus with the gift of land (Deuteronomy 26:8–9). In English legal history, land grants were sometimes accompanied by dramatic symbolic acts which impressed the grant on the memory of all those present.[16]

Finally, the declaration in Deuteronomy 26 is an example of how an entire nation came to acquire land. Although Israel is unique in claiming to receive its land as a direct gift from God, it remains the case that "all nations engage in telling highly coloured stories about their origins."[17] Sometimes we even find examples of countries revising their stories in order to provide a more satisfactory account. Such has recently been the case with Australia. This is because Australia's "property origins" story, which denied Aboriginal people rights to land, was felt to be in conflict with its identity as a liberal state. This prompted the High Court of Australia to find a new way of reading the country's conventional narrative, which was based on a belief that the colonized land was *terra nullius* (meaning "no-one's land"). This led to the watershed *Mabo* ruling,[18] which recognized indigenous rights to land and provided Australia with "a newly redemptive, liberal myth narrative."[19] Changing Australia's origin story led to a different understanding of the relationship between people and land. The relationship between people, land, and narrative is thus powerful and formative in both ancient and modern times.

---

11. Alain Pottage, *The Measure of Land*, MOD. L. REV. 57, 361–84, 361 (1994).
12. Ibid., 363.
13. Ibid., 361.
14. Ibid., 364.
15. Attwood, *Law of the Land*, p. 2.
16. Pottage, *Measure of Land*, p. 361.
17. Attwood, *Law of the Land*, p. 2.
18. Mabo v. Queensland (n. 2) [1992] COMMONWEALTH LAW REPORTS, 1.
19. Attwood, *Law of the Land*, p. 1.

B. Land as a network of relationships

Stories about land are important because they determine how it is used. In biblical Israel, "land-as-narrative" creates a network of relationships: (1) vertically, with God; (2) horizontally, with the needy; and (3) temporally, with past ancestors and future descendants.

First, land-as-narrative creates a vertical relationship between the Israelites and God. This is reflected in the climax of the ritual declaration in Deuteronomy 26:10:

> And behold, now I bring the first of the fruit of the ground, which thou, O LORD, hast given me. *(Moses speaking)*

This indicates the Israelites' dependence upon God. The different ecosystem of Canaan (mountains and rain) as opposed to Egypt (flat fields and irrigation) meant that the Israelites lived closer to the edge, agriculturally speaking, than they did in Egypt. As Davis observes, "[The Israelites] had only the slightest margin for negligence, ignorance or error. The Bible as we have it could not have been written beside the irrigation canals of Babylon or the perennially flooding Nile, any more than it could have emerged from the vast fertile plains of the North American continent. For revelation addresses the necessities of a place as well as a people."[20]

Second, land-as-narrative also creates horizontal relationships with those in need. In Deuteronomy 26:5–9, declaration of title results in giving away the first fruits to those who do not have access to their own agricultural land:

> [A]nd you shall rejoice in all the good which the LORD your God has given to you and to your house[hold], you, and the Levite, and the sojourner who is among you. (Deuteronomy 26:11; *Moses speaking*)

This was no mean sacrifice: there was always a risk of no further produce. But because the land was received as a gift, the fruit of the land had to be given away as a gift.

Finally, land-as-narrative creates a network of temporal relationships with the descendants of Abraham, past and future. The ritual declaration of Deuteronomy 26:5–10 begins by acknowledging the speaker's descent from the patriarchs. This means that the individual Israelite holds the land not simply on his own behalf but as part of a line. It also means that "[the land] is never the property of some kin unit in some point of time, but rather belongs to all units in all points of time in the past, present and future."[21] Biblical law thus shows "a relationship of multi-generational commitment and nurture."[22] From the perspective of

---

20. Davis, Scripture, Culture and Agriculture, p. 26.
21. Meir Malul, Knowledge, Control and Sex: Studies in biblical thought, culture and worldview (Tel Aviv-Jaffa: Archaeological Centre Publication, 2002), 452.
22. Davis, Scripture, Culture and Agriculture, p. 67.

cognitive anthropology, this means that the allotted portion or *nachalah* can be seen as "superorganic in the sense that it is not tied to any individual . . . but to the whole body of individuals—not only the present ones, but also the past and future members."[23] It means that no individual member ever has absolute right to the land.[24] The promised land is "an everlasting possession" (*achuzzat olam*; Genesis 17:8). As a result "no one of the individuals—who are all ephemeral, temporary, momentary—can claim to own any piece of [the 'everlasting'] property and the right to dispose of it in any way he likes."[25] Selling land so that it can never be redeemed under the jubilee legislation is like selling ancestors. Likewise, buying up large tracts of land is wrong because there is "no personal attachment to the soil on the part of the landowners."[26] This approach to land is condemned by prophets such as Micah:

> Woe to those who devise wickedness
> and work evil upon their beds!
> When the morning dawns, they perform it,
> because it is in the power of their hand.
> They covet fields, and seize them;
> and houses, and take them away;
> they oppress a man and his house,
> a man and his inheritance. (Micah 2:1–2; *God speaking*)

This understanding of the *nachalah* explains the conflict between Naboth, an Israelite farmer, and Ahab, an Israelite king:

> Now Naboth the Jezreelite had a vineyard in Jezreel, beside the palace of Ahab king of Samaria. And after this Ahab said to Naboth, "Give me your vineyard, that I may have it for a vegetable garden, because it is near my house; and I will give you a better vineyard for it; or, if it seems good to you, I will give you its value in money." But Naboth said to Ahab, "The LORD forbid that I should give [up to] you the inheritance of my fathers." (1 Kings 21:1–3)

For Ahab, land is a symbol of status and power and a means of accumulating capital. The valley of Jezreel was well-known for its fertile land; indeed, the word Jezreel means "God sows." To Ahab, Naboth's vineyard was nothing more than a piece of real estate that happened to be a prime spot for redevelopment. For Naboth, by contrast, land is a symbol of the ancestral promise and the place of encounter with God. His tart reply—"The LORD forbid that I should give [up to]

---

23. Malul, Knowledge, Control and Sex, p. 452.
24. Ibid.
25. Ibid.
26. Gunther H. Wittenberg, The Vision of Land in Jeremiah 32, in The Earth Story in the Psalms and the Prophets (Norman C. Habel ed., The Earth Bible, 5 vols.; Sheffield: Sheffield Academic Press, 2001), vol. IV, 129–42, 133.

you the inheritance of my fathers"—powerfully expresses "the theology of covenantal economics."[27] Naboth speaks "for the whole community-through-time of those who experience God's blessing as they live and work this one small piece of land . . . In complete contrast to Ahab, Naboth has a complex notion of property ownership."[28] Had Naboth agreed to the king, he would have effectively eliminated his own family. This is mirrored in the divine punishment delivered to Ahab by Elijah, namely, that every member of Ahab's family will be wiped out ("[God] will utterly sweep you away, and will cut off from Ahab every male, bond or free, in Israel . . ."; 1 Kings 21:21). This reflects the fate of Naboth's own family, if and when Ahab takes the land.

The standoff between Naboth and Ahab can be summed up as a clash of worldviews: land-as-covenant *versus* land-as-commodity. The conflict is symbolized by Ahab's plans to turn Naboth's vineyard into a vegetable garden. Vineyards are also an eloquent symbol of God's covenant relationship with Israel (Isaiah 5:1–7) and of establishing Israelites in the land (Micah 4:4). Wanting to turn a vineyard into a vegetable patch is a graphic illustration of the way in which Ahab trivializes the significance of Naboth's land and shows his contempt for the original divine allocation. Vineyards are "the work of decades, not a summer . . . a sign of permanence, an investment in the future of a place and a people."[29] We saw in Chapter 5 that Deuteronomy 20:10–20 forbade cutting down fruit trees in wartime, partly because fruit trees take generations to grow. Like the vineyard, fruit trees symbolize long-term commitment and future generations. It was precisely this sense of responsibility to previous and future generations that Ahab lacked.

In the end, the monarchy subverts Naboth's claim to his land by foul means. Naboth is framed for a capital offense and executed, aided, and abetted by his local townsmen (1 Kings 21:11–13; JPS). Here again, we see the interdependence of people and land. When the original divine allocation of land is subverted, the result is injustice among the people. Perverting the land perverts the people. "Misuse of the gift of the land, including maltreatment of those who work the soil, will ultimately undo every political structure, no matter how sophisticated, stable, and powerful it appears to be."[30] Treating land as a cash commodity results in false witnesses, judicial murder, and a community that turns upon itself. "It is not possible to subtract the essential economic functions from a community and expect mutual trust, goodwill, and aid among neighbours to remain."[31]

---

27. Davis, Scripture, Culture and Agriculture, p. 111.
28. Ibid.
29. Ibid., 112.
30. Ibid., 121.
31. Ibid., 114.

Having considered the basic assumptions underlying biblical land law, we are now in a position to consider some practical examples, including the laws of inheritance and disinheritance, as well as the spectrum of biblical Sabbath laws which have major implications for land use. This will be the focus of the rest of this chapter.

IV. FAVORED SONS, REBELLIOUS SONS

We begin with the biblical laws of inheritance and disinheritance. The modern law of property distinguishes between (1) testate succession, which is the division of property according to a will made during the owner's lifetime; and (2) intestate succession, which is the division of property according to law in the absence of a will. There is evidence of both these practices in the biblical laws of inheritance. We will see that Deuteronomy 21:15–17 approximates to testate succession while Numbers 27:1–11 approximates to what we would nowadays call intestate succession.

First, we consider the law in Deuteronomy 21:15–17, as follows:

If a man has two wives, the one loved and the other disliked [or "unloved"; JPS], and they have borne him children, both the loved and the disliked, and if the firstborn son is hers that is disliked, then on the day when he assigns his possessions as an inheritance to his sons, he may not treat the son of the loved as the firstborn in preference to the son of the disliked, who is the first-born, but he shall acknowledge the first-born, the son of the disliked, by giving him a double portion of all that he has . . . . *(Moses speaking)*

This approximates to testate succession because it refers to "the day when [the father] assigns his possessions as an inheritance to his sons" (Deuteronomy 21:16). Deuteronomy 21:15–17 also illustrates the practice of primogeniture (seniority of birth) in biblical law because it gives the eldest son (the firstborn) a double share of the father's inheritance. This contrasts with much of English legal history, where the firstborn son was entitled to the entire estate,[32] although some have argued that the Hebrew phrase for "a double portion" actually means two-thirds on account of its idiomatic usage in Zechariah 13:8. The purpose of the preferential share may have been to reimburse the firstborn heir for the duties he has to perform as head of the household upon the father's death. These might have included burial costs for the father, caring for his widow in her old age, and general "kinsman" (*go'el*) obligations, such as those relating to the redemption of land. However, although the eldest son is favored in regard to the inheritance, this favoritism does not carry over to an anointing for leadership.

---

32. J. H. Baker, An Introduction to English Legal History (Bath: Butterworths, 4th ed. 2002), 267–68.

Indeed, often the firstborn was overlooked in favor of the anointing of a younger son (e.g., David, the youngest of Jesse's sons, in 1 Samuel 16:13).[33]

Deuteronomy 21:15–17 also recognizes that fathers were tempted to give the preferential share to someone other than the firstborn. This makes sense against the background of the patriarchal narratives which recount the complete disinheritance of the first two generations of firstborn sons; Ishmael (Genesis 17:18–27) and Esau (Genesis 25:27–34). We also find, in Genesis 49:3–4, that Jacob refuses to give a preferential share to his firstborn, Reuben (Genesis 35:22) and gives it, instead, through Ephraim and Menasseh, to Joseph. Jacob's favoritism could, however, be justified in spite of Deuteronomy 21:15–17 because his reason was not that he disliked his wife but because Reuben had sexual relations with Jacob's concubine, Bilhah. So although removing the preferential share from a firstborn who proved unfit for family leadership may be justified, Deuteronomy 21:15–17 insists that the father in a polygamous marriage should not remove it for the relatively trivial reason of disliking the firstborn's mother.[34] In the New Testament, the issue is not, as it is in Deuteronomy 21:15-17, "who is entitled to inherit the promised land?," but "who are the legitimate heirs of the covenant?"[35]

Deuteronomy 21:15–17 presumes that property passes from fathers to sons. There are sound practical reasons why property could not have passed to both sons *and* daughters. In a simple case, if a ten-acre farm is divided among two sons and two girls, for example, each child will receive two and a half acres each. If one of the sons marries a woman who is in the same position, she will bring her two and a half acres into the marriage as well. The problem is that the husband's land is in one place, and his wife's land is in another location. Looking after the land would then involve a great deal of travel if, say, the properties are 10 miles apart; this is inefficient. The problems are multiplied if both sons *and* daughters continue to inherit in the following generation. The husband who marries a wife who also inherits under similar circumstances now has *four* different pieces of land to manage in four different locations. The result is chaos with tiny parcels of land in many different places because the man's inheritance has been diluted by his sister's inheritance. Consequently, for land to be used efficiently, it must be the case that *either* all men inherit *or* all women. In biblical

---

33. *See generally* ROGER SYRÉN, THE FORSAKEN FIRST-BORN: A STUDY OF A RECURRENT MOTIF IN THE PATRIARCHAL NARRATIVES, JOURNAL FOR THE STUDY OF THE OLD TESTAMENT SUPPLEMENT SERIES 133 (Sheffield: Sheffield University Press, 1993) for an exploration of the recurring motif of the "forsaken firstborn" in the patriarchal narratives.

34. BERNARD S. JACKSON, ESSAYS ON HALAKHAH IN THE NEW TESTAMENT (Leiden: Brill, 2008), 139–40.

35. *See* JACKSON, ESSAYS ON HALAKHAH, pp. 139ff which considers the role of Deuteronomy 21:15–17 in the parable of the prodigal son in Luke 15:11–32.

society, the practice was that sons inherited. This, inter alia, reflected the fact that men had primary responsibility for physically working the land.[36]

A. The emergence of feminist jurisprudence?

In contrast to Deuteronomy 21:15–17, which approximates to testate succession, the law in Numbers 27:1–11 approximates to what we would nowadays call intestate succession.

Numbers 27:1–11 deals with the problem of an Israelite man, Zelophehad, who died for his part in the wilderness rebellion (Numbers 13:25ff) but without leaving a male heir. The position differs from that of Deuteronomy 21:15–17 in which there is at least one male heir. Zelophehad's daughters petition Moses to inherit their father's property:

> Why should the name of our father be taken away from his family, because he had no son? Give to us a possession (*ahuzzah*) among our father's brethren. (Numbers 27:4)

The daughters' appeal does nothing to disturb the presumption that sons should inherit. Their request is that they should be able to inherit in the absence of sons, instead of the property being dispersed among Zelophehad's nearest male kin. The daughters' petition is emphatically vindicated by God; an emphasis captured in the King James Version, as follows:

> The daughters of Zelophehad *speak right: thou shalt surely give* [infinitive form] them a possession of an inheritance among their father's brethren; and *thou shalt cause* the inheritance of their father to pass unto them. (Numbers 27:7; KJV)

Numbers 27:1–11 thus approximates to intestate succession because here we see that customary rules and divine revelation are used to resolve the problem of inheritance, irrespective of the owner's personal wishes.

However, this is not the end of the matter. In Numbers 36, the Josephites (family heads of the clan to which Zelophehad belonged; Numbers 36:1) are concerned that if the daughters receive the inheritance but marry outside the tribe, the land will be absorbed into their husband's family and thus into another tribe. The jubilee laws (see below) do not address this problem (Numbers 36:4) because the reversion of the jubilee applies only to land that has been sold, not land that has been inherited (Leviticus 25). Unless the ruling in the case of the

---

36. Michael Schluter, Family, in JUBILEE MANIFESTO (Michael Schluter & John Ashcroft eds., Leicester: InterVarsity Press/Jubilee Centre, 2005), 154–74, 163–65; and cf. James Riddell, Jeswald Salacuse & David Tabachnik, *The National Land Law of Zaire and Indigenous Tenure in Central Badandu, Zaire*, Land Tenure Center Paper 92 (University of Wisconsin-Madison: Land Tenure Centre, 1987) for examples of some of the problems that arise under matrilineal succession in a West African context.

daughters of Zelophehad is qualified in some way, there is a danger that the land will be permanently alienated. This will upset the original divine allocation.

The Josephites' concern is also legitimated by God in somewhat similar terms to the daughters:

> And Moses commanded the people of Israel according to the word of the LORD, saying, "The tribe of the sons of Joseph is right. This is what the LORD commands concerning the daughters of Zelophehad, 'Let them marry whom they think best; only, they shall marry within the family of the tribe of their father. The inheritance of the people of Israel shall not be transferred from one tribe to another; for every one of the people of Israel shall cleave to the inheritance of the tribe of his fathers.'" (Numbers 36:5–7)

If the daughters wish to inherit their father's land, they are required to marry within the tribe. Presumably they are also free to marry outside their tribe, providing they do not also wish to inherit the land. The daughters become, as it were, temporary guardians of their father's property until a male heir inherits it. It is a kind of levirate marriage (cf. Deuteronomy 25:5–10, see further Chapter 10), although "instead of a wife marrying the deceased's kin, the daughters marry the deceased's kin."[37]

The daughters are hailed as heroines in some feminist circles because their request makes them the first innovators in the history of biblical law. However, there is a problem with seeing the daughters of Zelophehad as proto-feminists, not least because their request is framed in terms of the injustice done to their *father* (Numbers 36:4a), not the sisterhood. Some commentators are apt to see the limitation of Numbers 36 as an attempt by the patriarchal system to silence female voices.[38] But the instincts of both the daughters and the Josephites are very similar. Both are concerned with the problem of how to keep name (*shem*) and possession (*ahuzzah*) together in line with the original divine allocation. In this sense, both daughters and Josephites are on the same side. As a result, it is not hard to see why both received divine legitimation. Of course, it is possible to read the daughters' support for the original distribution of property as evidence of patriarchal bias on their part and a sign, perhaps, that the daughters were captive to patriarchal hegemony. On the other hand, it is far more likely that the daughters were motivated by entirely different cultural concerns to those of modern feminists and that their instinct to preserve their father's name was ultimately in their own best interests.

---

37. Dora Rudo Mbuwayesango, *Can daughters be sons? The daughters of Zelophehad in patriarchal and imperial society*, in RELATING TO THE TEXT: INTERDISCIPLINARY AND FORM-CRITICAL INSIGHTS ON THE BIBLE (Timothy J. Sandoval & Carleen Mandolfo eds., London: Continuum, 2003), 251–62, 261.

38. E.g., JIONE HAVEA, ELUSIONS OF CONTROL: BIBLICAL LAW ON THE WORDS OF WOMEN (Atlanta: Society of Biblical Literature, 2003), 54–59.

B. Divine revelation, human need

Together, Numbers 27:1–11 and Numbers 36 have important implications for our understanding of biblical law. They remind us that the rules promulgated as part of biblical law are not complete (see Chapter 1) nor were they ever complete, even for the Sinai generation.

The daughters challenge the presumption in customary law that they could not inherit their father's land; and they are successful. Customary law is negotiated in the light of divine revelation. There is a loose parallel here with the dynamic nature of adjudication in modern liberal society put forward by Ronald Dworkin, in which rules and principles are negotiated to produce a just outcome.[39] Yet, at the same time, the story of Zelophehad's daughters shows us that divine revelation is itself subject to continual inquiry. Nor is it immune to the need for further clarification and, where necessary, qualification. The law in Numbers 27:1–11 is qualified in Numbers 36. The Josephites are concerned that an interpretation of the divine revelation in Numbers 27:7–11 which allows the daughters to inherit *and* marry outside the tribe would conflict with the subsequent narrative development of the divine land grant in Numbers 33. The Josephites' legal reasoning shows us, once again, how law is interpreted in the light of narrative (see Chapter 1).

The Josephites' approach to biblical jurisprudence is confirmed by God in Numbers 36. The right interpretation of biblical law is the one that is consistent with God's purposes, as seen in the story of Israel as a whole, which includes the narrative of the divine land grant in Numbers 33. Again, this is not too far removed from Dworkin's interpretative approach which sees the right interpretation of law and legal theory as that which, inter alia, presents the law in its morally most appealing light.[40] Biblical law, like divine revelation in general, is understood in the light of its point or purpose, as disclosed by the biblical narrative as a whole.

Some scholars have argued that Numbers 27:1–11 is evidence that Torah "supplied only the groundwork on which the complete structure [of law] should be built."[41] However, we should question whether "building a complete structure" is a feasible ambition for biblical law or indeed any legal system. To speak of a complete structure implies that it is possible for us, as a matter of practical legal reasoning, to identify and articulate in advance all the possible situations in which a norm might be called into play. This means anticipating all the possible circumstances in which a modification may or may not be necessary. But as

---

39. Ronald Dworkin, Law's Empire (Oxford: Hart, 1986).

40. Ibid., 225–38.

41. Tal Ilan, *The Daughters of Zelophehad and Women's Inheritance: The Biblical injunction and its outcome, in* Exodus to Deuteronomy: A Feminist Companion to the Bible (Second Series) (Athalya Brenner ed., Sheffield: Sheffield Academic Press, 2000), 176–86, 178.

Numbers 36 indicates, this is hardly a very plausible view either of biblical law or of law in general. As we saw in Chapter 1, every legal system has to deal with the fact that "in many contexts, our knowledge of what constitutes appropriate behaviour depends upon a background of understandings that we could not fully articulate in advance of the situations that call them into play,"[42] including those situations that might form the basis for changing our understanding of a rule.

Instead of a complete structure of biblical law, we should perhaps think of an ongoing dialectic between divine revelation and situations of human need that require wisdom. This need may be met by further divine wisdom, in the case of oracular consultations, or divinely inspired wisdom, in the case of inspired human rulings (see Chapter 4). This dialectic—between divine revelation and situations of human need requiring wisdom—is exactly what we find in Numbers 27:1-11, where the problem is resolved on the basis of direct divine wisdom.

Seen from this perspective, the daughters do, of course, successfully challenge and overturn customary law, but they are not challengers of divine revelation. Instead, they are its facilitators because they present a situation of human need that is met by further divine wisdom (Numbers 27:8–11). It is therefore fitting that the daughters should be described in the Babylonian Talmud as "wise women" and "exegetes" of Torah (Baba Bathra 119b). Similarly, the response of the Josephites in Numbers 36 underlines the dynamic, incremental, nature of Torah. The Josephites want to reconcile their ethical presuppositions regarding the priority of the land grant (which is that "no inheritance should pass permanently outside the tribe") with the ruling in the case of the daughters ("daughters can inherit land in the absence of sons"). Again, biblical law develops in response to the human need for wisdom.

C. Wealth warning

We turn from the biblical laws of inheritance to those of disinheritance. As hinted in the case of Reuben, above, misbehavior on the part of a potential heir could result in the loss of part or all of the inheritance. Notably, the law of primogeniture in Deuteronomy 21:15–17 is followed by Deuteronomy 21:18–21, which concerns the identification and execution of "a stubborn and rebellious son." This literary juxtaposition suggests that in biblical law, a rebellious son could forfeit his inheritance. There are overlaps here with Deuteronomy 21:18–21. In my view, Deuteronomy 21:18–21 presents a narrative stereotype not only of a bad son but also of a bad heir who engages in recidivist apostate behavior ("This our son is stubborn and rebellious, he will not obey our voice; he is a glutton and a drunkard"; verse 20).[43] The charge of being "a glutton and a drunkard"

---

42. N. E. SIMMONDS, CENTRAL ISSUES IN JURISPRUDENCE (London: Sweet & Maxwell, 2002), 148.

43. JONATHAN P. BURNSIDE, THE SIGNS OF SIN: SERIOUSNESS OF OFFENCE IN BIBLICAL LAW, JOURNAL FOR THE STUDY OF THE OLD TESTAMENT SUPPLEMENT SERIES 364 (London: Continuum International, 2003), 71–78.

safeguards the son from malicious prosecution by his parents by establishing a different form of proof that can be verified by judges outside the family, in this case, the elders (verse 20).[44]

This is broadly consistent with the practice of disinheritance elsewhere in the ancient Near East (ANE). According to a wide range of ANE documents, including adoption and inheritance texts, children who disobey their parents in certain specified ways can lose their status as sons and heirs.[45] For example, the Laws of Hammurabi (LH) §§168–169 show that fathers had the power to disinherit their sons. They also indicate that this power could not be exercised in a capricious manner and was subject to judicial investigation, while the son himself had to be a repeat offender. This is similar to Deuteronomy 21:18–21, giving further support to the view that this biblical law is concerned with disinheritance.

Disinheritance in the Bible was not restricted to individuals but could also be applied to the people as a whole. The covenant between God and Israel stipulated the loss of land for disobedience (e.g., Deuteronomy 28:63). Jeremiah 3:19 crystallizes the key expectations that God had of Israel:

> I thought how I would set you [Israel] among my sons, and give you a pleasant land, a heritage most beauteous of all nations. And I thought you would call me, "My Father," and would not turn from following me. (*God speaking*)

It is clear from this that Israel is (1) adopted as a son, (2) promised an inheritance, and (3) expected not to rebel against his adoptive father. The condition that children should not rebel was a common clause in ANE adoption contracts, especially if the father had bequeathed a large or a valuable inheritance.[46] If the conditions laid down in the adoption agreement were broken, the inheritance was first to go. The conditional nature of Israel's inheritance—the promised land—is stressed throughout Deuteronomy. The book emphasises that obedience is necessary to obtain the inheritance in three main ways: first, by Moses's failure to enter the land (Deuteronomy 1:37); second, by the death of the Exodus generation in the wilderness (Deuteronomy 1:32-35); and third, by Moses's statement that entry into the land and continued occupation is dependent on obedience (Deuteronomy 4:1). Being an obedient son is central to inheritance, both individually and corporately. No one has an unconditional right to the land.[47]

---

44. Ibid., 68–71.

45. Joseph Fleishman, *Offences against parents punishable by death: Towards a socio-legal interpretation of Ex. 21:15, 17, in* THE JEWISH LAW ANNUAL VOL. X (Boston: The Institute of Jewish Law, 1992), 7–37.

46. Janet L. R. Melnyk, *When Israel was a child: Ancient Near Eastern Adoption Formulas and the Relationship between God and Israel, in* HISTORY AND INTERPRETATION, Journal for the Study of the Old Testament Supplement Series 173 (M. Patrick Graham et al., eds.; Sheffield: Sheffield Academic Press, 1993), 245–59, 251.

47. BURNSIDE, SIGNS OF SIN, 71–77.

To summarize, biblical law is familiar both with testate and intestate succession in its rules for inheritance. It is also familiar with the disinheritance of property, which seems to apply both to individuals and to the nation as a whole.

V. "RESTONOMICS"

One of the most important aspects of people and land in biblical law is the way in which the people are regularly required to suspend their claims upon the land. This is another logical outworking of the belief in divine ownership: if God alone owns the land, no single person has an unconditional right to it. The principal way in which biblical Israel routinely relinquished its claims upon the land is found in the biblical Sabbath laws. These include the laws relating to (1) the weekly Sabbath, which provides for one day's rest in seven for both people and land; (2) the sabbatical year, which provides for one year's rest for the land; and (3) the jubilee year, which provides for a further period of rest for the land every 50 years. We could call the provision of regular rest for people and land in the midst of economic cycles of production "restonomics."

The sabbatical and jubilee years are both extensions to, and more intense forms of, the weekly Sabbath. The sabbatical year is a sort of "Super-Sabbath," which I shall call "Sabbath-plus" to differentiate it from the regular Sabbath, while the jubilee year begins at the end of the seventh sabbatical year. It is another sort of Super-Sabbath which I shall call "Sabbath-squared" to differentiate it from the weekly Sabbath and the sabbatical year. The Sabbath laws thus create a spectrum of Sabbaths, ranging from the weekly Sabbath to the jubilee year. The most important laws for our understanding of people and land are the sabbatical and jubilee years, and these will occupy most of the rest of this chapter. (The implications of the sabbatical and jubilee years for social welfare are considered in Chapter 7).

A. Race memory

We saw in Chapter 5 that the institution of the Sabbath is presented as the climax of the story of universal creation (Genesis 1:1–2:4):

> And on the seventh day God finished his work which he had done, and he rested on the seventh day from all his work which he had done. So God blessed the seventh day and hallowed it, because on it God rested from all his work which he had done in creation. (Genesis 2:2–3).

The number seven was thus not a "magic number" for the Hebrews as it was for other peoples but rather a "holy number" because it evoked the seven days of creation. Observing the weekly Sabbath law requires "a memory that stretches back to the creation of the world."[48] Holding onto and acting upon this memory is not always easy, especially when Israel is under the pressure of fear. This includes the anxiety that human survival or productivity will be jeopardized as a result of Sabbath observance. Weekly Sabbath observance released people and land from work (Exodus 20:8–11) and reminded them that the land is something over which they must relinquish control:

> Remember the sabbath day, to keep it holy. Six days you shall labor, and do all your work; but the seventh day is a sabbath to the LORD your God; in it you shall not do any work, you, or your son, or your daughter, your manservant, or your maidservant, or your cattle, or the sojourner who is within your gates; for in six days the LORD made heaven and earth, the sea, and all that is in them, and rested the seventh day; therefore the LORD blessed the sabbath day and hallowed it. (Exodus 20:8–11; *God speaking*)

Consequently, the weekly Sabbath law reinforced Israel's worldview that all it has is a usufruct of property that belonged to God.

VI. "SABBATH-PLUS"

"Restonomics" meant not only "one day off in seven" but also "one *year* off in seven." This is the sabbatical year. The similarity between these sabbatical institutions is reinforced by the fact that they are proclaimed together. Interestingly, the law relating to the Sabbath year (Exodus 23:10–11) *precedes* that for the Sabbath day (Exodus 23:12) in the Covenant Code (Exodus 20:22/MT20: 19–22:33). In this context, it seems as though the sabbatical year was at least as important as the weekly Sabbath mentioned in the Decalogue:

> For six years you shall sow your land and gather in its yield; but the seventh year you shall let it rest and lie fallow, that the poor of your people may eat; and what they leave the wild beasts may eat. You shall do likewise with your vineyard, and with your olive orchard. (Exodus 23:10–11; *God speaking*)

> Six days you shall do your work, but on the seventh day you shall rest; that your ox and your ass may have rest, and the son of your bondmaid, and the alien, may be refreshed. (Exodus 23:12; *God speaking*)

There is a parallel between Sabbath day observance in the wilderness, when the people survived off an extra (double) portion of manna produced on the sixth day (Exodus 16:22) and Sabbath *year* observance in the *land*, when the people survived off the extra (albeit triple) portion produced during the sixth year (Leviticus 25:21). The Sabbath year can be characterized as "Sabbath-plus" to

---

48. Davis, Scripture, Culture and Agriculture, p. 79.

distinguish it from the weekly Sabbath, because it is a super-strength version of the Sabbath day. As with the Sabbath day, the sabbatical year makes it clear that "arable land is not for a moment private . . . [T]he seventh year simply clarifies what the land always is: God's domain."[49]

Significantly, it is *not* the people who are said to keep the sabbatical year but the *land*:

> in the seventh year there shall be a sabbath of solemn rest for the land, a sabbath to the LORD; you shall not sow your field or prune your vineyard. (Leviticus 25:4; *God speaking*)

The idea of "resting land," or a regular fallow year, is an important land management and environmental issue. There is a sense here in which the land, like the people, is in a relationship with God which is founded on some form of Sabbath observance. Like land, like people. Like the Sabbath day itself, the sabbatical year is rooted in the creation narrative. For example, Leviticus 25:6–7 states that:

> The sabbath of the land shall provide food for you (*lakhem leokhelah*), for yourself and for your male and female slaves and for your hired servant and the sojourner who lives with you; for your cattle also and for the beasts that are in your land all its yield shall be for food. (*God speaking*)

which, as Kawashima[50] points out, alludes to God's provision for human and beast in Genesis:

> Behold, I have given you every plant yielding seed which is upon the face of all the earth, and every tree with seed in its fruit; you shall have them for food (*lakhem yihyeh leokhelah*). (Genesis 1:29; *God speaking*)

The picture of Israelites and animals nibbling from a shared unworked food source (Leviticus 25:6–7) is manifestly Edenic and fecund. All creation is at rest and able to receive from its Creator without toil.

Leviticus 25:5 describes how the land should be left in "complete rest" (JPS) during the sabbatical year, with crops and vines growing as they pleased. The Hebrew phrase *innebhey nezirekha*, which is usually translated "your untrimmed vines," alludes to the Nazirite. This is the ordinary Israelite who chooses to refrain from certain behavior in order to "set himself apart for the LORD" (Numbers 6:2–8), thereby entering a state of ritual purity equalled only by the high priest (Exodus 28:36–38). The allusion suggests that the sabbatical year enables the land to enter into a degree of consecration that parallels the Nazirite and the high priest. To put it another way, it seems as though the "holy" properties of the

---

49. Ibid., 109.
50. Robert S. Kawashima, *The Jubilee year and the return of cosmic purity*, CATHOLIC BIBLICAL Q. 65, 370–89, 385 (2003).

Sabbath day (Genesis 2:3) are shared by the land itself throughout its sabbatical year. The holy status of the consecrated land is signified by the "untrimmed vines." Kawashima[51] sees the untrimmed vines as a metaphor for the land's holy status, but in my view, the association is primarily visual. There is a visual connection between the picture of a Nazirite who has an unkempt beard (Numbers 6:5) and the sight of straggly growth on the "face" of the land. This is not surprising: as we have seen repeatedly, land and people go together. If so, what we have here is an association between the law of the Nazirite and the sabbatical year. However, this is not expressed in terms of their underlying conceptual similarity (e.g., the "unworked" Nazirite is like the "unworked" grapes); rather, both have an underlying visual connection (straggly growth). If this is correct, we see once again that biblical law makes better sense in visual terms rather than as an abstract conceptual schema. Further support for this reading can be found in the parallel that Davis finds between the prohibition on cutting the edge of the field (Leviticus 19:9) and the edge of the human head and beard (Leviticus 19:27).[52] This too highlights the similarity between the male Israelite and the field. The farmer is "like" the farm.[53]

The use of "straggly growth" to communicate something about the status of land reminds us of the visual dimension of the law of property. As one modern geographer writes, "property requires forms of persuasive communication."[54] The power of "visual notices" cannot be underestimated.[55] The straggly growth of Leviticus 25:5 is a visual notice that persuasively reminds the Israelites that the land does not belong to them. In this way, even the countryside of biblical Israel told a story. Undressed vines were symbols that had the power to shape social relations. This is not as odd as it might sound. We can find examples in the English countryside. Blomley, for example, explores how the introduction of hedgerows in the sixteenth and early seventeenth centuries encouraged the enclosure movement and led to changes in the use of property in rural England. Hedgerows led to a shift away from traditional use rights such as gleanings and the "commons" towards exclusion and maintaining the private interests of property owners. Hawthorn hedges were "a form of organic barbed wire"[56] and became "the principal symbol of private ownership of land."[57] Hedges both kept people off the land and served as a visual reminder of the changes that were

---

51. Kawashima, *Jubilee year*, p. 384.
52. DAVIS, SCRIPTURE, CULTURE AND AGRICULTURE, p. 90.
53. Ibid., 91.
54. Nicholas Blomley, *Making private property: enclosure, common right and the work of hedges*, RURAL HIST. 18, 1–21, 13 (2007).
55. Ibid.
56. Ibid., 20.
57. Ibid., 13.

taking place in property ownership. Like Israelite vines, English hedges symbolized beliefs about property in culturally specific ways.

Finally, although the sabbatical year was a rest for the land, there is no specific reference to rest for the people. Of course, there is a rest for the people in the sense that if the land is at rest, then the people are freed from the need for intensive farming. They are only to harvest whatever the land "shall provide... for you" (25:6). In Leviticus 25:4–5, the paradigm case of reaping and harvesting refers to market activity rather than household activity. Even so, there is no indication in the text that the sabbatical year is meant to be a year off for the people. If the people are not supposed to engage in agricultural trade and are not supposed to rest either, then we should assume that the sabbatical year was an opportunity for the Israelites to engage in long-term investment that they might otherwise overlook, such as digging wells, planting trees, repairing fences, and repairing roads. These are all time-consuming tasks from which the Israelites would reap major benefits until the next sabbatical year. Of course, there is a sense in which this change of activity may itself be regarded as a rest because it does not characterize the Israelites' activity during nonsabbatical years. The sabbatical year may also create the necessity for forward planning in a hot climate where there may well be less inclination to plan ahead than in a colder climate.

To conclude, the sabbatical year is a more intense form of the weekly Sabbath, at least as far as the land is concerned.

VII. SQUARING THE SABBATH

The final sabbatical institution on the Sabbath spectrum is the jubilee year, which is reached as a result of counting "seven times seven years" (25:8). This is of great symbolic importance because the forty-ninth year is the square of the number seven. This means that if the sabbatical year can be described as "Sabbath-plus," then we can fairly describe the jubilee as "Sabbath-squared." It is a more intense form of Super-Sabbath than the sabbatical year because the jubilee does not only provide rest for land but also redemption. Given the importance of the jubilee year within biblical law, this section looks at a number of different aspects, including the primary functions of the jubilee, its contrast with Egyptian land tenure, and the relationship between law and narrative as seen in the Joseph cycle.

A. Family fortunes

The start of the jubilee was signalled by the sound of a ram's horn (*shofar*). This noise is associated with divine declarations of freedom, including Mount Sinai (Exodus 19:13), New Year's Day (Leviticus 23:24), and the day of future redemption (cf. 1 Corinthians 15:52). Similar proclamations of liberty are found elsewhere in the ANE, such as Mesopotamia where they were accompanied by the ceremonial raising of a golden torch.[58] One key difference is that whereas Israel's proclamation was supposed to take place every 49 years, Mesopotamian proclamations were random and coincided with the king's accession to the throne, although we cannot exclude the possibility of an additional cyclical liberty in Mesopotamia.[59] It is understandable that biblical Israel would favor cyclical, rather than ad hoc, liberty. Cyclical redemption reflects the value of the ancestral land and the need for regular reunions between chosen people and promised land. Regular 49-year cycles based on the number seven also evoked the original creation, tying together law and narrative. Boundaries are reset, and order emerges from chaos. It is fully consistent with the biblical belief that "God the Creator declared freedom for the created beings at the time of creation, and obedience to God was itself the result of that freedom."[60] From a modern economic point of view, having predictable property rights encourages "economic growth by maintaining incentives to work, save and invest."[61]

The jubilee laws served a number of related functions: (1) they reunited people with alienated land, (2) in doing so they allowed the poor to escape dependency, (3) they reunited people with their families, and (4) they eliminated personal debt. We will consider each in turn.

One of the principal functions of the jubilee laws of Leviticus was to deal with the problem of Israelites who had, for whatever reason, temporarily sold their ancestral property and become alienated from the land. This was important because for the most part, peoples of the ANE relied on access to land for economic security. Unlike peoples in the modern West, few had much in the way of liquid assets. Poor harvests, which may or may not have been the fault of families and individuals, may have resulted in debt for which the collateral, in many cases, would have been land. Without a change in fortunes, this land would be lost, possibly for good. In the jubilee year, alienated land was given back to the family who had lost it in the first place or to their descendants:

> [I]f he [referring back to the kinsman who has become poor, and who has to sell part of his property in verse 25] has not sufficient means to get it [that is, his property] back for himself, then what he sold shall remain in the hand of him who bought it until the year of jubilee; in the jubilee it shall be released, and he shall return to his property. (Leviticus 25:28; *God speaking*)

Land could, of course, be regained outside the jubilee year by being bought back by the next of kin (Leviticus 25:25). It could also be reclaimed as a result of an upswing in family fortunes that enabled the family to buy back the land

---

58. MOSHE WEINFELD, SOCIAL JUSTICE IN ANCIENT ISRAEL (Jerusalem: Magnes Press, 1995), 91 n. 70.
59. Ibid., 75ff.
60. Ibid., 17.
61. Paul Mills, *The divine economy*, CAMBRIDGE PAPERS 9, 1–4, 2 (2000).

themselves (Leviticus 25:26–27). For the family which did not have wealthy relatives or experience a change in fortunes, the jubilee was their ultimate "safety net." We can imagine the land as being on the end of an elastic band which "bounced back" to the original family every 50 years. Whatever the reasons for its loss, the family or its descendants would be given a second chance. This was important because as we have seen, land is fundamental to Israel's identity. Unlike the modern West, where people are primarily identified by their jobs (which are changeable), people in biblical society were identified primarily by their geographical roots. Land law in the Bible is concerned not simply with land but with constructing and maintaining personal identity.

In this way, the jubilee laws are designed to prevent land from being reduced to a capital asset. Treating land as a capital asset effectively abolishes the original divine allocation of land in Numbers 33; it also destroys family cohesiveness and any sense of geographical "belonging." In addition, it means that there is no incentive to care for the land. It is seldom recognized that the jubilee laws have significant environmental consequences. If the land is going to revert to you and your descendants every 50 years, you *have* to care for the land because it's all you've got—and it's all your descendants will ever have. There is no possibility of alienating the land, long-term, and having someone else's instead. The jubilee laws ensure that landowners think about how they are going to manage the land in the light of their descent relationships (their descendants). For all these reasons, agricultural land in biblical society was "literally invaluable. There is no record, biblical or inscriptional, of an Israelite voluntarily selling land on the open market, because—in contrast to their neighbours in Egypt and Mesopotamia—Israelites seem to have had no concept of arable land (*adamah*) as a commodity, to be bought and sold freely."[62] Ironically, by preventing land from being seen as a liquid asset, the jubilee laws confer upon the land its true value, which is different from—and far beyond—any market value because it is the land of promise.

A second function of the jubilee year, and related to the primary function of reuniting people and land, was to lift the disadvantaged out of dependency on others by reuniting them with the means of production. This is consistent with the Israelite ideal according to which:

they shall sit every man
under his vine and under his fig tree,
and none shall make them afraid. (Micah 4:4, *God speaking*; cf. 1 Kings 4:25)

Modern writers such as C. B. Macpherson, reflecting on the changing concept of property within capitalist systems, have forecast that "if property is to be consistent with any real democracy, the concept of property will have to be

---

62. Davis, Scripture, Culture and Agriculture, p. 39.

broadened... to include the right to a share in political power, and, even beyond that, a right to a kind of society or set of power relations which will enable the individual to live a fully human life."[63] Such breadth of vision takes, it is said, "the concept of property as the prerequisite of a free life" to a higher level.[64] This is exactly in keeping with the political ideal of the biblical prophets. The big political idea underlying the jubilee was that "a family should not have been totally without means of independent support for more than a generation."[65] As Davis writes, "There is to be no permanently landless underclass in Israel"[66] (and see Chapter 7 for the role of the jubilee in promoting social welfare). However, the purpose of reuniting people with the means of production is not limited to lifting people out of poverty. Instead, restoring the relationship between people and land is valued because it is a way of developing right relationships with other people. The grapevine and fig tree are symbols of abundance, community, and hospitality and hence of the "fully human life" to which Macpherson refers.

A third function of the jubilee year was to restore alienated families with their clans. The relationship between land and clan meant that the jubilee did not only restore land but also restored families. Since specific families and clans were identified with particular allocations of land, this meant that every 50 years, alienated persons returned, not just to the land, but also to the clan: "each of you shall return to his property and each of you shall return to his *family*" (Leviticus 25:10).

Finally, the jubilee not only reunited people with alienated land, it also "wiped the slate" clean of personal debts:

> [Your indebted kinsman] shall be with you as a hired servant and as a sojourner. He shall serve with you until the year of the jubilee; then he shall go out from you, he and his children with him, and go back to his own family, and return to the possession of his fathers. For they are my servants, whom I brought forth out of the land of Egypt; they shall not be sold as slaves. (Leviticus 25:40–42; *God speaking*)

Leviticus 25:47–55 provides for the redemption of indebted Israelites in the jubilee year who become the debt slaves of resident aliens.

The result was that every debtor could expect to be released from debt in his lifetime. This limited the collateral damage to the next generation. For alienated families and individuals, the jubilee meant they could go back home with a

---

63. C. B. Macpherson, *Capitalism and changing concept of property*, in FEUDALISM, CAPITALISM AND BEYOND (Eugene Kamenka & R. S. Neale eds., Canberra: Australian National University Press, 1975), 105–24, 120.
64. Ibid.
65. Paul Mills, *The economy*, in *Jubilee Manifesto* (Michael Schluter & John Ashcroft eds., Leicester: InterVarsity Press/Jubilee Centre, 2005), 216–33, 223.
66. DAVIS, SCRIPTURE, CULTURE AND AGRICULTURE, p. 39.

restored credit rating. It is not hard to imagine how, for some, the jubilee year could have resulted in a radical change of personal fortunes, for example, the former slave who returns as the "master of his long-lost property."[67]

B. A noble dream?

It is clear from all this that the jubilee is a more intense form of sabbatical institution than either the weekly Sabbath or sabbatical year, which is why we can place it further along the spectrum of Super-Sabbaths. This means that we can also see the weekly Sabbath and sabbatical year as "pre-jubilary" releases.[68] Within the kabbalistic tradition of the *Zohar*, there is a parallel between the 50 years of the Jubilee cycle and the 50 days that are said to have elapsed between the Exodus and the gift of Torah at Mount Sinai (Exodus 85b). This is an attractive reading because it means that the conclusion of each 49-year cycle marks the transition from debt and slavery to standing before God as a nation of equals.

The fact that the jubilee took place in the fiftieth year means that the seventh sabbatical year and the jubilee year were successive and not concurrent events. Observing the sabbatical laws thus seems to have resulted in *two* consecutive fallow years, although some scholars have suggested that the "fiftieth year" was just 49 days long.[69] This is based on the assumption that biblical Israel used a 364-day calendar (the so-called Jubilees calendar). If so, this might have meant that a two-month jubilee was needed every 49 years to align the calendar with the seasons. On the face of it, if the jubilee was only two months long, this might seem easier to practice (although modern perspectives about what is practical and "realistic" are not necessarily a reliable guide to what biblical peoples thought was realistic). There is a tendency in biblical scholarship to regard the jubilee legislation as an example of utopian planning that was never intended to have any practical application.[70] However, this is not how the jubilee is understood by the texts themselves. For one thing, although land is redistributed in the jubilee year, there is no absolutely no attempt to redistribute movable assets such as animals. If the law was idealistic, why not redistribute these as well? Second, Leviticus 26:41–43 understands exile, if it were to occur, as a compulsory observance of the land sabbatical laws. Biblical law thus attests to the view that God expected the Israelites to apply the land sabbatical law. 2 Chronicles 36:21 equates the 70 years that Israel spent in exile in Babylon with 70 years of nonobservance

---

67. Andrew G. Shead, *An Old Testament theology of the Sabbath year and jubilee*, REFORMED THEOLOGICAL REV. 61, 19–33, 33 (2002).

68. Ibid., 24.

69. Such as S. B. Hoenig, *Sabbatical years and the year of jubilee*, JEWISH Q. REV. 59, 222–36 (1969), followed by GORDON J. WENHAM, LEVITICUS, NEW INTERNATIONAL COMMENTARY ON THE OLD TESTAMENT (Grand Rapids: Eerdmans, 1979), 302, n. 4.

70. *E.g.*, KARL ELLIGER, LEVITICUS, HANDBUCH ZUM ALTEN TESTAMENT 4 (Tübingen: Mohr, 1966).

of the sabbatical years over 490 (cf. Leviticus 26:41–43). This could be seen as a convenient piece of numerology that helps to make sense of a national disaster; yet even this argument relies upon an understanding that the land sabbatical laws *could* have applied in practice. Milgrom[71] thinks that the sabbatical year was also observed in Second Temple times, while the ancient Jewish historian Josephus claims that the land sabbatical year was observed, at least in Roman times (Jewish War, I: 60).

There is no direct evidence that the jubilee took place which is, of course, a different question to whether it *could* have taken place. Milgrom concludes that "the jubilee law existed, was intended to be implemented and would have been implemented were it not for the typical and expected resistance from those who might be adversely affected,"[72] namely, the rich and the political elite. However, Fried and Freedman[73] find some evidence to suggest that the jubilee did apply in the period of the late monarchy and that it was well-known during the exile. Scholars have combined hints from the biblical narratives with dates from Roman history and projected a list of sabbatical and jubilee years from 1003 BC.[74] On the basis of this, Casperson suggests that major Temple construction and repair activities between 1000 BC and 500 BC (including those carried out by Solomon, Joash, Hezekiah, Josiah, and Zerubbabel) may have been timed to start during jubilee years. There is logic to this proposal; indeed the manpower released by the jubilee year may have been essential to provide the labour needed for monarchical building projects (cf. 1 Kings 5:13-16; 2 Chronicles 2:17-18).[75] And because the jubilee year promoted reconciliation (between God and Israel, Israel and the land, individual family members), restoring a Temple—a building whose function is to promote reconciliation, was an appropriate thing to do. In political terms, the jubilee would have been an auspicious time to embark on national projects, rather like the rash of building projects that marked the turn of the last millennium in the West.

Finally, the jubilee was an Exodus-type event. We recall that the Exodus was an act of divine intervention that kicked off with national level sacrifices (the Passover lambs) and had as its express purpose the liberation of an enslaved people to worship God. It also resulted in the people returning home to the land of the ancestral promise. Likewise, the jubilee began with national level sacrifices

---

71. Jacob Milgrom, Leviticus 23–27, Anchor Bible Commentary (New York: Doubleday, 2001), 2246.

72. Milgrom, Leviticus 23–27, p. 2251.

73. Ibid., 2257–71.

74. Lee W. Casperson, *Sabbatical, Jubilee, and the Temple of Solomon*, Vetus Testamentum 53, 283-96 (2003); *see also* Lisbeth S. Fried & David N. Freedman, *in* Leviticus 23–27, Jacob Milgrom, Anchor Bible Commentary (New York: Doubleday, 2001), 2257–70, 2269–70.

75. Casperson, *Sabbatical, Jubilee*, p. 289.

(the Day of Atonement) and liberated an enslaved people who could return home to their ancestral lands. In addition, the Exodus and the jubilee were divine interventions that broke a spiral of economic dependency. Given the sacral purpose of the Exodus, it is hardly surprising that the jubilee, too, has a sacral dimension, and so it is said to be a holy year (25:12). Nor is the jubilee the only example in Torah of an exile who is able to go home following a national purificatory event. We will see in Chapter 8 that the death of the high priest means the end of exile for the accidental killer who is allowed to leave the city of refuge and return home (Numbers 35:25).[76]

C. "Family economics" *versus* "Pharaonic economics"

There is a contrast between the jubilee laws of biblical Israel, which can be seen as an example of "family economics" and the system of land tenure practiced in ancient Egypt, which can be characterized as "Pharaonic economics." The jubilee laws can be characterized as family economics because they pressed the "reset" button that restored people to the original divine allocation of land. They also broke the power of the rich by preventing the growth of large estates. Without the jubilee, small indebted farms could be swallowed up by the rich, leaving the landless poor at the mercy of the employment practices of the landed rich, as condemned by the prophets:

> Woe
> to those who join house to house,
> who add field to field,
> until there is no more room,
> and you are made to dwell alone in the midst of the land.
> (Isaiah 5:8; *Isaiah speaking*)

This contrasts with the practice of amassing land which was characteristic of Pharaoh in ancient Egypt and which can thus be characterized as Pharaonic economics (at least, from the biblical writers' point of view). The Joseph story records the following plea by the Egyptians at the height of famine:

> Why should we die before your eyes, both we and our land? Buy us and our land for food, and we with our land will be slaves to Pharaoh; and give us seed, that we may live, and not die, and that the land may not be desolate. (Genesis 47:19)

Pharaoh is thus the archetypal "estate eater" who exploited other peoples' extremity to gain property for himself. As we have seen, the loss of property was a serious matter in Israel where land is part of the Abrahamic promise. Losing the land is tantamount to losing personal identity: it is also the betrayal of past

---

76. Kawashima, *Jubilee year*, p. 382.

and future generations. We should of course note that Pharaonic economics was not limited to Pharaoh: the Israelites themselves were capable of acting like Pharaoh and regularly succumbed to Pharaonic economics (e.g., 1 Kings 21:1–2).

There is thus a sharp contrast between the family economics of the jubilee land laws and the Pharaonic economics described in Genesis 47. This is not altogether surprising. Biblical law is frequently opposed to Pharaonic practices because, in terms of the story of the Pentateuch, it is with Pharaoh that Abraham and his descendants have had most dealings, rather than any other foreign leader. Pharaoh and the practices of Egypt are constantly invoked as a way of life that the Israelites are not to imitate: a warning that informs Israel's new life of freedom.[77]

Of course, this does not mean that the contrast between family economics and Pharaonic economics was an artificial one, engineered for propaganda purposes. The surviving evidence shows that there was a basic difference in the way land was held and used in Egypt, compared to biblical Israel. We saw, above, that the Hebrews were tribal groups who wanted to keep the land within the family. This was completely unlike the practice of land ownership in Egypt. Of course, the Egyptians had families who lived on land, but they had no sense of *belonging* to that land, as the Israelites did. For the Egyptians, various types of land were owned and administered by the state during the Middle Kingdom and Second Intermediate period (*circa* 2134–1540 BC).[78] Egypt (along with the Canaanite city-states) "were highly stratified, strongly militarised societies in which the whole land belonged (at least in name) to the monarch. In practical terms, that meant the wealth of the land flowed upward, away from the small farmers, serfs, and slaves who composed the overwhelming majority of the population, to the large landowners, the nobility, the great temples, and the crown."[79]

Support for this can be found in primary Egyptian texts such as the Wilbour Papyrus—a comprehensive survey of land allocation in Middle Kingdom Egypt (*circa* 2134–1786 BC). This shows that although individuals and groups of individuals ran Egyptian estates, probably as a reward for past service, including military service,[80] the land itself remained vested in Pharaoh. Individual sections within this papyrus are typically introduced by the formula "*Mine*-Land of

---

77. See generally Franz Volker Greifenhagen, Egypt on the Pentateuch's Ideological Map, Journal for the Study of the Old Testament Supplement Series (London: Continuum, 2002).

78. Richard Jasnow, *Middle Kingdom and Second Intermediate Period*, in A History of Ancient Near Eastern Law (Raymond Westbrook ed., Leiden: Brill, 2003), vol. I, 255–88, 276.

79. Davis, Scripture, Culture and Agriculture, p. 68.

80. Jasnow, *Middle Kingdom*, p. 330.

Pharaoh under the authority of [X]."[81] During the New Kingdom period (*circa* 1552–1069 BC), it is supposed that "ultimately . . . all the land . . . was in possession of the king [i.e., Pharaoh], who might theoretically remove it at any time."[82] So although the Egyptians could trace their family back, there is no sense of it being land that *must* be owned by a given family.

We can see this in a famous Egyptian lawsuit which is recorded in the Legal Text of Mose, an Egyptian man who served as the Treasury-Scribe of Ptah (an Egyptian god). This epic case lasted for a century; it began during the reign of Akhenaten (*circa* 1353–1336 BC), but it was not resolved until the time of Rameses II (1279–1213 BC). We know about this dispute because it is preserved on the north wall of the tomb chapel which was erected by the lawsuit's eventual victor, Mose, at Saqqara and now found in the Cairo Museum.[83] Mose's ancestors included a man called Neshi, who had received the original land some three hundred years earlier and it was Neshi's descendants who had cultivated this patch of land ever since. The problem was that someone within the family tried to split it up into so many parcels that the land would no longer be economically viable. What the Legal Text of Mose shows is that a single Egyptian family could trace their ancestry over three hundred years in relation to a single piece of land. However, although the Egyptians could prove that land belonged in their family for a long time, a close relationship between land and family was not part of the Egyptian worldview. Mose's land *could* have been alienated—and there was nothing intrinsically wrong with that. The issue in the lawsuit was not the alienation of the land itself but dividing it so that it would not be economically viable. The land could have been bought and sold if the whole family agreed. That is a major difference between the worldview of ancient Egypt and that of biblical Israel.

To conclude, the biblical land laws—and especially the jubilee—expose the differences between Israel and Egypt regarding land ownership and labor on the land. It is a clash between two different economic systems and two different ideologies regarding land tenure.

D. Joseph and the Amazing Technicolor Jubilee

In this penultimate section, we will consider another important link between the jubilee laws and biblical narrative that is seldom recognized. This is the relationship between law and narrative found in the Joseph cycle. We saw, above, that in the sabbatical year, the people rely on a miraculous threefold crop in the sixth year to sustain them during the seventh year, as well as the first year of the next sabbatical cycle, while they are waiting for that first year's yield to come

---

81. *See* ALAN H. GARDINER, THE WILBOUR PAPYRUS. VOLUME III: TRANSLATION (Oxford: Oxford University Press, 1948).

82. Jasnow, *Middle Kingdom*, p. 330.

83. KENNETH A. KITCHEN, RAMESSIDE INSCRIPTIONS: TRANSLATED AND ANNOTATED TRANSLATIONS. VOLUME III: RAMESES II, HIS CONTEMPORARIES (Oxford: Blackwell, 2000), 307–11.

in (Leviticus 25:19–22). The absence of crops during the seventh year is reminiscent of a famine, even though the conditions are the result of abstaining from agricultural activity, rather than natural causes.[84] Calum Carmichael notes an underlying pattern in which a divinely ordained bumper crop is followed by a divinely ordained famine. This is reminiscent of the story of Joseph in Egypt where God tells Joseph, via Pharaoh's dreams, that Egypt will experience seven bumper years followed by seven years of famine (Genesis 41). Carmichael argues that if the sabbatical laws were observed over a 49-year period, the Israelites will experience, over the course of seven sabbatical cycles, a total of seven famine-like years. And since the sixth year of each seventh sabbatical cycle is also a year of abundance, the Israelites will also experience seven "bumper" years as well. Forty-nine years is precisely the figure that takes us to the eve of the jubilee, or fiftieth, year (Leviticus 25:8). Every jubilee cycle thus constitutes a parallel to the Joseph story.[85] Of course, a succession of seven fallow years followed by seven consecutive bumper years would reenact the story better, but we are here speaking of a commemoration rather than an actual restaging. We have already noted, above, how the jubilee recalls deliverance from Egypt. But if Carmichael is correct, the sabbatical laws are a remembrance—not only of deliverance *from* Egypt—but also of deliverance *in* Egypt.

In the Joseph story, the conclusion of the cycle of seven years of bounty followed by seven years of plenty results in the Egyptians selling their land and themselves to Pharaoh, on a permanent basis:

> Then Joseph said to the people, "Behold, I have this day bought you and your land for Pharaoh . . . ." And they said, "You have saved our lives; may it please my LORD, we will be slaves to Pharaoh." (Genesis 47:23–25)

On one level, there is a striking similarity between the economic position of the Egyptians and that of the Israelites. We saw, above, that the Israelites, like the Egyptians, are permanent slaves of God and have no absolute rights over land. But there are major differences. The entire Egyptian population ends up being enslaved to a human master (Pharaoh) whereas in the jubilee year, the entire Israelite population is *freed* from slavery to a human master.[86] The Joseph story, in fact, highlights the exceptional economic privileges of the Israelites. For while the Egyptians become the slaves of Pharaoh (Genesis 47:13–26), Pharaoh makes an extraordinary bequest of land to the Israelites:

> Then Pharaoh said to Joseph, "Your father and your brothers have come to you. The land of Egypt is before you; settle your father and your brothers in

---

84. Calum M. Carmichael, *The Sabbatical/Jubilee cycle and the Seven-Year Famine in Egypt*, BIBLICA 80, 224–39, 228 (1999).
85. Ibid., 227ff.
86. Ibid., 231.

the best of the land; let them dwell in the land of Goshen . . . ." Then Joseph settled his father and his brothers, and gave them a possession (*ahuzzah*) in the land of Egypt, in the best of the land, in the land of Rameses, as Pharaoh had commanded. (Genesis 47:5–6, 11)

The term used for Pharaoh's gift of land is *ahuzzah*; the same term used for the ancestral land to which the Israelite returns in the jubilee year (Leviticus 25:10, 13, 41).[87]

Moreover, Carmichael's suggestion is fully in keeping with the stipulation that the jubilee year should begin on the Day of Atonement. It is against the backdrop of famine that Joseph first becomes reconciled to his brothers (Genesis 45:1–15) and later, after the end of the two seven-year cycles, forgives them (Genesis 50:15–21). In a dramatic reversal of all of the stories in Genesis, starting with Cain and Abel, of brothers who do *not* dwell peaceably on land, it ends with brothers who were formerly alienated from each other finally living together on the land.[88] This is precisely the objective of Leviticus 25. It is all the more remarkable in the light of the common biblical stories of fraternal conflict. The Israelite who observes the seven sabbatical cycles experiences the conclusion of the Joseph story, which finds poetic expression in Psalm 133:1:

Behold, how good and pleasant it is when brothers dwell in unity!

E. The joy of law

This reading, if correct, has important implications for our understanding of biblical law. First, if the jubilee laws were observed, an Israelite over the age of 50 could meaningfully be said to have lived through the experience of Israel in Egypt, by experiencing seven years of plenty and seven years of famine. Law is a way of enacting key elements of the story for those who have already identified themselves with it. It is not enough that the addressees of Leviticus should have experienced the Exodus firsthand for themselves. They should also experience secondhand the story of Joseph (although in fact the Exodus generation are never presented as doing so because they never entered the promised land). There is a good precedent for this reenactment, namely, the weekly Sabbath laws that commemorate creation. In terms of the actual *experience* of seven fallow years and seven bumper harvests, the sabbatical laws are arguably a more vivid re-creation than the weekly Sabbath remembrance. But perhaps this is to be expected. When law is theater, some productions will be more realistic than others.

Second, the structural similarities between Genesis 47 and Leviticus 25 suggest that the specific purpose of the jubilee law is to rejoice in the difference between being a slave of Pharaoh and a slave of Israel's God. This is consistent

---

87. Ibid.
88. Ibid., 234.

with the other Sabbath laws, including the weekly Sabbath and the sabbatical year. It is also consistent with the explicit anti-Egyptian agenda elsewhere in Leviticus (e.g., 18:3).[89] Israel, at this point in her history, is in a liminal state; and this is aptly reflected in her geographical location—in the wilderness—between Egypt and the promised land. She is betwixt and between. Law is designed, inter alia, to help Israel disengage from her Egyptian cultural heritage and assume a new cultural identity, in keeping with her Sinaitic vocation (see Chapter 2).

A third aspect of the function of the jubilee laws is to legitimize the lawgiver. After all, one of the recurring motifs in the Joseph story is how the various protagonists come to recognize that Joseph operates under divine direction (Genesis 45:8; 50:20) and divine instruction (Genesis 41:16, 25, 28, 32, 39). It is plausible to suggest, therefore, that the structural similarities between Genesis 47 and Leviticus 25 indicate that Moses, too, operates under divine direction (e.g., Exodus 3:10) and divine instruction (e.g., Numbers 12:8). Like Joseph, Moses had plenty of opponents and detractors among his own family. The jubilee laws legitimize the leadership's claim that the same God who worked through Joseph to deliver his people is also at work in Moses to the same end. The similarities between Genesis 47 and Leviticus 25 reinforce the thematic repetition apparent in the parallel biographies of Joseph and Moses ((1) cast away by family, (2) rescued by the house of Pharaoh, (3) becomes a prince of Egypt, (4) to deliver their people). There is a narrative symmetry between the economic arrangements of Genesis 47 and Leviticus 25. In Genesis 47, Israel goes down *into* Egypt under Joseph's leadership and settles in the land, whereas in Leviticus 25, Israel comes up *out of* Egypt under Moses's leadership and settles in the land.

VIII. DEVELOPING PROPERTY

We have noted the conflict in biblical Israel between "land-as-commodity" and "land-as-covenant." This resonates with similar ideological tensions regarding the role of land, which can be found in modern property jurisprudence.

To some degree, the biblical idea that people are bound to land by a narrative that creates a complex series of relationships and interdependencies (vertical, horizontal, and temporal) would have been familiar for much of the history of English land law. Early medieval English land law, especially, had no difficulty recognizing that land could be used to promote relationships. For example, Norman land tenure, which was rooted in the relationship between the Norman lord and his tenant, was "much more than a commercial bargain. It was a lifelong bond, comparable in some respects with marriage."[90] This contrasts with

---

89. Ibid., 232.
90. BAKER, ENGLISH LEGAL HISTORY, p. 225.

developments since the nineteenth century, in which land has increasingly been seen as a form of economic cash exchange. As far back as 1857, the Royal Commissioners on Land Transfers and Registration claimed that it was their ambition to enable owners "to deal with land in as simple and easy a manner . . . as they can now deal with moveable chattels or stock."[91] This parallels developments in the history of economics. In classical eighteenth and nineteenth-century economics, the three main factors of production are land, labor, and capital; however, with the rise of neoclassical economics from the late nineteenth century onwards, the factors of production are reduced to two: capital and labor. Land is no longer part of the picture because it has been reduced to a form of capital. This is reflected in modern social practice: most people nowadays only regard land as significant inasmuch as it is a capital asset or a pension fund.

In recent years, this approach has culminated in the Land Registration Act (LRA) 2002. This is a major step toward the comprehensive—and in many cases, compulsory—registration of land in England and Wales on the Land Registry. The idea is to facilitate electronic conveyancing and hence to make it even easier to trade in land. The LRA 2002 is a practical example of the idea that one of the objectives of land law reform should be to increase the marketability of land.[92] Indeed, the Land Registry's current 10-year strategic plan states that "Around £1million worth of property is processed every minute in England and Wales. We now want Land Registry to be at the heart of the most efficient property market in the world."[93] Land, on this view, is merely a temporal and convenient way of holding and transferring capital. Indeed, it can even be argued that in the interest of free economic movement, all rights to land not recorded on the Land Register should be abolished. From this perspective, narrative has no part to play in understanding land law: the model is land as a form of share dealing. By reducing the significance of land in this way, English land law has lost the sense that land creates relationships and interdependencies. Instead, English law now concentrates exclusively on what occurs within the physical boundaries of the user's property. There is little sense of an obligation to use the property for the benefit of the less fortunate; nor is there even much sense of the way in which properties are *physically* interconnected.

---

91. *Cited in* KEVIN GRAY & SUSAN FRANCIS GRAY, LAND LAW (Oxford: Oxford University Press, 5th ed. 2007), 51.

92. *See* Charles Harpum, *The Law Commission and the Reform of Land Law*, *in* LAND LAW: THEMES AND PERSPECTIVES (S. Bright & J. Dewar eds., Oxford: Oxford University Press, 1998), 150–79, 164.

93. http://www.landregistry.gov.uk/strategy/10yearplan/, accessed December 22, 2007.

At the same time, however, this "classic liberal image of property as a self-interested claim of unfettered power"[94] is undercut by the reality that "all property in land is held subject to—and is redefined by—a wide range of socially conditioned constraints."[95] Accordingly, scholars such as Kevin Gray and Susan Francis Gray have developed what they describe as a "relational view of land law."[96] This contends that "the beginning of truth about property is the realisation that property is not a *thing* but rather a *relationship* which one has with a thing."[97] Accordingly, "the law of property is not really about *things* but rather about *people*."[98] The function of land law is ultimately to regulate "an important range of socially defined relationships and morally conditioned obligations."[99] This approach is consistent with the idea that the very word "property" "reflects its semantically correct root by identifying the condition of a particular resource as being 'proper' to a particular person."[100] The word property may even be bound up with the idea of "propriety" with the result that "the notion of a 'property right' may ultimately have more to do with perceptions of 'rightness' than with any understanding of enforceable exclusionary title."[101] This modern exposition of the moral dimension of property resonates with the biblical ideology of land-as-covenant, according to which the use of land is inseparable from proper and right relationships with God and neighbor, not to mention ancestors and potential descendants.

In line with this modern restatement of the relational character of property, a number of modern property and environment lawyers have argued in recent decades for a radical rethink of property rights. Thus Sax's critique of the modern law of property stresses the way in which land gives rise to relationships: "Property does not exist in isolation. Particular parcels are tied to one another in complex ways, and property is more accurately described as being inextricably part of a network of relationships that is neither limited to, nor usefully defined by, the property boundaries with which the legal system is accustomed to dealing."[102] There are some indications that the legal conception of property in English law is presently moving away from a rights-based notion to one in which responsibilities and obligations are the basic elements of our understanding

---

94. Kevin Gray & Susan Francis Gray, *The idea of property in land*, in LAND LAW: THEMES AND PERSPECTIVES (S. Bright & J. Dewar eds., Oxford: Oxford University Press, 1998), 15–31, 41.
95. Ibid.
96. Gray & Gray, ELEMENTS OF LAND LAW, p. 4.
97. Gray & Gray, *Idea of property*, p. 15 (italics added).
98. Gray & Gray, ELEMENTS OF LAND LAW, p. 4 (italics original).
99. Ibid.
100. Gray & Gray, *Idea of property*, pp. 15–16.
101. Ibid., 16.
102. Joseph L. Sax, *Takings, private property and public rights*, YALE L.J. 181, 149–86, 152 (1971).

of property.[103] A relational approach to land law also includes responsibilities and obligations to subsequent generations. This is because it recognizes "the potential for contiguous claims."[104] These could inhibit owners from exploiting resources in ways that will interfere with the interests of future generations.[105] Again, this resonates with the biblical idea of the *nachalah* (inheritance) which embodies multigenerational relationships of commitment and nurture.

To sum up, there is a tension in the English law of property between different ideologies of land. The conflict is between the classic liberal ideology, which sees land as a source of ready cash and the more traditional view of land, which has its roots in early medieval English law and which emphasizes the essentially relational character of property. Both ideologies are present in English land law, although the liberal approach currently dominates. This mirrors to a considerable extent the conflict in biblical law between land-as-commodity and land-as-covenant, as well as the underlying opposition between Pharaonic economics and family economics.

A. There's no place like home

In addition to these connections between biblical law and modern property jurisprudence, biblical land law is relevant to several aspects of modern public policy, despite the fact that the emphasis of biblical land law is on rural land.

First, biblical land law meant that a person's geographical neighbors were also their relatives. This means that land tenure is not understood in purely material terms. It includes relational dimensions both in terms of people "belonging" to the land and the way in which the land itself supports and enables a wide range of temporal and horizontal relationships. Brueggemann claims that the "urban promise" of "mobility and anonymity which seemed so full of promise for freedom and self-actualisation"[106] has failed, with the ideal of "detached, unrooted lives of endless choice and no commitment"[107] being exposed for what it is. As a result, "it is now clear that a *sense of place* is a human hunger which the urban promise has not met."[108] This ties in with the need for land reform and housing schemes (see further, below). If the true value of land lies in the relationships and interdependencies it creates, then it is

---

103. Gray & Gray, *Idea of property*, pp. 39–51.

104. Sean Coyle & Karen Morrow, THE PHILOSOPHICAL FOUNDATIONS OF ENVIRONMENTAL LAW: PROPERTY, RIGHTS AND NATURE (Oxford and Portland, Oregon: Hart, 2004), 207.

105. Kevin Gray, *The ambivalence of property, in* THREATS WITHOUT ENEMIES: FACING ENVIRONMENTAL INSECURITY (G. Prins ed., London: Earthscan, 1993), 150–53.

106. Walter Brueggemann, *The Land*, Overtures to Biblical Theology Series (Philadelphia: Fortress Press, 1977), 4.

107. Ibid.

108. Ibid (italics original).

important to give land ownership to as many people as possible. The true value of land lies in its relational, as opposed to its economic, potential. Related to this, there is evidence that "people's primary sense of identification is to a very small local area . . . despite the fact that no discrete physical boundaries separate neighborhoods in the major cities."[109] This has implications for the spatial distribution of housing and community identity.

Nowadays, there is little overlap between our neighbors, relatives, and work colleagues, all of whom are located in different places. Maintaining relationships across such a broad geographical base is time consuming, and this means that time, for many of us, is our most precious commodity. By contrast, it was easier for biblical Israel to maintain a stable extended multigenerational family because it was rooted in a central place. Biblical society was characterized by "multiplex" relationships, that is, people whom one meets in a large number of different roles. (A multiplex relationship, in modern terms, might be a next-door neighbor whom you see at work and who also goes to the same health club). There are a number of ways in which public policy might recognize the relational and economic benefits of rootedness and family co-location. These might include tax breaks to encourage adult children to live closer to their aging parents, co-residence of members of an extended family within a given geographical area, and students to study closer to their local university.[110]

A second area of contemporary application is the importance of the Sabbath year for land. In biblical law, land is part of a morally purposive enterprise—the issue is not "what best protects my self-interest?" but "what is right?" The jubilee expresses the moral duty of landowners and society as a whole "to be responsible toward those who precede and follow us in this world."[111] Land must be "kindly used" "so that it may continue to be used from generation to generation."[112] Biblical law presents a challenge to modern law, which "reflects a view of property rights as *competing* with environmental value and concerns, rather than *emerging* from moral reflection upon mankind's place in the world."[113] Biblical law also presents the question of land tenure and land use as essentially a matter of justice, including intergenerational justice. There is some evidence of a move in this direction on the part of modern law in response to concern for the environment. Coyle and Morrow show that "legal regulation and protection of the

---

109. Michael Schluter & Roy Clements, *Reactivating the Extended Family: From Biblical Norms to Public Policy in Britain*, Jubilee Centre Paper No. 1 (Cambridge: Jubilee Centre, 1986), 48, *available at* www.seekjustice.co.uk.

110. Michael Schluter, *Roots*, in Christianity in a Changing World (Michael Schluter et al., eds., London: Marshall Pickering, 2000), 81–91; Schluter, *Family*, pp. 171–72.

111. Davis, Scripture, Culture and Agriculture, p. 141.

112. Ibid., 8.

113. Coyle & Morrow, Philosophical Foundations, p. 157 (italics original).

environment increasingly indicates a concern with justice and moral value, rather than a purely prudential concern with human interests."[114] Indeed, implementing ideas such as sustainable development "bring[s] into play . . . a conception of justice which includes respect for future generations"[115]—something that is better expressed using the language of responsibilities rather than rights.[116]

A final area of modern relevance is land reform and housing schemes. Just as biblical law aimed to give every family their own debt-free leasehold on a piece of property, so the modern land reform movement seeks to increase the number of people in society who own their property. Giving as many people as possible access to a piece of property is one way of promoting a form of equality in society without crushing incentives. The difficulty facing land reform in England is that, as we have seen, English land law does not have a concept of ownership or occupation that does not, at the same time, allow it to be treated as an economically transferable asset. At present, unless owners and occupiers can sell, they have no property right. Accordingly, giving people properties which they can turn into cash defeats the point of land reform. So although we might want to provide housing for those who cannot afford to buy in a grossly inflated market, we are hampered by the fact that we do not have a conception of property rights that is not economically fungible. One solution might be to use trust law to create an equitable right to the property. "Owners" thus become equitable beneficiaries who are entitled to use the property, although they cannot sell it.

One of the advantages of land reform—in addition to social justice—is that they can have the effect of invigorating local economies. This is certainly one of the potential effects of biblical land law. If individuals in biblical society cannot invest money in property in the longer term, the effect is to encourage a different use of money, including both "non-interest charitable lending and risk-sharing business finance (so distributing the profits or losses from commercial ventures more widely)."[117] What this actually amounts to is "the wide dispersion of economic power."[118] Biblical land law thus creates the pre-conditions for an "enterprise culture." This may partly underlie the success of the Asian "tiger economies," including South Korea, which undertook significant programs of land reform in the latter half of the twentieth century. In just two years (1952–1954) the percentage of land-owning South Korean farmers leapt from 50 percent to 94 percent.[119]

---

114. Ibid., 162.
115. Ibid.
116. Ibid., 174.
117. Mills, *The economy*, p. 230.
118. Ibid., *cf.* Macpherson's quote about democratizing property, above.
119. MILGROM, LEVITICUS, p. 2271.

To summarize, although the nature of the relationship between biblical Israel and the promised land is unique, some aspects of biblical land law remain relevant to modern property jurisprudence and land use.

IX. CONCLUSION

Land is unique among all forms of property in biblical law because it is the land of promise. It is the setting for the vocation of Israel as a chosen people. There are thus especially close connections between people, land, and narrative. This is reflected in biblical law. The fusion between law and narrative means that the biblical law of property is dynamic, not least in the area of inheritance. There is also a complex interaction between the narrative of Genesis and Exodus (including creation, the Joseph story, and the Exodus) and the various sabbatical laws. These include the weekly Sabbath, sabbatical year, and jubilee years, which together form a "spectrum of Sabbaths" of increasing intensity. The ideology of divine ownership has major implications for biblical land law. Israel's exercise of land use repeatedly presents her with the choice of whether she will serve the ancestral god of the ancestral lands. The laws, too, present a basic choice between Pharaonic economics (amassing land) and family economics (restoring land).

Selected reading
Walter Brueggemann, *The Covenanted Self: Explorations in Law and Covenant* (Minneapolis: Fortress, 1999), Chapter 9.
Walter Brueggemann, *The Land*, Overtures to Biblical Theology Series (Philadelphia: Fortress Press, 1977), Chapter 4.
Jonathan P. Burnside, *The Signs of Sin: Seriousness of Offence in Biblical Law*, Journal for the Study of the Old Testament Supplement Series 364 (London: Continuum International, 2003), Chapter 3.
Ellen F. Davis, *Scripture, Culture and Agriculture: An Agrarian Reading* (Cambridge: Cambridge University Press, 2008), Chapter 6.
Jeffrey A. Fager, *Land Tenure and the Biblical Jubilee: Uncovering Hebrew Ethics through the Sociology of Knowledge*, Journal for the Study of the Old Testament Supplement Series 155 (Sheffield: Sheffield Academic Press, 1993), Chapters 2 and 8.
K. D. Irani and Morris Silver eds., *Social Justice in the Ancient World* (London: Greenwood Press, 1995), Chapter 12.
Jan Joosten, *People and Land in the Holiness Code* (Leiden: E.J. Brill, 1996), Chapter 6.
Michael Schluter and John Ashcroft, *Jubilee Manifesto* (Leicester: InterVarsity Press/ Jubilee Centre, 2005), Chapters 9–12.
Michael Schluter and the Cambridge Papers Group eds., *Christianity in a Changing World: Biblical insight on contemporary issues* (London: Marshall Pickering, 2000), Chapter 13.
Moshe Weinfeld, *Social Justice in Biblical Israel and in the Ancient Near East* (Jerusalem: The Magnes Press, 1995), Chapter 8.

7. SOCIAL WELFARE

Should we help the poor, and if so, how? Is it right to use redistributive taxation as a means to this end, or is that unjust? And does a system of taxation and handouts destroy incentive for rich and poor alike? We will see that biblical law approaches the question of social welfare in a similar way to the relationship between "people and land." Accordingly, this chapter builds on the previous one by exploring how property was supposed to be *used*. It also adds to our understanding of the various sabbatical institutions by showing how they restore people as well as land. For this reason, the chapter will start by exploring the implications for social welfare of the Sabbath day, sabbatical year, and jubilee year. We will then turn to consider the ban on interest as well as the laws relating to tithes, food distribution, and gleanings. This raises the question of whether these laws promoted social welfare or social justice and whether there is any difference between the two. We will then be in a position to see how the biblical Sabbath laws were extended in the prophetic literature and the New Testament. Finally, we will consider the contemporary relevance of the biblical welfare laws. The language and some of the ideals of biblical law found broad ownership and entered popular consciousness on a global scale because of the "Jubilee 2000" and "Drop the Debt" campaigns. This naturally raises the question of the applicability of biblical law to modern social practice.

I. FREEDOM FROM DEMANDS

We saw in Chapter 6 that divine ownership powerfully shapes biblical understandings of property. No one in ancient Israel ultimately owns anything because all property is owned by God. This means that there are no freeholders, only leaseholders. This affects the biblical understanding of social welfare as well. From God's perspective, it means that even those who have access to property are "strangers and sojourners":

> The land shall not be sold in perpetuity, for the land is mine; for you are strangers and sojourners (*gerim wetoshabhim*) with me.
> (Leviticus 25:23; *God speaking*)

"Strangers and sojourners" refers to assimilating and nonassimilating immigrants who are, by definition, not descendants of Abraham. They typify vulnerable persons living on or beyond Israel's social margins who do not have any rights in land. Biblical law radically characterizes those who have access to property as somehow being like those who have no property at all. This encourages identification between those who have access to property and those who do not. It means that it is impossible to separate access to property from social welfare. Nor can we distinguish being a leaseholder and showing care for poor immigrants. Biblical law redraws the encounter between the "haves" and the "have-nots." The relationship between these two groups is not characterized, as it might be in modern property law, as a clash between private rights (my right to do as I please with my property) and public rights (other people's right to use my property in a particular way). Biblical law simply does not present the issues in this way. Rather, both groups are seen as two different kinds of sojourners with different degrees of access to property. It relativizes the claims. The biblical picture is one of shared dependence, which contrasts with the Western model of competition between contending claims.

Following Rose and Valverde,[1] instead of asking, "how does 'the law' regulate 'social welfare'?," we might ask, "how does a particular problem—say, what to do with sojourners who have nothing to eat—come to emerge as a particular concern of Torah?" The reason is because it triggers a salient aspect of Israel's national story and hence identity. Caring for sojourners is an issue in Torah because the Israelites were sojourners in Egypt (Genesis 15:13; Exodus 6:4). They were therefore to treat other sojourners as they had been treated. For example, they were to leave food on the ground for gathering in the gleaning laws, in a way that recalled how God had left food on the ground for gathering after the Exodus from Egypt (see further, below).

When it comes to thinking about social welfare it makes a big difference who we have in mind. We may see the typical recipients of social welfare as the feckless, perhaps, or those who fall into hardship through no fault of their own. In biblical Israel, stereotypically needy persons are characterized as "the sojourner, the fatherless, and the widow." These groups are repeatedly mentioned in legal (e.g., Deuteronomy 14:29), wisdom (e.g., Job 24:3), and prophetic texts (e.g., Jeremiah 22:3). What they have in common is the absence of an adult male relative or protector who is able and willing to act on their behalf. The absence of a male protector, in turn, points to the absence of a wider family unit. People without family were highly vulnerable in a society that did not have a comprehensive welfare system. It is this lack of family support which makes the sojourner, the fatherless, and the widow the special focus of Torah.

The cornerstone of the biblical social welfare laws is the sabbatical legislation. We saw in Chapter 6 that there are three main sabbatical institutions: the weekly Sabbath (one day off in seven), the sabbatical year (one year off in seven), and the jubilee year (another year off at the end of seven cycles of seven years). Together they form a spectrum of Sabbaths. In Chapter 6, we described the cessation of

---

1. Nikolas Rose & Mariana Valverde, *Governed by Law?*, Soc. & Legal Studs. 7, 541–55, 545 (1998).

work and the regular suspension of demands upon people and land as "restonomics." Each Sabbath institution has different implications for social welfare, and we shall consider each in turn.

The biblical Sabbath laws are found in both versions of the Decalogue:

Remember the sabbath day, to keep it holy.
Six days you shall labour, and do all your work;
but the seventh day is a sabbath to the LORD your God; in it you shall not do any work, you, or your son, or your daughter, your manservant, or your maidservant, or your cattle, or the sojourner who is within your gates;
for in six days the LORD made heaven and earth, the sea, and all that is in them, and rested the seventh day; therefore the LORD blessed the sabbath day and hallowed it. (Exodus 20:8-11; *God speaking*)

You shall remember that you were a servant in the land of Egypt, and the LORD your God brought you out thence with a mighty hand and an outstretched arm; therefore the LORD your God commanded you to keep the sabbath day. (Deuteronomy 5:15; *Moses speaking*)

The Sabbath promoted social welfare by protecting vulnerable workers. It ensured there were limits to how much they could be made to work. In this sense, the Sabbath laws ". . . are not really demands; they are a liberation from demands."[2] One day off in seven made the Sabbath "a tithe on time."[3] The list of beneficiaries in Exodus 23:12 includes the "son of your bond-maid," reflecting the youth and vulnerability of this dependent. Biblical law was cited by the former British Prime Minister Harold Macmillan in a 1986 House of Lords debate on the Shops Bill: "Let us remember that the great commandment that was handed down to God's chosen people was perhaps the greatest social reform in the history of civilisation; the concept that every man or woman, however humble, should have at least some period of rest."[4]

Somewhat unusually in biblical law, there is evidence of Sabbath observance *prior* to the Sinaitic revelation (Exodus 16:25–30). In narrative terms, this suggests the reassertion of a preexisting Sabbath tradition. Customary Sabbath observance may have been disrupted, perhaps by Pharaoh.[5] This is consistent with the sufferings described in Exodus 1:11–14 and Exodus 5:6–18, which included extremely harsh working conditions. It is notable that Moses's repeated

---

2. Gareth Lloyd Jones, *The Biblical Sabbath: An Oasis in Time*, SCRIPTURE BULL. 34, 14–23, 22–23 (2004).

3. ROLAND DE VAUX, ANCIENT ISRAEL: ITS LIFE AND INSTITUTIONS, (John McHugh trans., London: Dartman, Longman & Todd, 1961), 480.

4. *Hansard*, Shops Bill, January 21, 1986, p.160.

5. Pinchas Kahn, *The expanding perspectives of the Sabbath*, JEWISH BIBLE Q. 32, 239–44, 241 (2004).

request, which Pharaoh repeatedly refuses, is for the Israelites to have some time off work in order to worship God:

> Afterward Moses and Aaron went to Pharaoh and said, "Thus says the LORD, the God of Israel, 'Let my people go, that they may hold a feast to me in the wilderness.'" But Pharaoh said, "Who is the LORD, that I should heed his voice and let Israel go? I do not know the LORD, and moreover I will not let Israel go." Then they said, "The God of the Hebrews has met with us; let us go, we pray, a three days' journey into the wilderness, and sacrifice to the LORD our God, lest he fall upon us with pestilence or with the sword." But the king of Egypt said to them, "Moses and Aaron, why do you take the people away from their work? Get to your burdens." And Pharaoh said, "Behold, the people of the land are now many and you make them rest from their burdens!" (Exodus 5:1–5)

This might explain why Sabbath observance was such a priority as soon as the Israelites got their release (Exodus 16:23). It could also explain why Sabbath observance is tied to remembering the Exodus in Deuteronomy 5:12–15. We saw in Chapter 6 that there was a contrast between Pharaonic economics, which took the form of amassing land and family economics, which was about access to personalized land. There is a similar contrast in relation to employee protection. Here, Pharaonic economics is linked to harsh working conditions and slavery while family economics is reflected in time off for workers and Sabbath rest.

II. A WELFARE SYSTEM OR A WELFARE SOCIETY?

The restonomics approach of "one day off in seven" was extended to "one *year* off in seven," in other words, the sabbatical year. This promotes social welfare by requiring creditors to let go of outstanding debts owed by fellow Israelites at the end of the seventh year. This ancient "drop the debt" campaign is seen in the *shemittah* laws of Deuteronomy 15:1–11:

> Every seventh year you shall practice remission of debts.
> (*shemittah*; Deuteronomy 15:1; *Moses speaking,* JPS)

We saw, above, a relationship between the Exodus and the Sabbath laws. This set up a contrast between Pharaonic economics and family economics, raising the question whether hearers would follow Pharaoh or God. There is a very similar contrast between the Exodus and the *shemittah* laws, which also generates a contrast between Pharaonic economics and family economics. This is seen in a number of ways.

A. The hand of God and the fist of man

First, there is a binary opposition between the "shut hand" of Deuteronomy 15:7 and the "open hand" of verse 8. It is a contrast between two narrative stereotypes: the person with a closed hand who will not let go (verse 7) and the person with an open hand (verses 3, 8, and 11) who brings freedom. Who springs to mind when we think of these narrative stereotypes? Surely it is Pharaoh and God, although to my knowledge this has not been remarked on in relation to this passage. Pharaoh is repeatedly portrayed in the Exodus story as the person who, in the classic refrain, refused to "let the people go" (e.g., Exodus 8:32). By contrast, the "mighty hand" of God is typically portrayed as bringing the Israelites out of slavery "from the hand of Pharaoh king of Egypt" (e.g., Deuteronomy 7:8). The common identification in the ancient Near East (ANE) of "hand" with power underlines, once again, the nature of the choice before the Israelites: in relation to the poor, will they exercise their power like Pharaoh or like God?

Second, another striking aspect of this debt release (*shemittah*; Deuteronomy 15:1) is the juxtaposition between "heart" and "hand":

> If there is among you a poor man, one of your brethren . . . you shall not harden your *heart* or shut your *hand* against your poor brother.
> (Deuteronomy 15:7; *Moses speaking*)

This correspondence of heart and hand as symbols of will and action is found elsewhere in the ANE, including ancient Egyptian texts.[6] This is relevant in the light of the intertexuality with Pharaoh. Indeed, the juxtaposition of the hardened heart with the shut hand confirms the idea that Pharaoh is the narrative typification of the harsh creditor. After all it is Pharaoh who:

> . . . hardened his heart . . . and did not let the people go. (Exodus 8:32/ MT 8:28; and note that in this verse Pharaoh is the subject who explicitly hardens his own heart)

The verb used for hardening in Deuteronomy 15:7 (*'immetz*) is different from the normal verb used to describe the hardening of Pharaoh's heart in Exodus (*chazaq*; e.g., Exodus 4:21). But this does not undermine the argument because different verbs are used for the hardening of Pharaoh's heart, even in Exodus itself (thus Exodus 8:32, quoted above, uses the verb *kabhad*).

Third, according to Deuteronomy 15:9, the closed hand is also a product of the "base (*beliya'al*) thought in your heart." Although the meaning of the word *beliya'al* is uncertain, most modern scholars see it as a compound word related to a form of the root *ya'al*, which means "to profit/to benefit."[7] Given the other Pharaonic references in this passage, we may see an allusion to Pharaoh's desire

---

6. J. Bergman, Yad, in THEOLOGICAL DICTIONARY OF THE OLD TESTAMENT (G. Johannes Botterweck & Helmer Ringgren, eds.; David E. Green trans.; Grand Rapids, Mich.: Eerdmans, 1986), vol. V, 393–96, 396.

7. Benedikt Otzen, Beliyya'al, in THEOLOGICAL DICTIONARY OF THE OLD TESTAMENT, (G. Johannes Botterweck & Helmer Ringgren eds., David E. Green trans.; Grand Rapids, Mich.: Eerdmans, 1977), vol. 2, 131–36, 133.

to squeeze maximum profit from the Israelites' labor; the classic example, of course, being the "bricks without straw" episode (Exodus 5:1–21).

Finally, according to Deuteronomy 15:10, the closed hand is also related to the grudging heart. Again, in line with the argument so far, this may evoke the extreme reluctance with which Pharaoh let the Israelites go. According to the Exodus story, the Israelites were not released until after the seriousness of the tenth plague (Exodus 12:29–32) whereupon Pharaoh regretted the loss and sought to bring them back (Exodus 14:5–9).

To sum up the argument so far, Sabbath and "Sabbath-plus" laws employ a structural opposition between Pharaoh and God. Pharaonic economics here means holding onto debts while family economics means letting them go. Family economics inspires the Israelites to imitate God rather than Pharaoh. This argument has particular force given that those addressed are presented as Pharaoh's slaves. In rhetorical terms the Israelites' collective experience is used to generate a change of perspective. The precise technique used in Deuteronomy 15 can be found elsewhere in biblical law. Leviticus 25:43 states that the Israelite who holds power over an Israelite debt-slave must not "rule over him ruthlessly (*bepharekh*)" (JPS). This is a very rare word in the Hebrew Bible, but it is twice used to describe Pharaoh's rule over the Israelites (Exodus 1:13, 14).[8] Israel's experience of being on the receiving end of injustice encourages subsequent generations to be generous toward the poor. Law draws upon the Israelites' memory to reshape corporate and individual identity.

B. "Brothers", not "others"

Deuteronomy 15:1–11, like the book as a whole, has an impressive rhetorical structure that serves a particular purpose. This is worth examining more closely to assist our understanding of the character of biblical law. The connections between "hand," "heart," and also "eye" (verse 9) indicate that the social welfare laws are largely designed to change attitudes by making the hearers feel certain emotions. Commentators note the opposing potentialities in verse 4 which states: "There will be no poor among you" and verse 11 which predicts: "the poor will never cease out of the land." Some suggest that this contrasts life in the "true brotherhood of Israel" with the reality of life in the physical land.[9] This contrast is not explicit, however. What is explicit is the claim that freedom from poverty is conditional upon obeying "the voice of the LORD your God" (verse 5). Failure to do so (anticipated in verses 7–9) guarantees the continued existence of the poor.

---

8. Calum M. Carmichael, *The Sabbatical/Jubilee cycle and the Seven-Year Famine in Egypt*, BIBLICA 80, 224–39, 234 (1999).

9. *E.g.*, Martin J. Oosthuizen, *Deuteronomy 15:1-18 in Socio-Rhetorical Perspective*. ZEITSCHRIFT FÜR ALTORIENTALISCHE UND BIBLISCHE RECHTSGESCHICHTE 3, 64–91, 68 (1997), citing Lohfink with approval.

The *shemittah* laws artfully evoke sympathy for the "poor brother" (verses 7, 9). The language is very inclusive—it is "brothers" not "others." The emphasis here is on moral exhortation and not on setting out areas of legal entitlement. The affections have a role to play. Biblical law is not concerned with creating a welfare system but a welfare society. The verb "to open" (*patach*) is given double emphasis in the commandment to "open your hand" (*patoach tiphtach*; verse 8). There are more absolute infinitives (e.g., "open, open" in verse 8) in Deuteronomy 15:4–10 (five in all) than in any other commandment.[10] Any modern fundraiser would recognize the emotional plea. In common with other social justice laws in the Bible, there is also a naked appeal to self-interest (verses 5–6, 10). Even modern think tanks, which see a place for altruism in social welfare strategy, argue "the moral case is . . . more likely to prove acceptable if people can feel confident that it is not going to impede their own ambitions and aspirations."[11] Poetic justice, too, is present. Seeking the economic self-sufficiency of the poor results in increased economic power for the creditor:

> You shall give to him ["your poor brother," verse 9] freely, and your heart shall not be grudging when you give to him; because for this the LORD your God will bless you in all your work and in all that you undertake.
> (Deuteronomy 15:10; *Moses speaking*)

Moreover, the creditor's privileged economic status is not simply described in domestic political terms (as in verse 10) but also in international terms (see verse 6). The picture of Israel extending loans "to many nations" (verse 6) emphasizes Israel's fortunate position. Of course, international lending is a bigger risk to the creditor than domestic lending because, in the latter case, there is likely to be a stronger relationship between the parties. Yet Israel is expected to take that risk and to be a model of generosity to the nations. This can be seen as another way in which Israel fulfills its vocation to be a source of blessing to all the nations of the earth (Genesis 12:2–3).

Deuteronomy 15:1–11 has the same purpose as a stirring political speech, which is not surprising since that is exactly what the book of Deuteronomy is. The *shemittah* laws are full of irresistible sound bites. "There will be no poor among you" (verse 4). "You shall lend to many nations, but you shall not borrow; and you shall rule over many nations, but they shall not rule over you" (verse 6). Their political power cannot be underestimated. British readers might recall the compelling slogans of the Beveridge Committee Report that inspired the United Kingdom during the Second World War, such as "Freedom From Want" and

---

10. WALTER BRUEGGEMANN, THE COVENANTED SELF: EXPLORATIONS IN LAW AND COVENANT (Minneapolis: Fortress, 1999), 81.

11. RAYMOND PLANT, SOCIAL JUSTICE, LABOUR AND THE NEW RIGHT, FABIAN PAMPHLET 556 (London: Fabian Society, 1993), 17.

"Security for All."[12] Deuteronomy 15:1–11 is essentially a call to national solidarity. The purpose of law here is to get the people's backing for a rosy economic program founded on the generosity of God and man. It is a positive vision of social good.

C. The uses of capital

The focus of welfare is lending, not giving, although the remission of debt in the final year carries with it the possibility that the loan will eventually become a gift. Nevertheless, the emphasis is on repayment by the borrower, which helps to preserve the dignity of the poor and also encourages them to take responsibility. The ban on interest has a promise of widespread blessing attached ("that the LORD your God may bless you *in all that you undertake* in the land which you are entering to take possession of it"; Deuteronomy 23:20/ MT 23:21). Biblical "blessings and curses" are frequently seen as the outworking of human behavior, either positively or negatively. This is in keeping with the sort of worldview espoused by the book of Proverbs, for example, in which human behavior has moral consequences (e.g., Proverbs 6:27–29). Rewards and punishments are thus integral to particular forms of human behavior. The universal social blessing of Deuteronomy 23:20/ MT 23:21 reflects the belief that the ban on interest has positive implications for society. It is not concerned simply with the financial arrangements between two parties but with the social ramifications of how capital is used.

Capital can be used in different ways, with differing social consequences. For example, financial arrangements can be used as a way of enabling and thereby encouraging people to become autonomous. Or they can form a "social glue" that causes people to engage closely with one another. It is generally recognized that an interest-based economy encourages individualism. This is because it makes it possible to obtain a return on a loan without there being an ongoing relationship between the parties or a connection between the return on the loan and the use of the money. The global financial crisis of 2007–2009 illustrated once again the dangers of such a debt-based system. Families were encouraged to borrow heavily in the United States, United Kingdom, and elsewhere against inflated house values. Lenders themselves had low levels of capital to absorb losses and had often sold the loans on to be repackaged as securities. Once the music stopped, US house prices stopped rising and defaults mounted, securities had to be sold rapidly, banks became first illiquid and then insolvent, and governments were forced to become "borrowers of last resort" to prevent the complete collapse of the financial system. Reflecting on the crisis, the British

---

12. Beveridge Committee Report, State Provision for Social Need: The Beveridge Committee Report on the Welfare State (Microfiche. Public Record Office Class PIN 8 & Cab 87/76–82, 1942).

Chancellor of the Exchequer spoke of the need to return to "good, old-fashioned banking". "In crude terms [lenders] need to know who they're lending to, how much they're lending and what the risk is"[13]—an indication, perhaps, of how divorced the UK interest-based economy has become from relationships between borrowers and lenders.

By contrast, the biblical ban on interest encourages the use of capital to build relationships, especially between lender and borrower. This is because if one cannot lend at interest, the options are either to make an outright gift, to lend interest free, to rent/lease property, or to make an equity-based investment. The ban on interest pushes the lender toward sharing risk with the borrower. The lender shares in the profits of the enterprise if it is successful, as opposed to simply making a return from the use of his money, regardless of whether the business fails or succeeds. Thus, capital is used in biblical Israel in a way that encourages personal engagement between the parties, especially on the part of the provider. The ban on interest determines the shape and color of the whole of Israelite commerce and has far-reaching effects.

Deuteronomy 15:1–11 is also remarkable because through it we glimpse a problem that must have been widespread. This is the tendency to misinterpret and misapply biblical law, right from the moment it was first delivered. Thus, the lawgiver in verse 9 anticipates that the *shemittah* law will be subject to a narrow reading; it will apply in the early but not the later years of the sabbatical cycle. Remarkably, the lawgiver heads off this reading in the following terms:

> Take heed lest there be a base thought in your heart, and you say, "The seventh year, the year of release is near," and your eye be hostile to your poor brother, and you give him nothing, and he cry to the LORD against you, and it be sin in you. (Deuteronomy 15:9; *Moses speaking*)

This takes us back to some of the issues raised in Chapter 1 regarding the interpretation of biblical law and how we might choose between rival interpretations. Deuteronomy 15:9 excludes the reading that is prompted by "a base thought in your heart." By exposing the thoughts of the heart, Deuteronomy 15 also lays bare the workings of biblical law. Competing interpretations of biblical law are resolved on the basis of wisdom. Divining the correct interpretation of law is a question of character (see Chapter 4 for a biblical approach to Ronald Dworkin's "right-answer" thesis). While this approach to legal interpretation may be news to some Western lawyers, who are usually trained to rely upon a different set of hermeneutic skills, it is consistent with what we have seen thus far regarding the nature of biblical law. We saw in Chapter 3 that biblical law, in the context of the Sinaitic revelation, is a display of the character of God. If so, "being like Pharaoh" and having a profiteering heart will result in a badly

---

13. Daily Telegraph, September 13, 2007.

mistaken interpretation of the *shemittah* law. Equally, "being like God" and seeking other people's economic freedom will form the basis of a reliable interpretation. The warning in verse 9 ("Take heed") reminds us that the biblical laws were, right from the start, essentially contested materials. Interpretative questions were not and could not be settled from some neutral standpoint precisely because Deuteronomy 15 assumes a narrative context (escaping from Pharaoh).

Social welfare is a question of storytelling. The fusion between law and narrative has this inevitable consequence: interpreting the *shemittah* law properly means being part of the story, recognizing where you are in the story, and making sure you are imitating the right leading characters. With this in mind, it is very striking that the lawgiver makes the following command in relation to the *shemittah* law and the entire Deuteronomic legal collection:

> And Moses wrote this law [or "Teaching"; JPS], and gave it to the priests the sons of Levi, who carried the ark of the covenant of the LORD, and to all the elders of Israel. And Moses commanded them, "At the end of every seven years, at the set time of the year of release, at the feast of booths, when all Israel comes to appear before the LORD your God at the place which he will choose, you shall read this law [or 'Teaching'; JPS] before all Israel in their hearing." (Deuteronomy 31:9–11)

The *shemittah* law itself is read in a cultic setting during the "year of *shemittah*" when the whole of Deuteronomy is proclaimed, reminding the people of the story of Israel. It is the special responsibility of priests and elders to organize the septennial reading and to promote social welfare. The prominent role of the priests highlights the sacral aspect of the sabbatical year (see Chapter 6). Mesopotamian kings had a special form of responsibility for debt relief and issued retrospective decrees cancelling debts. The greatest profusion of sources comes from the Old Babylonian (early second millennium) period.[14]

D. Let my people go

We turn from the sabbatical year (once every seven years) to the jubilee year (once every 49 years). The jubilee laws are found in Leviticus 25:8–55 (see further Chapter 6). The jubilee year promotes social welfare by requiring masters to release debt slaves. There were three main kinds of slavery in ancient Israel: (1) Israelite-to-Israelite debt-slavery. Here, one Israelite becomes a slave to another in order to pay off a debt or as punishment for theft (Exodus 22:1/ MT 21:37). The value of the slave's labor over a period of time constitutes payment (up to a maximum of seven years according to Deuteronomy 15:1–3, though Leviticus 25:39–41 runs the period up to the jubilee; see further, below); (2) Non-

---

14. Raymond Westbrook, *Social justice in the Ancient Near East*, in SOCIAL JUSTICE IN THE ANCIENT WORLD (K. D. Irani & Morris Silver eds.; London: Greenwood Press, 1995), 149–63, 154–55.

Israelite to Israelite permanent slavery (Leviticus 25:44–46). Aliens could be acquired through capture in war or bought "from among the children of aliens resident among you" (verse 45; JPS). In contrast to "Israelite-to-Israelite debt slavery," this condition was permanent ("you may keep them as a possession for your children after you, for them to inherit as property for all time; verse 46); and (3) Israelite-to-non-Israelite debt slavery. Here, an Israelite becomes enslaved to a foreigner, typically to pay off a debt (Leviticus 25:47–54). Like (1) above, this was a temporary form of slavery subject to automatic release in the jubilee year (verses 50 and 54). Israelites were permitted to make debt slaves of other Israelites because debt slavery was a temporary status—but not to make them permanent slaves (verse 46). This, of course, reflects Israel's national identity; that of a people who had been released from slavery. Even debt slavery compromised Israel's identity, and for this reason, there was a need to intervene at regular intervals to let debt slaves go free:

> And if your brother becomes poor beside you, and sells himself to you, you shall not make him serve as a slave: he shall be with you as a hired servant and as a sojourner [or "bound labourer"; JPS]. He shall serve with you until the year of the jubilee. (Leviticus 25:39–40; *God speaking*).

According to Leviticus 25:47–54, the debt slave could gain his freedom by the same means possible for alienated land, that is, next of kin (verses 47–49); one's own means (verse 49), or if all else fails, the jubilee year (verses 39–40, 54). Like land, like people. Even while waiting for the jubilee year, the "hired servant" was to be paid (Leviticus 25:39, which provided financial incentives for low-income persons).

Biblical social welfare laws such as redemption and the jubilee put the onus on the extended family to care for its own members. As Mills writes, "it is only through the physical and prolonged proximity of extended family members and neighbours that society can deliver care of dependants without ever greater reliance on the state or on purchased 'care.'"[15] Finally, we saw in Chapter 6 how, in the jubilee year, alienated land was given back to the family who had lost it in the first place or to their descendants. This promoted social welfare by enabling the poor to escape dependency by reuniting them with the means of production.

The jubilee proclamation of release for slaves, like the debt release, is similar to a long tradition of royal proclamations of freedom in Mesopotamia. One of the key expressions found in surviving edicts is "to establish 'liberation'" (*andurarum shakanum*), which refers specifically to the return of property to its owner and to the manumission of persons.[16] There is evidence of such releases being performed from the middle of the third millennium to the end of the first

---

15. Paul Mills, *The divine economy*, CAMBRIDGE PAPERS 9, 1–4, 4 (2000).
16. Moshe Weinfeld, SOCIAL JUSTICE IN ANCIENT ISRAEL (Jerusalem: Magnes Press, 1995), 75.

millennium BC, though most of the documents that use the phrase "to establish *andurarum*" are from the Old Babylonian period (approximately before the middle of the second millennium BC).

Other parts of biblical law regulate the release of debt slaves, although these refer to the release of slaves following their *individual* period of service, rather than a universal release. The laws in Exodus 21:2–6 and Deuteronomy 15:12–18 are similar:

> When you buy a Hebrew slave, he shall serve six years, and in the seventh he shall go out free, for nothing. (Exodus 21:2; *God speaking*)

> If your brother, a Hebrew man, or a Hebrew woman, is sold to you, he shall serve you six years, and in the seventh year you shall let him go free from you. (Deuteronomy 15:12; *Moses speaking*)

This is a longer maximum period than that envisaged in the Laws of Hammurabi (*circa* 1750 BC):

> If an obligation is outstanding against a man and he sells or gives into debt service his wife, his son, or his daughter, they shall perform service in the house of their buyer or of the one who holds them in debt service for three years; their release shall be secured in the fourth year. (LH §117)[17]

Westbrook[18] suggests that the difference may have been more apparent than real inasmuch as both biblical and cuneiform sources may presuppose some discretion based on whether the debt slaves have paid off the capital of the debt. This may lie behind paragraph 14 of Codex Lipit-Ishtar (circa 1930 BC):

> If a man's slave contests his slave status against his master, and it is proven that his master has been compensated for this slavery two-fold, that slave shall be freed.[19]

and the motivation clause of Deuteronomy 15:18:[20]

> It shall not seem hard to you, when you let him go free from you; for at half the cost of a hired servant he has served you six years . . . . (*Moses speaking*)

Six years may well have been the typical length of time in which it took a debt slave to work off the capital of the typical debt. Of course, the biblical preference for six years rather than three may be an extension of the "six plus one" rhythm

---

17. Martha T. Roth, Law collections from Mesopotamia and Asia Minor (Atlanta: Scholars Press, 2nd ed. 1997), 103.
18. Westbrook, Social justice, p. 154.
19. Roth, Law Collections, pp. 28–29.
20. Westbrook, *Social justice*, p. 154.

of the creation narrative. On this basis, six years could have been an appropriate unit for working as a debt slave, after which there is rest and release.

On the face of things, Leviticus 25:39–46 is less favorable to the debtor than Exodus 21:2–11 and Deuteronomy 15:12–18. This is because Exodus and Deuteronomy both make provision for release after six years, whereas in Leviticus, there is no stated release after six years. Instead, the slave has to wait "until the year of the jubilee" (25:40) which could be 49 years away! Some scholars such as Bernard Jackson[21] claim that it is impossible to reconcile the text in Leviticus with those of Exodus and Deuteronomy. However, Gregory Chirichigno[22] argues that the difference lies in the fact that Exodus 21:2–11 and Deuteronomy 15:12–18 are only concerned with the sale of dependents into debt slavery, which would not entail any loss of land: hence a smaller debt and shorter service. By contrast, he argues that Leviticus 25:39–46 is concerned with the sale of the *whole* household into debt slavery which would involve the loss of land: hence a much heavier debt and longer service. It is appropriate to address household debt slavery in the context of Leviticus 25 because the jubilee laws are concerned with the redemption of both family *and* land. This could explain why the debtor of Leviticus 25:39–46 must wait for the jubilee year rather than the sabbatical year because only the jubilee restores alienated land (see Chapter 6).

Leviticus 25:39–46 differs from Deuteronomy 15:12–18 in another important respect. According to Deuteronomy 15:18, the Hebrew debt slave serves the creditor for six years "at half the cost of a hired servant." This implies that the debt slave is not to be categorized as "a hired servant." By contrast, Leviticus 25:39–40 makes it clear that he *is* to be thought of as "a hired servant" and not as a slave (". . . you shall not make him serve as a slave: he shall be with you as a hired servant and as a sojourner [or 'bound labourer'; JPS]"). This is because Leviticus 25:39–46 sets up a binary opposition between debt slaves in verses 39–43 (who are typically fellow Israelites) and war captive slaves in verses 44–45 (who are typically foreigners). A clear distinction is thus drawn between insiders (i.e., fellow Israelites) who are subject to, at most, temporary servitude (Leviticus 25:39–43) and outsiders (i.e., foreigners) who can be permanent slaves (Leviticus 25:44–46).[23] This concern to clarify the status of the debt slave is wholly in keeping with Levitical and scribal concerns for categorization (cf. "onomastica" and Mesopotamian lexical and other lists). We note that although Deuteronomy 15:12–18 does not juxtapose the insider/outsider distinction in the same way as

---

21. BERNARD S. JACKSON, WISDOM-LAWS: A STUDY OF THE MISHPATIM OF EXODUS 21:1-22:16 (Oxford: Oxford University Press, 2006), 87 n. 41.
22. GREGORY C. CHIRICHIGNO, DEBT-SLAVERY IN ISRAEL AND THE ANCIENT NEAR EAST, JOURNAL FOR THE STUDY OF THE OLD TESTAMENT SUPPLEMENT SERIES 141 (Sheffield: Sheffield Academic Press, 1993), 336.
23. JACKSON, WISDOM-LAWS, pp. 82–83.

Leviticus 25:39–46, there is nevertheless a distinction in Deuteronomy between debt slaves and war captive slaves as far as the women are concerned. There is a binary opposition between the female debt slave (the *ibhriyyah* of Deuteronomy 15:12 and the *amah* of Deuteronomy 15:17) and the war captive female slave (Deuteronomy 21:10–14).[24] This parallel underlines the difference between Leviticus 25:39–46 and Deuteronomy 15:12–18 in regard to slaves and their release. If one takes Jackson's view, namely, that Leviticus 25:39–46 cannot be reconciled with Deuteronomy 15:12–18, the categorization of the Hebrew debt slave in Leviticus 25:39–46 is a way of compensating, at the ideological level, for the increase in the period of slavery from 7 years to 49 years. Leviticus 25:39–46 changes the concept of slavery while prolonging its length. This contrasts with Chiricigno's argument (see above) which seeks to reconcile the two texts.

III. THE DEBT PENALTY

We turn from the Sabbath day, sabbatical year, and jubilee year to consider further laws concerned with social welfare. These include the ban on interest and laws relating to tithes, food distribution, and gleanings (although, as we have noted above, the ban on interest should not be seen purely, or even primarily, as a matter of social welfare but rather as a way of determining the shape and color of Israelite commerce).

First is the ban on interest (Exodus 22:25/MT 22:24, Leviticus 25:35–38, and Deuteronomy 23:19–20/MT 23:20–21). The ban is on any interest (and not merely excessive interest or usury as some translations wrongly state):

> Do not extract from him advance (*neshekh*) or accrued interest (*tarbit*), but fear your God. Let him live by your side as your kinsman. Do not lend him your money at advance interest, or give him your food at accrued interest. I the LORD am your God, who brought you out of the land of Egypt . . . .
> (Leviticus 25:36–38; *God speaking*; JPS)

The word translated interest (*neshekh*) refers to "that which is bitten off."[25] Interest was seen as "an increase 'bitten off' from the principal."[26] Jewish tradition distinguishes interest (*neshekh*) from increase (*tarbit*) by stating that *neshekh* is prepaid interest while *tarbit* is accrued interest. This is the approach taken in the translation, above. From the borrower's point of view, *neshekh* is worse than *tarbit*. It is to this form of interest that the laws usually refer. The beneficiary

---

24. JACKSON, WISDOM-LAWS, pp. 115–17, 302.
25. A. S. Kapelrud, *Neshek*, in THEOLOGICAL DICTIONARY OF THE OLD TESTAMENT (G. Johannes Botterweck, Helmer Ringgren & Heinz-Josef Fabry eds.; Douglas W. Stott trans.; Grand Rapids, Mich.: Eerdmans, 1999), vol. X, 61–65, 62.
26. Ibid.

of the ban is the fellow Israelite. Charging interest is a departure from the mutual aid that ought to characterize Israel's sense of brotherhood. However, the ban did not preclude charging interest to the nonresident alien (*nokhri*). This may have been because it was opposed to the paradigm case of the "brother" Israelite (Leviticus 25:36). Mills notes that the combination of a ban on interest and regular debt cancellation (see above) meant that "lending was done either for charitable purposes or for mutual favours between family, neighbours or business partners."[27] It also meant that "investment finance would have been channelled into alternative, risk-sharing and rental contracts rather than commercial loans."[28]

We saw that both the weekly Sabbath and *shemittah* laws drew a structural contrast between Pharaonic economics and family economics. The same is true of the ban on interest. Leviticus 25:37 makes it clear that lending at interest is a form of Pharaonic economics:

> Do not lend him your money at advance interest, *or give him your food* at accrued interest. (*God speaking;* JPS)

Food is a significant motif in the light of the Joseph story. This records the following plea by the Egyptians during a time of famine:

> "Why should we die before your eyes, both we and our land? *Buy us and our land for food*, and we with our land will be slaves to Pharaoh; and give us seed, that we may live, and not die, and that the land may not be desolate." So Joseph bought all the land of Egypt for Pharaoh; for all the Egyptians sold their fields, because the famine was severe upon them. The land became Pharaoh's; and as for the people, he made slaves of them from one end of Egypt to the other. (Genesis 47:19–21)

Genesis 47 describes the handing out of state rations to those "bought up" by Pharaoh. This is not quite the same thing as selling food for profit, but it does exploit the desperation of the needy in order to gain material advantage. Food for profit is thus related to the type of thing that Pharaoh or his representatives would do. The picture of Pharaoh as a totalitarian controller of food production reappears in Ezekiel 29. "State rations" from Pharaoh is in stark contrast to the motif of "food in abundance" associated with God:

> And God said, "Behold, I have given you every plant yielding seed which is upon the face of all the earth, and every tree with seed in its fruit; you shall have them for food." (Genesis 1:29)

---

27. Paul Mills, *Finance,* in JUBILEE MANIFESTO (Michael Schluter & John Ashcroft eds.; Leicester: InterVarsity Press/Jubilee Centre, 2005), 196–215, 206.

28. Ibid.

This contrast between Pharaonic economics (lending for profit) and family economics (giving freely) is sealed by the refrain: "I am the LORD your God, who brought you forth out of the land of Egypt to give you the land of Canaan, and to be your God" (Leviticus 25:38). For Israel, the practice of social welfare is about choosing not to be like Pharaoh and choosing to follow God.

IV. LAWS OF ABUNDANCE

Having noted the association between God and abundance (which, as we saw in Chapter 6, derives from a belief in divine ownership of the land), we move on to consider what I call "laws of abundance." These are the tithe laws (Deuteronomy 14:22–29), the Sukkot celebrations (Deuteronomy 16:13–15), and the law of gleanings (Leviticus 19:9–10; Deuteronomy 23:24/MT 23:25 and Deuteronomy 24:19–22).

A. The economics of joy

First, let's consider the tithe laws (Deuteronomy 14:22–29). We saw in Chapter 6 that ideas and stories about land determine how it is used. We also saw that "land-as-narrative" creates a network of interdependencies. The tithe laws are a good example of the "horizontal" responsibilities owed by those who have access to property. Deuteronomy 14:27 requires that the landless Levites are included in the ritual consumption of the tithe, which represents one-tenth of agricultural production, while Deuteronomy 14:28–29 requires that the triennial tithe benefits a broader group, including "the sojourner, the fatherless, and the widow."

Second, the annual *Sukkot* (Feast of Booths) celebrations (Deuteronomy 16:13–15) envisage the distribution of food to vulnerable groups:

> [Y]ou shall rejoice in your feast, you and your son and your daughter, your manservant and your maidservant, the Levite, the sojourner, the fatherless, and the widow who are within your towns. For seven days you shall keep the feast to the LORD your God at the place which the LORD will choose; because the LORD your God will bless you in all your produce and in all the work of your hands, so that you will be altogether joyful.
> (Deuteronomy 16:14–15; *Moses speaking*)

Sukkot was one of the three great pilgrimage festivals of the Hebrew year. At this celebration, the Israelites dramatized the Exodus from Egypt by living in temporary shelters. Again, making sense of the biblical social welfare laws means thinking about images and the story they tell so that it changes attitudes. Here we see that the social distribution of wealth occurs in the context of remembering the Exodus. It is another example of family economics. This distribution took place at a centralized location (16:15), unlike the tithe laws of Deuteronomy 14:28–29, where the food was distributed locally.

For critical theorists, Deuteronomy 16:13–15 is an example of a social welfare law that exacerbated the position of widows, strangers, and orphans. It discriminated against the very groups it was supposed to assist because travel to and from the location was dangerous. Vulnerable persons probably could not afford to travel anyway.[29] However, this interpretation unconsciously assumes a semantic reading of the text. It implies that the obligation to be joyful with the vulnerable is limited to the temporal and physical feast. A narrative approach to the text, on the other hand, conveys the image of travelling to and returning from the feast and so would involve assistance and provision at that stage also. It is part of the paradigmatic act of giving, viz., "every man shall give as he is able, according to the blessing of the LORD your God which he has given you" (Deuteronomy 16:17).

An interesting aspect of both the tithe laws and the *Sukkot* celebrations is the reference to sharing "before the LORD your God, in the place which he will choose, to make his name dwell there . . ." (14:23) and celebrating "before the LORD your God at the place which he will choose" (Deuteronomy 16:16). These turns of phrase refer to the central sanctuary (either the roving Tabernacle or to the Temple). It evokes the account of the elders eating in the Presence of God at Sinai (Exodus 24:11). Social welfare takes place in God's Presence. This association may help us to make sense of the connection in the prophets between social welfare and the light of God's Presence (referred to as the *Shekhinah* in postbiblical literature):

> if you pour yourself out for the hungry and satisfy the desire of the afflicted, then shall your light rise in the darkness and your gloom be as the noonday. (Isaiah 58:10, *God speaking*)

Elsewhere, in Deuteronomy 26:12–15, the triennial tithe given to vulnerable groups is expressly identified as the "sacred portion" (26:13). The sacerdotal quality of the act is accentuated by a formal oath in which the person tithing swears:

> I have not eaten of the tithe while I was mourning, or removed any of it while I was unclean, or offered any of it to the dead; I have obeyed the voice of the LORD my God . . . . (Deuteronomy 26:14, *Moses speaking*)

There is a binary opposition here between improper ritual misuse of the tithe (mourning/ uncleanness/sacrifice to the dead) and proper ritual use. This underlines the sacred character of social welfare.

The sacred dimension of the social welfare laws is also seen in the various sabbatical institutions (above), which are associated with the holy day of the

---

29. Harold V. Bennett, INJUSTICE MADE LEGAL: DEUTERONOMIC LAW AND THE PLIGHT OF WIDOWS, STRANGERS, AND ORPHANS IN ANCIENT ISRAEL (Grand Rapids, Mich.: Eerdmans, 2002), 118.

original Sabbath (in the case of the weekly Sabbath and the sabbatical year) or the Day of Atonement (in the case of the jubilee). This presentation of the biblical social welfare laws is important for our understanding of the character of biblical law. The sabbatical and jubilee years are not a "Seven Year Plan" or a "Great Leap Forward" in the style of some twentieth century social and economic reforms. They are arguably more radical than anything put forward by Chairmen Lenin and Mao because biblical law regards social reform as a sacred obligation. In the case of the jubilee, national purification precedes economic restoration. Welfare is spiritual, and spirituality involves social welfare. (The same is true of economics: we saw in Chapter 6 that land is integral to Israel's spirituality and so are the various sabbatical laws). The food distribution laws of Deuteronomy 14 and 16 illustrate that biblical law did not merely apply cultic terminology or cultic settings to socioeconomic problems, "they actually used this apparatus as a means of reasoning about, and attempting a solution to, the problem of poverty."[30] Sacral categories are not a means of escaping social problems but a way of addressing and resolving them. This means that they are capable of profound social application, both in biblical Israel and in modern society.[31] And given the role of narrative in shaping biblical Israel's social welfare, it invites us today to tell the right story—of full inclusion and participation that can transform people's lives while preserving individual responsibility.

B. Gleaning law from narrative

Finally, we consider the law of gleanings (Leviticus 19:9–10; Deuteronomy 23:24/ MT 23:25 and Deuteronomy 24:19–22). This is the last social welfare law we will consider before moving on to consider the development of the social welfare laws in the New Testament and their implications for modern social practice. "Gleanings" are the agricultural produce left behind by farmers—both accidentally (Deuteronomy 24:19) and intentionally (Leviticus 19:10)—to benefit the poor. It was a form of patronage and support and a publicly visible source of welfare. The gleaning laws covered several forms of produce, including olives and grapes, but those relating to grain were of particular practical importance. This is because ordinary people relied on wheat and barley as their primary sources of protein and of nutrition. As far as the poor were concerned, access to grain and gleanings was "literally a matter of life and death."[32]

---

30. Robert S. Kawashima, *The Jubilee year and the return of cosmic purity*, CATHOLIC BIBLICAL Q. 65, 370–389, 387 (2003).

31. *See* Mills, *Finance*, and Mills, *The economy*; Michael Schluter, *Welfare*, in JUBILEE MANIFESTO (Michael Schluter & John Ashcroft eds.; Leicester: InterVarsity Press/Jubilee Centre, 2005), 175–95 and further below.

32. ELLEN F. DAVIS, SCRIPTURE, CULTURE AND AGRICULTURE: AN AGRARIAN READING (Cambridge: Cambridge University Press, 2008), 125.

The gleaning laws presuppose abundance and trust in the God who makes the land fertile (see Chapter 6). The law has its roots in the manna story. The provision of manna in the wilderness is a picture of abundance:

> This is what the LORD has commanded: "Gather *(liqtu)* of it, every man of you, as much as he can eat; you shall take an omer apiece, according to the number of the persons whom each of you has in his tent." And the people of Israel did so; they gathered *(wayyilqetu)*, some more, some less. But when they measured it with an omer, *he that gathered much had nothing over, and he that gathered little had no lack*; each gathered *(laqatu)* according to what he could eat. And Moses said to them, "Let no man leave any of it till the morning." But they did not listen to Moses; some left part of it till the morning, and it bred worms and became foul; and Moses was angry with them. (Exodus 16:16-20)

The repetition of "evening . . . and morning" in Exodus 16:6–7 alludes to the story of universal creation, which emphasizes the abundant provision of God (e.g,. Genesis 1:11–13).[33] It is also a picture of social justice in the sense that it aims at an equitable distribution of resources: "he that gathered much had nothing over, and he that gathered little had no lack" (Exodus 16:18). From a semiotic perspective, therefore, observance of the gleaning laws visually alludes to the manna story. Both involve the sight of "food lying around on the ground." Reenacting the manna story creates the conditions for social justice, both symbolically and in practice.

Leaving food on the ground for the poor is the binary opposite of hoarding. This is another way in which the gleaning laws relate to the manna story. The "bread from heaven" had, as it were, a heavenly supermarket label stuck on it that instead of reading "This product may contain nuts" warned "This product is not to be kept." The "Use By" date was always "Today" (unless it was gathered on the eve of the Sabbath). Hoarding is prohibited, and hoarded food spoiled (Exodus 16:20). The gleaning laws even prohibit hoarding by the needy (Deuteronomy 23:24/MT 23:25). This is because, as we saw above, "hoarding food" was characteristic of Pharaoh because there was no abundance (Genesis 47:19). Davis[34] sees hoarding as a symptom of "Egypt's disease." The ban on hoarding was a complete break from life in Egypt: after all, the point of the Israelites' slave labor was to build storage cities for Pharaoh (Exodus 1:11). The ban on hoarding in Exodus 16:16 ensures that "no Israelite tent can be a silo; the Israelite camp cannot be a storage city."[35] Yet again, the social welfare laws reflect an opposition between Pharaonic economics (hoarding and want) and family economics (abandon and abundance).

---

33. Ibid., 74.
34. Ibid., 70.
35. Ibid., 76.

A further connection between the manna story and the gleaning laws is the fact that the verb translated "to gather" (*laqat*) can also be translated "to glean" (e.g., Ruth 2:7). The repetition of this verb in the manna story underlines how Israel is as dependent for its food upon the generosity of God as poor gleaners are upon the generosity of Israelite farmers.[36] Davis draws attention to Egyptian tomb paintings which show that "gleaners were the most vulnerable and often the most desperate participants in the ancient food economy."[37] We saw above that the biblical land laws present Israelite landowners, paradoxically, as "strangers and sojourners" (Leviticus 25:23). Here too, in the manna story, Israel is made to identify herself with those on the margins of society. "Even as the Israelites begin their journey to the land they will possess, they are put in the position of the most dependent members of the society they themselves will form."[38] There is sense here of "them" and "us": all are seen to be dependent on God, and all are kept in a position of humility.

Can we legislate generosity? Deuteronomy 15:12–15 certainly does so (see above). Elsewhere, "commanding kindness" takes the form of prohibitions (don't intensively harvest all the produce, don't collect a forgotten sheaf, and so on; Deuteronomy 24:19–21). These are backed up by the motivation clause of verses 22: "You shall remember that you were a slave in the land of Egypt; therefore I command you to do this." Observing this law involves identification with the story of Israel and the generosity of Israel's God. Once again, we find that narrative shapes and colors attitudes toward property (see Chapter 6). This being so, we could expect to find wide variations in care for the poor depending on the degree to which Israelites had internalized this story of God's generosity. This is in fact what we do find. Even in a small locality such as Bethlehem, we discover that Ruth is far better off in Boaz's fields than she is in anyone else's (Ruth 2:22). Boaz commands those under his authority: "Let her [Ruth] glean *even among the sheaves* . . ." (Ruth 2:15) which suggests that there were "restricted zones" for gleaning. Boaz (like God) is capable of commanding generosity, ordering his workers to "pull some [stalks] out of the heaps and leave them for her to glean . . ." (Ruth 2:16). One sign that Boaz has observed the law is the telling detail that Ruth "ate her fill" (2:14; JPS). The language evokes the tithe laws in Deuteronomy 26:12 which require that vulnerable groups should "eat their fill." Indeed, Ruth "had some left over" (Ruth 2:14), showing that Boaz has gone beyond the requirements of social welfare.

The book of Ruth offers further insights into the operation of the gleaning laws and allows us a rare glimpse of the relationship between law and practice.

---

36. In the same vein, a jar of manna was said to be kept in Israel as a reminder for future generations that the whole nation was—and remains—dependent on God for its welfare (Exodus 16:32–34).
37. Ibid., 75.
38. Ibid.

For one thing, Ruth allows us to hear "the female voice" in relation to the gleaning laws. Both Boaz (Ruth 2:8–9) and Naomi (Ruth 2:22) warn of the dangers faced by women of being molested while out in the fields. The big question, though, is: is the book of Ruth an example of the "proper" application of the biblical law of gleanings? In one sense it is; in another sense, it is not.

The first point to note is that although Boaz has a good reputation (Ruth 2:22), his treatment of Ruth was generous even by his standards. Other needy girls were not treated like this—a point to which Ruth explicitly refers (Ruth 2:11). Is it that Ruth embodies the notion of the "respectable" or "resourceful" poor? No. Boaz's characterization of her is significant:

> All that you have done for your mother-in-law since the death of your husband has been fully told me, *and how you left your father and mother and your native land and came to a people that you did not know before.*
> (Ruth 2:11; *Boaz speaking*)

On the face of things, Ruth falls within a semantic reading of the biblical laws: she is a "sojourner." But as Boaz sees, there is more to Ruth than that. This means that contrary to appearances, she does not fit the narrative typification of the sojourner. Rather, her narrative evokes the story of Abraham, ancestor of Israel:

> [T]he LORD said to Abram, *"Go from your country and your kindred and your father's house to the land that I will show you."* (Genesis 12:1)

Ruth's story is, if anything, even more extreme than Abraham's because Ruth does not actually respond to a call. She leaves Moab of her own volition—and contrary to the advice of an Israelite woman, Naomi![39] As if that were not enough, Ruth's story evokes the story of Rebekah, Jacob's wife (another of Israel's ancestors). Naomi's response to Ruth's story about meeting Boaz has striking similarities with the response of Abraham's servant's upon meeting Rebekah:[40]

> "Blessed be the LORD, the God of my master Abraham, who has not forsaken his steadfast love and his faithfulness toward my master. As for me, the LORD has led me in the way to the house of my master's kinsmen."
> (Genesis 24:27; *Abraham's servant speaking*)

> "Blessed be he [Boaz] by the LORD, whose kindness has not forsaken the living or the dead!" Naomi also said to her, "The man is a relative of ours, one of our nearest kin." (Ruth 2:20)

---

39. Irmtraud Fischer, *The Book of Ruth: A "Feminist" Commentary to the Torah?*, in RUTH AND ESTHER: A FEMINIST COMPANION TO THE BIBLE (Athalya Brenner ed., Sheffield: Sheffield Academic Press, 2nd series, 1999), 24–49, 43.

40. Ibid.

These responses signify broadly similar narratives: both Genesis 24 and Ruth 2 concern marriages within an extended family that are arranged by divine providence. Toward the end of the story, the elders' blessing upon Boaz and Ruth's marriage explicitly brackets Ruth with Israel's famous ancestresses (Rachel, Leah, and Tamar; Ruth 4:11–12). This confirms that Ruth does not fit the narrative stereotype of the sojourner.

For all these reasons, the account of the gleanings in *Ruth* may not be a straightforward application of the social welfare laws for the simple reason that Ruth was not a typical sojourner. She was treated in an extraordinary fashion because Ruth herself was extraordinary. This has implications for our understanding of biblical law. Once again, we see the interdependence of law and narrative. Boaz seems to have interpreted the gleaning laws in the light of the patriarchal narratives. The result was acts of spectacular generosity. *Ruth* is a hybridization of law and narrative that shapes and directs beliefs about how to help specific individuals in need.

V. SOCIAL WELFARE OR SOCIAL JUSTICE?

Are the biblical laws concerned with social welfare or social justice? Certainly among critical scholars, welfare is not synonymous with justice. "Assisting the poor is . . . a potent way of containing the most difficult sections of the population, and improving all other sections."[41] Critics of nineteenth century social reform legislation (including poor laws and housing) have characterized it as not being concerned with the poor but only with "protecting the labour market [and] unburdening the taxpayer."[42] On this view, social welfare is a way of making sure that the middle classes aren't threatened. When the purpose of welfare is to provide justice, it creates a different set of laws than if the purpose of welfare is to reduce risk to certain sections of the population.

Law is especially likely to be used as a subversive instrument where poverty and the poor assume a "menacing character"[43] and are "intensified to the level of *social danger*."[44] This is "the specter of the mob," "[the] magma in which are fused all the dangers which beset the social order."[45] Viewed from this perspective, writers in the field of governmentality (broadly speaking, the way in

---

41. *Marbeau* 1847, *cited in* Giovanna Procacci, *Social economy and the government of poverty, in* THE FOUCAULT EFFECT: STUDIES IN GOVERNMENTALITY (Graham Burchell, Colin Gordon & Peter Miller eds.; Chicago: University of Chicago Press, 1991), 151–68, 151.

42. Procacci, *Social economy*, p. 155.

43. Ibid., 158.

44. Ibid., 159, italics original.

45. Ibid.

which we govern ourselves and other people in a wide variety of different settings) have emphasized the "strategic advantages" of social welfare: "assistance becomes ... a sacrament of moralization, control and dissuasion."[46]

It is not clear that the biblical legal texts envisage a difference between welfare and justice. At a number of points, the biblical welfare laws are expressly connected to biblical pictures of justice, including Sabbath rest (Genesis 2:2, in the case of the sabbatical institutions) and the original divine allocation of land (Numbers 33, in the case of the jubilee). The land is distributed according to a simple basis of equality (large tribes get larger pieces, and small clans get smaller pieces; Numbers 33:54). A number of the social welfare laws are related to the Exodus event, either explicitly or implicitly. This is important because the Exodus is the paradigm act of justice in the Hebrew Bible (because it is the ultimate act of overthrowing an oppressor and delivering the weak). And although some texts, such as Leviticus 25:39–46, distinguish between "insiders" and "outsiders," it is not clear that the purpose of this categorization is to stigmatize the other. On the contrary, attitudes toward the use of property downplay the distinction between "native" and "sojourner" while the distinction between creditor and debt-slave is minimized in the *shemittah* laws by a rhetorical appeal to "brotherhood."

It is said that "Men in general respect most the institutions in which they participate."[47] There is a high degree of participation in social welfare in biblical Israel. Welfare is conducted by and in the community, not "top-down" by central government. It is a picture of what social welfare should be like: drawing marginalized persons back to full membership of the community. Social welfare is not simply a matter of minimal subsistence; rather it is about enabling human flourishing. Nor is it a matter of providing handouts but of full community inclusion. Such involvement has benefits for the community by giving it a role and an identity. Indeed it is fair to say that our failure to deal with welfare appropriately undermines our sense of community. Part of the problem with the modern British welfare system, for example, is its excessive centralization which neuters local government. The lack of a role for local government means that social welfare is administered at a national level by means of rules, which means it is often hard to be flexible or to meet the needs of individuals. In addition, there are few incentives for local government to solve local welfare problems because any benefits are dispersed nationally. Moreover, the State cannot love. It can provide money, but only people can provide love and a sense of belonging.

Another striking aspect of the social welfare laws is the multiplicity of narrative allusions and the way in which they embody the story of Israel, which is an invitation to participate in the grand design of God. Nowhere is this seen more

---

46. Ibid., 165.
47. *Alexandre de Laborde* 1821, *cited in* Procacci, *Social economy*, p. 166.

clearly than in the story of Ruth; the émigrée from Moab who gleans in a field and becomes the ancestress of King David and, in both Jewish and Christian tradition, the forerunner of the Messiah. We are therefore justified in not distinguishing in biblical law between the terms social welfare and social justice. Having said that, there are variations in the intensity of the different biblical laws. There is a distinction between the large-scale structural reforms of the jubilee, on the one hand, and the more ameliorative nature of the gleaning laws, on the other.

Modern lawyers might query whether the biblical social welfare laws attain the status of law in any meaningful sense. How could one enforce the laws of gleaning, for example? In the last century, we have seen how philosophers such as Michel Foucault have challenged traditional ideas of law that have been rooted in "sovereign-subject" relations and where the institution of law is the expression of sovereign power. This is displaced in favor of massively hybridized forms of power in which "the legal complex . . . [becomes] welded to substantive, normalizing, disciplinary and bio-political objectives" that can remold individual and collective action around certain desired ends.[48] From this perspective, François Ewald,[49] for example, opposes traditional ideas of "juridical" power (associated with monarchical law) with "normative" power (that is to say, an idea of law which is fused to the power of norms). The latter is a different sort of power because it is concerned with "a principle of valorization" or "normality" that allows us to distinguish between the normal and the abnormal and has its source in something other than monarchy or government.

The point is not to go into this in great detail but to recognize that, even in modern times, there are quite complex ideas about what law is and how law, combined with other power relations, affects everyday life and behavior. "The workings of law are always intermixed with extra-legal processes and practices."[50] If this is so, then it is not a very large step to recognize the social welfare laws as "law," even though the source of their power lies in narrative and personal identification and not in law enforcement officers.

VI. THE SABBATH SPECTRUM

We are now in a position to see how some of the biblical laws of social welfare, specifically the sabbatical laws, have been extended in the prophetic literature and the New Testament. We saw in Chapter 6 that there is a "spectrum of

---

48. Nikolas Rose & Mariana Valverde, *Governed by Law?*, Soc. & Leg. Studs. 7, 541–51, 543 (1998).
49. François Ewald, *Norms, discipline and the law*, Representations 30, 138–61, 138, 159 (1990).
50. Rose & Valverde, *Governed by Law*, 546.

Sabbaths" of increasing intensity. That there is a range of institutions of d[ecreas]ing scope shows that each Sabbath institution is limited in what it can d[o to] preserve freedom. Thus, the Sabbath day offers respite for a limited period but does nothing about debt. The sabbatical year offers relief for a longer period and addresses debt but does nothing about the alienation of land. The jubilee year addresses the alienation of land and national financial debt but does not address nonphysical debts (e.g., interpersonal forgiveness). And while the jubilee addresses debt slavery, it does not deal with other forms of bondage (e.g., physical infirmity and death).

It is within this thoroughly Jewish tradition of expanding sabbatical institutions that we can begin to make sense of the New Testament's application of the sabbatical laws. Jesus's program of "Torah-awareness" (in which Jesus intends to make clear God's requirements of Israel) is consistent with the dynamic development of Sabbath institutions in biblical law. As the New Testament sees it, Jesus is "lord of the Sabbath" (Matthew 12:8), and so being around Jesus is like living in a perpetual sabbatical year. Thus, the *shemittah* law of Deuteronomy 15 is given a different level of application in the "Lord's prayer" of Matthew 6, which Jesus presents as a pattern of how to pray to God:

> And forgive us our debts, as we also have forgiven our debtors.
> (Matthew 6:12; *Jesus speaking*)

Releasing debt takes place not every seven years but continually. Alongside this increased specificity goes the practice not merely of lending but of *giving*—and not only to fellow Israelites but also to *foreigners*:

> And if you lend to those from whom you hope to receive, what credit is that to you? Even sinners lend to sinners, to receive as much again. But love your enemies, and do good, and lend, expecting nothing in return; and your reward will be great, and you will be sons of the Most High; for he is kind to the ungrateful and the selfish. (Luke 6:34–35; *Jesus speaking*)

On top of all this, we find the continual release not only of financial debts but of nonmonetary debts as well. It is after Jesus's teaching of the "Lord's prayer" that Peter, one of Jesus's senior disciples, asks:

> ... "Lord, how often shall my brother sin against me, and I forgive him? As many as seven times?" Jesus said to him, "I do not say to you seven times, but seventy times seven." (Matthew 18:21–22)

Compared to the sabbatical laws, this is a considerable multiplication; not the number seven (as *per* the Sabbath day and sabbatical year) nor seven times seven (as *per* the jubilee year) but seventy times seven—a figure of speech for infinity. If the jubilee year is "Sabbath-squared," Jesus's approach to the Sabbath of forgiveness is a "perpetual Sabbath." The notion of release here appears to be related to the "seventy sevens" of Daniel 9:24 (i.e., 7 x 70 = 490 years) which, according to the calculations of one of the Dead Sea Scrolls (11Q Melchizedek) corresponds to the end of the tenth Jubilee cycle (50 x 10),[51] which is associated with fulfillment. The elapsing of seventy symbolic sabbatical years is also associated with the end of Israel's exile in Babylon (2 Chronicles 36:21). "Seventy times seven" forgiveness also reverses the "seventy-sevenfold" vengeance of Lamech (Genesis 4:24).

Jesus's disciples are expected to forgive on a constant basis. It is a continual "drop the debt" campaign that covers all debts, to all persons, all the time. By way of illustration, Jesus tells the parable of the unforgiving servant. The conclusion to this story, like the "Lord's prayer", shows that no distinction is made between nonmonetary and monetary debts for the purpose of release:

> Then [the servant's] lord summoned him and said to him, "You wicked servant! I forgave you all that debt because you besought me; and should not you have had mercy on your fellow servant, as I had mercy on you?" And in anger his lord delivered him to the jailers, till he should pay all his debt. So also my heavenly Father will do to every one of you, if you do not forgive your brother from your heart. (Matthew 18:32–35; *Jesus speaking*)

The master and servant relationship is a stock parallel for the relationship between God and Israel. Jesus's Torah-awareness has its roots in God's mercy, which is here presented as debt release. This parallels the Sabbath day, sabbatical, and jubilee years, all of which are rooted in the Exodus. Jesus's Torah-awareness also underlines the connection between nonmonetary and monetary debts. This is implicit in the link between Genesis 47:5–6, 11 (noting Joseph's forgiveness of his brothers; cf. 50:15–21) and Leviticus 25[52] (see Chapter 6). The connection between nonmonetary and monetary debts is also seen in the fact that the jubilee year (which releases Israelites from each others' monetary debts) begins with the Day of Atonement (which releases Israel from nonmonetary debts owed to God). It is because God has provided a way "to make atonement for the Israelites for all their sins once a year" (Leviticus 16:34) that individual Israelites have the moral capacity to release one another from financial debt.

The New Testament is not alone in showing an increase in the scope of sabbatical institutions. We see something similar in the prophetic use of the jubilee laws:

> The Spirit of the Lord GOD is upon me,
> because the LORD has anointed me
> to bring good tidings to the afflicted;

---

51. MOSHE WEINFELD, SOCIAL JUSTICE IN ANCIENT ISRAEL (Jerusalem: Magnes Press, 1995), 210–11.

52. Calum M. Carmichael, *The Sabbatical/Jubilee cycle and the Seven-Year Famine in Egypt*, BIBLICA 80 (1999), 224–39, 234.

he has sent me to bind up the brokenhearted,
to proclaim liberty to the captives,
and the opening of the prison to those who are bound;
to proclaim the year of the LORD's favor,
and the day of vengeance of our God;
to comfort all who mourn; (Isaiah 61:1–2; *the Anointed One speaking*)

Here, "a royal figure . . . one appointed by God upon whom the Holy Spirit rests"[53] proclaims freedom. Some scholars doubt that Isaiah 61 is a jubilary text. But the prophecy certainly contains a number of jubilee motifs which can be summarized in the following manner (Leviticus 25/Isaiah 61): (1) a divinely sanctioned announcement (trumpet/preaching), (2) contrition (the day of atonement/"the wounded of heart"), (3) holiness (a holy year/an anointed servant), (4) proclamation of liberty (slaves and debtors/captives and prisoners), (5) the end of exile (from land/cultic community), (6) restoration and return (to original disposition of land/to God's original creative intent), and (7) reversal of fortunes (e.g., slaves/mourners). It is thus reasonable to see in Isaiah 61 an expansion of Leviticus 25. Nor is it hard to see why the jubilee tradition lent itself as a message of hope to those experiencing exile in Babylon. It perfectly captured the sense of alienation and the desire to be restored to the lost ancestral land.

Isaiah 61 is thought to have its roots in prospective (i.e., future-oriented) Mesopotamian freedom proclamations. During the neo-Assyrian period, such decrees (called *andurarum*) allowed prisoners to be released and exiles to return home (cf. the decrees of Cyrus and Darius; Isaiah 45:1, Ezra 6:1–12).[54] To some extent, there is a parallel between the Jewish expansion of "Super-Sabbath" and the royal tradition of "proclaiming liberty," where granting freedom and restoring individual rights is seen as part of what it means for an individual to return to God. Political, economic, and spiritual freedom went together in the ANE, although there were of course enormous differences between ancient Israel and the rest of the ANE regarding the exercise of that freedom.[55]

The forward-looking aspect of Isaiah 61 points to a tension at the heart of the different sabbatical laws. On the one hand, the Sabbath, sabbatical year, and jubilee year all hark back either to Creation, the Joseph story, or the Exodus, while the notion of families returning every 50 years to a division of property that originally took place under Joshua is a very obvious case of turning the clock back. At the same time, however, the sabbatical laws are also forward-looking: the Sabbath day anticipates the sabbath year which anticipates the jubilee year. For this reason, the Sabbath laws lend themselves to an eschatological program.

---

53. WEINFELD, SOCIAL JUSTICE, p. 12.
54. Ibid., 12–13.
55. *See generally* WEINFELD, SOCIAL JUSTICE.

There are hints of this in Isaiah 61 because, apart from anything else, Isaiah was not envisaging a literal return to the land in the next jubilee year (and in the event the period of the exile was said to last 70 years; 2 Chronicles 36:21).

Isaiah's use of the jubilee tradition therefore points toward a jubilee event that lay outside and beyond the normal 50-year cycle. Already the jubilee came to contain a much bigger hope: not just the end of slavery and the redemption of land but the end of Israel's exile. And what the end of exile might mean was starting to look like a very large question. Some of the exilic prophets, such as Ezekiel, were beginning to characterize the end of exile with a corporate national "resurrection from the dead" (Ezekiel 37). The jubilee laws were being used to speak of a liberation that went beyond debt slavery to announce a greater restoration than the return to family land.

Naturally, if Isaiah could make creative use of the jubilee laws, so could others. For example, the entire Pseudepigraphic work the Book of Jubilees, written during the Second Temple period, presents the history of Israel as a series of jubilee cycles. The entry into Canaan is presented as occurring on the fiftieth cycle (the jubilee of jubilees). In the New Testament, the Gospels use the Isaianic jubilee to make sense of Jesus's emerging ministry, which, like the jubilee, is conceived in terms of "end of exile":

> And Jesus returned in the power of the Spirit into Galilee, and a report concerning him went out through all the surrounding country. And he came to Nazareth, where he had been brought up; and he went to the synagogue, as his custom was, on the sabbath day. And he stood up to read; and there was given to him the book of the prophet Isaiah. He opened the book and found the place where it was written, "The Spirit of the LORD is upon me, because he has anointed me to preach good news to the poor. He has sent me to proclaim release to the captives and recovering of sight to the blind, to set at liberty those who are oppressed, to proclaim the acceptable year of the LORD." And he closed the book, and gave it back to the attendant, and sat down; and the eyes of all in the synagogue were fixed on him. And he began to say to them, "Today this scripture has been fulfilled in your hearing."
> (Luke 4:14–21)

Even without the quotation from Isaiah 61, the links are clear. In keeping with the jubilee laws, Jesus himself "return[s] to his family" home after "proclaim[ing] liberty throughout the land to all its inhabitants" (Leviticus 25:10). Luke 4:23ff assumes a victorious "healing tour" prior to Jesus's arrival in Nazareth. Indeed, the reference to "a report concerning him [Jesus]" that "went throughout the surrounding country" (Luke 4:14) sounds similar to the proclamation of liberty "throughout the land to all its inhabitants" in Leviticus 25:10. What Jesus does is an extension of the things mentioned in Isaiah 58:6–7, which are themselves "the very acts performed by the king who grants freedom to his people."⁵⁶ Such things are appropriate to the year of the LORD's favor (Isaiah 61:1–2).

At one level, what we have here is a physical enactment of the jubilee year. But it is also an extension of Isaiah 61 and, in keeping with Jesus's program of Torah-awareness, it is a further prophetic extrapolation from the jubilee laws. Unlike Leviticus 25, alienation is not here conceived primarily in terms of separation from land and family but in terms of the multiple separations from God's creative intent, typified by disease and infirmity. Later on, Jesus's "jubilee manifesto" addresses the basic alienation that comes with sin and death by the promise of God's forgiveness and resurrection from the dead. Unlike Leviticus 25, the "return home" is not simply a return to land and family but a return to Israel's original vocation; that is, to the freedom of sonship and to intimacy with the ancestral God. All this was radical enough but along with this increased Torah-awareness went Torah-expansion and the suggestion that pagans would also benefit from the "Jesus jubilee"—and might indeed end up being its prime beneficiaries (Luke 4:23–27). In Luke's account, it was this aspect of the "Jesus jubilee" that led to the Nazarenes' spontaneous attempt on Jesus's life (4:28–30). In that sense, the jubilee laws serve the same function as Nazareth in this passage: both are the launch pad for Jesus's public ministry but do not seem to play an especially key role thereafter (4:23–30); a sign, perhaps, of the New Testament's radical continuity with the jubilee legislation but also of its radical discontinuity.

VII. THE ORIGINAL "THIRD WAY"?

The biblical laws of social welfare raise basic questions about the just distribution of resources. This question is at the heart of modern liberal political philosophy. On a global level, it is estimated that the richest 1 percent of adults owned 40 percent of the world's total assets in the year 2000. This study, which was the first of its kind to cover all countries and to include all major components of household wealth, also found that the richest 10 percent of adults accounted for 85 percent of total assets. By contrast, the bottom half of the world's adult population owned just 1 percent of global wealth.⁵⁷ A different study found that the three richest persons in the world have assets in excess of "the combined GDP [gross domestic product] of the 48 least developed countries."⁵⁸

---

56. Ibid., 18.
57. James B. Davies, Susanna Sandstrom, Anthony Shorrocks & Edward N. Wolff, THE WORLD DISTRIBUTION OF HOUSEHOLD WEALTH (United Nations University: World Institute for Development Economics Research, 2006).
58. United Nations Development Programme, HUMAN DEVELOPMENT REPORT 1998: CONSUMPTION FOR HUMAN DEVELOPMENT (Oxford: Oxford University Press, 1998), 30.

Modern liberal theories of social justice can be broadly categorized according to whether they tend to advocate notions of equality and those that favor some idea of liberty. Any account of "justice as equality" would include John Rawls's theory of social justice which, in simple terms, argues that social and economic inequalities can only be justified to the extent that they benefit the least advantaged.[59] The theory is based on two principles of justice: (1) "each person is to have an equal right to the most extensive scheme of equal basic liberties compatible with a similar scheme of liberties for others,"[60] and (2) "social and economic inequalities are to be arranged so that they are . . . reasonably expected to be to everyone's advantage."[61] To give a contemporary example, if the $2 million which author J.K. Rowling reportedly earns every three days cannot be said to benefit the least advantaged, then intervention is justified at a general level—typically in the form of taxation by the State—to achieve this. (Rawls thinks that a theory of justice only concerns the basic structure, and so his theory applies at the level of general taxation laws and not the individual case). Rawls's approach favors a "patterned distribution" of wealth, so called because it is a redistribution of wealth patterned after a particular idea of equality (although Rawls's theory is sensitive to process as well as outcomes in the distribution of wealth). It is typical of left-wing approaches to social justice because it favors a particular conception of equality over liberty.

Other liberal philosophers[62] object to this approach because they do not agree that other people's resources or abilities can be a common asset. They dispute the belief that everyone has a claim on what anyone makes out of exercising their talents. "Patterned" distributions of justice are thus incompatible with liberty. Again, to use the Rowling example, the author's massive wealth is justified, even if it is out of line with a favored pattern, provided her wealth is the result of entering freely negotiated contracts. In basic terms, this is typical of right-wing approaches to social justice because it favors liberty over equality.

Of course, the philosophical debate is far more nuanced and complex than this: nevertheless, it is striking that the biblical approach to property and social welfare eschews a simple preference for either equality or liberty. On the one hand, it is true that the jubilee year promotes equality by granting each family a measure of equality in their *access* to land every 50 years (cf. Numbers 33:54, although as we noted in Chapter 6, it is impossible to have equality in land distribution according to every possible variable, such as fertility, transport routes, mineral wealth, and so on). Indeed, the jubilee laws favor patterned distribution in the sense that they favor a periodic redistribution of land patterned after the

---

59. JOHN RAWLS, A THEORY OF JUSTICE (Oxford: Oxford University Press, rev. ed. 1999).

60. Ibid., p. 53.

61. Ibid.

62. Such as ROBERT NOZICK, ANARCHY, STATE AND UTOPIA (London: Blackwell, 1974).

original divine allocation. This is described both before and after the Conquest of the promised land (see Numbers 33:54 and Joshua 14–19, respectively). The difference is that whereas Rawls's redistribution is according to an abstract conception of equality (summarized in the two principles of justice above), the biblical redistribution of resources does *not* rely on an abstract idea of egalitarianism: "It shall be a jubilee for *you*, when *each* of you shall return to *his* property and *each* of you shall return to *his* family" (Leviticus 25:10). As Fager notes, the jubilee is "not . . . a call for communal ownership in which the welfare of the individual is subsumed under the welfare of the group as a whole"[63] but a declaration that "*this* person, who is a member of *this* family, has a right to occupy and reap the produce from *this* land."[64] The story of the original grant ensures that the claims of individuals, families, and clans remain distinct from those of wider social groups, such as the tribe. One of the problems with a Rawlsian approach to social justice is that the idea of equality is so abstract that it becomes difficult to implement and harder still to tell whether it is working or not (e.g., paying a company director extra money could be justified on the grounds that this might benefit the least advantaged in the longer term by helping to create a more prosperous economy, but how could we ever know this?). By contrast, the specificity of the jubilee concentrates the mind and demands a response.

On the other hand, it is equally true that the jubilee year promotes liberty. Inequalities are allowed to exist as a result of free contracts. The main constraint is that voluntary transfers of entitlement are not regarded as valid in the jubilee year if they arose as a result of indebtedness or debt slavery. But *within* each 49-year cycle, there is every incentive to work hard. People are allowed to prosper without interference during each sabbatical and 50-year cycle. In addition, it is important to remember that the jubilee laws only redistribute land. There is no redistribution of chattels, even in the jubilee year. Biblical Israel is thus an incentive-based, entrepreneurial economy in which it is possible for individuals and families to build up assets and hand on the benefits from one generation to the next. Biblical law provides for the just distribution of resources, while preserving an incentive-based economy—a combination that releases creativity and encourages an entrepreneurial spirit.

The biblical approach thus represents a modified version of modern liberal theories of social justice. Whereas modern political philosophy debates whether questions of equality or liberty are prior, biblical law subverts both under a prior assumption: what comes first is a gift. In contrast to the nonspecific narrative nature of some modern political philosophies (e.g., Rawls's theory which relies upon an artificial thought experiment to generate principles of justice), biblical

---

63. Jeffrey A. Fager, Land Tenure and the Biblical Jubilee: Uncovering Hebrew Ethics through the Sociology of Knowledge, Journal for the Study of the Old Testament Supplement Series 155 (Sheffield: Sheffield Academic Press, 1993), 118.

64. Ibid., 113, italics original.

law is rooted in a specific event (God's gift of the land). It is a story of a God who creates the world in six days and rests on the seventh and within that lies the telling of other stories, including the covenant with Abraham and the gift of land. The biblical laws form an approach to social justice that satisfies our concern for equality and liberty more fully than the current consensus in political philosophy.

A. It's the economy, stupid

Perhaps in part because the biblical approach transcends the politics of left and right, some of the biblical laws of social welfare have caught economists' eyes in recent years. As a result, "Leviticus 25 is a passage that makes *Das Kapital* look tame . . . it is no longer Morris, Keynes and Beveridge who inspire and change the world—it's *Leviticus*."[65] Several key aspects of biblical law have in recent years become part of our intellectual currency. The Drop the Debt and Jubilee 2000 campaigns, aimed at the cancellation of debt among Low Income Countries (LICs), were inspired by the biblical ban on interest. Gordon Brown, the United Kingdom's then-Chancellor of the Exchequer (and later Prime Minister) acknowledged the influence of his Christian upbringing on his worldwide campaign to secure debt relief for the world's poorest nations.[66] This is not altogether surprising; after all, "the principles that should govern economic organisation (the ownership of capital, work, incentives, finance, the monetary system, taxes and welfare) are not technology-specific."[67] New ideas are old ideas.

The leading role of Leviticus can be seen against the backdrop of the two main economic systems of the twentieth and twenty-first centuries: capitalism and Marxism. We can say, briefly but fairly, that capitalism excels at maximizing wealth production but is poor at wealth distribution. Greater rights in property mean that it is possible to move property around and invest it wherever the owner thinks it will be most productive; this provides incentive. The downside is that there is no universal access to property and, accordingly, some degree of concentration of wealth. The more property one has, the more one can do with it, and the more wealth one is likely to have. On the other hand, if one is poor and does not have access to property, it is hard to break out of the cycle. The result is a rich/poor divide and a section of the population that is disenfranchised because it does not have access to the means of production. The response to the problem, very often, is regulation by the State and some form of wealth redistribution by means of taxation to alleviate excessive poverty. By contrast, under Marxism, everything is owned by the State and most people, in theory, have access to the means of production. However, because there is collective ownership, there is little

---

65. Will Hutton, THE OBSERVER, October 3, 1999.
66. THE INDEPENDENT, January 15, 2005.
67. Paul Mills, *The divine economy*, CAMBRIDGE PAPERS 9, 1–4, 2 (2000).

incentive to the family or the individual to use the property to maximum advantage, with the result that overall production is low. In addition, the mechanisms for the transfer of information from consumers to producers are weak. Overall, the population is poor, although there is less of a gap between rich and poor.

In contrast to both capitalism and Marxism, biblical law presents a third way; access to the means of production *and* incentives to work hard. Whereas modern Western approaches to social welfare favor a system of redistributive taxation *after* the process of wealth creation, biblical law provides for a roughly equitable distribution of productive assets that can be maintained over a lifetime. To put it another way, biblical law addresses the question of social welfare by giving as many people as possible the capacity to produce and hence to look after themselves. The biblical emphasis is not, as it is in the United Kingdom, on allowing the poor to get poorer until eventually one has to pick up the pieces. Instead, the emphasis is on preventing people from getting caught in a generational "poverty trap" and having to rely increasingly upon taxpayers. The latter is, in my view, a more defensible approach to social justice. The equitable economic society is not one in which the state "confiscate[s] the results of people's labour and pass[es] it to those it deems deserving of assistance, but . . . [one that ensures] that everyone has access to the means of production and support."[68] Such an approach combines "the efficiency benefits of competitive market processes with a concern for fairness for those with lower incomes."[69]

A contemporary jubilee would give "every family access to an income-generating asset."[70] In biblical times, this was agricultural land; today it could be "a national investment fund . . . an equal share of which would be bestowed upon every citizen when reaching voting age and relinquished on death."[71] The recently established UK Children's Trust Fund which provides an endowment to every child at birth can be seen as the first step toward this.[72] The problem with this proposal is that it is rather too ephemeral: if all the money is spent, what then? As such, it is only a partial way of advancing the jubilee. Since the heart of the jubilee is the idea that everyone should have access to some property, any serious application of the jubilee must ultimately mean a commitment to global land reform, especially in the Third World.[73]

---

68. Mills, *The economy*, p. 232.
69. Mills, *The divine economy*, p. 2.
70. Mills, *The economy*, p. 233.
71. Ibid.
72. Ibid.
73. *See generally* Michael Schluter, *Family*, in JUBILEE MANIFESTO (Michael Schluter & John Ashcroft eds.; Leicester: InterVarsity Press/Jubilee Centre, 2005), 154-74; and Michael Schluter, *Welfare*, pp. 175–95. *See also* research by the U.S. Land Tenure Centre which, among other things, explores the relationship between land access and social welfare (http://www.nelson.wisc.edu/ltc/; accessed September 29, 2009).

VIII. CONCLUSION

The biblical laws of social welfare take a wide variety of forms, including the ban on interest, tithe and gleaning laws, and a range of Sabbath institutions. As in the biblical law of property, the biblical laws of social welfare present the Israelites with a choice between Pharaonic economics and family economics. Pharaonic economics is associated with harsh working conditions, slavery, holding onto debts, lending at interest, hoarding, state rations, and exploiting people for food. By contrast, family economics is associated with time off for workers, Sabbath rest, releasing debts, a ban on interest, abundance, and leaving food behind for the needy. The extension of "Super-Sabbath" institutions ("Sabbath-plus," "Sabbath-squared," and "perpetual Sabbath") shows the way that the biblical welfare laws can be creatively adapted and applied to very different situations, in both the prophetic literature and the New Testament. In modern terms, biblical law presents a third way that goes beyond the dichotomy between equality and liberty, promoting access to the means of production, releasing creativity, and preserving incentives. The goal is to create community solidarity with a strong sense of individual responsibility.

Selected reading

Walter Brueggemann, *The Covenanted Self: Explorations in Law and Covenant* (Minneapolis: Fortress, 1999), Chapter 9.

Walter Brueggemann, *The Land*, Overtures to Biblical Theology Series (Philadelphia: Fortress Press, 1977), Chapter 4.

Jonathan P. Burnside, *The Signs of Sin: Seriousness of Offence in Biblical Law*, Journal for the Study of the Old Testament Supplement Series 364 (London: Continuum, 2003), Chapter 3.

Jonathan P. Burnside, *The Status and Welfare of Immigrants: The place of the foreigner in biblical law and its relevance to contemporary society* (Cambridge: Jubilee Centre, 2001).

Ellen F. Davis, *Scripture, Culture and Agriculture: An Agrarian Reading* (Cambridge: Cambridge University Press, 2008), Chapter 4.

Jeffrey A. Fager, *Land Tenure and the Biblical Jubilee: Uncovering Hebrew Ethics through the Sociology of Knowledge*, Journal for the Study of the Old Testament Supplement Series 155 (Sheffield: Sheffield Academic Press, 1993), Chapters 2 and 8.

K. D. Irani and Morris Silver eds., *Social Justice in the Ancient World* (London: Greenwood Press, 1995), Chapter 12.

Jan Joosten, *People and Land in the Holiness Code* (Leiden: E.J. Brill, 1996), Chapter 6.

Michael Schluter and John Ashcroft, *Jubilee Manifesto* (Leicester: Intervarsity Press/Jubilee Centre, 2005), Chapters 9-12.

Michael Schluter and the Cambridge Papers Group eds., *Christianity in a Changing World: Biblical insight on contemporary issues* (London: Marshall Pickering, 2000), Chapter 13.

Moshe Weinfeld, *Social Justice in Ancient Israel and in the Ancient Near East* (Jerusalem: The Magnes Press, 1995), Chapter 8.

8. HOMICIDE AND VENGEANCE

According to the Bible, the first baby born on earth was a killer, and his brother was the first victim. Homicide stalks the pages of the Bible from the story of Cain and Abel onwards. Not surprisingly, the legal regulation of homicide, including the provision of asylum, is an important subject in biblical law. Homicide is also the ultimate act of violence, provoking strong public reactions in both ancient and modern times. This too makes it a significant subject for inclusion in this book. Nor would the study of biblical law be complete without an analysis of the *lex talionis*—Latin for "law of retaliation"—as commonly expressed in the formula "an eye for an eye, a tooth for a tooth" (e.g., Exodus 21:24). Yet ironically, these well-known stories and laws in the Bible are among the least well understood. This chapter provides an overview of the biblical laws of homicide and asylum and their relationship to key narratives. In doing so, it will help us to develop a picture of how biblical law might have operated in practice.

I. THE INTERPRETATION OF MURDER

We begin by reminding ourselves that homicide—in both ancient and modern law—covers a broad range of cases and degrees of culpability. We can recognize this most easily by considering the following modern scenarios:

(1) A man lies in wait on a walkway and drops a concrete block onto his chosen victim, who is walking below.
(2) A terrorist blows up a shopping center in order to make a political statement, in the course of which some people die—although he believed they would not.
(3) A man is taunted about his victimhood by his sexual abuser, whereupon he loses his self-control and kills his tormentor.
(4) A hospital patient dies when a tube on a ventilating machine becomes disconnected for four and a half minutes, during which time the anesthetist in charge has gone out for a bag of chips.
(5) A pedestrian is killed because the poor exercise of discretion by an administrative clerk has resulted in a badly located traffic sign.
(6) A motorist kills a number of cyclists when his car collides with them on an icy road.

Modern legal systems have ways of distinguishing between the seriousness of these different cases, even though the harm—death—is the same in each case. In English law, the scenarios can be differentiated as follows:

Case (1), above, is a classic case of murder, since the defendant has the intention to kill or cause serious harm.

Case (2) is a classic example of "oblique" intent, according to which the defendant can be guilty of murder if both he and the "reasonable person" foresee death or serious injury as a "virtually certain consequence" of his actions, even though his direct intent is to make a political statement.

Case (3) is a typical way in which the offense of murder may be reduced to the lesser offense of manslaughter by means of the defense of provocation.

Case (4) is an example of "gross negligent manslaughter," in the context of medical negligence.

Case (5) is an example of negligence which may be actionable under civil law but probably not under criminal law.

Case (6) is a fairly straightforward example of an accident, providing there is no evidence of careless driving or dangerous driving.

The existence of these different categories of homicide shows the way in which modern English law tries to differentiate between the seriousness of different killings on the grounds of culpability. This is understandable: empirical research on public perceptions of the seriousness of homicide has consistently shown that, for example, planned and deliberate killings are considered more serious than unplanned but nevertheless intentional killings.[1] Seen from the perspective of the victim's family and friends, however, the balance that is struck between harm and culpability is not always satisfactory. In practical terms the result, very often, is that many homicides which occur in road traffic cases, for example, are dealt with in a way that seems unduly lenient to many. Thus, in case (6), which is a real-life example from a newspaper, the motorist in question was merely fined £180 and given six penalty points on his driving license for killing four cyclists.

How does biblical law try to strike the balance between harm and culpability, and how does this compare with English law? We can address this question by reference to three sets of biblical homicide laws: Exodus 21:12–14, Deuteronomy 19:4–13, and Numbers 35:16–24.

As we do so, we must briefly note who has the power to take human life in biblical law. We will see that reference is made in Deuteronomy 19:4–13 and Numbers 35:16–24 to the "avenger of blood" (*go'el haddam*). This person is uniquely authorized to take the life of the killer in carefully defined circumstances

---

1. Sergio Herzog, *The effect of motive on public perceptions of the seriousness of murder in Israel*, BRIT. J. CRIMINOLOGY 44, 771–82 (2004).

(e.g., Numbers 35:19). The avenger is not *required* to kill him (see below) but if he does, the killing will be deemed permissible; it will not incur "bloodguilt." This is important because it means that the avenger's family will not be open to a further round of vengeance.

The homicide texts do not specify who can be an "avenger of blood." Some scholars have assumed that the avenger is a designated official[2] who was perhaps chosen because of his speed and athleticism. Supporting this is the argument that there would have been many occasions in which family members were unable to carry out the task or might have risked injury themselves.[3] Others have argued that the avenger of blood was a close family member and that responsibility for avenging shed blood in biblical law devolved, in order, on the son, brother, or next of kin. On this view, when kinship ends, there is no longer any *go'el*.

This latter argument is preferable for several reasons. First, the traditional system of revenge is thought to be rooted in the possession of common blood. To this extent, there is a more natural association between blood revenge and kinship than between vengeance and a "public official." This is apparently confirmed by the description of the "avenger of blood" pursuing the fugitive "in hot anger" (Deuteronomy 19:6)—a response that is more in keeping with a close relative than a civic official. Also, the story of the blood feud between Joab and Abner (two high-ranking military figures in King Saul's and King David's armies) shows that the *go'el haddam* is a family member ("Joab and Abishai his brother slew Abner, because he had killed their brother Asahel"; 2 Samuel 3:30; *narrator speaking*).

A. Homicide in Exodus

First, we consider the construction of homicide in Exodus 21:12–14. The opening phrase describes the killing in a neutral fashion: "He who fatally strikes (*makkeh*) a man . . ." (verse 12; JPS). The root (*nakhah*; "to strike" from which we derive the *hifil* participle *makkeh*) is often used to denote the outward act of inflicting a deadly blow, and so it is often used in the Bible as a term for homicide.[4] However, *makkeh* provides no indication of the killer's state of mind. This is unlike, for example, the Hebrew verb *ratsah*, which normally denotes "culpable killing by use of force"[5] and is usually—though not exclusively—translated

---

2. Anthony Phillips, Essays in Biblical Law, Journal for the Study of the Old Testament Supplement Series 344 (London: Continuum, 2002), 56.
3. Ibid.
4. J. Conrad, *Nkh*, in Theological Dictionary of the Old Testament (G. Johannes Botterweck, Helmer Ringgren & Heinz-Josef Fabry eds.; David E. Green trans.; Grand Rapids: Eerdmans, 1998), vol. IX, 415–23.
5. F. L. Hossfeld, *Ratsah*, in Theological Dictionary of the Old Testament, (G. Johannes Botterweck, Helmer Ringgren & Heinz-Josef Fabry eds.; David E. Green trans.; Grand Rapids: Eerdmans, 2004), vol. XIII, 630–40, 632.

"murder." (In Numbers 35:27, *ratsach* describes the action of the executioner who "kills" (*ratsach*) the killer and so commits a justifiable homicide).

The traditional interpretation of Exodus 21:12–14 is set out in Table 8, below.

In literary terms, Exodus 21:13–14 qualifies the general norm set out in verse 12. Verses 13 and 14 are not presented as "stand-alone" offenses and in fact make no sense at all apart from verse 12. Verse 13 contains two specifications ("If he did not do it by design," and "it came about by an act of God") which are linked in the Hebrew by a single letter (a *vav*). In modern translations, the *vav* is treated as a conjunctive ("but") so that the phrase "it came about by an act of God" is seen as an explanation of "if he did not do it by design" (see Table 8, below). The result is that verses 13 and 14 are thought to deal with two separate cases—and only two cases—as follows. Verse 13 is seen as a paradigm of "accidental killing." This is because it specifically negates the phrase "by design" (or "lie in wait"), which is the paradigm case of intention (see further, below). In these accidental circumstances, the killer is guaranteed asylum at God's altar (see further, below). By contrast, verse 14 is usually seen as the exact opposite of verse 13 because it is seen as a paradigm of premeditated killing. This is because it specifically uses the word *be'ormah* ("with guile"; KJV) which signifies a plot and hence premeditation. In these circumstances, the killer cannot rely on asylum for protection from the avenger of blood. On this traditional reading, Exodus 21:12–14 does not tell us anything about homicides that are neither accidental nor premeditated. In other words, it tells us nothing about homicides that occur on the spur of the moment (e.g., a sudden quarrel).

However, the traditional reading of Exodus 21:12–14 has been challenged on the grounds that while the letter *vav* in verse 13 can be translated "and," it can equally be translated "or." On this reading, the phrase "it came about by an act of God" is not an *explanation* of the phrase "if he did not do it by design" but rather

TABLE 8 TRADITIONAL DIVISION OF EXODUS 21:12–14 (JPS TRANSLATION)

Verse	Case	Text	Paradigm	Availability of asylum
Exodus 21:12	#1	"He who fatally strikes a man shall be put to death"	No indication of state of mind	N/A
Exodus 21:13	#2	"If he did not do it by design, *but* it came about by an act of God…"	Accident	Yes
Exodus 21:14	#3	"When a man schemes against another and kills him treacherously (*be'ormah*)…"	Premeditated	No

an *alternative* to it.⁶ This means that verse 13 does not concern a single case of homicide but *two* separate cases. If we read the two parts of verse 13 narratively and see the words as symbols for typical action, then the words "it came about by an act of God . . ." (verse 13b) can be read as a more graphic interpretation of the preceding phrase "he did not do it by design" (verse 13a). In other words, if verse 13a evokes the image of the "spur of the moment" killing, which is less blameworthy than "doing it by design," then verse 13b simply goes further by picturing the case of the nonnegligent accident.⁷

If we combine verse 13 with verses 12 and 14, we have four cases of homicide in Exodus 21:12–14 (see Table 9, below).

There are three reasons for favoring this alternative reading. First, it is consistent with the way in which the letter *vav* is used, just a few verses on, in Exodus 21:16. Here, it can *only* mean "or" ("Whoever steals a man, whether he sells him *or* is found in possession of him, shall be put to death").⁸ Second, the traditional reading results in superfluous drafting which is not characteristic of this particular legal collection (the Covenant Code; Exodus 21:1–22:16). Finally, it means that we have three focal points along the spectrum of intention, not just two. This is consistent with other ancient approaches, including Roman law which also has a threefold classification of crimes committed "from forethought, on

TABLE 9 ALTERNATIVE DIVISION OF EXODUS 21:12–14 (JPS TRANSLATION)

Verse	Case	Text	Paradigm	Availability of asylum
Exodus 21:12	#1	"He who fatally strikes a man shall be put to death"	No indication of state of mind	N/A
Exodus 21:13a	#2	"If he did not do it by design"	"Spur of the moment" killing	Yes
Exodus 21:13b	#3	"Or it came about by an act of God. . ."	Accident	Yes
Exodus 21:14	#4	"when a man schemes against another and kills him treacherously (be'ormah) . . ."	Premeditated	No

---

6. Bernard S. Jackson, Wisdom-Laws: A Study of the Mishpatim of Exodus 21:1–22:16 (Oxford: Oxford University Press, 2006), 124–25.
7. Jackson, Wisdom-Laws, p. 123.
8. Jackson, Wisdom-Laws, pp. 123–24.

impulse or by accident" ("*aut proposito, aut impetu, aut casu*"; Digest, 48.19.11.2).[9] This alternative reading has knock-on consequences for asylum as well. It authorizes flight to the altar for anyone who satisfies one of two independent conditions: *either* it was a "spur of the moment" killing, *or* he killed through an "act of God."

Before leaving Exodus 21:12–14, we should note the ambiguity of the Hebrew of Exodus 21:14: "...you shall take him from my altar, that he may die (*tiqqachennu lamut*)." We might assume that the phrase is prescriptive, but the Hebrew is compatible with a permissive interpretation ("he *may* be put to death").[10] This is because it is difficult in biblical Hebrew to distinguish at the linguistic level between permission and prescription. If the avenger of blood is *permitted* to put him to death, then he is equally allowed *not* to put him to death. This ambiguity is preserved in the structure of Exodus 21:12–14 itself. Verse 12 seems to tell the avenger of blood to put the killer to death (". . . [he] shall be put to death"; *mot yumat*) while the very next verse goes on to provide for asylum! So although verse 12 might sound mandatory, the context indicates that the killer is *not necessarily* put to death. The proper sense of verse 14 may actually be one of encouragement: "he should [normally] be put to death."[11] Unfortunately for us, biblical law does not have any clear or regular way of distinguishing between different modalities, such as "may," "must," and "it would be a good idea." These distinctions are part of the presupposition pool (see Chapter 1) that we need to recognize in order to reconstruct the social world of the texts.

B. Homicide in Deuteronomy

Next, we turn to the construction of homicide in Deuteronomy 19:4–13. This is summarized in Table 10, below.

Again, we find a basic opposition between accidental (verses 4–5) and premeditated homicide (verse 11; cf. Exodus 21:13b and 14). The "accidental homicide" ("without having been his enemy") is presented as the converse of the "premeditated homicide" ("a person who is the enemy of another"). However, unlike the case of accidental homicide in Exodus 21:13b, Deuteronomy 19:5–6 is not conceptualized as an "act of God." Instead, it is presented as a lack of premeditation, as evidenced by no previous enmity.[12]

Deuteronomy 19:4–13 seems to follow the same sequence of cases as Exodus 21:13b–14. A case of accidental homicide (Exodus 21:13a/Deuteronomy 19:4–5) is followed by flight to a place of refuge (Exodus 21:13b/Deuteronomy 19:5–7) and a case of premeditated homicide (Exodus 21:14/Deuteronomy 19:11). As in

---

9. BERNARD S. JACKSON, ESSAYS IN JEWISH AND COMPARATIVE LEGAL HISTORY (Leiden: E. J Brill, 1975), 91 n. 100.
10. JACKSON, WISDOM-LAWS, p. 132.
11. Ibid.
12. Ibid., 127.

TABLE 10 STRUCTURE OF DEUTERONOMY 19:4–13 (JPS TRANSLATION)

Verse	Text	Paradigm	Availability of asylum
Deuteronomy 19:4–5	". . . one who has killed another unwittingly, *without having been his enemy in the past*" (19:4) + stereotypical case of flying axe-head (19:5)	Accident	Yes
Deuteronomy 19:11	". . . a person *who is the enemy of another* lies in wait for him and sets upon him and strikes him a fatal blow. . ."	Premeditated	No

Exodus 21:13b–14, asylum is available in the case of accidental homicide but not in the case of premeditated homicide. However, the place of refuge has changed from the "altar" of Exodus 21:13–14 to the city of refuge of Deuteronomy 19:1–7. The other difference is that the text explicitly states that the avenger of blood can kill the accidental slayer *before* he reaches asylum (Deuteronomy 19:6).

The ability of the *go'el haddam* to kill the suspect before he reaches the city of refuge (Deuteronomy 19:6) is found in the context of creating three new cities of refuge (Deuteronomy 19:7). Further reference is then made to the need to:

> add three other cities to these three, lest innocent blood be shed in your land which the LORD your God gives you for an inheritance, and so the guilt of bloodshed be upon you. (Deuteronomy 19:9–10; *Moses speaking*)

This suggests that Deuteronomy, at least, seems concerned about what might happen if the *go'el* catches up with the alleged killer and kills him, only for it to turn out that the alleged killer was innocent. The reference to "innocent blood" (*dam naqi*) could refer to several different things. It could refer to the suspect who is completely innocent, in the sense that it is a case of "mistaken identity."[13] However, this is not the "paradigm case" envisaged by the law since the typical case of "pursuit by a *go'el haddam*" assumes some popular knowledge of who killed the victim. More likely, it refers to the non-premeditated killer—a category which spans, as we have seen in Table 9 above, the case of the accidental and the "spur of the moment" killing. We have also seen that the non-premeditated killer is left to the internal exile of a "city of refuge." This means that he is culpable to some degree; otherwise, why would he experience the penalty of internal exile? This suspect is not "innocent" in a straightforward "mistaken identity" sense and so, in this respect, the translation in Deuteronomy 19:9–10 as "innocent

---

13. For the alternative situation, where a factually innocent fugitive flees for asylum because of a false accusation of homicide, *see* Jonathan Burnside, *A "missing case" in the biblical laws of homicide and asylum?*, VETUS TESTAMENTUM 60, 288 – 291 (2010).

blood" needs to be qualified. Its typical referent is to "the blood of the non-premeditated killer."

At any rate, the concern in Deuteronomy 19:6ff is to maximize the chances of survival of the "innocent" person, even though he is likely to be culpable to some degree. It is not clear whether the *go'el haddam* must be careful not to spill "innocent blood" *or* that the *go'el haddam* is entitled to kill, regardless of whether the suspect is "innocent" or not and—if he is "innocent"—that he takes the risk of another cycle of violence. Overall, the provision of the extra cities, first in verse 7 and again in verse 9, implies that the *go'el haddam* ought *not* to kill the fugitive who is *en route* to the place of refuge, even though he is entitled to.

C. Homicide in Numbers

Finally, we turn to Numbers 35:16–24. This draws together Exodus 21:12–14 and Deuteronomy 19:4–13 while also expanding upon them both. Like Exodus 21:12–14 and Deuteronomy 19:4–13, Numbers 35:16–24 is partly structured around an underlying binary opposition that is concerned with legal consequences (asylum/no asylum). As Table 11 illustrates (below), Numbers 35 presents a group of cases in which the murderer should be handed over to the avenger of blood (verses 16–21; "the first series"), followed by another group in which the killer is protected from the *go'el haddam* (verses 22–23; "the second series"[14]; see Table 11, below). It is not necessary in biblical law for each series to be comprised of exactly the same number of cases, as long as each series is united by a distinctive theme.

TABLE 11 DOUBLE SERIES IN NUMBERS 35:16–24

	Case	Paradigm case	Asylum/ No asylum
THE FIRST SERIES	Case 1 (35:16)	Premeditated	No asylum
	Case 2 (35:17)	Premeditated	No asylum
	Case 3 (35:18)	Premeditated	No asylum
	Case 4 (35:20a)	Premeditated	No asylum
	Case 5 (35:20b)	Premeditated	No asylum
	Case 6 (35:21)	Premeditated	No asylum
THE SECOND SERIES	Case 7 (35:22a)	"Spur of the moment"	Asylum
	Case 8 (35:22b)	"Spur of the moment"	Asylum
	Case 9 (35:23)	Accidental	Asylum

---

14. JACKSON, WISDOM-LAWS, p. 127.

Numbers 35:16–24 thus confirms the alternative reading of Exodus 21:12–14 by making it clear that the spectrum of intention in biblical homicide law has three focal points (premeditated, "spur of the moment", and accidental). It also confirms (at verse 22 parts a and b) that the "spur of the moment" killer is eligible for asylum (cf. Exodus 21:13a). It is also fully consistent with Deuteronomy 19:4–13.

However, unlike the other legal materials, Numbers 35:16–24 develops this position in more detail. This elaboration takes the form of a chiasmus that straddles the two series[15] (see Table 12, below).

TABLE 12 CHIASTIC STRUCTURE IN NUMBERS 35:17–23[16]

Case	Chiasmus	Paradigm case	Asylum/No asylum
A (35:17)	STONE + INTENTION	If D kills V with a *stone* in his hand, the stone being (normally) sufficient to cause death	No asylum
B (35:20)	THROWS + INTENTION	If D kills V in an *ambush* by *throwing* something at V	No asylum
C (35:21)	ENMITY	If D kills V with his fists *"in enmity"* (JPS)	No asylum
C` (35:22)	NO ENMITY	If D stabs V "suddenly *without enmity*"	Asylum
B` (35:22)	THROWS + NO INTENTION	If D *throws* something at him "without lying in wait"	Asylum
A` (35:23)	STONE + NO INTENTION	If D kills V with a *stone*, even one that may normally cause death but "without seeing him" and without previous enmity or having sought him out	Asylum

As Table 12 shows, the terms used in the first series (at A/B/C) are explicitly negated by the second series (at C`/B`/A`).[17] This is what gives Numbers 35:17–23 its chiastic structure. Notably, the pivot of the chiasm (C/C`) is concerned with the presence or absence of enmity (verses 21–22). This is significant because we find the same opposition at the heart of Deuteronomy 19:4–13 (see Table 10, above). By putting "enmity" at the center of the homicide laws of Numbers 35:17–23, the draftsman underlines the fact that hatred is central to murder.

This more elaborate presentation of the biblical homicide laws in Numbers 35:16–24 modifies the paradigm cases of Exodus 21:12–14 and Deuteronomy 19:4–13, to some extent. Thus Numbers 35:16–18 includes different objective

---

15. Ibid., 128–30.
16. Summarizing JACKSON, WISDOM-LAWS, pp. 128–30.
17. Ibid., 128.

tests of premeditated killing, namely (1) striking someone with an iron object (verse 16), (2) with a stone (verse 17), and (3) with a wooden object (verse 18). These cases are doubly interesting because of their unusual drafting. Each test is followed by the formula: "he is a murderer (*rotseach hu*'); the murderer shall be put to death." This formula ("He is [X] + consequences") is rare in biblical law and is used "where the facts go beyond the normal image of the offence in question."[18] This could perhaps explain why the formula is used in Numbers 35:16–18. The normal paradigm case of homicide involves "lying in wait" and "being at enmity" (e.g., Exodus 21:14, Deuteronomy 19:11), whereas the paradigm cases in Numbers 35:16—18 do not involve evidence of ambush or prior hatred. Despite this, the formula makes it clear that the offender really is a murderer.

It is notable that whereas the new paradigm cases of premeditation in Numbers 35:17–18 refer to objects (stone and wood) "in the hand," there is no corresponding reference to the "instrument of iron" being "in the hand" (Numbers 35:16). This is interesting from a semiotic perspective. The implication is that instruments of iron have lethal connotations that stone and wood do not have. Innocent materials, such as stone and wood, only raise a presumption of intent if they are wielded "in the hand," which is, of course, the agent of action and intention. By contrast, an iron object is, in and of itself, sufficient to presume homicidal intent, regardless of how it is used. Iron is presented in the Pentateuchal texts as something that is in scarce supply. Moses is sufficiently impressed by King Og and his bedroom furniture, that he reminds his hearers: "Behold, his bedstead was a bedstead of iron" (Deuteronomy 3:11). Reference to this King Og is also made in Numbers 21:33. Iron is also presented as something that is used in military contexts (cf. 1 Samuel 17:7). Against this background, then, a person who used an "instrument of iron" against another could be presumed to have malicious intent. Similar presumptions and objective tests operate in English law. A can of lager and a "knuckleduster" (a weapon used in hand-to-hand combat) both have the potential to be deadly weapons; however, only the latter is prohibited from being carried in public.

The schematizing approach of Numbers 35:16–24, compared to Exodus 21:12–14 and Deuteronomy 19:4–13, may reflect "priestly" preoccupations. The concern for ritual observance occupies large portions of the book of *Numbers* (see, for example, Chapters 3–9). Indeed, the homicide laws themselves are concerned with ritual issues, for example, the references to "blood pollution," expiation, and defilement in Numbers 35:33–34. Rituals—and the worldview that makes sense of them—are dependent on things being properly identified and classified. Therefore, to the extent that Numbers 35 is a priestly text, it is not

---

18. BERNARD S. JACKSON, STUDIES IN THE SEMIOTICS OF BIBLICAL LAW, JOURNAL FOR THE STUDY OF THE OLD TESTAMENT SUPPLEMENT SERIES 314 (Sheffield: Sheffield Academic Press, 2000), 50.

altogether surprising that it takes a more schematic approach to the laws of homicide. We can see examples of the priestly concerns for categorization elsewhere in biblical law (e.g., Leviticus 20, see Chapter 11).

D. Mortal thoughts

Biblical law thus distinguishes between three different categories of homicide: (1) premeditated, (2) "spur of the moment," and (3) accidental. It is important to recognize that the distinction in biblical law between a premeditated killing and an unpremeditated but intentional ("spur of the moment") killing does not operate at the level of language because there is no consistent biblical term. This is despite some translations of the Bible imposing the terminological distinction "murderer" and "manslayer" onto the biblical text (e.g., the RSV). Instead, the distinction between the premeditated killing and the "spur of the moment" killing exists at the level of the underlying narrative typification (see Tables 9–12, above) as well at the level of remedy (that is, whether there is asylum or not). Asylum is available in the case of the "spur of the moment" killing but not in the case of the premeditated killing.

This difference at the level of remedy is significant for two reasons. First, it shows that the "spur of the moment" killing is conceptually closer to an accidental killing than to a premeditated killing. Of course, since the biblical texts provide only paradigms, it follows that each individual case would have had to be looked at in its totality. Some cases of "spur of the moment" killing might appear to be closer to the paradigm of premeditated killing, while others may seem closer to that of an accidental killing.[19] This is presumably how biblical law would have distinguished between the ancient equivalents of the six modern scenarios above. Indeed, we find that similar judgments of relative approximation to a given paradigm are made in the modern law of homicide. For example, a battered wife might claim that she killed her husband with acid on the "spur of the moment"; however, the fact that she went shopping for it the day before at a do-it-yourself store and had it already on hand might suggest that she is closer to the paradigm of premeditation.

Second, the difference in remedy illustrates the way biblical law tries to balance concerns for harm and culpability. When the avenger of blood fails to punish the killer for accidental or "spur of the moment" killings—or chooses not to do so—the effect is to treat the most culpable cases (i.e., those involving ambush) as the most serious (because they result in death) while the least blameworthy cases (i.e., the "flying axe-head") are treated as the least serious (although they still attract some punishment because they result in the internal exile of the city of refuge). This is similar to the basic position in modern English law.

---

19. JACKSON, WISDOM-LAWS, p. 145.

Here, the seriousness of the offense is related to the offender's subjective state of mind.

However, there are other times when biblical law strikes a very different balance from modern English law. These are the occasions when the avenger of blood chooses—and succeeds—in punishing the killer for accidental or "spur of the moment" killings. Here, the accidental and "spur of the moment" killings are treated as seriously as the premeditated killing because all result in the death of the killer. No account is taken of the offender's subjective state of mind in applying the penalty. In biblical law, the "spur of the moment" and the accidental killings have the potential to be treated as seriously as the premeditated killing. This is contrary to modern English law where greater value is placed on the offender's subjective state of mind than on the objective harm he has caused.

Moreover, in biblical law, whether greater attention is paid to the offender's subjective state of mind or to the harm that he has caused is entirely a matter of chance. The opportunities for the avenger of blood to take life are limited to the time it takes for the killer to reach the city of refuge (Deuteronomy 19:5–6) and any subsequent occasions when the killer leaves the city, prior to the death of the high priest (Numbers 35:26–28). Of course, from a biblical perspective, the success or failure of the avenger of blood may not be a matter of chance but of divine providence. From this perspective, it reflects the belief that both God *and* the avenger of blood determine the outcome (cf. the discussion of the duality of Genesis 9:5–6 in Chapter 4).

The fact is that in biblical law, *all* taking of blood—even the case of the non-negligent accident—entails some degree of culpability. This is because the city of refuge should not be conceived in exclusively positive terms as a place of sanctuary. It is also a place of internal exile and so, to this extent, it implies that some negative evaluation attaches to the killer's sojourn. It is an experience of imprisonment. Therefore, even the case of the flying axe-head must involve some degree of culpability; otherwise, why punish him at all by internal exile? The death of one human being by another human being always has penal consequences in biblical law, no matter how accidental the cause. This was also the case in English law for a considerable period. The Statute of Gloucester[20] formalized the procedure by which a royal pardon could be available to the person who killed in self-defense or by "misadventure." It reflects the fact that at one time, English law did not take account of attendant circumstances and treated all killings as capital offenses.[21]

From a modern perspective, there is something to be said for the extent to which biblical law has a sense of harm. The mother whose small child is run over by the driver of a car, while the driver was fishing around in his glove

---

20. 1278, 6 Edw. 1, c.9.
21. Anon, *Felony murder as a first degree offense: An anachronism retained*, YALE L.J. 66, 427–35, 428 (1957).

compartment, naturally feels that the killer should be treated as seriously as a cold-blooded murderer. We can also ask whether the typically low sentences associated with vehicular homicide take sufficient account of the harm that has been caused and if the possibility of severe penalties for even accidental killing might help to concentrate the minds, not just of the driving public, but of company executives who preside over deaths at work.[22] According to Numbers 35:22—28 and Deuteronomy 19:4–10, non-premeditated killers will experience *either* death *or* a massive disruption in their personal lifestyle, as a result of relocating to a city of refuge. This mirrors, to some extent, the impact of the killing upon the victim and the disruption caused to their family. Whatever else one makes of biblical homicide law, it is clear that it takes seriously the value of human life—both in terms of the need to protect the life of the offender, in certain circumstances—*and* the value of the victim's life.

II. HOW TO SAVE A LIFE

Having considered some of the ways in which persons may be liable for homicide in biblical law, we turn to consider possible mitigation from its legal consequences. This allows us to consider in more detail the operation of the various forms of asylum, including the altar and the city of refuge, mentioned above. Several other institutions exist through which a person who has committed a homicide may escape the death penalty, and these include ransom and pardon.

A. The wings of refuge

We begin with asylum. There are two main forms of asylum in ancient Israel: the altar and the city of refuge.

First, there is the divinely approved altar referred to in Exodus 21:13–14. This altar is personally identified with God ("My altar"; Exodus 21:14), and so it is likely to refer to the altar at God's Tabernacle. Because God is popularly seen as a God of refuge (e.g., Psalm 7:1), it is not surprising that God's altar would be seen as a place of refuge. The practice described in 1 Kings 1:50 of grasping "the horns of the altar," which were its highest points, may have been understood as a representative way of laying hold of God "the Most High":

> He who dwells in the shelter of the Most High,
> who abides in the shadow of the Almighty,
> will say to the LORD, "My refuge and my fortress..."
> ...

---

22. See generally C. M. V. Clarkson, *Kicking corporate bodies and damning their souls*, Mod. L. Rev. 59, 557–72 (1996).

he will cover you with his pinions,
and under his wings you will find refuge ....
(Psalm 91:1–4; *psalmist speaking*)

The "horns" or "projections" may have seemed like wings, and the asylum seeker would have been in their shadow. Thus, references in the Psalms to the "wings of refuge" and to "the shadow of [God's] wings" (Psalm 17:8) may describe, poetically, the legal act of seeking asylum.

According to Exodus 21:12–14, God's altar benefits nonintentional killers but not premeditative ones. In cases of premeditative killing, the altar excludes the avenger of blood ("you shall take him *from* My very altar ..."; Exodus 21:14; *God speaking*; JPS). The altar is a place that prolongs life (e.g., Mishnah Middot 3:4), so naturally "agents of death" are repelled. This is consistent with the operation of asylum in other texts (Numbers 35:9–34; Deuteronomy 19:1–13; Joshua 20:1–9). But to assume that asylum *only* benefits such persons is to take a semantic approach to the text. We argued in Chapter 1 that the biblical legal collections seem to provide us with a series of paradigm cases. If so, the laws of asylum consist of stereotypical images that draw on social knowledge of who is—and who is not—a legitimate asylum seeker.[23] They suggest that the typical image of an asylum seeker is "the person accused of a homicide." But because this is only a stereotypical image, it does not necessarily mean that asylum is restricted to such persons. Being accused of homicide is not a precondition of asylum. Other persons could also be granted access to asylum, provided they are close to the narrative paradigm.

They could include, for example, the person who is in mortal fear for his or her life (e.g., a fugitive in a nonhomicide but capital case). Bernard Jackson rightly claims that there is no reason why the owner of a homicidal ox could not have taken advantage of asylum, even though the case is "so far distant from the paradigm ... that the offender may have felt confident enough to stay at home and negotiate rather than run for his life."[24] Equally, one could imagine people seeking asylum in noncapital cases (e.g., theft) if, for whatever reason, they too are in fear of their lives. Of course, the further one moves away from the paradigm, the less likely it is that asylum will be available—and at the same time, the less likely it is that asylum will be required.

---

23. I have argued elsewhere that Israel's collective experience of the Exodus forms part of the social knowledge of who is a legitimate asylum seeker. In the Exodus from Egypt, Israel flees from the wrath of Pharaoh to find asylum in the wilderness. Israel is therefore not simply a nation of escaped slaves; she is also a nation of successful asylum seekers. See J. P. Burnside, *Exodus and Asylum: Uncovering the relationship between biblical law and narrative*, J. STUD. OLD TESTAMENT 34, 243 – 266 (2010), and Jonathan Burnside, *The relationship between slavery, homicide and asylum in biblical law*, ZEITSCHRIFT FÜR ALTORIENTALISCHE UND BIBLISCHE RECHTSGECHICHTE 15, 234 – 236 (2009).

24. JACKSON, WISDOM-LAWS, p. 126.

Evidence of this paradigmatic approach to the biblical asylum laws may be found in the asylum cases described in several biblical narratives. These include the flight of Adonijah and Joab to the altar in 1 Kings 1:49–53 and 1 Kings 2:28–34, respectively. Taking the story of Adonijah first, scholars have long struggled to make sense of why he flees to the altar when he does not appear to be a killer (despite Nathan's warning to Bathsheba (1 Kings 1:12) and Bathsheba's own plea for protection (1 Kings 1:21)). But this is to take a semantic approach to the texts which sees the accusation of homicide as a precondition of seeking asylum. On a narrative approach, the fact that Adonijah is in mortal fear for his life means he is sufficiently close to the paradigm of the asylum seeker (i.e., the person accused of homicide). This is because the salient element is fear for one's life and not the reason for the fear. Adonijah is also close to the typification of the legitimate asylum seeker (i.e., the nonintentional killer) because he has not (apparently) killed anyone at all. He is thus able to benefit from asylum. One of the advantages of this narrative reading is that there is no need to invent an additional category of persons to whom Exodus 21:12–14 applies (e.g., "political asylum"[25]).

By contrast, Joab fails to benefit from asylum because he falls within the stereotype of the intentional killer (1 Kings 2:31–32). According to the David story, the killing of Joab's brother Asahel by Abner on the battlefield in 2 Samuel 2:18–23 did not give rise to "legitimate blood revenge."[26] This meant that Joab's subsequent killing of Abner (2 Samuel 3:27) was *not* a legitimate vengeance killing but one that incurred bloodguilt (2 Samuel 3:28–30). As a bloodguilty "agent of death," Joab could not benefit from asylum (1 Kings 2:5), although he may have thought he was entitled to its protection. But while he may have thought the killing was justified, David and Solomon did not agree.[27]

The Joab story confirms that there was nothing to stop anyone from fleeing to the altar, including those who were not ultimately entitled to its protection. This is further reinforced by Exodus 21:14 ("you shall take him [the guilty person] *from* My very altar . . ."; JPS). People claimed asylum even though they were not justified in doing so. Some sort of legal procedure was necessary to discriminate between the premeditated and the non-premeditated killing. Once again, we are forced to consider how Exodus 21:12–14 might have operated in practice.

It is plausible to suggest that such cases were dealt with on the basis of traditional custom. The standoff between King Solomon and Joab in which Solomon's "right-hand man" Benaiah conveys both the refugee and the king's

---

25. Martin J. Mulder, 1 Kings (Peeters: Leuven, 1998), 78.
26. A. A. Anderson, 2 Samuel, Word Biblical Commentary (Dallas: Word Books, 1989), 60–61.
27. For a full account of this argument, *see* J. P Burnside, *Flight of the fugitives: Rethinking the relationship between biblical law (Exodus 21:12–4) and the Davidic succession narrative (1 Kgs. 1–2)* J. Biblical Literature 129, 417–430 (2010).

wishes (1 Kings 2:29–34) suggests that these cases were subject to some sort of case-by-case negotiation between the parties. In the early period, at least as represented by Exodus 21:12–14, there is the possibility that the premeditated killer may not die if there was a successful negotiation between the parties and the next of kin was able to offer sufficient ransom (see further, below). Of course, this could not be presumed. There might be cases where the family's feelings are so inflamed that they will not want any damages, and so they will execute him. That there seems to be some room for diversity in Exodus 21:12–14 may be confirmed by the fact that cases of homicide are dealt with differently later on in the Covenant Code (Exodus 21:1–22:16). In Exodus 21:23, the penalty for the woman killed accidentally in the course of a brawl is "life for life" (as normally interpreted) while in Exodus 21:29–30, the owner of a homicidal ox can escape death by means of a ransom. In neither case is there any mention of asylum at the altar, even though both are cases of unintentional homicide. This approach, which allows for some flexibility, is confirmed by the Hebrew of Exodus 21:14, which reads: "... you shall take him from my altar, that he may die (*tiqqahennu lamut*)" which, as we saw above, is consistent with a permissory interpretation ("he *may* be put to death").

B. Cities of God

The second main form of asylum in ancient Israel was the institution of "cities of refuge" which were apparently set up on entry to the Promised Land (Joshua 20:7, 8). This was important because the conquest and settlement narratives describe how the portable Tabernacle moved from place to place on entry to the promised land.[28] With the Tabernacle functioning as a roving semipermanent place of asylum, the result would have been that for some, God's altar at the Tabernacle would be close at hand while for others, it would be a long way away. Six of the forty-eight Levitical cities were supposed to be set aside as places of asylum (Numbers 35:6–8), with a further three to be established on the east side of the Jordan for the two and one-half tribes who were going to live there (Deuteronomy 4:41–43). The idea of having regional centers of asylum, spread out around the land with good road connections (Deuteronomy 19:3), maximized the people's chances of reaching asylum. In this way, the cities of refuge are something of a compromise with clan law. They do not prevent the killing of the unpremeditated slayer *en route* to the city, but they do protect him once he gets there. The idea is to try to save the life of the unintentional killer without completely abolishing blood vengeance. Cities of refuge helped to limit the customary practice of blood feuds and kept the avenger of blood on a leash.

---

28. Summarized in R. E. Friedman, *Tabernacle*, in ANCHOR BIBLE DICTIONARY (D. N. Freedman ed., 6 vols.; London: Doubleday, 1992), vol. VI, 292–300, 293–94.

There are several reasons why the refugee has to stay in the city of refuge until the death of the high priest. First, it may be an arbitrary penalty. If the time spent in the city is thought of as a form of exile or punishment (not unlike living in a low-security prison), the question arises: how long should he be kept there? The death of the high priest is as good a fixed point as any, not least because the Levitical cities, being sacerdotal institutions, stand in some sort of subordinate relationship to the high priest. We have already seen that arbitrariness is a feature of the asylum laws—whether the refugee manages to escape the avenger of blood and make it to the city is largely a matter of chance. Of course, as we noted above, in a theocratic system, it is perfectly possible that such random elements may be seen as coming from God's hand. This is especially true when it comes to the death of the high priest, since God controls the lives of people. In that sense, the refugee's term of imprisonment is fixed by God.

Second, the death of the high priest in ancient Israel may have been an opportunity to operate an amnesty. We know that amnesties were proclaimed for prisoners and debtors upon the coronation of Egyptian kings. An example can be found in the poem "Joy on the Accession of Ramesses IV" (*circa* 1150 BC) lines 9–10 of which read: "Those who had been imprisoned are now set free/ the one [once] fettered is [now] in joy."[29] In premonarchical ancient Israel, the high priest was effectively the national leader, and so his death could have paved the way for an amnesty. It is possible that Moses himself benefited from an amnesty and, indeed, a "city of refuge"-type experience.[30] According to Exodus 2:11–15, Moses commits an (apparently) "spur of the moment" killing and flees into exile in Midian to escape the vengeance of Pharaoh. It was common for fugitives in antiquity to head for the desert where they could not be chased or tracked. Despite the evidence that Moses "looked this way and that" to see if the coast was clear (Exodus 2:12), the killing is close to the paradigm of the "spur of the moment" killing because there is no evidence that Moses had any previous enmity toward the Egyptian. While in exile in Midian, Moses finds himself under the supervision of Jethro, who is a priest (Exodus 2:16–21). Being under the aegis of a man who represents God is the nearest thing in the circumstances to the Israelite city of refuge. Finally, Moses remains in exile until Pharaoh dies (Exodus 2:23). Confirmation that the Egyptian practice of amnesty extended to former outlaws may again be found in the Ramesses IV poem, above, lines 3–4 of which read: "Those who fled have returned to their city/ those who had hidden have come out [again]."[31] (Similar amnesties are not unknown in modern times. In 2007,

---

29. Kenneth A. Kitchen, Poetry of Ancient Egypt (Paul Åströms Förlag: Jonsered, Sweden, 1999), 217.

30. For an exploration of this and other forms of thematic repetition in the biblical narratives and the laws of asylum, *see* J.P. Burnside, *Exodus and Asylum*.

31. Kitchen, Poetry of Ancient Egypt, 217.

nearly 9000 prisoners were released from Moroccan prisons under a pardon granted by its monarch to mark the birth of his daughter).[32]

Finally, the death of the high priest seems to have sacrificial overtones. "As the High Priest atones for Israel's sins through his cultic service in his lifetime . . . so he atones for homicide through his death."[33] Numbers as a whole is far more interested in the question of atonement than, for example, Deuteronomy[34] and this is reflected, for example, in concerns about the ritual pollution of land (e.g., Numbers 35:33).[35] Therefore, it is not surprising that Numbers 35 should pay closer attention to this aspect of the city of refuge than Deuteronomy 19. The idea that the death of one human being could function as atonement is confirmed in the Talmud (Makkoth 11b; and see also Leviticus Rabbah 10:6). It is central to sacrifice in the New Testament (e.g., "[Jesus the 'high priest' of the 'new covenant'] entered once for all into the Holy Place, taking not the blood of goats and calves but his own blood, thus securing an eternal redemption"; Hebrews 9:12).

As in the case of altar refuge, some adjudicatory procedure is needed to decide whether the killer is entitled to remain in a city of refuge. In Deuteronomy 19:12, this function is apparently given to the elders in the refugee's own city and to a congregation ('*edah*) in Numbers 35:12, 24–25. In this sense, the laws of asylum are a step toward the institutionalization of homicide—the question of whether blood can be shed or not is too serious to be left for the next of kin to decide alone.

C. Ransom and pardon

Having touched on the relationship between asylum and ransom in Numbers 35, we now turn to consider ransom—and pardon—separately. As already hinted, a second means by which a killer may escape the death penalty is ransom (*kopher*). Exodus 21:28–30 shows that there was a period in biblical legal history when it was possible to ransom the killer's life, at the kin's discretion:

> If a ransom is laid on him [the owner of the homicidal ox], then he shall give for the redemption of his life *whatever* is laid upon him.
> (*God speaking to Moses*)

Ransom thus takes the form of money paid to the kin. The size of the payment is not restricted by legal norms—hence the reference to "whatever" in verse 30—but would have been regulated by social norms. This was seemingly

---

32. THE TIMES, March 3, 2007.
33. JACOB MILGROM, NUMBERS (Philadelphia: The Jewish Publication Society, 1990), 294; Pamela Barmash, HOMICIDE IN THE BIBLICAL WORLD (Cambridge: Cambridge University Press, 2005), 103.
34. BARMASH, HOMICIDE, p. 104.
35. MILGROM, NUMBERS, p. 291.

available irrespective of the type of homicide. By the time of Numbers 35:31–32, however, *kopher* was banned. Numbers 35 sees asylum and ransom (*kopher*) as competing institutions. Numbers 35:32 prohibits the use of *kopher* even in those cases where the accused has the right to the protection of the city of refuge. It is thus excluded even in cases of accidental and "spur of the moment" homicide as well as premeditated killings. The change is said to be related to the need for expiation: only blood can wipe out blood—whether the killer's own blood or that of the high priest (Numbers 35:33–34).

In the light of the earlier discussion regarding the scope for negotiation at the altar, it is striking that the ban on taking ransom is found precisely in a passage which recommends the use of cities of refuge. Ultimately, ransom is banned even as a payment to "buy off" exile in such cities (Numbers 35:32). This sets a further limit on the power of the next of kin.

The final way in which a killer could escape the death penalty is by royal pardon. This is evident in the exchange between King David and the woman of Tekoa (2 Samuel 14). She claims that one of her sons has killed another and that if the avenger of blood takes vengeance on her only surviving son, she will be left with no sons to continue the family name. There is no mention of asylum either at the altar or at the city of refuge, unless the woman's own house constituted a refuge of sorts (as implied by 2 Samuel 14:7). Her family's desire for vengeance was in conformity with the biblical norms on homicide; however, it appears that this desire could be overridden by the king (2 Samuel 14:8–11). The family positions itself on the paradigm (premeditated homicide), but when the king judges the case of the widow, as a whole, he decides that the paradigm is too far distant for justice to be done by applying the paradigm.[36] The killer is effectively granted a royal pardon.

III. FIRST BLOOD

We have seen that biblical law is schematizing in its presentation, although it remains to be seen whether matters are quite so clear when we consider the biblical homicide narratives. We will explore this question by reference to the most famous homicide narrative of all, namely, that of Cain and Abel (Genesis 4:1–16). In doing so, we will find that biblical law does not map easily onto biblical narrative, at least in the primeval period. Indeed, the story is "perhaps the most elliptically described murder in literature."[37] This raises the question of the relationship between biblical law and narrative.

---

36. Jackson, Wisdom-Laws, p. 157.
37. Ellen Van Wolde, *The story of Cain and Abel: A narrative study*, J. Stud. of Old Testament 52, 25–41, 35 (1991).

The traditional rabbinic view is that the killing took place in the context of a quarrel between Cain and Abel (Midrash Genesis Rabbah 22:16), which might support the idea that it was "spur of the moment". Against this, there is no evidence of the verb *'amar* ("to say") being used in Bible in the sense of "to argue."[38] More damagingly, we need to reckon with the fact that the killing is *not* presented as following on immediately from whatever Cain is supposed to have said to Abel. Instead, Cain's "speaking" and Cain's "killing" are separated by "two time-extending words/phrases ['and it was,' 'when they were'] and one geographical word/phrase ['in the field'] that all function to dissociate the controversy [if there was one] from the crime."[39] Indeed, the very existence of these "three space-taking, time-stretching words . . . placed between the 'speaking against' and the killing"[40] point toward the argument that Cain's killing was premeditated. They provide "an opportunity for [Cain's] resentment to build"[41] following God's disfavor of Cain's offering (Genesis 4:3–5).

Indeed, there are several points at which the narrative suggests prior enmity between Cain and Abel—and hence premeditation. First, Cain receives a warning from God about his anger and what it might lead to (4:6–7). The phraseology is interesting: God warns Cain that "at the door sin is stretched out" (Genesis 4:7).[42] The words "stretched out" evoke the image of Abel "stretched out [dead] on the ground."[43] There is clear cause and effect. The implication is that if Cain continues to indulge his hostile feelings toward Abel, death will result.

Second, there is some evidence of verbal hostility between Cain and Abel prior to the killing. Verbal aggression, practiced over time, may provide evidence of enmity, which is central to the biblical paradigm of murder. Thus, we find that while Genesis 4:8a is usually translated "Cain said to (*'el*) his brother Abel," the word *'el* can also be translated "against," resulting in "Cain spoke against his brother Abel."[44] There are several advantages to this reading. It means that there is a parallel between Cain "speaking against" Abel and Cain "rising against" Abel. It also sheds light on God's warning in verse 7 that "sin is couching at the door (*lappetach*) [literally, 'opening']." The word *lappetach* is frequently used in the Bible to refer to opening a mouth (e.g., Numbers 16:32). God is specifically warning Cain that "evil speech leads to murder."[45] The emphasis upon prior

---

38. Pamela Tamarkin Reis, *What Cain said: A note on Genesis 4:8*, J. STUD. OLD TESTAMENT 27, 107–13, 111 (2002).

39. Ibid.

40. Reis, *What Cain said*, p. 112.

41. Ibid.

42. Craig Kenneth M. Craig, Jr., *Questions outside Eden (Genesis 4:1–16): Yahweh, Cain and their rhetorical interchange*, J. STUD. OLD TESTAMENT 86, 107–28, 116 (1999).

43. Ibid.

44. Reis, *What Cain said*, pp. 112–13.

45. Ibid., 113.

enmity, at different times and places to the actual killing, underscores Cain's premeditation. From this perspective, Cain's act seems to develop over time, just as God warned it would (Genesis 4:7). "The act of murder, unthinkable at one stage, becomes inevitable at another."[46]

Pamela Reis's proposed translation is, in my view, congruent with the fact that the Masoretic Text of Genesis 4:8 does not report what Cain said to, or about, Abel. This "speaking without content,"[47] as Ellen Van Wolde calls it, is highly significant because elsewhere in Genesis 4:1–16, we are told the content of the parties' speech. "Speaking without content" suggests that the semantic content of the speech was itself "empty." "This 'empty' speaking would then suggest, or testify to, the negation of the existence of the other as an equal, as a brother, and it can be seen as pointing ahead to the actual elimination of the other."[48] But although we do not know what exactly Cain says to Abel, we do know what Cain says to God. Cain's notorious response: "Am I my brother's keeper?" (Genesis 4:9) is a further indication of the way in which Cain's speech "negates . . . his relationship with his brother."[49] Van Wolde's claim regarding "empty" and negative speech confirms Reis's argument that Cain speaks against his brother and that this is linked to the subsequent killing.

Reis's proposed translation gains further force if we see the cry of Abel's blood (Genesis 4:10) as drawing together the themes of Cain's "evil speech" and the violence to which it led. It is further bolstered by the connection Jesus makes in the "Sermon on the Mount" (Matthew 5:1–7:29) between angry speech and murder:

> You have heard that it was said to the men of old, "You shall not kill [=Exodus 20:13/ Deuteronomy 5:18]; and whoever kills shall be liable to judgment [cf. *Targum Onqelos/Targum Pseudo-Jonathan*]." But I say to you that every one who is angry with his brother shall be liable to judgment; whoever insults his brother shall be liable to the council, and whoever says, "You fool!" shall be liable to the hell of fire. (Matthew 5:21–22; *Jesus speaking*).

The composite citation ("You have heard that it was said . . .") is thought to draw both on the Decalogue and well-known Targumic paraphrases of Genesis 9:6.[50] Jesus radically extends the teaching on Torah in relation to murder to include anger and angry speech, which is the root of murder. Given Jesus's emphasis on the early chapters of Genesis (see further Chapter 12), it is plausible to suggest that Jesus has Genesis 4:1–16 in mind.

---

46. Ibid.
47. Van Wolde, *Cain and Abel*, p. 34.
48. Ibid., 34–35.
49. Ibid., 35.
50. Serge Ruzer, *The technique of composite citation in the Sermon on the Mount (Matt. 5:21–22, 33–37)*, Revue Biblique 103, 65–75 (1996).

Finally, we should also reckon with the description of the offense itself:

when they were in the field, Cain rose up against his brother Abel, and killed him. (Genesis 4:8)

Whereas God wanted Cain to experience "uplift" (4:7; JPS), Cain instead "rose up against his brother." It is the wrong kind of ascent.[51] The sudden "rising up" indicates that Cain has been "lying low" in the field. This is exactly the narrative paradigm of a predator ambushing its prey. It is fully consistent with the biblical paradigm of the premeditated killing which specifically focuses upon ambush (Numbers 35:20; Deuteronomy 19:11).

However, the view that Cain's killing was premeditated does not square very well with God's treatment of Cain, making him "a fugitive and a wanderer on the earth" (Genesis 4:12). God's punishment is different from the typical punishment that is given to the premeditated killer in biblical law. Indeed, God's treatment of Cain is closer to the treatment given to the "spur of the moment" killer, inasmuch as Cain's punishment is a form of exile. Yet, even here there are differences between God's treatment of Cain and that given to the "spur of the moment" killer. It is clear that prior to God's intervention, Cain is in a worse position than the "spur of the moment" killer in biblical law because Cain can be killed by a stranger ("whoever finds me will slay me"; Genesis 4:14). By contrast, the "spur of the moment" killer can only be killed by the *go'el haddam*. However, after God's intervention, Cain becomes an outlaw who has been given total immunity. As a result, his is an entirely different form of exile to that found in biblical law: it is "external exile" in the form of "wandering" as opposed to "internal" exile in a city of refuge.[52]

To sum up, the narrative leans in favor of Cain's killing being premeditated while God's punishment of Cain is different from the treatment given to both premeditated and "spur of the moment" killings in biblical law, although it is closer to the latter than to the former. This suggests that the biblical laws of homicide, vengeance, and asylum do not always map easily onto biblical narrative, at least that of the primeval period (Genesis 1–11). This may be because this epoch "depicts a social context . . . which conspicuously lacks the institutions of the later Israel."[53] Cain's lenient treatment is perhaps most consistent with the theme of God's repeated mitigation in his dealings with humanity throughout the primeval history.[54]

Nevertheless, the relationship of the Cain and Abel narrative to biblical law is an important one because it shows a number of connections between law and

---

51. Craig, *Questions outside Eden*, p. 116.
52. Bernard S. Jackson, *Homicide in the Bible: A review article*, ZEITSCHRIFT FÜR ALTORIENTALISCHE UND BIBLISCHE RECHTSGESCHICHTE 12, 362–74, 369 (2006).
53. Ibid.
54. *See* Joze Krašovec, *Punishment and mercy in the primeval history*, EPHEMERIDES THEOLOGICAE LOVANIENSES 70, 5–33 (1994).

narrative in the form of thematic repetition. Thus, we find the "mark" of protection (Genesis 4:15) which contains "an implicit protest against blood-feud."[55] This may evoke God's subsequent protection of non-premeditated killers by means of asylum because Cain is, in effect, his own place of asylum. Second, there is the theme of exile. Genesis 4:16 describes Cain settling "in the land of Nod [understood as 'wandering']." Here, the combination of "settling" and "wandering" paints a picture of exile.[56] Again, the image of Cain going into exile for his crime and subsequently building a "city" (Genesis 4:17) evokes the use of the city of refuge for non-premeditated killers. Other examples of thematic repetition in Genesis 4:1-16 and later biblical texts include God favoring the younger brother (Genesis 4:4–5; cf. the preference of Jacob over Esau), conflict between brothers leading to fratricide (Genesis 4:8; cf. 2 Samuel 14:6), the cry of the victim with none to save them from violence (Genesis 4:10; cf. Deuteronomy 22:24, 27), and the notion of blood polluting the ground (Genesis 4:10–11; cf. Numbers 35:33–34). Consequently, although there is no straightforward "one-to-one" correspondence between the Cain and Abel narrative and biblical law, there is considerable evidence of thematic repetition.

IV. "V" FOR VENDETTA?

How does the concern for saving life in the asylum laws, together with God's clemency in the case of Cain, square with the role of vengeance elsewhere in biblical law? In particular, what sense should we make of the biblical laws that speak of "eye for eye, tooth for tooth, hand for hand, foot for foot, burn for burn, wound for wound, bruise for bruise" (Exodus 21:24–25; JPS)? These laws are commonly referred to as the *lex talionis* (Latin for "law of retaliation"). It is an important question because these are the best-known laws of the Bible—and among the most misunderstood.

At a general level, the *lex talionis* expresses the ideal of poetic justice, namely, that the punishment should fit the crime. This was popular in both biblical and ancient Near Eastern (ANE) texts. In the Psalms, frequent appeals are made to God to do to oppressors what they have done to others (and conversely to reward those who behave uprightly):

God is a righteous judge . . .
Behold, the wicked man conceives evil, and is pregnant with mischief,
and brings forth lies.
He makes a pit, digging it out,
and falls into the hole which he has made.

---

55. THOMAS L. BRODIE, GENESIS AS DIALOGUE: A LITERARY, HISTORICAL AND THEOLOGICAL COMMENTARY (Oxford: Oxford University Press, 2001), 154.
56. BRODIE, GENESIS AS DIALOGUE.

His mischief returns upon his own head,
and on his own pate [or "skull"] his violence descends.
(Psalm 7:11, 14–16/ MT 7:12, 15–17; *David speaking*).

This expresses the biblical belief that consequences, whether in the form of rewards or punishments, are inherent to the form of behavior practiced.[57] This idea is also reflected in the New Testament where final judgment is said to operate on the basis of talion:

> For we must all appear before the judgment seat of Christ, so that each one may receive good or evil, according to what he has done in the body. (2 Corinthians 5:10; *Paul speaking*)

"Mirroring punishment" is also found in ANE legal collections. This is expressed both negatively and positively. An example of the former (in which the offense is replicated upon the offender) is found in the Middle Assyrian Laws:

> If a man sodomises his comrade and they prove the charges against him and find him guilty, they shall sodomise him . . . . (Tablet A §20)[58]

An example of the latter (in which the penalty reflects an attempt to reverse the harm) is found in the Hittite Laws:

> If a free man sets fire to a house, he shall rebuild [the house]. And whatever perished in the house—whether it is persons, [cattle, or sheep], it is damage (?). He shall make compensation for it.[59]

Yet although the *lex talionis* can be said to express the general ideal of poetic justice, we need to consider more carefully how these laws were applied in biblical society.

A. Fearful symmetry?

Much turns on the meaning of the word "for" in such phrases as "eye for eye, tooth for tooth" (Exodus 21:24). Daube notes that the Hebrew word translated "for" (*tachat*) "frequently refers to one thing's taking the place of another and . . . to one thing's being given in place of another by way of compensation,"[60] pointing to a number of examples. First, the master who destroys a slave's eye "shall let him go free on account of (*tachat*) his eye" (Exodus 21:26; JPS)—and the same applies to a tooth (Exodus 21:27). The slave is thus compensated for the loss of

---

57. *See generally* Tikva Frymer-Kensky, *Tit for Tat: The principle of equal retribution in Near Eastern and Biblical law*, BIBLICAL ARCHAEOLOGIST 43, 230–34 (1980).

58. MARTHA T. ROTH, LAW COLLECTIONS FROM MESOPOTAMIA AND ASIA MINOR (Atlanta: Scholars Press, 2nd ed. 1997), 160.

59. Ibid., 229.

60. DAVID DAUBE, STUDIES IN BIBLICAL LAW (Cambridge: Cambridge University Press, 1947), 103–04.

his eye or tooth.[61] Likewise, the owner of the bovicidal ox "must restore ox for (*tachat*) ox" (Exodus 21:36; JPS), which is also a case of compensation. Third, according to Exodus 22:1/MT 21:37, the person who steals an ox or a sheep "shall pay five oxen for an ox, and four sheep for a sheep," although notably this goes beyond mere compensation to include a punitive element. This shows the importance, within biblical law, of the idea of compensation within the institution of retaliation itself.[62] It is, moreover, a subtle and nuanced idea of compensation: "the five-fold restitution of an ox may well represent an attempt to take into account the higher working capacity of that animal,"[63] while in Exodus 21:19, compensation for a wound involves paying for the loss of the victim's time.

The idea that there might be "cognitive equivalences between retaliation and restitution"[64] is not surprising. After all, taking the life of the person who has killed your family member "does restore the original proportion of power between the two persons or families concerned. The difference between [retaliation] and restitution proper is that it restores the original relation in a negative way, by depriving the wrongdoer of the same thing of which he has deprived the person wronged; while restitution is positive and gives back to the person wronged that which the wrongdoer has appropriated."[65] We can pick up on David Daube's reference to "positive restitution" at this point and distinguish between "positive talion" (which refers to live substitution or to some other form of compensation) and "negative talion" (which refers to equivalent physical harm). The distinction between positive and negative talion gives symmetry to the *lex talionis*; "giving an eye" as opposed to "taking an eye." (It is, in my view, unhelpful to describe physical mutilation as physical talion because the substitution of a live ox for a dead one is every bit as physical as killing someone else's ox).

The result is that to reflect the preposition *tachat* accurately, we should read verses such as Leviticus 24:18, 20 as "life *in the place of* life ... fracture *in the place of* fracture, eye *in the place of* eye, tooth *in the place of* tooth." This is so contrary to the way in which these verses have been presented to us in popular culture that some may find this reading counterintuitive. We are conditioned to reading "life for life" as though it means "death for death." But the context of Leviticus 24:18, for example, is explicitly concerned with restitution. The phrase *nephesh tachat nephesh*, which is commonly translated "life for life," can *only* mean a live substitution:

> He who kills a beast shall make it good, life for life.
> (*God speaking to Moses*)

---

61. Ibid., 104.
62. Ibid., 102–47.
63. Ibid., 133.
64. Bernard S. Jackson, *Lex Talionis: Revisiting Daube's Classic*, Society of Biblical Literature Meeting, Denver 2001,http://www.law2.byu.edu/biblicallaw/papers/jackson_bs_lex_talionis.pdf, accessed January7, 2008, p. 7.
65. DAUBE, STUDIES, p. 128.

Daube[66] finds support for this reading in the Hittite Laws §1–4, which are thought to date from the Old Hittite period (*circa* 1650–1500 BC). Here, four substitutes are given in the place of the person killed in a quarrel (Hittite Law §1), and two are given if the victim is a slave (Hittite Law §2). Notably, the number substituted depends on the nature of the killing and the victim's social status. The idea that people can be replaced is not unusual: even today, we remind stressed executives who need a holiday that "no one is irreplaceable." Although biblical law envisages the live substitution of people and animals, modern medicine raises the possibility of even more imaginative forms of live substitution. For example, there have been calls in the Philippines for a law that would commute a death sentence to life imprisonment if the convicted person agreed to donate a bodily organ for transplant.[67] This approach has as much claim to being inspired by the biblical provision of "life for life" as the more usual connotation of the *lex talionis*, namely, "death for death."

Jackson[68] finds a closer ANE parallel to live substitution in biblical law in the form of the Middle Assyrian Laws, which are thought to date anywhere between 1191 and 1076 BC. Tablet A §50 compensates the pregnant woman who is assaulted and then loses her unborn child. The relevant phrasing reads, "and they shall treat him [the assailant] as he treated her; he shall make full payment of a life for her foetus (*napsate umalla*)."[69] Live substitution makes sense in this context: "the services of a dependent member of the household have been lost," and so the assailant must provide a replacement.[70] There is a parallel here with Exodus 21:22 which also concerns an assault on a pregnant woman and results, it is thought, in a miscarriage. Moreover, this is followed by an extensive talionic formula (Exodus 21:23–25) which includes the phrase "life for life" (*nephesh tachat nephesh*). The same Semitic root is present in both the Akkadian word *napsate* and the Hebrew word *nephesh*. Thus, Exodus 21:22–25 lends itself to the idea of live substitution, and this is supported by other laws from the ANE.

Perhaps significantly, the context of Exodus 21:22–25 is nonintentional behavior. The assault upon the pregnant woman does not seem to be deliberate (Exodus 21:22). This too is consistent with the ANE. Several of the Hittite laws of talion are concerned with harm that takes place in the context of a quarrel (§1, 2), while several others are the result of an accident (§ 3, 4). Likewise, Jackson[71] has argued that the Middle Assyrian Laws are also concerned with nonintentional homicide. This means that cases of live substitution, in both biblical and ANE law, are concerned with nonintentional behavior. By contrast, the typical case of

---

66. Ibid., 116.
67. THE DAILY TELEGRAPH, June 23, 2000.
68. Jackson, *Lex talionis*, p. 4.
69. ROTH, LAW COLLECTIONS, p. 173.
70. JACKSON, WISDOM-LAWS, p. 233.
71. Jackson, *Lex talionis*, p. 4.

homicide in the Bible is premeditated and we have no evidence in biblical or ANE law (as yet) that live substitution is used in those cases.

One of the remarkable features of the *tachat* formula is its emphasis upon different parts of the body and the visual manifestation of different kinds of physical harm:

> ... the penalty shall be life for life, eye for eye, tooth for tooth, hand for hand, foot for foot, burn for burn, wound for wound, bruise for bruise.
> (Exodus 21:23–25; *God speaking to Moses;* JPS).

This extended formulation is interesting from a semiotic perspective because it emphasizes the visual representation of the harm. This is, of course, what talion does: it is a visual manifestation of the offender's offense on the offender's own body.[72] Its power comes from being iconic. Those who live and work with the offender "will continually be reminded of the offence, both of its iniquity and of the consequences of performing it."[73] Of course, the effect would be equally powerful if the application of talion resulted in a live substitution: the surrogate person or animal is a constant visual reminder of the one who has been killed.

It is because of the visual impact upon the observer that Deuteronomy 19:21 specifically exhorts:

> Your *eye* shall not pity; it shall be life for life, eye for eye, tooth for tooth, hand for hand, foot for foot. (*Moses addressing the people*)

It is the eye that is the focus of the exhortation and not, for example, the "heart." Punishment is in the eye of the beholder. This emphasis upon the visual may also explain why the Laws of Hammurabi, like biblical law, use eyes and teeth as examples of talion (e.g., §§ 196, 200, respectively). No doubt the choice reflects both the value and the vulnerability of these particular body parts. But it probably also reflects the fact that eyes and teeth are part of the face—and it is when talion is applied to the face that it typically has the greatest visual impact.

B. Ultraviolence

The expression of talion in the Bible is not limited to the *tachat* formula but is also expressed, according to Jackson,[74] using the word *ka'asher*, as in the following text:

> Adoni-bezek [a Canaanite king] fled; but they [the Israelites] pursued him, and caught him, and cut off his thumbs and his great toes. And Adoni-bezek said, "Seventy kings with their thumbs and their great toes cut off used to pick

---

72. Jackson, Studies, p. 290.
73. Ibid.
74. Jackson, *Lex talionis*, pp. 4–5.

up scraps under my table; as *(ka'asher)* I have done, so God has requited me" . . . . (Judges 1:6–7)

This language is comparable to that found in the law of the false witness:

you shall do to him as *(ka'asher)* he schemed to do to his fellow . . . . (Deuteronomy 19:19; *Moses addressing the Israelites;* JPS)

and in the general expression of the talionic principle in Leviticus 24:19:

When a man causes a disfigurement in his neighbour, as *(ka'asher)* he has done it shall be done to him. (*God speaking to Moses*)

Jackson has argued that the two formulas may be distinguished in the following way: "the *ka'asher* formula implies (only) *qualitatively* equivalent retribution, but without any concern for *quantitative* equivalence."[75] This is seen in the case of Adoni-bezek, who applies the *ka'asher* formula to similar nonfatal bodily injuries *without* referring to the fact that there is a difference in the quantum of the punishment (70 kings as opposed to one).[76] By contrast, the *tachat* formula is concerned *both* with qualitative *and* quantitative proportionality.

The importance of proportionality—and of distinguishing between qualitative and quantitative harm—can best be seen with reference to the story of Lamech, who boasts:

. . . I have slain a man for wounding me,
And a lad for bruising me.
If Cain is avenged *(yuqqam)* sevenfold,
Then Lamech seventy-sevenfold.
(Genesis 4:23–24; *Lamech speaking*)

For Jackson, Lamech's boast is objectionable not only because of the lack of quantitative proportionality (being avenged "seventy-sevenfold") but also because "he sees in purely quantitative terms what is in fact a qualitative difference—between nonfatal and fatal injuries."[77]

Both talionic formulas—the *tachat* formula and the *ka'asher* formula—function together in Leviticus 24; the former appearing at verse 18 and three times in verse 20 and the latter at verses 19, 20, and 23. Indeed, Leviticus 24 has been shown to have a detailed chiastic structure which is centered upon "fracture for *(tachat)* fracture, eye for *(tachat)* eye, tooth for *(tachat)* tooth" (Leviticus 24:20).[78] The literary presentation of Leviticus 24 thus physically presents the *tachat* formula *within* the *ka'asher* formula. It is plausible to conclude, then, that "the (qualitative) *ka'asher*

---

75. Ibid., 5.
76. JACKSON, WISDOM-LAWS, p. 191.
77. Ibid., 198.
78. Ibid., 447–48.

principle is to be qualified by the (quantitative) *tachat* formula."[79] In other words, the biblical requirement for qualitative proportionality—"an eye for an eye," not "an eye for a tooth"—is further tempered by the requirement for quantitative proportionality, that is, *"no more than* an eye for an eye."

This insistence upon qualitative *and* quantitative equivalence is radical in the light of the Lamech boast in Genesis 4:23–24, above. Genesis 4:24 uses the verb *naqam*, to avenge or take vengeance, which is also used in Exodus 21:20, where it refers to the punishment of the master who abuses his slave ("he shall be punished *(naqom yinnaqem))*." Both Genesis 4:23–24 and the Covenant Code show that vengeance can easily get out of hand. This underlines the importance of proportionality both in the Covenant Code and elsewhere in biblical law. It is also broadly consistent with the limits on vengeance we have seen elsewhere in the biblical laws of homicide and asylum.

Other texts go further and directly discourage the practice of vengeance. Leviticus 19:18 reads:

> You shall not take vengeance *(lo-tiqqom)* or bear a grudge against your countrymen. Love your fellow as yourself: I am the LORD.
> *(The LORD speaking to Moses;* JPS).

It is thought that the verb for vengeance in verse 18 *(naqam)* may be related to the Akkadian verb "to slaughter," in which case the verse should read: "Do not slaughter the sons of your people." If so, it is a polemic against killing the offender's children as punishment for the offender himself.[80] This text can be compared with Exodus 21:20–21 which concerns a fatal assault (verse 20) by a master upon his *'amah*, which is commonly thought to refer to a debt slave[81]:

> When a man strikes his slave, male or female, with a rod and the slave dies under his hand, he shall be punished [or "avenged"; *yinnaqem*].
> (Exodus 21:20; *God speaking*)

Westbrook[82] draws on what he sees as a parallel case in the Laws of Hammurabi (LH §116) to argue that vengeance takes the form of vicarious punishment, which means that the master's son can be killed by the slave's family, in place of the slave. The difficulty with this view is that we have no evidence of vicarious punishment elsewhere in the Covenant Code (Exodus 21:1–22:16). In particular, we do not find it at Exodus 21:31, where the penalty for the ox who kills a free

---

79. Ibid., 447–48.
80. For a general discussion of transgenerational punishment, *see* BERNARD M. LEVINSON, LEGAL REVISION AND RELIGIOUS RENEWAL IN ANCIENT ISRAEL (Cambridge: Cambridge University Press, 2008), 53–94.
81. JACKSON, WISDOM-LAWS, p. 249.
82. RAYMOND WESTBROOK, STUDIES IN BIBLICAL AND CUNEIFORM LAW (Paris: Gabalda, 1988), 89–100.

man's son or daughter is monetary payment and not the death of the owner's son or daughter (Exodus 21:30).[83] However, if Westbrook is correct in his reading of Exodus 21:20 (which sees this verse as allowing vicarious punishment), then Leviticus 19:18 (which prohibits vicarious punishment) can be seen as a rejection of the practice of vicarious revenge.

Notably, Jesus uses the "eye for eye, tooth for tooth" (Exodus 21:24) formula to teach not only the rejection of retaliation but also the acceptance of injustice without revenge or redress (Matthew 5:38–42). In doing so, Jesus commends the person who is entirely freed from personal animosity. This explains why Exodus 21:24 flows into Leviticus 19:18 in Jesus's teaching: it is because the latter rejects the practice of vengeance. Leviticus 19:18 itself is extended by Jesus to cover not merely the absence of malice but proactive "love for enemies" (Matthew 5:43–48). An example of "love for enemies" can be found in Exodus 23:4–5, which refers to the duty to assist even your enemy's beast. Jesus's teaching again has links with the primeval history: it is consistent with God's advice to Cain about overcoming hatred (Genesis 4:7) while Lamech's boast is subverted into a call to unlimited forgiveness (see Matthew 18:21–35, which uses the "seventy times seven" motif at verse 22).

To summarize, it is misleading to think of the *lex talionis* and biblical law as giving free rein to vengeful practice. There is not one talionic formula, but two, both of which have proportionality as their goal. Against the backdrop of "ultraviolence," as seen in other biblical texts, even the literal application of the *lex talionis* radically insists on the need for restraint. To this extent, the *lex talionis* is consistent with other biblical texts that set limits to bloodshed, including the laws of homicide and asylum. They are also congruent with those texts that are opposed to the practice of vengeance altogether. Nevertheless, proportionate retaliation is permitted, although this can also be understood in terms of compensation. Whether the response took the form of positive or negative talion depends on the narrative paradigm of the case in question. However, the fact that negative talion may have been permitted did not prevent the parties from negotiating terms. Ultimately, the phrase "eye for eye, tooth for tooth" operates on two levels: it creates an initial presumption of physical mutilation but, at the same time, it functions as a symbol of some more general equivalence, which could be substitution or some other form of compensation.[84] It is probable that in cases of nonfatal injuries resulting from a fight, the victim was entitled to threaten the offender with talionic punishment. But that punishment was always negotiable, and the further the circumstances were from the typical case, the less likely that *talio* would even be demanded, let alone enforced.

---

83. *Cf.* WESTBROOK, STUDIES, p. 99.
84. JACKSON, WISDOM-LAWS, p. 195.

V. CONCLUSION

Biblical law distinguishes between three different kinds of homicide: premeditated, "spur of the moment", and accidental. As in modern law, the biblical laws of homicide cover a broad range of cases and degrees of culpability. The laws of asylum illustrate how biblical law tries to strike a balance between harm and culpability. Asylum is available in the case of the "spur of the moment" but not the premeditated killing. However, in biblical law, even an accidental killing can be treated as seriously as murder. Biblical law takes seriously the value of human life—both the value of the victim's life and the need to protect the life of the offender, in certain circumstances. This is consistent with the limits that are set to blood vengeance—and to other forms of vengeance—as expressed in the *lex talionis*, which is concerned with both quantitative and qualitative proportionality. Biblical law insists radically upon restraint. This chapter has also emphasized the need to understand the meaning of the biblical laws in terms of their application. Apparently categorical language regarding the execution of an offender is immediately qualified by reference to an institution of refuge, while expressions of negative talion did not exclude the possibility of negotiation.

Selected reading

Pamela Barmash, *Homicide in the Biblical World* (Cambridge: Cambridge University Press, 2005), Chapter 5.

Jonathan Burnside, "Exodus and Asylum: Uncovering the relationship between biblical law and narrative," *Journal for the Study of the Old Testament* 34, 243–266 (2010).

David Daube, *Studies in Biblical Law* (Cambridge: Cambridge University Press, 1947), Chapter 3.

Bernard S. Jackson, *Wisdom-Laws: A Study of the* Mishpatim *of Exodus 21:1–22:16* (Oxford: Oxford University Press, 2006), Chapter 4.

Bernard S. Jackson, *Lex Talionis: Revisiting Daube's Classic,* Society of Biblical Literature Meeting, Denver 2001, http://www.law2.byu.edu/biblicallaw/papers/jackson_bs_lex_talionis.pdf, accessed January 7, 2008.

Bernard S. Jackson, *Studies in the Semiotics of Biblical Law,* Journal for the Study of the Old Testament Supplement Series 314 (Sheffield: Sheffield Academic Press, 2000), Chapter 10.

Johnson Lim Teng Lim, *Grace in the Midst of Judgment: Grappling with Genesis 1–11* (Berlin: Walter de Gruyter, 2002), Chapter 8 (Cain and Abel).

9. THEFT AND BURGLARY

Who is a thief? This is not always an easy question to answer. It is sometimes hard to tell at what point a person can be said, with certainty, to have "stolen" something. Much depends on what balance the law strikes between an objective approach to the law of theft (that is, doing something observably wrong with property belonging to another) and a subjective approach (that is, one based on the defendant's state of mind). The European Retail Theft Barometer 2006, which is the world's largest survey of retail crime, found that the top item stolen from food stores in the United Kingdom and Europe is "perfumes and fine fragrances."[1] Imagine, then, that you are shopping in a typical modern grocery store. Do you commit a theft the moment you put some designer fragrance in your shoulder bag, with the intention of not paying for it? Or is it a theft when you put the fragrance into the store's shopping basket, with the intention of not paying for it, even though the store allows you to put things in its shopping basket? Or is it a theft when you start using the item as if it belongs to you—by spraying it on yourself as you stroll around the shop—before you have reached the cash register?

This chapter explores the construction of theft and burglary in biblical law. We will see that in contrast to the modern English law of theft, which is predominantly subjective, biblical law takes an objective approach. In other words, a person is a thief in biblical law if he has observably interfered with another person's property, for example, by selling it or by having it in his possession. A further contrast with modern law is that the first case of theft in the Covenant Code (Exodus 20:22/MT 20:19–23:33) is actually that of "stealing another human being." Subsequent laws, including the theft of animals are, in some ways, variations upon the case of "kidnap." We will also see that understanding the biblical laws of theft and burglary means exploring the relationship between biblical law and narrative, as well as comparative laws on theft from the ancient Near East (ANE). We will also look at a juridical parable which strangely uses the biblical laws of theft to address quite different problems of adultery and murder. Finally, we will conclude by exploring the potential penalties in biblical law for theft and burglary, which have considerable contemporary resonance.

---

1. JOSHUA BAMFIELD, EUROPEAN RETAIL THEFT BAROMETER: MONITORING THE COSTS OF SHRINKAGE AND CRIME FOR EUROPE'S RETAILERS (Nottingham: Centre for Retail Research, 2006).

1. WHO'S THE THIEF?

We begin by addressing the central problem of "who is a thief" in relation to modern English law. Other countries have, of course, different rules and emphases, and even the English law of theft is apt to change, as we will see. However, it is worth setting out the English position because it shows some of the basic choices that legal systems have when framing a law of theft. This will help us to appreciate the nature of the choices that are made in biblical law.

In modern English law, theft is defined as the appropriation of property belonging to another with the intention to permanently deprive the other of it. But what does it mean to "appropriate" something? Section 3(1) of the Theft Act 1968 states that "any assumption by a person of the rights of an owner amounts to an appropriation . . . ." The crucial question is: what does it mean to "assume the rights of an owner"?

One approach is to give an objective definition to appropriation. This would mean, for example, that to be a thief one has to do something that is objectively inconsistent with the rights of the owner. On this view, one would not be a thief merely by having a secret intention to steal something. This used to be the approach taken by English law. For example, in the case of *Morris*,[2] Mr Morris went into a supermarket and switched the price labels on two items, intending to buy the more expensive item for the price of the less expensive one. He put the item into the supermarket's shopping cart and was subsequently charged with theft. The question was whether what he had done amounted to an appropriation. The House of Lords held that there is an appropriation as soon as the defendant usurps the owner's rights by doing something that is unauthorized by the owner. On the facts, Mr Morris usurped the rights of the supermarket by switching the labels, and so he was guilty of theft. Equally, he would also have been guilty of theft if he put the items into his own shopping bag instead of into the cart, without intending to pay for them, since this would also have usurped the rights of the owner. But he would not have been guilty of theft if he put the items into his shopping trolley while harboring the secret intention of stealing them. This is because he is not objectively usurping the rights of the owner. Indeed, he is objectively respecting the rights of the owner by doing exactly what he is expected to do, which is putting the goods into the cart. This objective approach to the law of theft is quite narrow. In fact, when the law is defined in these terms, fewer defendants are likely to be guilty of theft.

In recent years, however, English law has moved away from an objective approach to the law of theft and toward a more subjective approach. Here, the person who merely has a secret intention to steal goods may be said to have appropriated them, even if he has not actually done anything that is objectively

---

2. [1984] Appeal Cases 320.

inconsistent with the rights of the owner. According to the European Retail Theft Barometer 2006, the second most-stolen item from grocery stores in the United Kingdom and Europe is alcohol.[3] Imagine the typical shoplifter who goes into the local supermarket and puts a bottle of whiskey in his basket with the intention of stealing the item. It could be argued that as soon as he puts the whiskey in his basket, he has already treated the item as his own simply because he has already resolved to steal it. He is a thief because he has already subjectively assumed the rights of an owner, even though his criminal intentions are secret, and he has not actually done anything objectively to usurp the rights of the supermarket.

The classic case of this subjective approach is that of *Lawrence v. Metropolitan Police Commissioner*.[4] Mr. Lawrence was a taxi driver in London. An Italian student, who was on his first visit to England, approached Lawrence, showing him a piece of paper on which an address was written. The defendant said it was a very expensive journey, but in fact, it was only fifty pence. The student took out his wallet and offered one pound for the fare. Lawrence said it was more expensive than that and, with the wallet still open, helped himself to six pounds more—and off they sped across London. Lawrence was charged with theft, even though the student had consented to him taking the six pounds. It was held that Lawrence appropriated the money when he took it from the student's wallet. The fact that the student had consented was irrelevant. This subjective approach is much broader than the objective approach. The result is that when the law is defined in these terms, more defendants are likely to be guilty of theft.

It is this subjective approach that English law has favored in recent years. Thus, in the case of *Hinks*,[5] Mrs. Hinks became friendly with a man of limited intelligence who had been left some money by his father. Mrs. Hinks was alleged to have influenced this man to have withdrawn sums amounting to £60,000 from his building society account and deposit them in her bank account. Although she claimed these deposits were loans or gifts, she was convicted of theft. As in *Lawrence*, the courts held that an appropriation of goods could occur even when the owner consented to the property being taken. However, this case goes further than that of *Lawrence v. Metropolitan Police Commissioner* because there was no deception or false representation by Mrs. Hinks. (It should be noted that in English law, undue influence is not in itself a crime although "obtaining by deception" is an offense under sections 15–16 of the Theft Act 1968). The decision in *Hinks* supports the view of Lord Keith (who gave the leading judgment in the earlier case of *Gomez*[6]). He held that simply taking an article off the shelf of a supermarket and putting it into a trolley amounted to an appropriation

---

3. Joshua Bamfield, European Retail Theft.
4. [1972] Appeal Cases 626.
5. [2000] 3 *Weekly Law Reports* 1590.
6. [1992] 3 *Weekly Law Reports* 1067.

and was therefore a theft, provided the defendant had the requisite intention to steal.

However, this subjective approach is problematic. Imagine that you are reading this book in a coffee shop, and I decide that I like your bookmark, which is lying on the table. If I simply move my hand toward your bookmark, with the intention of stealing it, I have arguably committed theft. The decisions in *Hinks* and *Gomez* are simply extraordinary. The result is that modern English law elevates the subjective element of dishonesty at the expense of the objective element of doing something that is inconsistent with the rights of the owner. It virtually endorses the idea that criminal liability can be imposed on the basis of the defendant's blameworthy state of mind. (Of course, the defendant's state of mind must be proved "by reference to all the evidence," according to section 8(b) of the Criminal Justice Act 1967, and establishing an intention to steal on the basis of minimal action on the defendant's part is problematic). The English law of theft distances itself from the traditional requirement of the criminal law that a completed criminal offense should result in harm and/or confer some benefit on the offender. Here, we see that the English law of theft is closely concerned with expressing moral judgments, even though liberal jurisprudence claims that law should not be concerned with morality.

It is of course possible that English law will have changed again by the time you read this book. The point, however, is that the recent history of the law of theft in English law shows that very different answers can be given to the question of who is a thief? What approach does biblical law favor?

II. TO CATCH A THIEF

In contrast to the modern English law of theft, biblical law takes an objective approach to the problem, viz., the biblical tests require that the offender do something observably wrong in relation to another person's property. The typical ways in which this can be shown to occur is either (1) evidence that you have what belongs to another in your possession, or (2) evidence that you had it at one time, and that you have since disposed of it. The former is known as "hot possession" and, by extension, the latter can be called "lukewarm possession," because the trail has not yet gone cold.

A. Human traffic

Our first encounter with the law of theft in the biblical legal collections concerns stealing a person:

> Whoever steals a man, whether he sells him or is found in possession (*beyado*) of him, shall be put to death. (Exodus 21:16; *God speaking*)

Subsequent cases of the law of theft, which include stealing an ox or a sheep (Exodus 22:1–4/MT 21:37–22:3), are presented, in some ways, as variations upon the case of "stealing a person," which modern law classifies as "kidnapping." We will consider cases of animal theft further, below. Both Exodus 21:16 and Exodus 22:4/MT 22:3 use objective tests of lukewarm possession (sale) and hot possession (that is, when the thief is caught with the stolen item literally "in his hand"; *beyado*). We will explore these tests further, below.

The patriarchal narratives are consistent with Exodus 21:16, which presents kidnapping as a form of theft. Thus, when Jacob secretly leaves the service of his father-in-law, Laban, with his own wives (Genesis 31:20–21), Laban accuses Jacob of stealing his daughters ("What have you done, that you have . . . carried away my daughters like captives of the sword?"; Genesis 31:26). Likewise, Joseph's brothers commit the offense of "man stealing" when they sell Joseph into slavery (Genesis 37:25; and cf. Joseph's own description of the offense as having been "stolen out of the land of the Hebrews"; Genesis 40:15). Both patriarchal stories concern family members (daughters and brothers), which suggests that the family status of the kidnapped person is relevant (for example, because they are children). Like Exodus 21:16, the Laws of Hammurabi also specify the death penalty for kidnapping although, as we will see, capital punishment was a common penalty in the Laws of Hammurabi for theft in general (see further, below). LH §14 refers to the kidnap of "the young child of another man," which is also consistent with the emphasis in the biblical materials on dependent family members.

The seriousness of "people stealing" is emphasized in the following text from Deuteronomy. This is not surprising because Deuteronomy as a whole places great stress on "brotherhood":

> If a man is found stealing one of his brethren, the people of Israel, and if he treats him as a slave or sells him, then that thief shall die; so you shall purge the evil from the midst of you. (Deuteronomy 24:7; *Moses speaking*)

A literal translation of verse 7 reads: "If a man is found stealing the life of a man (*ish gonebh nephesh*) . . ." where *nephesh* can mean the life of an individual. This underlines the gravity of the offense: kidnapping, in this sense, is akin to murder. The seriousness of Deuteronomy's presentation is underscored by the use of the rare formulation *ki-yimmatse*, which can be translated "if there be found . . . ." This phrase occurs only at the head of four biblical laws, all of them in Deuteronomy (the others being 17:2; 21:1 and 22:22). David Daube[7] claims that the formula cannot simply mean "caught red-handed." After all, this is clearly not the case in Deuteronomy 24:7, where the thief has sold the victim already. Instead, Daube argues that the solemnity of the expression and its location at the head of the statute is designed to emphasize "the fearfulness of the resulting appearance in the eyes of the beholder—[including] God, above all."[8]

---

7. David Daube, *To be found doing wrong*, STUDI IN ONORE DI EDOARDO VOLTERRA 2, 1–13, 4–5 (1969).
8. Ibid, 7.

As such, the unusual formula functions as a linguistic "register" of the seriousness of this particular offense. This is consistent with other "shame-cultural" elements in Deuteronomy (e.g., Deuteronomy 25:5–10) because things are shameful depending on how they are seen in the eyes of others.[9] An association between theft and exposure is also found in Proverbs 6:30–31:

> A thief is not held in contempt
> For stealing to appease his hunger;
> Yet if caught he must pay sevenfold;
> He must give up all he owns (*Solomon speaking;* JPS).

As Daube[10] notes, people do not despise a thief when he steals in secret and gets away with it. Like the adulterer, with whom the thief is compared in the immediate context (Proverbs 6:29, 32–35), the thief gives into temptation to meet his appetite but loses everything when he is caught. Like adultery, theft and shame go together because theft is a secretive act, and shame results when the secret is made known.

B. The cook, the thief, the sheep, and its owner

We turn from the theft of persons to the theft of animals. The key text is Exodus 22:1–4/ MT 21:37–22:3). Exodus 22:1/MT 21:37 introduces a norm by the Hebrew word *ki*, followed by three further norms, each of which are introduced by the Hebrew word *'im* (verses 2, 3, and 4). Exodus 22:5/MT 22:4 moves onto a different norm introduced by *ki*.[11] This means that Exodus 22:1–4/ MT 21:37–22:3 can be treated as a single thematic unit, despite its range of interests. However, for the sake of simplicity, we will explore Exodus 22:1 and 4/ MT 21:37 and 22:3 first, which concern theft, and then consider Exodus 22:2–3/ MT 22:1–2, which concern burglary.

First, Exodus 22:1/ MT 21:37:

> If a man steals an ox or a sheep, and kills it or sells it, he shall pay five oxen for an ox, and four sheep for a sheep. (*God speaking*)

As in Exodus 21:16, biblical law uses an objective test. According to Exodus 22:1/MT 21:37, a person is a thief if he steals something and kills it or sells it. It is an objective test. This means that simply approaching a herd of cattle in suspicious circumstances but not handling or taking away the animals will not be theft. Likewise, to use the supermarket examples at the start of the chapter, it is not theft in biblical law to put a fragrance into a supermarket shopping basket with the intention of not paying for it. Exodus 22:1/ MT 21:37 is an

---

9. Ibid.
10. Daube, *To be found*, p. 12.
11. Bernard S. Jackson, Wisdom-Laws: A Study of the Mishpatim of Exodus 21:1–22:16 (Oxford: Oxford University Press, 2006) 291.

objective test but it is not "hot possession" because the thief does not have the stolen item (that is, the live ox or sheep) in his possession. However, there is evidence that he previously had the stolen items in his possession because the property was disposed of by means of sale or slaughter ("lukewarm" possession). "Selling" and "killing" were the normal way of disposing of an animal because, in a small agricultural community, a thief would not ordinarily use the stolen beast for drawing a cart or plough but would try to get rid of it as quickly as possible.[12] The idea that proving the sale of stolen property could be conclusive evidence of theft appears in ANE sources, including Laws of Hammurabi (LH) §§9, 265 and Middle Assyrian Laws Tablet A (MAL A) §1.

Daube[13] regards the existence of two different evidentiary tests: (1) sale/slaughter, and (2) possession, as indicating two stages in the development of the biblical laws of theft, with the former (Exodus 22:1–3/ MT 21:37–22:2) reflecting early practice and the latter (Exodus 22:4/ MT 22:3) indicating later practice, which was subsequently added as an appendix. According to Daube, this explains the literary presentation of the passage, which otherwise seems illogical. However, we should not expect biblical legal texts to conform to modern ideas about the importance of "strict logic."[14] In any case, Exodus 22:1–4/ MT 21:37–22:3 makes sense as a literary unit in its current form. Of course, it may have been the case that evidence by sale/slaughter was the most common form of evidence, and this may be the reason why this is dealt with first. However, this is not a reason for thinking that hot possession could not have been a valid form of evidence at the same time.[15]

Why might biblical law have favored an objective approach? The answer may lie in the fact that, were a person to be exposed as a thief, he would typically be required to make multiple restitution, which might well have resulted in his becoming a slave (Exodus 22:3/ MT 22:2; see further, below). This being so, it was important that a person should not be treated as a thief unless it is possible to show that he is one. In addition, objective tests are easier to apply than subjective tests. To this extent, objective tests enable the biblical laws of theft to function as "self-executing rules," that is, rules that can be applied by the parties themselves.[16]

Exodus 22:1/ MT 21:37 suggests that oxen and sheep were the typical animals stolen. Losing an ox, particularly, was a significant deprivation for the owner. In Babylonia in the fifth century BC, one ox was worth more than half the value of

---

12. David Daube, Studies in Biblical Law (Cambridge: Cambridge University Press, 1947), 90.

13. Ibid., 89–96.

14. Ibid., 90.

15. Bernard S. Jackson, Theft in Early Jewish Law (Oxford: Clarendon Press, 1972), 47.

16. Jackson, Wisdom-Laws, p. 29.

a typical slave (40 shekels compared to 60 shekels).[17] Stealing an ox deprives the victim of his livelihood, and this includes future as well as present benefits. This is also part of the reason why theft is serious in biblical society. It contrasts with the typical modern examples of theft from supermarkets (fragrance, alcohol) and individual households (luxury electronic goods).

C. "Hot possession" and biblical narratives

We turn from "lukewarm possession" in Exodus 22:1/ MT 21:37 to "hot possession" in Exodus 22:4/ MT 22:3:

> If the stolen beast is found alive in his possession (*beyado*), whether it is an ox or an ass or a sheep, he shall pay double. (*God speaking*)

As in Exodus 21:16, biblical law uses the objective test of hot possession. A person is a thief if the stolen item is found in his possession (literally "in his hand"; *beyado*).

There are a number of examples of hot possession in the biblical narratives, starting with the Jacob and Joseph cycles. First, hot possession is taken as conclusive evidence of theft in the shepherding contract between Jacob and Laban:

> my honesty will answer for me later, when you come to look into my wages with you. Every one that is not speckled and spotted among the goats and black among the lambs, if found with me, shall be counted stolen.
> (Genesis 30:33; *Jacob speaking*)

The parties themselves agree on the use of the conclusive test. They are also the ones who apply it. As noted above, one of the advantages of hot possession is that it is a self-executing rule that does not require institutional adjudication.

Later in the Jacob story, hot possession is, once again, taken as conclusive evidence of theft between Jacob, Laban, and their households. Jacob is accused of stealing Laban's household idols (*teraphim*) although unbeknown to either of them, the real culprit is one of Jacob's wives, Rachel (Genesis 31:22–42). Genesis 31:22ff describes Laban's "hot pursuit" of Jacob, and his subsequent formalized search of Jacob's possessions is common to many ancient legal systems.[18] "Pursuit and search" extends the period in which you can catch the thief redhanded. The temporal references (three days to discover Jacob had gone, followed by seven days' hot pursuit; Genesis 31:22–23) suggests that Laban was only just in time. Genesis 31 suggests a formal procedure for dealing with the suspect. This centers upon an accusation that a specific item has been stolen, followed by a search for that item. There is no general accusation, nor is there a

---

17. JOE M. SPRINKLE, BIBLICAL LAW AND ITS RELEVANCE (Lanham: University Press of America, 2006), 95.
18. DAUBE, STUDIES, p. 201; JACKSON, THEFT, pp. 216–17.

general search for anything that might have gone missing. We are told that Laban brings his "relatives" with him (Genesis 31:23). No doubt it was common for the pursuer to be accompanied. Relatives would be useful witnesses if the property is found and useful warriors if the encounter turned nasty. It is not surprising that the search was formalized by customary law. This is because "pursuers were far more likely to abuse the suspect's household than the owner of stolen property who was a member of the same settled community as the thief, and who would, therefore, have to face the suspected thief, and other members of the common community, in the future."[19] A similar pattern of pursuit and search is found in Genesis 44:4–17, where Joseph's steward pursues the brothers for suspected theft of Joseph's goods. Once again, we find a specific complaint followed by a search for the missing item (Genesis 44:4–12).

In both cases, the object of the theft is characterized as "sacred property." In Genesis 31:30, Jacob is accused of stealing Laban's "gods" (*elohim*, though it is interesting that Jacob refers to them dismissively as *keley-beytekha* or "household objects" (Genesis 31:37). In modern language, Jacob's dismissal is the difference between referring to "gods" and "goods". Likewise, Joseph's brothers are accused of stealing Joseph's divination cup (Genesis 44:5). The theft of sacred property seems to be an aggravating factor.[20] This is apparent in several of the ANE legal collections (LH §§ 6 and 8, both of which involve the theft of property "belonging to the god", while MAL Tablet A §1 concerns theft "from the sanctuary in the temple"[21]).

Finally, hot possession is also taken as conclusive evidence of the theft of Joseph's silver cup in Genesis 44:9, even though the brothers know they are innocent. The cup had been planted in Benjamin's sack by Joseph's house steward, on Joseph's instructions (Genesis 44:1–2). There is a parallel here between what Joseph does to his brothers and what the brothers did to Joseph (Genesis 37:25–35). In both stories, a brother wrongfully turns another into a slave, and there is deceitful use of physical evidence (Joseph's coat and the cup; Genesis 37:31–33; 44:1–2). Joseph places the brothers in an analogous situation to that in which he was put himself:

> What shall we say to my lord [i.e. Joseph]? What shall we speak? Or how can we clear ourselves? God has found out the guilt of your servants; behold, we are my lord's slaves, both we and he also in whose hand (*beyado*) the cup has been found. (Genesis 44:16; *Judah speaking*)

---

19. JACKSON, THEFT, p. 217.
20. DAUBE, STUDIES, p. 101 n. 28; JACKSON, THEFT, pp. 63–67, 167–70.
21. MARTHA T. ROTH, LAW COLLECTIONS FROM MESOPOTAMIA AND ASIA MINOR (Atlanta: Scholars Press, 2nd ed. 1997), 155.

Genesis 44:16 uses the same term (*beyado*) as Exodus 22:4. Likewise, Joseph accepts the brothers' evidentiary test, although he rejects the brothers' proposed penalty (multiple slavery) in favor of making Benjamin alone his slave:[22]

> But he [Joseph] said, "Far be it from me that I should do so! Only the man in whose hand (*beyado*) the cup was found shall be my slave; but as for you, go up in peace to your father." (Genesis 44:17)

This is similar to the acceptance of an objective test between Jacob and Laban (Genesis 31:32). Of course, hot possession cuts both ways. If possessing the stolen property is conclusive of guilt, it follows that the failure to find the property is conclusive of the defendant's innocence. There is some confirmation for this in the biblical text. The books of Samuel describe how the prophet Samuel is forced, by popular demand, to step down as Israel's national leader and make way for Israel's first king (1 Samuel 8). He has been sacked from the top job. Not surprisingly, he uses his farewell speech as an opportunity to justify his record in office. In doing so he throws down a challenge that uses similar language to the laws of theft:

> [*Samuel speaking*] "Here I am; testify against me before the LORD and before his anointed. Whose ox have I taken? Or whose ass have I taken? Or whom have I defrauded? Whom have I oppressed? . . . ." They said, "You have not defrauded us or oppressed us or taken anything from any man's hand." And he said to them, "The LORD is witness against you, and his anointed is witness this day, that you have not found anything in my hand (*beyadi*)." And they said, "He is witness." (1 Samuel 12:3–5)

It is very unlikely that Samuel's oral declaration before "all Israel" (1 Samuel 12:1) is made up specially for the occasion. It is likely that he is drawing on an established oral declaration formula that has its roots in establishing innocence of theft when there is suspicion. This is followed by a formal acknowledgment of innocence on the part of those who might have had cause for suspicion. The whole event is observed by divine and human witnesses. In Samuel's case, the purpose of the ritual is to clear his name from any suspicion that he personally had to step down because of corruption.

If formal declarations of innocence were indeed made before God, this amounts to a recognition that hot possession will not deal with every case. Despite a thorough search, the suspect may still be guilty. The implication is that God will punish the lying thief.

The use of a divine as well as a human witness is consistent with the laws of theft. For example, the bailee who is accused of having stolen property that was placed in his safekeeping is said to "come near (*weniqrabh*) to God"

---

22. JACKSON, WISDOM-LAWS, p. 298.

(Exodus 22:8/MT 22:7), terminology that is elsewhere associated with an oracular consultation (e.g., Numbers 27:1, 5).[23]

It is also consistent with the biblical narratives. Judah cries, "God has found out the guilt of your servants" (Genesis 44:16) when Joseph's cup is discovered. (This is, of course, a craftily assembled piece of writing. Judah is referring to the theft. However, from the narrator's point of view, the cup actually uncovers the brothers' crime against Joseph from years before, because it places them in Joseph's shoes. Judah speaks more truly than he realizes). But why does Judah think God has an interest in the theft? Perhaps the reference to divine interest reflects the nature of the stolen object, in this case, a "divining cup" and hence sacred property? Or perhaps we should regard Judah's declaration as hyperbole, in keeping with his request for multiple enslavement, which is rejected by Joseph (Genesis 44:16–17)? In my view, it is likely that Judah's outburst reflects a more widespread belief about God's involvement in theft cases, rather than just this case in particular. There is similar evidence from the ANE legal collections that suspects in theft cases testified before deities (e.g., LH §§9, 265 and MAL Tablet A §1).

But why is God presented as having a specific interest in theft cases, as opposed to cases of lying? Perhaps the test of hot possession was thought to be divine in origin inasmuch as "it was believed that God would enable the property to be discovered, if it had been stolen."[24] This general belief has, in my view, some textual basis in Torah where "uncovering things that are secret" is a divine speciality. This is, in fact, one of the points of the Joseph story. The brothers kept what they did from Jacob for many years, but eventually their guilt became known. God's special interest in "secret acts" is expressly stated in Deuteronomy 29:29/ MT 29:28:

> Concealed acts concern the LORD our God; but with overt acts, it is for us and our children ever to apply all the provisions of this Teaching.
> (*Moses speaking;* JPS)

We noted, above, that secrecy is the essence of theft. It follows then, that cases which involve the uncovering of secret things should be referred to God (and cf. Numbers 5:11–31). This includes cases where the objective test for theft has failed to produce a conviction.

To summarize, the biblical law of theft uses objective tests of lukewarm and hot possession. This contrasts with the modern English law of theft, which is subjective and almost amounts to punishing people for their thoughts. In fact, on this point, English law takes a more extreme position than the Eighth Commandment: while this prohibits "coveting" other people's possessions (Exodus 20:17), it does not prescribe a penalty. Rather ironically, modern English law is more moralistic than biblical law.

---

23. JACKSON, THEFT, p. 242.
24. Ibid., 45.

D. Protecting the innocent

It is immediately apparent from the cases we have considered so far that hot possession is an arbitrary test in at least two respects. For one thing, "no other evidence seems to count, not even eyewitness testimony of the accused thief's act, in the absence either of hot possession or disposal by way of slaughter and sale."[25] Second, "the evidence appears to create conclusive presumptions of guilt, notwithstanding the possible availability of evidence to the contrary."[26] The advantage of having such arbitrary rules is that first, they make proof of an offense easier and, second, that they provide remedies which can be readily implemented by the parties without the intervention of adjudicatory agencies. The disadvantage of arbitrary rules is that they can lead to individual cases of injustice, especially for the person who buys stolen goods and the person who has been framed.

First, we consider the problem of the person who buys stolen goods. Under the hot possession test, the buyer is identified as a thief because he is in possession of the stolen goods, even though he is not responsible for the original theft. One of the justifications for hot possession is that it puts the onus on the purchaser to be satisfied or take care that the items he is purchasing are not stolen goods; otherwise, he risks paying multiple restitution. At this level, making the buyer liable in cases of hot possession is not unreasonable (and we can imagine how a modern test of hot possession might affect Internet auction sites). In addition, we should recall that we are dealing with an agricultural economy where it is much easier for a person to tell whether an item belongs to someone else. Even today in agricultural communities, Farmer Jones can say that he saw one of Farmer Smith's sheep walking down the road. It is likely that in biblical society, animals were marked in some way. The branding of livestock is attested in antiquity and was even interfered with and faked, according to a case in the *Varzy Papyrus* from the Egyptian Twentieth Dynasty, at the time of the assassination attempt on Ramesses III, *circa* 1150s BC.[27] LH §265 is concerned with the shepherd who is given an animal for shepherding, changes its brand, and sells it on. Recognizing an ox is thus like recognizing a car number plate (cf. Genesis 30:33). In this context, a hot possession rule is not unfair.

What about those cases where the buyer could not have known that he was receiving stolen goods? We do not have any specific indication of how this was addressed in biblical law: as we saw in Chapter 1, biblical law is not comprehensive. However, the problem is tackled in the Laws of Hammurabi (§9). This is worth exploring because it is a good example of the way in which ANE law can be used to generate hypotheses and shed light on the biblical material.

---

25. JACKSON, WISDOM-LAWS, p. 293.
26. Ibid.
27. ALAN H. GARDINER, RAMESSIDE ADMINISTRATIVE DOCUMENTS (Oxford: Oxford University Press, 1948), xviii–xix.

In LH §9, the person who is labelled a thief because of hot possession can avoid liability by claiming and proving that he is a bona fide purchaser. Proof takes the form of witnesses to the sale, on the part of both the buyer and the seller. If both sets of witnesses are believed—and the owner's witnesses make a declaration before a god (which we discussed above)—then that is taken as evidence that the seller was himself the thief. It is possible that this was also the practice in biblical society. Moreover, if witnesses could be used to rebut the guilt implied by hot possession, then it follows that hot possession itself might not always have been a necessary test. If so, then a victim of theft might also succeed if the theft was observed by eyewitnesses, but it was not possible to obtain evidence of hot possession. The same reasoning can also apply to lukewarm possession; accordingly, "sale or slaughter is not to be taken as absolutely prohibiting any other method of proof."[28] Even so, an element of arbitrariness remains if, for example, the bona fide purchaser is unable to produce the witnesses.[29]

We argued in Chapter 1 for responsible comparative study between ANE and biblical legal materials. In this case, we are justified in comparing LH §9 with the Covenant Code because the evidence on which the seller of the stolen property is convicted as a thief is the same as one of the evidentiary tests found in Exodus 22:1/MT 21:37, namely, proof of sale.[30] At the same time, if we are to avoid "parallelomania" between the ANE and biblical legal materials, we should recognize that there are important differences between LH and the Covenant Code. LH §9 is concerned with "lost property"[31] which probably refers, not to animal theft (as in the Covenant Code), but to "moveable property in general"[32] which, crucially, is "the subject-matter of normal commercial relations, for which there is an established commercial procedure of transfer."[33] By contrast, there is no indication that the animal theft of the *Mishpatim* is subject to "a normal set of formalities of transfer."[34] Second, LH §9 refers to "the judges"[35] who examine the case. The fact that judges are required in LH §9 to examine the witnesses shows that there is some discretionary element involved in the process of fact construction. By contrast the *Mishpatim* does not make any reference to judges. Indeed, as we have seen, the arbitrariness of hot possession reflects the absence of judicial determination of the issue. The test is agreed by the parties themselves and is applied by them directly.[36]

---

28. JACKSON, THEFT, p. 48.
29. JACKSON, WISDOM-LAWS, p. 295.
30. JACKSON, THEFT, p. 42; WISDOM-LAWS, p. 296.
31. ROTH, LAW COLLECTIONS, p. 83.
32. JACKSON, WISDOM-LAWS, p. 296.
33. Ibid.
34. Ibid.
35. ROTH, LAW COLLECTIONS, p. 83.
36. JACKSON, WISDOM-LAWS, p. 296.

We turn from the problem of the person who buys stolen goods to the problem of the person who has been framed. Under the hot possession test, a person can be framed for an offense as a result of having stolen property "planted" on his person. Another justification for hot possession is that people have to take care of *whatever* they have in their possession (and we can imagine today how this might apply to possessions that are not acquired as a result of fair trading policies or which may be the product of child slave labor). In Genesis 44, Benjamin is supposed to know, at all times, what is in his sack. The problem in Benjamin's case is that he does not know that something has been planted. Should he have kept on checking? At what point should he have stopped doing an inventory?

In certain respects, the modern English law of possession is not too far removed from that of biblical law. In *Lewis*,[37] the defendant, Mr. Lewis, was sole tenant of a house which was found to contain sachets of Class B controlled drugs which were hidden inside a cassette case underneath some clothing. Mr. Lewis claimed that he never intended to live in the house, that his tenancy was merely a contrivance to obtain social security benefits, and that the drugs belonged to those who frequented the house in his absence. Lord Justice May recognized that "the question of what constitutes 'possession' is an elusive concept at [English] common law"[38] and varied with the circumstances and the intent of the statute that created the particular offense. In this case, the relevant statute was section 5(1) of the Misuse of Drugs Act 1971, which states that "it shall not be lawful for a person to have a controlled drug in his possession." The court accepted the principle laid down in *Warner v. Metropolitan Police Commissioner*[39] that the key issue is whether the defendant was "knowingly in control of a thing in circumstances which have involved an opportunity (whether availed [by him] or not) to learn or discover, at least in a general way, what the thing is."[40] In Mr. Lewis's case, it did not matter that he did not have actual knowledge that the drugs were there, provided they were present at a place that was under his control. The point is that in English law, the physical element of possession could be satisfied even though, as in this case, the defendant did not know the item was there and might indeed have had some difficulty in finding it even if he had carried out a search. This is not too far removed from Benjamin's position of being "knowingly in control" of the contents of his sack, even though he did not know that the silver cup was there. Of course, there can be no doubt that the decision in *Lewis* reflects the seriousness of the item in question (Class B drugs) although, as we have seen, the sacred nature of the property in Genesis 44 may have been an aggravating feature in that case as well. The point is that even modern criminal law accepts a certain degree of potential

---

37. (1988) 87 *Criminal Appeal Reports* 270.
38. At p. 275.
39. (1968) *Criminal Appeal Reports* 373.
40. Lord Morris at p. 404.

unfairness regarding the meaning of possession. This is because otherwise it is difficult to prove, from an evidentiary perspective, the defendant's precise state of mind in relation to the object.

III. A THIEF IN THE NIGHT

Having considered Exodus 22:1 and 4/MT 21:37 and 22:3, we now turn to the middle section of Exodus 22:1-4/MT 21:37–22:3. From a modern legal perspective, this is strictly termed burglary, and not theft, although it is still a species of theft and is dealt with as such under the Theft Act 1968.

> If a thief is found breaking in [or "tunnelling" (bammachteret); JPS], and is struck so that he dies, there shall be no bloodguilt for him; but if the sun has risen upon him, there shall be bloodguilt for him. He shall make restitution; if he has nothing, then he shall be sold for his theft.
> (Exodus 22:2–4/MT 22:1–3; *God speaking*)

We noted above that the whole of Exodus 22:1–4/MT 21:37–22:3 holds to a continuous line of thought.[41] The "thief" of Exodus 22:2/MT 22:1 is the same as that of Exodus 22:1/MT 21:37.[42] Therefore, Exodus 22:1–2/MT 21:37–22:1 does not refer to breaking into a house but breaking into a sheepfold. Interestingly, the JPS translates this as "tunnelling," implying that the *modus operandi* of burglary is to tunnel under the wall rather than make a hole in the wall and break through it. It is however possible that the law envisages a tunnelling through the wall. After all, Israelite walls could be substantial, and if made with stones and plaster, one would have to "dig through" to gain access. This seems to have been a common form of entry by thieves. Forcible entry is also envisaged in ANE law (see LH §125).[43]

The "animal stealing" described in Exodus 22:1/MT 21:37 suggests that the typical purpose of the "break-in" of Exodus 22:2/MT 22:1 was to steal the householder's ox or sheep. It seems therefore that the thief is tunnelling into the area occupied by the animals, perhaps the sheepfold.[44] It was not unusual for an Israelite family to share their home, or at least their courtyard, with their most valuable animals, eliding the distinction between "breaking into a sheepfold" and "domestic burglary."

From a modern perspective, the drafting of Exodus 22:1–4/MT 21:37–22:3 seems strange. While Exodus 22:2/MT 22:1 makes no explicit reference to when the burglary occurs, timing is an issue in the following verse which denies the legitimacy of killing the burglar during the day. From this, we infer that the

---

41. JACKSON, THEFT, pp. 205ff.
42. Ibid., 49 ff.
43. JACKSON, THEFT, pp. 51–53, 154–56.
44. Ibid., 49–50; WISDOM-LAWS p. 297, n. 21.

householder can only rely on self-help at night. It is oddly styled because first we are given the impression that self-help is always available, and then we are told it is not.[45] It is a problem that arises when we read biblical law "semantically" or literally but is resolved when we read it "narratively," as we are supposed to (see Chapter 1).

A narrative reading asks, "what is the typical situation evoked by the words 'tunnelling thief'"? We know from elsewhere in the Bible that thieves typically tunnelled into other people's houses at night:

> There are those who rebel against the light,
> who are not acquainted with its ways,
> and do not stay in its paths.
> The murderer rises in the dark,
> that he may kill the poor and needy;
> and in the night he is as a thief.
> The eye of the adulterer also waits for the twilight,
> saying, "No eye will see me";
> and he disguises his face.
> In the dark they dig through (*chatar*) houses;
> by day they shut themselves up;
> they do not know the light.
> For deep darkness is morning to all of them;
> for they are friends with the terrors of deep darkness.
> (Job 24:13–17; *Job speaking*)

According to Job, the image of "acting like a thief" is a combination of secret nocturnal activity that involves crossing territorial boundaries. (This is not unlike adultery, as the text explicitly notes. We noted the links between theft and adultery in Proverbs 6:29–35, above). Job's image of the thief as someone who "dig[s] through (*chatar*) houses" in verse 16 uses the same terminology as that found in Exodus 22:2/MT 22:1, which refers to the thief "breaking in" (*bammachteret*).[46] This typical image of the thief is part of the presupposition pool of Exodus 22:2–3/MT 22:1–22:2. It means that the typical situation evoked by the words in Exodus 22:2/MT 22:1 is one in which the thief tunnels at night. There is therefore no tension with the subsequent part of the rule which contrasts the legitimate action of the householder at night with the illegitimate action of the householder by day.[47] The image of acting like a thief represents the core of the message. This means that the further one departs from the typical case, the less

---

45. Jackson, Wisdom-Laws, p. 310.
46. Bernard S. Jackson, Studies in the Semiotics of Biblical Law, Journal for the Study of the Old Testament Supplement Series 314 (Sheffield: Sheffield Academic Press, 2000), 75–77.
47. Jackson, Studies, pp. 75–81.

sure we can be that "the same message is intended to apply, or would be regarded as applicable by the audience."[48] For example, killing a thief who was breaking in at dusk would probably have been regarded as questionable and would have led to negotiations for compensation between the householder and the deceased thief's family.

This picture of the meaning of Exodus 22:2–3/MT 21:1–22:2, as illuminated by Job 24:13–17, is confirmed by Jeremiah as follows:

As a thief is shamed when caught,
so the house of Israel shall be shamed
. . .
Also on your skirts is found
the lifeblood of guiltless poor;
you did not find them breaking in (*bammachteret*).
Yet in spite of all these things
you say, "I am innocent . . . ."
(Jeremiah 2:26, 34–35; *Jeremiah speaking*)

Here, Jeremiah applies Exodus 22:2/MT 22:1 not to the specific burglar but to Israel as a whole. In Jeremiah 2:35, Israel has claimed innocence before God. Jeremiah wishes to show that this claim is not justified. He does this by comparing Israel to the burglar who has been caught "in the act" of breaking in (verse 26) before comparing Israel to the property owner who kills without justification (verse 34). Israel did not kill the poor when they were caught tunnelling, in which case there might have been an excuse for killing them. Instead, they killed innocent people who were, impliedly, "assaulted out in the open."[49] The inversion in Jeremiah 2 of the justifiable killing in Exodus 22:2–3 makes Israel's claim to innocence all the more reprehensible.

As with the objective tests of lukewarm and hot possession, there is value in having a conclusive objective test about when a householder can use self-help, based on the time of day. In biblical society, an unjustified killing can give rise to reciprocal action by the "avenger of blood" (the *go'el haddam*), who is usually the deceased's next of kin (see Chapter 8). Having a "bright-line" rule means that "the kin of the deceased can know, without an adjudication whether the killing had been justified or not."[50] If it happens by night, the householder is in the clear; but if it happens by day, the householder stands to lose his own life at the hands of the *go'el haddam*. Exodus 22:2-3/MT 22:1-2 implies that if a break-in

---

48. Jackson, Wisdom-Laws, p. 311.
49. Michael Fishbane, Biblical Interpretation in Ancient Israel (Oxford: Clarendon Press, 1985), 314.
50. Jackson, Wisdom-Laws, p. 297.

occurs during the day, the homeowner is expected to summon help and take the thief alive.[51]

However, as we saw above with reference to comparative ANE materials, the operation of objective tests such as hot possession did not rule out the possibility of denying guilt in the light of other witness evidence (e.g., the bona fide purchaser). By the same token, there may well have been circumstances when the owner was not liable for killing the daytime thief (for example, if he was attacked). Unfortunately, the Laws of Hammurabi dealing with burglary do not make reference to the time of day and so do not shed any further light on this issue (LH §21, 125). It may have been the case that the owner could settle with the kin in such circumstances, even though the kin had no right to blood vengeance.[52]

Exodus 22:2–3/MT 22:1–2 has influenced the history of the English common law. The famous eighteenth-century jurist Blackstone wrote, "If any person attempts . . . to break open a house in the night-time, . . . and shall be killed in such attempt, the slayer shall be acquitted and discharged."[53] Blackstone explicitly cites Exodus 22:2 by way of support.[54] Legal historians note that "it was settled by the 1450s that burglary was a nocturnal crime."[55] Later law went beyond Blackstone to allow the killing of burglars even if did not take place a night. A nineteenth-century legal textbook records that in 1811, a certain septuagenarian (Mr. Purcell of Cork Co.) was knighted for killing four burglars with a carving knife. As late as 1924, in the case of *Hussey*, the Lord Chief Justice approved the view that "in defence of a man's house, the owner or his family may kill a trespasser who would forcibly dispossess him of it."[56] Here, the householder could kill during the day to defend his property—the very opposite of Exodus 22:3/MT 22:2.

In recent years, however, there has been greater tendency to define what degree of force defenders can legitimately use. The court of appeal in *Owino*[57] held that in determining whether a defendant acted in self-defense, the jury must decide, first, whether the defendant honestly believed that the circumstances required him to use force to defend himself from an attack or threatened attack, and second, whether the force used was reasonable in the circumstances as he believed them to be (subsequently affirmed in section 76(6) and (7) of the Criminal Justice and Immigration Act 2008). But what constitutes "reasonable

---

51. Jackson, Theft, p. 208.
52. Jackson, Theft, pp. 208–09.
53. Sir William Blackstone, Commentaries on the Laws of England, 4 vols., (London: Strahan and Cadell, 10th ed. 1787), vol. IV, p. 180.
54. Ibid., 181.
55. J. H. Baker, An Introduction to English Legal History (Bath: Butterworths, 4th ed. 2002), 532; *see also* Sir James Fitzjames Stephen, A History of the Criminal Law of England, 3 vols. (London: Macmillan, 1883), vol. III, p. 150.
56. (1924) 18 *Criminal Appeal Reports* 160.
57. (1996) 2 *Criminal Appeal Reports* 128.

force" is for the jury to decide. The decision in R. v. Martin[58]—where a householder was initially given a life sentence for killing a nocturnal burglar—divided the United Kingdom. Of a record 270,000 readers who responded to a tabloid poll ("Should Martin be locked up for life?"), only 10,800 supported the verdict. Exodus 22:2–3 was cited with approval in the national press.[59] Today, the need for clear guidance is seen as a matter of political importance. At the time of writing, the Lord Chancellor and Secretary of State for Justice has announced a review of the law of self-defense in England and Wales in order better to protect those who intervene in criminal situations.

IV. PAYBACK

This section considers the penalties for animal theft in biblical law. (The penalties for "human traffic" and burglary have been considered in previous sections). The penalties for animal theft take the form of multiple restitution, although the level depends on the value of the animals and whether the original creatures can be returned or not.

In cases of lukewarm possession, where there has been disposal of the goods, either by sale or slaughter, the penalty is fivefold restitution, in the case of an ox, and fourfold restitution, in the case of a sheep (Exodus 22:1/MT 21:37). Multiple restitution reflects the importance of animals in an agricultural society, together with the fact that the owner's assets are unrecoverable. The variation between an ox and a sheep may reflect their relative value; to some extent, a distinction also found in the Hittite Laws (HL §178–179).

In cases of hot possession where there has not (yet) been any disposal of goods, the penalty is double restitution, regardless of whether it is an ox or a sheep (Exodus 22:4/MT 22:3). The lower penalty, together with the lack of any distinction between the animals, may reflect the fact that the victim gets his animal(s) back and therefore does not need to be compensated to the same degree. Nevertheless, some punishment is required; after all, the thief who is caught red-handed is "no less morally guilty than his counterpart of Exodus 21:37 (MT) . . . merely less successful."[60] The difficulty with this view is that sentimental attachment to animals becomes less plausible the greater the size of the owner's flocks and herds.[61] The lesser penalty may reflect the fact that if you are successful in catching the thief red-handed, then presumably the thief will not have had your animal for very long. If so, the loss to the owner of the use of the

---

58. (2001) EWCA Crim. 2245, October 30, 2001.
59. *See* Jonathan Burnside, *Licence to kill?*, CAMBRIDGE PAPERS 11, 1–4 (2002), available at http://www.jubilee-centre.org/cambridge_papers; accessed September 30, 2009.
60. JACKSON, THEFT, p. 133.
61. Ibid., 134.

animal is not as great as it is in a case of lukewarm possession, and so the owner needs to be compensated less. By contrast, a case of lukewarm possession is, by definition, "further down the line." Here, the owner needs more compensation for the increased loss of the use value of his animal. It may also be the case that it is harder, in evidentiary terms, to prove cases of lukewarm possession than it is to prove cases of hot possession. If so, it may be legitimate to have larger compensation to reflect the greater evidentiary burden that the victim has to discharge. The variation takes account of the victim's increased time and trouble.

Multiple restitution is potentially a very heavy penalty that could conceivably wipe out all of a thief's assets. This is recognized in Proverbs:

> A thief is not held in contempt
> For stealing to appease his hunger;
> Yet if caught he must pay sevenfold;
> He must give up all he owns. (Proverbs 6:30–31; *Solomon speaking;* JPS)

Here, the level of multiple restitution is expressed as the higher figure of "sevenfold." This penalty does not appear to be limited to animal theft. Jackson suggests that it refers to "a royal practice which punished thieves more severely than the traditional law."[62] If the reference to sevenfold is not to be understood in purely symbolic terms, for example, as perfect restitution (cf. Psalm 79:12), it is reasonable to conclude that there was "a degree of discretion" as to the upper limit of the penalty for theft.[63]

Of course, it is possible that the thief may not have sufficient resources to make restitution, in which case "he shall be sold for his theft (*genevah*)" (Exodus 22:1/MT 21:37). "Can't pay, won't pay" is not a slogan familiar to the Covenant Code or *Mishpatim*. Instead, the law envisages a form of debt slavery, the idea of which is introduced at the start of the *Mishpatim* itself (Exodus 21:2–4).[64] However, the phrase "he shall be sold for his theft (*genevah*)" can equally be translated "he shall be sold for the thing stolen." There is an important difference between the two. If it means "theft," then the thief is sold in order to secure repayment of the value of the stolen property *plus* multiple restitution (viz., he is sold as punishment for his theft). If it means "for the thing stolen," then the thief is sold only "to secure repayment of the value of the stolen property,"[65] namely, the stolen animal. Jackson[66] argues that since the word *genevah* is used in the very next verse—where the animal is "found alive in his possession [literally 'in his hand']"; Exodus 22:4/MT 22:3)—sale of the thief must refer to "the thing stolen," rather than to the more conceptual "theft." This means that the insolvent

---

62. JACKSON, THEFT, p. 152.
63. Ibid.
64. JACKSON, WISDOM-LAWS, p. 300.
65. Ibid., 299.
66. Ibid., 299–300.

thief is only sold in order to secure repayment for the value of the stolen animal: he is not sold in order to make multiple restitution. It is also possible that the thief might have sold "a member of his family rather than himself."[67]

The sale appears to create a form of (temporary) debt slavery which means that the enslaved thief (or a member of his family) goes free after six years (Exodus 21:2, see further Chapter 7). If so, what is being exchanged is not the value of the thief on the slave market but the value of his labor for six years.[68] There is evidence that debt slavery was used as a penalty for theft in Genesis 44. Judah declares to Joseph:

> ... Behold, we are my LORD's slaves, both we and he also in whose hand the cup has been found. (Genesis 44:16)

On the face of it, it seems like an extremely generous offer: not only the value of Benjamin's labor but also that of all the brothers. It is generous even if we assume that a high monetary and ritual value was placed on the divining cup. Jackson claims that "there is no good reason why the brothers should have proposed a greater penalty than that which they conceived the law to require."[69] However, it is possible that Judah's offer reflects a standard bartering approach between the guilty party and the victim. This involves offering far too much in the knowledge that it gives the other party the chance to offer something realistic and thus appear generous (cf. Abraham's negotiations regarding the cave of Machpelah; Genesis 23:3–20). For example, if I rip your coat I can offer to mend it or, if I am really sorry, I might offer to buy you a new one. Since offering more is a sign of sincerity it is likely that you will say, "it's OK, that's not necessary." I might then be "let off the hook" and only have to mend it. It is a sort of reverse psychology. A bartering approach, in which the offender offers more as a sign of wanting to put things right and the victim accepts less as a sign of being merciful, may have been a commonly-accepted way for the parties to demonstrate wisdom and progress towards restoring the relationship. A similar pattern to Judah's offer in Genesis 44:16 – in which the defendant offers an excessive penalty – can be seen in Jacob's dealings with Laban. Jacob promises Laban that "anyone with whom you find your [stolen] gods shall not live" (Genesis 31:32). But had Rachel been found with the stolen gods Laban would not have been bound to kill her – and since she was his daughter, he would not have wanted to anyway!

This bartering approach may lie behind Joseph's rejection of Judah's offer:

> Far be it from me that I should do so! Only the man in whose hand the cup was found shall be my slave; but as for you, go up in peace to your father. (Genesis 44:17)

---

67. Ibid., 302.
68. Ibid.
69. JACKSON, THEFT, p. 166.

At the very least, the practice described in Genesis 44 indicates that the victim has a say in determining the appropriate penalty. This is reflected in the *Mishpatim* where the phrase "he shall be sold for his theft" (Exodus 22:1/MT 21:37) can equally be translated, "he *may* be sold for his theft."

Such texts remind us that the penalties in the biblical laws of theft were subject to negotiation. Exodus 22:3/MT 22:2 is a further example of a self-executing rule which, in keeping with the nature of such rules, is arbitrary in its effects.[70] There is no guarantee that "the value of the thief or of his labour for the period involved will happen to coincide with the value of the stolen animal, or of the multiple restitution if that is involved ... [A]ny shortfall is the price which is to be paid for the ability to resolve the matter without requiring institutional assistance."[71] If the shortfall is to the thief's disadvantage, with the result that he has to pay more than the usual amount of compensation, he can hardly complain since he has "brought the situation on himself."[72] Burglars can't be choosers. The rabbis argued that the thief could be sold only when his value equated exactly with that of the stolen animal, which effectively abolished the operation of the rule on a technicality.[73]

Compared to surviving ANE legal collections, the biblical materials appear lenient. The Hittite Laws have an extensive series of theft laws, covering the theft of a wide range of animals (HL §57–59, 63–70, 80–81, 91–92, 119–120, and 130); plant life (HL § 101, 103, 108, and 124) and other materials (HL §110, 121–122, 125–129, 131, and 143). The Hittite Laws provide details of older penalties and subsequent (more lenient) reform, although even some of the reforms are well in excess of biblical penalties, including tenfold restitution for an ox (HL §63) and fifteenfold restitution for a sheep (HL §59). The contrast between biblical and ANE law is even greater in the Laws of Hammurabi which typically present capital punishment as the penalty for theft (e.g., LH § 7, 9, and 10). On those occasions when multiple restitution is permitted, as in the case of shepherding (LH §265), the multiple is tenfold, regardless of whether they are cattle or sheep. In MAL Tablet C §8, restitution is supplemented by additional penalties, which include corporal punishment.

The biblical profile of the "poverty-stricken thief" (cf. Proverbs 6:30) contrasts with the "common shoplifter" who accounts for a vast number of cases of theft in modern law. Farrington[74] contends that if all persons in England and Wales

---

70. Jackson, Wisdom-Laws, pp. 29, 300.
71. Ibid., 301.
72. Ibid.
73. Ibid., 301–02.
74. David P. Farrington, What has been learned from self-reports about criminal careers and the causes of offending?, Report for the Home Office (London: Home Office, 2001), 17.

were interviewed in a self-reported offending survey, the total number of shopliftings should be around nine million incidents per year. Although obtaining profiles of the typical shoplifter are notoriously difficult, because detections may reflect the personal biases of store detectives, a small but well-constructed observational study of shoplifting made the interesting finding that shoplifters typically bought an item in the store and that "the average amount spent in the store by the . . . shoplifters was much greater than the value of the items which they stole."[75]

If the findings of this small study are true more widely, it might help to explain the success of "retail civil recovery" schemes in the United States. This is a specific administrative process that allows retailers to gather restitution directly from shoplifters. The practice is necessary in jurisdictions where only a small proportion of shoplifters caught by retailers are convicted of an offense (only 3 percent of shoplifters convicted in Scotland in 1995–1996).[76] In the United States, a variety of state laws provide for a charge of between one and five times the cost of goods (if lost or damaged), plus exceptional damages, plus costs. Normally, the retailer or third party makes a basic charge of $250 but depending on whether this is contested by the thief and the law that applies in a given state, the figure could be as large as $1500 (as for example in New York state). This means that the basis of the law in the United States is not strictly biblical inasmuch as item costs are only charged if the goods are not recovered. However, the operation is somewhat equivalent in that the average value of merchandise stolen is about $60, which means that a $250 charge roughly amounts to fourfold restitution. In the United Kingdom, civil recovery schemes are limited by the operation of tort law. Here, claims are based on the actual costs of goods, plus costs of arrest, plus costs of litigation and debt recovery. The claim is justified in terms of the actual costs to the retailer and others resulting from the tort. By coincidence, this usually turns out to be two to three times the cost of the goods.[77] There is no indication of biblical law being cited as an inspiration for these developments. Nevertheless, it seems as though we are rediscovering, in modern times, the appeal of subjecting a thief's assets to multiple restitution—especially when applied to those who have the ability to pay.

---

75. Abigail Buckle & David P. Farrington, *An observational study of shoplifting*, BRIT. J. CRIMINOLOGY 24, 63–73, 68 (1984).

76. Joshua Bamfield, *Retail civil recovery: Filling a deficit in the criminal justice system?* INT'L J. OF RISK, SECURITY & CRIME PREVENTION 34 (1998), 257–67, 261.

77. Bamfield, *Retail civil recovery*; JOSHUA BAMFIELD, MAKING SHOPLIFTERS PAY: RETAIL CIVIL RECOVERY (London: The Social Market Foundation, 1997); Bamfield, personal communication.

V. THE LAW OF THEFT IN THE PARABLE OF NATHAN

To what extent, if at all, are these legal sources reflected in the narratives? A good example of the law of theft being applied outside the legal collections is the parable told by the prophet Nathan to King David, on God's instructions (2 Samuel 12:1–4). It is relevant to our study of theft because the parable involves the taking of a ewe lamb, and it imposes a fourfold penalty. This recalls Exodus 22:1/MT 21:37. However, the application of the law of theft is far from straightforward because the real-life situation to which the parable applies concerns homicide and adultery. This seems very far removed from the paradigm case of Exodus 22:1/MT 21:37.

It is worth summarizing briefly the wider circumstances into which the law of theft is being applied. King David has committed adultery against one of his soldiers, Uriah the Hittite, whilst Uriah is away fighting one of David's wars. Uriah's wife, Bathsheba, becomes pregnant with David's child. To avoid exposure, David recalls Uriah from the front. He thinks Uriah will take the opportunity, while on home leave, to have intercourse with Bathsheba and so "cover up" David's offense. However, the plan fails because Uriah is too principled to break solidarity with his fellow soldiers, who do not enjoy conjugal luxuries. David thus improvises "Plan B" by arranging Uriah's murder. This looks like an accident, leaving the path clear for David to take Uriah's wife (2 Samuel 11).

Following the birth of David and Bathsheba's child, the prophet Nathan brings a (fictional) case to David for adjudication. The case involves a rich man taking a ewe lamb from a poor man under outrageous circumstances (2 Samuel 12:1–4). David passes judgement on the offender (the sentence being the death of the offender plus fourfold repayment of the sheep). This judicial decision clears the way for a declaration of divine judgment upon David (2 Samuel 12:7–14).

The precise nature of the interplay between the different parties (including God, David, Bathsheba, Uriah, Joab, and Nathan) raises a whole range of questions that are beyond the scope of this short section. Nor are we in a position to provide an in-depth analysis of the parable itself.[78] What we will consider is the unusual application of the law of theft to the question of adultery and homicide and what this means for our understanding of biblical law in general.

---

78. *See* Erik Eynikel, *The parable of Nathan (2 Samuel 12:1–4) and the theory of semiosis*, in RETHINKING THE FOUNDATIONS: HISTORIOGRAPHY IN THE ANCIENT WORLD AND IN THE BIBLE (Steven L. McKenzie & Thomas Römer *eds.*; Berlin: Walter de Gruyter, 2000), 71–90; and Uriel Simon, *The poor man's ewe lamb: An example of a juridical parable*, BIBLICA 48, 207–42 (1967).

A. The fact of fiction

As far as this chapter is concerned, the key question is: why does Nathan apply the biblical law of theft to a real-life case involving murder and adultery? To answer this question, we need to step back for a moment and consider the nature of the challenge facing Nathan. He did not need to persuade David cognitively that his actions were blameworthy. David's cover-ups were proof that he knew he had done wrong. Rather, Nathan's challenge was the harder one of getting David to connect emotionally with the gravity of what he had done. It is clear from the exchange between David and his military intelligence (2 Samuel 11:19–25) that David is emotionally disconnected. The giveaway is that while David has a reputation for flying into a rage if his men's lives are lost unnecessarily, the death toll on this occasion, which includes the death of Uriah the Hittite, leaves him cold (2 Samuel 11:25).[79]

Nathan's challenge is how to penetrate David's "defensive detachment." His strategy is to present a case that externalizes exactly David's attitude toward Uriah. By objectifying the issue, Nathan hopes to get David to put the right label on his behavior. Perhaps this will force him to identify and reconnect with the reality of what he has done. This may in turn be a catalyst for his repentance.

Accordingly, Nathan presents what seems to be a real-life case to the king for adjudication—but which is in fact a fiction. This type of fictional case may fairly be described as a "juridical parable"; "a realistic story about a violation of the law, related to someone who had committed a similar offence, with the purpose of leading the unsuspecting hearer to pass judgement on himself."[80] We have seen an example of this in Chapter 4, regarding the case brought by the woman of Tekoa. The deception is "designed to overcome man's own closeness to himself, enabling him to judge himself by the same yardstick that he applies to others."[81]

Accordingly, the juridical parable needs several ingredients to be successful: (1) *disguise* (namely, the ability to smuggle itself past the judge by posing as a real case), (2) *revelation* (the disclosure that the case is fictional and that its true application is to a different set of facts), and (3) *personal identification* (making a direct link between the parable and the personal circumstances of the judge).[82] In some ways, the juridical parable is rather like a stealth bomber—a type of military aircraft which is practically invisible to enemy sensors. Accordingly, it is capable of reaching and destroying its target without prior detection.[83] This is exactly what

---

79. Simon, *Poor man's ewe lamb*, pp. 231–32.
80. Ibid., 220–21.
81. Ibid., 221.
82. *Cf.* the different presentation of Simon, *Poor man's ewe lamb*, p. 223.
83. *Cf.* Roy Clements, A Sting in the Tale (Leicester: Inter-Varsity Press, 1997), 7, who applies the analogy to the parables of Jesus.

Nathan does when he declares "That man is you!" to an unsuspecting David (2 Samuel 12:7; JPS).

As the stealth bomber imagery reminds us, the juridical parable is *not* an allegory. Allegories are symbolic, and they are characterized by a "point-for-point" correspondence between the real-life situation and the representation. The problem with even a subtle allegory, in Nathan's context, is that these symbolic correspondences risk showing on the radar. An allegory would never get past David's defenses. By contrast, the judicial parable is stealthier. As Erik Eynikel writes, "a parable has only one major point of correspondence between the situation in the parable and that of the hearer."[84] Given that the problem in David's case was the inability to feel or connect with the gravity of what he had done, it is fair to say that the main point of correspondence between Nathan's parable and David's real-life situation is the callousness of the rich man and David, both of whom "had no pity" (2 Samuel 12:6). The rich man's gain was minimal compared with the suffering he caused to the poor man. Likewise David's gain was minimal compared with the suffering he caused to Uriah, his immediate family (including Bathsheba), and his extended family.[85] It is precisely this major point of correspondence that successfully generates an emotional response on the part of David, who "flew into a rage against the [rich] man" (2 Samuel 12:5; JPS).

We should not be surprised that juridical parables have a strong affective component, nor that they are crafted with the aim of creating a particular feeling in the audience. For a start, *any* legal case invites a judgment and judgments always involve an emotional component (cf. Freudian psychoanalysis which asserts that the id always makes a contribution to the sense-making exercise).[86] Second, emotions are particularly likely to come to the fore when, as here, they involve evaluations of seriousness. Third, the juridical parable is presented in such a way as to emphasize not the breaking of a rule, but the violation of a person. There is more emotion in criticizing someone in the context of interpersonal relationships (e.g., the story of a rich man and a poor man) than exists in a formal statement of the offense (e.g.,"A rich man shall not steal a household pet from a poor man"). Norms are inherently less emotional than stories.

All this means is that we should not go looking for "point-for-point" correspondences between the parable and the real-life case. This fails to recognise the strengths—and the limits—of the juridical parable.

---

84. Eynikel, *Parable of Nathan*, p. 86.
85. Simon, *Poor man's ewe lamb*, p. 230.
86. Bernard S. Jackson, Making Sense in Law: Linguistic, Psychological and Semiotic Perspectives (Liverpool: Deborah Charles Publications, 1995), 273–85.

B. The dish of the day

It follows from the above, then, that the creator of a judicial parable can afford to describe a situation that is less serious than the real-life situation. However, it is vital that the emotional dilemma remains the same; otherwise, it is too easy for the audience to claim that the parable is too far distant from the real-life case.[87] Emotion embeds the parable in the real-life situation. As we turn to consider the parable itself, we can see that Nathan constructs the story in such a way as to emphasize David's callousness toward Uriah.

Modern scholars, however, have taken different views regarding Nathan's construction of the parable. David Daube[88] argues that the primary referent of the parable is to Saul (the rich man) who treats David (the poor man) badly by refusing to give him back his wife Michal (the lamb). However, there is no need for such an arbitrary reading when the text itself supplies us with a coherent explanation from Nathan himself. Nathan's accusation, "You are the man" is explained on the grounds that:

> ". . . You have put Uriah the Hittite to the sword; you took his wife and made her your wife and had him killed by the sword of the Ammonites. Therefore the sword shall never depart from your House—because you spurned Me by taking the wife of Uriah the Hittite and making her your wife."
> (2 Samuel 12:9–10; *God speaking via Nathan the prophet;* JPS)

David's attitude is identified with that of the rich man because: (1) he "put Uriah the Hittite to the sword" and (2) "took his wife." The principal connection is the similar attitude of David and the rich man. Although the parable supports the charges of both homicide and adultery, it is clear from Nathan's explanation that the parable focuses on the taking of Uriah's life. God's judgment in verses 9–10 makes repeated reference to the "sword." This signifies that in terms of seriousness, what David did to Uriah in taking his life is worse than what he did to Uriah by taking his wife. Homicide is more serious than adultery (cf. Deuteronomy 22:26, where a case of rape is described as being "like" homicide—a formulation that is itself dependent on the fact that homicide is seen as the more serious offense; see Chapter 11). Taking Uriah's life is the primary issue, and taking his wife is the secondary issue. This is reflected in Nathan's construction of the parable, which focuses on the taking of Uriah's life. This is contrary to Daube's view that the parable is problematic because it does not contain "any hint at the ghastly elimination of Uriah,"[89] as well as Bernard Jackson's claim that "the parable alludes in no way to the murder of Uriah."[90]

---

87. Simon, *Poor man's ewe lamb*, p. 226.
88. David Daube, *Nathan's parable*, NOVUM TESTAMENTUM 24, 275–88 (1982).
89. Ibid., 276.
90. JACKSON, THEFT, p. 147.

Commentators are apt to regard Bathsheba as either the exclusive or primary referent of the lamb in the parable,[91] with several noting that the Hebrew word for daughter (*bat*) reminds us of the name "Bathsheba."[92] However, there are a number of indications in the text that Uriah is the lamb who is slaughtered. This is contrary to Uriel Simon's claim that there is an "absence of slaying in the narrative."[93] The killing of the lamb is not explicitly stated, but it is implicit in the fact that the lamb is being served as "the dish of the day."

First, there is a parallel between the lamb which "used to *eat* of his morsel, and *drink* from his cup, and *lie* in his bosom" (2 Samuel 12:3) and Uriah who protests to David: "shall I then go to my house, to *eat* and to *drink*, and to *lie* with my wife?" (2 Samuel 11:11).[94] Second, in my view, there is also a parallel between the characteristics of the lamb and Uriah. The lamb is presented as a trusting creature, nestling in the bosom. Uriah, too, is trusting to a fault; otherwise David could hardly have entrusted him with his own death warrant (2 Samuel 11:14–15). Third, there is, in my view, a spatial parallel between the ewe and Uriah. The ewe is "served up" before the traveller (2 Samuel 12:4) while Uriah is "served up" before the Ammonites (2 Samuel 11:15, 16), although the verbs are not identical in the Hebrew.

Fourth, there is an opposition in the parable between hospitality and enmity. Hospitality has a dark undertone in the parable because the meal was the product of a callous killing, which we normally associate with enmity (see Chapter 8). This reflects the hospitality that David showed Uriah. Uriah should have felt safe at David's table but in fact he was far from safe. Instead of "wining and dining" him, David "wines and dices" him.

Finally, the parable notes that the rich man's theft saves him some money ("he was unwilling to take one of his own flock or herd . . ."; 2 Samuel 12:4). Given the compact nature of the piece, Daube claims that this should be given its "due weight."[95] Although Daube himself does not find any indication of Uriah's murder in the parable, this detail does in fact provide further support for identifying the ewe with Uriah. Had David confessed to the adultery, the likelihood is that he would have had to pay considerable damages to Uriah. By taking Uriah "out of the picture," David managed to save himself a sum of money.

Seeing Uriah as the primary referent of the lamb results in Uriah nestling in Bathsheba's bosom, rather than the other way around. For some, this is

---

91. *E.g.*, RANDALL C. BAILEY, DAVID IN LOVE AND WAR: THE PURSUIT OF POWER IN 2 SAMUEL 10–12, JOURNAL FOR THE STUDY OF THE OLD TESTAMENT SUPPLEMENT SERIES 75 (Sheffield: Journal for the Study of the Old Testament Press, 1990), 106; JACKSON, THEFT, pp. 147–48.

92. J. P. FOKKELMAN, NARRATIVE ART AND POETRY IN THE BOOKS OF SAMUEL. VOLUME I: KING DAVID (2 SAMUEL 9-20 & 1 KINGS 1-2) (Assen: Van Gorcum, 1981), 79; ROBERT P. GORDON, 1 & 2 SAMUEL: A COMMENTARY (Exeter: Paternoster Press, 1986), 256.

93. Simon, *Poor man's ewe lamb*, p. 226 n. 1.

94. Ibid., 229.

95. Daube, *Nathan's parable*, p. 279.

counterintuitive since it seems to place Bathsheba in a stronger position within the marriage. But there are grounds for thinking that Uriah was indeed "the weaker party in comparison with Bathsheba's family."[96] Bathsheba was the "daughter of Eliam" (2 Samuel 11:3) and thus the granddaughter of Ahithopel (2 Samuel 23:34) who was also David's esteemed counselor (2 Samuel 16:23). Bathsheba belonged to a prominent family and her bathing spot was clearly proximate to the royal palace. In addition, emphasizing Uriah's place at Bathsheba's bosom underscores the sexual nature of their relationship which is, of course, what David usurps.

By making *Uriah* the primary referent of the "lamb", Nathan is able successfully to re-create David's attitude toward him. This reading does not, however, exclude the possibility that the ewe lamb can be identified with Bathsheba, in a secondary sense. This possibility arises because the text says that David "took" Bathsheba (2 Samuel 11:4) and that the rich man "took" the lamb (2 Samuel 12:4).

To conclude, then, it is in my view a mistake to see the lamb as referring exclusively or even primarily to Bathsheba. In fact, it refers primarily to Uriah. The parable is primarily concerned with the taking of Uriah's life and secondarily with the taking of Uriah's wife—the two offenses being connected in any case. This is reflected in God's judgment in 2 Samuel 12:9–10. Consequently, the lamb in the parable has Uriah as its primary referent and Bathsheba as its secondary one. Seen from one perspective, the lamb is Uriah, who is taken from Bathsheba's bosom while seen from another viewpoint, the lamb is Bathsheba who is taken from Uriah's bosom. The change in perspective is possible because it is a juridical parable and not an allegory. Its purpose is to establish a correspondence between the attitude of the rich man and David. Either way, seeing the lamb as referring primarily to Uriah or secondarily as referring to Bathsheba serves the same end, namely, David's callousness toward Uriah. This is the central issue, and the parable is deliberately constructed to make this point.

We are now in a position to understand Nathan's application of the biblical laws of theft.

C. Nathan's brilliance

Nathan's brilliance lies in how he flies the stealth bomber. Or to put it another way, it is seen in how he applies the law of theft to a case of murder and adultery. Nathan has to "strike a careful balance between getting too close to the parable's application and being too remote from it"[97] (cf. the widow of Tekoa in Chapter 8). This explains Nathan's choice of the law of theft to address cases of adultery and

---

96. J. W. Wesselius, *Joab's death and the central theme of the succession narrative (2 Samuel 9–1 Kings 2)*, VETUS TESTAMENTUM 40 (1990), 336–51, 347, n. 15.

97. Simon, *Poor man's ewe lamb*, p. 221.

homicide. He has to construct a story that involves a "taking" and a "killing." But to get past David's defenses, he has to tell a story that is not obviously about either adultery or homicide.

Bearing in mind that the salient elements in David's offenses are taking and killing, Nathan understandably turns to the paradigm case of lukewarm possession in Exodus 22:1/MT 21:37 to construct his story. This is because the core elements of lukewarm possession are, of course, all about a taking and a killing. As we have seen, lukewarm possession is the most serious form of animal theft because the animal has been sold or slaughtered. In the context of Nathan's parable, it is impossible for the poor man in the parable to recover the personality of the lamb "[who] was like a daughter to him" (2 Samuel 12:3). This is true in the case of Uriah, who is "slaughtered."

Exodus 22:1/MT 21:37 lends itself well to a judicial parable about homicide. To bring out the parallel in modern language, Exodus 22:1/MT 21:37 concerns someone who wants to get rid of "the merchandise", exactly the kind of code favored by a Mafia boss who wants to kill someone. Like the thief who has disposed of incriminating evidence, David thinks he has committed the perfect crime. Equally, Exodus 22:1/MT 21:37 lends itself to a judicial parable about adultery because it involves the taking of that which belongs to another; a connection which, we saw, is also made in Proverbs 6:29–35. A case of lukewarm possession is thus perfect for Nathan's needs. It is far enough removed from the real-life scenario to get under David's radar, but at the same time, it successfully combines the requisite elements of homicide and adultery. Combining these elements enables Nathan to re-create David's callousness toward Uriah and allows the bomber to hit the target.

By addressing homicide and adultery in terms of theft, Nathan limits both the scope of the offense in the parable and makes it less serious.[98] This strategy is followed by another prophet who challenges a king. For example, King Ahab's wrongdoing in freeing an "enemy of the state" (King Ben-hadad of Aram; see 1 Kings 20:1–34) is addressed by means of a far less serious parable concerning a careless guard (1 Kings 20:35–43).[99]

Nathan's final masterstroke is to find a way of presenting this story as something that could have happened in real-life *and* as something that could credibly be brought to the king for adjudication. The story is factually plausible. Even today, among the Bedouin—desert-dwelling pastoralists found throughout the Middle East—there is evidence that such a case could arise. Among this group, it is permissible to commit *adayieh*, viz., "stealing" an animal from another person's flock in order to prepare a feast for a guest. However, this is only legitimate if, among other things, the stolen animal does not fall within the "protected" category.

---

98. Ibid., 223.
99. Ibid., 224.

An example of the protected animal is "the ewe which has a bell or beads attached to its neck." This is "a sign that the owner has a special affection for it."[100] The factual plausibility of the story is important because David "will only be caught in the trap . . . if he truly believes that the story told him actually happened."[101]

Second, the story has also to be one that would plausibly require David's intervention. But are we to imagine David really spent his time adjudicating such cases? This case "was presented to David not by a litigant but by a prophet in the role of a champion of an oppressed poor man"[102] (and see Chapter 4). His status as a poor man is the key because the king is supposed to champion justice on behalf of the poor (e.g., Proverbs 29:14).

The only remaining question is: why does David go beyond fourfold damages and call for the man's death? This is because "the parable does not place the emphasis on the actual stealing"[103] but on the rich man's cruelty. The imposition of a fourfold penalty was "as nothing compared with the loss of the poor man"; under these circumstances, multiple restitution is "grossly inadequate."[104] Even setting aside the sentimental attachment between the poor man and the ewe, it is the case that, elsewhere in the Bible, taking a poor man's goods is equivalent to taking his life (e.g., Deuteronomy 24:6). This idea is found elsewhere in the ANE. *The Protests of the Eloquent Peasant*, a Middle Kingdom Egyptian text states, "Do not plunder of his property a poor man . . . His property is the [very] breath of a suffering man, and he who takes it away is one who stops up his nose."[105]

Even so, David's judgment upon the rich man's attitude appears to leave the punishment up to God. David does not order that the rich man should be "put to death" but rather states that he is a *ben-mawet* (literally, "son of death"; 2 Samuel 12:5), which is usually translated "deserves to die." This is exactly how David's judgment is understood when the judgment is applied to David himself. David deserves to die by God's hand, but he is spared because of his repentance (2 Samuel 12:13). As for the fourfold penalty, we might normally assume that the penalty took the form of live substitution (four live sheep for the single sheep that was slaughtered). However, the penalty could equally take the form of four dead sheep for a single dead sheep, and this is how it is applied in David's case. In the place of Uriah (the single dead sheep), we have the death of four of David's sons (the four dead sheep). These are David's first child born to Bathsheba (2 Samuel 12:15–19), Amnon (2 Samuel 13:28–29), Absalom (2 Samuel 18:14),

---

100. Ibid., 228.
101. Ibid., 221.
102. Ibid.
103. Ibid., 230.
104. John Mauchline, 1 and 2 Samuel, New Century Bible Commentary (London: Oliphants, 1971), 253–54.
105. James B. Pritchard, Ancient Near Eastern Texts Relating to the Old Testament (Princeton: Princeton University Press, 1950), 409.

and Adonijah (1 Kings 2:24–25). J. W. Wesselius[106] rightly notes that these are "all the four sons who are ascribed to [David] in the Succession Narrative" (2 Samuel 9:1–1 Kings 2).

What does this mean for our understanding of theft in biblical law and of biblical law generally? The object of the parable is to get David to acknowledge the seriousness of the offense, connect with the emotion of it, feel the weight of it, and so be the catalyst for a change of attitude. This opposition between emotional attachment and emotional detachment is reflected in Nathan's parable, which depicts the emotional warmth of the poor man for his ewe lamb and the emotional indifference of the rich man who could not care less about taking it away. Nathan's inventive application of the laws of theft thus illustrates the educative character of biblical law. It shows how the laws of theft can be used to address very different scenarios of homicide and adultery because biblical law is inherently didactic and can be applied beyond the presenting issue.

VI. CONCLUSION

The biblical laws of theft take an objective approach to the question of "who is a thief" by applying objective tests of hot possession and lukewarm possession. These tests are seen to apply both in biblical law and biblical narratives. The use of objective texts may reflect the seriousness of the offense in biblical law. This means that a person should not be exposed for being a thief unless it is clear that he is one. There is a risk that objective tests could lead to individual acts of injustice, although we should not discount the possibility of admitting evidence that would acquit the innocent, as was possible in the relevant Laws of Hammurabi. The biblical laws of theft and burglary confirm the importance of reading biblical law narratively, as opposed to semantically. Similarly, the application of the laws of theft to cases of murder and adultery further underline the creative and didactic character of biblical law.

Selected reading

Jonathan Burnside, "Licence to kill?" *Cambridge Papers* 11 (2002), 1–4, available at http://www.jubilee-centre.org/cambridge_papers; accessed September 30, 2009.

David Daube, Studies in Biblical Law (Cambridge: Cambridge University Press, 1947), 202–220.

Bernard S. Jackson, *Wisdom-Laws: A Study of the* Mishpatim *of Exodus 21:1–22:16* (Oxford: Oxford University Press, 2006), Chapter 9.

Bernard S. Jackson, *Theft in Early Jewish Law* (Oxford: Clarendon Press, 1972), Chapter 7.

Uriel Simon, "The poor man's ewe lamb: An example of a juridical parable," *Biblica* 48 (1967), 207–242.

---

106. Wesselius, *Joab's death*, p. 347, n.15.

10. MARRIAGE AND DIVORCE

There are times when biblical law seems as alien as a walk on the moon. At other times, it is as familiar as a leaf through *Hello!* magazine. Sometimes it manages to be both at the same time. Nowhere is this truer than the laws of marriage, divorce, and remarriage. Some of its marital arrangements will seem surreal. And yet the everyday human dramas that surround the search for intimacy—and what happens when it all goes wrong—remain exactly the same. Perhaps the most surprising thing is how few formal rules there are and how much is taken for granted in preexisting custom. The subject is thus a good example of the way in which biblical law regulates and is dependent on custom. Understanding biblical law in this area involves drawing on a wide range of legal materials, including evidence of local custom, shared ancient Near Eastern (ANE) conventions, formal rules, and rabbinic traditions. The biblical laws relating to marriage and divorce also form the basis for considering sexual practices that deviate from marriage, principally adultery, and these will be considered in Chapter 11. The present chapter focuses on marriage, divorce, and remarriage in the Hebrew Bible; materials relating to these issues from the Dead Sea Scrolls and the New Testament are the subject of Chapter 12.

I. FAMILY CIRCLES

Modern family law scholars attest to the difficulty of thinking about the legal regulation of marriage and the family from a purely doctrinal or positivist perspective. The growing importance of sociolegal studies to family law over the past 20 years shows the need to understand family relations and law within a wider social context.[1] This is also true of biblical law, and so we will begin with a brief overview of the place of the family within the wider social structure of biblical Israel.

Multidisciplinary reconstructions of the social world of biblical Israel suggest that family was conventionally understood as a series of increasingly large kinship circles, beginning with the smallest social unit, the "father's house" (*beyt'abh*) and moving outwards in ever-increasing circles to include clan and tribe. Textual support for this is found in Joshua 7:14–18 where Joshua calls the nation of Israel forward by tribe, clan, and household in order to identify a particular

---

1. *E.g.*, Susan S. Boyd, *Legal regulation of families in changing societies*, in THE BLACKWELL COMPANION TO LAW AND SOCIETY, (Austin Sarat ed.; Oxford: Blackwell, 2005), 255–70, 255.

individual. The family in ancient Israel is thus an example of a "patrilineal, segmentary, lineage system."[2]

The "father's house" is frequently referred to in biblical law (e.g., Deuteronomy 22:21). Its basic form is suggested by archaeological excavations of Late Bronze Age (*circa* 1600–1200 BC) and Iron I Age (*circa* 1200–920 BC) Palestine, which show the existence of family compounds. Each compound seemed to be occupied by an extended family of up to 12 individuals and consisted of several individual houses.[3] It is thought that each compound made up a single father's house. The extended family consisted of blood relatives, together with women who had married into the family. Ethnographic research suggests that a family head oversaw these living arrangements (cf. the "head" of the "father's house" referred to in 1 Chronicles 24:31).[4] If the family extended to three generations, then the family head would normally be the grandfather. However, it is thought that, under premodern conditions, probably less than 30 percent of families extended to three generations.[5]

This inner family circle expanded to include the clan or household (*mishpachah*). The clan grew with the death of each head of the father's house and upon the consequent division of the family into separate households, each with its own share of land. Each new father's house remained connected to the others by sharing a deceased ancestor. The biblical laws of redemption, according to which land and persons could be 'bought back," extend as far as the "cousin . . . or a near kinsman belonging to his family (*mishpachto*)."[6] This marks the circumference of the clan and thus the limits of our knowledge about the size of the biblical family (Leviticus 25:49). We do not know exactly what degrees of kinship are involved here, and so the size of the typical clan remains imprecise.

Beyond that, the next family circle is the Israelite tribe (*shebhet* or *matteh*). According to the patriarchal narratives, each tribe is descended from one of the sons of Israel. The tribes of Israel (*shibhtey yisrael*; e.g., Genesis 49:28) are of course the ultimate "family circle" in ancient Israel.

---

2. Victor H. Matthews, *Family relationships*, in DICTIONARY OF THE OLD TESTAMENT: PENTATEUCH: A COMPENDIUM OF CONTEMPORARY BIBLICAL SCHOLARSHIP (T. D. Alexander & D. W. Baker eds., Leicester: Apollos, 2003), 291–99, 292.

3. CAROL MEYERS, DISCOVERING EVE: ANCIENT ISRAELITE WOMEN IN CONTEXT (Oxford: Oxford University Press, 1988).

4. Lawrence E. Stager, *The archaeology of the family in Ancient Israel*, BULL. AM. SCH. ORIENTAL RES. 260, 1–36, 18–23 (1985).

5. Ibid., 20.

6. RAYMOND WESTBROOK, PROPERTY AND THE FAMILY IN BIBLICAL LAW, JOURNAL FOR THE STUDY OF THE OLD TESTAMENT SUPPLEMENT SERIES 113 (Sheffield: Sheffield Academic Press, 1991), 20.

II. SCENES FROM A MARRIAGE

The student of biblical law may be surprised to learn that biblical law rarely addresses the subjects of marriage and divorce head-on. Most of our knowledge is indirect. There is no systematic account of marriage in biblical law, despite the importance attached to heterosexual union at the start of the canon (Genesis 2:22–24). This reflects the fact that marriage, being so common, was largely regulated by custom. Most marriages in the ANE were probably oral ceremonies anyway.

Despite these limitations, we can draw on other biblical texts to gain some sense of what might have been said in biblical marriage ceremonies. Hugenberger[7] has argued that the paradigmatic marriage of Adam and Eve contains the following marriage formula:

> This [one] at last
> is bone of my bones
> and flesh of my flesh. (Genesis 2:23; *Adam speaking*)

while Hosea 2:16/MT 2:18 suggests that Israelite couples used the legal formula, "You are my wife," and "You are my husband."[8]

Marriage is explicitly called a covenant (*berit*) in the Hebrew Bible (e.g., Ezekiel 16:8). This is because it is "an elected, as opposed to natural, relationship of obligation established under divine sanction."[9] There is evidence from elsewhere in the ANE that marriage took the form of a contract, sometimes even a written one. A Sumerian tablet from Ur, dating perhaps to the eighteenth-century BC, provides that, in the absence of such a contract, the man does not owe any financial obligations toward the woman in the event of the relationship ending, even though he had intercourse with her.[10]

The biblical materials see the marriage covenant as the subject of divine interest (e.g., Malachi 2:14; Proverbs 2:16–17) which presumably reflects God's role in the paradigmatic marriage of Genesis 2:22–24. This presents heterosexual monogamy as the divine norm for Adam by creating just one Eve, as opposed to

---

7. Gordon Paul Hugenberger, Marriage as a Covenant: A study of biblical law and ethics governing marriage, developed from the perspective of Malachi (Leiden: E.J. Brill, 1994), 164–67.

8. Mordechai A. Friedman, *Israel's response in Hosea 2:17b: "You are my husband"*, J. Biblical Literature 99, 199–204 (1980).

9. Hugenberger, Marriage as a Covenant, p. 342.

10. Daniela Piattelli, *The marriage contract and bill of divorce in ancient Hebrew law*, in The Jewish Law Annual Volume 4 (B. S. Jackson ed.; Leiden: Brill, 1981), 66–78, 74.

extra Eves or additional Adams. The rationale for marriage, as given in Genesis 2:24, also emphasizes the singular (one man/one woman):

> Hence *a* man leaves his father and mother and clings to *his wife*, so that they become one flesh.

The "leaving" here is not spatial because marriage was typically patrilocal (although there are examples of matrilocal marriages, such as Jacob's marriage to Leah and Rachel; Genesis 29:27–30). Instead, the departure is psychological: the wife is prioritized over parents. The ideal of monogamy is reflected in other biblical texts (e.g., "Your wife [singular] will be like a fruitful vine within your house . . ."; Psalm 128:3). That said, biblical society is aware of the practice of polygamy, and this is reflected in biblical law (e.g., Exodus 21:10).

The narratives present polygamy in a negative light. The first polygamous character in the Bible is Lamech, who is a byword for lack of self-control (Genesis 4:23–24). Many famous faces from Israel's past had more than one wife, including Abraham, Jacob, David, and Solomon; however, the narratives expose the rivalries and jealousies that frequently arise from multiple marriages. Of course, where such marriages were allowed, it was polygamy for men, not polyandry for women. A married man could have multiple marriage partners without committing adultery against his first wife. However, a married woman could only have a sexual relationship with one husband. Polygamy may have reflected the realities of gender imbalance in biblical society (i.e., more women than men, perhaps as a result of wars, though Myers notes[11] that on the basis of Palestinian tomb studies, female mortality rates in childbearing years far exceeded that of males). In practice, polygamy was rare, owing to the expense. Only rich people and kings were polygamists in Israel, and even then this was discouraged (Deuteronomy 17:17). Qumran texts and early rabbinic interpretation are generally skeptical about polygamy, while the New Testament insists on monogamy (e.g., 1 Timothy 3:2, 12, 5:9, and see further Chapter 12).[12]

A. The urge to merge

Procreation was an important part of biblical marriage, to judge from Genesis 1:28. It is also reflected in the ideals of the patriarchs and their wives, who passionately express their desire for children (e.g., Genesis 30:1). This longing is widely shared: at a popular level, Jephthah's daughter and her friends bewail the fact that she will never marry and have children; and this became a regular mourning ritual (Judges 11:37–40). At the same time, the biblical texts are

---

11. Carol Myers, *The roots of restriction: Women in early Israel*, in THE BIBLE AND LIBERATION, (Norman K. Gottwald ed.; Orbis: Maryknoll, 1983), 289–306, 295.

12. *See generally* LOUIS M. EPSTEIN, MARRIAGE LAWS IN THE BIBLE AND THE TALMUD (Cambridge, Mass.: Harvard University Press, 1942), 3–33; DAVID INSTONE-BREWER, DIVORCE AND REMARRIAGE IN THE BIBLE (Grand Rapids: Eerdmans, 2002), 59–72.

unabashed in their portrayal of marriage as a celebration of romantic love, especially in The Song of Songs. Marriage is also presented as a spiritual relationship: the Hebrew Bible uses marriage as a picture of the relationship between God and Israel (Hosea 1–3), while the New Testament speaks of the marriage between Jesus and the people of God (Ephesians 5:22–33; Revelation 21:9ff). In addition, biblical marriage can also be seen as an economic alliance between two families which pooled wealth and ensured there were legitimate heirs.[13]

The basic form of Israelite marriage involves the "giving" of a bride by her parents and the "taking" of a bride by the groom. The conventional marriage procedure was as follows:

agreement between the parties	→	bridal payment/betrothal present (*mohar*)	→	inchoate (i.e., embryonic) state of marriage	→	marriage completed by intercourse

However, to fill in the details we need to draw on a variety of texts.

First, there is an agreement between the parties representing the two families that the bride will be given in marriage to the groom. The father of the groom typically opened negotiations with the father of the bride, even in cases where the son chose the woman himself (e.g., Genesis 34:4; Judges 14:1–5). This reminds us of the androcentric character of biblical marriage: men typically took the initiative. The bride is "the object of the agreement rather than a party thereto."[14] As part of the deal, the groom agrees to make a betrothal payment (*mohar*; see further, below) to the bride's father. The *mohar* was normally in silver (Exodus 22:16/MT 22:15) although it could take more exotic forms, such as King Saul's request for 100 Philistine foreskins (1 Samuel 18:25). This agreement superficially acknowledged the fact that David's family had comparatively little money (and cf. Jacob's seven years' labor for each wife; Genesis 29:18–20, 27, 30).[15]

The next stage is the delivery of the *mohar* by the groom to the bride's father. This may be more than agreed: David ultimately presents Saul with 200 Philistine foreskins (1 Samuel 18:27). Upon delivery of the *mohar*, the parties embark on a period of betrothal, which was really a kind of inchoate or embryonic marriage. There does not seem to have been, in biblical law, a period of what we would nowadays call "engagement." From this point on, the betrothed woman is referred to as a "wife" with the status and protection of a fully married woman (Deuteronomy 22:23–24). No distinction is made between betrothed and married

---

13. Raymond Westbrook, Biblical law, in AN INTRODUCTION TO THE HISTORY AND SOURCES OF JEWISH LAW, 9 (N. S. Hecht, B. S. Jackson, S. M. Passamaneck, D. Piattelli & A. M. Rabello eds.; Oxford: Oxford University Press, 1996), 1–17, 10.

14. Westbrook, Biblical law, p. 11.

15. Allen Guenther, A typology of Israelite marriage: Kinship, socio-economic, and religious factors, J. STUD. OF OLD TESTAMENT 29, 387–407, 394 (2005).

women in cases of rape or seduction by a third party (Deuteronomy 22:22–27). In the early period, it seems to have been customary to allow a year between betrothal and marriage. During this period, the parties could not have sexual relations with each other. However, if the woman had relations with anyone else, it would be adultery (see further Chapter 11).

The final stage is the completion of the marriage. This is marked by a banquet thrown by the father of the bride (Genesis 29:22), which accompanies the consummation of the marriage. Consummation signifies legal completion of the marriage.[16] This is consistent with frequent references in the Bible to the husband's "going in" to his wife, which alludes both to entering the bedchamber and penetrating the woman (e.g., Ruth 4:13). There are good reasons for thinking that sexual intercourse was the complementary "oath sign" that formally ratified the "one-flesh" covenant of marriage.[17]

Once married, husbands were expected to provide a certain basic minimum of support for their wives. The threefold provision of Exodus 21:10 seems to reflect stereotypical standards of care in the ANE, according to which caregivers were expected to provide food, clothing, and *'onatah* (e.g., Laws of Lipit-Ishtar §27, Middle Assyrian Laws Tablet A (MAL A) §36). The word *'onatah* is a *hapax legomenon* (that is, a word which appears only once, in this case in the Hebrew Bible). The general view of rabbinic and biblical studies is that it refers to conjugal rights, although some scholars such as Shalom Paul[18] see it as referring to oil, or cosmetics.

There is evidence that fathers gave their daughters property upon their marriage (e.g., Laban's gifts of Zilpah and Bilhah to Leah and Rachel, respectively, in Genesis 29:24, 29, and Caleb's gift of land to his daughter Achsah, in Joshua 15:18–19). This went with the woman in the case of a divorce and provided her with some financial independence. The property (*shilluchim*) is usually regarded as a "dowry" (e.g., 1 Kings 9:16),[19] although this is questioned by Bernard Jackson[20] who notes that husbands did not seem to have any rights over this property (cf. Genesis 16:6). In addition, there are grounds for seeing the *mohar* itself as an "indirect dowry,"[21] which helped the wife and children in the event of a divorce, as opposed to simply benefiting the father of the bride.

---

16. Westbrook, *Biblical law*, p. 11.
17. Hugenberger, Marriage as a Covenant, p. 343.
18. Shalom Paul, Studies in the Book of the Covenant in the Light of Cuneiform and Biblical Law, Supplements to *Vetus Testamentum* 17 (Leiden: Brill, 1970), 56–60.
19. *See generally* Westbrook, Property and the Family, pp. 142–64.
20. Bernard S. Jackson, *The "institutions" of marriage and divorce in the Hebrew Bible.* Unpublished paper, p. 10, n. 60.
21. Jackson, *"Institutions" of marriage and divorce*, p. 6.

B. Made in heaven?

Choosing a bride meant striking some sort of balance between endogamy (marrying within a social group) and exogamy (marrying outside a social group). The patriarchal narratives show a marked preference for endogamy over exogamy. Abraham married his half-sister Sarah (Genesis 20:12), just like his brother Nahor, who married his half-sister, Milcah (Genesis 11:29). Abraham casts the net a little wider when finding a wife for his son Isaac; nevertheless, Isaac ends up getting married to his cousin's daughter, Rebekah (Abraham's brother's granddaughter; Genesis 24:15). Since God is presented in Genesis 24 as running a divine dating agency, the Isaac/Rebekah "love-in" merely highlights the virtues of endogamy (Genesis 24).

The next generation of courting couples take a different tack—with disastrous results. Esau chooses two wives: unfortunately, both came from non-Israelite stock, and the result was domestic strife (Genesis 26:34–35). To avoid any more ghastly in-laws, his brother Jacob is sent off to Abraham's family roots in Upper Mesopotamia and told to find a wife from among his father's kin group (Genesis 28:1–5). Jacob duly marries his cousins whereupon Esau falls into line and marries a cousin, also (Genesis 28:6–9; Genesis 29:10–28). Endogamy rules, OK.

The patriarchal narratives reflect a general belief among nomadic tribes that endogamy helps to preserve corporate identity. This concern is heightened in Abraham's case by the knowledge that his descendants would inherit the promised land. It was of prime importance that Abraham's descendants would not get "bred out" as a result of intermarriage with other families who might not be prepared to abide by the covenant between Abraham and God. Accordingly, later biblical law prohibited marriage with a number of people-groups (Exodus 34:11–16). Several scholars have shown the powerful way in which biblical law shapes national and personal identity.[22] This includes the biblical laws of marriage. Indeed, there is evidence that marriage laws are particularly important at times when national identity is being formed, for example, at the entrance to the Promised Land (Deuteronomy 7:1–4) or when it is under threat, for example, during the time of Ezra (Ezra 9–10).[23]

Given the conservative tendencies underlying marriage in biblical times, it is easy to imagine the problems that might arise when a marriage is desired on either, or both, sides but where there is significant social or religious distance between the parties. Allen Guenther[24] suggests that in such cases, there was a

---

22. *E.g.*, CHERYL B. ANDERSON, WOMEN, IDEOLOGY AND VIOLENCE, JOURNAL FOR THE STUDY OF THE OLD TESTAMENT SUPPLEMENT SERIES 394 (London: Continuum, 2004); FRANZ VOLKER GREIFENHAGEN, EGYPT ON THE PENTATEUCH'S IDEOLOGICAL MAP, JOURNAL FOR THE STUDY OF THE OLD TESTAMENT SUPPLEMENT SERIES 361 (London: Continuum, 2002).

23. Philip F. Esler, *Ezra-Nehemiah as a narrative of (re-invented) Israelite identity,* BIBLICAL INTERPRETATION 11, 413–26 (2003).

24. Guenther, *Typology of Israelite marriage,* pp. 390–96.

procedure for requesting or offering to contract a marriage. This is signified by the verb *chatan* which does not by itself signify marriage but rather "the act of establishing an affinity relationship with a view to marriage or inter-marriage."[25]

One example of "outsiders" who might be subject to such a treaty is of course non-Israelites. An example of this may be found in Genesis 34 where Hamor requests that Jacob "intermarry" (*wehitchattenu*) with the Shechemites (Genesis 34:9). We note in passing that although the would-be groom is very much in love, the object of the intermarriage proposal is to set up a "free-trade" agreement (Genesis 34:8–10, 20–23). Marriage in the Bible frequently has significant economic implications.

On the other hand, the "outsiders" may be socially inferior Israelites who were seen by their superiors as "not our class" (e.g., the rich man who falls in love with a peasant girl). Again, some sort of "parity treaty with negotiation of terms and formal procedures" may have been required.[26] We see the operation of this kind of *chatan* agreement in the David story where a common shepherd, who is even overlooked by his own family, becomes son-in-law to the king (1 Samuel 18:17–29).

Such love matches do not always work, however. Genesis 34 is a classic example of the dangers of *chatan*-type marriages. The story of Dinah and Shechem (see further, below) is quickly followed by Jacob's household dumping its "alien gods" and rededicating itself at Bethel, all of which climaxes in an appearance by God, who renews the blessing upon Jacob (Genesis 35:2–4, 6–7; 9–12). As far as the wider Jacob cycle is concerned, therefore, Genesis 34 is proof that exclusivism triumphs in the face of polytheistic and multiethnic temptations.[27] Some differences are just too great to be overcome.

III. ANYTHING FOR LOVE?

An overview of recent studies found that "modern family law is characterised by complexity, fragmentation and a variety of processes."[28] If this is true even in modern law, it is not altogether surprising that biblical law should also be characterized by complexity, lack of systemization, and a range of procedures. Some of the different kinds of marriages and processes that exist in biblical law are helpfully identified by Guenther.[29]

---

25. Ibid., 395.
26. Ibid.
27. Ellen Van Wolde, *Love and hatred in a multiracial society: The Dinah and Shechem story in Genesis 34 in the context of Genesis 28-35*, in READING FROM RIGHT TO LEFT (J. Cheryl Exum & H. G. M. Williamson eds.; Journal for the Study of the Old Testament Supplement Series 373; London: Continuum, 2003), 435–49, 444–47.
28. Boyd, *Legal regulation*, p. 257.
29. Guenther, *Typology of Israelite marriage*.

First is the *yabham*-type marriage, otherwise known as "sex with your sister-in-law" (Deuteronomy 25:5–10). Here, the brother of a man who dies without any sons is obliged to impregnate his widow. The verb *yabham* refers to the duty of the brother-in-law. The purpose is to raise a son who will continue the deceased's lineage and inherit the estate. It is an exceptional form of marriage that would not have been permitted under normal circumstances (cf. Leviticus 18:16). Indeed, there is every indication that the duty was not a popular one on the part of the brother, although widows had, of course, a vested interest in obtaining an heir.[30] The duty prevents the deceased's "name" or title to his landed inheritance from being extinguished, and it keeps the ancestral estate within the immediate family. It is thus another example of the way in which marriage, family, and property go together in biblical law (see Chapter 6). Refusal to perform the duty results in a highly symbolic shaming ceremony in which the man's sandal is removed. Since the earth is associated with fertility, particularly in agricultural societies, the sandal may be regarded as a fertility symbol because it has contact with the ground. The removal of the man's sandal thus signifies that the privilege of intercourse with his brother's wife is taken away from him.[31]

Second is the *chataph*-type marriage. This is derived from the verb "to catch" or "to seize" (*chataph*). In Judges 21:20–23, men from the tribe of Benjamin whose wives had been killed in Israel's civil war were given permission by their community elders to "seize" (*wachataphtem*) a wife from among a group of unmarried women in a given location (Judges 21:21). The reason why it is a seizing and not the usual "giving and taking" is because of the unusual circumstances of the war. This had resulted in a self-imposed curse by the tribes of Israel on anyone who gave a wife to the tribe of Benjamin (Judges 21:18). The only way around this was to allow the men of the tribe of Benjamin to seize a wife, under certain conditions. As a result, it is an example of a marriage that takes place without the customary *mohar*. The exceptional nature of this sort of marriage is reflected in the local opposition (Judges 21:22), although this sense of outrage probably has little in common with the objections of modern feminists[32] and more to do with the absence of a *mohar*.[33] The story is in keeping with the overall structure of Judges, in which each episode narrates a further stage in

---

30. Dvora E. Weisberg, *The Widow of Our Discontent: Levirate Marriage in the Bible and Ancient Israel*, J. STUD. OLD TESTAMENT 28 (2004), 403-29.

31. JONATHAN P. BURNSIDE, THE SIGNS OF SIN: SERIOUSNESS OF OFFENCE IN BIBLICAL LAW, JOURNAL FOR THE STUDY OF THE OLD TESTAMENT SUPPLEMENT SERIES 364 (London: Continuum International, 2003), 107–14.

32. E.g., Alice Bach, *Rereading the body politic: Women and violence in Judges 21*, in JUDGES: A FEMINIST COMPANION TO THE BIBLE 4 (Athalya Brenner, ed.; Sheffield: Sheffield Academic Press, 2nd series 1999), 143–59.

33. Jackson, "*Institutions*" *of marriage and divorce*, p. 3.

Israel's moral decline. Seen in this light, the *chataph*-type marriage is another outrageous aspect of the nadir of Judges 19–21.

A third variation on the basic form of marriage is the *hoshibh*-type marriage (e.g., Ezra 10:2; Nehemiah 13:23). This is a special form of the verb *yashabh* which means "to cause to dwell or stay." Guenther[34] suggests that it refers to cohabitation that may result in formal marriage, citing MAL A §34 as an example of the relationship between cohabitation and marriage in the ANE.

We conclude that there is a fair degree of complexity in biblical law. This is consistent with the complex picture that we find regarding marriage in other ANE legal collections.[35]

IV. WEDDING LISTS

In contrast to the biblical legal materials, later Jewish law shows a significant increase in systematization in relation to betrothal and marriage. The Mishnah is one of the earliest collections of rabbinic interpretation and is thought to have been completed by around 200 AD. The third order of the Mishnah (*Nashim*, which means "women" or "wives") contains the tractates *Ketubot* ("Marriage deeds"), *Gittin* ("Bills of divorce"), and *Kiddushin* ("Betrothals"). The systematic presentation of the Mishnah raises the question: to what extent is this later development consistent with customary practice in biblical times?

Mishnah Kiddushin sheds light on the historical development of marriage in biblical and later Jewish law. First, it specifies that a woman is "acquired" (becomes a wife) in three ways: (1) through money, (2) a contract, or (3) sexual intercourse:

> By three means is the woman acquired [by the man] . . . . She is acquired by money, by document or by intercourse . . . . (Mishnah Kiddushin 1:1)[36]

It is generally thought that the reference to "money" and "document" in Mishnah Kiddushin 1:1 refers to betrothal or to inchoate marriage. As such, Mishnah Kiddushin is not too far removed from the account given above of the formation of marriage in biblical law. There we saw that the following were all integral to the process of getting married: (1) the *mohar*, (2) formal agreement between family representatives, and (3) sexual intercourse.

Second, Mishnah Kiddushin illuminates the historical development of marriage in biblical law by indicating that there is, substantively, a close parallel

---

34. Guenther, *Typology of Israelite marriage*, pp. 401–02.
35. *E.g.*, INSTONE-BREWER, DIVORCE AND REMARRIAGE, pp. 1–15.
36. THE MISHNAH, translated from the Hebrew with an introduction and brief explanatory notes by Herbert Danby (Oxford: Oxford University Press, 1933), 321.

between the means by which the woman is acquired and the acquisition of property.[37] This is reflected in a subsequent portion of Mishnah Kiddushin:

> Property for which there is security can be acquired by money or by writ or by usucaption [i.e. an act of possession; *hazakah*] .... (1:5)[38]

Both women and property can be acquired through: (1) money, (2) documentation, and (3) use. In the case of women, such use may take the form of sexual intercourse. Tosefta Kiddushin 1:3 (a parallel compilation of laws omitted from the Mishnah) implies that intercourse must be consensual. But Mishnah Kiddushin 1:5 indicates that land can also be acquired through *hazakah*, which means the exercise of strength in relation to an object. In the case of land, this involves a physical act of taking possession, such as digging up part of the land (cf. the act of taking physical control of land through *mancipatio* in Roman law). There is a parallel here between "taking possession of land," understood as "penetrating Earth and depositing seed" and "taking possession of a woman" by means of intercourse.[39] It is for this reason that "ploughing is the primary androcentric metaphor for sexual intercourse in the ancient world"[40] (cf. the sexual connotations of Samson's reference to "ploughing with his heifer"; Judges 14:18). Jackson[41] speculates that Mishnah Kiddushin 1:1, which refers to the "woman acquired by intercourse," may historically be associated with "robbery marriage" (*raubehe*; i.e., marriage by rape or capture). It is certainly possible that marriage by capture was the origin of intercourse as a source of betrothal. We have already seen an example of *raubehe* in the *chataph*-type marriage of Judges 21:20–23.

A. Sexual terrorists

However, a more subtle example of *raubehe* is that of Amnon and Tamar. According to the story in 2 Samuel 13, Amnon becomes sexually obsessed with his half-sister Tamar and contrives a situation in which it is possible for him to have intercourse with her by force. Unlike the Dinah story in Genesis 34 (see below), the context makes it clear that this is rape: "[Amnon] would not listen to her voice, overpowered her, pressed her down, and had sex with her"[42] (2 Samuel 13:14).

---

37. Jackson, *"Institutions" of marriage and divorce.*
38. THE MISHNAH, DANBY TRANSLATION, p. 322.
39. Alan H. Cadwallader, *Swords into Ploughshares: The End of War?* in THE EARTH STORY IN THE NEW TESTAMENT (Norman C. Habel & Vicky Balabanski eds., Earth Bible Series, 5 vols.; London: Continuum, 2002), vol. V, 57–75, 62.
40. Ibid.
41. BERNARD S. JACKSON, WISDOM-LAWS: A STUDY OF THE MISHPATIM OF EXODUS 21: 1-22:16 (Oxford: Oxford University Press, 2006), 373.
42. Translation by Ellen Van Wolde, *Does 'inna denote rape? A semantic analysis of a controversial word*, VETUS TESTAMENTUM 52, 528–44, 540 (2005).

Amnon's behavior is characteristic of the "scoundrels (*hannebhalim*) of Israel" and thus inappropriate for the king's son (verse 13). The word *hannebhalim* shares the same root as *nebhalah* ("vile thing"), which is how Tamar characterizes Amnon's behavior in verse 12:

> Don't, brother. Don't force me. Such things are not done in Israel! Don't do such a vile thing! (*nebhalah*; JPS)

Nebhalah is a complex word which is probably best translated as "abomination," or by similar terms that signal "a breach or derangement of the bonds that unite human beings with each other or with God."[43] It is a graphic term for relational disorder. The significance of *nebhalah* lies in its ability to threaten communal society. It results in "the break up of an existing relationship whether between tribes, within the family, in a business arrangement, in marriage or with God."[44]

In Amnon's case, his behavior makes him one of the *hannebhalim* because "he is someone who has seriously damaged the community of Israel through a sexual transgression."[45] This is merely one indication of the way in which, in biblical thought, sexual relationships can be used either to create community or to destroy community (see further Chapter 11). Sexual order helps to create relational order, and sexual disorder leads to relational disorder. ("Order" is here used in the sense of things occupying their proper place before God and does not primarily refer to order in a hierarchical sense). In anthropological terms, *nebhalah* is often used of behavior that is "antistructural"[46] because it contravenes accepted social, and in this case sexual, norms. To this extent, *nebhalah* may be antonymous to Wisdom notions of an ordered world that consists of right relationships.

As far as Tamar is concerned, however, her lack of consent is *not* the worst feature of the case. This is striking from a modern point of view. The rape is understood by Tamar as an attempt by Amnon to marry her by force. Her primary fear is *not* that she will be raped but that she will be subject to "marriage by capture." This is why she argues with Amnon that marriage by rape is not necessary because marriage with David's consent is possible (2 Samuel 13:13). Accordingly, her response to Amnon's sexual advances is to plead with him to open negotiations with the king:

> Please, speak to the king; he will not refuse me to you. (2 Samuel 13:13; JPS)

---

43. J. Marböck, *Nabal, nebala*, in THEOLOGICAL DICTIONARY OF THE OLD TESTAMENT (G. Johannes Botterweck, Helmer Ringgren & Heinz-Josef Fabry eds.; David E. Green trans.; Grand Rapids, Mich.: Eerdmans, 1998), vol. IX, 157–71, 171.

44. Anthony Phillips, *Nebalah—a term for serious disorderly and unruly conduct*, VETUS TESTAMENTUM 25, 237–42, 241 (1975).

45. Marböck, *Nabal, nebala*, p. 163.

46. Meir Malul, KNOWLEDGE, CONTROL AND SEX: STUDIES IN BIBLICAL THOUGHT, CULTURE AND WORLDVIEW (Tel Aviv-Jaffa: Archaeological Centre Publication, 2002), 299.

However, Amnon refuses to listen to her. He commits *nebhalah* and behaves like one of the *hannebhalim* by making Tamar his wife without first opening negotiations with King David and securing his consent. Amnon's "marriage by capture" has the effect of transferring Tamar from the legal domain of her "father's house" to his "house." However, as soon as he has "married" her, he loathes her (verse 15) and instantly "sends her away," using the normal term for a divorce:[47]

> ... Amnon said to her, "Get out!" She pleaded with him, "Please don't commit this wrong; to send me away would be *even worse than the first wrong you committed* against me." But he would not listen to her. He summoned his young attendant and said, "Get that woman out of my presence, and bar the door behind her." (2 Samuel 13:15–17; JPS)

The language of divorce confirms that a marriage has taken place, in this case, *raubehe*. It also means that Tamar suffers the quickest marriage and divorce in history. From her perspective, the shame of being immediately divorced was even worse than being the object of *raubehe* in the first place (2 Samuel 13:16). This is why Tamar sees the second wrong as worse than the first wrong, her "marriage by capture." Significantly, when she is thrown out of Amnon's house, she does not return to her father's house but to her brother Absalom's house. This is because following the enforced marriage and the divorce, she has no ties either to her father or to a husband.[48] She is effectively without any form of status (cf. Abraham's "sending away" of Hagar; Genesis 21:14). All she can do is head for the nearest male kin who can offer her any kind of protection, namely, her brother Absalom. Tamar ends up in the worst possible position—a "desolate woman" (2 Samuel 13:20). This is not a comment on her psychological state but an evaluation of her social status. She is cast into a position that is "not acknowledged by the classificatory rules of structured society ... [an] outcast and disenfranchised [entity]."[49]

V. DANGEROUS LIAISONS

We have seen that the conventional marriage procedure in ancient Israel took the following form:

agreement → *mohar* → inchoate state of marriage → marriage completed by intercourse

---

47. Jackson, Wisdom-Laws, p. 373.
48. Van Wolde, *Semantic analysis*, p. 540.
49. Malul, Knowledge, Control and Sex, p. 167.

This section explores what happens when the conventional marriage procedure is subverted. We will consider three cases: Genesis 34 (the "rape" of Dinah), Exodus 22:16–17 (consensual intercourse with an unbetrothed girl of marriageable age), and Deuteronomy 22:28–29.

A. Bride and prejudice

The sexual encounter described in Genesis 34 is problematic for several reasons. This is seen in the reaction of Dinah's brothers:

> The men were distressed and very angry, because he [Shechem] had committed an outrage (*nebhalah*) in Israel by lying with Jacob's daughter—a thing not to be done. (Genesis 34:7)

Why is Shechem's act characterized as *nebhalah*? There are several possible reasons. The first is that Dinah did not consent to the sexual act, although the text is not entirely clear on this point. Some modern Bibles translate verse 2 as ". . . [Shechem] took her [Dinah] and raped her (*wayeannehah*)" (NIV) and even give Genesis 34 the overall heading of "The Rape of Dinah." This approach is enshrined in the Latin Vulgate translation of the Bible and is followed by a number of modern scholars.[50] On the other hand, some scholars translate the special form of the verb *'anah* in verse 2 (*yeannehah*) as "debased" rather than "raped," arguing that *'anah* is an evaluative term that signifies a downward movement in a social sense.[51] The verb reflects the consequences of the sexual act and the debasement of the woman from a social-juridical point of view.[52] This approach is followed by the English Standard Version which translates the relevant verb in verse 2 as "humiliated her." Such divergent translations are possible because the text itself is ambiguous as to whether Dinah consented or not.

Assuming that the sexual act was nonconsensual, could Shechem's act of *nebhalah* have been a case of marriage by capture? After all, we saw above that Amnon's *nebhalah* behavior toward Tamar took the form of *raubehe*. However, it seems unlikely that this is the case with Shechem.[53] This is because, on the surface, Shechem and his family ask Jacob's permission after the intercourse. Indeed, Shechem is apparently fearful that Jacob will refuse permission ("only give me the maiden to be my wife"; Genesis 34:12), which implies that Dinah is not already his wife as a result of "robbery marriage."

---

50. DANNA NOLAN FEWELL & DAVID M. GUNN, GENDER, POWER AND PROMISE (Nashville: Abingdon Press, 1993), 81ff; Mignon R. Jacobs, *Love, honour, and violence: Socioconceptual matrix in Genesis 34*, in PREGNANT PASSION: GENDER, SEX, AND VIOLENCE IN THE BIBLE (Cheryl A. Kirk-Duggan ed.; Atlanta: Society of Biblical Literature, 2003), 11–35, 14ff.

51. Van Wolde, *Semantic analysis*.

52. Van Wolde, *Love and hatred*; *Semantic analysis*.

53. Contra Joseph Fleishman, *Why did Simeon and Levi rebuke their father in Genesis 34:31?*, J. NORTHWEST SEMITIC LANGUAGES 26, 101–16 (2000).

Setting the question of Dinah's consent to one side—since the subject is indeterminate on the basis of the text—there are at least two further reasons why Shechem's behavior was seen by Dinah's brothers as *nebhalah*. First, we can see Genesis 34 as a case of premarital intercourse in which the normal customary steps in the formation of a marriage are subverted. Added to this, we have the further complication that Shechem is a foreign prince. The introduction of these power dynamics to an already delicate situation ensures that resolving the irregularity will be even more problematic than usual (cf. Exodus 22:16–17/MT 22:15–16). To cap it all, Shechem is a Hivite and hence a non-Israelite. Sexual relations between a daughter of Israel and a non-Israelite fly in the face of Israel's preference for endogamy, as seen in earlier patriarchal narratives. This is reflected in the brother's objection: "We cannot . . . give our sister to a man who is uncircumcised, for that would be a disgrace to us" (Genesis 34:14). We will consider each of these problems in turn.

First, Shechem's act can be understood as a case of an incorrect marriage procedure in which the man takes the initiative and has sexual intercourse with a woman to whom he is not legally related.[54] Shechem has intercourse with Dinah (verse 2) before opening negotiations via Hamor (verse 4) and without prior agreement with Jacob. Thus, instead of:

agreement → *mohar* → inchoate state of marriage → marriage completed by intercourse

we have:

intercourse → inchoate state of marriage → agreement (?) → *mohar* (?)

At this point in the biblical period, intercourse is not regarded as inherently creating *kiddushin* (betrothal). However, it is an act that should, in the normal course of events, lead to serious negotiation over the creation of *kiddushin*. Genesis 34:26 refers to the brothers taking Dinah out of Shechem's house. Mignon Jacobs thinks that this "implies that Dinah was in some sense already married to Shechem,"[55] although she does not identify this as inchoate marriage. At any rate, it was possible to rectify this unusual situation, provided there was willingness on both sides regarding the *mohar*. This is why "Hamor the father of Shechem went out to Jacob to speak with him" (34:6). Shechem subsequently offers to pay any "marriage present (*mohar*) and gift" to the family to set the matter right (34:12). The magnitude of his offer indicates his desire to compensate for the harm done. At this point, the reader expects negotiations between the house of Jacob and the house of Hamor leading to a settlement and damages.

---

54. Ellen Van Wolde, *The Dinah story: rape or worse?*, OLD TESTAMENT ESSAYS 15, 225–39, 235 (2002).

55. Jacobs, *Love, honour, and violence*, p. 14.

These would have been payable to Jacob and not to Dinah because it is Jacob's lack of consent that is at the heart of the offense.

This reading of the text explains why the sons object: "Should he treat our sister as a harlot?" (Genesis 34:31). The point is not that Dinah has acted like a prostitute but that Shechem has treated her like one. This makes sense when we recall that prostitutes in biblical Israel were typically women who were not under the authority of a father or husband[56] (cf. the two prostitutes in 1 Kings 3:16–28 who petition King Solomon because they lack any male family members who can sue for justice on their behalf). The prostitute is the stereotypical woman with whom a man can have sexual intercourse without needing to consider the impact upon her father or family. Once again, we find that sexual intercourse in biblical Israel is typically regarded as something that affects third parties and is not simply a matter of consent between the parties to the sexual act (see further Chapter 11). Shechem's offense is to treat Dinah as though she is not under the authority of her father and as though his behavior has no effect on Jacob's family honor. This is what the sons object to. Their protest is pointedly placed at the very end of the chapter and confirms that this is indeed the heart of the matter.

Second, Exodus 22:16–17/MT 22:15–16 (see further, below) indicates that negotiations between the man and the father could be fraught: indeed, a very angry father could demand a *mohar* and still not give his daughter in marriage. If negotiations (as envisaged under the later law of Exodus) could be difficult between two Israelite men, how much more difficult might we expect them to be between an Israelite and a non-Israelite? This is a further reason why Shechem's act provokes the brothers' wrath.[57] Genesis 34 is distanced even further from the scenario of Exodus 22:16–17/MT 22:15–16 because there is a significant power differential between the parties: a nomadic, landless chieftain's daughter has sexual relations with a settled, landed prince. So although we would ordinarily expect the father to be the one who "holds all the cards" in the ensuing negotiations (as is the case in Exodus 22:16–17/MT 22:15–16), this may not be so in Genesis 34. A clue that the balance of power is not weighted solely in Jacob's favor is the fact that Dinah, although apparently not yet married, remains at Shechem's house. She may be staying there voluntarily, or she may not. Either way, she is a potential hostage if things go badly.[58] This might explain Jacob's curious passivity, summed up in the detail: "Jacob kept silent" (verse 5).[59] Perhaps he felt in no position to refuse. It all goes wrong, however, when the sons of

---

56. Robin Parry, Old Testament Story and Christian Ethics: The Rape of Dinah as a Case Study, Paternoster Biblical Monographs (Milton Keynes: Wipf & Stock, 2004), 176.

57. Gordon Wenham, Story As Torah, Old Testament Studies (Edinburgh: T&T Clark, 2000), 113–17.

58. Parry, Old Testament Story, p. 149.

59. Ibid., 173–74.

Jacob—in contrast to their father's indifference—embark on a course of vengeance rather than negotiation. This leads to conflict between Jacob and his sons and conflict between the house of Jacob and the other peoples of the land (Genesis 34:30–31).

There may be some implied criticism of Dinah's independent behavior,[60] but overall, the narrator reserves his chief ire for Shechem for treating her "like a harlot," Jacob for his timidity, and the sons for their disproportionate response to the original offense (cf. Jacob's curse on Levi and Simeon; Genesis 49:5–7). In this way, the story draws together some of the issues we have already seen, including the need for proper order in the process of forming a marriage and the desirability of endogamy over exogamy.

B. Love My Way

The central problem of Genesis 34—regulating incorrect marriage procedure— is also addressed in Exodus and Deuteronomy. Several of the laws address different aspects of the problem when the man takes the initiative and has sexual intercourse with a woman to whom he is not legally related. Exodus 22:16–17/ MT 22:15–16 deals with the situation where a man has "jumped the gun" and had consensual intercourse with the woman *before* securing her father's consent and negotiating a bridal price. This subverts the normal procedure in which the *mohar* was usually agreed between families prior to intercourse. Verse 16/MT 22:15 indicates that the groom must put right his relationship with the woman, if her father consents. The man has to regularize her status. Accordingly, it is not best characterized as a rape case but one in which the normal sequence of events leading to marriage is subverted.

The woman is described as a *betulah* in verses 16–17/MT 22:15–16, and there are good reasons for thinking that this refers to a woman of marriageable age who is typically, but not necessarily, a virgin.[61] This subversion of the normal marriage sequence places the man in a vulnerable position. An angry father might well demand a higher *mohar* than otherwise (cf. Shechem's offer in Genesis 34:11–12). Alternatively, a very angry father could have demanded a *mohar* and still not given his daughter in marriage (Exodus 22:17/MT 22:16). If so, it would have amounted to colossal damages for premarital sex, which may have totalled years of the man's annual salary (cf. Jacob's service to Laban, above). The damages are apparently paid to the father (Exodus 22:17/MT 22:16). This is presumably because he is prevented from giving primary consent to the marriage (cf. Genesis 34:8, 11–12).

---

60. *E.g.*, Van Wolde, *Dinah story*.
61. Gordon J. Wenham, *Betulah: A girl of marriageable age*, Vetus Testamentum 22, 326–48 (1972).

We note in passing that the biblical marriage laws show some concern for the woman's status and protection. For example, in the slave laws of Exodus 21:7–11, the female debt slave (*'amah*) cannot be used for sexual services by her master without a change of status.[62] Cognitive anthropology might see this as a way in which legal control attaches to "verbs of knowledge," including sexual activity.[63] Biblical law lends some support to the view that "carnal knowledge is . . . a legal ceremonial act" that confers "status upon a formerly statusless person."[64]

In contrast to Exodus 22:16–17/MT 22:15–16, which is concerned with seduction and hence with consensual intercourse between the parties, the law in Deuteronomy 22:28–29 deals with *non*consensual intercourse. The paradigm case concerns a man who "seizes . . .and lies" with a *betulah* (verse 28), that is, a woman of marriageable age who is typically a virgin. Unlike the previous case, Deuteronomy 22:28–29 could be described as a rape law. However, we must be careful not to allow the categories of modern criminal law to eclipse the literary presentation of the biblical laws themselves. In fact, Deuteronomy 22:28–29 is part of a wider body of laws (Deuteronomy 22:23–29), which in turn is headed by the law of adultery in Deuteronomy 22:22. As a result, Deuteronomy 22:28–29 should be seen, not primarily as a rape law but as a variation of the law of adultery in Deuteronomy 22:22.[65] This is perfectly in keeping with my analysis of the literary structure of Leviticus 20 which deals with a wide range of sexual offenses.[66] As we will see in Chapter 11, sexual offenses are classified within the Bible as variations on the central case of adultery.

Yet, although Deuteronomy 22:28–29 concerns nonconsensual intercourse, the resolution is to some extent similar to that of Exodus 22:16–17/MT 22:15–16. Compensation is paid, once again, to the father rather than to the woman. The difference between Deuteronomy and Exodus is that whereas Deuteronomy 22:28–29 makes the payment to the father explicit, Exodus 22:16–17/MT 22:15–16 leaves it implicit. We also learn in Deuteronomy 22:29 that the guide price for the *mohar* payable under these circumstances is 50 shekels of silver, whereas in Exodus 22 there is no figure. Such variations are typical of the differences between the legal collections of Exodus and Deuteronomy, with the latter tending to be more specific. Given the circumstances (in which the man has intercourse

---

62. Jackson, Wisdom-Laws, p. 89.
63. Malul, Knowledge, Control and Sex, p. 302.
64. Ibid.
65. *Cf.* H. C. Washington, *Lest he die in the battle and another man take her: Violence and the construction of gender in the laws of Deuteronomy 20-22, in* Gender and Law in the Hebrew Bible and the Ancient Near East, (V. H. Matthews et al. eds.; Journal for the Study of the Old Testament Supplement Series 262 (Sheffield: Sheffield Academic Press, 1998), 185–213, 208.
66. Jonathan P. Burnside, *Strange Flesh: Sex, semiotics and the construction of deviancy in biblical law,* J. Stud. Old Testament 30, 387–420, 395–97 (2006).

before securing the father's consent and negotiating a bride-price), it is reasonable to suppose that the typical value of the *mohar* would normally have been less than 50 shekels and that the difference payable on this occasion constitutes a fine. The ballpark figure of 50 shekels may be taken to reflect "customary expectations"[67] which would have provided the starting point for negotiations, especially in light of the fact that there had been no consultation prior to this point. Fifty shekels was a heavy penalty in a society where this figure was the going rate for redeeming or "buying back" an Israelite male in his prime (Leviticus 27:3). The valuations of Leviticus 27 also show that this was the maximum value placed on anyone in ancient Israel's labor pool.[68]

A further difference between Deuteronomy 22:28–29 and Exodus 22:16–17/ MT 22:15–16 is that in the event of a marriage, Deuteronomy 22:28–29 prohibits divorce, whereas Exodus 22:16–17/MT 22:15–16 is silent. This can be seen as a form of "mirroring" punishment: the rash young man is prevented from capricious treatment in the future. From a modern perspective, it seems outrageous that the woman is further subjugated by marrying her rapist.[69] However, we must be careful not to import Western ideas about women's rights into biblical law. For one thing, in a polygamous society, the practical implications of being married are not as great as in a nonpolygamous society. The man need not have intercourse—or even contact—with the woman again. But he does have to support her. It is another example of "the effect of non-marital sex on personal status."[70] Biblical law protects the woman by giving her support and the status of a wife who cannot be divorced. Had this not been the case, the woman could have ended up being both raped *and* divorced—the unfortunate position of Tamar in 2 Samuel 13:16–20.

That being said, we should not exclude the possibility that the father had the right to refuse to give his daughter. After all, if he could refuse the seducer in Exodus 22:17/MT 22:16, there is no reason in principle why he could not have refused the rapist in Deuteronomy 22:28–29. If so, the position in Deuteronomy 22:28–29 is similar to MAL A §55 which gives the father the option to refuse to give his unbetrothed daughter to the offender as a wife, while at the same time receiving "triple silver"[71] in damages. As in biblical law, primary consent in the Middle Assyrian Laws belongs to the father, not the daughter (cf. Laws of Eshnunna (LE) §26 which refer to "the consent of her [the girl's] father and mother"—in a slightly different case of violation). Finally, the fact that primary consent belongs to the father does not preclude the possibility of the woman

---

67. JACKSON, WISDOM-LAWS, p. 371 n. 22.
68. Carol L. Meyers, *Procreation, production and protection: Male-female balance in ancient Israel*, J. AM. ACAD. RELIGION 51, 569–93, 585 (1983).
69. Jacobs, *Love, honour, and violence*, p. 24.
70. JACKSON, WISDOM-LAWS, p. 91 n. 65.
71. ROTH, LAW COLLECTIONS, p. 175.

saying to her father that she does not wish to live with this man (unlike Tamar, who was apparently willing to remain as a wife to Amnon).

VI. BREAKING UP

The biblical law on divorce is, if anything, even sketchier than the biblical laws of marriage. Biblical law does not set out the different grounds for divorce, nor the living arrangements, nor the financial settlements for postdivorce family life. It is left unsaid, once again, because the customary practice was well-known. The Mishnah provides some evidence of an oral formula for the *sepher keritut* ("a bill of divorcement"; Deuteronomy 24:1):

> The essential formula in the bill of divorce is: "Lo, thou art free to marry any man." R. Judah says: "Let this be from me thy writ of divorce and letter of dismissal and deed of liberation, that thou mayest marry whatsoever man thou wilt".... (Mishnah Gittin 9:3)[72]

However, we do not know if any particular form of communication was mandatory. Nevertheless, as with the laws of marriage, we can fill in the gaps to some extent by drawing on other biblical texts and ANE materials. The law of divorce, like the law of marriage, was largely a matter of custom and had much in common with the ancient Near East.

A. Go on now go, walk out the door

One of the problems with reconstructing the biblical laws of divorce is that biblical law is not concerned with divorce itself so much as with regulating its abuse. The primary focus of Deuteronomy 24:1–4, for example, is not divorce but palingamy, that is, the conditions under which a woman can remarry. This means that in seeking to reconstruct the biblical practice of divorce, we must be careful not to over-extrapolate from cases such as this that are primarily concerned with something else. Nevertheless, we can draw some conclusions about divorce in biblical Israel from Deuteronomy 24:1–4.

First, divorce is presented in Deuteronomy 24:1 as being "a private and unilateral legal act of the husband"[73] in contrast to the mutuality of the marriage formula. On the basis of Hosea 2:2/MT 2:4, it is thought that the customary divorce formula used the words, "You are not my wife, and I am not your husband." This negates the customary marriage declaration.[74] Deuteronomy 24:1 suggests that divorce could be initiated without reference to third parties, contrary

---

72. The Mishnah, Danby translation, p. 319.
73. Reuven Yaron, *On divorce in Old Testament times*, Revue Internationale des Droits de L'Antiquité 3, 117–28, 128 (1957).
74. Friedman, *Israel's response*, p. 199.

to Driver who assumes that "the case . . . must be brought before some public functionary."[75] This prompts us to consider whether the character of the drafting is "semantic" or "narrative." On the former reading, only a man can divorce a woman. However, on a narrative approach, while divorce by a man may still be the typical case, it does not necessarily exclude unilateral divorce by a woman. A variety of ANE legal texts indicate that it was possible for the wife to divorce her husband, under certain circumstances, although this could prove risky if she failed to impute sufficient blame to him.[76] For example, Laws of Hammurabi (LH) §142 allows a married woman to divorce her husband provided she is "without fault," and he is "wayward [that is, a womaniser] and disparages her greatly."[77] However, such cases should be seen as exceptional: according to LH §143, the wife is executed if she fails to establish sufficient grounds for a divorce. Divorce by Jewish women became much easier in the Persian period, as indicated by the Elephantine papyri (a collection of manuscripts hailing from a Jewish community at Elephantine in Egypt and thought to date from around the fifth century BC).[78]

Second, the reference in Deuteronomy 24:1 to the husband finding some fault with his wife suggests that there must be valid grounds for divorce or, at the very least, that the husband has to justify his course of action.[79] However, the reference in verse 3 to his rejecting the woman implies that it is ultimately his decision. Third, it is clear from Deuteronomy 24:1–4 that the whole point of a *sepher keritut* was to enable the woman to remarry. Surviving Jewish divorce certificates from the fifth century BC use the wording, "You are allowed to marry any man you wish" (cf. Mishnah Gittin 9:3, cited above and MAL A §33). Even if this was not actually written down, such permission is at the heart of the "bill of divorcement" (*sepher keritut*). Without it, the woman risked being charged with adultery if she had a relationship with another man.

Fourth, verse 3 uses the verb "to hate" (*sane'*) which sometimes has the additional technical meaning of "to divorce." This indicates an association in biblical thought between divorce and dislike. In Judges 15:2, Samson's father-in-law mistakenly assumes that Samson "had taken a dislike (*ki-sano senetah*)" (JPS) to his wife, as a result of which the father-in-law felt justified in giving her to another man. The verb *sane'* is the standard term for divorce in the Elephantine

---

75. S. R. Driver, A Critical and Exegetical Commentary on Deuteronomy (Edinburgh: T&T Clark, 3rd ed. 1906), 272.

76. See generally E. Lipiński, *The wife's right to divorce in the light of an ancient near eastern tradition*, in The Jewish Law Annual Volume 4 (B. S. Jackson ed.; Leiden: Brill, 1981), 9–26.

77. Roth, Law Collections, p. 108.

78. See Instone-Brewer, Divorce and Remarriage, pp. 75–80.

79. E. Neufeld, Ancient Hebrew Marriage Laws (London: Longmans, 1944), 176–79.

papyri.[80] Verse 3 combines the verb "to hate" with the verb "to send away," which is a technical divorce formulation, although the verbs are also used together in a nontechnical sense (e.g., Genesis 26:27).

Finally, it seems that handing the bill of divorce to the woman, combined with physical expulsion, is sufficient to terminate the marriage, although this was not sufficient in later Jewish law (witness, for example, the various marriage contracts from among the Elephantine papyri).[81] "Sending away" implies expulsion from the marital house. The woman, and not the man, would normally have left because most marriages were patrilocal. Had it been a matrilocal marriage, the husband would have departed.

B. Limits to remarriage

Biblical law regulates the practice of divorce in a number of ways. First, Exodus 21:10–11 deals with the female slave who is given by the master to his son for sexual services. If he takes another wife and refuses to give the slave-wife food, clothing, and 'onah (whether sexual attention or cosmetics), then she is released from the marriage "without payment" (Exodus 21:11). This ambiguous phrase could mean either that she does not have to purchase her freedom, or it may mean that the man does not have to give her a sum of money to compensate for her lack of property: a slave-wife would not have received property from her father upon entering the marriage.[82] It is reasonable to suppose that neglect on the grounds listed in Exodus 21:10–11 also provided a basis for divorce for free women in ancient Israel.[83] Exodus 21:10–11 also formed the basis of rabbinic grounds for divorce (e.g., Mishnah Ketuboth 5:6–8).

At the same time, biblical law set limits to the operation of divorce. Several texts forbid the husband from divorcing his wife, for example, where he has brought false charges against her (Deuteronomy 22:19) and where he has had intercourse with the woman without her consent or that of her father (Deuteronomy 22:29). Just as there are limits to marriage in biblical law (e.g., Leviticus 18 and 20 prohibit marrying affines; see Chapter 11), so there are limits to divorce, in certain circumstances.

The biblical laws of divorce lead naturally into laws about remarriage because, as we have seen, the bill of divorce was functionally equivalent to a permission to remarry. Just as there are limits to marriage *and* divorce in biblical law, so there are limits to *re*marriage.

---

80. Yaron, *On divorce*, p. 118.
81. Emil G. Kraeling, The Brooklyn Museum Aramaic Papyri: New Documents of the Fifth Century B.C. from the Jewish Colony at Elephantine (New Haven: Yale University Press, 1953).
82. Instone-Brewer, Divorce and Remarriage, p. 23.
83. Ibid., 99–103.

Biblical law sets limits to divorcées' ability to remarry. Deuteronomy 24:1–4 deals with the problem of the divorced woman who wishes to return to her first husband, after having been divorced from her second. The circumstances of her first divorce are that the husband finds "something obnoxious" (*'ervat dabhar*; JPS) about her. This literally means "nakedness of a thing." However, we do not know exactly what it refers to. The word translated "nakedness" (*'ervah*) is frequently used in sexual contexts to refer to genitalia (e.g., Exodus 20:26). Thus, it is reasonable to suppose that the husband's objection has something to do with sexual relations. It is notable that the only other case of *'ervat dabhar* in the Bible refers to the sight of uncovered excrement (Deuteronomy 23:13–14). Both laws are concerned with how things look to the offended parties and how this creates feelings of revulsion.[84] They are described in terms of how they are presented to the senses. It is the sensory perception of the *'ervat dabhar* that creates the disturbance.

At any rate, whatever the *'ervat dabhar* is, it is the reason why the first husband cannot take her back. ANE law distinguishes between grounds for divorce which allow the woman to exit the marriage with her property intact and those grounds which cause her to forfeit it (e.g., LH §§138, 141–142, 149).[85] It has been suggested that a similar distinction operates here.[86] The distinction is between an "objective" ground for divorce based on blameworthy behavior by the woman (which causes her to lose her *mohar*) and a "subjective" decision to divorce on the part of the husband, which does not imply any bad conduct by the woman (which means she can keep her *mohar*). Raymond Westbrook[87] sees the phrase, "he finds something obnoxious about her" (Deuteronomy 24:1) as referring to some objective blameworthy fault on the part of the wife which causes her to lose her *mohar*. However, when the second husband rejects her, this refers merely to a subjective decision on his part, which does not imply any bad conduct on the part of the woman. Under these conditions, the woman is allowed to exit the marriage with her *mohar*. She is now, on the face of it, an eligible divorcée with money from her second marriage.

The reason, then, why the first husband cannot take her back is because "having profited from the claim that she was unfit to be his wife, he cannot now act as if she were fit to marry him because circumstances have made her a more profitable match."[88] Taking back the first wife is described as "abhorrent" (*toebhah*) because the word is also used to describe swindlers (Deuteronomy 25:15–16).

---

84. David Daube, *To Be Found Doing Wrong*, STUDI IN ONORE DI EDOARDO VOLTERRA 2, 1–13, 8 (1969).
85. *See generally* WESTBROOK, PROPERTY AND THE FAMILY.
86. Raymond Westbrook, *The prohibition of restoration of marriage in Deuteronomy 24:1-4*, SCRIPTA HIEROSOLYMITANA 31, 387–405 (1986).
87. Ibid.
88. Ibid., 405.

The word *toebhah* is applied to a range of activities which the Hebrew Bible sees as disgusting, detestable, or loathsome. It is very notable that like the phrase *'ervat dabhar*, the word *toebhah* is strongly correlated with the senses.[89] The first husband might have been sickened by the woman but, in taking her back, *we* are repelled by what *he* does!

There are further limits on divorcées' ability to remarry. They may not marry a high priest (Leviticus 21:14) or a priest (Leviticus 21:7; Ezekiel 44:22) because priests are "holy to their God" (Leviticus 21:7). There is also some indication of prejudice against divorcées outside the priestly texts. Proverbs 30:21, 23 reads:

> Under three things the earth trembles; under four it cannot bear up:
> ... an unloved (*senuah*) woman when she gets a husband ...

which is thought by some scholars to refer to the remarriage of a divorcée.[90]

Turning to the ANE, we find that the position is broadly similar to biblical law in that remarriage was possible for divorcées, with some exceptions. LH §134 lets a woman remarry if her husband is captured, presumably in war, and he has not left her with sufficient resources with which to await his return. Notably, should the husband come back, the wife must return to the first husband, together with any children of the second marriage (LH §135). Babylonian men were not to be dissuaded from war by the thought of losing their wives. On the other hand, the unpatriotic man who deserts his city cannot claim his wife back from her second husband (LH §136).

VII. DECONSTRUCTING MARRIAGE

Biblical law champions the good of marriage and the value of lifelong fidelity. This conversely leads to a strong repudiation of adultery and its various forms (see further Chapter 11). In many respects, the dynamics of biblical family law and modern family law are like "chalk and cheese." Family law in the West has undergone revolutionary changes over the past 20 years. As a result, it may seem almost impossible to relate our current understandings of family law to biblical law because biblical law is so radical. If so, it shows how different societies can look at issues of marriage and divorce from fundamentally different starting points.

It has been said that "marriage performs critical social tasks and produces valuable personal and social goods that are far harder or impossible to achieve through individual action, private enterprise, public programmes or alternative

---

89. BURNSIDE, SIGNS OF SIN, pp. 204–06.
90. Yaron, *On divorce*, p. 118.

institutions."[91] Statistically, the benefits of marriage, as opposed to cohabitation and lone parenting, are well-documented across a wide range of indices, including benefits to children and building social capital.[92] Despite this, marriage has been deconstructed in the United Kingdom as the major determinant of family relationships, and this is reflected in social trends.

The number of persons choosing to marry in England and Wales has fallen to the lowest levels since records began in 1862, standing at 40 percent fewer than the early 1970s.[93] It is estimated that by 2031, the proportion of unmarried men will rise to 46 percent, compared with 35 percent in 2003.[94] The number of divorces in England and Wales has risen from 2.1 per thousand of married persons in 1961[95] to 12.3 in 2006,[96] while the proportion of children born outside marriage in England and Wales has risen from 6.3 percent in 1961[97] to 45 percent in 2008.[98] In some parts of the United Kingdom as many as 68.5% of babies were born out of marriage in 2008.[99] The United Kingdom has one of the highest divorce rates in Europe and over one-third of all marriages in England and Wales in 2008 were remarriages.[100]

Alongside this, there have been major challenges both to the ways in which law reinforces heterosexual family norms and the normativity of the nuclear family.[101] The conjugal rainbow now includes heterosexual marriages

---

91. Patricia Morgan, *The value of marriage*. Re: *Katherine Zappone and Ann Louise Gilligan v Revenue Commissioners, Ireland and the Attorney General* High Court Record No. 2004 19616P, unpublished paper, undated, 8 pp, p. 1.

92. *See generally* Jill Kirby, BROKEN HEARTS: FAMILY DECLINE AND THE CONSEQUENCES FOR SOCIETY (London: Centre for Policy Studies, 2002).

93. OFFICE FOR NATIONAL STATISTICS, SOCIAL TRENDS *31* (London: The Stationery Office, 2001), pp. 46–47; OFFICE FOR NATIONAL STATISTICS, STATISTICAL BULLETIN: MARRIAGES IN ENGLAND AND WALES *2008* (London: Office for National Statistics, 11 February 2010), p. 122.

94. OFFICE FOR NATIONAL STATISTICS, POPULATION TRENDS *121: REPORT: 2003-BASED MARITAL STATUS AND COHABITATION PROJECTIONS FOR ENGLAND AND WALES* (London: Palgrave Macmillan, 2005), p. 79.

95. OFFICE FOR NATIONAL STATISTICS, SOCIAL TRENDS *31* (London: The Stationery Office, 2001), p. 48.

96. OFFICE FOR NATIONAL STATISTICS, POPULATION TRENDS 136: MARRIAGES AND DIVORCES DURING 2006 AND ADOPTIONS IN 2007: ENGLAND AND WALES (London: Office for National Statistics, 2009), p. 121.

97. OFFICE FOR NATIONAL STATISTICS, SOCIAL TRENDS *31* (London: The Stationery Office, 2001).

98. OFFICE FOR NATIONAL STATISTICS, *STATISTICAL BULLETIN: WHO IS HAVING BABIES? (2008)* (London: Office for National Statistics, 2009).

99. *The Sunday Times*, 18 April 2010.

100. OFFICE FOR NATIONAL STATISTICS, *STATISTICAL BULLETIN: MARRIAGES IN ENGLAND AND WALES 2008*, p.2.

101. Boyd, *Legal regulation*.

and homosexual partnerships, "donor babes," and gay adoptions, as well as unmarried mothers who bring up their children with the help of gay friends or straight colleagues who want to be "unlive-in" dads. It is, perhaps, "ironic that, as personal relationships have been freed from many traditional constraints, they are often represented as more tortuous and problematic than ever before."[102]

Despite this, the human yearning for marriage and children remains as strong as ever. Heterosexual marriage is "still a majority behaviour, a majority situation in which children are reared and the aspiration of at least 80% or more of the population."[103] The desire for marriage and children also means that some of the stranger aspects of the biblical marriage laws are not so difficult to understand after all. So biblical law makes room for polygamy—how licentious! Yet modern law and policy both encourages and facilitates "polygyny with women in sequential or contemporaneous unions."[104] So biblical law allows a man to impregnate his dead brother's sister—how bizarre! But we allow women to be impregnated from beyond the grave with their dead husband's frozen sperm. Even Tamar's gambit with Judah in Genesis 38 is echoed by the modern woman who chooses a "coparent" from an online sperm bank. With this in mind—revolutionary social change combined with unchanged human instincts—what points of connection, if any, can we find between biblical and modern law?

First, we find *a shared preoccupation with defining the boundaries of the family*. Biblical law promotes a clear sense of belonging by structuring the family as a series of kinship circles and by seeking to balance endogamy and exogamy. Modern law and public policy also reflects a preoccupation with defining—and redefining—the boundaries of the family, although these are much looser than ancient Israel. There has been a radical shift away from definitions based on the traditional heterosexual nuclear family and toward the subjective and sentimental language of "care."[105] In the "new formless families ... people do not marry or have any time for institutionally founded ties, they simply 'care.'"[106] The term "family" has become "a sponge concept ... that can include two friends who live together, the people who work in an office, a local unit of the Mafia, and the

---

102. FRANK FERUDI, PARANOID PARENTING (London: Penguin, 2001), p. 105.

103. Patricia Morgan, *Consequences: The failure of social re-engineering and the wider impact of family fragmentation*, paper presented at Jubilee Centre Sexual Offences Reform Conference, Lucy Cavendish College, University of Cambridge, December 15, 2005, 46 pp., p. 3.

104. Ibid., 26.

105. *E.g,.* F. WILLIAMS, RETHINKING FAMILIES (London: Calouste Gulbenkian Foundation, 2004).

106. MORGAN, CONSEQUENCES, p. 21.

family of man."[107] Identifying the boundaries of the family is for us a deeply contested issue.

Second, we find *recognition that there are economic incentives to getting married and economic disincentives to divorce*. Biblical law recognizes and affirms that marriage is, to an important extent, an economic contract which involves pooling wealth and which requires proper economic support and provision. This is recognized by modern critical legal scholars. Rather than demanding the abolition of marriage, feminists such as Carol Smart note that "it would be far more effective to undermine the social and legal *need* and support for the marriage contract."[108] There is increasing recognition that it is difficult to sustain the institution of marriage "unless it confers privileges and imposes obligations on those who choose to marry that are different from those imposed on people who elect to cohabit or associate in some other way."[109]

Third, we find *shared concerns regarding consent, equality, and protection*, although, again, these are structured differently in biblical and modern law. In relation to *consent*, much depends on whose permission we are talking about. In biblical law, primary consent belongs to the father. We have seen that he is the one to whom damages are given because his consent was not sought in advance. By contrast, in modern law, consent is a matter for the parties to the sexual act, provided they are of age. Biblical law thus has a "thick" concept of consent in relation to third parties because it goes beyond individual consent to include the consent of the father of the woman in question and, by extension, other family members who have an interest in negotiating terms of marriage. It recognizes that sexual intercourse has implications that go beyond the two parties to include third parties and the community as a whole. Modern law, by contrast, has a "thin" understanding of consent in relation to third parties because it is limited to the parties to the sexual act. We will explore this more fully in Chapter 11, which is concerned with sexual offenses.

In relation to *equality*, we note that the term "equality" in moral and political philosophy serves to identify certain classes within which it is not possible to make distinctions. In biblical law, we find that there is equality between betrothed and married women because they are classes of persons within which it is not possible to make distinctions for the purpose of applying criminal sanctions. Both are liable for punishment if they have sexual relations with a third party. Modern law structures its concerns for equality differently, for example, by seeking to minimize distinctions between married persons and unmarried cohabitants and,

---

107. D. Popenoe, *American family decline, 1960–1990: A review and appraisal*, J. MARRIAGE & FAM. 55, 527–41, 529 (1993).

108. CAROL SMART, THE TIES THAT BIND: LAW, MARRIAGE AND THE REPRODUCTION OF PATRIARCHAL RELATIONS (London: Routledge & Kegan Paul, 1984), 225, italics original.

109. MORGAN, CONSEQUENCES, p. 44.

latterly, between opposite-sex cohabitants and same-sex cohabitants through the use of registered domestic partnerships.

We have also seen that *protection* is relevant to the structure of marriage and divorce in biblical law, particularly in relation to women, who are protected by various means (including betrothal, the financial provision of a dowry, and limiting the capricious behavior of would-be husbands). Modern law structures its concerns for protection differently, for example, by making it easier for women to leave abusive marriages. However, it is often difficult to compensate women for the financial disadvantage and need which they typically experience upon divorce.[110]

Fourth, there is a shared preoccupation with heterosexual ideology although again, this is worked out rather differently. Biblical law is heteronormative, and this is reflected in its response to homosexual behavior (see Chapter 11). Modern law, in fact, reflects similar concerns even while it seeks to deconstruct heteronormativity. It is perhaps ironic that the focus on marriage and the desire for a "parallel universe" of same-sex civil partnerships indirectly affirms the primacy of heterosexual marriage. For this reason, some scholars have questioned "the centrality of the quest for marriage rights by lesbians and gay men."[111]

Fifth, both biblical and modern law recognize, in different ways, the fallacy of privatizing family law. Marriage, divorce, and remarriage had a very clear public aspect in biblical law. Sexual relations with the wrong family could lead to a local war, and marrying foreign women was not in the national interest. In a related way, modern scholarship in family law has "challenged notions that the family was—or could be—an unregulated private sphere."[112] Although there remains a popular sense that the State should stay outside the family, "the history of legal regulation of family relations challenges any rigid notion of the public/private divide emanating from liberalism."[113]

Finally, both biblical and modern societies recognize that there is a corporate dimension to marriage, divorce, and remarriage. We noted that in Genesis 34, it is not only Dinah who is debased by her encounter; it also affects her father, her brothers, and her entire community. This is because marriage and sexual relations forge legal relationships between persons and their families and create new political and economic alliances. Likewise in modern societies, it must equally be the case that radical changes to the laws of marriage, divorce, and remarriage of the sort that we have seen in recent decades also have profound social consequences,[114] although the full effects of this monumental social experiment have yet to be seen.

---

110. Boyd, *Legal regulation*, p. 259.
111. Ibid., 260.
112. Ibid., 256.
113. Ibid.
114. Summarized in KIRBY, BROKEN HEARTS.

VIII. CONCLUSION

Understanding the biblical laws of marriage and divorce means drawing on a wide range of legal materials. This includes evidence of local custom, shared ancient Near Eastern conventions, formal rules, and rabbinic traditions. There is a great deal of complexity in the biblical legal arrangements. This is reflected in the wide range of marriages and accompanying processual features. The typical marriage followed a conventional procedure, and problems arose when this was subverted. Biblical law also regulates the practice of divorce and sets limits to its operation. It also restricts the ability of divorcées to remarry. Biblical law is aware of the importance of marriage in determining the identity of individuals and groups. Marriage is a covenant that is the subject of divine interest, yet at the same time, economic concerns are never far away. The biblical laws of marriage, divorce, and remarriage have a corporate dimension and thus have a clear public aspect. They are not purely "private" matters. Biblical law shows concern for issues of consent, equality, protection, gender, and heterosexual ideology, although these are expressed differently from similar interests in modern law. The present protracted struggles over family relations, gender relations, and heteronormative definitions of marriage are just some of the ways in which modern family law conflicts with biblical law, while at the same time attesting—indirectly—to its continuing importance.

Selected reading

Jonathan P. Burnside, *The Signs of Sin: Seriousness of Offence in Biblical Law*, Journal for the Study of the Old Testament Supplement Series 364 (London: Continuum International, 2003), Chapter 3.

Allen Guenther, "A typology of Israelite marriage: Kinship, socio-economic, and religious factors," *Journal for the Study of the Old Testament* 29 (2005), 387–407.

David Instone-Brewer, "Deuteronomy 24:1–4 and the origins of the Jewish divorce certificate," *Journal of Jewish Studies* 49 (1998), 230–243.

Bernard S. Jackson, *Wisdom-Laws: A Study of the* Mishpatim *of Exodus 21:1–22:16* (Oxford: Oxford University Press, 2006), Chapter 12.

Carol Meyers, *Discovering Eve: Ancient Israelite Women in Context* (Oxford: Oxford University Press, 1988), Chapter 6.

Ellen Van Wolde, "Does 'inna denote rape? A semantic analysis of a controversial word," *Vetus Testamentum* 52 (2005), 528–544.

11. SEXUAL OFFENSES

Israel's vocation is to be "a kingdom of priests and a holy nation" (Exodus 19:6), which means that she is committed to becoming the sort of people whose prime characteristic is a concern for right relationships. We saw in Chapter 1 that Israel's vocation to be "the people of God" is something that "comes into being as the precipitate of innumerable well-conducted relationships between individual and individual,"[1] as well as between each individual and God and the surrounding creation order. Israel's vocation is to show the nations what a relationally well-ordered society looks like. In such a society, sex has a crucial role. "Relational order," as opposed to "relational chaos" involves a concern for "sexual order," as opposed to "sexual chaos."[2] We saw in Chapter 10 that biblical law assumes certain conventions in regard to the formation of marriage, and when this sequence gets muddled up or is ignored, all kinds of problems result. For example, we saw that Tamar describes Amnon as one of "the scoundrels (*nebhalim*) in Israel" (2 Samuel 13:13) and his sexual behavior as "a vile thing (*nebhalah*)" (2 Samuel 13:12). We saw that this language reflects the biblical understanding that sexual transgressions threaten communal society. The ideas of relational chaos and sexual chaos are thus firmly rooted in the biblical texts.

This chapter brings this contrast between sexual order and sexual chaos to the fore. We begin by looking in detail at Leviticus 20, which is, as we will see, one of the most controversial texts in the whole of biblical law, from a modern standpoint. We will find that biblical law provides us with a positive understanding of well-ordered sexual relationships in the form of heterosexual marriage. This in turn shapes our understanding of departures from the norm and explains why they are prohibited. In other words, biblical law provide us with an understanding of what is good in sexual relationships, and from that flows everything else. What we would today call "sexual offenses" are labelled "deviations from the covenant of heterosexual marriage." As a result, adultery is the archetypal sexual offense in the Bible because it is the paradigm case of sexual relations outside marriage. Likewise, other forms of sexual deviancy are characterized, in biblical law, as forms of adultery. This is reflected in a number of biblical laws. In contrast to modern law, which regards consent as the sole issue in determining legitimate sexual relationships, biblical law seeks to channel sexual energy in such a way as to create community. Biblical law provides us with a different

---

1. Bernard Harrison, *The strangeness of Leviticus*, JUDAISM 48, 208–28, 218 (1999).
2. Again, as we saw in Chapter 10, "order" is here used in the sense of things occupying their proper place before God and does not primarily refer to order in a hierarchical sense.

sexual ethic, one which achieves coherence by placing relational and sexual order, rather than consent, at its core.

I. THE GOOD SEX GUIDE

We begin by exploring Leviticus 20—a founding text for this chapter because it sets out a range of sexual offenses in a schematized way. It is a controversial text to choose as a starting point because the typical reading of Leviticus 20 sees it as a "text of terror."[3] This is because Leviticus 20, among other things, makes male homosexuality a capital offense. It is after all a page from Leviticus, concerning homosexuality, which Sir Ian McKellen, star of *The Lord of the Rings*, admits to tearing from hotel Bibles on a regular basis because he finds it offensive to homosexual persons.[4] However, what Leviticus 20 is actually concerned with is setting out a positive vision of what the Bible sees as necessary to well-ordered sexual relationships in order to optimize relational order. Relational order consists of the following dimensions: (1) covenantal order, (2) species order, (3) gender order, (4) generational or "descent" order, and (5) kinship order. Leviticus 20 indicates that sexual relationships are not meant to be—and cannot be—haphazard and arbitrary. On the contrary, Leviticus 20 assumes there is a contrast between covenantal sex, expressed as the covenant of heterosexual marriage, and casual sex, which refers to every other kind of sexual relationship, since these do not express heterosexual marital commitment. Relational order, covenantal sex, and sexual faithfulness are seen as the answer to the question of how to channel sexual energy in a way that creates community. Leviticus 20 is thus a detailed study of the place of sexual relations in relational order. It also depicts the relational consequences of sexual chaos. Leviticus 20 shows that the shockwaves spread out and impact on the following relationships: (1) the betrayed husband or wife, (2) the cohesion of the community, (3) the future of the nation, and (4) the relationship between the people and God, all of which are interconnected.

Leviticus 20 is well ordered in terms of its literary presentation; likewise, its substantive content presents a picture of relational and sexual order.[5] The form reflects the content. However, my argument is contrary to those of most

---

3. The phrase is used by Phyllis Trible, Texts of Terror: Literary Feminist Readings of Biblical Narratives (Minneapolis: Fortress Press, 1984), although Trible herself does not discuss Leviticus 20 in her book.
4. http://www.mckellan.com/epost/m021110.htm#1, accessed October 5, 2009.
5. *See further* J. P. Burnside, Rethinking "sexual" offences in biblical law: The literary structure of Leviticus 20, in Jewish Law Association Studies XVI: The Boston 2004 Conference Volume (E. Dorff ed.; Binghampton: Global Academic Publishing, 2007), 37–55.

commentators who regard Leviticus 20 as a miscellaneous collection that lacks any kind of literary presentation.[6] Lester Grabbe concedes that original authors or redactors "may have arranged the material according to a logical pattern"[7] but offers no suggestion as to what this might be. However, we are about to see that Leviticus 20 is characterized by a high degree of internal structure, even by the standards of biblical law. First, we will see that Leviticus 20 is patterned on the Decalogue, viz., the order of Leviticus 20:5–21 echoes the sequence of taboos in the Decalogue (e.g., Exodus 20:3–14). Second, we will see that the overall chapter (20:2–27) is arranged chiastically and can be broken down to three main sections (verses 3–6; 9–16; 17–21). We will also see that the first and third of these sections (verses 3–6; 17–21) are themselves arranged chiastically and that the middle section (effectively, verses 10–16) is presented as a series of binary oppositions. This all adds up to a complex presentation on the subject of what we today call sexual offenses.

II. THE DECALOGUE PATTERN IN LEVITICUS 20

The first thing to notice about the overall structure of Leviticus 20 is the way in which verses 5–21 echo the sequence of taboos in the Decalogue (e.g., Exodus 20:3–14, see Figure 5 below).

There is a "Decalogue pattern" in Leviticus 20 because the Decalogue provides "narrative typifications" of key commands and prohibitions (such as "serving other gods," "honoring father and mother," and "adultery"). These then form the basis of more detailed elaboration in Leviticus 20 (viz., "Molech worship," "cursing parents," and "adultery," as well as "forms of adultery," see further B., below). In other words, the biblical construction of what we would today call

"Serving other gods" (e.g., Exodus 20:3–5)
→ "honouring father and mother" (e.g., Exodus 20:12)
→ "adultery" (e.g., Exodus 20:14)

"Molech worship" (verses 2–5)
→ "cursing parents" (verse 9)
→ "sexual offences" (verses 10–21)

FIGURE 5. THE "DECALOGUE PATTERN" IN LEVITICUS 20

---

6. *E.g.*, W. H. BELLINGER, JR., LEVITICUS AND NUMBERS, New International Bible Commentary (Peabody MA: Hendrickson, 2001), 124; PHILIP J. BUDD, LEVITICUS, NEW CENTURY BIBLE COMMENTARY (Grand Rapids: Eerdmans, 1996), 289.

7. LESTER L. GRABBE, LEVITICUS, OLD TESTAMENT GUIDE (Sheffield: Sheffield Academic Press, 1997), 80.

sexual offenses uses well-established categories such as "idolatry," "dishonoring parents," and "adultery." It is a good example of the well-known philosophical principle: "entities should not be multiplied beyond necessity" (otherwise known as "Ockham's razor"). Biblical society did not need to create an additional category of sexual offenses because it already had the building blocks of the Decalogue to work with. Leviticus 20 thus reaffirms the centrality of the Decalogue in biblical law (see Chapter 2). There are three "Decalogue headings" in Leviticus 20: "idolatry," "cursing father or mother," and "adultery." Each determines how sexual deviancy is constructed and understood in biblical society. We will look at each category in turn.

A. Understanding sexual deviancy

The first Decalogue heading is *idolatry*. In Leviticus 20:2–5, this takes the form of worshipping the Ammonite deity Molech. Leviticus classifies Molech-worship as idolatry—it is an extended case of what we already know. The offender is portrayed as giving "his seed (*mizzaro*) to Molech" (20:4). This uses the word *zera*, which can mean semen as well as offspring. The precise nature of this activity is disputed:[8] some have claimed that the practice refers to a form of child sacrifice, in which case the law is designed to protect children from abuse. Nevertheless, although Molech-worship is not usually treated as a sexual offense in other biblical texts,[9] it is clear that either way, Molech-worship in Leviticus 20:4 involves some emission of semen. Consequently, the key elements of Leviticus 20:2–5 are: (1) the presence of a foreign god and (2) sexual activity. For this reason, it cannot simply be characterized either as a sexual offense or as an offense against Israel's religion. It is both. This gives an added point to, and may receive support from, the prophetic marriage metaphor according to which Israel's rebellion against God is characterized as adultery (Hosea 3:1). The punishment for the Molech-worshipper is to be stoned *and* "cut . . . off from among his people" (Leviticus 20:3, and the same applies to the medium or wizard; Leviticus 20:6, 27). This "double whammy"—punishment by human beings *and* God (see Table 14 at III., below)—indicates that these offenses are seen as the most serious offenses in Leviticus 20.

The second Decalogue heading in Leviticus 20 is *cursing father or mother* (verse 9). This is the negative image of the Decalogue commandment, "Honour your father and your mother . . ." (Exodus 20:12). The verb for cursing takes the *piel* form ("to be slight . . . trifling . . . [and of] little account"). This is one of the key terms for cursing, which appears in Exodus 22:28/MT 22:27 ("You shall not revile God, nor

---

8. John Day, Molech: A God of Human Sacrifice in the Old Testament, University of Cambridge Oriental Publications (Cambridge: Cambridge University Press, 1990).

9. James E. Miller, *Notes on Leviticus 18*, Zeitschrift für die Alttestamentliche Wissenschaft 112, 401–03 (2000).

curse a ruler of your people . . .") and later in Leviticus itself (Leviticus 24:11, 14, 15, and 23). Darrell Bock's overview of the use of this and related terms concludes that cursing is understood broadly to include actions as well as words that indicate a lack of respect;[10] hence Jacob Milgrom[11] cites with approval the rendering by *Targum Neofiti* "holds cheap the honour." The underlying idea in Leviticus 20:9–21 is the offender's rejection of the authority of father and mother. "Dishonouring parents" is thus the heading for the sexual misdemeanors that follow (verses 10–21). The man, or rather, the son, who does any of the things listed in 20:10–21 "curses" or "holds lightly" the ones who brought him to life. This indicates that, in biblical law, sexual offenses are partly defined in terms of how they impact the offender's family.

This structural connection between cursing parents and sexual deviance seems unusual from a modern point of view. However, it is not surprising given what we know about the formation of Israelite marriage in Chapter 10. We saw that one of the features of the normal sequence of marriage is obtaining the consent of the father of the bride. This shows respect for parents. We also saw in Chapter 10 that biblical law views departures from this sequence as problematic. If respect for parents is part of the *normal* sequence of heterosexual marriage, and if sexual deviancy is understood as a departure from what is normative, then it follows that the biblical characterization of adultery, and other sexual relationships opposed to marriage, will include the idea of disrespecting or cursing parents. Even in the modern world, family and respect for parents can function as legal "building blocks." "Family" and "respect for parents" are key components of the African Charter on Human and Peoples Rights, Article 29 of which states: "The individual shall . . . have the duty . . . to preserve the harmonious development of the family and to work for the cohesion and respect of the family [and] to respect his parents at all times . . . ."

The structural link between verse 9 (cursing parents) and verses 10–21 (sexual offenses) may also reflect the reality that, in practical terms, parents are deeply affected by the sexual misbehavior of their children (including adultery) because they are the ones who, in most cases, have to deal with the emotional, organizational, and possibly lineage implications. Adultery and sexual wrongdoing affects parents because managing the fallout of sexual wrongdoing makes demands on time and resources across the whole nexus of family relationships. If adultery takes place in a marriage, and this leads to a divorce, this will have knock-on effects on parents and siblings who may have the increased burden of looking after dependent family members. For example, Amnon's sexual wrongdoing in relation to Tamar causes David great emotional grief and simultaneously places

---

10. DARRELL L. BOCK, BLASPHEMY AND EXALTATION IN JUDAISM: THE CHARGE AGAINST JESUS IN MARK 14:53–65 (Grand Rapids: Baker Books, 2000), 42.
11. JACOB MILGROM, LEVITICUS 17–22, Anchor Bible Commentary (New York: Doubleday, 2000), 1745.

additional welfare responsibilities upon Amnon's half-brother Absalom (2 Samuel 13:20–21).

Sexual deviancy on the part of children may also have generational consequences for parents (such as whether or not they have access to their grandchildren and whether or not the family line continues). Should we find the connection between Leviticus 20:9 and verses 10–21 surprising, it may be because we do not sufficiently value descent relationships (e.g., relationships between parents and children, grandparents, and grandchildren). As Dench and Brown write, "In order to uphold marriage, it is essential to recognise and promote descent [relationships] . . . It is descent which epitomises the enduring shared interests which family life expresses."[12] Descent relationships are one of the reasons why marriage is important; therefore, it follows that they are an important aspect of the seriousness of adultery.

B. Forms of adultery

The third Decalogue heading in Leviticus 20 is *adultery* (verse 10). This is the only prohibited sexual relationship mentioned in the Decalogue. In view of the Decalogue pattern in Leviticus 20, it is not surprising that adultery is the first sexual relationship to be prohibited in this text. It is used as an overall heading for all the sexual offenses listed in verses 10–21. This is because adultery is the paradigm case of consensual relations outside marriage. The emphatic place of adultery within the structure of Leviticus 20 is seen in verse 10, where the Hebrew repeats the verb for adultery (*na'ap*):

> Now [as for] a man who commits adultery *(yinaph)* with a man's wife,
> who commits adultery *(yinaph)* with his neighbour's wife,
> both the adulterer *(hanno'eph)* and the adulteress *(hanno'ephet)* shall be put to death. (*God speaking*; own translation)

The repetition of the verb, as shown by the literal translation and the explicit labelling of the guilty parties as adulterer and adulteress, fixes the narrative typification of adultery in the minds of hearers and readers. It makes it clear that adultery is the overall category for what follows in verses 10–21.

That said, there is an important terminological distinction between verse 10 and verses 11–21. Although the standard verb for adultery is emphasized in verse 10, it is entirely absent from rest of the sequence (20:11–21). Other verbs are used instead to signify sexual union (see Table 13, below).

Contrary to other readings of this text, I argue that verse 11 refers to sexual relations with the father's wife *after* the father has died or divorced her. This is because the verb used is *shakhabh*, which is the normal verb for sexual relations.

---

12. Geoff Dench & Belinda Brown, *Towards A New Partnership Between Family and State (The Grandmother Project)*, Institute of Community Studies Working Paper No. 7 (2004), 11.

TABLE 13 USE OF VERB FOR ADULTERY IN LEVITICUS 20:10–21

Verse	Offense	Verb	Use of verb for adultery	Classification
20:10	Relations with neighbor's wife	na'ap	Yes	Adultery
20:11	Relations with father's wife	shakhabh	No	Nonadultery (but a "form of adultery")
20:12	Relations with daughter-in-law	shakhabh	No	Nonadultery (but a "form of adultery")
20:13	Male homosexuality	shakhabh	No	Nonadultery (but a "form of adultery")
20:14	Relations with both wife and wife's mother	laqach	No	Nonadultery (but a "form of adultery")
20:15	Bestiality (man and beast)	shakhabh	No	Nonadultery (but a "form of adultery")
20:16	Bestiality (woman and beast)	shakhabh	No	Nonadultery (but a "form of adultery")
20:17	Relations with sister	laqach	No	Nonadultery (but a "form of adultery")
20:18	Relations with menstruant	shakhabh	No	Nonadultery (but a "form of adultery")
20:19	Relations with mother's sister/father's sister	'ara	No	Nonadultery (but a "form of adultery")
20:20	Relations with uncle's wife	shakhabh	No	Nonadultery (but a "form of adultery")
20:21	Relations with brother's wife	laqach	No	Nonadultery (but a "form of adultery")

Had sexual relations occurred while the father was still alive, it would be a case of adultery (*na'aph*). Verse 11 indicates that sexual relations with the father's widow is a capital offense *even when* the father is dead. This point is easily demonstrated by reference to verse 20. This concerns the man who has sexual relations (*shakhabh*, again) with his uncle's wife. Verse 20 follows the same formal pattern as verse 11 ("lies with" + "uncovering the nakedness" + penalty). This indicates that verse 11 should be read in the same way as verse 20, which cannot be a case of adultery because the penalty in that verse is noncapital for the guilty parties ("they shall die childless"). It makes no sense to claim that relations with the wife of your (living) neighbor is capital (20:10) but that relations with the wife of your (living) uncle is noncapital. Therefore, Lev. 20:20 must refer to sexual relations that take place after the uncle is dead or has divorced his wife. Verse 20 indicates that *even if* your uncle is dead or divorced, you must not engage in sexual relations with his widow or divorcée, and there are divine penalties for doing so. It is not a case of adultery because the woman is no longer married, but it is a *form* of adultery. In the same way, verse 21 envisages the brother who has sexual relations with his brother's wife *after* his death or divorce. Again, if he was still alive and married, the offense would have to be treated at least as seriously as adultery. (An exception to this is found in Deuteronomy 25:5–10).[13]

Why are sexual relations with the father's wife a capital offense even if the father is dead or divorced? There may be a clue in the reference to the "father's wife" (*'eshet'abiw*) instead of the "mother" (*'em*). In biblical Israel, "father's wife" need not refer to the offender's mother because polygamy was tolerated, and women (perhaps frequently) died in childbirth. Leviticus 18 explicitly distinguishes between sexual relations with the mother (18:7) and sexual relations with the father's wife (18:8). Given the many thematic associations between Leviticus 18 and 20 (see further, below), it is likely that the same distinction is intended in 20:11, which would exclude the mother. The paradigm case of 20:11 thus appears to be another wife in a polygamous marriage or a concubine. With this is mind, Leviticus 20:11 immediately evokes narratives of upstart sons who have sexual relations with their father's sexual partners (e.g., Reuben's intercourse with Jacob's concubine Bilhah; Genesis 35:22; 49:4 and Absalom's public intercourse with David's concubines; 2 Samuel 16:21–22). Underlying both of these stories is the son's desire to usurp the father's position. Leviticus 20:11 thus provides some protection for women against this sort of power play.

Consequently, I would argue that verses 11–21 are not to be classified as adultery as such (see Table 13 above). This is because they do not conform to the paradigm case of adultery. They are, instead, further negations of what Leviticus 20 regards as a normal sexual relationship. However, although they are not cases of adultery, they fall under the subheading of it. They are thus forms of adultery. They are extended cases of what we already know, namely, the Decalogue prohibition against adultery. We have already seen this elsewhere in biblical law. The laws of Deuteronomy 22:28–29 (intercourse with an unbetrothed woman) can be seen as a variation upon the law of adultery in Deuteronomy 22:22 (intercourse with a married or betrothed woman).[14]

---

13. *See* JONATHAN P. BURNSIDE, THE SIGNS OF SIN: SERIOUSNESS OF OFFENCE IN BIBLICAL LAW, JOURNAL FOR THE STUDY OF THE OLD TESTAMENT SUPPLEMENT SERIES 364 (London: Continuum International, 2003), 79–120.

14. *Cf.* H. C. Washington, *"Lest he die in the battle and another man take her": Violence and the construction of gender in the laws of Deuteronomy 20–22*, in GENDER AND LAW IN THE HEBREW BIBLE AND THE ANCIENT NEAR EAST (V. H. Matthews et al., eds.; Journal for the

A more extended version of this classificatory approach can be found in the New Testament. Jesus classifies "looking at a woman lustfully" as "adultery of the heart" and thus as a further "form of adultery."

> You have heard that it was said, "You shall not commit adultery." But I say to you that every one who looks at a woman lustfully has already committed adultery with her in his heart. (Matthew 5:27–28; *Jesus speaking*)

There is thus no need to create another category such as "sexual fantasy": the general prohibition against adultery is enough. There is also evidence in the New Testament of how adultery can be followed by a form of adultery in a list of wrongs:

> For out of the heart come evil thoughts, murder, *adultery, fornication*, theft, false witness, slander. (Matthew 15:19; *Jesus speaking*)

Adultery is followed by fornication, which is implicitly classified as a form of adultery within an overall Decalogue pattern. If this reasoning is correct, then Leviticus 20:10–21 can be seen as a more detailed elaboration of the Decalogue prohibition against adultery.

To sum up, understanding sexual deviancy in the Bible means taking seriously the major classificatory headings in Leviticus 20. These are "idolatry," "dishonouring parents," and "adultery." In terms of the aetiology of sexual deviancy, then, biblical law sees the primary issue as being one of idolatry, which raises the question of the offender's relationship with God. The secondary issue is dishonoring parents, which raises the question of the offender's relationship with his father and mother. Leviticus 20 thus establishes an order of priorities regarding the offender's relationship to divine and parental authority. Sexual deviancy in Leviticus 20 is thus presented as raising two key questions: first, what does this or that behavior suggest about the offender's relationship with God and, second, what does it suggest about the offender's relationship with his or her parents? Leviticus 20 suggests that sexual deviancy in biblical law is an expression of spiritual and familial dysfunction. Consequently, there are limits to sexual expression. Leviticus 20 thus contrasts with the modern tendency to affirm sexual minorities in the name of "cultural liberty," which is defined by the United Nations Development Program as "the capability of people to live as they would like and to have the opportunity to choose from the options they have—or can have."[15]

Study of the Old Testament Supplement Series 262; Sheffield: Sheffield Academic Press, 1998), 185–213, 208.

15. United Nations Development Programme, Human Development Report 2004: Cultural liberty in today's diverse world (New York: United Nations Development Programme, 2004), 13.

III. WHO PUNISHES WHOM?

The second main thing to note about the overall structure of Leviticus 20 is that the chapter (20:2–27) is arranged chiastically and can be broken down into three main sections (verses 3–6; 9–16; 17–21).[16] This is another important aspect of the orderliness of Leviticus 20. It is another way in which the chapter sets out a positive vision of well-ordered sexual relationships. Aside from the Decalogue pattern in Leviticus 20, I argue that the key to unlocking the internal structure—and hence the meaning of Leviticus 20—is to realize that Leviticus 20 mirrors Leviticus 18 to a large extent. This is not in itself an original observation: it is obvious even to the most casual reader that Chapters 18 and 20 have as their theme "sexual offenses and other customs in neighboring nations" and that many of the paradigm cases are the same (e.g., 18:8–20:11; 18:9–20:17; 18:15–20:12; 18:17a–20:14; 18:19–20:18; 18:20–20:10). It is also widely recognized that whereas Leviticus 20 states the penalties for each prohibited sexual act, Leviticus 18 does not. What has not been noticed, to the best of my knowledge, is the possibility that the penalties of Leviticus 20 hold the key to the entire structure. This can be seen in Table 14, below. It summarizes the different offenses in Leviticus 20 and identifies who is responsible for meting out the particular punishment.

It is clear from Table 14, then, that Leviticus 20 has a complex internal structure based on who has responsibility for punishing the offender. This is arranged chiastically, as shown in Fig. 6, below.

A		Humanity	(verse 2)
B		God	(verses 3–6)
	C [centre]	Humanity	(verses 9–16)
B'		God	(verses 17–21)
A'		Humanity	(verse 27)

FIGURE 6. THE OVERALL CHIASTIC STRUCTURE OF LEVITICUS 20

According to verse 2, *humanity* is responsible for meting out punishment ("... [the offender] *shall be put to death*; the people of the land shall stone him with stones). This contrasts with verses 3–6, where *God* is responsible ("I myself will *set my face against* that man, and will *cut him off from among his people* ..."). Short versions of these phrases ("shall be put to death") and ("set My face against" and "cutting off from among their people") recur throughout the chapter. They signify punishment either by humanity or punishment by God. This means that humanity is also responsible for "putting to death" in verses 9–13 and 15–16. Verse 14 refers to a burning, rather than to a simple stoning, and hence is phrased differently ("they shall be burned with fire"); however, the implication is

---

16. *See further* Jonathan P. Burnside, *Strange Flesh: Sex, semiotics and the construction of deviancy in biblical law,* J. STUD. OLD TESTAMENT 30, 387–420 (2006).

TABLE 14 RESPONSIBILITY FOR PUNISHING HUMAN BEINGS IN LEVITICUS 20

Verse	Offense	Description of punishment	Punisher
20:2	Molech-worship	"*shall be put to death*; the people of the land shall pelt him with stones"	Humanity
20:3	Molech-worship	"I myself will *set my face against* that man and will *cut him off from among his people*"	God
20:4–5	Turning a blind eye	"I will *set my face against* that man and against his family, and will *cut them off from among their people*, him and all who follow him"	God
20:6	Mediums and wizards	"I will *set my face against* that person and will *cut him off from among his people*"	God
20:9	Cursing parents	"*shall be put to death*"	Humanity
20:10	Adultery	"*shall be put to death*"	Humanity
20:11	Relations with father's wife	"*shall be put to death*"	Humanity
20:12	Relations with daughter-in-law	"*shall be put to death*"	Humanity
20:13	Male homosexuality	"*shall be put to death*"	Humanity
20:14	Relations with wife and mother	"*shall be burned with fire*"	Humanity
20:15	Bestiality (man)	"*shall be put to death*"	Humanity
20:16	Bestiality (woman)	"*shall be put to death*"	Humanity
20:17	Relations with sister	"shall be *cut off*"	God
20:18	Menstruant	"shall be *cut off from among their people*"	God
20:19	Relations with mother's sister/father's sister	"they shall bear their guilt" (JPS)	God
20:20	Relations with uncle's wife	"they shall bear their guilt: they shall die childless" (JPS)	God
20:21	Relations with brother's wife	"they shall remain childless" (JPS)	God
20:27	Mediums and wizards	"*shall be put to death*; they shall be stoned with stones"	Humanity

that humanity is also responsible. Likewise, the repetition of "cutting off" seems to indicate that God is responsible for punishing in verses 17–18 because *karet* ("cutting off") is a characteristically divine form of punishment.[17] Other characteristically divine forms of punishment include bearing iniquity (verse 19), dying childless (verse 20), and being childless (verse 21).

What all this means is that Leviticus 20:2–27 can be divided into three main sections. These are verses 3–6 (section B, above), verses 9–16 (section C, above, which is the center of the chiasm), and verses 17–21 (section B', above). This is a breakthrough in understanding both the structure and the content of this passage because when we look at each of these sections individually, we find that each section, in turn, has its own internal literary structure. If we look at verses 3–6 (section B, above) we find that it has a chiastic structure. We also find that verses 17–21 (section B', above) have a chiastic structure, while verses 10–16 (section C) is a series of binary oppositions (see further, below). These three sections are set within a surrounding frame (verses 2 and 27), which we can lay aside for the time being. They are also connected by several hortatory passages (20:7–8; 22–26) that connect sections B and B' to the Decalogue.

We will look at each section in turn, starting with section B (verses 3–6). We will deal with sections B and B' rather briefly and spend most of our time on section C. This is because section C is the center of the chiasm and is thus the most complex and important.

IV. SEX, HARM, AND SOCIETY

Starting with section B, we noted in Table 14 above, that Leviticus 20:3–6 is a single unit because God is responsible for punishing this group of offenses. I argue that this section has a chiastic literary structure because the object of the punishment moves from the individual offender (in verse 3) to the "offender plus *mishpachah*" (in verse 5) and back to the individual offender again (in verse 6; see Figure 7, below).

The word *mishpachah* (here translated "kin") is usually thought to refer to a "suprahousehold social unit" or "protective association of families" and is "generally understood to be coterminous with the inhabitants of a village."[18] This means that the pivot of the chiasm is the punishment of "the man *and* his group of nuclear households" (*mishpachah*). Special emphasis is placed on the fact that the man's behavior has serious consequences not only for him but also for his *mishpachah* ("... I will set my face against that man *and against his family*").

---

17. Jacob Milgrom, Numbers (Philadelphia: The Jewish Publication Society, 1990), 405–08.
18. Carol Myers, *The family in early Israel*, in Families in Ancient Israel, (Leo G. Perdue et al, eds.; Westminster: John Knox Press, 1997), 1–47, 37.

D		Punishment of offender *alone*	"I myself will set my face against *that man*, and will cut *him* off from among his people . . ." (20:3; *God speaking*)
E [centre]		Punishment of offender *and his mishpachah* (i.e., group of families)	". . . I will set my face against *that man and against his family* (*mishpachah*), and will cut them off from among their people, him and all who follow him . . ." (20:5; *God speaking*)
D'		Punishment of offender *alone*	". . . I will set my face against *that person [lit. soul]*, and will cut *him* off from among his people." (20:6; *God speaking*)

FIGURE 7. THE CHIASTIC STRUCTURE OF LEVITICUS 20:3–6

This observation is not unique to the structure of Leviticus 20. We saw above, in relation to the second Decalogue heading of "cursing father and mother," that biblical law defines sexual offenses partly in terms of how they impact the offender's family.

The negative social impact of sexual wrongdoing is a recurring theme in the biblical materials. According to Genesis 26:6–11, it is even recognized by non-Israelites. Here, Isaac passes off his wife as his sister with the result that the Philistines, under the leadership of Abimelech, nearly end up committing inadvertent adultery. Abimelech complains to Isaac:

> . . . What have you done to us! *One* of the people might have lain with your wife, and you would have brought guilt upon *us*. (Genesis 26:10)

Abimelech suggests that divine punishment might be visited not merely upon the adulterer himself but upon the whole society. Other biblical texts, such as Leviticus 18:24–30, present sexual wrongdoing as an act that defiles a whole group, not just the parties to the sexual act. It pollutes both people and land and attracts divine wrath upon the whole area where the sexual acts took place.[19] As far as the biblical materials are concerned, private acts have public consequences. Again, biblical law applies this concept of harm not only to Israel but also to "the nation" as a whole (Leviticus 20:23). It is because "the nation which I am casting out before you" has committed deviant sexual acts that it is said to be subject to God's judgment and ejected from the promised land. Consequently, Leviticus 20 does not present a purely ritual understanding of the harm that results from certain forms of sexual behavior. Nor is this understanding limited to the internal cult of Israel. Instead, it is presented as a universal understanding of harm that applies to all.

---

19. Raymond Westbrook, *Adultery in Ancient Near Eastern Law*, REVUE BIBLIQUE 97, 542–80, 568 (1990).

A. All in the family?

We turn from the literary structure of verses 3–6 (section B) to that of verses 17–21 (section B' in Figure 6, above). Verses 17–21 consist of six cases, all of which refer to "uncovering nakedness,"' viz., sexual intercourse. Sections B and B' are parallel units because in both sections, God is responsible for meting out punishments for these offenses (see Table 14, above). Section B' is also similar to section B because it too has a chiastic structure. This chiasm moves from "taking" and "lying" in the first two cases (verses 17–18) to a pair of cases that contain no reference to either "taking' or "lying" (verse 19) and then to two final cases that refer to lying and taking (verses 20–21; see Figure 8, below).

F		[♂ and ♀]	♂ said to uncover nakedness of ♀	*takes*	(v. 17)
G		[♂ and ♀]	♂ said to uncover nakedness of ♀	*lies*	(v. 18)
	H [centre]	[♂ and ♀]	♂ said to uncover nakedness of ♀	*(neither takes nor lies)*	(v. 19)
		[♂ and ♀]	♂ said to uncover nakedness of ♀	*(neither takes nor lies)*	(v. 19)
G'		[♂ and ♀]	♂ said to uncover nakedness of ♂	*lies*	(v. 20)
F'		[♂ and ♀]	♂ said to uncover nakedness of ♂	*takes*	(v. 21)

FIGURE 8. THE CHIASTIC STRUCTURE OF LEVITICUS 20:17–21

According to this, the center of the chiasm is 20:19. This concerns two cases: the mother's sister and the father's sister. Although the English language does not discriminate between these identities, subsuming both under the term "aunt", many cultures do distinguish between the two, including biblical Israel.[20] These cases receive special emphasis because they are "hard cases." They are also the only cases in verses 19–21—and the entire chapter—not to have a designated punishment. This is explained by the motive clause in verse 19: "for that is to make naked one's near kin." The reference to "near kin" indicates that they are hard cases because they are right on the boundary of what constitutes near kin or family in early Israel, as far as sexual ethics is concerned. Family units must have a boundary, and there must come a point when that boundary is reached. The cases in Leviticus 20:19 are therefore at the limit of what is classified as wrongdoing. This means that it is hard to find the right punishment, and so none is given. Even so, the behavior is not recommended ("they shall bear their iniquity"). As in verses 3–6, above, (where the offender's behavior was said to impact his *mishpachah*), ideas about the family help to structure the biblical understanding of sexual offenses.

---

20. *See* Madeline McClenney-Sadler, *A synopsis of key findings*, in *Re-covering the daughter's nakedness: A formal analysis of Israelite kinship terminology and the internal logic of Leviticus 18*, paper presented to Society of Biblical Literature Annual Meeting (2002), http://www.law2.byu.edu/Biblical_Law/papers/missingdaughter.pdf, accessed April 22, 2005.

V. FROM FOREPLAY TO HORSEPLAY

Having dealt briefly with the literary structure of sections B (verses 3–6) and B' (verses 17–21), we now turn to that of section C (verses 9–16). Verses 9–16 are the center of the chapter as a whole (see Figure 6, above), and so we would expect it to be the most complex and interesting section. As a result, it requires much closer analysis. My argument is that the sexual offenses in verses 10–21 are developed through a series of paired "binary oppositions." Each pair of oppositions is placed in an orderly fashion at a relative distance from the paradigm of normal sexual relations. This is another important way in which Leviticus 20 presents us with a picture of relational and sexual order. Leviticus 20:10–21 is also structured around binary oppositions relating to punishment. These indicate that the most serious offense in the sequence is the man who has relations with both a woman and her mother (Leviticus 20:14).

Turning to section C as a whole, we have already seen that verses 10–16 cannot be regarded as a self-contained group of sexual offenses. We have already seen that verse 9 (which prohibits cursing father and mother) is part of the Decalogue pattern in Leviticus 20 and forms the heading for verses 10–21 (contra Noth[21] who claims that verse 9 "does not fit on to what follows"). This is confirmed by the fact that, in purely drafting terms, 20:10–21 is a continuation of 20:9. Verse 9 begins with *ki-ish'ish'asher* ("If anyone"; JPS), and each of the verses in 10–21 follow with either *weish'asher* ("If a man"; JPS) or *weishshah'asher* ("If a woman"; JPS). The sole exception is verse 19, which is singled out as a "hard case," as we have already seen (see Figure 8, above). It is thus impossible to formally exclude verse 9 from an understanding of verses 10–21 because it is the first verse in a series. The fact that verse 9 is the heading for verses 10–21, determines how we read the sexual taboos themselves.

The key question now is: how are the sexual offenses in verses 10–21 organized, and what is the relationship between adultery in verse 10 and the various forms of it in verses 11–21? The answer is that they are developed through an extended series of binary oppositions. A binary opposition is "a pair of terms conventionally regarded as opposites" (e.g., hot/cold; on/off).[22] Binary oppositions are frequently used as a means of structuring biblical thought. They are also frequently used in biblical law.[23] By structuring thought through related oppositions, binary oppositions allow us to establish categories, construct sense, and create order.

My argument is that there are two sets of binary oppositions in Leviticus 20:10–16: the first set concerns the identity of the sexual parties (see Table 15, below), and

---

21. MARTIN NOTH, LEVITICUS (Norwich: SCM Press, 1977), 149.
22. BERNARD S. JACKSON, MAKING SENSE IN LAW: LINGUISTIC, PSYCHOLOGICAL AND SEMIOTIC PERSPECTIVES (Liverpool: Deborah Charles Publications, 1995), 510.
23. *E.g.*, BURNSIDE, SIGNS OF SIN, pp. 222–23; JACKSON, WISDOM-LAWS, p. 270.

the second set concerns the punishments that are given (see Table 16, below). First, we consider the set of binary oppositions that relate to the identity of the sexual parties (see Table 15, below). There are a total of six in all, and each column presents a different pair of oppositions.[24]

The biblical paradigm of normal sexual relations is that of marriage between a man and a woman (assuming they are not prohibited to each other for any reason). Adultery—which is the general heading for this section (verse 10)—is the archetypal sexual offense in the Bible because it is the paradigm case of sexual relations outside marriage. Each pair of oppositions in this sequence (verses 10–16) is placed, in order, at relative distance from the paradigm of normal sexual relations. Each represents a further deviation from the norm of

TABLE 15 BINARY OPPOSITIONS REGARDING IDENTITY OF SEXUAL PARTNER(S) IN LEVITICUS 20:10–16[24]

Verse	Verse content	#1	#2	#3	#4	#5	#6
20:10	"If a man *commits adultery* with another man's wife, if he commits adultery with his neighbour's wife. . ."	Outside family (Non-kin)	—	♂♀	No Marriage	♂♀	♂ initiates
20:11	"The man who *lies* with his *father's* wife. . ."	Inside family (Kin)	Father	♂♀	No Marriage	♂♀	♂ initiates
20:12	"If a man *lies* with his *daughter-in-law*. . ."		Son	♂♀	No Marriage	♂♀	♂ initiates
20:13	"If a man *lies* with a *male* as with a woman. . ."			♂♂	No Marriage	♂♀	♂ initiates
20:14	"If a man *takes* a *wife* and her mother also. . ."				Marriage	♂♀	♂ initiates
20:15	"If a man *lies* with a *beast*. . ."					♂	♂ initiates
20:16	"If a woman *approaches* any *beast* and lies with it. . ."						♀ initiates

---

24. Burnside, *Strange Flesh*, p. 414.

heterosexual marriage. Leviticus 20:10–16 is thus a sophisticated play on a series of binary oppositions, as follows:

(1) Outside family/inside family
(2) Father/son
(3) Heterosexual intercourse/homosexual intercourse
(4) Nonmarriage/marriage
(5) Sex between human beings/sex between human beings and animals (bestiality)
(6) Man initiates/woman initiates

We can unpack this further, as follows:

→ Leviticus 20:10 is opposed to the narrative typification of normal sexual relations because it concerns relations between one man and one woman who is already married to another man.
→ Leviticus 20:11 is further opposed to the paradigm because the woman in question is *a family member*, as opposed to the wife of a neighbor (column 1).
→ Leviticus 20:12 offers a further variation on the "same family" complication; *going "down" to the next generation* instead of "up" to the previous one (column 2).
→ Leviticus 20:13 is even further opposed to the narrative typification of normal sexual relations because it is no longer one man and one woman but *one man and another man* (column 3).
→ Leviticus 20:14 is yet further opposed to the narrative typification because it is no longer one man and one sexual partner but *one man and two sexual partners*, specifically a marriage between two partners who have the closest possible blood tie (column 4). Anthropologists note that this sexual encounter is widely abhorred. From a structural perspective, the reason for this may be, not that mother and daughter come into sexual contact with the same man but that they come into contact with each other through the same man.[25]
→ Leviticus 20:15 is still further opposed to the normal narrative typification because it concerns relations between *a man and an animal* (column 5).
→ Finally, Leviticus 20:16 is further opposed to the narrative typification of normal sexual relations because it concerns relations between a human and an animal in which *the woman takes the initiative*, and the male submits (column 6). In verse 15, the man has sexual relations with a beast. However, he is still behaving "like a man" in terms of his sexual role.

---

25. Françoise Héritier, Two Sisters and Their Mother (New York: Zone Books, 1999).

By contrast, in verse 16, the woman "approaches" the beast and behaves "like a man." Yet although she performs the role of a man, she also performs the role of a woman by being the submissive partner. She too behaves like a beast. The beast, on the other hand, behaves like a beast, but it also behaves "like a man." That is why it is the last in the series. It is the most extreme case of confusion imaginable—so much so that it is impossible to tell the woman and the beast apart.

The idea that sexual wrongdoing can be opposed to the norm of marriage is also found in the New Testament. We will see in Chapter 12, which explores marriage and divorce in the New Testament, that a feature of Jesus's teaching on marriage and divorce is his appeal to the Eden story (Matthew 19:4–6; Mark 10:5–9). A key feature of this is the lack of any alternative marital relationship for Adam and Eve. This is important from the point of view of how the New Testament thinks about marriage. The calling or the vocation of marriage is such that one *cannot* consider any alternative. As in Leviticus 20, the whole problem with adultery—and sexual wrongdoing in general—is that it takes the form of an alternative, and hence impermissible, sexual relationship to the covenant of heterosexual marriage. This is at the heart of what the Bible understands by a "sexual offense."

A. Public acts and public consequences

Finally, we turn to the second set of binary oppositions in Leviticus 20:10–16. This relates to the punishments listed in verses 10–16. All of these are capital; however, there are different registers of capital punishment in biblical law, including burning, stoning, or being shot with an arrow (Exodus 19:13).[26] This raises the question as to why these sexual offenses are punished so severely.

We should probably start by recognizing that, as a matter of evidence, capital offenses in biblical law required the existence of "two or more [lit. 'three'] witnesses" (Deuteronomy 17:6; JPS). Given the essentially private nature of sexual activity, this provision cuts down the practical operation of the death penalty for sexual offenses. In addition, we saw in Chapter 8 that although the formulation "... [so-and-so] shall be put to death" (*mot yumat*) might sound mandatory to our ears, biblical law does not have any clear or regular way of distinguishing between different modalities, such as "may," "must," and "it would be a good idea." The idea that the death penalty for adultery may not, in practice, always be mandatory is reflected in other biblical texts, such as Proverbs 6:32–35 which speaks of the vengeful husband refusing ransom from the adulterer for the adultery. This is a case of the exception proving the rule because it implies that it was possible, at least in some cases, for the sexual offender to commute the death penalty to a monetary payment.

---

26. *See further* BURNSIDE, SIGNS OF SIN, p. 23.

Nevertheless, it remains the case that biblical law sees the death penalty as a potentially suitable response for some sexual relationships, at least in those cases where there was sufficient evidence and where the offended party wished to prosecute. The seriousness of adultery and forms of it reflects the importance of marital faithfulness in biblical thought. As we saw in Chapter 10, marriage is explicitly called a covenant (*berit*) in the Hebrew Bible (e.g., Ezekiel 16:8), and the marriage covenant is the subject of divine interest (e.g., Malachi 2:14; Proverbs 2:16–17). It is also a picture of the relationship between God and Israel (Hosea 1–3). Against this background, sexual relationships that are opposed to marriage are viewed very seriously. The fact that we do not regard these offenses as serious is probably because we do not see relationships as significant nor adultery as one of the worst breaches of trust and relational devotion. We are so committed to living in what Dale Kuehne calls the "iWorld" of postmodern individualism that we are insensitive to the relational concerns of the "rWorld," which is based on the belief that "humans are made for relationships and that we find our deepest fulfillment not when seeking self-fulfillment but when living and engaging in the full constellation of healthy human relationships."[27]

There are two main oppositions in verses 10–16 (see Table 16, below). First, there is an opposition in the form of the punishment, between "stoning" and

TABLE 16 BINARY OPPOSITIONS REGARDING PUNISHMENT IN LEVITICUS 20

Verse	Verse content	Form of punishment	Execution formula
20:10	"... the adulterer and the adulteress shall be put to death"	Stoning	Human offender "put to death"
20:11	"... both of them shall be put to death"	Stoning	Human offender "put to death"
20:12	"... both of them shall be put to death. . ."	Stoning	Human offender "put to death"
20:13	"... they shall be put to death. . ."	Stoning	Human offender "put to death"
20:14	"... they shall be burned with fire, both he and they. . ."	Burning	Human offender "put to death"
20:15	". . .he shall be put to death. . ."	Stoning	Human offender "put to death"
20:16	". . .you shall kill the woman. . ."	Stoning	Human offender "killed"

---

27. Dale Kuehne, Sex and the iWorld: rethinking relationship beyond an age of individualism (Grand Rapids: Baker Academic Press, 2009), 95.

"burning." Second, there is an opposition in the execution formula between human offenders who are said to be "put to death" and those who are said to be "killed."

The first opposition is between stoning and burning. With the exception of 20:14, all the capital cases in Leviticus 20 are dealt with by stoning. The key question is: why does Leviticus 20:14—which concerns marriage between a man and a woman and her mother—have the most serious of all the punishments in Leviticus 20:10–21? This is explained by the *only* motive clause in the whole of Leviticus 20:10–21: "that there be no depravity among you (plural)" (JPS). Elsewhere in biblical law, burning is purgative (e.g., Leviticus 21:9). Somehow the community is tainted by the offense, unlike the rest of 20:10–16, and needs to be purged. The reason why the community is tainted is because this is the only case in verses 10–16 that involves marriage—and marriage is a public event. The offenders are walking around as a marital threesome. The community is complicit by allowing the marriage. Community complicity means community purging.

We note in passing that Leviticus 20:14 is a particularly interesting case from the point of view of the structure of sexual offenses. It is a case of "perverse polygamy." In other words, it is a normal marriage between a man and a woman with a secondary marriage grafted on that violates blood ties. We have already noted how sexual prohibitions in biblical law helped to define the family (see Tables 13 and 15, above). Here we see that the prohibitions also help to define marriage. According to Leviticus 20:14, some marriages are wrong, and certain marriages are a form of adultery. We will return to this theme in Chapter 12.

Finally, we note that there is also an opposition in the execution formula between "putting to death" and "killing" that mirrors the opposition between "men" and "beasts." The designated formula for the judicial execution of human beings is that they should be put to death, whereas the execution formula for beasts is that they should be killed. Whatever the exact reason for the difference in Hebrew thought, putting to death and killing represents a distinction between species. They are the appropriate execution formulas "according to their kind." In verse 16, *both* the woman *and* the beast are "put to death" *and* "killed." Why are both formulas applied to both parties? Surely it is sufficient if only one execution formula is applied? The use of both formulas emphasizes the seriousness of the offense. The woman who acts like a man *and* a beast is punished *both* like a man *and* like a beast. She is said to be put to death *and* killed. The beast who acts like a man is punished *both* like a beast *and* like a man. Accordingly, it is said to be killed *and* put to death. You cannot tell which is which, and so they are treated the same. This is reflected in the execution formulas.

To sum up, Leviticus 20 presents us with a positive understanding of relational order that consists of the following dimensions. It presents a picture of right relationships between (1) God and humanity (covenantal order), (2) humanity and animals (species order), (3) men and women (gender order), (4) parents and children (generational or "descent" order), and (5) siblings (kinship order). Leviticus 20 thereby demonstrates that sexual relationships are not meant to be—and cannot be—haphazard and arbitrary. It is thus a detailed study of the place of sexual relations in relational order. It also shows the relational consequences of sexual chaos. Leviticus 20 shows that the shockwaves spread out and impact on the following relationships: (1) the betrayed husband or wife; (2) the family unit to which the offender belongs (see Figure 5, above), (3) the future of the nation as a whole (Leviticus 20:22), and (4) the relationship between the people and God (Leviticus 20:26), all of which are interconnected.

VI. SLEEP WITH ME

Some of the key ideas in Leviticus 20 are also found in other biblical laws. In Exodus 20:14, for example, adultery is confirmed as the paradigm case of sexual relations outside marriage. In addition, a literary unit such as Deuteronomy 22:13–27 characterizes sexual offenses in terms of adultery and forms of it. We will look at these additional biblical laws before turning to consider how modern law seeks to regulate sexual offenses.

First, as we have already seen, other biblical laws present adultery as the paradigm case of sexual relations outside marriage. The classic expression of the prohibition of adultery is, of course, found in the Decalogue:

> You shall not commit adultery. (Exodus 20:14; *God speaking*)

In biblical law, as elsewhere in the ancient Near East (ANE), adultery is understood as consensual sexual intercourse between a married woman and a man who is not her husband. It does not matter whether the man himself is married or unmarried:

> If a man is found lying with the wife of another man, both of them shall die, the man who lay with the woman, and the woman . . . .
> (Deuteronomy 22:22; *Moses speaking*)

Adultery is seen in androcentric terms as an infringement by a third party of the husband's marital rights over his wife.[28] It is *not* adultery if a married man has intercourse with an unbetrothed woman. This is because there is no husband whose marital interests are threatened. Nowadays, this strikes us as an unfair asymmetry between men and women: in one case, the sexual relationship is classed as "adultery" whereas in the other, it is merely "an affair." However, this may reflect the view that in biblical society, men are the protectors of women. It may also be because married men needed to be sure of the paternity of their offspring who will, after all, inherit the family property. According to this

---

28. Westbrook, *Adultery*, p. 551.

conception of adultery, the husband is wronged by two parties: his wife and her lover. Accordingly, he has redress against both if he wishes.

As already noted, it is difficult to distinguish in Hebrew between the mandatory "[he] *shall* die" and the permissive "[he] *may* die." Consequently, in Deuteronomy 22:22, it is up to the husband whether he wants to prosecute the offenders or not. Likewise, the penalty is a matter for the husband's discretion. But although the offender *may* be able to negotiate an appropriate settlement with the victim, it seems as though the adulterer could not always presume upon this. As we have seen, Proverbs 6:34–35 warns the would-be adulterer that the husband may refuse to accept *kopher* (monetary payment) in damages. It is open to the husband to choose to take vengeance upon the offender and kill him. In these circumstances, however, the husband must kill his wife as well (e.g., Deuteronomy 22:22, above, where the adulterer's death is conditional upon the death of the adulteress). Examples of other possible penalties against the wife may be found in Jeremiah 3:8 (divorce) and Ezekiel 16:39 (a public shaming ritual).

Raymond Westbrook claims that the biblical laws are structured in this way to avoid the danger that the husband acquiesces in his wife's behavior and/or that the offense is procured by entrapment. "If [the adulteress] is not punished for adultery when her clients are, the corrupt couple can easily blackmail their victims on a false claim as much as on a real one."[29] However, this is not something that is anywhere envisaged in the biblical texts themselves. Indeed, the laws always imagine that both parties are guilty unless there is evidence of duress by the man, as in Deuteronomy 22:25–26.

VII. SECRETS AND LIES

There are further dimensions to adultery in biblical law. We saw in Chapter 10 that there are several stages to the formation of marriage in biblical society. One of these is the period of betrothal, which follows payment of the *mohar* (brideprice). During this stage, which lasts until consummation and legal completion of the marriage, the betrothed woman is referred to as a "wife" with the status and protection of a fully married woman. The parties could not have sexual relations with each other, and if the woman had relations with anyone else, it would be considered adultery. An unusual example of this is found in Deuteronomy 22:13–21, which is part of a wider literary unit concerned with "sexual offenses" (Deuteronomy 22:13–29; see Table 17, below).

In Deuteronomy 22:13–21, a newly wed husband brings a charge against his parents-in-law regarding his bride, claiming that she was not a *bethulah* at the time of the marriage (verse 14). The word *bethulah* is traditionally understood to

---

29. Ibid.

refer to a woman who is a virgin. Consequently, the husband's claim is understood to mean that his bride was not a virgin on their wedding night. If the parents want to rebut this charge they must produce a *simlah* (cloth) that bears evidence of the bride's *bethulim* (verse 15). This is usually understood to mean that the parents must produce evidence of their daughter's virginity, namely a perforated hymen, on the wedding night bedsheets. If the parents are not able to produce such evidence, the penalty for the bride is death (Deuteronomy 22:20–21). On this traditional reading, biblical law is said to set an extremely high value on premarital virginity.

We will see further below that a better approach is to interpret the word *bethulah*, not as meaning a "virgin" but as "a girl of marriageable age," viz., a menstruant who may or may not be a virgin. In keeping with this, the *bethulim* can be interpreted as evidence of menstruation.[30] This in turn means that the *simlah* is understood to refer to a menstrual cloth. If the parents want to rebut the husband's charge, they must produce evidence that their daughter was menstruating during the period of betrothal and could not therefore have been pregnant on the wedding night.

This is because there are a number of reasons for doubting the traditional reading of Deuteronomy 22:13–21.[31] First, the literary structure of Deuteronomy 22:13–29 suggests that the primary concern of Deuteronomy 22:13–21 is *not* whether the girl was a virgin at the time of the offense but whether or not she was betrothed (see Table 17, below).

Table 17 shows that all the cases in Deuteronomy 22:13–29 are concerned with the status of the woman, whether married, betrothed, or unbetrothed. As we have already seen, offenses against married and betrothed women amount to the same thing in biblical law, so the third column (status of woman) really boils down to an opposition between "women who are pledged to a man" (cases 1–5) and "women who are not" (case 6). Within this overall structure, virginity is simply not a salient issue.

Second, the traditional view implies that any intercourse by an unmarried woman is capital. But we have already seen in Chapter 10, there is no penalty in biblical law for the unbetrothed girl who engages in consensual relations (Exodus 22:16–17/MT 22:15–16). In this case, a man seduces an unbetrothed woman, and they have consensual relations without her father's permission. We saw in Chapter 10 that this case concerns the man who "jumps the gun" and has consensual intercourse with the woman *before* securing her father's consent and negotiating a bridal price. There is, of course, a heavy penalty *for the man* if the girl's father refuses to let her be married. The man has to pay the bride price but does not get the bride.

---

30. Gordon J. Wenham, *Betulah: A girl of marriageable age*, VETUS TESTAMENTUM 22, 326–48 (1972).
31. BURNSIDE, SIGNS OF SIN, pp. 137–155.

TABLE 17 SUMMARY OF CASES PRESENTED IN DEUTERONOMY 22:13–29

	Verse(s)	Status of woman	Punishment (if any)	Execution site
Case 1	22.13–19	Married (presumably following betrothal)	Damages (100 shekels) No divorce	N/A
Case 2 [subsidiary to 1]	22.20–21	Married (presumably following betrothal)	Woman executed	*At door of father's house*
Case 3	22.22	Married	Man and woman executed	*No location specified*
Case 4 [Relations in town]	22.23–24	Betrothed *bethulah* (consents to intercourse)	*Man and woman executed.* Man said to have "violated his neighbour's wife"	At city gate
Case 5 [Relations in open country]	22.25–27	Betrothed *bethulah* (raped)	Man executed Woman exempted	*No location specified*
Case 6	22.28–29	Unbetrothed *bethulah* (raped)	Damages (50 shekels) No divorce	N/A

Why are consensual relations capital in Deuteronomy 22:13–21 but not in Exodus 22:16–17/MT 22:15–16? This is because the *bethulah* is "betrothed" in Deuteronomy 22:20–21, whereas the *bethulah* in Exodus 22:16–17 is not betrothed. This makes it clear that the woman's offense in Deuteronomy 22:20–21 is to have had intercourse *during the period of betrothal*. This makes the offense one of adultery. The seriousness of the offense in Deuteronomy 22:20–21 thus revolves around marital status, not virginity.

Third, if the combination of the *simlah* and the *bethulim* are really evidence of virginity, it is impossible to make sense of the husband's behavior. If his claim is proven false, he will incur a severe punishment (Deuteronomy 22:18–19). Therefore, he cannot know in advance whether the parents will be able to produce the *bethulim* or not. Whatever the *bethulim* are, "the husband is prepared to gamble very heavily that the girl's parents cannot produce it."[32] And if the *simlah* are the bedsheets, no one knows better than he does whether they are stained or not! If they *are* stained, there is no point in the husband bringing an accusation. He already knows that his parents-in-law can produce the evidence (Deuteronomy 22:17).

---

32. Wenham, *Betulah*, p. 334.

Fourth, a perforated hymen on the wedding night is not a very reliable virginity test. While it is typically the case that virgins have intact hymens and bleed the first time they have sexual relations, it is not medically speaking true of all virgins. This is extremely important in the context of Deuteronomy 22:13–21 because this is the *only* case in biblical law where physical evidence is conclusive of guilt in a capital case. All other capital cases require witnesses (Deuteronomy 17:6–7). Therefore, whatever the *simlah* is, it must be a reliable form of evidence that ensures innocent parties are not executed.

As already indicated, a better approach is to interpret the word *bethulah* not as a "virgin" but as "a girl of marriageable age," viz., a menstruant who may or may not be a virgin. In keeping with this, the *bethulim* can be interpreted as evidence of menstruation.[33] Accordingly, the husband's complaint ("I did not find the *bethulim* in her"; Deuteronomy 22:13) is that his wife showed no signs of menstruation in the month following marriage. We are presumably to imagine that, upon betrothal, the woman wore distinctive clothing, which was probably provided by her husband-to-be. The fact that a woman is clothed by a man indicates that she belongs to him (cf. the description of the Babylonian *bethulah* in Isaiah 47:1–3). There is evidence in the biblical texts that a woman's social status is indicated by her clothing (e.g., 2 Samuel 13:18). It is likely that betrothed as well as married women wore special clothes since the violation of a betrothed woman (Deuteronomy 22:23–27) was treated as seriously as that of a married woman (Deuteronomy 22:22). In the case of the *bethulah* of Deuteronomy 22:13–21, it seems that her clothing had contact with the lower part of her body during the period of her betrothal and so would provide dateable evidence of menstruation.[34] When the period of betrothal is over and the daughter begins cohabiting with her husband, the *simlah* is handed over to her parents. If it contains the stains of menstruation, the parents can subsequently adduce it as datable proof that their daughter was not pregnant prior to the marriage (Deuteronomy 22:17).

This means that Deuteronomy 22:13–21 is not concerned with virginity but with paternity. In particular, it is concerned with the paternity of an unexpected pregnancy that occurs immediately after marriage. This means that the *bethulim* are not so much tokens of virginity as a nonpregnancy test. Uncertainty as to paternity is a serious matter in biblical Israel, where lineage is defined in terms of the father. The husband must be certain that his children are his own. Exactly the same concerns underlie Numbers 5:11–31 where a husband who suspects that his wife has been unfaithful can require her to undergo a divine "test."

---

33. Ibid., 331.
34. BURNSIDE, SIGNS OF SIN, pp. 150–52.

A. Pretty woman

Of course, if paternity—and not virginity—is the issue in Deuteronomy 22: 13–21, proof of menstruation at the time of marriage is just as good as proof of virginity. We have evidence for this concern elsewhere in biblical law. In Deuteronomy 21:10–14—the case of the "war captive woman"—a "beautiful woman" who is captured in war must spend "a full month" (Deuteronomy 21:13) mourning for her parents before her would-be husband can have sexual access. One might have expected a shorter mourning period of perhaps seven days (as is the case, for example, in Genesis 50:10 and 1 Samuel 31:13) or even a thirty-day mourning period (as it is in Numbers 20:29 and Deuteronomy 34:8). The reason for waiting a full month is presumably so that there is enough time for the woman to complete her menstrual cycle.[35] As with Deuteronomy 22:13–21, the purpose of the law is to ensure paternity. Significantly, there is a parallel between Deuteronomy 21:10–14 and Deuteronomy 22:13. The former has the sequence:

"taking" the woman (21:11) → "going into her" (21:13) → and "taking no delight in her" (21:14)

while the latter has the sequence:

"taking a wife" → "going into her" → and "spurning her" (22:13).

In my view, this strengthens the similarities between the two cases.[36]

There are several advantages, therefore, to reading Deuteronomy 22:13–21— the case of the slandered bride—in terms of paternity. First, it means that it does not matter whether the woman is a *virgo intacta* or not. The parents are able to produce datable evidence of menstruation because the *simlah* is identifiably the same one that the young woman wore during betrothal. When betrothal is over and the daughter begins cohabiting with her husband, the *simlah*—and any evidence of menstruation—is handed over to her parents. This explains why the husband has to take a gamble and risk punishment if he is proved wrong (Deuteronomy 22:18–19). He has no access to the evidence and does not know for certain whether his suspicions can be rebutted. The use of clothing to prove or disprove sexual contact and the gamble on whether or not the other party is able to produce it is not unknown even today. President Clinton gambled on whether Monica Lewinsky could produce the infamous "little black cocktail dress" to prove they had an intimate relationship.

How does the fact that the *bethulah* had not menstruated at some time in the past few months constitute proof that she was not pregnant at the time of the

---

35. Washington, *"Lest he die,"* p. 206.
36. BURNSIDE, SIGNS OF SIN, p. 144.

marriage? After all, it is well-known that irregular periods are the norm for the first years of menstruation, and it is also true that stress (including stress induced by a forthcoming marriage) can result in skipped periods. However, if the girl had begun to menstruate regularly and if the betrothal period was, say, several months, it would be very unusual if the girl did not have a period during that time. Moreover, if the daughter did have a tendency to skip periods, then one would expect her parents to negotiate a longer probationary period. Certainly, as a question of proof, the failure to menstruate during the period of betrothal is a fairer evidentiary test than the broken hymen demanded by the traditional approach.

Finally, if we read Deuteronomy 22:13–21 as being concerned with paternity, it also explains why the woman is executed at the front door of her father's house (Deuteronomy 22:21). This is a unique location for a capital offense in biblical law. It signifies that the father is in some way responsible for her behavior, unlike the father of the woman who has consensual relations during betrothal and who is executed at the city gate (Deuteronomy 22:23–24, above). Perhaps the father made a special pledge to the groom that his daughter would not be pregnant by another man on her wedding night. This might have been necessary if, for example, his daughter was known to have had a previous sexual history, for example, as a professional prostitute. The location of the execution—at the entrance (*petach*) to her father's house—may also signify the offense. In Genesis 38:14, when Tamar pretends to be a prostitute in order to entrap Judah, we are told that she "sat down at the entrance (*petach*) to [the place of] Enaim."

It is plausible to suggest that when the father put his daughter out to prostitution, she advertised her trade by sitting at the "entrance" (*petach*) to her father's house. This is consistent with other ANE laws and legal documents where an extraordinary site of execution reflects the nature of the offense (e.g., Laws of Hammurabi §§ 21, 25, 256; Hittite Laws §166). The location is clearly punitive because it lays the blame quite literally at the father's door. The family has an execution site for a doormat, and they are scarred and shamed every time they go in and out of that house. The implication is that the girl is having sexual relations under his roof while betrothed. This implies that it is prostitution, and that he is benefiting from it. The father is thus responsible because of his undertaking to guarantee the groom's paternity, while the woman is responsible because she is the one having consensual sex.

VIII. SEX IN THE CITY

What happens in cases of betrothal, where a man other than the groom has intercourse with a woman who is betrothed but who is not yet married? According to Deuteronomy 22:23–27, intercourse with a betrothed woman is treated as seriously as if she was married. Indeed, the offender is expressly said to have "violated another man's wife" (Deuteronomy 22:24). This means that relations with a betrothed woman is also characterized as adultery.

Significantly, the liability of the woman varies according to the location of the act: both parties are deemed guilty if it takes place in a town (verses 23–24), whereas only the man is guilty if it takes place in "the open country" (verses 25–27). This is because the woman's consent, and therefore her guilt, is determined by an objective test. (The man is of course guilty in either case because he is having relations with a betrothed woman and is thus violating the interests of the groom). If it was a case of "sex in the city," the intercourse is deemed to be consensual because it is assumed that, had she cried for help, she would have been rescued (verses 23–24). The setting is conclusive of guilt because it is densely populated. By contrast, if it is a case of "sex in the country," then the intercourse is deemed to be nonconsensual because it is assumed that even if she had protested, there is no guarantee she would have been heard (verses 25–27). Here, the setting is not conclusive of guilt.

The use of objective tests in making evidentiary presumptions relating to consent is not unknown in English law. According to section 74 of the Sexual Offences Act 2003, a person is said to consent, for the purpose of any nonconsensual sexual offense, "if he agrees by choice, and has the freedom and capacity to make that choice." This agreement may be express or implied and may be evidenced by words or conduct, past or present. In the light of this, sections 75 and 76 lay down evidential and conclusive presumptions as to the absence of consent. For example, section 75 of the Sexual Offences Act 2003 deems the victim to have withheld consent if asleep or unable to communicate consent or if the victim was subject to violence or unlawful detention. Nevertheless, there may be exceptions according to section 75(2)(d). For example, Richard Card[37] suggests that consent to sex by a sleeping partner may be implied, on the basis of previous practice, if the couple routinely engaged in "sleepy sex."

Lack of consent functions as a defense to a charge of adultery in Deuteronomy 22:25–27. Here, biblical law draws a parallel between rape and murder:

> ... this case [that is, the rape case] is like that of a man attacking and murdering his neighbour (*re'ehu*; Deuteronomy 22:26; *Moses speaking*).

This is the only example in biblical law where an explicit parallel is drawn between two different cases by means of the formula, "this case is like . . . ." However, we should not understand this verse as commenting on the effects of rape upon the victim (e.g., "when you are raped, you feel your life is over"). This is because the word translated "his neighbor" (*re'ehu*) is a masculine singular noun. The rape in Deuteronomy 22:25–26 is like murder because it involves the attack of one man upon another man. There is a parallel between the spatial

---

37. Richard Card, Sexual Offences: The New Law (Trowbridge: Jordan, 2004), 31.

movement of throwing down a man and killing him (= murder) and the social "throwing down" of the husband by debasing the betrothed woman (= rape). The analogy refers not to the consequences of the rapist's actions upon the betrothed woman but upon the groom's "social relationships with other men."[38]

This is in keeping with the argument, above, that the seriousness of adultery is tied to its impact on other male interests. As such, it reflects the cultural and social conventions of ancient Israel. Here, as Ken Stone has shown, one of the ways men relate to other men is by means of their relations with women.[39] Although Stone does not discuss Deuteronomy 22:25–26, it is in fact a prime example of his general thesis that sexual wrongdoing in biblical texts can be interrogated according to what they tell us, not primarily about relationships between men and women, but relationships between men. This in turn reflects the fact that in the biblical economy, women do not have economic independence, and so do not have political independence, either. Women live, for the most part, under the protection of men—and this means they are vulnerable to becoming pawns in political power-plays when men fail to treat women honorably (e.g., 2 Samuel 16:20–22). It is a further aspect of the presupposition pool of biblical Israel, noted in Chapter 1.

IX. CONSENT *VERSUS* COMMUNITY

To a modern sensibility, biblical law seems harsh, not just regarding homosexuality, but also adultery, incest, and bestiality. The "politics of recognition" demands formal recognition of the distinctive perspective of sexual minorities.[40] Not surprisingly, texts such as Leviticus 20, which set limits to sexual choice—backed up, even worse, by references to the death penalty—will find themselves labelled as "texts of terror." There is a tendency to assume that because the contemporary social context is in some ways hostile to biblical sexual ethics, biblical law must at best be irrelevant or, at worst, should be actively excluded from the debate. However, when we compare biblical law with recent sexual offenses reform in England and Wales, we will find that biblical law is not irrelevant. On the contrary, we will see that consent is not the only way of thinking about sexual offenses in modern society. Biblical law provides us with the idea of relational and sexual order. This means that biblical law is highly relevant to modern debates. It provides us with a complex vision of relational and sexual order that

---

38. Ellen Van Wolde, *Does 'inna denote rape? A semantic analysis of a controversial word*, VETUS TESTAMENTUM 52, 528–44, 536 (2005).
39. KEN STONE, SEX, HONOUR, AND POWER IN THE DEUTERONOMISTIC HISTORY, JOURNAL FOR THE STUDY OF THE OLD TESTAMENT SUPPLEMENT SERIES 234 (Sheffield: Sheffield Academic Press, 1996), 47.
40. UNITED NATIONS DEVELOPMENT PROGRAMME, HUMAN DEVELOPMENT, p. 29.

has, at its heart, a positive vision of well-ordered sexual relationships, something which our society struggles to articulate.

We will begin by looking at the recent overhaul of sexual offenses legislation in England and Wales. This will allow us to make explicit comparisons with biblical law. We will see that modern English law is based on a set of moral beliefs about harm, the nature of the family, consent, equality, and protection. Of these, perhaps the most prominent is the idea of consent, which can be broadly understood in terms of "free agreement." But although we have recently had major sexual offenses reform in England and Wales, there are still major problems with modern law; in particular, our excessive focus on consent as a means of structuring sexual offenses. We will also see that modern law is based on very narrow conceptions about harm, the family, consent, equality, and protection, and that this, too, is problematic. Biblical law makes a helpful contribution because it illustrates an alternative developed, integrated model that is based on relational order. This holds the modern, consent-based approach up to the light and poses questions and challenges.

A. "Promoting public good"

At the turn of the millennium, English law experienced the biggest overhaul of its sexual offenses legislation in almost 50 years. The Sexual Offences Act 2003 radically reformed the Sexual Offences Act 1956. These reforms are of wider relevance than just England and Wales because they are broadly consistent with changes that have either been introduced or mooted in other Western jurisdictions.[41] By looking at this legislation more closely, we can examine the presuppositions that underlie the construction of a modern public sexual ethic.

The Sexual Offences Act 2003 implemented most of the recommendations of the Sex Offences Review Group set up by the Home Office. The Group reported with a document titled "Setting the Boundaries," which outlined its thinking on a number of key points, including harm, family, consent, equality, and protection. These are all key building blocks in the construction of a public sexual ethic. We will explore each of these issues, in turn, from a modern and a biblical point of view and consider whether biblical law provides us with a more coherent sexual ethic.

First, we consider underlying beliefs about *the nature of harm*. The Group took as its starting point the view that "the criminal law does not condone or advocate any form of sexual behaviour, but is based on principles of preventing harm and promoting public good."[42] It thus adopted a classic liberal standpoint by claiming

---

41. Home Office Research, Development and Statistics Directorate, Setting the Boundaries: Reforming the Law on Sex Offences, Sex Offences Review Group, 2 vols. (London: Home Office Communications Directorate, 2000), vol. II, 257–64.

42. Sex Offences Review Group, Setting the Boundaries: Reforming the Law on Sex Offences, 2 vols. (London: Home Office Communications Directorate, 2000), vol. I, 98.

to exclude considerations of excellence or value. Personal moral concerns are subordinated to a shared public conception of justice that is said to be objective. However, as Simmonds notes, "the neutrality of a liberal legal order is neutrality at the level of justification, not of effect."[43] Not everyone in a liberal society has an equal chance to pursue his or her own conception of a good sex life, and in this sense, the classic liberal approach to the criminal law is not neutral. Some people are able to indulge their conception of a good life without hindrance (e.g., consensual homosexual intercourse in private), while others are restrained (e.g., consensual homosexual intercourse in public). This moral stance is reflected in the Act.

The Act's morality is thus clearly based on the "harm" principle. The Group states that "judgement[s] on what is right and wrong should be based on an assessment of the harm done to the individual (and through the individual to society as a whole)."[44] The harm or welfare principle accordingly sets limits to the principle of autonomy. In identifying harmful sexual activity, the review team claimed to take account of the views of victims of sexual offenses (who tended to be women) and academic research.[45] Naturally, taking this as a basis for our understanding of harm makes a number of hidden assumptions. As Kleinhams points out, "any such assessment must recognise that definitions of 'harm' have their own ambivalence, slipping between physical and moral terms of harm depending on who maintains the power to define exactly what constitutes a harm."[46] The Group took the view that constraining sexual autonomy was only necessary where the sexual activity was nonconsensual or not legally valid because it involved children or the very vulnerable who required protection.[47] In other words, sexual choice may not be exercised in cases of abuse where the welfare principle clearly outweighs the principle of autonomy. But this is a very minimalist position. It means that modern law treats a number of forms of sexual behavior as "victimless crimes" (e.g., adultery and private consensual homosexual behavior above the age of consent).

Like modern law, biblical law explicitly acknowledges the role of harm in shaping our understanding of sexual offenses. However, whereas modern law has a limited understanding of harm and constrains sexual choice only in clear cases of abuse and lack of consent, biblical law is based on a much more expansive category of harm. Sexual wrongdoing harms not only the offender himself but also his *mishpahah*, or group of nuclear households (see Figure 7, above).

---

43. N. E. SIMMONDS, CENTRAL ISSUES IN JURISPRUDENCE (London: Sweet & Maxwell, 2002), 72.
44. SEX OFFENCES REVIEW GROUP, SETTING THE BOUNDARIES, Vol. I, iv.
45. Ibid.
46. Martha-Marie Kleinhams, *Criminal justice approaches to paedophilic sex offenders*, SOC. & AND LEGAL STUDS. 11, 233–55, 240 (2002).
47. SEX OFFENCES REVIEW GROUP, SETTING THE BOUNDARIES, Vol. I, iv.

The shockwaves of relational disorder expand and impact the following relationships: (1) the betrayed husband or wife, (2) the cohesion of the community, (3) the future of the nation, and (4) the relationship between the people and God, all of which are interconnected.

B. The "nuclear family" and the "unclear family"

Second, we consider underlying beliefs about *the nature of the family*. This follows directly from the Sex Offences Review Group's beliefs about the nature of harm. The Group's moral stance on the question of harm inevitably influences its view of the family and the value that should be placed on its protection. For example, the Group acknowledged that "an adult's right to exercise sexual autonomy in their private life is not absolute, and society may properly apply standards through the criminal law which are intended *to protect the family as an institution*" (italics added).[48] Naturally, the extent to which sexual choice may be circumscribed through law in order to "protect the family" is a matter of degree. Where one draws the line says much about how one defines the family and sees threats to the family and the extent to which one takes either seriously. We have already seen that constraining sexual autonomy was only thought to be necessary where the sexual activity was nonconsensual or not legally valid because it involved those who required protection.[49] This is a very minimalist position. The fact that constraints upon choice are limited only to clear cases of abuse and lack of consent suggests that the Group did not attach very much weight to the institution of the family or its need for protection.

This minimalist approach to the family is underlined in several other parts of the Sexual Offences Act 2003. First, the Act abolished the traditional blood tie of incest and replaced it with the new crime of "familial child sex offences." This drew in a wider range of relationships than blood relationships (sections 25 and 26 of the Act) and was presented as an attempt to reflect the looser structure of modern families. This is consistent with the general trend toward reordering kinship relations "according to an ever-widening set of possibilities in which the bare facts of biology are incidental to the primary business of making and maintaining relationships of one kind or another."[50] Following a decision of the European Court of Human Rights, it is now lawful for a father-in-law to marry his daughter-in-law, which means that the same must also apply between a son and his mother-in-law.[51] According to modern anthropologists, this results in "scrambled parenthood." It leads to "a conflict between generationality and

---

48. Ibid.
49. Ibid.
50. Bob Simpson, *Scrambling parenthood: English kinship and the prohibited degrees of affinity*, ANTHROPOLOGY TODAY 22, 3–6, 6 (2006).
51. Chamber Judgment, B and L v. The United Kingdom, 462a 13.09.05; http://www.echr.coe.int/echr/, accessed October 5, 2009.

chronology" and makes "fathers and sons sexually interchangeable."[52] "We are faced not so much with the nuclear family but a striking example of the "unclear" family . . . wherein what we encounter is not so much a kinship universe as a kinship multiverse, replete with black holes and parallel modes of time reckoning . . ."[53] Such radical changes to the traditional understanding of the family means that the law increasingly has to rely on legal definitions of what is "sexual" in order to give meaning to "sexual offenses," instead of relying on definitions of the family. Under section 78 of the Act, offenses are sexual because of "penetration, touching or any other activity" which a reasonable person would consider to be sexual because of "its nature . . . its circumstances or the purpose of any person in relation to it . . ."

Like modern law, biblical law explicitly claims to be based on certain assumptions about the family to construct its sexual offenses. However, whereas modern law has a minimalist understanding of family and only allows it to influence sex offenses law to a limited degree, biblical law is based on a far stronger and more expansive conception of *mishpahah*, or group of nuclear households. Accordingly, ideas about the family almost entirely structure the biblical laws concerning sexual behavior. We have seen that Leviticus 20:9–21 defines the "sexual" entirely in terms of the "family." In particular, "sexual offenses" are characterized as "forms of adultery" that deviate from the norm of heterosexual marriage. Consistent with this strong view of the family and the importance of its protection, biblical law, unlike modern law, places more limits on sexual behavior. Indeed, Leviticus 20:3–6 emphasises that applying the penalties for sexual offenses is essential to preserving the survival of the biblical family unit (see Figure 7, above).

To summarize, modern law shows that where there is a weak understanding of family and the significance of marriage, regulating sexual behavior means defining with increasing specificity what we mean by "sexual" and, therefore, "sexual offenses." By contrast, where there is a clear understanding of what marriage and the family is, there is no need to define what is meant by "sexual." This is the case in biblical law. Here, the sexual is defined in relation to marriage and family because there is a strong understanding of the centrality of family and marriage to relational and sexual order. Indeed, there is no need for a separate category of sexual offenses. Biblical law has a clear understanding of the good and from that flows everything else. There is a contrast between covenantal sex and casual sex. Accordingly, there is a need in modern law for a positive understanding of well-ordered sexual relationships that gives shape to the departures and which therefore explains why certain sexual offenses are criminal. This in turn should lead into an understanding of what is a well-ordered sexual relationship, that is, the covenant of heterosexual marriage.

---

52. Simpson, *Scrambling parenthood*, p. 5.
53. Ibid., 7.

C. "Who gives a . . . ?"

Third, we consider underlying beliefs about *the nature of consent*. This is important because the main provisions of the Sexual Offences Act 2003 cohere around three related themes: consent, equality, and protection.[54] These themes provide a useful framework within which to consider the specific policies of modern law and how they compare with biblical law.

Consent undergirds the whole of the Act because its underlying goal is to protect persons from nonconsensual sexual activity. The result is a structure of sexual offenses that is based on respect for private life and thus "broadly permits consensual acts in private."[55] This concern for consent reflects the beliefs of the 1957 Wolfenden Committee that "the criminal law should not intrude unnecessarily into the private life of adults."[56] The emphasis upon consent is also one of the implications of incorporating the ECHR into English law, especially in regard to Article 8 (the right to a private life). This in turn is related to the harm principle on the basis that most consensual sexual acts between adults in private are perceived as harmless, whereas sexual acts that are not consensual, or where consent is not legally valid, are seen as harmful (e.g., those involving children and other "very vulnerable people").[57] Concern for consent is thus entwined with concerns for privacy and autonomy. Lack of consent is entwined with paternalist concerns about harm and welfare.

The Act reflects the modern belief that consent is confined to the actors concerned. It may be the case that the wife is deeply affected when the husband has a sexual relationship with the *au pair*. However, her consent is neither necessary nor relevant as far as modern law is concerned, which is only interested in the free and informed agreement of the parties directly involved in the sexual act itself, provided they are of age. This widely held assumption is typified by Lord Thomas of Gresford in his speech at the second reading of the Sexual Offences Bill:

> It is important to set out a principle at the beginning: that sex between two consenting adults and, in our culture, in private is a healthy, life-enhancing, pleasurable activity. That should be recognised as in my view a great amount of deviant behaviour takes place because it is not recognised due to guilt, inadequacy and immaturity.[58]

---

54. Jonathan Burnside, Consent versus community: What basis for sexual offences reform? (Cambridge: Jubilee Centre, 2006), 9, available at http://www.jubilee-centre.org/Resources, accessed October 5, 2009.
55. Sex Offences Review Group, Setting the Boundaries, Vol. I, p. 98.
56. Ibid., iv.
57. Ibid.
58. *Hansard*, House of Lords Debates, col. 779, February 13, 2003.

Yet despite the claim in modern law that private sexual acts do not have public consequences, it remains the case that third parties *do* have an interest in consensual sexual behavior. Following *B & L v. The United Kingdom* (see footnote 51, above), the marriage between a father-in-law (B) and his daughter-in-law (L) has major structural implications for third parties. From the perspective of L's son, his own biological father is subject to "a kind of structural invisibility"[59] as his biological grandfather (B) drops down a generation to become a "dad." It also means that his biological grandfather becomes the husband of his mother. And if the son should gain a male sibling as a result of the union of his mother and her husband (who is also his biological grandfather), this child would simultaneously be a brother, a half-brother, or an uncle.[60] The result is sexual and relational chaos within networks of primary kin.

What is true in cases of intergenerational marriage between in-laws is also true of sexual relationships more widely, namely, that what happens in a sexual relationship impacts many people beyond the parties to the sexual act. This is, of course, a staple theme of classic literature (*Anna Karenina, The Great Gatsby*) and famous movie adaptations (*Dr. Zhivago, The English Patient, Brokeback Mountain*), not to mention nearly every soap opera running around the world. Affairs have the capacity to destroy marriages and families, and usually it is the children who lose the most when a man leaves his wife and children for another woman—or a man. Members of the immediate and the extended family may end up siding with one party over the other, leading to permanent loss of contact with a former member of the family. In some cases, grandparents and grandchildren may never see each other again. The long-term impact of sexual relationships also affects local communities. Nor can we ignore the cost to the taxpayer of promiscuity outside marriage and the increase in sexually transmitted infections.[61] There is a social cost for sexual chaos.

Like modern law, biblical law acknowledges the role of consent in ordering sexual behavior. However, unlike modern law, the biblical concern for consent goes beyond the parties involved in the sexual act to include the consent of certain family members. Biblical law thus uses a different and more expansive conception of consent. It means that in biblical law, "the morality of a decision regarding sexual practice can only adequately be judged when the interests of third parties are taken into account."[62] Biblical law offers a public sexual ethic

---

59. Simpson, *Scrambled parenthood*, p. 5.
60. Ibid.
61. HEALTH PROTECTION AGENCY, ANNUAL REPORT AND ACCOUNTS (London: The Stationery Office, 2007), 75–76, 126.
62. Jason Fletcher, *Foreword, in* CONSENT VERSUS COMMUNITY: WHAT BASIS FOR SEXUAL OFFENCES REFORM?; Jonathan Burnside (Cambridge: Jubilee Centre, 2006), 5, http://www.jubilee-centre.org/Resources, accessed October 5, 2009.

that is less individualistic than modern law and which is positively oriented toward the community as a whole.

Ultimately, there is a choice to be made between two approaches. On the one hand, there is "covenant sex" which is characterized by commitment between the parties and the formal recognition that sexual relations have the power to make or break communities. Here, the key question is how to channel sexual energy in such a way as to create community. On the other hand, there is "casual sex" which is characterized by low levels of commitment and sexual relations with almost anyone you like, provided there is consent. A society based on covenant sex is not straightforward and requires support. At the same time, however, there is an increasing need to recognize that casual sex has an impact on all of us who are obliged to live with the social consequences. If we are to move away from relational chaos toward relational order, part of the challenge will be to develop appropriate ways of addressing the impacts of the pursuit of personal sexual agendas upon third parties. Sexual relationships are not meant to be—and cannot be—haphazard and arbitrary. They are far too significant and complex to be reduced to personal pleasure; and when we try to do so, we risk creating many losers.

D. Sexual order *versus* sexual chaos

Fourth, we consider underlying beliefs about *the nature of equality*. Like consent, equality is a major organizing theme of the Sexual Offences Act 2003. However, "equality" is a slippery term—equality in relation to what?—and nowhere is this truer than when applied to sexual ethics. The concern for "actual equality" breaks down at certain points in the Act itself; for example, "cottaging" (homosexual behavior in a public toilet) is a male crime that has no female equivalent. However, actual equality is not the sense in which the term equality operates in this debate. In moral and political philosophy, equal consideration serves to identify certain classes within which it is not possible to make distinctions. As applied to the classification of sexual offenses, equality means identifying classes of sexual behavior within which it is not possible to make distinctions for the purpose of applying criminal sanctions. The Act treats consensual homosexual and heterosexual intercourse above the age of consent as equal in the sense that it does not regard any distinction between them as justified in criminal law. This is in keeping with the aspirations of the Sex Offences Review to develop a system of penalties in which homosexual offenses were no higher than for equivalent heterosexual ones.[63]

But while the modern aspiration to equality appears to be "value free" ("I just want what you have"), it is in fact unavoidably founded on moral claims. In this case, "equalizing" heterosexual and homosexual offenses is based on the moral

---

63. Sex Offences Review Group, Setting the Boundaries, Vol. I, pp. 100–01.

belief that there is an equivalence between heterosexual and homosexual intercourse. Indeed, pursuant to its own moral beliefs, the Act sets limits to equality by regarding distinctions between some forms of intercourse and *other* kinds of sexual behavior as valid. Thus, while the Act claims that homosexual intercourse is not a criminal offense, it does claim that necrophilia (sex with human remains) and voyeurism should be regarded as criminal offenses. The Act's vision of equality is necessarily founded on a series of moral distinctions.

Like modern law, biblical law has a conception of equality that is founded on a series of moral distinctions. However, the moral basis of these distinctions is different from those of modern law. Many categories of sexual behavior, including homosexual relationships, are not treated on an equal basis to marital relationships. On the other hand, biblical law is similar to modern law in that *homosexual offenses are not treated any more severely than heterosexual offenses*, such as adultery. At the level of penalty, there is no difference between adultery and homosexual intercourse in biblical law. As in modern law, distinctions are made between permitted and prohibited relationships, although in biblical law, these boundaries are intended to establish a positive understanding of relational order based on the following: (1) covenantal order, (2) species order, (3) gender order, (4) generational or "descent" order, and (5) kinship order. Consequently, biblical law, as with modern law, has a conception of equality; however, it is based on a different set of moral distinctions.

E. Safe sex

Fifth, we consider *the nature of protection*. Like consent and equality, protection is a major organizing theme of the Sexual Offences Act 2003. The Act is ostensibly concerned to protect vulnerable groups, including children, and aims to do so by means of a range of provisions.[64] The sexualization of children, together with actual sexual violence against children and cultural anxiety regarding child/adult relationships, creates a social context in which the language of "protection" becomes paramount when constructing a public sexual ethic. However, this concern for protection is somewhat undercut by the decision to lower the age of consent from 18 to 16 which, as I have argued elsewhere, removes the net effect of protection for 16–18 year olds.[65]

Like modern law, biblical law is characterized by a concern for protection, including child protection. Looking at the subject of child welfare more broadly, if we were to construct a sexual ethic from scratch that was best for children, the evidence suggests that we would tend to favor a stable monogamous family unit

---

64. BURNSIDE, CONSENT VERSUS COMMUNITY, pp. 12–14.
65. Jonathan Burnside, *The Sexual Offences (Amendment) Act 2000: The head of a "kiddy-libber" and the torso of a "child-saver"?*, CRIM. L. REV. 425–34, 431, (2001).

characterized by fidelity and mutual respect between husband and wife.[66] We would also think it desirable for this unit to have the support of an extended family committed to preserving sexual boundaries and distinctiveness. This is exactly the sexual ethic presupposed by the laws of Leviticus 20 (and Leviticus 18). We do not find any specific "child protection" laws in the Bible—although the book of Proverbs as a whole can be read as a counsel on positive parent-child relationships. Nevertheless, as we saw above, the prohibition of Molech-worship shows some concern to protect children from parental abuse (Leviticus 20:2–5).

We also saw that the community as a whole risked punishment if it failed to deal with such offenders (Leviticus 20:4). Protection is also relevant in biblical law, particularly in relation to women, who are protected by means of betrothal or marriage. In addition, we have seen that punishment for sexual offenses was designed to protect the social institutions of marriage and the extended family (or *mishpachah*; see Figure 6, above). It was also designed to protect the nation as a whole, including its vocation (Leviticus 20:24) and covenant relationship with God (Leviticus 20:26). Consequently, biblical law, as with modern law, understands protection, but it is a different and more expansive conception.

In addition to these familiar categories of consent, equality, and protection, biblical law uses different categories altogether which are not present in modern law. We saw that in Leviticus 20, these included "idolatry," "honoring parents," "adultery," and "forms of adultery." In particular, the schematization of Leviticus 20:9–16 has striking modern relevance. Leviticus 20:9–16 presents the following behaviors as progressively distant from the norm: (1) homosexual relations (20:13); followed by (2) marriage between a man, a woman, and her daughter (Leviticus 20:14); and (3) relations between humans and animals (Leviticus 20:15–16). Remarkably, a similar sequence appears to be underway in certain Western jurisdictions. The legalisation of homosexual relations and the introduction of same-sex civil partnerships is seen, in some quarters, as paving the way for three-way civil partnerships and this, in turn, is said to create pressure for the legalization of bestiality. This mirrors the Levitical sequence of 20:13–16.

Civil unions between three persons became legal in the Netherlands in 2005, which was seen by some as the "legalization" of polygamy in all but name. Although the first "three-party marriage" in the Netherlands involved a man and two women, there is no conceptual reason why the next three-way union could not be between two men and one woman, or even between three men—including a man, a father, and his son. In the United States, the case is being made by

---

66. Social Justice Policy Group, Breakthrough Britain: Ending the costs of social breakdown (London: Centre for Social Justice, 2007).

practitioners and academics for the legalization of bestiality.[67] Singer[68] argues that the liberation movements that have so far extended rights to women, black persons, Spanish-Americans, and homosexuals should now benefit animals and that, indeed, the pursuit of equality should allow sexual contact between humans and nonhuman species. The alternative is "species-ism."[69] These aspirations are entirely in keeping with the assumptions underlying "cultural liberty" and the desire to affirm sexual minorities[70] (see p. 355 above).

To sum up, we can compare the underlying beliefs and assumptions in modern law regarding harm, the nature of the family, consent, equality, and protection with biblical law. It is simply not the case that modern law is concerned with these ideas and categories while biblical law is not. However, biblical law uses different conceptions of these categories from those found in modern law. In addition, biblical law uses different categories altogether that help to build a picture of relational and sexual order.

F. Relational order *versus* relational chaos

To draw this chapter to a close, we note that there is a close and complex relationship between social context and law reform which has led us to think in certain ways about the nature of harm, the family, consent, equality, and protection. This in turn has led us to identify certain people as being relevant in giving consent (and not others), or as deserving equality (and not others), or as requiring protection (and not others). This identification has now become embedded in the criminal law. This is how we have ended up constructing a sexual ethic that is contentious in terms of its ideas about harm, the family, consent, equality, and protection. The value of looking at biblical law, then, is that it forces us to shift context and question the seeming normality of what appears to be the social consensus of late-modern liberal society. The result is that a text such as Leviticus 20— which many would like to actively exclude from the debate—actually turns out to be of profound relevance. Although biblical law shares many of the same categories as modern law, biblical law offers a more expansive conception. The Sexual Offences Act 2003 points beyond itself to a loss within our social consciousness of how we understand the significance of sexual behavior. This is something we are all caught up in because it affects all of us, both individually and collectively as a society.

---

67. Mark Steyn, *Animal lovers*, THE SPECTATOR, August 11, 2001, 20–21.
68. Peter Singer, *All animals are equal, in* ANIMAL RIGHTS AND HUMAN OBLIGATIONS, (Tom Regan & Peter Singer eds.; New Jersey, 1989), 73–74, 148–62, also at http://www.utilitarian.net/singer/, accessed October 5, 2009.
69. Peter Singer, *Heavy petting* (2001), http://www.utilitarian.net/singer/, accessed October 5, 2009.
70. UNITED NATIONS DEVELOPMENT PROGRAMME, HUMAN DEVELOPMENT, p. 13.

Biblical law points beyond consent to a positive vision for society that is founded on relational order. It presents a picture of sexual order such that our spontaneous understanding of family, for example, produces a conception of equality that has a different moral basis; one that protects vulnerable individuals as well as defending the institution of marriage and the life of the nation as a whole. In contrast to the rather sterile category of "consent," there is a community aspect to sexual ethics in the Bible. It shows us how it is possible to construct a more coherent public sexual ethic—one that seeks to channel the desire for intimacy in such a way as to create community. The covenant of heterosexual marriage is the central image of good sexual relationships, and everything else is defined in relation to that.

In this way, the ability of biblical law to put forward a vision of the good challenges not only the *content* of modern law but also its mode of *presentation*. Leviticus 20 is remarkable because it presents an overview of sexual deviancy *while at the same time* evoking the pattern of the original creation. Diane Kelsey McColley's work on Milton's *Paradise Lost* and its subsequent influence upon the visual arts speaks of the need in Western civilization to "reimagine Eden and so re-Edenise the imagination."[71] Biblical law has a positive part to play in this challenge. After all, we saw in Chapter 7 how Leviticus has captured our cultural imagination regarding economic freedom. Imagine if it also revolutionized our understanding of sexual freedom?

X. CONCLUSION

This chapter has considered a range of problematic sexual relationships in biblical law, including rape, adultery (whether with married or betrothed women), as well as various "forms of adultery," including incest, homosexual sex, and bestiality. Adultery and forms of adultery are schematized in biblical law by being presented as a series of oppositions to the norm of marriage. There is no category of "sexual offenses" as such in the Bible: instead, prohibited sexual relationships are understood in terms of preexisting categories of idolatry and dishonoring parents. Biblical sexual ethics are structured around a clear understanding of harm and the family, which leads to constraints on sexual behavior. By contrast, the primary limits in modern law are set by a concern for consent, equality, and protection. Private acts are not, for the most part, thought to have public consequences. In addition, biblical law defines consent, equality, and protection more expansively, with the result that the wider community has an interest in sexual behavior that is seen as harmful. What people do with each other

---

71. Diane Kelsey McColley, A Gust for Paradise: Milton's Eden and the Visual Arts (Chicago: University of Illinois Press, 1993), xi.

sexually is not a matter for themselves only: it has implications for their families, other families, and society as a whole.

Selected reading

J. P. Burnside. "Rethinking 'sexual' offences in biblical law: The literary structure of Leviticus 20," in *Jewish Law Association Studies XVI: The Boston 2004 Conference Volume*, E. Dorff ed. (Binghampton: Global Academic Publishing, 2007), pp. 37–55.

Jonathan P. Burnside, "Strange Flesh: Sex, semiotics and the construction of deviancy in biblical law," *Journal for the Study of the Old Testament* 30 (2006), 387–420.

Robert A. J. Gagnon, *Zeitschrift für die Alttestamentliche Wissenschaft*, "The Old Testament and homosexuality: A critical review of the case made by Phyllis Bird," 117 (2005), 367–394.

Mark Gray, "Amnon: A chip off the old block? Rhetorical strategy in 2 Samuel 13:7–15. The rape of Tamar and the humiliation of the poor," *Journal for the Study of the Old Testament* 77 (1998), 39–54.

Raymond Westbrook, "Adultery in Ancient Near Eastern Law," *Revue Biblique* 97 (1990), 542–580.

12. NEW LAWS FOR A NEW AGE

So far in this book, we have explored a number of substantive legal topics in order to gain a sense of how biblical law operates, both as a system and as applied (see "How to use this book"). It's now time for us to consider more directly some of the ways in which biblical law has been interpreted by Jewish communities in the biblical period. This is important because it allows us to see how biblical law has been applied in the context of different social groups. We can thus explore a significant aspect of biblical law as a legal phenomenon, namely, the way in which it is used to define a given community that accepts its norms as authoritative. As we do so, we'll find that what's interesting about this is the way in which the application of biblical law plays out very differently, depending on the nature of the group in question. In particular, we'll see that the differences in application between these groups can be explained, in part, by the fact that each is telling a different story of what it means to "be Israel." Once again, we find that law and narrative are closely intertwined.

The question of how biblical law plays out in different communities in the biblical period is a complex one that could be approached from many different angles. The simplest approach is probably to take a single substantive topic and to see how the issues have been interpreted by different communities, which are roughly contemporaneous. As far as a given time is concerned, there are advantages in looking at Israel's history toward the end of the "Second Temple" period. This is the stretch in Israel's history that covers the rebuilding of the Temple in Jerusalem, which was completed in 516 BC, to the destruction of its Herodian manifestation in AD 70. For much of this time, Israel was without full political independence: conditions which helped to incubate intense debates about the application of biblical law toward the end of this period. Within the scope of this chapter, we cannot take more than a few Jewish groups as examples. Therefore, it will focus on those for which we have good extant materials. This means concentrating on the community at Qumran—by the shores of the Dead Sea—and the followers of Jesus of Nazareth.

I. IN THE SHADOW OF THE TEMPLE

Both of these groups have plenty of shared concerns, including for example, purity and behavior on the Sabbath. Depending on the topic, we could draw different conclusions about how these groups interpreted biblical law. A study of the purity and Sabbath laws would tend to emphasize the exclusivity of the Qumran group as opposed to the inclusivity of the Jesus group. However—and again to keep things simple—it makes sense to choose a topic that we have already explored in previous chapters. For this reason, we will choose marriage and divorce as our substantive issues and see how these are handled by the Qumran authors and by Jesus.

Before we do so, we need to sketch briefly the background to the Second Temple period. The story of Israel is a complex one.[1] Israel's triumph on entering the land was marred in subsequent generations by the social chaos described in the book of Judges, while the early flowering of Israelite monarchy under Saul, David, and Solomon quickly gave way to the divided kingdoms of Israel and Judah in 930 BC. The northern kingdom of Israel, with its capital in Samaria, was conquered by the Assyrian kings Shalmaneser V and Sargon II in 722 BC, and its peoples lost to history. The southern kingdom of Judah, with its capital in Jerusalem, capitulated to the Babylonian king Nebuchadnezzar II in 597 BC. Its peoples were deported to Babylon between 597 and 586 BC, whereupon the original Temple built by Solomon, was burned. From 537 BC on, there would be successive waves of Israelite repatriation to Jerusalem which culminated in the building of the Second Temple.

However, Israel's return from captivity in Babylon was a mixed blessing. Her fortunes were only partially restored. The people—at least what was left of them—were back in the land, but they were still under Persian oversight. Even when the time of the Persians had passed, Israel remained under the thumb of successive pagan overlords, culminating in Rome.[2] It was a long period of national frustration, which served only to deepen the desire for freedom. This hope was articulated by a variety of Jewish groups who gave differing accounts of where Israel had gone wrong and what she had to do to put things right with her ancestral God. Among these competing visions of what Israel's future would look like, there was talk of a new messianic age. Common to all factions, however, was a concern for the proper interpretation and application of biblical law, which is the focus of this chapter.

II. SECRETS FROM THE DESERT

We begin by exploring attitudes toward biblical law among the community that lived at Qumran, on the shores of the Dead Sea. Our insight into this group is derived from the Dead Sea Scrolls which were discovered by accident at Qumran in 1947. Of course, "we have little way of knowing which of the sectarian laws found in the scrolls were the product of the Qumran community and which had been inherited from previous pre-Qumranic contexts or were shared with other

---

1. See Time line p. xxiii–xxiv.
2. See Time line p. xxiii–xxiv.

Jewish groups."³ Therefore, we must be careful not to overgeneralize. We can draw conclusions only about the interpretation of biblical law as it appears in the Dead Sea Scrolls in their final form.⁴ In addition, "there is no reason to assume that the Qumran documents, deposited in the caves over a lengthy period of time, . . . derive from a group or groups that had a unified sense of the way in which scripture was to be read or a single conception of the message that it was to convey."⁵ Nevertheless, we can still ask the question: what do the Dead Sea Scrolls tell us about the interpretation of biblical law during the Second Temple period?

A. The joy of sect

In order to begin to answer this question, we need to build up a picture of how the group saw itself as an interpretative community. It is clear that the sect, like others in Israel, were still waiting for the end of exile. (Even in our own day, we are familiar with breakaway religious groups whose identity is based around a particular interpretation of the apocalypse, for example the Branch Davidians led by David Koresh until 1993). The Second Temple had been built, but national restoration had not followed. Since God had destroyed the first Temple and sent Israel into exile for disobeying his commandments, many concluded that Israel's continuing exile was the result of her failure fully to observe Torah. This was the urgent challenge of the age. The Qumran group reobligated themselves to following the "revealed" (*niglot*) laws of Moses that were given to Israel at Mount Sinai, but they also obligated themselves to follow, for the first time, an ever-increasing body of "hidden" (*nistarot*) laws, which they were privileged to discover through divinely inspired study sessions and exegesis.⁶

> Whoever approaches the Council of the Community (*yachad*) shall enter the Covenant of God in the presence of all who have freely pledged themselves. He shall undertake by a binding oath to return with all his heart and soul to every commandment of the Law of Moses in accordance with all that has been

---

3. Steven D. Fraade, *Looking for legal midrash at Qumran*, in BIBLICAL PERSPECTIVES: EARLY USE AND INTERPRETATION OF THE BIBLE IN THE LIGHT OF THE DEAD SEA SCROLLS, (M. E. Stone & E. G. Chazon eds.; Leiden: Brill, 1998), 59–79, 75 n. 56.

4. Moshe J. Bernstein & Shlomo A. Koyfman, *The interpretation of biblical law in the Dead Sea Scrolls: Forms and methods*, in BIBLICAL INTERPRETATION AT QUMRAN, (Matthias Henze ed., Grand Rapids: Eerdmans, 2005), 61–87, 64.

5. Moshe J. Bernstein, *Interpretation of Scriptures*, in ENCYCLOPEDIA OF THE DEAD SEA SCROLLS, (Lawrence H. Schiffman & James C. Vanderkam eds.; Oxford: Oxford University Press 2000), vol. I, 376–83, 376.

6. Gary A. Anderson, *Law and lawgiving*, in ENCYCLOPEDIA OF THE DEAD SEA SCROLLS, (Lawrence H. Schiffman & James C. Vanderkam eds., 2 vols.; Oxford: Oxford University Press, 2000), vol. I, 475–77, 476.

revealed of it to the sons of Zadok, the Priests, the Keepers of the Covenant and Seekers of His will . . . . (The Community Rule 5:7ff)[7]

The choice of the word "community" (*yachad*) to describe their gathering is significant because it conveys the sense of "being one."[8] They were united—and unique. They are correctly described as sectarian because they had "separated themselves to a large degree, both theologically and physically, from the current priestly establishment in Jerusalem."[9] There is considerable evidence that the community modeled itself on Israel encamped at Mount Sinai.[10] They were the exclusive members of God's covenant with Israel: those outside the community were "the men of injustice who walk in the way of wickedness" (The Community Rule 5:11).[11] The *yachad* was "a temporary substitute for Jerusalem"[12] and was opposed to the corrupt Hellenism of Second Temple Judaism. The group had a strong sense of eschatology, believing that their actions would hasten the transition between the present age and the next.

Even this brief sketch enables us to see why the interpretation of biblical law was important. It was not a way of passing the time for a bunch of armchair apocalypticists. Instead, it was central to Israel's political and spiritual survival—the two being inseparable in any case.

We will now turn to look at a range of issues regarding marriage and divorce in the Dead Sea Scrolls. We will begin by looking at some of the ways in which Qumran law regulated marriage, by reference to the cases of the war captive bride and the slandered bride. We will then consider how the Qumran group sought to restrict sexual relations, including possible limits on marriage. We will then turn to consider some further restrictions, including incest and prohibitions on divorce. This approach allows us to work systematically through various sources of law. These include, first, the Temple Scroll which is the longest and probably the oldest document at Qumran. As the name suggests, it is mainly concerned with the Temple and cultic activities. Next we will consider the manuscript known

---

7. *The Complete Dead Sea Scrolls in English*, edited by Geza Vermes, revised edition (London: Penguin, 2004), 104.

8. Heinz-Josef Fabry, *Yahad*, in Theological Dictionary of the Old Testament, (G. Johannes Botterweck & Helmer Ringgren, eds.; David E. Green trans.; Grand Rapids: Eerdmans, 1990), vol. VI, 40–48, 48.

9. Hannah K. Harrington, *Biblical law at Qumran*, in The Dead Sea Scrolls After Fifty Years: A Comprehensive Assessment, (Peter W. Flint & James C. Vanderkam eds.; 2 vols.; Leiden: Brill, 1998), vol. I, 160–185, 160.

10. James C. Vanderkam, *Sinai revisited*, in Biblical Interpretation at Qumran, (Matthias Henze ed.; Grand Rapids: Eerdmans, 2005), 44–60, 48.

11. Vermes, Dead Sea Scrolls, p. 104.

12. Elisha Qimron, *Celibacy in the Dead Sea Scrolls and the Two Kinds of Sectarianism*, in The Madrid Qumran Congress, (Julio Trebolle Barrera & Luis Vegas Montaner eds.; Leiden: Brill, 1992), vol. I, pp. 287–94, 288.

as *Miqsat Ma'ase Ha-Torah* (usually shortened to *MMT*), which means "Some Observances of the Law." The style of this document suggests some kind of public letter which may have been addressed to religious leaders in charge of the Temple in Jerusalem. A final source is the Damascus Document, so-called because of its references to "the New Covenant in the land of Damascus" (e.g., Damascus Document 6:19).[13] This is a sort of legal anthology which the Qumran community thought should apply to all Jews in the land of Israel. At points, we will compare these documents with each other; however, we will need to remember that they are different documents, intended for different audiences, and probably written with different purposes in mind.

B. Deleting Moses

We begin by considering how Qumran law regulated marriage in the case of the "war captive bride." This law is set out in the Temple Scroll (63:10–15). It is based on Deuteronomy 21:10–14, although there is no explicit quotation. Qumran law modifies the biblical text in several significant ways. In Deuteronomy, it is the woman herself who discards her old identity (by trimming her hair, paring her nails, and discarding her clothes), whereas in the Temple Scroll, the man does these things to her. This is because the Qumran interpreter understands verse 12, which begins with the phrase, "you shall . . .," to mean that the soldier performs the actions.[14] Qumran legal interpretation can be very literal.

The Qumran author also adds to Deuteronomy 21:10–14 by limiting what the woman can touch and eat. These additions recall the rituals required of new entrants to the Qumran community (The Community Rule 5:16; 6:17, 20–21; 7:19–20). The sect also had seven-year "quarantine" provisions for "straying" members (Damascus Document 12:5–6) who were required to serve some kind of "probationary period."[15] The writer of the Temple Scroll thus makes a connection between Deuteronomy 21:10–14, which governs the admission procedure for entry to the covenant community of Israel and the entry requirements for his own congregation. Accordingly, extra laws are grafted onto Deuteronomy to bring it into line with the sect's worldview.

Finally, and most remarkably of all, we discover that the Qumran author changes the third person reference to God in the MT (". . . and the LORD your God delivers them into your hands"; verse 10) into a first person verb (". . . and

---

13. VERMES, DEAD SEA SCROLLS, p. 134.
14. Lawrence H. Schiffman, *Laws pertaining to women in the Temple Scroll*, in THE DEAD SEA SCROLLS: FORTY YEARS OF RESEARCH, (Devorah Dimant & Uriel Rappaport eds.; Leiden: Brill, 1992), 210–28, 218–19.
15. Schiffman, *Laws pertaining to women*, p. 220.

I deliver them into your hands"; Temple Scroll 63:9ff).[16] Re-presenting commands that were mediated by Moses into commands given directly from God to the people is a characteristic of the Temple Scroll and makes it "a very unusual form of rewritten Bible."[17] The effect is to "eliminate the intermediacy of the lawgiver Moses and present the whole as direct divine revelation."[18] Ironically, the Temple Scroll asserts that "much more of the Pentateuch derives directly from God than the Pentateuch itself [claims]."[19] Biblical law is thus re-presented to promote Qumranic ideology. Elbowing Moses to one side is consistent with the sect's belief in their ability to discern the "hidden" laws (*nistarot*). After all, if they are capable of receiving direct divine inspiration, who needs Moses?

C. Loose talk and Loose Women

Reading further on down the Temple Scroll, we find another example of how Qumran law regulated marriage, this time in the case of the "slandered bride" (cf. Chapter 11). Temple Scroll 65:7–16 faithfully parallels Deuteronomy 22:13–21 (apart from some small variations). However, an additional piece of manuscript, known as 4Q159—one of a collection of Qumran ordinances on biblical law—differs significantly from the biblical text.

We saw in Chapter 11 that there are several problems with the traditional view that Deuteronomy 22:13–21 punishes the daughter for her loss of virginity. We argued that since not all virgins have intact hymens or bleed the first time they have sexual relations, the "cloth" cannot be used to provide *conclusive* evidence in a capital case. We also noted that the traditional view does not explain why this girl is stoned at the entrance to her father's house when this does not happen to other betrothed girls who misbehave (Deuteronomy 22:23–24). As a result, we argued that Deuteronomy 22:13–21 is concerned with whether or not the parents can produce evidence of their daughter's menstrual stains and hence evidence of whether or not she was pregnant at the time of the marriage.

4Q159, interestingly enough, gets around both of these problems. First, there is no examination of a cloth by town elders (cf. Deuteronomy 22:17). Jeffrey Tigay notes that a feminine adjective is used in relation to the examination, which indicates that the examiners are female. Accordingly, he thinks it "virtually

---

16. Vermes, Dead Sea Scrolls, p. 218.
17. Moshe J. Bernstein, *Pentateuch interpretation at Qumran*, in The Dead Sea Scrolls After Fifty Years: A Comprehensive Assessment (Peter W. Flint & James C. Vanderkam eds.; Leiden: Brill, 1998), 128-59, 154.
18. Ibid.
19. Ibid., 155.

certain"[20] that the bride herself is the subject of the examination. Second, there is no reference at all to the woman being stoned at the entrance to her father's house.

This being so, it is perfectly possible that Qumran law *was* concerned with the loss of virginity, unlike the text in Deuteronomy. If so, it would represent an escalation in the seriousness of the offense. It means that whereas the loss of virginity goes unpunished in biblical law, it merits the death penalty in Qumran law. Such intensification when compared with biblical law is not inconceivable, given the escalating concern for purity at Qumran.[21] On the other hand, it may be the case that Qumran law, like the underlying biblical law, was concerned with the question of paternity. If so, the purpose of the medical examination might have been to check the woman's menstrual cycle and/or for signs of pregnancy.

III. SLEEPING WITH THE ENEMY

Further restrictions on marriage are spelt out in the laws of *Miqsat Ma'ase Ha-Torah* (*MMT* B 75–82):

> And concerning fornication practised by the people, they should be s[ons of] holiness, as it is written, {Israel} is holy (Jeremiah 2:3). And concerning [his clea]n animal, it is written that it shall not be mated with a different kind. And concerning [his clothes], it is written that they shall [not be of mixed] material. And he shall not sow his field and vine[yard with two kind]s. For they are holy and the sons of Aaron are most h[oly]. And you know that some of the priests and [the people mingle] [and they] unite and defile the [holy] seed and also their [seed] with whores . . . .. (MMT B 75–82)[22]

These laws are consistent with other laws in MMT which "ramp up" the holiness quotient when compared with biblical law. Thus, whereas biblical law regards the high priest as "most holy" and the priests as "holy,"[23] MMT regards the Israelites as "holy" and the priests as "most holy." From a Qumranic perspective, the rhetoric is a way of maximizing holy personnel, both in terms of their

---

20. Jeffrey H. Tigay, *Examination of the accused bride in 4Q159: Forensic medicine at Qumran*, J. ANCIENT NEAR EASTERN SOC'Y 22, 129–34, 131 (1993).
21. Harrington, *Biblical law*, pp. 182–84.
22. VERMES, DEAD SEA SCROLLS, p. 227.
23. P. P. JENSON, GRADUATED HOLINESS, JOURNAL FOR THE SOCIETY OF THE OLD TESTAMENT SUPPLEMENT SERIES 106 (Sheffield: Journal for the Society of the Old Testament Press, 1992).

numbers and their degree of sanctity. This reclassification has considerable implications for marriage. In particular, the biblical requirement that the high priest marry within "his own kin" (Leviticus 21:14) is now extended to all priests.

Although MMT B 75–82 uses the phrase, "it is written . . . " to indicate its scriptural basis, it does not cite the underlying biblical laws of Leviticus 19:19. The Qumran author thus offers us another implicit interpretation of biblical law. MMT B parallels the ban on fornication with the ban on mating different kinds of animals, before moving on to other prohibited "mixings." The legal interpreter uses biblical law in a metaphorical sense to promote a sectarian agenda. In keeping with this flexible approach, the writer inverts the order of the mixings in Leviticus 19:19 by putting clothing before seed. This rearrangement, of course, links in with the charge that the priests are defiling their "seed."

The Qumran legislators are selective in their use of biblical law. In this case, it is notable that MMT B 75–82 draws on Leviticus 19:19 rather than the somewhat similar laws of Deuteronomy 22:9–11. It is likely that the author was familiar with Deuteronomy 22:9 because he incorporates the Deuteronomic prohibition on mixing seed in field *and* vineyard, whereas Leviticus 19:19 just refers to a field (although the writer may, of course, have been relying on a variant reading of Leviticus 19:19).

There are two reasons why the Qumran exegete would have preferred Leviticus 19. First, Leviticus 19:19 belongs to a wider section (19:1–37) which begins with the command to be "holy" (19:2) and closes with the command to "faithfully observe all My laws and My rules" (19:37). This call to be separate chimes with the argument in MMT B 75–82.[24] The Qumran writer chooses the interpretation that will amplify his message.

Second, we note that the following verse—Leviticus 19:20—regulates the sexual relationship between a free man and a betrothed slave woman. There is thus a precedent in biblical law itself for juxtaposing Leviticus 19:19 with sexual relations. However, although Leviticus 19:20 only prohibits this sexual relationship, Qumran law uses Leviticus 19:19 as a springboard to prohibit sexual relations between *all* Israelites and non-Israelites. It is thus a good example of the way in which the community at Qumran takes biblical categories (here, prohibited mixings) and radically expands their application. Critical theorists might argue that this is simply a way of trying to derive biblical authority for a sectarian position that has no basis in the Bible. This is, however, to miss the point. As far as the Qumran author is concerned, there is no distinction between the sectarian laws of MMT B 75–82 and the biblical law of Leviticus 19:19.

---

24. David Rothstein, *Gen. 24:14 and marital law in 4Q271 3: Exegetical aspects and implications*, DEAD SEA DISCOVERIES 12, 189–204 (2005).

IV. ANOTHER BRICK IN THE WALL

We turn to another manuscript—the Damascus Document—which also contains a polemic about fornication. This time it is directed against the so-called "builders of the wall," which seems to have its roots in the biblical text of Ezekiel 13:10.[25] The immediate context (Ezekiel 13:9–16) concerns a wall that has been built by the people and which is then daubed over with plaster by false prophets. Ezekiel prophesizes that this wall will be brought down by the wrath of God. The Qumran group uses this imagery to attack the "safe orthodoxy' of those living outside the community who are doomed because they are following a false commandment.[26] The "builders of the wall" refers to "all-Israel-outside-Qumran."

> The "builders of the wall" (Ezekiel 13:10) . . . are caught in fornication twice by taking two wives in their [*masculine* possessive pronominal suffix] lifetime, whereas the principle of creation is "Male and female created he them" (Genesis 1:27). Also, those who entered the Ark went in two by two (Genesis 7:7–9). (Damascus Document 4:20–5:1).[27]

The key question is what is meant by "taking two wives in their [masculine form] lifetime"? The ambiguous phrasing ensures that the subject is deeply contested among Qumran scholars,[28] and there is, at present, no consensus in sight. Geza Vermes[29] summarizes the key positions as being: (1) a ban on concurrent polygamy (i.e., more than one wife at the same time) as well as remarriage following divorce (consecutive polygamy); (2) a ban on concurrent polygamy but not divorce; (3) a ban on divorce but not concurrent polygamy; and (4) a ban on consecutive polygamy, that is, any second marriage, even after the death of the first wife.

The scriptural references in Damascus Document 4:20–5:2 uphold the ideal of monogamy: "[*one*] male and [*one*] female created he them." Likewise, the reference to "two by two" in Genesis 7:7–9 also points toward monogamy. The references to Genesis 1:27 and 7:7–9 indicate Qumranic antipathy toward polygamy, although whether the sectarians are objecting to concurrent or consecutive

---

25. Philip R. Davies, The Damascus Covenant, Journal for the Study of the Old Testament Supplement Series 25 (Sheffield: Sheffield Academic Press, 1982).
26. Davies, Damascus Covenant, p. 113.
27. Translation Vermes, Dead Sea Scrolls, p. 197.
28. *E.g.*, Charlotte Hempel, The Damascus Texts (Sheffield: Sheffield Academic Press, 2000), 82–83; Adiel Schremer, *Qumran polemic on marital law: CD 4:20-5:11 and its social background*, in The Damascus Document: A Centennial of Discovery, (Joseph M. Baumgarten, Esther G. Chazon & Avital Pinnick eds., Leiden: Brill, 2000), 147–60, 147–52.
29. Geza Vermes, *Sectarian matrimonial halakah in the Damascus Rule*, J. Jewish Studies 25, 197–202, 197 (1974), followed by Bernard S. Jackson, Essays on Halakhah in the New Testament (Leiden: Brill, 2008), 173–74.

polygamy remains to be determined. P. Winter[30] argues that there would have been no need to express the ban using the masculine form if the goal was to prohibit concurrent polygamy while Bernard Jackson[31] contends that Damascus Document 4:20–5:2 bans consecutive polygamy. This is in keeping with the sect's asceticism. A ban on consecutive polygamy "reinforces the view that marriage, where permitted, is itself a concession, required for pragmatic reasons in order to support the eschatological project . . . the ideal remains celibacy."[32] If this reading is correct, it amounts to a radical reinterpretation of biblical law, which permits both concurrent polygamy and remarriage for ordinary Israelites (see Chapter 10).

Regardless of whether the polemic is directed against concurrent or consecutive polygamy, we can draw some conclusions about Qumranic legal method. First, we note that law is derived from carefully chosen narratives. Genesis 1:27 and 7:9 are selected because they set a "precedent for monogamy."[33] Notably, the Qumran exegetes do not see the need to include the full quotation to make their point. The "two by two" quotation continues with the words "male and female." These words are not cited even though they actually make the connection with Genesis 1:27. They explain why these verses *together* define marriage *exclusively* in terms of two heterosexual persons.[34] The Qumran writers assume that the audience is sophisticated enough to make these connections for themselves. The Ark story also suggests that monogamy is normative, even for beasts. This suits the Qumran writer's polemical style because it implies that anyone who engages in polygamy behaves worse than a beast. Law and narrative are used to promote a sectarian agenda.

However, it is not simply a question of law and narrative; there is also the question of *which* narratives. The Qumran exegetes draw on Genesis to condemn fornication rather than, say, stories from The Book of Kings that question the wisdom of polygamy (e.g., 1 Kings 11:3–4). In this respect, Damascus Document 4:20ff is typical of a Qumranic tendency to privilege the first half of the book of Genesis (cf. some biblically based apocryphal works at Qumran, including Jubilees and the Genesis Apocryphon).[35]

---

30. P. Winter, *Sadoqite fragments IC 20, 21 and the exegesis of Genesis 1:27 in late Judaism*, ZEITSCHRIFT FÜR DIE ALTTESTAMENTLICHE WISSENSCHAFT 68, 289–302, 77 (1956).

31. JACKSON, ESSAYS ON HALAKHAH, pp. 173–81.

32. Ibid.

33. Jeffrey L. Rubenstein, *Nominalism and realism in Qumranic and Rabbinic Law: A reassessment*, DEAD SEA DISCOVERIES 6, 157–83, 162 (1999).

34. Evald Lövestam, *Divorce and remarriage in the New Testament* in THE JEWISH LAW ANNUAL (B. S. Jackson ed., Leiden: Brill, 1981), vol. IV, 47–65, 50–51.

35. Bernstein, *Pentateuch interpretation*, p. 137.

A. Kings and Courtesans

The section of the Damascus Document we have just been considering (4.20–5.1) continues with a provision relating to the king. This explicitly cites Deuteronomy 17:17:

> And concerning the prince it is written, "He shall not multiply wives to himself" (Deuteronomy 17:17). (Damascus Document 5:2)[36]

The introductory formulation can be seen as referring to a special rule for the king. Some scholars have taken Damascus Document 5:2 to mean that the king should be monogamous.[37] However, if the formulation is setting out a different rule for the monarch, which is not permitted for the rank and file, then the provision may allow for consecutive polygamy (Damascus Document 4:20–5:1). This makes sense as a way of ensuring that the king will produce heirs, otherwise "the eschatological leadership would disappear with him."[38] If this reasoning is correct, then the real issue is the extent of the multiplicity. He may have wives but not too many (cf. Mishnah Sanhedrin 4:2, which places the maximum at 18). The king is in a class of his own in this respect. However, there are limits even for the king.

Further monarchical provisions relating to marriage are found in a different manuscript, the Temple Scroll. The so-called "Law of the King" (56:12–59:21) states:

> He [the king] shall not acquire many wives that they may not turn his heart away from me. (Temple Scroll 56:18–19)[39]

This time, Deuteronomy 17:17 is not cited. Notably, the Qumran exegete departs from the original text of Deuteronomy 17:17 which reads ". . . [the king] shall not have many wives, *lest his heart go astray*." Temple Scroll 56:18–19 is therefore not a paraphrase but an exegesis of Deuteronomy 17:17. As far as the commentator is concerned, the problem with polygamous marriages is not the marriages themselves but the sort of wives the king marries. This interpretation seems to be derived from Deuteronomy 7:4 "for they [foreign women] will turn your children away from Me to worship other gods . . . ."[40] At Qumran, Deuteronomy 17:17 is understood in the light of Deuteronomy 7:4. This is a classic example of the way in which "the Temple Scroll interprets the laws of the Pentateuch as it paraphrases, rewrites and rearranges them."[41]

---

36. Translation VERMES, DEAD SEA SCROLLS, p. 132.
37. E.g., the list provided by Schremer, *Qumran polemic*, p. 148 n. 3.
38. JACKSON, ESSAYS ON HALAKAH, p. 181.
39. Translation VERMES, DEAD SEA SCROLLS, p. 133.
40. Schiffman, *Laws pertaining to women*, p. 213.
41. Bernstein, *Pentateuch interpretation*, p. 142.

A little further down the same Scroll, we find further provisions relating to the king:

> ... He [the king] shall not marry as wife any daughter of the nations, but shall take a wife for himself from his father's house, from his father's family. He shall not take another wife in addition to her, for she alone shall be with him all the time of her life. But if she dies, he may marry another from his father's house, from his family. (Temple Scroll 57:15–19)[42]

Some scholars claim that the Qumran author here draws upon the biblical text of Leviticus 18:18.[43] This prohibits the taking of a woman and her sister, which was understood in the Qumran tradition to refer to "a woman and another." On this basis, they argue that Temple Scroll 57:15–19 prohibits (concurrent) polygamy. However, Leviticus 18:18 is not cited in Temple Scroll 57:15–19, and this is significant. After all, if the Qumran legislators understood Leviticus 18:18 as an explicit ban on polygamy and if they sought to ban polygamy in the Damascus Document, why would they not cite Leviticus 18:18 in support of this (assumed) position in the Temple Scroll?[44] In addition, if the phrase "He shall not take another wife in addition to her" refers to polygamy, then the following phrase "for she alone shall be with him all the time of her life" is redundant.[45] It therefore seems as though Temple Scroll 57:15–19 does not prohibit concurrent polygamy on the part of the king but divorce. The king is not allowed to divorce his wife; but if she dies, he is allowed (commanded?) to take a new wife.[46] Again, this is something which the ordinary member of the community is not allowed to do (Damascus Document 4:20–5:1).

B. All in the Family?

Further restrictions on marriage are found in the Damascus Document, this time marriage between uncles and nieces:

> And each man marries the daughter of his brother or sister, whereas Moses said, "You shall not approach your mother's sister; she is your mother's near kin" (Leviticus 18:13). But although the laws against incest are written for men, they also apply to women. When, therefore, a brother's daughter uncovers the nakedness of her father's brother, she is (also his) near kin. (Damascus Document 5:7–11)[47]

---

42. Translation VERMES, DEAD SEA SCROLLS, p. 214.
43. E.g., Schiffman, *Laws pertaining to women*, p. 216.
44. JACKSON, ESSAYS ON HALAKAH, pp. 176–78.
45. Ibid., 181 n. 61.
46. Ibid., 181.
47. Translation VERMES, DEAD SEA SCROLLS, p. 133.

At Qumran, the practice of uncles marrying nieces is understood to be implicitly condemned by Leviticus 18:13, even though the biblical text does not explicitly state this. Unlike other examples so far, we have a citation formula ("Moses said . . .") followed by a *verbatim* quote of the law in question. And also, for once, we have an explicit methodology. This takes the form of reasoning by analogy. The Qumran author here recognizes gender equality, which we will return to in the New Testament texts (see below). It is thus an excellent example of what Moshe Bernstein calls a "simple sense"[48] reading, as opposed to the "extreme eisegesis" we sometimes find in Qumran law.

Why does the Damascus Document go out of its way to provide us with such an explicit citation and interpretation? Bernstein[49] notes that explicit textual support is often used in respect of laws that are the subject of dispute between the Qumran community and its opponents. In other words, the more contentious the issue, the more important it is to show that God is on your side. Flavius Josephus tells us that there were a number of uncle-niece marriages during this period (e.g., Jewish Antiquities 12:186–189), particularly in the royal court (e.g., Jewish Antiquities 17:19). There are good reasons for thinking that uncle-niece marriages reflect Second Temple practice, especially among the Pharisees. Permission for uncle-niece marriages is also found in rabbinic texts (Tractate Yevamot 62b–63a). Some scholars go so far as to say that the incest laws are one of the few examples where we see "direct criticism of the *halakhic* practices of the Pharisees."[50] Adopting a simple sense reading merely highlights the folly of the opposition.

This prohibition in the Damascus Document is not explicitly stated in biblical law. If one takes a legal (i.e., literal) approach to biblical law, one could claim that Qumran law extends the biblical laws of incest. On the other hand, if one takes a narrative approach to biblical law, there is nothing necessarily new about the Qumran interpretation. The ban on uncles marrying nieces is simply part of the paradigm case of Leviticus 18:13. If so, the difference between the Damascus Document and Leviticus is the fact that the Qumran writer felt the need to spell out the prohibition.

Within the overall literary context of the Damascus Document, the uncle-niece ban is part of the condemnation of the "builders of the wall" (see Damascus Document 4:19–5:1, above). This raises the question whether there is any relationship between the ban on "taking two wives in their lifetime" and the ban on uncle-niece marriage. According to Tractate Yevamot (part of the Babylonian Talmud which is concerned with levirate marriage), the simultaneous marriage of a man to a woman *and* his niece was a matter of real practical concern

---

48. Bernstein, *Interpretation of Scriptures*, p. 378.
49. Ibid.
50. Lawrence H. Schiffman, *The Pharisees and their legal traditions according to the Dead Sea Scrolls*, DEAD SEA DISCOVERIES 8, 262–77, 271 (2001).

(e.g., Mishnah Yevamot 1:2).[51] It may thus be the case that the prohibitions mentioned in the Damascus Document are "closely related to one another and are, in fact, two aspects of the same phenomenon."[52]

This incest ban is also prohibited in the Temple Scroll:

> A man shall not take the daughter of his brother or the daughter of his sister for this is abominable. (Temple Scroll 66:15–16)[53]

This goes further than the Damascus Document by adding the concluding words, "for this is abominable." This evokes the comparable judgement upon male homosexuality in Leviticus 18:22 ("it is an abomination"). Here, the Qumran interpreter borrows from other biblical laws to express his belief that uncle-niece marriage is as immoral as sex between men.

C. A Biblical Law Frappuccino

We turn finally to the end of the Temple Scroll, which deals with a number of sexual offenses. They include, first of all, the rape of the betrothed woman (66:4–9). The case parallels Deuteronomy 22:25–27 (see Chapter 10), although the source is not cited. But whereas the paradigm case of Deuteronomy 22:25 describes the location of the offense as being "the open country," the Temple Scroll specifies "a distant place hidden from the city." This implicit interpretation expands on the Pentateuchal text, making it clear that the location is one where the woman's cry of help cannot be heard.

Immediately after that, we find the following law, which purports to be about seduction:

> When a man seduces a virgin who is not betrothed, but is suitable to him according to the rule, and lies with her, and he is found out, he who has lain with her shall give the girl's father fifty pieces of silver and she shall be his wife. Because he has dishonoured her, he may not divorce her all his days. (Temple Scroll 66:8–11)[54]

This illustrates another characteristic of the Temple Scroll, namely, the tendency to gather in one place disparate laws that are united by a similar theme. Here, the laws of Exodus 22:15–16 and Deuteronomy 22:28–29 are blended into one. The result is a sort of biblical law frappuccino. The Qumran synthesizer begins with the language of Exodus 22:15 but drops the reference to "seizing" which is present in Deuteronomy 22:28. The rest of the law then flows into the remainder of Deuteronomy 22:28–29. A further consequence of the blending is

---

51. Schremer, *Qumran polemic*, pp. 154–57.
52. Ibid., 157.
53. Translation VERMES, DEAD SEA SCROLLS, p. 220.
54. Ibid., 219–20.

that the ban on divorce in Deuteronomy is also applied to seduction in Exodus. The idea seems to be "to produce a 'better organised' Torah than the Mosaic one."[55] Rather than seeing the literary presentation and canonical organization of the biblical texts as a guide to interpretation and understanding, the Qumran author sees it as an obstacle. The proper interpretation of biblical law requires rearrangement.

The problem with this attempted merger is that the two cases are different. Exodus 22:15–16 is concerned with seduction (which implies manipulation and persuasion), whereas Deuteronomy 22:28–29 deals with what we would nowadays call rape (which involves physical force; see Chapter 10). The Qumran interpreter is most likely aware of the difference because he omits the reference to "seizing." What then is gained from joining two different cases? Presumably some claim to equivalence between the two cases is being made, although in what direction is hard to tell. Seduction is regarded as seriously as rape and vice versa. It is possible that the Qumran author objects to "post-rape marriage" and wishes to reduce it down to a case of seduction where, presumably, he thinks it *is* fair to make the woman marry the man. At any rate, it is fair to say that while biblical law preserves the distinction between two different offenses, Qumran law abolishes them.

V. BIBLICAL LAW AT QUMRAN

To sum up, what do the Dead Sea Scrolls tell us about the interpretation of biblical law toward the end of the Second Temple period? It is clear that although the Qumran writers regard the biblical texts as authoritative, they still feel free to reinterpret them and represent them. Indeed, it is *because* they see the texts as speaking directly to their own time—and because they see their group as uniquely placed to understand them—that they have an interpretative approach which strikes us moderns as somewhat flexible. Sometimes there is an explicit—and indeed *verbatim*—citation of Scripture, while at other times, there is no indication of the underlying biblical text. Sometimes there is a paraphrase: at other times, an exegesis. Then again, there may be an implicit interpretation which in turn may be at odds with the underlying text. Occasionally the reading is a literal one; more often it is fluid, pictorial, and associative. Finally, there is evidence of considerable discretion and flexibility: texts are chosen because they suit the sect's worldview and agenda, while others are discarded. These interpretive norms seem remarkable to us because their idea of authority is different to what we have seen elsewhere in our discussion of biblical law. This is because

---

55. Bernstein, *Interpretation of Scriptures*, p. 380.

Qumranic perceptions of legitimate interpretative authority are at every point shaped by the community's eschatological worldview.

Metaphor and narrative are used at Qumran to reshape the traditional boundaries of biblical law, along with various interpretative methods, such as reasoning by analogy. These interpretations expand the scope of biblical law to cover new situations while advancing ideological claims about the community and its legitimacy as authoritative interpreters of Torah. They also promote a sectarian agenda which highlights the distinctiveness of the Qumran community against other religious groups in Israel. The Qumran texts are an excellent example of what happens when authority is located in an interpretative community. The Qumran community believes that it is in possession of its own authority to be able to present its Jewish tradition—and biblical law—in new and binding ways.

VI. LAW IN THE HANDS OF JESUS

We turn from the Qumranic application of biblical law to marital issues to explore Jesus's handling of the laws relating to marriage, divorce, and remarriage. There is a wide diversity of positions within the Christian church on how to read Jesus's teaching on this subject. They range from Roman Catholic/ extreme Protestant positions which see marriage as indissoluble, through to those that permit remarriage during the lifetime of the former spouse in exceptional circumstances (e.g., the Church of England). The spectrum also includes more liberal positions in other denominations which regard remarriage as a matter of individual conscience. In some cases, this is tantamount to the view that marriage is something that can be ended at will. The controversy surrounding this issue in recent decades (divorce only became legal in the Republic of Ireland in 1997) means that it provides a good illustration of the central issue in this book, namely, how do we understand and apply biblical law?

Certainly, the early church in the first five centuries was near unanimous in its view that remarriage following divorce for any reason is adulterous.[56] Its view of the divorce and remarriage texts remained the standard position of the Western church until the sixteenth century, when a more liberal view was put forward by the theologian Erasmus in 1519. This was subsequently adopted by Protestant theologians such as Jean Calvin, Martin Luther, and William Tyndale. The Erasmian/Protestant view differs from the position of the early church by

---

56. Summarized in GORDON J. WENHAM & WILLIAM E. HETH, JESUS AND DIVORCE (Carlisle: Paternoster Press, 2002), 19–44.

allowing divorce and remarriage for adultery and desertion, a position enshrined in the influential Westminster Confession of Faith (1648).[57]

We will explore the question of how to understand divorce and remarriage by reference to the various Gospel accounts of Matthew, Mark, and Luke, as well as Paul's *First Letter to the Corinthians*. This will show us how the biblical laws relating to divorce and remarriage were handled by Jesus and his followers and in a way that contrasts with the community at Qumran. Again, we will see that the way in which biblical law is interpreted depends on the wider story being told of what it means to "be Israel," at this point in her history. For simplicity's sake, we begin with the more straightforward accounts in the Gospels of Mark and Luke, before dealing with the more complicated case of Matthew.

In the Gospel According to Mark, Jesus's teaching on the subject is prompted by a test question from the Pharisees: "Is it lawful for a man to divorce his wife?" (Mark 10:2). This indicates, as the Dead Sea Scrolls attest, that divorce was heavily debated in Second Temple times. Jesus responds tactically with a counter-question ("What did Moses command you?"; Mark 10:3) which transforms the "doorstep interview" into a dialogue. The resulting exchange illustrates the differences between Jesus and the Pharisees regarding the interpretation of Torah:

> [The Pharisees] said, "Moses allowed a man to write a certificate of divorce, and to put her away." But Jesus said to them, "For your hardness of heart he wrote you this commandment. But from the beginning of creation, 'God made them male and female'. 'For this reason a man shall leave his father and mother and be joined to his wife, and the two shall become one flesh'. So they are no longer two but one flesh. What therefore God has joined together, let not man put asunder."(Mark 10:4–9)

As far as Jesus is concerned, the Pharisees' emphasis upon the permissory nature of Deuteronomy 24:1 exposes "hardness of heart" both on the part of the Pharisees and the original recipients of this law from Moses. The term "hardness of heart" (*sklerokardia*) is also used in Mark 16:14 to describe the disciples' initial refusal to believe in the evidence of Jesus's resurrection. Its use in Mark 10:5 implies "lack of faith, ignorance [and] blindness"[58] on the part of Jesus's questioners and the original recipients of the law. It implies that those who do not know that "one must not put away one's wife are somehow lacking in insight into the fundamental message, are failing in the faith itself."[59] This is not the first time that a link has been made between character and the ability to discern

---

57. A summary of the contrasts between the early church and the Protestant/Erasmian positions is provided in WENHAM & HETH, JESUS AND DIVORCE, pp. 85–86.

58. Quentin Quesnell, *Made themselves eunuchs for the kingdom of heaven (Matthew 19:12)*, CATHOLIC BIBLICAL Q., 335–58, 352 (1968).

59. Ibid.

the correct interpretation of biblical law (cf. Deuteronomy 15:9; see Chapter 7). "The tactics of Jesus's argument have the effect of achieving a striking identification between his questioners and the law of Deuteronomy 24:1: "What did Moses command *you*? . . . With a view to *your* hardness of heart Moses wrote this commandment *for you*." They are firmly associated with that commandment which Jesus abrogates . . . ."[60] As N. T. Wright confirms, "Jesus was not debating with the Pharisees on their own terms, or about the detail of their own agendas. Two musicians may discuss which key is best for a particular Schubert song. Somebody who proposes rearranging the poem for a heavy metal band is not joining in the discussion, but challenging its very premises."[61] As we saw in relation to Qumran law, the interpretation of marriage and divorce laws is a way of clarifying group identity.

My argument is that implicit in Jesus's teaching at this point is a distinction between legality and morality, that is, between what is halakhically permissible in Jewish law and what is morally right. This distinction is implicit in Jesus's words themselves. It is the difference between Jesus saying "[Moses] wrote you this commandment" (Mark 10:5) and "Let not man put asunder" (verse 9). In my view, Jesus makes the radical claim that *it is halakhically permissible to divorce in circumstances when it is not morally right to do so.*

Jesus's approach to the question of divorce and remarriage contrasts with that of the Pharisees because the starting point for Jesus's understanding is not Deuteronomy but Genesis. The quotation from Genesis 1:27, which emphasizes the separateness and the "two-ness" of the man and the woman, is a foil for the quotation from Genesis 2:24, which expresses the fusion and 'one-ness" of marriage. But although Jesus starts with Genesis, he goes beyond it. He makes "a man's and a woman's becoming one flesh *the reason* why the man should not divorce the woman."[62]

We saw above that Genesis 1:27 is also used as an authority in the Damascus Document concerning marriage and, possibly, divorce. However, the Damascus Document is at best only a partial parallel to Jesus's approach.[63] For starters, Jesus combines Genesis 1:27 with Genesis 2:24—which the Qumran interpreters did not do. He then produces from these texts something new. "Jesus does not limit himself . . . to the way in which the quoted statements were intended to

---

60. David R. Catchpole, *The Synoptic divorce material as a traditio-historical problem*, Bull. of the John Rylands University Library of Manchester, 57, 92–127, 126 (1974).

61. N. T. Wright, Jesus and the Victory of God (London: SPCK, 1996), 378.

62. Robert H. Gundry, Mark: A Commentary on His Apology for the Cross (Grand Rapids: Eerdmans, 2000), 532; italics added.

63. Catchpole, *Synoptic divorce material.*

be taken."⁶⁴ There is a freedom and a creativity in Jesus's approach to the law that is different to Qumran. This gives us an important insight into Jesus's handling of Torah. "The exposure of the will of God by Jesus came not by way of straight deduction from the law of Moses, but either totally independently of that law or by means of a dialectic within, and between, different parts of it."⁶⁵ In fact, what is remarkable about Jesus's exegetical technique is this: Jesus combines two distinct and unrelated texts that have nothing to do with divorce, and this leads to something new that *does* address the issue. This method actually mirrors the *content* of the texts themselves (two-ness leading to one-ness and a new entity).

The theological argument which Jesus presents from these materials is thus that the marriage relationship is permanent and indissoluble. Marriage is "the establishing (by God) of that one-ness which is the goal of creation."⁶⁶ Jesus's account of marriage sees God not just as a witness (per Malachi 2:14 and Proverbs 2:16–17) but the One who joins the couple together. There is a binary opposition between God and man and between "joining together" and "putting asunder." Divorce is wrong because it undoes God's work.⁶⁷ The use of the word "let . . ." in the phrase "let not man put asunder" (Mark 10:9) implies that the divine fusion *can* be reversed, although it should not be. Divorce is an act of "anti-creation." It thus stands in opposition to Jesus's kingdom work which seeks the restoration of God's creative intent.

This means that Jesus's teaching on marriage and divorce—like that at Qumran—has an eschatological dimension. David Catchpole writes that "in the antithesis between Deuteronomy 24:1 and Mark 10:9 there is expressed an underlying antithesis between the old age and the new."⁶⁸ There is a presupposition that the "new age" represented by Jesus and his kingdom is already breaking in and that this will see the renewal of creation. "Where there is hardness of heart, divorce is inevitable and lawful. But where the kingdom has been preached . . . it is now possible to attain to the purposes of the Creator. In the kingdom, divorce is not so much forbidden as it is unnecessary. There is now another way of dealing with it."⁶⁹ Jesus's teaching concerns more than simply "divorce laws": it "belongs inside the central concerns of the mission of Jesus and the proclamation of the present impact of that kingdom."⁷⁰

---

64. GUNDRY, MARK, p. 532.
65. Catchpole, *Synoptic divorce material*, p. 127.
66. Ibid., 125.
67. Ibid., 123.
68. Ibid., 126.
69. L. D. Hurst, *Ethics of Jesus, in* DICTIONARY OF JESUS AND THE GOSPELS, (Joel B. Green & Scot McKnight eds.; Leicester: InterVarsity Press, 1992), 210–22, 219.
70. Catchpole, *Synoptic divorce material*, p. 125.

Jesus's division between law and ethics—between that which is legally permissible and that which is morally right—is one expression of the coming kingdom. As applied to divorce and remarriage, the distinction raises the possibility that *legal divorce can lead to moral adultery*. This is exactly the issue that Jesus goes on to address with his disciples, in private:

> And he [Jesus] said to them [the disciples], "Whoever divorces his wife and marries another, commits adultery against her [that is, the divorced wife because she is still his spouse]; and if she divorces her husband and marries another, she commits adultery." (Mark 10:11–12)

As far as Jesus is concerned, the kingdom of God is associated with clear standards on the absolute commitment of marriage. The private setting gives Jesus's teaching "special emphasis."[71] It signifies that obedience on this issue is a crucial part of the disciples' identity. As at Qumran (despite the difference in substantive content), Jesus's teaching on divorce and remarriage is presented as being a core part of the disciples' identity. The same is true of Paul's teaching on divorce (see below). We will see that Paul distinguishes between Christian spouses, for whom divorce is not presented as being an option, and mixed marriages (Christian and not-Christian) for whom, in his view, divorce is an option, although even here it is a last resort (1 Corinthians 7:15).[72]

Jesus's teaching to his disciples in Mark 10:11–12 reappears in Luke's Gospel. Here, once again, it is given special emphasis as private instruction:

> Every one who divorces his wife and marries another commits adultery, and he who marries a woman divorced from her husband commits adultery. (Luke 16:18; *Jesus speaking*)

This teaching is also repeated by the apostle Paul in the *First Letter to the Corinthians*:

> To the married I give charge, not I but the Lord, that the wife should not separate from her husband (but if she does, let her remain single or else be reconciled to her husband)—and that the husband should not divorce his wife. (1 Corinthians 7:10–11)

This is one of very few places where Jesus's words are quoted in the New Testament outside the Gospels. (The variation in terminology here simply reflects the difference in perspective).

Jesus's private instruction spells out the implications of his theological argument. *If marriage is an indissoluble, two-in-one-flesh communion then the remarriage of a legally divorced partner must constitute moral adultery*. Again, we need to

---

71. WENHAM & HETH, JESUS AND DIVORCE, p. 62.
72. Catchpole, *Synoptic divorce material*, p. 126.

recognize that Jesus is making a distinction between what is legal and what is ethical, in line with Mark 10:5–9.

A. Traditional Radicalism

Jesus's citation of Genesis is, at one level, deeply traditional. But it is also extremely radical. Jesus's teaching on marriage and divorce is thus an example of what we might call "traditional radicalism." Mark 10:1–12 is revolutionary for four reasons.

First, Jesus distinguishes between legal and moral divorce. The person who legally divorces thinks he or she has a legal and a moral right to remarry. But Jesus states that the person who legally divorces and remarries is committing moral adultery. Such a person thinks they are morally free to remarry; but, in fact, they are not because the divorce is morally ineffective. In this sense, the divorce has been legally operative but not morally effective. The person who divorces and remarries still ends up committing adultery because the marriage bond is not broken. Jesus's teaching thus radically cuts down the operation of divorce because it denies its effectiveness. At the same time, Jesus's teaching expands the use of adultery to cover cases of legal divorce. Jesus is saying that it is possible for someone to legally divorce and to legally remarry but that this constitutes moral adultery.

Second, by labelling remarriage after a divorce "adultery," Jesus increases the scope of the offense of adultery (cf. the way in which the Qumran interpreters expanded the scope of the offense of fornication; see above). From the point of view of biblical law, this is not without precedent. We saw in Chapter 11 that biblical law sees adultery as an expansible category. In Leviticus 20, for example, we saw that the Decalogue heading of "adultery" in verse 10 gives rise to a series of sexual relationships that can be characterized as "forms of adultery" (verses 11–21). Indeed, we saw that one of the sexual relationships in this list actually takes the form of marriage (Leviticus 20:14, which concerns the man who marries a woman and her mother). This means that even in biblical law, we can identify a marriage that is nevertheless classified as a form of adultery.

Third, as part of this expansion, Jesus also extends the range of victims. We saw in Chapter 11 that a man is typically thought of as committing adultery against the *husband* of the woman with whom he has sexual relations (see Chapter 11). In Mark 10:1–12, Jesus radically extends the breadth of the typical understanding of adultery by saying that it can also be committed against his own *wife*. This means that the adultery by the husband is also an offense against *himself*. It follows from this extension that husbands and wives are treated equally for the purpose of adultery. The husband's behavior constitutes adultery against his wife and vice versa (cf. 1 Corinthians 7:3–4). On the subject of sexual equality, we should note that Mark 10:12 takes it for granted that wives could divorce their husbands (10:12). This is not surprising because it is consistent with a narrative reading of Deuteronomy 24:1–4 (see Chapter 11). Mark also refers to

Herodias, who had divorced her husband, Philip, in order to marry Herod Antipas (6:17).

Finally, Mark 10 is revolutionary because, at a stroke, Jesus abolishes polygamy. Jesus's reasoning—that marrying another after divorce constitutes adultery—presupposes monogamy because if polygamy was legitimate, there would no problem with remarriage to another woman. Again, there are parallels with the Qumran texts to the extent that these also prohibit polygamy.

B. Outlawing Moses?

So far, Jesus's teaching on marriage and divorce is consistent with the kind of thing that Jesus *would* say: it is clear, radical, and revolutionary. We have seen elsewhere how Jesus intensifies the jubilee in the form of "releasing debts" and forgiveness (see Chapter 7). It also fits the way that Jesus's teaching conflicts with first-century Jewish practice (e.g., Mark 7:9–13, 14–15). Likewise, it coheres with Jesus's use of Torah, generally, inasmuch as Jesus's direct quotation of biblical law in his ethical teaching is "minimal"[73] and prefers instead "the authority of an early ideal."[74]

Does Jesus's handling of Torah in Mark 10:1–12 abolish Moses? Jesus's treatment of Deuteronomy 24:1–4 reflects a complex attitude. He makes a "careful distinction between what God had said (in Genesis) and what Moses had said (in Deuteronomy)."[75] He also allows God's creative intention to question "the tacit approval of divorce within the Mosaic tradition."[76] For some commentators, this constitutes an abolition of the law. As Catchpole avers, "What Moses commanded, the historical Jesus rejects."[77] After all, it is Jesus himself who calls Deuteronomy 24:1 a "command" (10:3) and not merely a concession, per the Pharisees (10:4).

In the light of this, it is very striking that Jesus's teaching in Luke's Gospel follows directly on from the claim that:

> . . . it is easier for heaven and earth to pass away, than for one dot of the law to become void. (Luke 16:17; *Jesus speaking*)

Why did Luke include Jesus's divorce teaching at this point? This may have been because the liberal attitudes of Jesus's contemporaries toward marriage and divorce were seen as a prime example of the way in which "the law' *was*

---

73. D. J. Moo, Law, in Dictionary of Jesus and the Gospels, (Joel B. Green & Scot McKnight eds.; Leicester: InterVarsity Press, 1992), 450–61, 454.

74. John Kampen, *The Matthean divorce texts reexamined*, in New Qumran Texts & Studies (George J. Brooke ed., with Florentino García Martínez; Leiden: Brill, 1994), 149–67, 166.

75. Moo, Law, p. 453.

76. Ibid., 455.

77. Catchpole, *Synoptic divorce material*, p. 120.

being ignored and set aside. From that perspective, Jesus's strict teaching on marriage and divorce is not best seen as an example of "annulling" the law but of upholding it. In this sense, then, Jesus's teaching is not new.

Jesus's handling of Deuteronomy 24:1–4 emphasises the importance of creation in thinking about biblical law. As Hurst writes, "There is a law of God built into creation—lifelong fidelity—to which Deuteronomy is but an afterthought. If Jesus goes on to say that remarriage after divorce is adultery, it would not represent for him new legislation."[78]

If we put all this together, we find that there is a tension at the heart of Jesus's approach to the biblical material on marriage and divorce. It is both new and not new. It is radical and traditional. This may be part of the reason why we find Jesus's teaching on this subject difficult. It is hard to see exactly what Jesus is doing. Is he setting the law to one side, or is he upholding it? Jesus's strange division between law and ethics in Mark 10:5–9 exposes the tension. On the one hand, Jesus ethicizes the law by showing us the point of the rule. But on the other hand, Jesus relativizes the law by downplaying its significance in the light of Genesis.

Jesus's distinction in the Gospels of Mark and Luke between what is legally permissible and what is morally right inevitably raises the following questions. Can there ever be a moral divorce? That is, can a person be free to divorce in a way that is morally right? This is exactly the question addressed in Matthew's Gospel.

VII. ADULTERY—BUT NOT AS WE KNOW IT

The Gospel According to Matthew is widely recognized as being the most Jewish of the four Gospels and the one most sensitive to Jewish concerns. We might therefore expect some variation in expression, particularly if there was any anxiety that Jesus's teaching on marriage and divorce "outlawed Moses." It is therefore not surprising to find a different formulation of Jesus's teaching to that found in Mark and Luke.

Jesus's teaching is discussed in two places in Matthew's Gospel (Matthew 5:31–32 and 19:1–12). The first discussion occurs in the context of a discussion about adultery in the Sermon on the Mount. The Sermon is not "new law," as is sometimes thought, but a description of life in the kingdom of God.[79] For Jesus, ethics is primarily descriptive: it illustrates how men and women will behave in the kingdom. This lifestyle involves "a higher standard of ethical observance

---

78. Hurst, *Ethics of Jesus*, p. 219.
79. Ibid., 220.

than can ever be enforced by law"[80] no doubt because it is a question of vocation. We shall return to this question of calling in relation to marriage, below.

The teaching on divorce in the Sermon on the Mount is sandwiched between a prohibition of adultery and an exhortation to truth telling. Both point to a way of living that in practice makes divorce less likely to occur.[81] In regard to adultery, Jesus gives two examples of violations of the seventh commandment "which his audience would never contemplate as adulterous,"[82] namely, looking at another for the purpose of lust (verse 27–30) and divorce (verses 31–32). This context confirms that, as in Mark and Luke's Gospel, Jesus's teaching on divorce radically extends the scope of adultery:

> It was also said, "Whoever divorces (*apolyse*) his wife, let him give her a certificate of divorce." But I say to you that every one who divorces (*apolyon*) his wife, except on the ground of unchastity (*porneia*), makes her an adulteress; and whoever marries a divorced woman commits adultery (*moichatai*). (Matthew 5:31–32; *Jesus speaking*)

However, the reference to *porneia* in Matthew's Gospel appears to qualify the absolute prohibitions of Mark and Luke. Although some have argued that *porneia* here has a broad meaning (including "anything that causes the breakdown of a marriage"), its use in conjunction with *moicheia*, which means adultery, indicates that its use in verse 32 refers to adultery.[83] Gordon Wenham and William Heth[84] note that *porneia* is used in the Septuagint and the New Testament as an umbrella term that covers any and all types of unlawful sexual activity, including those found in Leviticus 18 and 20. We have seen in Chapter 11 that the sexual offenses listed in Leviticus 20:10–21, for example, can be classified as adultery and forms of adultery. Attempts to limit *porneia* to specific kinds of offenses, such as incest,[85] are unconvincing because it is not clear that the word is being used with such precision.

A. Permission to remarry?

Jesus's qualification in Matthew's Gospel means that there are some circumstances in which it is possible to speak of a moral divorce. It is possible for a disciple of Jesus to divorce in a way that is morally right, namely, when the

---

80. Ibid.
81. TOM WRIGHT, MATTHEW FOR EVERYONE, 2 vols. (London: SPCK, 2002), vol. I, 47.
82. John J. Kilgallen, *To what are the Matthean exception-texts (5:32 and 19:9) an exception?*, BIBLICA 61, 102–05, 103 (1980).
83. *See generally* DAVID INSTONE-BREWER, DIVORCE AND REMARRIAGE IN THE BIBLE (Grand Rapids: Eerdmans, 2002), 275–79.
84. WENHAM & HETH, JESUS AND DIVORCE, p. 137.
85. James R. Mueller, *The Temple Scroll and the Gospel Divorce Texts*, REVUE DU QUMRAN 10, 247–56, 256 (1980).

other party has committed *porneia*. In fact, there is an argument for saying that Jewish law did not simply permit the husband of an adulterous wife to divorce her but actually *required* him to do so.[86] But whether or not the divorce is mandatory or permissive, Jesus's exception (on the grounds of *porneia*) seems to mean that the spouse who is *not* responsible for the breakup can remarry, whereas the spouse who is responsible for breaking up the marriage is forbidden to remarry.

Some scholars go further to argue that it is *never* possible for either spouse to remarry.[87] They argue that Jesus's exception clause in Matthew *only* qualifies the phrase "every one who divorces his wife." This means that while the innocent spouse who has not committed *porneia* may obtain a divorce, she can never remarry because "whoever marries a divorced woman commits adultery" (Matthew 5:32). They argue that the verb "divorces" in verse 5:32a does not include the right to remarry. This leads them to construct the exception clause in the following terms:

> "(1) A man may not put away his wife unless she is guilty of adultery;
> (2) Whoever marries another after putting away his wife commits adultery."[88]

Their position can be summarized thus: "putting away for reasons other than unchastity is forbidden; and remarriage after every divorce is adulterous."[89] On this reading, there is no tension between what Jesus says in Mark and Luke and what Jesus says in Matthew. In all three Gospels, Jesus represents God's intention that there should be no exceptions to the ban on remarriage. The church is God's new creation and so it should be living according to the "one flesh" ideal set out in Genesis 1 and 2.

There are several difficulties with the view that Jesus's words constitute a ban on remarriage, *even* in the case of adultery. First, it assumes that Jesus gives the verb "divorce"' in verse 32a a highly restrictive meaning. Wenham and Heth[90] argue that Jesus limits the meaning of divorce to "separation from bed and board." Indeed, their construction of Matthew's exception clause only makes sense on this supposition. However, this would have been contrary to Jewish assumptions at the time. Of course, we have seen that Jesus does challenge contemporary Jewish ideas about divorce, but this is not in itself sufficient grounds for thinking that Jesus redefines the meaning of divorce in the way that Wenham and Heth imply. Their argument requires that they attach two different meanings to the verb "divorces" in verses 31 and 32. Thus, verse 31, which draws on Deuteronomy 24:1–4, uses the verb "to divorce" in the sense of "divorce with the

---

86. Jackson, Essays on Halakah, pp. 203, 208–10.
87. Wenham & Heth, Jesus and Divorce.
88. Ibid., 117.
89. Ibid.
90. Ibid., 129–35.

right to remarry" ("Whoever divorces (*apolyse*) his wife, let him give her a certificate of divorce"). However, on their view, verse 32 uses the verb in the sense of "separation and no right of remarriage" ("But I say to you that every one who divorces (*apolyon*) his wife, except on the ground of unchastity, makes her an adulteress; and whoever marries a divorced woman commits adultery"). Wenham and Heth argue that since the word *apolyein* has a general meaning that does not convey the specifics of whether one could or could not remarry, the word can mean two different things, according to context.[91] However, given the sharpness of the distinction that is being made, one would expect this to be flagged somewhere in the text itself.

Second, if, as Wenham and Heth argue, the verb "divorces" in verse 32a refers only to "separation from bed and board," how can divorce alone make the woman "an adulteress"? They explain Jesus's saying by claiming that "divorce, except for unchastity, is tantamount to committing adultery."[92] But Jesus says that she is an adulteress, not that she is nearly an adulteress. The reference to "an adulteress" surely implies that she has contracted a second marriage. Again, the view that "divorce" in verse 32 refers to separation with no right of remarriage seems implausible.

My argument is that the exception clause reminds us, once again, of the importance of the distinction Jesus makes between that which is legally permissible and that which is morally right. In Matthew's Gospel, Jesus seems to be saying that while it is possible to legally divorce in circumstances when it is not morally right to do so; it is sometimes possible to legally divorce in a way that is morally right—when one party commits *porneia*. However, the person who wrongfully divorces—for reasons other than *porneia*—and who legally remarries, commits moral adultery.

B. Healing and Teaching

Matthew returns to the subject of marriage and divorce later in his Gospel (Matthew 19:1–12). It is characteristic of Matthew to mention topics or to quote sayings twice (e.g., 3:2=4:17; 3:10=7:19; 3:12=25:29).[93] Wenham and Heth helpfully note that in such cases, Matthew "tends to abridge so that some of his remarks can only be understood in the light of the fuller text."[94] This creates the sensible presumption that the exception clause "except for *porneia*" should be understood in the same way in both passages.

Nevertheless, there are important differences between the contexts of the two sayings. Matthew 5:31–32 does not record any interaction with Jesus's listeners, whereas Matthew 19:1–12 begins with a debate with the Pharisees (cf. Mark 10).

---

91. Ibid., 133–34.
92. Ibid., 71.
93. Ibid., 49.
94. Ibid.

Matthew opens his second pericope on divorce by tracking Jesus's movement into:

> ... the region of Judea beyond the Jordan and large crowds followed him [Jesus], and he healed them there. And Pharisees came up to him and tested him by asking, "Is it lawful to divorce one's wife for any cause?" (Matthew 19:2–3)

It is striking that Jesus's teaching on divorce occurs in the context of physical healings. The restoration of persons to God's original creative intent is consistent with the teaching that follows, which is a call to return to the ideals of Genesis. There is an implied contrast between "healing," which implies wholeness, and "putting asunder," which implies woundedness. The context further underlines Jesus's tension with the Pharisees whose preoccupation with grounds for divorce—and hence "uncreation"—is opposed to Jesus's concern for wholeness and "recreation."

There is also a contrast between the setting of Jesus's teaching in Matthew's Gospel and that of Mark. In Matthew, the implications of Jesus's teaching are made public, whereas in Mark, they are private. We also find that the Pharisees' opening question is different. Instead of the general "Is it lawful for a man to divorce his wife?" (Mark 10:2), we have the more pointed "Is it lawful to divorce one's wife for any cause?" (Matthew 19:3). This phrase alludes to sharp rabbinic debates in Jesus's day regarding the meaning of Deuteronomy 24:1–4; a record of which survives in postbiblical rabbinic accounts:

> The School of Shammai say: A man should not divorce his wife unless he found in her a matter of indecency, as it is said: "For he finds in her an indecent matter." And the School of Hillel say, Even if she spoiled his dish, since it says "For he finds in her an indecent matter." (Mishnah Gittin 9:10)

To judge from surviving writings, the liberal Hillelite position appears to have been dominant in the first century (e.g., Josephus Antiquities 4:253), and it seems that the Pharisees in Matthew 19:3 assume this majority position.

Jesus rejects the Pharisees' basic assumption that Deuteronomy 24:1–4 should be the starting point of the debate and takes them back, as we have seen, to Genesis. We have already considered how this tactic could be seen as rejecting the authority of Moses. This is why the Pharisees respond by asking why Moses had authority to permit divorce in the first place ("Why then did Moses command one . . . ?"; Matthew 19:7). Jesus responds by identifying their interpretation as a symptom of hard-heartedness. It is in this context that we find the repetition of the so-called "Matthean exception":

> And I say to you: whoever divorces his wife, except for unchastity, and marries another, commits adultery. (Matthew 19:9)

As in Matthew 5:31–32, Jesus is saying that while it is possible to legally divorce in circumstances when it is not morally right to do so, it is sometimes possible to legally divorce in a way that is morally right. Once again, the person who wrongfully divorces—that is, for reasons other than *porneia*—and who legally remarries, commits moral adultery.

Why does Matthew include Jesus's exception when Mark and Luke do not? The answer seems to lie in Matthew's general sensitivity toward Jewish concerns. Insofar as the word *porneia* covers adultery, there is enough evidence to indicate the possibility that the *porneia* exception reflects a Jewish movement toward a mandatory divorce of the adulterer's wife.[95] If so, it is only to be expected that Matthew would include information that was relevant to his primarily Jewish audience.

VIII. ADULTERERS CANNOT BENEFIT

We have seen that Jesus's teaching in Mark and Luke appears to absolutely prohibit divorce and remarriage, while Jesus's teaching in Matthew appears to grant an exception on the grounds of *porneia*. How do we make sense of this apparent discrepancy? Understanding the New Testament's handling of biblical law is not too far removed from the general problem we have been considering throughout this book, namely, how do we do biblical law? Once again, we find that we have a choice between adopting a rule-based literal approach or a narrative paradigmatic one. Can the texts be resolved by either, or both, of these approaches?

First, if we approach Jesus's teaching as a set of rules and in a legalistic fashion, then we will encounter problems because Jesus's teaching in Mark and Luke does not refer to any exceptions, whereas Matthew does. This implies that the absolutist position in Mark and Luke's Gospels is not the whole story, an impression that is confirmed by Paul's additional exception in First Corinthians. Even the prohibitive language of Mark 10:5–9 is undercut by the phraseology of Mark 10:9—"let not man put asunder"—which implies that human beings have the power to end a marriage.

However, even on a rule-based approach, there is a possible way of harmonizing the texts. Matthew 5 states that if the husband legally divorces his wife for a reason other than *porneia*, it is a wrongful divorce and hence ineffective. The result is that when the woman legally remarries, she commits moral adultery. On the other hand, if the husband divorces the woman for *porneia*, he is not guilty of causing her to be an adulteress, either (a) because she is an adulteress already (since *porneia* is the reason why he is divorcing her); or (b) because she committed the *porneia*, and so she is responsible for his ending the relationship.

---

95. LÖVESTAM, DIVORCE AND REMARRIAGE, p. 61; JACKSON, ESSAYS ON HALAKAH, pp. 203, 208–10.

Either way, she is not free to remarry because the marriage has come to an end through her own fault.

In my view, it follows that what Matthew's Gospel adds to Mark and Luke is the possibility that one spouse can divorce the other if the other spouse is at fault in ending the marriage. The spouse who has committed *porneia* is responsible for it and cannot remarry, whereas the party who has not committed *porneia* is free to remarry. It is a true divorce—legally and morally—but only for the party who is not at fault.

A. The nuclear option

This fits with Mark and Luke's Gospels where Jesus says that neither spouse, as one party to the marriage, has power to bring it to an end. This is because if you do something to end it, you can never remarry. What Matthew adds is that if the marriage is formally dissolved because of what the other person has done, then the innocent party is not prevented from remarrying.

This is also compatible with Paul, who identifies at least one other circumstance other than *porneia*—desertion:

> To the rest I say, not the Lord, that if any brother has a wife who is an unbeliever, and she consents to live with him, he should not divorce her. If any woman has a husband who is an unbeliever, and he consents to live with her, she should not divorce him . . . But if the unbelieving partner desires to separate, let it be so; in such a case the brother or sister is not bound. For God has called us to peace. (1 Corinthians 7:12–13, 15; *Paul speaking*)

To put it another way, while there are justifiable grounds for divorce, it is not possible for you to rely upon them if you are responsible for bringing about the end of the marriage. This means that, in effect, the commission of *porneia* or the act of desertion are informal modes of divorce. Adultery and desertion are equivalent to ending a marriage. There is a power to divorce—but it should never be used ("let not man put asunder . . ."). Adultery and desertion are the "nuclear option"; however, it is best not to have your finger on the button.

Jesus's teaching in Matthew's Gospel envisages the moral—but not the legal—possibility that one party is "as if they are married," and the other party is not. What this means is that the person who is not responsible for breaking up the marriage is allowed to enter another one. However, the person who is responsible for the divorce is not free to remarry because this person is regarded as morally married, even though there has been a legal divorce. There is an element of poetic justice here. The party who takes marriage seriously and is not responsible for the divorce can have another marriage; but the party who despises the marriage and precipitates a divorce is not allowed to enter into another one.

The irony is that the person who breaks up the marriage cannot benefit from his or her wrong. The divorce is morally ineffective—for them. They are still regarded as married and so cannot remarry. Some might argue that this reading suffers from the same objection as that levied against Wenham and Heth, above, inasmuch as this too involves a "double sense." It means that "divorce" for the innocent party means "divorce with the right of remarriage," whereas "divorce" for the guilty party means "separation with no right of divorce." However, my argument is that this difference in meaning reflects a distinction that is present in Matthew 5:31–32, where Jesus distinguishes between that which is legally valid and that which is morally effective. As I have argued above, Jesus's response to the Pharisees assumes that divorce can be legally permissible but morally ineffective. This is why a legally permissible divorce can result in moral adultery.

If we put together Jesus's teaching in Matthew, Mark, and Luke, we can, in my view, reach the following conclusions. Jesus is saying that the legal act of divorce can be a wrongful repudiation of marriage. But there are some circumstances in which the legal act of divorce is not a wrongful repudiation of marriage if the other party is at fault. In these circumstances, divorce gives legal effect to the fact that the marriage has been repudiated. (This is a different way of harmonizing the Gospels to that suggested by Instone-Brewer[96]).

Of course, we can think of different ways in which marriage can be repudiated. The question is: when is it ethically appropriate to make use of that legal power to divorce? This is the question Jesus addresses in Matthew's Gospel. Jesus proclaims that if you make use of it in certain circumstances, then it is not wrongful; but if you do it in other circumstances, then it is wrongful. The bottom line is that you cannot benefit from your wrongdoing.

This approach ties in with rabbinic practice which did not, on the face of it, allow marriage between the guilty party and the suspected paramour (Sotah 5:1; and even if marriage was possible, the husband could not have sexual relations with her. In a polygamous context, this would not have been such a problem, for the husband). This is broadly consistent with Jesus's teaching; that adulterers cannot benefit from their wrong.

It might be objected that this approach is unfair since no party is ever wholly responsible for breaking up a marriage. But this merely recognizes that there are ups and downs in any marriage and, since this is the case, it is all the more important not to add to it through *porneia* or desertion. Jesus's teaching thus provides protection for both parties in the marriage because there is never any incentive to end it by *porneia*. Instead, there is every incentive to stay in the marriage precisely because it is "the only one you've got." This means that Jesus's exception in Matthew's Gospel does not encourage *porneia* as a way of getting out of a failed marriage. Nor does Luke punish the wife who has been wrongfully divorced by her husband.

---

96. INSTONE-BREWER, DIVORCE AND REMARRIAGE, pp. 133–88. For criticisms of Instone-Brewer's approach, SEE JACKSON, ESSAYS IN HALAKAH, pp. 193–96, 203–11.

Although Jesus's teaching makes sense in terms of rules, a strictly casuistic approach leaves too many questions unanswered. Jesus identifies *porneia* as providing a moral ground for divorce, and Paul—dealing with a situation that Jesus never had to deal with —identifies a further ground of desertion. This raises the question of whether there are any additional grounds for divorce, such as emotional and material neglect (cf. Exodus 21:10–11). Another question is the status of the second marriage. What about the man who wrongfully divorces and legally remarries? Jesus claims that this is adultery. But what is the true status of the "morally adulterous marriage"? Is the fact that the parties are married sufficient to distinguish it from a "straightforward" adulterous relationship? If so, is it a full marriage? Or is it a defective marriage? Or is it really a form of serial polygamy?

The danger of a legalistic approach to Jesus's teaching is that it takes us back to the very debate that the Pharisees wanted to have with Jesus—and which Jesus sets to one side. The problem with a casuistic approach is that we end up adding exception after exception and one clarification clause after another. Ironically, we end up reading Jesus like Moses at the very point where Jesus separates himself from Moses.

To conclude, Jesus's teaching sets out a very clear rule; but that does not necessarily mean that all of its ramifications are worked out. This is indicated by the way in which Paul identifies desertion as an additional ground. It raises the possibility that Jesus is not advocating a casuistic approach and might instead be envisioning a calling. If so, the rule and its implications are to be understood and applied in the light of the calling.

B. Ethics and Calling

Another way of resolving the different accounts might simply be to reject a casuistic approach. It may simply be a misreading of the material to think about reconciling the texts in terms of their exceptions. Instead, we could try to resolve Jesus's teaching by taking a narrative paradigmatic approach.

It is sometimes said that the problem we have with Jesus's teaching in the Gospels of Mark and Luke is that it appears to be "an overstatement in which universal language [regarding divorce] is used to teach a non-universal truth."[97] However, we have already had reason to question whether the Bible does in fact reflect any straightforward commitment to universalism (see Chapter 3). What we found instead was evidence of norms known to everyone to whom they apply and that this was not inconsistent with some form of moral pluralism. We also saw that the expression of moral virtues, consistent with a particular call and commitment, could vary from one person to the next. In that regard, it is notable

---

97. R. H. Stein, *Divorce, in* Dictionary of Jesus and the Gospels, (Joel B. Green & Scot McKnight eds.; Leicester: InterVarsity Press, 1992), 192–99, 195.

that Jesus's teaching on marriage and divorce does appear to be presented in terms of a response to a calling.

C. The shock of Torah

This is explicit in Jesus's debate with his disciples in Matthew 19:10–12, which immediately follows Jesus's debate with the Pharisees in Matthew 19:3–9. The disciples protest at Jesus's teaching (19:10) by saying, "it is not expedient to marry" (verse 10). This triggers a peroration from Jesus on the subject of eunuchs (19:12) which is prefaced by Jesus's remark: "Not all men can receive this saying (*ton logon touton*), but only those to whom it is given" (19:11). This clearly introduces the idea of a calling. But to what does the calling refer?

It seems clear the "saying" in verse 11, and hence the calling, refers to Jesus's teaching on marriage and divorce in verses 4–9.[98] The ones who "can accept" Jesus's teaching because it has been "given" to them are those who obey Jesus's teaching in relation to marriage and divorce. Those who can respond to the call of marriage should do so. This is consistent with Jesus's use of Genesis, which implies a "universal" calling to marriage. Matthew 19:4–6 confirms that the "default" position is marriage, and Jesus sets out three reasons why people might not marry and might discern that they have a calling not to marry (verse 12).

This reading contrasts with those who argue that the "saying" refers to the disciples' outburst in verse 10: "it is not expedient to marry." If this is correct, and the referent of Jesus's saying is to the disciples' reaction, then it follows that the calling of which Jesus speaks is celibacy. This is how verse 12 has traditionally been understood.[99] However, the problem with this reading is that it does not square with Jesus's teaching regarding Genesis. In the light of this, it is bizarre to interpret Jesus as saying that singleness is the default position. This interpretation is also inconsistent with a subsequent conversation that Jesus has with the disciples later, in Chapter 19. Here, the disciples are witness to another radical exchange between Jesus and a third party (verses 16–22) where the disciples, once again, express astonishment at his teaching (verse 25). On this occasion, it is clear that Jesus's response in verse 26 ("With men this is impossible...") does not refer back to the disciples' shocked reaction in verse 25 ("Who then can be saved?") but rather continues his teaching in verses 23–24 on the subject of wealth.[100] It is almost certain, then, that the same is true earlier in Chapter 19 as well. This means that Jesus's "saying" in verse 11 refers not to the disciples' outburst in verse 10 but rather continues Jesus's teaching in verses 4–9 on the subject of marriage.

---

98. *E.g.,* David Patte, The Gospel According to Matthew: A Structural Commentary on Matthew's Faith (Philadelphia: Fortress Press, 1987), 266.
99. Ibid., 268.
100. Wenham & Heth, Jesus and Divorce, p. 58.

Consequently, we can see that Jesus's teaching on marriage and divorce in Matthew 19:3–9 is anchored in the belief that marriage is a calling (19:11–12).

D. Forsaking all others

Indeed, Jesus's use of the Eden narrative in Matthew 19:4–6 and Mark 10: 5–9 indicates that marriage is understood in terms of a calling. The picture emphasizes three things: (1) God, (2) the couple, and (3) work in the forest of Eden (Genesis 2:15–25). "Marriage is instituted by the Creator in the context of meaningful work . . . the purpose of sex is not in principle the promotion of interpersonal relationship."[101] The Eden story presents a very positive image of marriage: it is a picture of mutual dependency in the service of something greater than the couple themselves. Another striking feature of Eden is the lack of any alternative marital relationship for Adam and Eve. As presented, there are no other human beings around. There is no alternative marriage for them to jump into or reason for them to abandon the marriage they have got. This is important from the point of view of calling. The call of marriage is such that one cannot consider any alternative. The "question of intent"—asked at wedding ceremonies in the Church of England—captures this well. It asks whether the parties are willing to "forsake all others as long as you both shall live?" The marriage should be as if there were no others, as was the case in Eden. This ties the question of calling ("am I called to that sort of exclusive relationship?") to the narrative image.

E. "Let everyone lead the life which the Lord has assigned to him . . . "

The same belief—that marriage is a vocation—is also explicit in Paul's teaching. Paul starts by repeating Jesus's "command" that "a wife must not separate from her husband . . . And a husband must not divorce his wife" (1 Corinthians 7:10–11). He then delivers, on his own authority, an additional exception which is not mentioned by Jesus in Matthew's Gospel, namely, that the believer in a mixed marriage may consent to divorce by an unbeliever (1 Corinthians 7:12–15). Paul is able to insist both on a prohibition upon divorce and on an exception. This is similar to the combined view of the Gospels. Again, Paul locates this teaching in the context of a calling:

> Only, let every one lead the life which the Lord has assigned to him, and in which God has called him. This is my rule in all the churches.
> (1 Corinthians 7:17; *Paul speaking*)

Putting Jesus and Paul together, it seems as though one way of making sense of the apparent dissonance regarding marriage and divorce is to recognize that

---

101. CHRISTOPHER ASH, MARRIAGE: SEX IN THE SERVICE OF GOD (Leicester: InterVarsity Press, 2005), 21.

the New Testament situates its regulations in the context of a calling. Even in Mark and Luke's Gospels, Jesus's teaching on marriage and divorce occurs in the broader context of what it means for Israel to fulfill her vocation as the people of God. Likewise Jesus's teaching in Matthew 5 occurs in the context of describing those who are members of the Kingdom of God. This is not too far removed from the character of Torah itself. We saw in Chapter 2 that the priestly covenant of Exodus 19 is understood primarily in terms of a vocation ("you shall be to me a kingdom of priests and a holy nation"; 19:6). In particular, it is clear that obedience to Jesus on the subject of divorce and remarriage was one of the key ways in which the new Israel, which was being formed around Jesus, would fulfill its vocation. The "Kingdom of God" would be a work of new creation (cf. the parallels between the creation of the world and the creation of Israel at Mount Sinai, noted in Chapter 2). The coming of the Kingdom of God in the *eschaton* (the "end times" or the "end of the present age") is bound up with the fulfillment of God's purposes for creation. Jesus's reference to Genesis in Mark 10:6–8 understands marriage in the light of creation. This means that Jesus's teaching on divorce and remarriage is not some kind of ethical "optional extra" but is central to his eschatological thinking. As Catchpole writes: "Jesus presupposes . . . that the End time, which will see a renewal of the Beginning time, has already dawned."[102] To this extent, it is fair to say that the debate between Jesus and the Pharisees reflects "a more basic ideological debate on the status of marriage itself in the imminent eschatological age."[103] Eschatology also helps us to make sense of Paul's allowance for divorce in the case of the non-Christian who deserts a Christian spouse. Divorce is here allowable precisely because the initiative is taken by someone who is *not* identified as a follower of Jesus. Paul's teaching is eschatological in its outlook because it presumes and implements "a distinction between those who are in Christ and those who are not. For Christian couples, divorce is excluded, but for 'mixed couples' it is a reluctantly allowed possibility."[104]

The idea that Jesus's disciples were defined by their behavior in relation to divorce and remarriage and that this was a way of fulfilling their vocation as the people of God during the "last days" has parallels with the Qumran sectarians. Of course, there are major substantive differences in the content of Dead Sea Scrolls and the New Testament in relation to divorce and remarriage. Nevertheless, it is true that the members of the Qumran community saw themselves as fulfilling Israel's vocation in the "end times," even to the extent of camping out in the desert in a manner that evoked Sinai and that their high standards in relation to divorce and remarriage anticipated the coming Messianic age. Jackson understands the differences between the Dead Sea Scrolls and the New

---

102. Catchpole, *Synoptic divorce material*, p. 125.
103. Jackson, Essays in Halakah, p. 211.
104. Catchpole, *Synoptic divorce material*, p. 126.

Testament on divorce and remarriage in the light of sectarian rivalry, which expressed itself in "'holier than thou" claims regarding permissible sexual relationships."[105] Jackson's approach is not too far removed from my argument that divorce and remarriage in the New Testament is understood in terms of a vocation. Some groups, like the Qumran community and the followers of Jesus, see themselves as distinct from others and as endorsing higher standards, and this can be identified with having a sense of calling.

Within the overall context of a calling, it is self-evident that the "call" to faithful marriage precludes the option of divorce. No one who is concerned with responding to the call to marriage could possibly be interested in whether there is an exception on the grounds of *porneia*, or of having an unbelieving spouse or indeed a range of other grounds that may be permissible but are not articulated. Inherent in the concept of a marriage is the belief that one cannot ditch it. It is simply not possible to speak of marriage in a provisional way. The idea that marriage is a calling also helps to explain why the person who wrongfully divorces is not given a second chance. The person who is to blame for the marriage failing and who has successfully destroyed "what God has joined together" has, by definition, demonstrated a lack of calling to marriage.

Even so, as far as the New Testament is concerned, the outworking of this calling means taking account of problems raised in two particular cases. These are (1) the social pressure to divorce in cases of *porneia* (which seems to be an issue for Jewish believers), and (2) desertion by the unbeliever (which is a problem for believers in a mixed marriage). Or to put it in different language, even in the run-up to the *eschaton*, concessions sometimes have to be made. As noted, above, in relation to the Dead Sea Scrolls, certain exceptions were made for the king, even though these did not apply to ordinary members of the community. Even in eschatological teaching, there is an element of eschatological pragmatism.[106] This is true, albeit in different ways, both for the Dead Sea Scrolls and the New Testament.

To conclude, there are various ways in which we can make sense of Jesus's teaching. They include a rule-based literal approach and a totally different narrative paradigmatic approach. From one perspective, Jesus can be read as giving very limited conditions under which couples can divorce (in which case it can all become very legalistic). From another, Jesus sets out an image of what marriage is about, which emphasizes that it is a vocation and a calling. My argument is that there are possibilities for reconciling the different accounts in Mark, Luke, and Matthew under either approach.

What implications does this have for our understanding of the nature of biblical law? I have argued that Jesus's approach in the Gospels of Matthew and Mark

---

105. Jackson, Essays in Halakah, p. 224.
106. Jackson, Essays in Halakah, pp. 223–25.

ties the rule about marriage and divorce to a central narrative image which is rooted in the idea of a calling. Further support for this approach is found in Paul's teaching. Indeed Paul *explicitly* juxtaposes the idea of a calling (". . . let every one lead the life . . . which God has called him") with that of a rule, or a command ("This is my *rule* in all the churches").

Understanding divorce and remarriage means holding onto both the sense of vocation and the rules. There are dangers with an exclusively legalistic approach because we end up being prescriptive about things that Jesus was not prescriptive about. Rules are not enough. They need to be understood in the light of God's calling; otherwise we will end up having debates around the Pharisees' agenda. But at the same time, rules are needed to give form and shape to the calling. Without them, the "calling" risks becoming overly subjective. It is a mistake to become fixated on either rules or calling. Rules are one mode of expressing reality, and calling is another. Both are needed to express the reality of marital commitment.

IX. CONCLUSION

Toward the end of the Second Temple period, biblical law was interpreted and applied in a way that often strikes modern interpreters as tendentious. At times it seems to border on eisegesis rather than exegesis. We find considerable fluidity between genres that are nowadays regarded as distinct, and we discover that the early chapters of Genesis were crucial to legal interpretation. This difference may be partly explained by the fact that the first-century AD was a time when much emphasis was placed by exegetes on understanding what the God of Israel was doing and requiring *now*, rather than on trying to reconstruct interpretations of "what people thought" in the past. The Qumran community believed that the God of Israel was present and active in the life of their unique community: the New Testament writers, by contrast, believed that Jesus of Nazareth was the means by which God was bringing about the restoration of Israel and the cosmos, in line with God's original creative intent.

Yet, despite these fundamental differences, we can say that the laws of marriage, divorce, and remarriage were important to both groups as a means of championing a particular attitude toward Moses, the purposes of God, and the eschaton. They also helped to define the identity of both religious groups, particularly in relation to their opponents, and they formed part of a call to renewed and intensified Torah-obedience. Indeed, for both the Qumran community and Jesus's disciples (in different ways), their behavior on the question of divorce and remarriage was central to their identity. The many differences between Qumran and Jesus show the considerable pluralism that existed within Second Temple Judaism on this single issue. Furthermore, there is evidence of considerable diversity within each group. It is far from clear that the Dead Sea Scrolls speak with a single voice on the subject of divorce, and even Jesus's disciples are shocked by Jesus's teaching. Our study of divorce and remarriage in the shadow of the Second Temple reminds us that this was a period of great diversity and conflict. It was a time when all the parties believed they were playing for high stakes. This is the background for the topic of the following chapter: the trials of Jesus.

Selected reading
Moshe J. Bernstein and Shlomo A. Koyfman, "The interpretation of biblical law in the Dead Sea Scrolls: Forms and methods." In *Biblical Interpretation at Qumran*, Matthias Henze ed. (Grand Rapids: Eerdmans, 2005), pp. 61–87.
David R. Catchpole, "The synoptic divorce material as a traditio-historical problem," *Bulletin of the John Rylands University Library of Manchester*, 57 (1974), 92–127.
Bernard S. Jackson, *Essays on Halakhah in the New Testament* (Leiden: Brill, 2008), Chapter 8.
Lawrence H. Schiffman, *Reclaiming the Dead Sea Scrolls* (Philadelphia: Jewish Publication Society, 1994), especially Chapter 15.
Gordon J. Wenham and William E. Heth, *Jesus and Divorce* (Carlisle: Paternoster Press, 2002), especially Chapters 2 and 6.
James C. Vanderkam, "Sinai revisited." In *Biblical Interpretation at Qumran*, Matthias Henze ed. (Grand Rapids: Eerdmans, 2005), pp. 44–60.

13. THE TRIALS OF JESUS

The trial of Jesus is a key aspect of law and legality in the Bible and, indeed, the question of the legality of Jesus's trial is a perennial topic of debate. It is the most notorious trial in history, and its importance—regardless of one's personal worldview—cannot be underestimated. The trial of Jesus also shows how particular biblical laws, such as blasphemy, false prophecy, and false teaching were understood in the late Second Temple period and how they interfaced with other legal traditions, such as Roman law and custom.

The trial of Jesus is central to the story of Jesus. Everything in the Gospels leads up to it, and everything in the New Testament flows from it. Yet the Gospels depict not the *trial* of Jesus but the *trials* of Jesus. There is more than one trial in both the Jewish and Roman proceedings, and there is also a trial before Herod. The multiple judicial scenes reflect the seriousness and difficulty of the issues.

This chapter explores the battle within Jewish tradition between, on the one hand, those who wanted to secure Jesus's conviction and, on the other, Jesus's popular following. It also investigates the conflict regarding the charges, if any, that could be brought. Was Jesus a true prophet or a false prophet; who could decide, and on what basis? We also explore the conflict between the Jewish legal tradition and an external legal system (Rome). Could a capital charge be constructed that would be valid in both Jewish and Roman law? We will also consider the ceding of jurisdiction by a Roman governor (Pilate) to a neighboring native puppet ruler (Herod); the relationship between customary law and Roman law in the form of the "Passover amnesty," and finally, the influence of the popular vote (the crowd) upon Pilate's executive action in sentencing Jesus. How did this unique confluence of personalities and events produce an unjust decision in a capital case? How should we make sense of the collective failure of Jewish, Roman, Herodian, and popular justice? And finally, being alert to the connections between law and theology, what implications does this have for modern cases of miscarriage of justice?

I. GOSPEL TRUTH?

We begin with a nonlegal problem: the nature of the Gospel records themselves. The claim is made, in some circles, that the Gospels ought to come with an epistemological "health warning."[1] They should be handled with extreme care, it is

---

1. *E.g.*, HAIM COHN, THE TRIAL AND DEATH OF JESUS (London: Weidenfeld and Nicholson, 1970), xiv–xix.

said, because they advance an interpretation of historical events, namely, that Jesus of Nazareth is the one in whom and through whom Israel's covenant God is at work to renew the world. But this desire to treat the Gospels as somehow different from any other historical text, or potential source of knowledge, does not recognize that the sort of knowledge we can reasonably claim to have of historical events is ultimately of the same order and subject to the same qualifications as knowledge in general. As N. T. Wright observes, "some critics have made a great song and dance about the fact that the details of Jesus's life . . . cannot be proved 'scientifically'; philosophical rigour should compel them to admit that the same problem pertains to the vast range of ordinary human knowledge, including the implicit claim that knowledge requires empirical verification."[2]

A more nuanced "critical realist" epistemology "acknowledges the *reality of the thing known, as something other than the knower* . . .[hence 'realist'], while also fully acknowledging that the only access we have to this reality lies along the spiralling path of *appropriate dialogue or conversation between the knower and the thing known* [hence 'critical']."[3] Human beings are not "bath sponges" that simply "soak up" sense data[4]; instead, we reflect upon external phenonema and aim to make sense it of by drawing on a larger framework or "set of *stories* about things that are likely to happen in the world."[5] Dismissing the Gospels as "history—with a spin on it" fails to recognize that *all* knowledge and *all* history has a "spin on it."

Another aspect of the "spin" is recognizing that we can never have exhaustive knowledge. We know in part. The only nonsuspect knowledge is exhaustive knowledge, and an exhaustive account of any period of history is not possible. The Gospels are —as they claim to be—a selection from the total available material on the life of Jesus (cf. John 21:25); what is being "spun" is what the authors think we most need to know (Luke 1:1–4; John 20:30–31). There is nothing surprising about this: our understanding of *any* period of history is going to be partial. Consequently, the Gospels are not suspect because they are nonexhaustive. Likewise, it is possible for us to know something without needing to have complete knowledge.

As a matter of historical knowledge, therefore, there is no difference in principle between picking up the Gospels and picking up the Pentateuch. We have seen in previous chapters how understanding biblical law means reconstructing, as best we can, the social context and worldview within which these texts made sense. We study law and narrative in the light of other law and narrative. That is

---

2. N. T. Wright, THE NEW TESTAMENT AND THE PEOPLE OF GOD (London: SPCK, 1993), 34.
3. Ibid., 35; italics original.
4. Ibid., 83.
5. Ibid., 37; italics original.

to say, we make sense of things in the light of other things that we have already made sense of and about which we are prepared to revise our beliefs, if necessary, in the light of additional data. Something can be a matter of interpretation yet still be the stuff of public truth.

The Gospels are no different. Right from the start of the Gospel According to Saint Matthew, the story of Jesus is placed in the wider context of the story of Israel and, as the Gospel goes on, the story of Jesus, at point after point, retells and reshapes the story of Israel. The Gospels do not aim to give us the same effect that we would receive from following Jesus around with a camcorder—and nor should we expect them to. The things that Jesus said and did had to be interpreted and, as we will see in the trials of Jesus, there was a real and fierce dispute regarding the sense that should be made of Jesus and his activities. The real question, then, is not whether the Gospels interpret events but whether their interpretation, like that of any hypothesis, passes the sort of test that is usually applied to hypotheses in any field, namely: (1) does it gather in all the relevant facts and explain the detail? (2) does it do so with a certain degree of simplicity? and (3) does it shed light on areas beyond its immediate concern?[6] Or, to put it another way, does the overall story that the Gospels tell about the world as a whole make more sense, in their "outline and detail, than other potential or actual stories that may be on offer"?[7]

This means that if we want to understand the trials of Jesus, we need to get to grips with some of the different ways in which people in the first century AD tried to make sense of Jesus and his ministry. As readers, we are engaged with a text that is written by other people who are making sense of their world. We need to look at the events that led up to the trials of Jesus because the construction of specific charges took place against this shared background of social knowledge (viz., knowledge of social situations which is informed by our social and historical context).

Precisely because the Gospels represent a selection from the sum of their knowledge, based on what each Gospel writer thinks is important, the Gospel accounts of the trials of Jesus are somewhat different from each other.[8] All the Gospels agree that the trial, death, and resurrection of Jesus are momentous events—but the Gospel writers also think that their differences in presentation are significant. Those who try to set the variations against each other invariably do not pause to consider how these differences work out with regard to the wider literary presentation. For example, Mark uniquely, interweaves the trial of Jesus by the Sanhedrin with the trial of Peter by a servant girl (14:53–72). Peter is portrayed as being on a downward spiral ("below in the courtyard"; 14:66) while

---

6. WRIGHT, NEW TESTAMENT, p. 42.
7. Ibid.
8. Summarized in BERNARD S. JACKSON, ESSAYS ON HALAKHAH IN THE NEW TESTAMENT (Leiden: Brill, 2008), 33–37.

Jesus is on an upward trajectory (above the courtyard, in the priest's house). Mark highlights the architecture because he wishes to draw out themes of honor and shame: Jesus is more and more exalted while Peter is more and more humiliated. Likewise, Luke is the only Gospel writer who includes the trial before Herod. This is because Luke finds significance in the moment—foreshadowed earlier in his Gospel (e.g., 13:31)—when the two "kings of the Jews" finally meet. Examples can be multiplied and although it would take longer to demonstrate, the differences are frequently explicable in terms of the wider accounts the Gospels are serving. This chapter, however, will tend to take a homogeneous approach to the Gospels, partly to reduce complexity and partly to enable us to focus on the structural issues.

II. DODGING BULLETS

The story of the trials forms a remarkably large part of each of the Gospels, so much so that the Gospels are sometimes described as "Passion narratives with an extended introduction." This means that we cannot understand the trials without grasping the events leading up to them. Although the trials of Jesus moved very quickly—it was only a matter of hours between Jesus's initial arrest and his execution—the Gospels indicate that they were the culmination of a long period of mounting opposition. It was an open secret that Jesus was in the crosshairs of the religious establishment:

> Some of the people of Jerusalem therefore said, "Is not this the man whom they seek to kill?" (John 7:25)

The surprise was not that Jesus was a marked man but that he was still alive. To the annoyance of the religious leaders, his continued existence seemed to imply their approval of his teaching and his apparently Messianic status:

> ... here he is, speaking openly, and they say nothing to him! Can it be that the authorities really know that this is the Christ [Messiah]? (John 7:26)

It is no surprise, then, that the Gospels record a number of assassination plots (e.g., John 7:1, 7:19) and attempts (John 8:59; 10:31–33), some of which even date from the start of Jesus's public ministry (Luke 4:28–29). Some are courtesy of the local lynch mob, such as the inhabitants of Jesus's hometown (Luke 4:28–29), but more often the instigators are what we could loosely call the "religious authorities." They include the chief priests, the "teachers of the law," the "elders," the Pharisees, and the Herodians. Combinations of these groups are presented as trying to bring about the arrest and/or execution of Jesus (e.g., Mark 3:6, 11:18, 12:12; John 7:32). Some of these factions were not natural bedfellows, to judge from the power struggles going on in Jerusalem at that time. But if the Gospels are correct, it is an example of the way in which criminal allegations can help to build a consensus against a person among those who might otherwise be rivals; it seems Jesus was defined as "other" by various factions that coalesced to silence his voice. John repeatedly refers to "the Jews" as a source of deadly opposition (e.g., John 8:57–59). This term—contentious in the eyes of some for its apparent anti-Semitism—refers not to Jewish people in general since John, along with Jesus and the rest of his followers, are themselves ethnic Jews. In the Passion narrative, the term refers to Jewish authorities who either act as spokespersons for the nation (e.g., John 11:49–54) or who "express hostility toward the Jewish Jesus"[9] and his followers (e.g., John 5:18).

III. THE STIGMATA OF JESUS

Given the importance of the trials of Jesus, one might have thought that, 21 centuries on, everyone would be clear as to what the charges were and why, precisely, Jesus was executed. Yet that is not the case. It has even been argued, perhaps implausibly, that the charges at Jesus's trials all revolved around magic and sorcery.[10] The confusion arises because, for a start, there is no single charge. All kinds of allegations are thrown around during the Jewish and the Roman trials and continue to be made at the place of crucifixion. They include such diverse charges as false prophecy, false teaching, leading the disciples astray, blasphemy, forbidding payment of taxes, threatening the Temple, and claiming some kind of kingship, although this too is expressed in different ways (see further, below). What do they all mean, and are they in any way related? We will see that this diversity of charges is not simply "bad history" by the evangelists but is, in some way, historically plausible. Again, we can make better sense of the charges if we place them in the context of previous assassination attempts. Some of these flashpoints generate remarkably similar charges to those that later surfaced at Jesus's trials.

One of the issues in modern miscarriages of justice is why factually innocent people who become victims of a false allegation attracted the false charge in the first place. Do such victims carry certain stigma compared with "normal" members of the public that makes the false charge seem plausible in the first place? There are often reasons why a false allegation seems to have the "ring of truth" (e.g., people believed to be Irish Republican sympathizers who are accused of

---

9. Martinus C. De Boer, *The narrative function of Pilate in John*, in NARRATIVITY IN BIBLICAL AND RELATED TEXTS, (G. J. Brook & J. D Kaestli (Leuven: Leuven University Press, 2000), 141–158, 147–48.

10. John W. Welch, Law, magic, miracles and the trial of Jesus, http://66.102.1.104/scholar?hl=en&lr=&q=cache:0LY2NCQ2as0J:www.law2.byu.edu/Biblical_Law/CurrentPapers/MagicSBL1205.pdf+john+welch+law+magic, accessed May 5, 2007.

planting terrorist bombs).[11] The same is true of people with "behavioral abnormalities" that lead them to be marginalized within their local communities. They too are easy prey for malicious allegations and wrongful convictions.[12] To be sure, miscarriages of justice appear to be shrouded in legitimacy.

By looking at the earlier Gospel accounts, we can build up a picture of the stigma that attached to Jesus and made the charges at his trials seem plausible. Some of the charges are more complex than others, and so we will be spending most of our time on the charges of false prophecy and false teaching, rather less on blasphemy, and with only brief comments on the others.

A. True or false?

First, we consider why Jesus might have attracted the charges of false prophecy and false teaching. To do this, we must understand what these charges were.

It is obvious that a charge of "false prophecy" only makes sense in a culture that has a lively expectation of *true* prophecy. This was the case in biblical Israel. Moses's farewell speech to the Israelites in Deuteronomy prophesies that:

> The LORD your God will raise up for you a prophet like me from among you, from your brethren—him you shall heed—just as you desired of the LORD your God at Horeb on the day of the assembly, when you said, "Let me not hear again the voice of the LORD my God, or see this great fire any more, lest I die." (Deuteronomy 18:15–16)

The "prophet like Moses" has authority to speak "words" in God's "name" which the people are to obey (Deuteronomy 18:18–19). In terms of family likeness, the "prophet like Moses" was never more like Moses than when mediating between God and the people and drawing Israel back to her true vocation, as revealed at Mount Sinai, to be "a kingdom of priests and a holy nation" (Exodus 19:6). Rabbinic tradition identified at least three such persons as "prophets like Moses" (Abraham, Micaiah, and Elijah, although this was on the basis that each had the authority to issue a command that was contrary to Mosaic law; Babylonian Talmud Sanhedrin 89b).[13]

In such a culture, it was vital to distinguish between the true and the false prophet. The fact that the prophet claims to speak words in God's name implies that there is already a built-in test. In the Bible, the name of a person is bound up with his or her character and reputation. Part of the test, then, is whether the prophets' words are the sort of thing that the God of Moses *would* say (Deuteronomy 18:20). As for the so-called prophet who prophesies things which

---

11. *See* B. WOFFINDEN, MISCARRIAGES OF JUSTICE (London: Hodder & Stoughton, 1987).

12. *See*, for instance, J. ROSE, S. PANTER & T. WILKINSON, INNOCENTS: HOW JUSTICE FAILED STEFAN KISZKO & LESLEY MOLSEED (London: Forth Estate, 1998).

13. *See* JACKSON, ESSAYS ON HALAKAH, pp. 17–8.

never happen, that person is obviously a nonstarter; no-one need worry about *him*. Making false prophesies is explicitly a falsification of the status of the prophet (Deuteronomy 18:21–22).

B. Can the devil speak true?

The real problem is the person whose prophesies *do* come true *and* who performs the "signs and wonders" Moses was famous for *but* whose overall teaching does not have the effect of drawing Israel back to her true vocation but leads her, instead, toward idolatry:

> If a prophet arises among you, or a dreamer of dreams, and gives you a sign or a wonder, and the sign or wonder which he tells you comes to pass, and if he says, "Let us go after other gods," which you have not known, "and let us serve them," you shall not listen to the words of that prophet or to that dreamer of dreams . . . . (Deuteronomy 13:1–3/MT 13:2–4; *Moses speaking*)

In the Masoretic Text of the Hebrew Bible, the chapter division is marked by Deuteronomy 12:32 rather than Deuteronomy 13:1, which implies that Deuteronomy 12:32–13:1/MT 13:1–2 are to be read together. Deuteronomy 12:32/MT 13:1 concerns the importance of not adding to or subtracting from Torah. Reading Deuteronomy 12:32–13:5/MT 13:1–6 as one, Bernard Jackson[14] reconstructs the underlying logic as follows: ordinary Israelites have no authority to change the law, but a true "prophet like Moses" may do so, if he proves his status by means of "signs and wonders." However, even a prophet who proves his status by means of "signs and wonders" is really false if he commands idolatry. To be a false prophet, one has first to be a prophet. But according to Deuteronomy 13:1–3/MT 13:2–4, making prophesies that come to pass and performing signs and wonders are not by themselves sufficient; indeed, Jesus himself confirms that miracles and prophecy are not in themselves proof of God's activity (Matthew 7:21–23). There is also a test as to the content of the prophet's teaching (Deuteronomy 13:1–3/MT 13:2–4). This in turn begs the question of what is the nature of the prophet's relationship to the Mosaic law? It is for this reason that the charges of being a "false prophet" and a "false teacher" are closely related.

Indeed, there is internal evidence that Jesus himself did not make a formal distinction between signs and teaching. On the contrary, the content of the signs and wonders was itself sufficient to address the charge of being a false teacher. This is apparent when Jesus's authority is questioned by the disciples of John the Baptist:

> And when the men had come to him [Jesus], they said, "John the Baptist has sent us to you, saying, 'Are you he who is to come, or shall we look for

---

14. Ibid., 19.

another?'" . . . And he answered them, "Go and tell John what you have seen and heard: the blind receive their sight, the lame walk, lepers are cleansed, and the deaf hear, the dead are raised up, the poor have good news preached to them. And blessed is he who takes no offence at me." (Luke 7:20–23)

It is notable that even John the Baptist—Jesus's first cousin—has doubts about the eschatological nature of Jesus's ministry. But Jesus's response to doubters is not simply to point to "acts of power" as proof that he can do *something*. Instead, Jesus points to the didactic purpose of the signs and the wonders. They occur in the context of "preaching good news to the poor" (verse 22). They teach that making people whole and acting on behalf of the poor and marginalized is what Torah is all about. The signs and wonders are, in part, performative teaching. They demonstrate not only Jesus's power but also something about the character of Jesus's teaching. One cannot split off the display of the signs from the content of the teaching: the report to John concerns what is "seen" *and* "heard" (verse 22).

C. Raising Lazarus

Even from this brief sketch, it is possible to see why Jesus gained the stigma—we could even say stigmata—of being labelled a false prophet and a false teacher. These charges would later facilitate his false conviction. All the Gospels attest to numerous performances of "signs and wonders," of which the most controversial was the raising of Lazarus (John 11). In the Gospel According to Saint John, this started the chain of events that led to Jesus's arrest:

> So the chief priests and the Pharisees gathered the council [Sanhedrin], and said, "What are we to do? For this man performs many *signs*. If we let him go on thus, *every one will believe in him* . . . ." (John 11:47–48)

The reference to "signs" confirms that the key issue for the Sanhedrin is false prophecy. A charge of false prophecy could be brought if either (a) the Sanhedrin thought Jesus was a false prophet, or (b) the Sanhedrin thought Jesus may be a true prophet and accused him of being a false prophet to protect their own power and authority. Either way, false prophecy was a capital offense in biblical law (Deuteronomy 13:5/MT 13:6). The controversy lay not simply in the performance of the miracles; after all, Israel had a long tradition of miracle makers. Rather, the problem lay in their effects, namely, "leading Israel astray." This brings us onto the question of why Jesus had the stigma of being a false teacher.

Jesus's claims to be an authoritative mediator of Torah, like Moses, would mean that he had the ability to set out the definitive exposition of the law (cf. Matthew 7:28–29). Sometimes this virtually amounted to the promulgation of a new law. But there was a fine line between this and the accusation that Jesus was abolishing "the law and the prophets." This accusation was expressly denied by Jesus (Matthew 5:17), but the fact that people said it is evidence that Jesus risked the stigma of being labelled a false teacher. The Gospels indicate that there was a real debate about the effects of Jesus's teaching during his lifetime:

> And there was much muttering about him [Jesus] among the people. While some said, "He is a good man," others said, "No, he is leading the people astray." (John 7:12)

Jesus was also accused of leading his own disciples astray (e.g., Mark 2:23–28). Jews were scandalized by Jesus's radical attitude toward contemporary interpretations of the Sabbath and purity laws (Matthew 12:1–14; Mark 7:1–23) as well as other Jewish traditions, which he stated negated Torah (Mark 7:8–13). Confirmation that Deuteronomy 18:15 was one of the issues at the heart of Jesus's trial can be found in Peter's sermon, delivered at the Beautiful Gate of the Temple after Jesus's resurrection. Here, Deuteronomy 18:15 is quoted to refute the judgment made at Jesus's trial (Acts 3:22–23).

There is another way in which Jesus's status as an authoritative and distinctive teacher may be relevant to the subsequent trials. Pilate apparently discerns that the "chief priests" handed Jesus over to him "out of envy" (Matthew 27:18). In the light of this, it is notable that one of the plots to kill Jesus is said to emerge in the context of Jesus's popular teaching:

> The Jews marvelled at it [Jesus' teaching], saying, "How is it that this man has learning, when he has never studied?" (John 7:15)

Those at the top of the religious tree were uncomfortable with an "unknown" who was teaching with authority and seemed to know Torah better than they did; who could perform "signs and wonders," and who had a massive popular following to boot (". . . look, the world has gone after him"; John 12:19). The religious authorities were faced with someone who was better at the things that made them special. There is nothing historically implausible about the suggestion that this might be a powerful reason for wanting to be rid of Jesus. This adds further weight to the idea that Jesus was a target of false allegations due to his apparent threat to the powerful if it became widely accepted that he was a true prophet.

D. Character assassination

Next, we consider why Jesus might have attracted the charge of blasphemy. Again, to do this, we must understand the roots of this charge in biblical law.

There is no single word for blasphemy. Instead, there is a general conception that is derived from a range of verbs for saying derogatory things, such as "reviling" and "cursing." We see this in Exodus 22:28 /MT 22:27:

> "You shall not revile (*teqallel*) God, nor curse a ruler of your people."
> (*God speaking*)

The root of the verb "to revile" (*qillel*) reflects the basic meaning of to "be light" (or "belittle") and is the opposite of the verb "to honor" (*kabhad*). However, in the *piel* form, which is how it appears in Exodus 22:28/MT 22:27, it can mean to "curse."[15] The term seems to have referred primarily "to utterances, as opposed to acts."[16] This is confirmed by the case of the blasphemer in Leviticus 24:10–23, which concerned a half-Israelite/half-Egyptian man who "blasphemed the Name, [literally, 'names the name'], and cursed" (Leviticus 24:11). Although there is some debate as to what his offense actually consists of, the two expressions—blasphemy and cursing—are usually seen as two parts of the same act. It seems as though the offender "blasphemed the divine name by using it illegitimately in some way (perhaps in a false accusation or a curse) . . . [with the result] that he "degraded" or "dishonoured" (God)."[17] Notably, the promulgation of the law of blasphemy (Leviticus 24:15–16) is immediately followed by promulgation of the law of homicide (Leviticus 24:17). Blasphemy is "character assassination."

By the time of Jesus, however, blasphemy was understood much more broadly to include acts as well as speech, especially acts that are directed against the things that God has ordained, including the Temple (e.g., 1 Maccabees 2:6–8 and cf. 2 Maccabees 8:4).[18] This contrasts with later rabbinic sources which interpret blasphemy much more restrictively and hence leniently (the blasphemer is only guilty "if he pronounces the name of God distinctly"; Mishnah Sanhedrin 7:5). Clearly, there were radical changes in Jewish law between the Second Temple period and the later codification of Jewish law in the Mishnah (which was completed *circa* AD 200).

Jesus was, in fact charged, with blasphemy a number of times *before* his trials. In the Gospel According to Saint Mark, Jesus promises a paralytic "your sins are forgiven," which the watching scribes regard as "blasphemy!" because "Who can forgive sins but God alone?"(Mark 2:5–7). There are also several implicit charges of blasphemy in John's Gospel. John 5:18 claims that ". . . the Jews sought all the more to kill him [Jesus], because he not only broke the sabbath but also called God his Father, making himself equal with God." (This is an implicit charge since John does not actually call it blasphemy). Several further incidents result in a near lynching. In one case, Jesus claims "before Abraham was, I am" (John 8:58) and in another, Jesus's opponents explicitly state that they are stoning him "for blasphemy; because you, being a man, make yourself God" (John 10:33) and because Jesus claimed, "I am the Son of God" (John 10:36). Although all

---

15. J. Scharbert, *Qll*, in THEOLOGICAL DICTIONARY OF THE OLD TESTAMENT, (G. Johannes Botterweck, Helmer Ringgren & Heinz-Josef Fabry eds.; David E. Green trans.; Grand Rapids: Eerdmans, 2004), vol. XIII, 37–44.

16. DARRELL L. BOCK, BLASPHEMY AND EXALTATION IN JUDAISM: THE CHARGE AGAINST JESUS IN MARK 14:53–65 (Grand Rapids: Baker Books, 2000), 34.

17. Rodney R. Hutton, *The case of the blasphemer revisited (Lev. XXIV 10-23)*, VETUS TESTAMENTUM 49, 532–41, 541 (1999).

18. *See generally* E. P. SANDERS, JEWISH LAW FROM JESUS TO THE MISHNAH (London: SCM Press, 1990), 57–67.

Israelites, in some way, saw themselves as "sons of God" (e.g., Hosea 11:1), Jesus's claim is different to that of the ordinary Israelite because Jesus uses the definite article. Certainly, the tone and context of these claims is understood by those hearing Jesus to assert some kind of special status or equivalence before God. The context indicates that Jesus understood the phrase specifically as "the-one-whom-the-Father-consecrated-and-sent-into-the-world." This could plausibly be said to denigrate God by reducing God to the status of a man. Such claims are consistent with Jesus's practice of saying "I say unto you . . ." (e.g., Matthew 5:2–7:29) instead of "Thus says the LORD . . ." which was the practice of the former prophets (e.g., Exodus 4:22).

Once again, we have a background of social knowledge in which Jesus was perceived and labelled by some of being a blasphemer.

E. Jesus's tax bombshell

Jesus was also stigmatized following attempts to entrap him over the question of paying taxes to Caesar (Mark 12:13–17; Luke 23:2). This question was asked in Jerusalem since that was where taxes were paid to Caesar.[19] Jesus's response—"Render to Caesar the things that are Caesar's, and to God the things that are God's" (Mark 12:17)—was a "double-whammy" tax bombshell. On the one hand, it could be read as supporting the payment of taxes but, on the other hand, it could be read as a coded call to revolution ("you'd better pay Caesar back as he deserves!"; cf. 1 Maccabees 2:66–68).[20] The stigma had currency.

The Roman tax question in Jerusalem has parallels with the Temple tax question in Capernaum (Matthew 17:24–27). Jesus's response (telling Peter to catch a fish) is similarly equivocal: the tax is paid but, at the same time, it is trivialized and subverted. So too is the Temple. This leads us to the final charge.

F. Putting a time bomb under the Temple

Finally, the stigma of being the sort of person who would destroy the Temple may have been rooted in Jesus's prophecy regarding his resurrection, where the reference to the destruction of his body is (mis)understood by others as referring to the destruction of the Temple (e.g., John 2:19). However, there are plenty of other examples in which Jesus does explicitly prophecy the destruction of the Temple (e.g., Luke 19:41–44). Most dramatically of all is Jesus's prophetic symbolic act of destroying the Temple, which was "an acted parable of judgment."[21] Overturning the tables of the money changers temporarily suspended the Temple's activities because it meant that people could not purchase sacrifices and bring them before the priests. It was a temporary suspension of the Temple's

---

19. BOCK, BLASPHEMY AND EXALTATION.
20. N. T. WRIGHT, JESUS AND THE VICTORY OF GOD (London: SPCK, 1996), 505.
21. Ibid., 416.

functions that pointed toward its destruction and the ultimate cessation of all its activities.[22] This, too, was a trigger for the trials of Jesus: following this "the chief priests and the scribes . . . sought a way to destroy him" (Mark 11:18). Again, this means that by the time of Jesus's trials, it was plausible to suggest that Jesus was a threat to the Temple and its operations.

In summary, by the time of Jesus's trials, he had the stigmata of being labelled a false prophet, a false teacher who led Israel astray and a blasphemer as well as an all-round troublemaker who forbade the payment of taxes and who threatened the reputation of the Temple. All of this is relevant as we turn from these antecedents to the trials of Jesus themselves.

IV. MORAL PANICS

We have already seen that, according to John's Gospel, the raising of Lazarus triggered a gathering of the Sanhedrin. This was effectively the first trial of Jesus. Under Caiaphas, the high priest, the Sanhedrin reached the decision—in Jesus's absence—that Jesus should die (John 11:49–53).

The decision in John 11 is historically plausible given the febrile political climate of Israel at the time. As we saw in the previous chapter, Second Temple Judaism was characterized by the emergence of a number of rival Jewish sects, some of which were opposed to the religious establishment in Jerusalem and some of whom wanted revolution against Rome. Unsurprisingly, the Temple establishment kept tabs on these movements, with the general policy of "spot it and stop it" (cf. the early investigation of John the Baptist; John 1:19–27 and the plot to kill the resurrected Lazarus; John 12:10). This was exactly the kind of social climate in which rumors could quickly spread about false prophecy and false teaching. The danger of such rumors is a "moral panic." One of the hallmarks of moral panics, which apply as much today as then, is that they are thought to justify extreme measures on policy grounds.

The plausibility of some of the Gospel accounts is supported by a historical account external to the New Testament, namely, that of the Jewish Roman historian Josephus. A reference to the outcome of the trials of Jesus is found in Jewish Antiquities (XVIII:63–64), but of greater interest for present purposes is the account in the Slavonic version of Flavius Josephus's Jewish War. This is a translation into old Russian which has been preserved in a number of medieval manuscripts, which some argue goes back to Josephus's first draft of his translation from the Aramaic. The Slavonic version differs from the Jewish War as we have it in a number of respects, including a passage that highlights the motivations of

---

22. Ibid., 423–24.

the priesthood.[23] On this account, Jesus was put at the head of a popular Jewish revolt against the Romans. When the priesthood heard about this, they decided the best course of action was to "shop" Jesus to Pilate and the Romans "lest he [Pilate] hear [it] from others, and we be robbed of our substance and ourselves slaughtered and our children scattered."[24] This comes close to the view expressed in some of the Gospels. Of course, there are differences between this account and the gathering of the chief priests and Pharisees described in John 11:47–48. However, there is a parallel inasmuch as both state that the original impetus for handing Jesus over to the Romans came from a priesthood that was worried about the threat that Jesus posed both to their own position and to "national security."

V. BEFORE THE SANHEDRIN

To keep things simple, the processual aspects of the Jewish and Roman trials will be considered separately from their substantive content. Thus, we begin by considering the key stages in the Jewish proceedings before moving on to consider the specific charges. The same approach will be taken in relation to the Roman trials, which will also enable us to draw parallels between the two sets of proceedings.

Following Jesus's capture, there appear to have been three main elements in the Jewish proceedings (see Table 18, below).

First, Jesus was taken to the palace of the high priest, which would have been located among the upper class residences of the Upper City in Jerusalem, an

TABLE 18 KEY STAGES IN THE JEWISH PROCEEDINGS

THE JEWISH PROCEEDINGS	Preliminary nocturnal interrogation by Annas	John 18:13, 19–24
	Nocturnal "trawl for evidence" before Caiaphas and the religious establishment/ Sanhedrin	Matthew 26:57–68; Mark 14:53, 55–65; Luke 22:54
	Dawn Sanhedrin gathering + formal legal decision	Matthew 27:1; Mark 15:1a; Luke 22:66–71

---

23. FLAVIUS JOSEPHUS, THE JEWISH WAR, translation by H. St. J. Thackeray, Loeb Classical Library (Cambridge, Mass.: Harvard University Press, 1997), 648–50.
24. Ibid., 650.

archaeological example of which has been uncovered.²⁵ The position of the high priest had become a political appointment although the nature of the function he performed was essentially religious and not political. At the time of Jesus, the high priest (Caiaphas) and his predecessor (Annas) were from the same family, forming a kind of religious dynasty (cf. Luke 3:2). It was not unusual, then, for Jesus to be the subject of a preliminary interview by Annas, who would still have carried a great deal of political influence. Jesus arrives bound and fettered for a nighttime examination at which he is physically abused (John 18:12–13, 19–24). "The atmosphere is not that of a trial but of a roughshod interrogation by a notable examiner to get incriminating evidence."²⁶

The second stage—the examination before Caiaphas—follows naturally since it is almost certain that Annas and Caiaphas lived in the same palace. Caiaphas is joined by other religious leaders; a quorum which some texts suggest is to be identified with the Sanhedrin itself (e.g., Matthew 26:57, 59). The Gospel writers claim that the purpose of this meeting was to seek "false testimony against Jesus that they might put him to death" (Matthew 26:59 = Mark 14:55). Modern miscarriage of justice cases would identify this as a "trawl for evidence," which is particularly liable to occur when there is a limited period of time for prosecuting authorities to come up with a charge.²⁷

The third and final stage is the formal decision reached by the Sanhedrin on the charges to be brought against Jesus. Luke 22:66 suggests a change in location from the night before (which according to various sources may have been located in another building outside the upper city on the Western slope of the Temple Mount, or outside the Temple, or in the Hall of Hewn Stones inside the inner forecourt of the Temple). Again, this followed naturally from the previous stage because the Sanhedrin met at dawn and formally drew together the events of the previous night.

However, the decision reached was not a capital sentence. The Gospel writers report that "They all condemned him *as deserving* death" (Mark 14:64) rather than "they all condemned him *to* death." The most likely reason for this is that the Sanhedrin, which was under Roman jurisdiction, did not have power to execute. That power vested in Rome, as John 18:31 indicates. The Sanhedrin could only come up with "an indictment to continue the process."²⁸

But why go to all to this trouble and involve Rome? Why not make Jesus the subject of an impromptu lynch party? After all, this is what happened to Stephen,

---

25. Nahman Avigad, *Herodian mansions in Jerusalem*, in JERUSALEM: 5,000 YEARS OF HISTORY. Special Issue of LES DOSSIERS D'ARCHEOLOGIE, March (1992), 56–65.

26. B. Corley, *Trial of Jesus*, in DICTIONARY OF JESUS AND THE GOSPELS (Joel B. Green & Scot McKnight eds.; Leicester: InterVarsity Press, 1992), 841–54, 854.

27. *See, e.g.,* RICHARD WEBSTER, THE SECRET OF BRYN ESTYN: THE MAKING OF A MODERN WITCH HUNT (Oxford: The Orwell Press, 2005).

28. BOCK, BLASPHEMY AND EXALTATION, p. 191.

one of Jesus's disciples, on a charge of blasphemy before the Sanhedrin (Acts 7:54–59). One reason is fear on the part of the religious establishment that they might trigger "tumult among the people" because of Jesus's popular following (e.g., Matthew 26:5). It was better to turn their problem into Rome's problem and make Jesus someone else's security issue. Bringing on the "big Roman guns" would also have been seen as the best way of finishing off the Jesus movement (cf. the concern to prevent any posthumous theft of the body; Matthew 27:62–66). In addition, for Jesus to be executed by the Romans signified complete separation from the religious authorities.[29] For the religious leaders, it was the perfect solution—a public death for which they were not responsible. Jesus would be executed before the masses, but they could distance themselves from it in the eyes of the people.

Finally, there were advantages for the chief priests in seeing Jesus executed by means of crucifixion because this had greater symbolic power than, say, stoning. First, crucifixion was seen by Jews in the Second Temple period as an expression of Deuteronomy 21:22–23 (cf. the apostle Paul's rendition of this verse in the New Testament as "cursed be every one who hangs on a tree"; Galatians 3:13). It decisively showed Jesus's rejection by the chief priests who represented the nation. At the same time, crucifixion was a uniquely Roman punishment. Crucifixion by Rome would therefore be the culmination of the rejection of Jesus by both Israel *and* Rome.

VI. FRAMING THE CHARGES

We turn from the processual aspects of the Jewish proceedings to the charges themselves. So far we have seen a perception on the part of the religious authorities that Jesus was an internal threat to Israel's beliefs and social order. He represented a challenge from within to what it meant for Israel to be the people of God. This "offense," of course, did not exist as such, but it did map quite easily onto some traditional offenses in biblical law, including those of false prophecy, false teaching, an attack on the Temple, and blasphemy. These were the specific charges that were brought against Jesus during the Jewish proceedings, and we can note their presentation briefly, as follows.

First, the interrelated charges of false prophecy, false teaching, and leading Israel astray. This is apparent in the interrogation before Annas. Jesus is questioned "about his disciples and his teaching" (John 18:19). Here we see that the focus is not only upon Jesus's relationship to the Mosaic law but his effects upon his disciples' behavior.

---

29. Walter Grundmann, Jesus der Galiläer und das Judentum (Weimar, 1940), 162.

Second, the charge of threatening to destroy the Temple (Mark 14:57–59). The witnesses reach a semantic agreement regarding the form of words that Jesus was supposed to have used, but they cannot seem to decide what Jesus meant. However, the Gospels report Jesus as saying only that the Temple will be destroyed, not that Jesus would perform this act himself. Jesus's silence implies that there is no case to answer. The witnesses in Mark 14:58 misunderstand the referent of Jesus's original saying in John 2:19, which the Gospel writers explain as a reference to Jesus's physical body, not the Temple. But, as we have seen above, Jesus already had a reputation for verbally and physically attacking the Temple. Small wonder, then, that the saying of John 2:19 was misunderstood.

Bernard Jackson[30] argues that the Temple charge is one of the reasons why the trial of Jesus is structurally similar to the trial of Jeremiah—an observation that is in fact captured in the eleventh window of King's College Chapel, Cambridge, which juxtaposes the trials of Jesus and Jeremiah. Since the plan of the Chapel windows is thought to be based on a long-standing scheme, it seems as though Jackson's thesis has an impressive medieval pedigree. Jeremiah was notorious among his contemporaries for his warning that Israel had turned away from the Sinai covenant and from her vocation and that Solomon's Temple would be destroyed by Israel's enemies. Jesus was likewise unpopular for prophecying an act of God's judgment on the Temple because it had become the center of revolution and exclusivism instead of a "blessing to the nations" (Matthew 21:13).

A. Is it a monster?

Finally, the charge of blasphemy. This is triggered by Jesus's answer to the high priest's question: "I adjure you by the living God ['I put you to the oath'] tell us if you are [claiming to be] the Christ, the Son of God" (Matthew 26:63). According to the Mishnah, the practice of imposing an oath is a standard juridical technique (e.g., Mishnah Shabuot). Caiaphas is challenging Jesus to confess or deny whether he has made that claim. It is not a question regarding the truth of the claim. Caiaphas's question may have been a standard one that was put to would-be Messianic pretenders.

Jesus's answer—and the only occasion on which he is presented as speaking to Caiaphas or to the Sanhedrin—subverts their idea of what Israel's Messiah would be and do:

> You have said so. But I tell you, hereafter you will see the Son of man seated at the right hand of Power, and coming on the clouds of heaven. (Matthew 26:64; *Jesus speaking*)

Jesus's words, "You have said so" may simply mean "your willingness to say this is justified."

---

30. Jackson, Essays on Halakah, 43–47.

His "confession" juxtaposes elements from Psalm 110:1 (the assumption of kingship at the "right hand" of God) and Daniel 7:13–14 (the "son of man" figure who is presented before God, vindicated before his enemies, and who is given all power and authority). There are several reasons why this would have been regarded as blasphemy.

First, blasphemy prohibited disrespect not only to God but also, as we saw above, to "a ruler of your people" (Exodus 22:28/MT 22:27). This was later extended to parents (Leviticus 20:9). The close association between "cursing God" and "cursing rulers and parents" "may well reflect the view that to speak against God's rulers is to speak against the wisdom of God who chose them."[31] This adds another level to the blasphemy charge in the Jewish proceedings because Jesus's statement actually constituted his sharpest attack yet on the religious establishment. As the "son of man" figure, Jesus claims to exercise "the judicial power of God on behalf of the righteous."[32] He "challenges and warns his accusers that the real authority is not the Jewish council, but Jesus, who will preside over them one day."[33] In that sense, the remark would have been seen as a challenge to "[the Sanhedrin's] claims for divinely appointed leadership and responsibility for Israel."[34]

But there is more. Daniel 7, which Jesus cites, was a popular text in Jesus's day. It begins by describing four great beasts that come out of the sea (verses 2–7). Daniel's writing belongs to the apocalyptic genre, which means that the imagery is representational. Daniel was not imagining Godzilla and three chums wading out of the Mediterranean. Rather, the sea symbolizes evil, as elsewhere in the Bible, and the monsters symbolize kings and/or kingdoms that war against Israel (as verse 17 confirms). The creatures attack the "son of man" figure, who stands for Israel, but he is finally vindicated.[35] From even this brief summary, we can see why Daniel 7 was popular in the first century: people read it primarily "in terms of the vindication of Israel after her suffering at the hands of the pagans"[36]—principally the Romans.

If Jesus identifies himself as the "son of man," it follows with devastating logic that those who are attacking him are the monsters. Caiaphas is not the chief priest—he is the chief beast.[37] Indeed, the delivering up of Jesus to "the high priest; and all the chief priests and the elders and the scribes" (Mark 14:53)—the Big Four, in other words—may well allude to Daniel's four "beasts from the sea." This is not the first time Jesus had said such things, having previously told the

---

31. Bock, Blasphemy and Exaltation, 35–36.
32. Ibid., 202.
33. Ibid., 207.
34. Ibid., 208.
35. Wright, New Testament, pp 289–97.
36. Ibid., 292.
37. Wright, Victory of God, pp. 525–26, 606.

scribes: "You are of your father the devil . . ." (John 8:44). In today's culture, the effect is rather like calling someone a "paedo." Jesus's comments were shocking in the extreme.

However, there was a third reason why the blasphemy charge was clear-cut. The claim to "come on the clouds" involves a claim to divinity. In the Hebrew Bible, clouds are associated with the divine (e.g., Numbers 10:34) and "riding on clouds" is something that God does (e.g., Psalm 104:3; Isaiah 19:1). Jesus's confession goes further than Caiaphas's notion of kingship by saying: "I am not just a 'King David' style Messiah-figure, who will cleanse the Temple and get rid of the Romans—I am someone who will be the judge of the world and who will have everything at my feet."

Jesus thus redefines Caiaphas's question and radically extends his Messianic claim to include "[sharing] the very throne of Israel's god . . . [as] one of the central figures in a theophany [i.e., manifestation of God]."[38] This was blasphemy because the essence of the charge, as we saw above, is that it belittles or dishonors God by, for example, reducing "God's unique stature."[39] The Sanhedrin did not necessarily doubt that the figure of whom Jesus spoke could exist or might appear in the future. The problem was that ". . . Jesus was making this identification with himself in a *self-claim* to share authority with God."[40] We must remember that it was not necessarily blasphemous to claim to be the Messiah; plenty of people before and after Jesus made such claims and, their delusions were exposed when they were executed by the Romans. It *was*, however, blasphemous to claim to be the sort of Messiah who would do *this*. The blasphemy lies in what Jesus says it means for him to be Messiah. Against Jesus's preexisting label and stigma of "being a blasphemer," it was all the Sanhedrin needed. Confession is, perhaps, the most powerful form of evidence and, as evidence goes, this was explosive.

B. A "kingship" matrix

Table 19, below, summarizes the main lines of interest on the part of accusers and accused.

The question is: *why, out of all of the possible charges that* could *have been brought against Jesus did these* particular *charges emerge?* This is a question of sense construction which means we have to ask: who is making sense and to whom? There are several different groups in the trials of Jesus: the religious establishment, Pilate, Herod, the crowd, and the condemned revolutionaries. Each constructs a particular kind of sense. The religious establishment had to make sense of Jesus and his activities for an internal Jewish audience. For this group, the charge

---

38. Ibid., 643.
39. Bock. Blasphemy and Exaltation, p. 205.
40. Ibid., 202; italics original.

TABLE 19 SUMMARY OF LINE OF QUESTIONING IN THE JEWISH PROCEEDINGS

	Charges and questions	Jesus's response
LINE OF QUESTIONING IN JEWISH PROCEEDINGS	False prophecy/Leading disciples astray (John 18:19)	Notes public context of ministry (John 18:20–21)
	False teaching (John 18:19)	Notes public context of teaching (John 18:20–21)
	Destruction of Temple (Matthew 26:61; Mark 14:57–58)	Silence (Matthew 26:63; Mark 14:61)
	Question under oath "Tell us if you are the Messiah, the Son of God" (Matthew 26:63); "Are you the Messiah, the Son of the Blessed One?" (Mark 14:61); "If you are the Messiah . . . tell us" (Luke 22:67); "Are you then the Son of God?" (Luke 23:70)	Jesus makes statement under oath—which redefines the charge on his terms (Matthew 26:64; Mark 14:62; Luke 22:67–69); Jesus agrees to redefined terms (Luke 23:70)
	Blasphemy (derived from Jesus's statement under oath) (Matthew 26:65; Mark 14:63–64)	No indication

sheet intuitively made sense because Jesus had already acquired the appropriate stigmata during his public ministry. The charges emerged naturally from the nocturnal trawl for evidence because they were already plausible.

But there is more to it than that. The charge sheet also seemed plausible because the offenses related to each other. This is often referred to in contemporary miscarriage of justice circles as "guilty by the weight of false allegations." Each allegation alone does not stand up to critical scrutiny and has no evidential basis; however, together a plethora of false allegations can make a compelling case, especially in a climate of "no smoke without fire." (This is not unrelated to the problem of *testes singulars* in Jewish law.[41] This is the situation where there is only a single witness to a given offense, as opposed to multiple witnesses. The question is whether and, if so, in what circumstances, one can rely on a combination of inadequate evidence to a series of separate but *related* offenses).

Moreover, unlike the offense profile of a modern day recidivist who tends to commit a whole range of crimes, the charges against Jesus are all of the same type. They are all concerned with *rival kingship*.

We have already seen that the charges of false prophecy, false teaching, and "leading Israel astray" are all inversions of the "prophet like Moses" and thus of

---

41. See JACKSON, ESSAYS ON HALAKAH, pp. 59–87.

true leadership. Moses was, of course, Israel's leader or king in those premonarchical days. Likewise, Jesus's Temple action is concerned with kingship because it assumed the authority to destroy and rebuild. The building of the Temple by the true king was an idea that went all the way back to Solomon. Finally, the charges of blasphemy are related to kingship inasmuch as they involve claims on Jesus's part to being some sort of Messiah. The cohesion of the charges against Jesus is confirmed by the mockery described in the Jewish proceedings (see Table 20, below). This draws together the charges of false prophecy, deception, and the false messianic claim.

As Jackson notes, the condemnation of Jesus's words in Matthew 26:65–66 is immediately followed by "a contemptuous challenge to the *prophetic* status of Jesus . . . ."[42] Jesus's blindfolding may reflect a *midrash* on Isaiah 11:3, according to which the Messiah could judge by smell without the need of sight (Babylonian Talmud Sanhedrin 93b). It was a traditional test of Messianic status to which Jesus declined to submit. Ironically, Mark's Gospel interleaves the trial of Jesus, which takes place above the courtyard, with the trial of Peter, which takes place in the courtyard. One of its purposes is to show that at the exact time Jesus is charged with being a false prophet, Jesus is, in fact, shown to be a true prophet because he accurately prophecizes Peter's betrayal (Mark 14:30; cf. 14:66–72).

According to the Jewish authorities and their interpretation of the biblical laws relating to blasphemy, false prophecy, and false teaching, Jesus was justly handed over to the Romans, and his death was not a miscarriage of justice. However, from Jesus's own perspective, and that of the Gospel writers, the actions of the religious authorities proved their opposition to God and to the "Son of Man." The understanding of the Jewish leaders regarding God and the vocation of Israel and consequently of Torah and Jesus himself was wrong

TABLE 20 SUMMARY OF FORMS OF MOCKERY IN JEWISH PROCEEDINGS

FORM OF MOCKERY IN JEWISH PROCEEDINGS	
	"Prophesy to us, Christ. . ." (Matthew 26:67–68; Mark 14:65; Luke 23:63–65)
	Alleged status as worker of "signs and wonders" (Mark 15:31–32)
	Alleged status as "Messiah, this King of Israel" (Mark 15:32)

---

42. Bernard S. Jackson, *The Prophet and the Law in Early Judaism and the New Testament*, JEWISH LAW ASSOCIATION: THE PARIS CONFERENCE VOLUME, S.M. Passamaneck & M. Finley eds., Jewish Law Association Studies, VII (Atlanta, Scholars Press, 1994), 67–112, 86.

at every point. Accordingly, the leaders failed to interpret and apply Torah correctly and so, from this perspective, the trial before the Sanhedrin was a miscarriage of justice.

VII. "CRUCIFIED UNDER PONTIUS PILATE"

The charges against Jesus do not only have to make sense for a Jewish audience; they have also got to make sense for a Roman audience. This brings us, then, to the Roman proceedings. As we turn to these, we will see that there are a large number of structural parallels between the Jewish and the Roman proceedings, as follows: (1) both follow the pattern of interrogation → condemnation → mockery (which is far more severe in the Roman proceedings); (2) both apply corporal punishment and abuse before there is a conviction; (3) both judges make ironic declarations that go to the heart of the trial (Caiaphas in John 11:49–52 and Pilate in John 19:19–22); (4) both Caiaphas and Pilate are presented as acting from utilitarian motives; in particular, both want Jesus dead in order to avert a rebellion and so they can keep their jobs; (5) both proceedings are presented as showing lack of concern for innocent blood (cf. Matthew 27:4, 24) and (6) in both cases, Jesus answers his accusers only to turn upside down their ideas of kingship.

The claim is sometimes made that the Gospels are written in such a way as to put blame for the death of Jesus on the Jewish people and to exonerate the Romans. Accordingly, a former Justice of the Supreme Court of Israel avers that "the Roman governor had to be thoroughly whitewashed"[43] by the Gospel writers in order to protect the interests of Gentile Christians who were living under the threat of Roman persecution. But if this had been the goal of the Gospel writers, we would have to conclude they made a poor job of it. Pilate comes out of the Gospel records at least as badly as Caiaphas. The structural parallels noted above, and explored further below, make it perfectly plain that *both* Jewish *and* Roman authorities play an active part in the prosecution and execution of Jesus. Nor, as we will see, is there much to choose between them as examples of a miscarriage of justice.

Consequently, the idea that the Gospel records "incriminate the Jews and exonerate the Romans" is about as far removed from the texts as it is possible to get. The structural parallels between the Jewish and the Roman proceedings demonstrate the Gospel writers' even-handedness. We find a similar approach in the book of Acts:

"Why did the Gentiles rage, and the peoples imagine vain things? The kings of the earth set themselves in array, and the rulers were gathered together, against the Lord and against his Anointed" [quoting Psalm 2:1–2]—for truly

---

43. *E.g.*, COHN, TRIAL AND DEATH, p. xvi.

in this city there were gathered together against thy holy servant Jesus, whom thou didst anoint, both Herod and Pontius Pilate, with the Gentiles and the peoples of Israel, to do whatever thy hand and thy plan had predestined to take place. (Acts 4:25–28; *Peter speaking*)

Here the apostle Peter explicitly presents the death of Jesus as an act in which all are complicit: both Jewish and Gentile political leaders and Jewish and Gentile peoples. Interpreters—Jewish and non-Jewish—who seek to derive anti-Semitism from the trials of Jesus are advocating a point of view that is not recognized by the New Testament. "The theological stance of the Gospels indicts us all."[44] One of the few points at which we can find any relative judgment in the Gospels is Jesus's claim to Pilate that "he who delivered me to you has the greater sin," which can only refer to Caiaphas and/or the Sanhedrin (John 19:11 and cf. Luke 24:20). But is this a remarkable thing to say? Surely it is the case that in any chain of events that leads to a miscarriage of justice, the person or agency that initially seeks to prosecute somebody on an unfounded charge bears the greater blame.

The main stages in the Roman proceedings are summarized in Table 21, below.

The first stage is handing Jesus over to Pilate in the *Praetorium*, Pilate's official residence in Jerusalem. This may have been located in the Antonia Fortress (a Roman military garrison located on the north-western corner of the Temple Mount) or, more likely, Herod's palace. Pilate's official position (confirmed by archaeological inscription)[45] was *praefectus Iudaeas* (prefect of Judea) in which capacity he commanded a troop of around 500–1000 Roman soldiers between AD 26–AD 36/37. Pilate was a military man notorious for bloody repression and a lack of sensitivity to the Jewish community (e.g., Josephus Antiquities, 18.3 l.55–62; 18.4 l.85–89). The trial before Pilate would have followed the procedures of the *cognitio extra ordinem* ("adjudication outside the order"). This covered crimes that fell outside the *ordo iudicorum publicorum* (i.e., the normal range of offenses).[46] However, as Harries points out, although such cases were "extraordinary" inasmuch as they gave the governor the chance to decide on matters not covered by "civil, praetorian or public criminal law . . . they were not 'extraordinary' in the sense of being 'exceptional.'"[47] In these cases, judgment would have been given by the Emperor or, as in Jesus's case, by an imperial agent acting on

---

44. Corley, *Trial of Jesus*, p. 854.

45. Jerry Vardaman, *A new inscription which mentions Pilate as Prefect*, J. BIBLICAL LITERATURE 81, 70–71 (1962).

46. A. N. SHERWIN-WHITE, ROMAN SOCIETY AND ROMAN LAW IN THE NEW TESTAMENT (Oxford: Clarendon Press, 1963), 24ff.

47. JILL HARRIES, LAW AND CRIME IN THE ROMAN WORLD (Cambridge: Cambridge University Press, 2007), 30.

TABLE 21 KEY ELEMENTS IN THE ROMAN PROCEEDINGS

THE ROMAN PROCEEDINGS	1	Jesus handed over to Pilate	Matthew 27:2; Mark 15:1b; Luke 23:1; John 18:28–32
	2	Jesus before Pilate in the *Praetorium*	Matthew 27:11–14; Mark 15:2–5; Luke 23:2–6; John 18:33–38
	3	Jesus before Herod Antipas	Luke 23:7–12
	4	Jesus before Pilate—again	Luke 23:13–16
	5	Jesus scourged	Matthew 27:26; Mark 15:15; John 19:1
	6	"Passover privilege" exercised	Matthew 27:15–18, 20–23; Mark 15:6–15; Luke 23:18–25; John 18:39–40
	7	Pilate washes his hands	Matthew 27:24
	8	Jesus handed over for crucifixion	Matthew 27:26; Mark 15:15; Luke 23:25; John 19:16

his behalf.[48] Pilate would have presided over the case *cum potestate* (with power) and had considerable discretion.

The opening exchange between the religious establishment and Pilate sets the tone for the rest of the proceedings. Pilate asks for the charges—and the Sanhedrin do not give any. Instead, they tell Pilate, who is supposed to adjudicate on the case, what the penalty is! The scene is set for a trial of strength. The Gospels present Pilate as being unwilling to get involved in the case. According to John 19:12, it is not until quite late on in the Roman proceedings that Pilate "sought to release" Jesus. What, then, is Pilate doing up until then by protesting Jesus's innocence? Presumably, Pilate is simply being "bolshy" by doing the opposite to what the religious establishment wanted him to do. This is hardly surprising since Pilate never wants to do what the Jewish leaders want him to do.

---

48. Olga Tellegen-Couperus, A Short History of Roman Law (London: Routledge, 1993), 93.

Pilate makes the threefold declaration: "I find no crime in him" (e.g., John 18:38). "In the original Greek, the *ego* is always at the start of the phrase, suggesting that whatever the priests and crowd might think, he proudly and passionately disagreed."[49] At least until near the end of the trial, Pilate is not "pro-Jesus"; he is simply "anti-Caiaphas." Siding with Jesus had advantages for Pilate: it put the ball back in the chief priests' court and challenged them to come up with more evidence. It was also a way of reminding them who was boss. This is entirely consistent with Pilate's behavior elsewhere in the Gospels (including the Jewish protest regarding the charge upon which Jesus is found guilty; John 19:21–22) and other historical accounts.

The second stage, according to Luke, is the trial before Herod Antipas (Luke 23:6–12). King Herod was Tetrarch of Galilee, where Jesus exercised his ministry. This trial reflects the custom of transferring jurisdiction from the *forum delicti* (the province where the offense was committed) to the *forum domicilii* (the province where the offender had permanent residence).[50] Roman prefects also used a *consilium* (body of legal advisers or friends) to help them reach a verdict.[51] However, the real reason for this development was probably that Pilate wanted to make Herod complicit in his dealing with a hard case.

Unfortunately for Pilate, Herod declined to pass judgment. Nevertheless, Pilate presented this as supporting his position that Jesus should be acquitted (Luke 23:15). The third stage thus sees Jesus back before Pilate and Pilate continuing to protest Jesus's innocence. The problem for Pilate is that Jesus is no help whatsoever in constructing a defense. And if Pilate cannot prove Jesus innocent, why should the religious authorities accept Pilate's findings?

Round about this point, according to John, the trial enters its next stage as Pilate has Jesus scourged. Scourging could be administered as an independent penalty, followed by release, or as the first part of a capital sentence. John's Gospel presents this as an attempt to release Jesus (19:1–6). This is consistent with Pilate's attempts to find some kind of "third way: not to kill Jesus, not to release him, but to take a middle course."[52] If Jesus was acquitted, he might have seen the scourging as a way of protecting himself from any subsequent criticism. He "covered his back" by savaging an innocent person's.

The fifth stage concerns the exercise of the "Passover privilege" (*privilegium paschale*). The Romans had a tradition of amnesty on special occasions, which in this case seems to have been tailored to acknowledge local customs, namely, the Jewish tradition of Passover. The Passover privilege saw the release of a prisoner by Pilate in a manner that evoked the release of the Jewish people by God. Mark's

---

49. Ann Wroe, Pilate: The Biography Of An Invented Man (London: Vintage, 1999), 252.
50. Sherwin-White, Roman Society, pp. 29–30.
51. Harries, Law and Crime, p. 28.
52. Wroe, Pilate, p. 231.

Gospel suggests that the crowd came to the *Praetorium* to petition the release of someone whom they already had in mind, Barabbas (Mark 15:6–7). There is no particular reason to think that they were there specifically to witness the trial of Jesus. Pilate appeals to this crowd in the final disposition of the case. Like the referral to Herod, Pilate could defer to the acclamation of the people (*acclamatio populi*). Perhaps he handed the choice to the crowd because he did not want to make it himself?[53] It was an irreversible step because "by placing [Jesus and Barabbas] on the same level, [as] two criminals who could be taken or left,"[54] *Pilate indicates, for the first time, that he finds Jesus worthy of execution.* The order of events exposes the miscarriage of justice. The Passover privilege was an act of mercy, but mercy assumes that the offender is already guilty of a crime. But it is *after* putting Jesus up before the crowd that Pilate asks: "what evil has he done?" (Mark 15:14). The order of events is completely wrong. They demonstrate that, as with the trial before the Sanhedrin, Jesus's trial before Pilate is a miscarriage of justice.

The peculiar placing of Jesus with Barabbas without any formal finding of fault is consistent with the fact that none of the Gospel writers record an official declaration of guilt at the end of the process. All we are told is that Pilate "delivered [Jesus] to be crucified"; Matthew 27:26; Mark 15:15). This may be for the simple reason that Pilate never actually made any verbal declaration. As with the *acclamatio populi*, Jesus's guilt is purely a matter of inference from Pilate's actions. This only heightens the miscarriage of justice. It is as though Pilate cannot bring himself to say that Jesus is guilty—because he knows he is innocent.

Pilate may have thought that by putting a scourged Jesus up against Barabbas, the crowd might have pity and choose Jesus. Perhaps he thought he could force his choice upon the crowd. If so, he makes the mistake of thinking that Jesus is more popular among the crowd than he really is. Barabbas, unlike Jesus, fitted the stereotypical image of the Messiah and was thus the preferred choice. Barabbas evokes the "freedom fighter" of modern times whose violent crimes attract no real censure—a sort of revolutionary "poster boy." Indeed, Barrabas is called a *lestes*, an insurrectionist (John 18:40). This is not too far removed from the current climate of what might be termed "gangster chic," in which there is tolerance, and perhaps even affection, for notorious gangsters such as Frank ("Mad Frankie") Fraser, one of the henchmen for the 1960s London gang, The Krays. This favor is not extended to people such as Basil Williams-Rigby and Mike Lawson, both found to have been falsely accused of sexually abusing male pupils in their care.[55] Even in modern times, we do not expect subtlety from

---

53. Ibid., 237.
54. Ibid., 238.
55. *See* R. v Williams-Rigby and Lawson [2003] England and Wales Court of Appeal, Criminal Division 693; http://www.bailii.org/ew/cases/EWCA/Crim/2003/693.html, accessed October 6, 2009.

popular justice. Faced with a choice between Jesus, who was far removed from the popular paradigm of a Messiah and a "celebrity criminal," which one was the crowd going to choose? The crowd was not able or willing to recognize the false nature of the charges against Jesus. Nor, like the Sanhedrin and Pilate, were they willing to recognize Jesus's claims to kingship.

Pilate's appeal to the crowd is a serious political miscalculation because it means he is now bound by their decision. He has given them the authority, and he cannot take it back, at least not without provoking a riot for which he would be to blame. All that is left for him, then, is "to satisfy the crowd" (Mark 15:15). He even has to ask the people what he should do with Jesus. He ends up being a rubberstamp twice over: for the Sanhedrin *and* the crowd. The thing he most wants to avoid he has to do. From a Roman perspective, Pilate completely mishandles the situation. His job is to deal with threats against Rome, but he releases the person who he knows is the greater danger.

Pilate does this because of threats to his own position: "If you release this man, you are not Caesar's friend . . ." (John 19:12). Intrigues at court meant Pilate was in a vulnerable position at this point in his career. Pilate does *not* have a reputation for being a "friend of Caesar." Jesus is ultimately condemned less for the false charges against him than for the true charge against Pilate. Jerusalem at Passover was full of people from across the Empire, including those of high rank who could carry tales of Pilate to the Emperor. "Here his past missteps and miscalculations come back to haunt him: for even if he wanted to be merciful in this case, he dared not be, if it would lead to a blistering report to Rome of everything else he had done."[56] It is Pilate's version of Caiaphas's logic: better that one man should die than that Pilate's job should be threatened.

In the penultimate stage, Pilate symbolically distances himself from the crowd's decision by washing his hands. It is a futile gesture. "He was still the hangman, and so could not excuse himself from making the same choice [as the crowd]."[57]

The final stage is handing Jesus over to be crucified. Pilate sits down on the judgment seat at the *Lithostraton* (stone pavement) and writes out the *titulus* (the charge upon which the offender has been found guilty). In Jesus's case, it is "The King of the Jews," written in Hebrew, Latin, and Greek. This brings us naturally to the social construction of the charges in the Roman, Herodian, and popular proceedings.

---

56. WROE, PILATE, p. 260; CF. PHILO OF ALEXANDRIA, PHILO WITH AN ENGLISH TRANSLATION, translated by F.H. Colson & G.H. Whitaker, Loeb Classical Library (London: Heinemann, 1939), Philo, *Leg.* 302f.

57. WROE, PILATE, p. 238.

VIII. "WHAT CHARGES DO YOU BRING AGAINST THIS MAN?"

We have seen that the charges against Jesus have to make sense not only for a Jewish audience but also for a Roman one. The Romans were not interested in internal Jewish religious disputes unless they threatened the *Pax Romana* (the law and order of the Empire). Each of the main charges (false prophecy/teaching and blasphemy) could be spun in a Roman direction. The formal *accusatio* before Pilate presents the charges in political terms:

> We found this man perverting our nation, and forbidding us to give tribute to Caesar, and saying that he himself is Christ a king.
> (Luke 23:2; *chief priests speaking*)

This "spin doctoring" by the Sanhedrin presents the charge of false prophecy/teaching as "perverting the nation" and the blasphemy charge as "sedition." The charge of "forbidding tribute to Caesar," which the Gospel writers do not mention as part of the trial proceedings, would have sounded plausible in the light of the stigma as a troublemaker and lawbreaker that Jesus had already acquired on the tax issue (see above). More importantly, it fitted the stereotype of Jesus as an opponent of Caesar. False prophecy and blasphemy were not capital offenses in Roman law, but challenging the Emperor fell within the provisions of *laesa maiestas* (offenses against the majesty of the emperor; Digest 48.4).[58] *Laesa maiestas* was punishable by crucifixion in the case of non-Roman citizens. They were among the most serious offenses that could be committed under Roman law and covered a wide range of potentially seditious acts or speech.[59] The Sanhedrin spell it out for Pilate by saying: "he himself is Christ *a king*." This is reinforced by the claim:

> We have a law, and by that law he ought to die, because he has made himself the Son of God. (John 19:7)

Indeed, the very coin which was the subject of the earlier tax dispute bore a superscription that proclaimed Caesar Tiberius in divine terms as the adopted son of the "divine Augustus." Jesus thus seems to fit the stereotype of the insurrectionist against Rome.

There is, therefore, clear continuity between the charges in the Jewish and Roman proceedings, both of which cohere around the idea of *kingship*. This is seen in Table 22, which summarizes the main areas of concern in the Roman proceedings. It confirms that for Pilate, the salient aspect is kingship.

---

58. *See generally* Floyd Seyward Lear, *Crimen Laesae Maiestatis in the Lex Romana Wisigothorum*, SPECULUM 4, 73–87 (1929).

59. ROBERT SAMUEL ROGERS, CRIMINAL TRIALS AND CRIMINAL LEGISLATION UNDER TIBERIUS (Connecticut: American Philological Association, 1935), 190–96.

TABLE 22 SUMMARY OF LINES OF QUESTIONING IN THE ROMAN PROCEEDINGS

		Charges and questions	Jesus's response
LINE OF QUESTIONING IN ROMAN PROCEEDINGS	PILATE	Kingship: "Are you the king of the Jews?" (Matthew 27:11; Mark 15:2; Luke 23:3)	"Yes, it is as you say" (Matthew 27:11; Mark 15:2; Luke 23:3)
		As above (John 18:33)	Jesus redefines meaning of kingship (John 18:34–37)
		Origins: "Where do you come from?" (John 19:9)	Silence (John 19:9)
	CHIEF PRIESTS AND ELDERS	Sundry accusations by "chief priests and elders" (Matthew 27:12; Mark 15:3)	Silence (Matthew 27:12–14; Mark 15:4–5)
		Opposing payment of taxes (Luke 23:1) Claim "to be Christ, a King" (Luke 23:1) False/seditious teacher (Luke 23:5)	No response recorded
	HEROD	Unrecorded questions (Luke 23:9)	Silence (Luke 23:9)

"The title 'The King of the Jews' only occurs on the lips of Pilate or his soldiers...".[60] It is central to the social construction of the offense by the Romans. When Pilate asks Jesus, "Are you the King of the Jews?" and Jesus replies, "You have said so" (Luke 23:3), it parallels Jesus's exchange with Caiaphas regarding Jesus's messianic claims. When Jesus speaks, in both the Jewish and the Roman proceedings, it is to make his judge reconsider the nature of the charge and their assumptions about kingship. Jesus is successful in getting *both* his judges to have the debate on his terms. Caiaphas, the "chief beast," has to engage with Jesus's understanding of his kingship in terms of Daniel 7. Likewise, Pilate has to grapple with a "kingship [that] is not of this world (*kosmos*)" (John 18:36), which is effectively "Daniel 7 for Gentiles." Jackson[61] characterizes the criminal trial as "a contest between competing narratives, which will be resolved on the criteria of relative similarity to narrative typifications." Ultimately, Pilate's problem is that he is unable to fit Jesus's claim to kingship into the narrative typification presented to him by the religious authorities. Even though Pilate

---

60. De Boer, *Pilate in John*, p. 151.
61. Bernard S. Jackson, *"Anchored narratives" and the interface of law, psychology and semiotics*, LEGAL & CRIMINOLOGICAL PSYCHOL. 1, 17–45, 28 (1996).

does not know exactly what Jesus's kingship amounts to, it is *not* a political threat to Rome.

The form of mockery in the Roman proceedings confirms that the key issue is kingship. Likewise, the mockery in the Herodian proceedings suggests that here, too, the key issue is kingship (see Table 23 below).

TABLE 23 DIFFERENT FORMS OF MOCKERY IN THE ROMAN PROCEEDINGS

FORM OF MOCKERY IN ROMAN PROCEEDINGS	BY SOLDIERS	Kingship (crown of thorns, robe, staff) (Matthew 27:27–31; Mark 15:16–20; John 19:1–3, 5).
	BY HEROD	Kingship (robe) (Luke 23:11)

In the lay proceedings, the form of mockery gives some idea of how different groups made sense of the judicial proceedings and the trials of Jesus. The response of one of the revolutionaries (*lestai*) who was crucified next to Jesus echoes the charge brought by the Sanhedrin, while the crowd's response focuses on the destruction of the Temple. This is a plausibly populist response because the Temple stood at the heart of national identity and was something which Jesus was widely thought to have threatened (see Table 24, below).

TABLE 24 DIFFERENT FORMS OF MOCKERY IN THE LAY PROCEEDINGS

FORM OF MOCKERY IN LAY PROCEEDINGS	BY LESTAI	Kingship "Aren't you the Messiah?" (Luke 23:39)
	BY CROWD	Destruction of Temple (Mark 15:29)

These constructions of the charges against Jesus may, of course, have reflected how the judicial proceedings had been "spun" to them by the religious authorities in the crowd (Mark 15:31). After all, Jesus's crucifixion is also, for them, the legal vindication of *their* stance that he was not the messiah. The mocking of the chief priests at the crucifixion site might also have been a way of signifying to the crowd that they need have no fear of the one who cannot perform a sign or wonder to save himself (cf. Deuteronomy 18:22). From this perspective, crucifixion symbolized the impotence of the false prophet.

IX. MISCARRIAGES OF JUSTICE THEN AND NOW

Aspects of the trials of Jesus are common to modern cases of miscarriage of justice. They include the maliciously brought prosecution, the false charges motivated by professional jealousy, the trawling for evidence, the prosecutors and judges who see the injustice but go along with the conviction to protect personal interests, and the readiness to process a capital case quickly in the absence of proper debate for reasons of political expediency. Many of the most notorious British criminal trials of the twentieth century, including the cases of Derek Bentley,[62] Ruth Ellis,[63] and Timothy Evans[64] share some or all of these aspects. In that sense, the forces that propelled Jesus onto a cross continue to operate. *Plus ça change, plus le même chose*; everything changes, but everything stays the same.

There are parallels, too, in the social construction of the charges. From a Jewish standpoint, Jesus is presented as a "threat from within." Such threats are regarded as more insidious and dangerous than threats from without and are hence more liable to miscarriages of justice. Even at the start of the twenty-first century, we have seen how moral panics around Islamic terrorism in the United States and the United Kingdom are thought to justify extreme measures in the name of homeland security. The ritual humiliation, abuse and torture of Jesus prior to a conviction, is echoed in the treatment of Abu Ghraib prisoners by the U.S. military. At the same time, however, miscarriages of justice are rarely overt. Both the Jewish and the Roman proceedings manifest concern for procedural justice. For modern miscarriages of justice to occur they must, by definition, have the pretence of legality.

We might not think that the specific charges against Jesus, such as false teaching and "leading people astray," have much relevance today. We should think again. Many modern miscarriage of justice cases concern teachers or former teachers who have been falsely accused of sexually abusing their pupils.[65] This is probably one of the most serious charges that can be brought in the current social climate, especially where it involves allegations of paedophilia. There is a structural similarity with the charges against Jesus in that both are concerned with the abuse of a position of trust. "Leading disciples astray" is an abuse of the teacher/pupil relationship. And since parents trust teachers (or rabbis) with their children, it is, perhaps, the most significant trust relationship that a

---

62. See J. PARRIS, SCAPEGOAT: THE INSIDE STORY OF THE TRIAL OF DEREK BENTLEY (London: Duckworth, 1991).

63. R. HANCOCK, RUTH ELLIS: THE LAST WOMAN TO BE HANGED (London: Weidenfeld & Nicolson, 1963).

64. L. KENNEDY, TEN RILLINGTON PLACE (London: Gollancz, 1961).

65. *See, e.g.*, Anver Daud Sheikh v The Crown [2006] EWCA Crim. 2625.

person can betray. The modern press presents "abusive teachers" as a national issue (per Caiaphas) because of the "sacredness" of children.

The same is true of the charges of false prophecy, which are accompanied by questions about the source of Jesus's power. The claim that Jesus was "in league with the devil" is of course identical to the ancient "witch hunt," which has continuities also with modern witch hunts. Again, we do not have to look very far for modern parallels; witness the "satanic abuse" scares in the United Kingdom in the 1980s in Nottingham, Rochdale, and the Orkneys. A Joint Enquiry Team set up in relation to the Nottingham allegations concluded that the entire case showed "how 'evidence' can, for want of a better term, be 'created.' That is to say you start with nothing except your own beliefs and end up with the story that you expected and wanted to hear before you started" (Nottinghamshire County Council).[66] The parallels with the trials of Jesus are close.

The Jewish and Roman proceedings are not well-integrated. The religious establishment turn Jesus into Rome's problem while Pilate tries to offload Jesus, variously, onto the Sanhedrin, Herod, and the crowd. This makes it easy for each judicial body to try and avoid responsibility. The tendency to deflect responsibility is a frequent theme of miscarriage of justice cases: whether it is the witnesses, the police, the trial judge, or the court of appeal. Only the brigand on the cross takes responsibility ("we are receiving the due reward of our deeds") and recognizes the miscarriage of justice taking place under his nose ("this man has done nothing wrong"). He is the only person to whom Jesus says, "Truly, I say to you, today you will be with me in Paradise" (Luke 23:41, 43).

Pilate goes through the pretence of "hand washing," but who does he think he's fooling? Modern "rituals of expiation" for miscarriages of justice include the posthumous pardon in a capital case[67] or, more usually, a photocall outside the Royal Courts of Justice in London, combined with a massive compensation payout. It is debatable whether such cleansing rites are any more convincing than Pilate's pail of water. Critical criminologists would argue that such rituals do not preserve the integrity of the system: they indict it.

Finally, one of the remarkable features of the trials of Jesus is the way in which Jesus consistently turns the tables on his judges. They judge themselves by their judgment of him. The same is true, to a degree, of the innocent victim of a miscarriage of justice. He or she sits in the dock but "actually sits" in the judge's chair.

The victim of a miscarriage of justice judges the justice process.

---

66. *Cited in* WEBSTER, SECRET OF BRYN ESTYN, p. 90.
67. *See* R. PATTENDEN, ENGLISH CRIMINAL APPEALS 1884-1994: APPEALS AGAINST CONVICTION AND SENTENCE IN ENGLAND AND WALES (Oxford: Clarendon Press, 1996).

X. THE SILENCE OF THE LAMB

Although the trials of Jesus share many features with modern miscarriages of justice, there are some aspects that remain unique. From a miscarriage of justice perspective, the most difficult problem is Jesus's silence. Roman law gave the accused an opportunity to defend himself (cf. Acts 25:15–16), and there were a number of formal opportunities for Jesus to do so. But he did not take them:

> ... when he [Jesus] was accused by the chief priests and elders, he made no answer. Then Pilate said to him, "Do you not hear how many things they testify against you?" But he gave him no answer, not even to a single charge. ... (Matthew 27:12–14)

Jesus's silence evokes the silence of the "servant" figure of *Isaiah*, which is integrated into the overall prophetic message of judgment and return from exile found in Isaiah 40–55:

> He was oppressed, and he was afflicted,
> yet he opened not his mouth;
> like a lamb that is led to the slaughter,
> and like a sheep that before its shearers is dumb,
> so he opened not his mouth. (Isaiah 53:7)

The right to silence in criminal proceedings has long been held as an invaluable safeguard against wrongful convictions.[68] It is, perhaps, unsurprising that the recommendation by the United Kingdom Royal Commission on Criminal Justice to restrict the right to silence to criminal suspects and defendants was met with universal dismay by the miscarriage of justice community.[69]

In modern miscarriage of justice cases, people sometimes remain silent because they believe the judicial process itself will expose the false allegation. After all, how could they be convicted for something they have not done? This confidence can be misplaced, however. Silence should be regarded as an "unsafe anchor" on which to ground a criminal conviction. However, as a matter of substantive social knowledge, silence is interpreted as agreement and with having something to hide. For this reason, in miscarriage of justice cases, it is important *not* to remain silent in the face of a false allegation and to construct a defense. All that is needed for a wrongful conviction is circumstantial evidence. As Mike Lawson, who overturned his conviction following a false allegation of sexual abuse on a former pupil when he was master of an approved reformatory for delinquent schoolboys observed, "If you're accused of an imaginary crime,

---

68. Stephen Greer, *The right to silence, defence disclosure, and confession evidence*, J.L. & Soc'y 21, 102–18 (1994).

69. *See, e.g.*, Stephen Greer, *Miscarriages of criminal justice reconsidered*, Mod. L. Rev.57, 58–74 (1994).

allegedly committed on an unspecified date years ago, then of course it's virtually impossible to defend yourself."[70]

Interestingly, although people typically assume guilt following the silence of the accused, Pilate, remarkably, does *not* assume Jesus's guilt. Instead Pilate "wondered greatly" (Matthew 27:14). Behavior seems strange to us when we cannot attribute a motive. However, Jesus's behavior becomes intelligible in the light of the wider Gospel accounts. The Gospels repeatedly present Jesus as working in cooperation with God both to avoid (John 7:1) and to be delivered from (John 7:30) fatal encounters. Jesus is successful in "dodging the bullets" "because his hour had not yet come" (John 7:30). Jesus's "hour" (John 16:32, 17:1) is the time of his capture and trials. It is also "the hour of darkness" (Luke 22:53). Such language recalls the massing of the "four beasts" against the "son of man" in Daniel 7. Evil is broken and defeated only when the beasts have gathered in maximum force.

As we have seen, this story from Daniel 7 is *the only account Jesus himself gives of the trials from his perspective.* The idea that evil is broken and defeated only when it is at its height goes back a long way in the Bible to the covenant with Abram (as he then was). There, God's judgment was delayed because "the iniquity of the Amorites is not yet complete" (Genesis 15:16). Delay makes sense inasmuch as only the battle that exhausts the utmost resources on both sides can be said to be conclusive. On this reading, the chief priests' attempts to prosecute Jesus are destined to succeed, and all of Pilate's attempts to release Jesus are doomed to fail, although the Gospels present the parties as possessing full responsibility for their actions. Jesus is presented as cooperating with God in regard to the circumstances of his own mortal death (cf. John 10:17–18). Indeed, *Jesus* is the one who causes the high priest's prosecution to succeed by making an explosive statement, and *Jesus* is the one who dooms Pilate's attempts at release by remaining silent.

Despite this, Jesus's strategy is not best understood as some weird "death wish." Even in modern times, we can imagine situations, such as tales of wartime heroism, in which people are prepared to lose their lives because they believe it will accomplish something. Such deaths are not best described as "quasi-suicides," even though the people in question knew that they would die. As far as the Gospels are concerned, Jesus's death makes sense within the context of several Jewish retellings of Israel's story, which anticipated the end of Israel's exile and her restoration.

Exile and restoration come into the picture because, as a result of Israel's "deal with God" at Mount Sinai and repeated at Moab (see Chapter 2), Israel would receive the blessings of the covenant if she obeyed God and the curses of

---

70. Mike Lawson (2003), http://www.richardwebster.net/print/xjubilation.htm, accessed October 6, 2009.

the covenant if she did not (Deuteronomy 29–30). Chief among the consequences for failing to fulfill her vocation was exile from the promised land. This exile was not only physical but spiritual since the land was an integral part of God's covenant with Abraham and hence of God's purposes with Israel. As far as the prophets were concerned, Israel went into exile in Babylon because of idolatry (e.g., Ezekiel 8–11). Accordingly, Israel's exile was understood as exile from God because of Israel's sin. It was a national "death," so much so that when Ezekiel prophecied Israel's return from exile and restoration to the land, he presented it as resurrection from the dead (Ezekiel 37:1–14).[71]

According to exilic and postexilic writings, including *Daniel, Isaiah,* and the Maccabean martyrs, "the great themes of exile and restoration and of the kingdom of god and the kingdom of the world, would reach their climax in a great moment of suffering and vindication."[72] Consequently, "we can credibly reconstruct a mindset in which a first-century Jew could come to believe that YHWH would act through the suffering of a particular individual in whom Israel's sufferings were focused: that this suffering would carry redemptive significance; *and that this individual would be himself.*"[73] Jesus believed that he was the representative of Israel and the people of God and that by going into the exile of death and returning from it in the resurrection, Israel's spiritual exile would come to an end and her real "return from exile" would begin.

This theme of substitution is established at the outset of the trials of Jesus at the initial Sanhedrin gathering:

> "You do not understand that *it is expedient for you that one man should die for the people, and that the whole nation should not perish."* He [Caiaphas] did not say this of his own accord, but being high priest that year *he prophesied that Jesus should die for the nation, and not for the nation only, but to gather into one the children of God who are scattered abroad.* (John 11:50–52)

As far as John is concerned, Caiaphas, as high priest, was capable of prophecying and thus spoke truer than he knew. To take on the fate of rebellious Israel, as typified by the revolutionary zealot, Jesus had to be executed in the place of such a person. According to the Gospels, this is what happens when Jesus dies on a cross between two political rebels and in the place of Barabbas. This is part of the reason why, from the point of view of the Gospel writers, the Romans needed to be involved in the trials of Jesus:

> Pilate said to them [the Sanhedrin], "Take him yourselves and judge him by your own law." The Jews said to him, "It is not lawful for us to put any man

---

71. WRIGHT, NEW TESTAMENT, p. 322.
72. WRIGHT, VICTORY OF GOD, p. 465.
73. Ibid., 593; italics original.

to death." This was to fulfil the word which Jesus had spoken to show *by what death he was to die*. (John 18:31–32)

It was central to Jesus's vocation that he be executed by crucifixion under *Roman* criminal jurisdiction, as opposed to being killed by a lynch mob or by the Sanhedrin. This is because crucifixion was a uniquely Roman punishment and one that was routinely applied to insurrectionists. As far as Jesus was concerned, Israel was courting exactly this fate as a result of her attitude toward Rome. Throughout his ministry, Jesus repeatedly called Israel back to her vocation to be "a light to the nations" (e.g., Isaiah 42:6–7; Matthew 5:14) and warned that if she continued on her collision course with Rome she would ultimately incur Roman wrath (e.g., Luke 23:27–31). As mentioned above, it was central to Jesus's sense of vocation, based on retellings of Israel's story, that he would be the one who would take the place of rebellious Israel and that his redemptive suffering would be the means by which God would bring Israel—and the world—back from exile. Accordingly, since the punishment for political insurrection typically took the form of crucifixion, it was important that Jesus's death should be upon a Roman cross.[74] In this way, Jesus's death would be a substitute for rebellious Israel.

Moreover, there is a deep connection between Jesus's death upon a cross and his claims to kingship. This is because the Gospels present Jesus's crucifixion as the moment, ironically, when Jesus becomes Israel's king. To put it another way, we can say that there is a close connection between the outcome of Jesus's trial and the question of kingship, which lies at the heart of the trial.

We have seen that *kingship* is the dominant motif throughout the Jewish, Roman, Herodian, and popular proceedings of the trials of Jesus. All are united by a lack of understanding regarding the nature of Jesus's kingship. Jesus's kingship is not what anyone in the Gospels thought it would look like, not least—Jesus's disciples. Two of them ask, "Grant us to sit, one at your right hand and one at your left, in your glory" (Mark 10:37).

> But Jesus said to them, "You do not know what you are asking. Are you able to drink the cup that I drink, or to be baptized with the baptism with which I am baptized?" And they said to him, "We are able." And Jesus said to them, "The cup that I drink you will drink; and with the baptism with which I am baptized, you will be baptised; but to sit at my right hand or at my left is not mine to grant, but it is for those for whom it has been prepared." (Mark 10:38–40)

It is on the cross, with one revolutionary on his right and one on his left, that Jesus is enthroned as Israel's king.[75] We may note, in the light of the universal

---

74. Ibid., 594–604.
75. Tom Wright, Mark for Everyone (London: SPCK, 2001), 141–42.

misunderstanding of Jesus's kingship in his trials, that Jesus prays for the forgiveness of his accusers on the grounds that they do not know and that they do not understand (Luke 23:34). This is consistent with the manner in which ancient kings pronounced a general amnesty on acceding to their thrones (cf. Chapters 7 and 8).

Second, judgment in the New Testament is seen as taking place as persons respond to the claims of Jesus's kingship. Judgment is presented as a process of division, between those who recognize Jesus's kingship and those who do not (cf. Exodus 7–12, where judgment is also presented as a process of division, between those who recognize the claims of Moses and those who do not). This is particularly apparent in some of the parables, but it is a dominant theme in John's Gospel, where the trials of Jesus are counterpointed with the trial of the world (e.g., John 3:31–32).[76] The world thinks it is judging Jesus when, in fact, the world is being judged *by* Jesus, and this is seen in the world's response to him. In fact, "the trials *of* Jesus" could equally be called "the trials of the religious establishment, Pilate, the crowd, and the revolutionaries *by* Jesus."[77] The process of division is most apparent at the crucifixion scene itself; the revolutionary who hangs on one side of Jesus reviles his kingship while the other brigand, hanging on the other side of Jesus's cross, accepts it (Luke 23:39–43 and cf. John 12:31–32):

> And he [the revolutionary] said, "Jesus, remember me when you come into your kingdom." And he [Jesus] said to him, "Truly, I say to you, today you will be with me in Paradise." (Luke 23:42–43)

This revolutionary is the only person in the Passion narratives who recognizes that Jesus, on the cross, is king. In this way Jesus, enthroned upon the cross, exercises the kingly prerogative of judgment.

Finally, we noted in Chapter 4 that central to the idea of "justice as a calling" was the belief that there could be an essential continuity between the divine and the human and that this has the potential to bring divine justice on earth. From the perspective of the New Testament, the partnership between God and Jesus—expressed in Jesus's total obedience to death on a cross—may be seen as the ultimate divine-human partnership. Appropriately, it is this partnership that is said to result in a unique act of divine justice (Romans 3:25–26).

---

76. Andrew T. Lincoln, *Trials, plots and the narrative of the fourth gospel*, J. STUD. NEW TESTAMENT 56, 3–30 (1994).

77. ANDREW T. LINCOLN, TRUTH ON TRIAL: THE LAWSUIT MOTIF IN THE FOURTH GOSPEL (Peabody, Mass.: Hendrickson, 2000), 137.

XI. CONCLUSION

The trials of Jesus are synonymous with the Passion narratives, and because the Gospels themselves are Passion narratives with an extended introduction, we cannot understand the trials without reference to the events leading up to them. Each of the main charges in the Jewish and Roman proceedings is introduced and developed in advance of the trials. The construction of the charges takes place against this background of contingent social knowledge. They include the charges of false prophecy, false teaching, leading Israel astray, blasphemy, forbidding payment of taxes, and threatening to destroy the Temple. Any number of charges could have been brought at the Jewish proceedings, but these particular charges were chosen because Jesus had already acquired a reputation and stigmata in relation to them. They also made intuitive sense because they cohered around the theme of kingship. This is arguably the dominant motif of the trials. The charges were also suitable because of their salience both for the religious establishment and for the Romans.

The Gospels are evenhanded in their account of the miscarriages of justices that occur, and there are structural parallels between the Jewish and Roman proceedings. There are also parallels between the trials of Jesus and modern miscarriages of justice. Despite this, the trials of Jesus are unique because they are rooted in Jesus's particular worldview and his sense of vocation. The Gospels present the trials as being a retelling and reshaping of the story of Israel, especially those aspects which are concerned with the vindication and restoration of the true Israel or "son of God" over Israel's enemies by means of suffering. As far as the Gospels are concerned, the trials of Jesus were not the trials of Jesus at all. They were the trial of the religious authorities. They were the trial of Pilate. They were the trial of Herod. They were the trial of the people. They were the trial of the world—of all of us—and according to the Gospels, we are judged by our response. They leave us with the question: on which side of Jesus's cross do I hang?

Selected reading

Roger P. Booth, "'We have a law . . .'; The Trials of Jesus of Nazareth," *Denning Law Journal* (1991), 1–19.

Darrell L. Bock, *Blasphemy and Exaltation in Judaism: The Charge against Jesus in Mark 14:53–65* (Grand Rapids: Baker Books, 2000), Chapter 4.

Bernard S. Jackson, *Essays on Halakhah in the New Testament* (Leiden: Brill, 2008), Chapters 2 and 3.

Frank J. Matera, "Responsibility for the death of Jesus according to the Acts of the apostles," *Journal for the Study of the New Testament* 39 (1990), 77–93.

N. T. Wright. *Jesus and the Victory of God* (London: SPCK, 1996), Chapter 12.

N. T. Wright. *The New Testament and the People of God* (London: SPCK, 1993), Chapter 4.

CONCLUSION: LAW IN THE PURPOSE OF GOD

Throughout this book we have seen how, in biblical law, individual legal precepts, bodies of law, judicial decisions, literary units, narratives, prophecy, and wisdom are all interconnected. This interconnectivity is reflected in the definition of biblical law we advanced in the Introduction, which sees "biblical law" as an integration of different instructional genres of the Bible, which together expresses a vision of society ultimately answerable to God. Previous chapters explored the general outlines of biblical law including its character, covenant, law outside Israel, and the vocation to pursue justice. They also looked at individual issues such as humanity and the environment, people and land, social welfare, homicide and vengeance, theft and burglary, marriage and divorce, and sexual offenses, as well as how different interpretive communities understood biblical law during the late Second Temple period (*circa* 537 BC–AD 70). At the end of this journey, what overall conclusions can we derive from this account about the purpose of biblical law?

It's an important question to ask because law always serves a purpose. Without purpose, law is a burnt-out field. It is without meaning for those who engage in it or those who are subject to it. The question is: *whose* purpose does law serve, and *what* purpose is it serving? Many different answers have been given to this question by legal philosophers in respect of modern law.[1] But how might we answer this question with reference to biblical law?

A. Spiritual jurisprudence

Unlike modern law, the purpose of biblical law is explicitly wrapped up in God's plans for Israel, humanity, and the world. This means that when we are thinking about the purpose of biblical law, we are thinking about law in the purpose of God. This is hardly surprising; we have seen over and over again that law is central to the biblical story and that biblical law has to be understood in a theological context.

On the basis of the material covered in this book, it is possible to identify the following five dimensions of law in the purpose of God. We can say that biblical law:

(1) Provides a vision of the good for humanity and the world
(2) Expresses and develops wisdom so that it can be applied to situations of human need

---

1. *See*, for example, RONALD DWORKIN, LAW'S EMPIRE (Oxford: Hart, 1986), pp. 50–52, 225ff; JOHN FINNIS, NATURAL LAW AND NATURAL RIGHTS (Oxford: Clarendon Press, 2001), pp. 3–4, 59ff; and LON L. FULLER, THE MORALITY OF LAW (New Haven and London: Yale University Press, 1969).

(3) Orders human behavior practically and holistically
(4) Advances the story of God's relationship with Israel and humanity
(5) Settles a vocation upon Israel and humanity

We shall explore each of these in turn.

B. "The temptation to do good"

First, *biblical law provides a vision of the good for humanity and the world.* There is a tendency to think of law and legal systems in narrow and technical ways; however, within any holistic conception of political philosophy, law is always embedded in a conception of the "good life" and the "just community." Law cannot be and never has been value neutral. Law and politics is always parasitic upon an idea of the just society[2] which will either be subject to competing claims or to a consensus. Law embodies a cultural vision of the good. The same is true in biblical law. Biblical law presents itself as a framework within which we can rightly understand who we are and live our lives to the full. It gives society "a pole of attraction" (as Philip Allott[3] writes in relation to justice and society). It offers us the temptation to do good.[4]

It is important to recognize this because, for some people, the image of biblical law has been tainted by, for example, the nature of the Christian church's engagement in society. Christians have often found it easier to agree on what they are against than on what they are for, and so the image has been allowed to grow of biblical law being about "killjoys, bans and prohibitions." However, this view is entirely at odds with how the Bible itself sees Torah, which is as an energizing vision of the good. This is classically expressed in the so-called "Great Psalm," Psalm 119, which is a sustained song of praise about the majesty and supremacy of Torah.[5] It includes the declaration:

> . . . I shall walk at liberty, for I have sought thy precepts (verse 45).

As far as the psalmist is concerned, biblical law does not restrict human freedom; instead it is the necessary precondition to human liberty. Biblical law claims to provide us with a broad framework in which we can understand who we are and live our lives to the fullest. Biblical law sees itself as providing categories to allow people to flourish in every different area of human activity, as well as to sustain the environment we are all dependent on.

---

2. FINNIS, NATURAL LAW.
3. PHILIP ALLOTT, EUNOMIA: NEW ORDER FOR A NEW WORLD. (Oxford: Oxford University Press, 1990), 83.
4. *Cf.* PHILIP ALLOTT, INVISIBLE POWER: A PHILOSOPHICAL ADVENTURE STORY (Xlibris Corporation, 2005), 145.
5. DAVID NOEL FREEDMAN, PSALM 119: THE EXALTATION OF TORAH (Eisenbrauns: Winona Lake, 1999).

Modern society attests to the value of a vision for the good. We recognize that people are driven by vision and values and that mobilizing support means accessing that domain and dimension of people's lives. Business and management literature shows that people are subject to a complex range of motivations and that most people do not always respond to the prospect of financial gain.[6] Individuals might offer a complex account of their life and the good they are trying to do, which is what ultimately gives them their motivation. Inspiring and energizing people, therefore, means recognizing that there are times when people should connect with those values. Likewise, incentives and the creation of social norms are recognized by social psychologists as key instruments of change. In this context, biblical law is more in touch with the reality of people and relationships and how to effect change than modern law; it also is in tune with developments in other disciplines.

This positive vision is seen right at the start of the Pentateuch, where God's sovereignty over creation in Genesis 1:1–25 is the paradigm for humanity's rule over the earth in Genesis 1:26 (see Chapter 5). This particular vision of the good in Genesis 1:26 means that humanity is supposed to reflect God's character by subduing any forces of chaos that might challenge the creation. Humanity's role is also to maintain the optimum conditions in which life can flourish. God is said to look upon creation and pronounce it first "good" (e.g., Genesis 1:12) and "very good" (Genesis 1:31). It follows, then, that Genesis 1:26 is a vision of the good that "discerns and abets goodness wherever it may be found."[7] Visions of the good are not inflexible but, rather, are capable of infinite expansion. Accordingly, humanity's vocation to "rule" the earth in Genesis 1:26 gains an added dimension in Genesis 1:28 where it is expanded to "master . . . and rule" (JPS) and further, in Genesis 2:15, where humanity is also called "to till . . . and tend" (JPS). Biblical law issues the challenge to imagine what Diane Kelsey McColley calls "the endlessly diverse and expansible"[8] forms of goodness. We concluded in Chapter 5 that biblical law presents us with a positive vision for the environment that is rooted in reflection upon mankind's place within the vertical hierarchy of creation and that without this complex vision, we will seriously underestimate the complexity of our duties in relation to the environment and to nonhuman creatures.

This vision of the good for humanity and the world is seen more clearly in the law given to Israel at Mount Sinai. It too is a positive vision because it reflects the character of the God who acts in history to bring Israel out of slavery so that she

---

6. *E.g.*, REGINE BIRUTE & ROGER LEWIN, THE SOUL AT WORK: UNLEASHING THE POWER OF COMPLEXITY SCIENCE FOR BUSINESS SUCCESS (Texere Publishing, 1999).

7. Applying the language of DIANE KELSEY MCCOLLEY, A GUST FOR PARADISE: MILTON'S EDEN AND THE VISUAL ARTS (Chicago: University of Illinois Press, 1993), p. 5 on a different topic.

8. Ibid., xvi.

can embark on a relationship with the ancestral deity (Exodus 5:1). We saw in Chapter 2 that the ten "proclamations" of the Decalogue, which bring Israel into being, parallel the "ten utterances" of Genesis 1:3–29 that establish creation. There is a parallel between God's acts in creation and God's acts in redemption, viz., saving Israel, since both are ultimately concerned with providing the optimum conditions for life and freedom. The primary purpose of the law at Mount Sinai is to preserve Israel's relationship with God and her newfound freedom. The point is nicely captured by a fourteenth-century *aggadah* (homiletic exegesis of the Talmud) which interprets Exodus 32:16 as follows:

> . . . [T]he day of the Giving of the Torah . . . was the liberation of Israel's souls. . . It is to this that [the Sages] were alluding when they commented on the verse "[The tablets were God's work, and the writing was God's writing,] incised upon the tablets" (Exodus 32:16) as follows: "Read it not as 'incised' (*harut*) but as 'freedom' (*herut*)."
> (*Menorat Hamaor* 3, lit. "The Candlestick of Light")

The law at Mount Sinai is, above all, an invitation to know, respond to, and reflect the character of God who is abounding in goodness, mercy, and compassion (Exodus 33:19). The idea that biblical law expresses a vision of the good for Israel (and thus for humanity and the world; Deuteronomy 4:6–8) is supported not only in the rabbinic tradition (see above) but also in the New Testament (e.g., Matthew 12:10–13 and Luke 13:10–16 on the legitimacy of healing on the Sabbath).

We have discussed some aspects of this vision of the good in previous chapters. We saw in Chapter 4, for example, that Israel's judges were to recall the Exodus by fighting to overthrow the oppressor and liberate the oppressed—and that if they reached their judicial decisions based on their knowledge of the character of God, they had the potential to mediate actual divine decisions. We also saw in Chapter 5 how biblical law requires humanity to suspend its claims over creation on a regular basis and to limit its take upon the environment, in a way that promotes sustainability. Furthermore, we saw in Chapter 6 how biblical law provides a democratic concept of property that includes the right to a share in political power, and, beyond that, to a set of power relations that enables the individual to live a fully human life. In addition, the biblical *nahalah* (inheritance) provides us with a relational approach to land law that embodies relationships of commitment and nurture. Moreover, we saw in Chapter 7 how biblical law presents the question of land tenure and land use as essentially matters of justice, including intergenerational justice. In doing so, it daringly presents us with a vision of a world that minimizes debt. We also saw that the biblical social welfare laws balance equality and liberty by setting limits to the extent to which the needy could be disadvantaged and giving them regular access to the means of production. This is just one of the ways in which biblical law presents us with the materials from which we can construct a worldview that is very different to modern ideas for social organization, whether Marxism, socialism, or capitalism.[9]

Moving into what we would now regard as criminal law, we saw that biblical homicide law takes seriously the value of human life, both in terms of the need to protect the life of the offender, in certain circumstances (hence the generous provisions with regard to asylum), *and* the value of the victim's life (with the result that *all* taking of blood—even the case of the non-negligent accident—entails some degree of culpability; see Chapter 8). We also saw that the *lex talionis* insists on the importance of proportionality and restraint when dealing with punishment. As far as what we call "sexual offenses" are concerned, biblical law provides us with a vision of the good in the form of well-ordered sexual relationships, that is, the covenant of heterosexual marriage. Here as elsewhere, an understanding of the good provides us with our starting points, from which flows everything else.

By providing a vision of the good for humanity and the world, biblical law is able to accommodate complexity. Thus, adjudication in the Bible goes beyond the assertion that there is a creative moment in all legal activity which distinguishes it from morality to claim (so it seems) that the creative moment in the act of judgment takes the form of divine inspiration. As a result, human beings stand in relation to the divine by virtue of their judicial office (e.g., Psalm 82). We have also seen, at a number of points, that modern law does not presently have sufficiently rich or deep categories to do justice to such matters as land and sexual relationships. Here, we need a more complex vision of the good. Thus, biblical law sees land as more than simply a fungible asset; rather, it is something that creates a network of interdependencies, vertically (with God), horizontally (with the needy), and temporally (with past ancestors and future descendants; e.g., the tithe laws of Deuteronomy 14:22–29). Likewise, sexual relationships are seen to be relationally and morally complex. Accordingly, a biblical typology of sexual offenses is based on more than simply consent between the parties: instead, it draws upon beliefs about how sexual relationships can be used to make or break communities.

At various points, this overall vision of the good is thrown into relief by Israel's experience of oppression and evil. In biblical law, this is expressed in the contrast between life under God's rule and life under Pharaoh's rule. We saw in Chapter 6 that there is a sharp contrast between the "family economics" of biblical law and the "Pharaonic economics" of Egyptian rule. Finally, the vision of the good advanced by biblical law is one that provokes engagement. We saw in Chapter 6, for example, that there was a process of negotiation between customary law and divine revelation in relation to the daughters of Zelophehad (Numbers 27:1–11)

---

9. *See* further MICHAEL SCHLUTER & JOHN ASHCROFT EDS., JUBILEE MANIFESTO, (Leicester: InterVarsity Press/Jubilee Centre, 2005).

and the Josephites (Numbers 36:1–12). Visions of the good are subject to challenge and refinement. This is partly why the legacy of biblical law is so different from that of Roman or Germanic law. The long-term influence of biblical law has been much more continuously refreshed by imaginative re-engagement with the texts.

To sum up, then, biblical law provides us with a vision of the good for humanity and the world. Israel submits to Torah because, like God's commands in the creation narrative, Torah provides the optimum conditions for life and freedom, understood as that which enables the person to live an authentically human life *both* as a human being made in the image of God *and* as the object of God's redemptive acts in history. This means that the public vision of biblical law has a constructive role to play in modern liberal democracies, pointers to which have been found in most chapters in this book. In this sense, biblical law not only helps to understand the past and the present (see Introduction)—it is also a guide to the future.

C. The growth of wisdom

Second, law in the purpose of God *expresses and develops wisdom so that it can be applied to situations of human need*. This follows on from the previous point: biblical law expresses wisdom because it provides a vision of the good. We have seen that there are parallels between biblical law and proverbial wisdom (cf., for example, Deuteronomy 16:18–19 and Proverbs 24:23). Many of the values of biblical law are also expressed in Proverbs (cf., for example, Leviticus 20:10 and Proverbs 7:24–27). Like law itself, one of the functions of wisdom is to provide an understanding of what to do in specific circumstances while Israel herself is presented as a concrete expression of true wisdom (e.g., Deuteronomy 4:6–8).

Biblical law also develops wisdom within the individual, the household, and society so that it can be applied to situations of human need. The study of biblical law, primarily in a domestic context, should result in the formation of a person's character and lead to the acquisition of wisdom (see Chapter 4). This means that biblical law operates mainly at the level of what William Spohn calls "virtue and character ethics."[10] The tension between divine and human justice takes the form of an ongoing process of knowing God, receiving wisdom, and allowing that to develop character and insight. This, in turn, means that adjudication is a progressive experience with judges who are committed to pursuing wisdom and justice travelling in a "virtuous spiral" that brings them closer to God, who is the source of all wisdom. It is because biblical law expresses and fosters wisdom that adjudication can be a partnership between the divine and the human. The Bible

---

10. William Spohn, What Are They Saying About Scripture and Ethics? (Paulist Press, 1996), 107.

bears witness to a number of specific examples of continuity between divine and human acts of judgment (see Chapter 3).

Acquiring wisdom is crucial because biblical law is not comprehensive. We saw in Chapters 1 and 4 that all legal systems have to deal with the fact that "in many contexts, our knowledge of what constitutes appropriate behaviour depends upon a background of understandings that we could not fully articulate in advance of the situations that call them into play."[11] Biblical law deals with this problem by offering rules that are limited in number but which are designed to promote wisdom. This results in considerable creativity in the application of biblical law to situations of human need. For example, we saw in Chapter 9 how Nathan's juridical parable inventively applies the laws of theft to the very different scenarios of homicide and adultery.

This purpose of law—inculcating wisdom in order to shape individual character—is not as strange as it sounds. Today, there is an explicit and acknowledged political agenda around changing people's attitudes and values and improving a whole swathe of relationships within society between parents and children, our relationship with the environment, care for relatives, care for our bodies, and even whether or not our children go to school. This desire on the part of government to change attitudes and social behavior is coupled with an increasing recognition that society and social organizations are complex systems whose outcomes cannot be determined by simple "command and control" mechanisms. As a result, politicians have found modern law to be a very limited instrument when it comes to tackling issues such as obesity, marriage failure, antisocial behavior, and so on.

Instead of simply relying on legislation, government has come to see that a whole range of mechanisms are needed. Major political initiatives such as the Labour Government's "Respect" agenda (which pledged to create a "culture of respect") comes quite close to the expansive concerns of biblical law. At one level the respect program looks like modern law (and involved some 44 parliamentary bills). At another level, it looks like biblical wisdom inasmuch as it provides a prosocial way of looking at the world and incorporates a wide range of strategies for seeking to change individual and social behavior. (As the then–Prime Minister Tony Blair said: "Bringing a proper sense of respect and responsibility to others is not the job of Government and Parliament alone. Parents, local communities and local people must join law makers and law enforcers to make a difference including partnerships with parents, local communities and local people."[12]) From a political point of view, the idea that law can be an effective means of

---

11. N. E. Simmonds, Central Issues in Jurisprudence (London: Sweet & Maxwell, 2002), 148.

12. The Rt. Hon. Tony Blair, House of Commons Hansard Debates, May 17, 2005, col. 48.

social engineering is not at all unusual: the problem lies in the fact that modern law often does not achieve that. Again, it is instructive to reflect on how biblical law seeks to change behavior in pursuit of a vision of the good that sometimes involves the use of spiritual language.

To sum up, although biblical law is not complete, its role in the purpose of God is to teach wisdom, which is complete. The application of wisdom to new situations requires creativity and imagination, and this is another aspect of the interplay between God, justice, and society.

D. Pragmatism and integrity

Third, biblical law *orders human behavior practically and holistically.* It is more accurate to claim that biblical law "orders" rather than, say, "regulates" human behavior because the model for law as a mediating factor in the relationship between God and Israel is not, as it might be today, governmental and hierarchical: instead, biblical law has a complex, diffusionist, approach to power which involves a wide range of formal and informal social authorities (see Chapter 4). To say that biblical law orders human behavior is to assert that biblical law places great emphasis on self-order and on sorting problems out at a grassroots level. In this sense, the word "order" is used in the eunomic sense of the good self-order of society and the individual, and not in the deontic mode of a command (whether in the form of prohibition or permission).

The idea that biblical law orders human behavior practically and holistically follows on from the previous point, namely, that biblical law expresses and develops wisdom within the individual, household, and society so that it can be applied to situations of human need. It is because biblical law is an expression of wisdom, which is both practical and universal, that it can both shape and integrate human behavior.

Self-order is seen in the many ways Israelites are supposed to exercise positive concern and restraint to keep relationships healthy. Biblical law promotes an attitude of forbearance toward enemies that makes litigation unlikely (cf. Exodus 23:1–8; see Chapter 1), and it restrains the degree to which an Israelite can profit from another's hardship and indebtedness (Leviticus 25:39–41; see Chapter 7). Self-order is in keeping with the biblical emphasis on the need for Torah to be internalized so that it becomes a source of memory and reflection (e.g., Psalm 19:7–8/MT 19:8–9). The emphasis on sorting out problems at a grassroots level is reflected in the general arrangements for the administration of justice (see Chapter 6). This puts justice in the hands of the many, not the few, because justice is seen as a communal responsibility (e.g., Zechariah 7:9–10). This is in keeping with the belief that justice is the vocation of Abraham's descendants (see Chapter 3). As a result, Israel's judicial relations are broadly based. This is consistent with the covenant ratification ceremony at Sinai in which all Israel is required to approve the laws and judgments presented to them (Exodus 21:1). Likewise, the whole people are taught the law (Exodus 24:12; Deuteronomy

17:10–11) and receive the same general instructions to avoid partiality and bribes as do the appointed judges (Exodus 23:1–8).

The deep connections between biblical law, order, and wisdom mean that law in the purpose of God *orders human behavior practically.* Biblical law is not only a morally purposive enterprise (because it pursues a vision of the good), it is also a pragmatic one. Wisdom is above all practical. God is seen as the source of all wisdom because there is nothing more practical than creating a universe from nothing! The relationship between biblical law and wisdom reminds us that biblical law does not exist purely as an "ideal type" but is meant to be applied by as many people as possible. One of the ways in which biblical law practically orders human affairs is by formulating self-executing rules that enable the "rough and ready" resolution of disputes[13] (e.g., Exodus 22:2–3/MT 22:1–2; see Chapter 9). Being able to resolve problems practically without recourse to third parties is itself a hallmark of wisdom (Proverbs 25:7–10). Biblical law is also pragmatic because it is acutely aware of the faults due to human nature. If it was not realistic, it would not see the need to challenge vested interests and human greed (e.g., Deuteronomy 15:9–10; see Chapter 7).

The substantive connections between biblical law, order, and wisdom also means that law in the purpose of God not only orders human behavior practically but also holistically. We saw that one of the reasons for studying biblical law is to gain a sense of how it all fits together. Biblical law has a high degree of interconnectivity. For example, we saw in Chapter 4 that a broadly based system of land ownership (Numbers 36:7, 9) made it possible to have a widespread network of local justice with judges being appointed over military units as small as "tens" (Exodus 18:25). Land tenure and land use is integrated into the pursuit of justice while sexual offenses are also integrated into concerns about land since they, along with other forms of social malpractice, have the capacity to drive the people from the land (see Chapter 11).

To summarize, biblical law is interconnected at a number of levels, which means that it has the capacity to order human behavior practically and holistically.

E. A metanarrative through time and space

Fourth, *biblical law advances the story of God's relationship with Israel—and hence with humanity.* The relationship between God, justice, and society is shaped at every point by the specific story of God's involvement with Israel and the world. As a result, to speak of this narrative is to speak very precisely of the specific, historical acts of a particular God who has a definite character. There is nothing vague about narrative.

---

13. Bernard S. Jackson, Wisdom-Laws: A Study of the Mishpatim of Exodus 21:1-22:16 (Oxford: Oxford University Press, 2006), 29–30.

Biblical law advances the story of God's relationship with Israel and, in so doing, advances the story of God's relationship with humanity. We saw in Chapter 1 that there is a relationship between the universalism of the primeval history (Genesis 1–11) and the particularism of Genesis 12ff. The link is the call of Abram (later Abraham; Genesis 12:1–3) who, along with his descendants, will be the means of blessing "all the families of the earth" (Genesis 12:3). This signifies that, somehow, resolving the outstanding problems of Genesis 1–11 will have something to do with Abraham and his family, although this story is not resolved within the Pentateuch itself.[14]

One of the key ways in which biblical law advances the story of God's relationship with Israel and humanity is through covenant. We saw in Chapter 2 that covenant is a universal form of divine relating and the primary mode of interaction between God and human beings (cf. Genesis 9:1–17). Each of the biblical covenants marks a turning point in the story of God's relationship with humanity and Israel. Each covenant event shows God becoming bound to the other party's problems so they, in turn, can be bonded to God's promises.[15] This individuality is reflected in the multiple variations of the covenant formula and the different types of covenant ceremony. The result is a great deal of dynamism in biblical law, as the law is used to keep the story moving along. Even the covenant at Sinai itself—which is popularly seen as "God handing down a monolithic set of laws to Israel"—is really a constant juxtaposition of law and narrative in which the law is broken almost as soon as it has been given. New laws and covenants are needed to keep the relationship between God, Israel, and the world on track. Biblical law also advances the story of Israel by containing narrative allusions, especially to the Exodus, which provide Israel with the motivation to follow the law. Subsequent developments in the story of Israel, such as the Babylonian exile, are understood in terms of biblical law: specifically, the failure to uphold the covenant at Sinai.

It is because biblical law develops the story of Israel in these ways that we have to pay attention to its literary presentation. We have seen throughout this book that biblical law is expressed with a great deal of artistry at both the level of metanarrative and in the detail of individual pericopes. "Holy writ" is brilliantly writ. For example, the chiastic structure of Numbers 35:17–23 provides us with a threefold classification of homicide[16] (see Chapter 8), and the internal structure of Leviticus 20 provides a series of binary oppositions for different sexual offenses (see Chapter 11).

---

14. David J. A. Clines, The Theme of the Pentateuch, Journal for the Study of the Old Testament Supplement Series 10 (Sheffield: Sheffield Academic Press, 1978).

15. *Adapting* Walter Brueggemann, The Covenanted Self: Explorations in Law and Covenant (Minneapolis: Fortress, 1999), 7.

16. Jackson, Wisdom-Laws, 128.

But although biblical law advances the story of God's relationship with Israel, this does not mean that there is always agreement within Israel as to what that story is. This leads to highly divergent readings of biblical law within the biblical period. We saw in Chapter 7 that the followers of Jesus traced a through-line from the jubilee laws of Leviticus 25 through to Isaiah 61 and thence to Jesus's healing ministry as described in Luke 4. The result is that Jesus's disciples are expected to forgive on a constant basis in a continual "drop the debt" campaign covering all debts, from all persons, all the time (Matthew 18:32–35), although this understanding was not common (Matthew 18:21). Similarly, we saw in Chapter 12 that considerable pluralism existed within Second Temple Judaism on the subject of marriage and divorce. This in turn reflected different ideas about what God was doing and requiring of Israel. These conflicts resulted in the trials of Jesus where Jesus's handling of biblical law and narrative is directly opposed to that of the Jewish leaders, precisely because of deep disagreement about what it means for Israel to fulfil her vocation (see Chapter 13).

To sum up, biblical law advances the story of God's relationship with Israel—and hence with humanity. This means that biblical law is intensely dynamic, flowing from the call of Abraham, to be a blessing to the nations. This brings us to the final sub-section.

F. The vocation of society

Finally, *biblical law settles a vocation upon Israel and humanity*. Allott has argued that "national identity" can take either genetic or generic forms.[17] In the genetic form, the nation sees the source of its identity in a unique story which involves, say, being the recipients of "the special favor of a god or gods" (as is the case with biblical Israel[18]). This contrasts with the generic form, according to which "the nation sees the source of its identity in its idea of the special character of its land, its people, its institutions, its values, its traditions" (for example, the United States of America[19]). If so, biblical Israel's national identity takes, not simply the genetic form, but also the generic form inasmuch as the land is identified as the promised land, and the national character is understood as a commitment to Sinai as a way of life. Yet whether Israel's national identity is understood in genetic or generic forms, her identity is rooted in the call of Abraham and hence in a sense of vocation. This calling is to be the one nation that uniquely bears witness to the character of God in the world.

As a result, it is not possible to understand biblical law, or its purpose, without reference to vocation, and the one is dependent on the other. By settling a

---

17. Philip Allott, *The nation as mind politic*, J. INT'L LAW & POLS. 24, 1361–98, 1374 (1992).
18. Ibid.
19. Ibid.

vocation on both Israel and humanity, biblical law reminds us of the importance of vocation within an overall understanding of ethics. As far as biblical law is concerned, vocation is the context for thinking about justice and society. Rules are not enough—they need to be understood in the light of their point, or a calling. Without a sense of purpose or vocation, rules risk collapsing into legalism. At the same time, however, rules are needed to give form and shape to a calling; for without rules, the vocation risks becoming overly subjective. It is a mistake to become fixated on either rules or calling. Rules are one mode of expressing reality and relationships, and calling is another. We saw in Chapter 12 that both rules and calling are needed to express marital commitment, for example.

First, biblical law *settles a vocation upon Israel*. The covenant at Sinai is vocational: "you shall be to me a kingdom of priests and a holy nation (*goy*)" (Exodus 19:6). Israel is "set apart" to serve the nations in the same way that a priest is "set apart" to serve other people. One of the ways in which Israel will bless the nations is by obeying Torah and so becoming a certain quality of people (Deuteronomy 4:6). In this way, like a priest officiating in the Temple, Israel holds out the knowledge of God to the rest of the world. This is fully in keeping with God's covenant with Abraham, which called Abraham to be an international blessing (Genesis 12:3). Biblical law fulfills its purpose when Israel carries out her mission to the nations. She is God's showcase to the world: the car "showroom" at which the nations can "test drive" Israel's God.

Again, we see that the purpose of biblical law is to fulfill a vocation and that individual rules have to be understood in the light of their point or, in this case, Israel's calling. The purpose of biblical law is to shape the identity and personality of biblical Israel so that Israel reflects the character of God. This corporate identity, of being the people of God, is something that is given at Mount Sinai (Exodus 19:6), but it is also something that develops over time as Israel acts in ways that are consistent with God's acts in history, principally revealed in the Creation and the Exodus. Israel reflects the character of God—and thus fulfills her vocation—when the inputs into biblical society (God's acts and revelation in regard to Israel) match up to the outputs (Israel's internal and external acts of justice which together constitute the relational society). This is how God, justice, and society work together in biblical law.

Israel's vocation brings into sharper focus *the vocation of humanity*. We saw in Chapter 5 that the creation narrative defines humanity's relationship to the environment in terms of a vocation (Genesis 1:26) and that there is a parallel between God's speech in Genesis 1:26—which creates a chosen species—and God's speech in Genesis 15—which creates a chosen people. Both chosen species and chosen people have a vocation inasmuch as they are designed to represent God to others. Biblical law reminds humanity of its vocation as made in the image of God, and for the same reason, as we saw in Chapter 3, we can meaningfully speak of natural law in the Bible.

To conclude, we find two principal vocations threaded through the Hebrew Bible—the vocation of humanity and the vocation of Israel, the two being closely related. As far as the Bible is concerned, law, justice, and society can only be understood correctly in the light of an understanding of God's vocation for individuals and communities and nations.

G. Conclusion

In the Bible, law is fully integrated with theology instead of being (as it may be for us) a substitute for religion. From the perspective of biblical law, the modern separation of "sacred" and "secular" is a false antithesis. In biblical law, theological categories are a means of thinking about—and finding solutions to—a variety of social and legal problems. The sacred is not a way of avoiding difficulties but a means of resolving them and so enhancing human and environmental well-being. Biblical law shows us what law looks like when it is part of the purposes of God. Unlike "law in the purpose of lawyers" or "law in the purpose of clients" or "law in the purpose of the State," "law in the purpose of God" is grounded in the Person and character of Israel's God. Biblical law is transcendent because it is rooted in a sense of purpose. Transcendence in the law is neither a luxury nor an irrelevance. If the legal profession is to remain as a vocation, as opposed to a trade that pays by the hour, it needs to have a transcendent point of reference and to champion a vision of the good. Where we do not have this sense of a bigger picture, we have a trivialized and reduced understanding of law. We will also find ourselves living in a maimed and diminished society, one in which our full humanity is not taken seriously. And where we rightly encounter splendor and grandeur in the law, biblical law reminds us this is because law, at its best, is about something else.

If it is the case that humanity has a vocation to seek justice, because it is made in the image of God, then each one of us has a vocation to see and to play our part in seeing, law in the purpose of God. Law appeals to a sense of order; therefore, to the source of all order it must go. We have dropped the golden thread of biblical law. It is time to pick it up once again and weave it back into our understanding of justice. And this is not just a job for lawyers. In fact, it is too important to be left for lawyers alone. It is the vocation for *all* of us in society—under whatever law we are subject. Biblical law grants us the possibility of seeing law—not just "law in the Bible"—but the whole phenomenon of *law*, in the purpose of God. We are not simply talking about "State law in the purpose of God" but law in whatever form you as a reader encounter it; whether as national law, international law, or religious law. We can see it all as biblical law does. Indeed, we need to see it as biblical law does. The outworking of that is down to each of us, and this is not a vague or impossible thing. We cannot think about the fifth dimension of biblical law—that biblical law settles a vocation upon humanity—without thinking about the previous four dimensions. Biblical law challenges us to see how *our* law settles a vocation upon humanity; how *our* law advances the divine story of blessing to the nations; how *our* law orders human behavior practically and holistically; how *our* law expresses and develops wisdom within the individual, household, and society so that it can be applied to situations of human need; and how *our* law provides us with a vision of the good. With that, we come full circle to the start of the book. The ultimate reason for studying biblical law is that it is an exemplar of how to see law in the purpose of God. That is its power and its enduring challenge.

BIBLIOGRAPHY

ANCIENT AND MEDIEVAL SOURCES

Babylonian Talmud, Tractate Baba Bathra, translated into English with notes, glossary, and indices by Israel W. Slotki under the editorship of I. Epstein, Hebrew-English edition (London: Soncino Press, 1976), vol. II.

Babylonian Talmud, Tractate Shabbath, translated into English with notes, glossary, and indices by R. Freedman under the editorship of I. Epstein, Hebrew-English edition (London: Soncino Press, 1976), vol. II.

Babylonian Talmud, Tractate Sanhedrin, translated by Jacob Shachter and R. Freedman, Hebrew-English edition (London: Soncino Press, 1969).

Babylonian Talmud, Tractate Yevamot, translated into English with notes, glossary, and indices by Israel W. Slotki under the editorship of I. Epstein, Hebrew-English edition (London: Soncino Press, 1984).

Josephus, Flavius, *The Jewish War*, translation by H. St. J. Thackeray, Loeb Classical Library (Cambridge, Mass.: Harvard University Press, 1997).

Josephus, Flavius, *Jewish Antiquities*, translation by H. St. J. Thackeray, Ralph Marcus, Loeb Classical Library (Cambridge, Mass.: Harvard University Press, 1998).

Justinian I, Emperor of the East, *The Digest of Justinian*, Latin text edited by Theodor Mommsen with the aid of Paul Krueger, English translation edited by Alan Watson (Philadelphia: University of Pennsylvania, 1985).

Cicero, Marcus Tullius, *De Re Publica: Selections*, Cambridge Greek & Latin Classics (Cambridge: Cambridge University Press, 1995).

Midrash Rabbah Genesis, translated by H. Freedman and Maurice Simon (London: Soncino Press, 1939), vol. I.

Midrash Rabbah Eccelesiastes, translated A. Cohen (London: Soncino Press).

Philo of Alexandria, *Philo with an English translation*, translated F.H. Colson, G.H. Whitaker, Loeb Classical Library (London: Heinemann, 1939).

Plato, *The Republic*, edited by G.R.F. Ferrari, translated Tom Griffith, Cambridge Texts in the History of Political Thought (Cambridge: Cambridge University Press, 2000).

Rashi, *Commentary on the Torah, Devarim/Deuteronomy*, translated, annotated, and elucidated by Yisrael Isser Zvi Herczeg (New York: Mesorah Publications, 1998), vol. V.

The Holy Scriptures in the King James and Revised Standard Version (Nashville: Abingdon Press, 1955).

The Mishnah, translated from the Hebrew with introduction and brief explanatory notes by Herbert Danby (Oxford: Oxford University Press, 1933).

The Tosefta, translated from the Hebrew with a new introduction by Jacob Neusner (Peabody, Mass.: Hendrickson Publishers, 2002).

The Complete Dead Sea Scrolls in English, edited by Geza Vermes, revised edition (London: Penguin, 2004).

The Zohar, translation and commentary by Daniel C. Matt (Stanford: Stanford University Press, 2004), vols. I–III.

MODERN SOURCES

Agnon, S. Y., *Present at Sinai: The giving of the Law,* translated Michael Swirsky (Philadelphia: The Jewish Publication Society, 1999).
Allott, Philip, *Invisible Power: A Philosophical Adventure Story* (Xlibris Corporation, 2005).
Allott, Philip, *The Health of Nations: Society and Law beyond the State* (Cambridge: Cambridge University Press, 2002).
Allott, Philip, "The true function of law in the international community," *Indiana Journal of Global Legal Studies* 5 (1998), 391–413.
Allott, Philip, "Kant or won't: theory and moral responsibility" (The British International Studies Association Lecture, December 1995), Review of International Studies 23 (1997), 339–357.
Allott, Philip, "The nation as mind politic," *Journal of International Law and Politics* 24 (1992), 1361–1398.
Allott, Philip, *Eunomia: New Order for a New World.* (Oxford: Oxford University Press, 1990).
Anderson, A. A., *2 Samuel,* Word Biblical Commentary (Dallas: Word Books, 1989).
Anderson, Cheryl B., *Women, Ideology and Violence.* Journal for the Study of the Old Testament Supplement Series 394 (London: Continuum, 2004).
Anderson, Gary A., "Law and lawgiving," in *Encyclopedia of the Dead Sea Scrolls,* eds. Lawrence H. Schiffman and James C. Vanderkam, 2 vols. (Oxford: Oxford University Press, 2000), vol. I, pp. 475–477.
Anon, "Felony murder as a first degree offense: An anachronism retained," *Yale Law Journal* 66 (1957), 427–435.
Aquinas, Saint Thomas, *Summa theologiae: A concise translation,* edited by Timothy McDermott, (London: Eyre and Spottiswoode, 1989).
Ash, Christopher, *Marriage: Sex in the Service of God,* (Leicester: InterVarsity Press, 2005).
Attwood, Bain, "*The Law of the Land* or the law of the land? History, law and narrative in a settler society," *History Compass* 2 (2004), 1–30.
Austin, John, *The Province of Jurisprudence Determined,* Cambridge Texts in the History of Political Thought (Cambridge: Cambridge University Press, 1832/1995).
Avigad, Nahman, "Herodian mansions in Jerusalem," in *Jerusalem: 5,000 Years of History.* Special Issue of *Les Dossiers D'Archeologie,* March (1992), 56–65.
Avishur, Yitzhak, "The narrative of the revelation at Sinai (Ex. 19–24)," in *Studies in Historical Geography and Biblical Historiography,* eds. Gershon Galil and Moshe Weinfeld (Leiden: Brill, 2000), pp. 197–214.
Bach, Alice, "Rereading the body politic: Women and violence in Judges 21," in *Judges: A Feminist Companion to the Bible 4,* ed. Athalya Brenner, second series (Sheffield: Sheffield Academic Press, 1999), pp. 143–159.
Bailey, Randall C., *David in Love and War: The Pursuit of Power in 2 Samuel 10–12,* Journal for the Study of the Old Testament Supplement Series 75. (Sheffield: Journal for the Study of the Old Testament Press, 1990).
Bailey S. J. "Hebrew Law and its influence on the Law of England," *Law Quarterly Review* 47 (1931), 533–535.
Baker, J. H., *An Introduction to English Legal History,* fourth edition (Bath: Butterworths, 2002).
Bamfield, Joshua, *European Retail Theft Barometer: Monitoring the Costs of Shrinkage and Crime for Europe's Retailers* (Nottingham: Centre for Retail Research, 2006).

Bamfield, Joshua, "Retail civil recovery: Filling a deficit in the criminal justice system?" *International Journal of Risk, Security and Crime Prevention* 34 (1998), 257–267.
Bamfield, Joshua, *Making Shoplifters Pay: Retail Civil Recovery* (London: The Social Market Foundation, 1997).
Barmash, Pamela, *Homicide in the Biblical World* (Cambridge: Cambridge University Press, 2005).
Baron, Salo Wittmayer, *A social and religious history of the Jews: Ancient Times: Volume I*, second edition (New York: Columbia University Press, 1952).
Barr, James, "A puzzle in Deuteronomy," in *Reading from Right to Left*, eds. J. Cheryl Exum and H. G. M. Williamson, Journal for the Study of the Old Testament Supplement Series 373 (Sheffield: Sheffield Academic Press, 2003), pp. 13–24.
Barr, James, "Biblical law and the question of natural theology," in *The Law in the Bible and in its Environment*, ed. Timo Veijola, Publications of the Finnish Exegetical Society 51 (Helsinki: Finnish Exegetical Society, 1990), pp. 1–22.
Barton, John, *Ethics and the Old Testament* (London: SCM, 1998).
Barton, John, "Ethics in the book of Isaiah," in *Writing and Reading the Scroll of Isaiah*, eds. Craig C. Broyles and Craig A. Evans (Leiden: Brill, 1997), pp. 67–77.
Barton, John, *Amos' Oracles Against the Nations: A study of Amos 1:3–2:5* (Cambridge: Cambridge University Press, 1980).
Barton, John, "Natural law and poetic justice in the Old Testament," *Journal of Theological Studies* 30 (1979), 1–14.
Bauckham, Richard, *The Book of Acts in Its Palestinian Setting*, (Grand Rapids: Eerdmans, 1995), The Book of Acts in Its First Century Setting, Volume 4.
Bechtel, L. M., "What if Dinah is not raped?," *Journal for the Study of the Old Testament* 62 (1994), 19–36.
Bell, Duran, "The structure of rights in the context of private property," *Journal of Socio-Economics*, 24 (1995), 608–621.
Bellefontaine, Elizabeth, "Customary law and chieftainship: Judicial aspects of 2 Samuel 14:4–21," *Journal for the Study of the Old Testament* 38 (1987), 47–72.
Bellinger, Jr., W. H., *Leviticus and Numbers*, New International Bible Commentary, (Peabody MA: Hendrickson, 2001).
Ben-Menahem, Hanina, "Postscript: The judicial process and the nature of Jewish law," in *An Introduction to the History and Sources of Jewish Law*, eds. N. S. Hecht, B. S. Jackson, S. M. Passamaneck, D. Piattelli and A. M. Rabello (Oxford: Oxford University Press, 1996), pp. 421–437.
Bennett, Harold V., *Injustice Made Legal: Deuteronomic Law and the Plight of Widows, Strangers, and Orphans in Ancient Israel* (Grand Rapids, Mich.: Eerdmans, 2002).
Bergman, J., "Yad," in *Theological Dictionary of the Old Testament*, eds. G. Johannes Botterweck and Helmer Ringgren, translated David E. Green (Grand Rapids, Mich.: Eerdmans, 1986), vol. V, pp. 393–396.
Berman, Harold J., *Law and Revolution: The Formation of the Western Legal Tradition* (Cambridge, Mass.: Harvard University Press, 1983).
Berman, Harold J., *Law and Revolution II: The Impact of the Protestant Reformations on the Western Legal Tradition* (Cambridge, Mass.: Harvard University Press, 2003).
Bernstein, Moshe J. and Shlomo A. Koyfman, "The interpretation of biblical law in the Dead Sea Scrolls: Forms and methods," in *Biblical Interpretation at Qumran*, ed. Matthias Henze (Grand Rapids: Eerdmans, 2005), pp. 61–87.

Bernstein, Moshe J., "Interpretation of Scriptures," in *Encyclopedia of the Dead Sea Scrolls*, ed. Lawrence H. Schiffman and James C. Vanderkam (Oxford: Oxford University Press, 2000), vol. I, pp. 376–83.

Bernstein, Moshe J., "Pentateuch interpretation at Qumran," in *The Dead Sea Scrolls After Fifty Years: A Comprehensive Assessment*, eds. Peter W. Flint and James C. Vanderkam (Leiden: Brill, 1998), pp. 128–159.

Berry, Wendell, *The Unsettling of America: Culture and Agriculture*, third edition (San Francisco: Sierra Club, 1996).

Beveridge Committee Report, *State Provision for Social Need: The Beveridge Committee Report on the Welfare State* (Microfiche. Public Record Office Class PIN 8 and Cab 87/76–82, 1942).

Biran, A., "Dan," in *The New Encyclopaedia of the Holy Land*, eds. Ephraim Stern et. al. (London: Simon and Schuster, 1993), pp. 323–332.

Bird, Phyllis, "The harlot as heroine," in *Women In The Hebrew Bible*, ed. Alice Bach (New York: Routledge, 1999), pp. 99–117.

Birute, Regine and Roger Lewin, *The Soul At Work: Unleashing the Power of Complexity Science for Business Success* (Texere Publishing, 1999).

Bjarup, Jes, "Continental perspectives on natural law theory and legal positivism," in *The Blackwell Guide to the Philosophy of Law and Legal Theory*, eds. Martin P. Golding and William A. Edmundson (Oxford: Blackwell, 2005), pp. 287–299.

Blackstone, Sir William, *Commentaries on the Laws of England*, 4 vols., tenth edition, (London: Strahan and Cadell, 1787), Vol. IV.

Blenkinsopp, Joseph, "Structure and meaning in the Sinai-Horeb narrative (Exodus 19–34)", in *A Biblical Itinerary*, ed. Eugene E. Carpenter, Journal for the Study of the Old Testament Supplement Series 240 (Sheffield: Sheffield Academic Press, 1997), pp. 109–125.

Blomley, Nicholas, "Making private property: enclosure, common right and the work of hedges," *Rural History* 18 (2007), 1–21.

Bock, Darrell L., *Blasphemy and Exaltation in Judaism: The Charge Against Jesus in Mark 14:53–65* (Grand Rapids: Baker Books, 2000).

Bockmuehl, Markus, *Jewish Law in Gentile Churches* (Grand Rapids: Baker Academic, 2000).

Boon, Andrew, "Good lawyers, good people?," *Westminster Law* 4 (2002), 3.

Bottoms, Anthony E., "Some sociological reflections on restorative justice," in *Restorative Justice and Criminal Justice: Competing or Reconcilable Paradigms?*, eds. Andrew von Hirsch et al. (Oxford: Hart, 2003), pp. 79–113.

Bovati, Pietro, *Re-Establishing Justice: Legal terms, concepts and procedures in the Hebrew Bible*, translated Michael J. Smith, Journal for the Study of the Old Testament Supplement Series 105 (Sheffield: Sheffield Academic Press, 1994).

Bowes, David, "The real Kindergarten Cop," *Relational Justice Bulletin* 16 (2002), 4–5.

Boyd, Susan S., "Legal regulation of families in changing societies," in *The Blackwell Companion to Law and Society*, ed. Austin Sarat (Oxford: Blackwell, 2005), pp. 255–270.

Braaten, Laurie J., "Earth community in Hosea 2," in *The Earth Story in the Psalms and the Prophets*, ed. Norman C. Habel (Sheffield: Sheffield Academic Press, 2001), pp. 185–203.

Brett, Mark G., "Earthing the human in Genesis 1–3," in *The Earth Story in Genesis*, eds. Norman C. Habel and Shirley Wurst (Sheffield: Sheffield Academic Press, 2000), pp. 73–86.

Brettler, Marc Zvi, "The many faces of God in Exodus 19," in *Jews, Christians and the Theology of the Hebrew Scriptures*, eds. Alice Ogden Bellis and Joel S. Kaminsky (Atlanta: Society of Biblical Literature, 2000), pp. 353–367.

Brettler, Marc Zvi, *God Is King: Understanding an Israelite Metaphor*, Journal for the Study of the Old Testament Supplement Series 76 (Sheffield: Sheffield Academic Press, 1989).

Brodie, Thomas L., *Genesis as Dialogue: A Literary, Historical and Theological Commentary* (Oxford: Oxford University Press, 2001).

Brown, Gillian and George Yule, *Discourse Analysis* (Cambridge: Cambridge University Press, 1983).

Brown, William P., "The law and the sages: A re-examination of *Torah* in *Proverbs*," in *Constituting the Community: Studies on the Polity of Ancient Israel in Honour of S. Dean McBride Jr.*, eds. John T. Strong and Steven S. Tuell (Eisenbrauns: Winona Lake, 2005), pp. 251–280.

Bruckner, James K., *Implied Law in the Abraham Narrative: A Literary and Theological Analysis*, Journal for the Study of the Old Testament Supplement Series 335 (Sheffield: Sheffield Academic Press, 2001).

Brueggemann, Walter, *The Covenanted Self: Explorations in Law and Covenant* (Minneapolis: Fortress, 1999).

Brueggemann, Walter, *Theology of the Old Testament* (Augsburg: Fortress Press, 1997).

Brueggemann, Walter, *Genesis*, Interpretation Bible Commentary (Louisville: John Knox Press, 1982).

Brueggemann, Walter, *The Land*, Overtures to Biblical Theology Series (Philadelphia: Fortress Press, 1977).

Brunner, Emil and Karl Barth, translated Peter Fraenkel, *Natural Theology* (London: Geoffrey Bles, 1946).

Buckle, Abigail and David P. Farrington, "An observational study of shoplifting," *British Journal of Criminology* 24 (1984), 63–73.

Budd, Philip J., *Leviticus*, New Century Bible Commentary (Grand Rapids: Eerdmans, 1996).

Bullmore, Michael A., "The four most important biblical passages for a Christian environmentalism," *Trinity Journal* 19 (1998), 139–162.

Burnside, J. P., "Flight of the fugitives: Rethinking the relationship between biblical law (Exod. 21:12–14) and the Davidic succession narrative (1 Kgs. 1–2)," *Journal of Biblical Literature* 129 (2010), 417–430.

Burnside, J. P., "Exodus and Asylum: Uncovering the relationship between biblical law and narrative," *Journal for the Study of the Old Testament* 34 (2010), 243–266.

Burnside, J. P., "What shall we do with the Sabbath-gatherer?" A narrative approach to a "hard case" in biblical law (Numbers 15:32–36)," *Vetus Testamentum* 60 (2010), 45–62.

Burnside, Jonathan, "A 'missing case' in the biblical laws of homicide and asylum?," *Vetus Testamentum* 60 (2010), 288–291.

Burnside, Jonathan, "The relationship between slavery, homicide and asylum in biblical law," *Zeitschrift für Altorientalische und Biblische Rechtsgeschichte* 15 (2009), 234–236.

Burnside, J. P., "Rethinking 'sexual' offences in biblical law: The literary structure of Leviticus 20," in *Jewish Law Association Studies XVI: The Boston 2004 Conference Volume*, ed. E. Dorff (Binghampton: Global Academic Publishing, 2007), pp. 37–55.

Burnside, Jonathan P., "Strange Flesh: Sex, semiotics and the construction of deviancy in biblical law," *Journal for the Study of the Old Testament* 30 (2006), 387–420.

Burnside, Jonathan, *Consent versus community: What basis for sexual offences reform?* (Cambridge: Jubilee Centre, 2006), available at http://www.jubilee-centre.org/ Resources/resourcecatalogue.php?cat=16.

Burnside, Jonathan, "Criminal justice," in *Jubilee Manifesto*, eds. Michael Schluter and John Ashcroft (Leicester: InterVarsity Press, 2005), pp. 234–254.

Burnside, Jonathan P., *The Signs of Sin: Seriousness of Offence in Biblical Law*, Journal for the Study of the Old Testament Supplement Series 364 (London: Continuum International, 2003).

Burnside, Jonathan, "Licence to kill?," *Cambridge Papers* 11 (2002), 1–4, available at http://www.jubilee-centre.org/cambridge_papers/index.php.

Burnside, Jonathan, "The Sexual Offences (Amendment) Act 2000: The head of a "kiddy-libber" and the torso of a "child-saver"?, *Criminal Law Review* (2001), 425–434.

Burnside, Jonathan, "Justice, seriousness and relationships," in *Christian Perspectives on Law and Relationism*, eds. Paul Beaumont and Keith Wotherspoon (Carlisle: Paternoster Press, 2000), pp. 19–51.

Burnside, Jonathan and Nicola Baker (eds.), *Relational Justice: Repairing the Breach* (Winchester: Waterside Press, 1994).

Cadwallader, Alan H., *Swords into Ploughshares: The End of War?*, in *The Earth Story in the New Testament*, eds. Norman C. Habel and Vicky Balabanski, Earth Bible Series, 5 vols. (London: Continuum, 2002), vol. V, pp. 57–75.

Callicott, J. B., "Genesis and John Muir," in *Covenant for a New Creation: Ethics, Religion and Public Policy*, eds. C. S. Robb and C. J. Casebolt (Maryknoll: Orbis, 1991), pp. 107–140.

Capps, P. and H. Olsen, "Legal autonomy and reflexive rationality in complex societies," *Social and Legal Studies* 11 (2002), 547–567.

Card, Richard, *Sexual Offences: The New Law* (Trowbridge: Jordan, 2004).

Carmichael, Calum M., *Law and Narrative in the Bible* (London: Cornell University Press, 1985).

Carmichael, Calum M., "The Sabbatical/Jubilee Cycle and the Seven-Year Famine in Egypt," *Biblica* 80 (1999), 224–239.

Carr, David M., *Writing on the Tablet of the Heart: Origins of Scripture and Literature* (Oxford: Oxford University Press, 2005).

Carroll, R. P., "Inscribing the covenant: Writing and the written in Jeremiah," in *Understanding Poets and Prophets*, ed. A. Graeme Auld, Journal for the Study of the Old Testament Supplement Series 152 (Sheffield: Sheffield Academic Press, 1993), pp. 61–75.

Carroll, Robert P., *From Chaos to Covenant: Uses of Prophecy in the Book of Jeremiah* (London: SCM Press, 1981).

Carpenter, Eugene, "Exodus 18: Its structure, style, motifs and function in the Book of Exodus," in *A Biblical Itinerary*, ed. Eugene E. Carpenter, Journal for the Study of the Old Testament Supplement Series 240 (Sheffield: Sheffield Academic Press, 1997), pp. 91–109.

Casperson, Lee W., "Sabbatical, Jubilee, and the Temple of Solomon," *Vetus Testamentum* 53 (2003), 283–296.

Catchpole, David R., "The synoptic divorce material as a traditio-historical problem," *Bulletin of the John Rylands University Library of Manchester*, 57 (1974), 92–127.

Charpin, Dominique, Francis Joannes, Sylvie Lackenbacher and Bertrand Lafont, *Archives Épistolaires de Mari I/2*, Archives Royales de Mari XXVI/2 (Paris: Editions Recherche sur les Civilisations, 1988).

Chirichigno, Gregory C., *Debt-Slavery in Israel and the Ancient Near East*, Journal for the Study of the Old Testament Supplement Series 141 (Sheffield: Sheffield Academic Press, 1993).
Clarkson, C. M. V., "Kicking corporate bodies and damning their souls," *Modern Law Review* 59 (1996), 557–572.
Clements, Roy, *A Sting in the Tale* (Leicester: Inter-Varsity Press, 1997).
Clements, R. E., "The concept of abomination in the Book of Proverbs," in *Texts, Temples and Traditions*, eds. Michael V. Fox, Victor Avigdor Hurowitz, Avi Hurvitz, Michael L. Klein, Baruch J. Schwartz and Nili Shupak (Winona Lake: Eisenbrauns, 1996), pp. 211–225.
Clines, David J. A., *The Theme of the Pentateuch*, Journal for the Study of the Old Testament Supplement Series 10 (Sheffield: Sheffield Academic Press, 1978).
Clines, D. J. A., "The Image of God in Man," *Tyndale Bulletin* 19 (1967), 53–103.
Cohn, Haim, *The Trial and Death of Jesus* (London: Weidenfeld and Nicholson, 1970).
Connolly, William E., *Why I Am Not a Secularist* (Minneapolis: University of Minnesota Press, 1999).
Conrad, J., "*Nkh*," in *Theological Dictionary of the Old Testament*, eds. G. Johannes Botterweck, Helmer Ringgren and Heinz-Josef Fabry, translated David E. Green (Grand Rapids: Eerdmans, 1998), vol. IX, pp. 415–423.
Corley, B., "Trial of Jesus," in *Dictionary of Jesus and the Gospels*, eds. Joel B. Green and Scot McKnight (Leicester: InterVarsity Press, 1992), pp. 841–854.
Coyle, Sean and Karen Morrow, *The Philosophical Foundations of Environmental Law: Property, Rights and Nature* (Oxford and Portland, Oregon: Hart, 2004).
Craig, Jr., Kenneth M., "Questions outside Eden (Genesis 4:1–16): Yahweh, Cain and their rhetorical interchange," *Journal for the Study of the Old Testament* 86 (1999), 107–128.
Crüsemann, Frank, *The Torah: Theology and Social History of Old Testament Law* (Edinburgh: T & T Clark, 1996).
Curtis, Adrian, "God as 'Judge' in Ugaritic and Hebrew Thought," in *Law and Religion: Essays on the place of the law in Israel and early Christianity*, ed. Barnabas Lindars (Cambridge: James Clarke, 1988), pp. 3–12.
Curtis, Sarah, "Lepers or learners," *Relational Justice Bulletin* 16 (2002), 4–5.
Daube, David, "Nathan's parable," *Novum Testamentum* 24 (1982), 275–288.
Daube, David, "To Be Found Doing Wrong," *Studi in Onore Di Edoardo Volterra* 2 (1969), 1–13.
Daube, David, *Studies in Biblical Law* (Cambridge: Cambridge University Press, 1947).
Davies, D. S, *The Bible in English Law* (London: Jewish Historical Society of England, 1954).
Davies, James B., Susanna Sandstrom, Anthony Shorrocks and Edward N. Wolff, *The World Distribution of Household Wealth* (United Nations University: World Institute for Development Economics Research, 2006).
Davies, Philip R., *The Damascus Covenant*, Journal for the Study of the Old Testament Supplement Series 25 (Sheffield: Sheffield Academic Press, 1982).
Davies, W. D., *Torah in the Messianic Age and/or the Age to Come*, Journal of Biblical Literature Monograph Series, Volume VII (Philadelphia: Society of Biblical Literature, 1952).
Davis, Ellen F., *Scripture, Culture and Agriculture: An Agrarian Reading* (Cambridge: Cambridge University Press, 2008).

Day, John, *Molech: A God of Human Sacrifice in the Old Testament*, University of Cambridge Oriental Publications (Cambridge: Cambridge University Press, 1990).
De Boer, Martinus C., "The narrative function of Pilate in John," in *Narrativity in Biblical and Related Texts*, eds. G. J. Brooke and J-D Kaestli (Leuven: Leuven University Press, 2000), pp. 141–58.
Dell, Katharine, *Get Wisdom, Get Insight: An Introduction to Israel's Wisdom Literature* (London: Darton, Longman and Todd, 2000).
Dench, Geoff and Belinda Brown, *Towards A New Partnership Between Family and State (The Grandmother Project)*, Institute of Community Studies Working Paper No. 7 (2004).
Lord Denning, *The Influence of Religion on Law* (Newport: Starling Press, 1989).
De Vaux, Roland, *Ancient Israel: Its Life and Institutions*, translated John McHugh (London: Dartman, Longman and Todd, 1961).
Dever, W. G., "Gezer," in *The New Encyclopaedia of the Holy Land*, eds. Ephraim Stern et al. (London: Simon and Schuster, 1993), pp. 496–506.
Douglas, Mary. "Purity and danger: An analysis of concept of pollution and taboo" (London: Routledge, 2005).
Dozeman, Thomas B., "Spatial form in Exod. 19:1-8a and in the larger Sinai narrative," in *Narrative Research on the Hebrew Bible*, eds. Miri Amihai, George W. Coats and Anne M. Solomon, Semeia 46 (Atlanta: Scholars Press, 1989), pp. 87–101.
Driver, S. R., *A critical and exegetical commentary on Deuteronomy*, third edition (Edinburgh: T&T Clark, 1906).
Du Bois, François, "Water rights and the limits of environmental law," *Journal of Environmental Law* 6 (1994), 73–84.
Durkheim, Emile, *Selected Writings*, edited, translated, and with an introduction by Anthony Giddens (Cambridge: Cambridge University Press, 1972).
Dworkin, Ronald, "Thirty years on: Review of Jules Coleman *The Practice of Principle*," *Harvard Law Review* 115 (2002), 1655–1687.
Dworkin, Ronald, *Law's Empire* (Oxford: Hart, 1986).
Dworkin, Ronald, *Taking Rights Seriously* (London: Duckworth, 1977).
Eichler, B. L., "Literary structure in the Laws of Eshnunna," in Francesca Rochberg-Halton ed., *Language, Literature and History: Philological and Historical Studies Presented to Erica Reiner* (New Haven: American Oriental Society, 1987), pp. 71–84.
Eliot, T. S., *The Complete Poems and Plays of T. S. Eliot* (London: Faber and Faber, 1969).
Elliger, Karl, *Leviticus*, Handbuch zum Alten Testament 4 (Tübingen: Mohr, 1966).
Epstein, Lee and Jack Knight, "Courts and judges," in *The Blackwell Companion to Law and Society*, ed. Austin Sarat (Oxford: Blackwell, 2005), pp. 170–194.
Epstein, Louis M., *Marriage Laws in the Bible and the Talmud* (Cambridge, Mass.: Harvard University Press, 1942).
Ereant, Gill and Nat Segnit, *Warm words: How are we telling the climate story and can we tell it better?* (London: Institute for Public Policy Research, 2006).
Esler, Philip F., "Ezra-Nehemiah as a narrative of (re-invented) Israelite identity," *Biblical Interpretation* 11 (2003), 413–426.
Ewald, François, "Norms, discipline and the law," *Representations* 30 (1990), 138–161.
Eynikel, Erik, "The parable of Nathan (2 Samuel 12:1–4) and the theory of semiosis," in *Rethinking the Foundations: Historiography in the Ancient World and in the Bible*, eds. Steven L. McKenzie and Thomas Römer (Berlin: Walter de Gruyter, 2000), pp. 71–90.
Fabry, Heinz-Josef, "*Edah*," in *Theological Dictionary of the Old Testament*, eds. G. Johannes Botterweck, Helmer Ringgren and Heinz-Josef Fabry, translated David E. Green (Grand Rapids: Eerdmans, 1999), vol. X, pp. 468–481.

Fabry, Heinz-Josef, "Yahad," in *Theological Dictionary of the Old Testament*, eds. G. Johannes Botterweck and Helmer Ringgren, translated David E. Green (Grand Rapids: Eerdmans, 1990), vol. VI, pp. 40–48.
Fager, Jeffrey A., *Land Tenure and the Biblical Jubilee: Uncovering Hebrew Ethics through the Sociology of Knowledge*, Journal for the Study of the Old Testament Supplement Series 155 (Sheffield: Sheffield Academic Press, 1993).
Farrington, David P., *What has been learned from self-reports about criminal careers and the causes of offending?*, Report for the Home Office (London: Home Office, 2001).
Faulkner, David, "Turning prisons inside-out," *Relational Justice Bulletin* 16 (2002), 1–3.
Ferudi, Frank, *Paranoid Parenting* (London: Penguin, 2001).
Fewell, Danna Nolan and David M. Gunn, *Gender, Power and Promise* (Nashville: Abingdon Press, 1993).
Fields, Weston W., *Sodom and Gomorrah: History and Motif in Biblical Narrative*, Journal for the Study of the Old Testament Supplement Series 231 (Sheffield: Sheffield Academic Press, 1997).
Finnis, John, *Natural Law and Natural Rights* (Oxford: Clarendon Press, 2001).
Fischer, Irmtraud, "The Book of Ruth: A Feminist Commentary to the Torah?," *Ruth and Esther: A Feminist Companion to the Bible*, ed. Athalya Brenner, second series (Sheffield: Sheffield Academic Press, 1999), pp. 24–49.
Fishbane, Michael, *Biblical Interpretation in Ancient Israel* (Oxford: Clarendon Press, 1985).
Fitzjames Stephen, Sir James, *A History of the Criminal Law of England*, 3 vols. (London: Macmillan, 1883), vol. III.
Fleishman, Joseph, "Why did Simeon and Levi rebuke their father in Genesis 34:31?," *Journal of Northwest Semitic Languages* 26 (2000), 101–116.
Fleishman, Joseph, "Offences against parents punishable by death: Towards a socio-legal interpretation of Ex. 21:15, 17," in *The Jewish Law Annual Vol. X* (Boston: The Institute of Jewish Law, 1992), pp. 7–37.
Fletcher, Jason, "Foreword," in *Consent versus community: What basis for sexual offences reform?*, Jonathan Burnside (Cambridge: Jubilee Centre, 2006), p. 5, http://www.jubilee-centre.org/Resources/resourcecatalogue.php?cat=16.
Fokkelman, J. P., *Narrative Art and Poetry in the Books of Samuel. Volume I: King David (2 Samuel 9–20 & 1 Kings–2)* (Assen: Van Gorcum, 1981).
Fraade, Steven D., "Looking for legal midrash at Qumran," in *Biblical Perspectives: Early Use and Interpretation of the Bible in the Light of the Dead Sea Scrolls*, eds. M. E. Stone and E. G. Chazon (Leiden: Brill, 1998), pp. 59–79.
Freedman, David Noel, *Psalm 119: The Exaltation of Torah* (Eisenbrauns: Winona Lake, 1999).
Freeman, M. D. A., *Lloyd's Introduction to Jurisprudence*, eighth edition (London: Sweet and Maxwell, 2008).
Fretheim, Terence E., "The reclamation of creation," *Interpretation* 45 (1991), 354–365.
Fried, Lisbeth S., "You shall appoint judges: Ezra's mission and the rescript of Artaxerxes," in *Persia and Torah: The theory of imperial authorisation of the Pentateuch*, ed. James W. Watts (Atlanta: Society of Biblical Literature, 2001), pp. 63–89.
Fried, Lisbeth S. and David N. Freedman, in *Leviticus 23–27*, Jacob Milgrom, Anchor Bible Commentary (New York: Doubleday, 2001), pp. 2257–2270.
Friedman, Mordechai A., "Israel's Response in Hosea 2:17b: You are my husband," *Journal of Biblical Literature* 99 (1980), 199–204.

Friedman, R. E., "Tabernacle," in *Anchor Bible Dictionary*, ed. D. N. Freedman, 6 vols. (London: Doubleday, 1992), vol. VI, pp. 292–300.

Frymer-Kensky, Tikva, "Tit for Tat: The principle of equal retribution in Near Eastern and Biblical law," *Biblical Archaeologist* 43 (1980), 230–234.

Frymer-Kensky, Tikva, "The Atrahasis Epic and its significance for our understanding of Genesis 1–9," *Biblical Archaeologist* 40 (1977), 147–155.

Fuller, Lon L., *The Morality of Law* (New Haven and London: Yale University Press, 1969).

Gaballa, G. A., *The Memphite Tomb-Chapel of Mose* (Warminster: Aris and Phillips, 1977).

Gardiner, Alan H., *The Wilbour Papyru, Volume III: Translation* (Oxford: Oxford University Press, 1948).

Gardiner, Alan H., *Ramesside Administrative Documents* (Oxford: Oxford University Press, 1948).

Gardner, Anne, "Ecojustice: A study of Genesis 6:11–13," in *The Earth Story in Genesis*, eds. Norman C. Habel and Shirley Wurst (Sheffield: Sheffield Academic Press, 2000), pp. 117–129.

Garland, David, *The Culture of Control* (Oxford: Oxford University Press, 2001).

Garner, Robert, *Animal Ethics* (Cambridge: Polity Press, 2005).

Gray, Kevin and Susan Francis Gray, "The idea of property in land," in *Land Law: Themes and Perspectives*, eds. S. Bright and J. Dewar (Oxford: Oxford University Press, 1998), pp. 15–31.

Gray, Kevin, "The ambivalence of property," in *Threats Without Enemies: Facing Environmental Insecurity*, ed. G. Prins (London: Earthscan, 1993).

Grabbe, Lester L., *Leviticus*, Old Testament Guide (Sheffield: Sheffield Academic Press, 1997).

Ginsberg, H. L., "Ugaritic myth, epics, and legends," in James B. Pritchard ed., *Ancient Near Eastern Texts Relating to the Old Testament* (Princeton: Princeton University Press, 1950), pp. 129–155.

Gordon, Robert P., *1 & 2 Samuel: A Commentary* (Exeter: Paternoster Press, 1986).

Gravett, Sandie, "Reading "rape" in the Hebrew Bible: A consideration of language," *Journal for the Study of the Old Testament* 28 (2004), 273–277.

Gray, Kevin and Susan Francis Gray, *Land Law*, fifth edition (Oxford: Oxford University Press, 2007).

Gray, Kevin and Susan Francis Gray, *Elements of Land Law*, fourth edition (Oxford: Oxford University Press, 2005).

Greenberg, Moshe, "Three Conceptions of the Torah in Hebrew Scriptures," in *Studies in the Bible and Jewish Thought* (Philadelphia: Jewish Publication Society, 1995), pp. 11–24.

Greer, Stephen, "The right to silence, defence disclosure, and confession evidence," *Journal of Law and Society* 21 (1994), 102–118.

Greer, Stephen, "Miscarriages of criminal justice reconsidered," *The Modern Law Review* 57 (1994), 58–74.

Greifenhagen, Franz Volker, *Egypt on the Pentateuch's Ideological Map*, Journal for the Study of the Old Testament Supplement Series 316 (London: Continuum, 2002).

Grundmann, Walter, *Jesus der Galiläer und das Judentum* (Weimar, 1940).

Guenther, Allen, "A typology of Israelite marriage: Kinship, socio-economic, and religious factors," *Journal for the Study of the Old Testament* 29 (2005), 387–407.

Gundry, Robert H., *Mark: A Commentary on His Apology for the Cross* (Grand Rapids: Eerdmans, 2000).

HM Treasury, *The Stern Review on the Economics of Climate Change* (Cambridge: Cambridge University Press, 2006).
Habel, Norman C., "Editorial preface," in *The Earth Story in the New Testament*, eds. Norman C. Habel and Vicky Balabanski, Earth Bible Series, 5 vols. (Sheffield: Sheffield Academic Press, 2002), vol. V, pp. ix–xii.
Habel, Norman C., "Is the wild ox willing to serve you?," in *The Earth Story in Wisdom Traditions*, eds. Norman C. Habel and Shirley Wurst (Cleveland: Sheffield Academic Press, 2001), pp. 179–189.
Habel, Norman C., "Geophany: The Earth story in Genesis 1," in *The Earth Story in Genesis*, eds. Norman C. Habel and Shirley Wurst (Sheffield: Sheffield Academic Press, 2000), pp. 34–48.
Harland, P. J., "Review of John Barton *Ethics and the Old Testament*," *Vetus Testamentum* 49 (1999), 135–136.
Hancock, R., *Ruth Ellis: the last woman to be hanged* (London: Weidenfeld & Nicolson, 1963).
Harpum, Charles, "The Law Commission and the reform of land law," in *Land Law: Themes and Perspectives*, eds. S. Bright and J. Dewar (Oxford: Oxford University Press, 1998), pp. 150–179.
Harries, Jill, *Law and Crime in the Roman World* (Cambridge: Cambridge University Press, 2007).
Harrington, Hannah K., "Biblical law at Qumran," in *The Dead Sea Scrolls After Fifty Years: A Comprehensive Assessment*, eds. Peter W. Flint and James C. Vanderkam, 2 vols. (Leiden: Brill, 1998), vol. I, pp. 160–185.
Harris, Rivkah, *Ancient Sippar: A Demographic Study of an Old-Babylonian City (1894–1595 B.C.)* (Belgium: Nederlands Historisch-Archaeologisch Instituut Te Instanbul, 1975).
Harris-Abbott, Troy, "On law and theology," *American Journal of Jurisprudence* 35 (1990), 105–127.
Harrison, Bernard, "The strangeness of *Leviticus*," *Judaism* 48 (1999), 208–228.
Hauge, Martin Ravndal, *The Descent from the Mountain: Narrative Patterns in Exodus 19–40*, Journal for the Study of the Old Testament Supplement Series 323 (Sheffield: Sheffield Academic Press, 2001).
Havea, Jione, *Elusions of Control: Biblical law on the words of women* (Atlanta: Society of Biblical Literature, 2003).
Health Protection Agency, *Annual Report and Accounts* (London: The Stationery Office, 2007).
Hempel, Charlotte, *The Damascus Texts* (Sheffield: Sheffield Academic Press, 2000).
Héritier, Françoise, *Two Sisters and Their Mother* (New York: Zone Books, 1999).
Herzog, Sergio, "The effect of motive on public perceptions of the seriousness of murder in Israel," *British Journal of Criminology* 44 (2004), 771–782.
Hillel, Daniel, *The Natural History of the Bible: An Environmental Exploration of the Hebrew Scriptures* (New York: Columbia University Press, 2006).
Hills, Alison, *Do Animals Have Rights?* (Cambridge: Icon Books, 2005).
Hoenig, S. B., "Sabbatical years and the year of jubilee," *Jewish Quarterly Review* 59 (1969), 222–236.
Hoffmeier, James K. *The Archaeology of the Bible* (Oxford: Lion, 2008).
Hoftijzer, J., "David and the Tekoite woman," *Vetus Testamentum* 20 (1970), 419–444.
Holladay, William L., "The structure and possible setting of the new covenant passage, Jer. 31:31-34," in *Palabra, Prodigio, Poesia*, ed. Vicente Collado Bertomeu, Analecta Biblica 151 (Roma: Editrice Pontificio Istituto Biblico, 2003), pp. 185–189.

Home Office Research, Development and Statistics Directorate, in *Setting the Boundaries: Reforming the law on sex offences*, Sex Offences Review Group, 2 vols. (London: Home Office Communications Directorate, 2000), vol. II, pp. 257–264.

Hossfeld, F. L., "Ratsah," in *Theological Dictionary of the Old Testament*, eds. G. Johannes Botterweck, Helmer Ringgren and Heinz-Josef Fabry, translated David E. Green (Grand Rapids: Eerdmans, 2004), vol. XIII, pp. 630–640.

House of Commons International Development Committee, *Department for International Development Annual Report 2007. First Report of Session 2007–08* (London: The Stationary Office Limited, 2007), volume II, also available at http://www.publications.parliament.uk/pa/cm200708/cmselect/cmintdev/64/64ii.pdf (accessed October 5, 2009).

Hugenberger, Gordon Paul, *Marriage as a Covenant: A study of biblical law and ethics governing marriage, developed from the perspective of Malachi* (Leiden: E.J. Brill, 1994).

Hurowtiz, Victor Avigdor, "True light on the Urim and Thummim," *Jewish Quarterly Review* 88 (1998), 263–274.

Hurst, L. D., "Ethics of Jesus," in *Dictionary of Jesus and the Gospels*, eds. Joel B. Green and Scot McKnight (Leicester: InterVarsity Press, 1992), pp. 210–222.

Hutton, Rodney R., "The case of the blasphemer revisited (Lev. XXIV 10-23)," *Vetus Testamentum* 49 (1999), 532–541.

Hutton, Will, "The Jubilee line that works," *The Observer*, October 3, 1999.

Ilan, Tal, "The Daughters of Zelophehad and Women's Inheritance: The Biblical injunction and its outcome," in *Exodus to Deuteronomy: A Feminist Companion to the Bible (Second Series)*, ed. Athalya Brenner (Sheffield: Sheffield Academic Press, 2000), pp. 176–186.

Instone-Brewer, David, *Divorce and Remarriage in the Bible* (Grand Rapids: Eerdmans, 2002).

Jackson, Bernard S., *Essays on Halakhah in the New Testament* (Leiden: Brill, 2008).

Jackson, Bernard S., "Human law and divine justice in the methodological maze of the Mishpatim," in *Jewish Law Association Studies XVI: The Boston 2004 Conference Volume*, ed. E. Dorff (Binghampton: Global Academic Publishing, 2007), pp. 101–122.

Jackson, Bernard S., "Law in the ninth century: Jehoshaphat's 'judicial reform,'" *Proceedings of the British Academy* 143 (2007), 357–385.

Jackson, Bernard S., "Gender critical observations on tripartite breeding relationships in the Hebrew Bible," in *A Question of Sex? Gender and Difference in the Hebrew Bible and Related Literature*, ed. D. Rooke (Sheffield: Sheffield Academic Press, 2007), pp. 39–52.

Jackson, Bernard S., "The 'institutions' of marriage and divorce in the Hebrew Bible," Unpublished paper (20 pages).

Jackson, Bernard S., "On Neusner's theology of *halakhah*," *Dine Israel* (2007), 257–292.

Jackson, Bernard S., *Wisdom-Laws: A Study of the* Mishpatim *of Exodus 21:1–22:16* (Oxford: Oxford University Press, 2006).

Jackson, Bernard S., "Homicide in the Bible: A review article," *Zeitschrift für Altorientalische und Biblische Rechtsgeschichte* 12 (2006), 362–374.

Jackson, Bernard S., "The practice of justice in Jewish law," *Daimon* 4 (2004), 31–48.

Jackson, Bernard S., "Historical observations on the relationship between letter and spirit," in *Law and Religion: Current Legal Issues*, eds. Richard O'Dair and Andrew Lewis (Oxford: Oxford University Press, 2001), pp. 101–110.

Jackson, Bernard S., "The Jewish view of natural law," *Journal of Jewish Studies* 52 (2001), 136–145.
Jackson, Bernard S., *Lex Talionis: Revisiting Daube's Classic*, Society of Biblical Literature Meeting, Denver 2001, http://www.law2.byu.edu/biblicallaw/papers/jackson_bs_lex_talionis.pdf (accessed January 7, 2008).
Jackson, Bernard S., *Studies in the Semiotics of Biblical Law*, Journal for the Study of the Old Testament Supplement Series 314 (Sheffield: Sheffield Academic Press, 2000).
Jackson, Bernard S., "The original oral law," in *Jewish Ways of Reading the Bible*, ed. G. W. Brooke, Journal of Semitic Studies Supplement X (Oxford: Oxford University Press, 2000), pp. 3–19.
Jackson, Bernard S., "Law, wisdom and narrative," in *Narrativity in Biblical and Related Texts*, eds. G. J. Brooke and J.-D. Kaestli (Leuven: Leuven University Press, 2000), pp. 31–51.
Jackson, Bernard S., "Literal meaning: Semantics and narratives in biblical law and modern jurisprudence," *International Journal for the Semiotics of Law* 13 (2000), 433–457.
Jackson, Bernard S., "'Law' and 'Justice' in the Bible," *Journal of Jewish Studies* 49 (1998), 218–229.
Jackson, Bernard S., "Justice and righteousness in the Bible: Rule of law or royal paternalism?," *Zeitschrift für Altorientalische und Biblische Rectsgeschichte* 4 (1998), 218–262.
Jackson, Bernard S., "'Anchored narratives' and the interface of law, psychology and semiotics," *Legal and Criminological Psychology* 1 (1996), 17–45.
Jackson, Bernard S., *Making Sense in Law: Linguistic, Psychological and Semiotic Perspectives* (Liverpool: Deborah Charles Publications, 1995).
Jackson, Bernard S., "Modelling biblical law: The covenant code," *Chicago-Kent Law Review* 70 (1995), 1745–1827.
Jackson, Bernard S., "The Prophet and the Law in Early Judaism and the New Testament," *Jewish Law Association: The Paris Conference Volume*, eds. S.M. Passamaneck and M. Finley, Jewish Law Association Studies, VII (Atlanta, Scholars Press, 1994), 67–112.
Jackson, Bernard S., "On the nature of analogical argument in early Jewish law," *The Jewish Law Annual* 11 (1993), 137–168.
Jackson, Bernard S., *Law, Fact and Narrative Coherence* (Liverpool: Deborah Charles Publications, 1991).
Jackson, Bernard S., "Ideas of law and legal administration: A semiotic approach," in *The World of Ancient Israel: Sociological, anthropological and political perspectives*, ed. R. E. Clements (Cambridge: Cambridge University Press, 1989), pp. 185–202.
Jackson, Bernard S., "The ceremonial and the judicial: Biblical law as sign and symbol," *Journal for the Study of the Old Testament* 30 (1984), 25–50.
Jackson, Bernard S., *Essays in Jewish and Comparative Legal History* (Leiden: E. J Brill, 1975).
Jackson, Bernard S., "Reflections on Biblical Criminal Law," *Journal of Jewish Studies* 24 (1973), 29–37.
Jackson, Bernard S., *Theft in Early Jewish Law* (Oxford: Clarendon Press, 1972).
Jacobs, Mignon R., "Love, honour, and violence: Socioconceptual matrix in Genesis 34," in *Pregnant Passion: Gender, Sex, and Violence in the Bible*, ed. Cheryl A. Kirk-Duggan (Atlanta: Society of Biblical Literature, 2003), pp. 11–35.

Jasnow, Richard, "Middle Kingdom and Second Intermediate Period," in *A History of Ancient Near Eastern Law*, ed. Raymond Westbrook, 2 vols. (Leiden: Brill, 2003), vol. I, pp. 255–288.
Jasnow, Richard, "New Kingdom," in *A History of Ancient Near Eastern Law*, ed. Raymond Westbrook, 2 vols. (Leiden: Brill, 2003), vol. I, pp. 289–359.
Jenkins, Simon, *Thatcher & Sons: A Revolution in Three Acts* (London: Penguin, 2007).
Jenson, P. P., *Graduated Holiness*, Journal for the Society of the Old Testament Supplement Series 106 (Sheffield: Journal for the Society of the Old Testament Press, 1992).
Joosten, Jan, "Covenant theology in the holiness code," *Zeitschrift für Altorientalische und Biblische Rectsgeschichte* 4 (1998), 145–164.
Kahn, Pinchas, "The expanding perspectives of the Sabbath", *Jewish Bible Quarterly* 32 (2004), 239–244.
Kampen, John, "The Matthean divorce texts re-examined," in *New Qumran Texts and Studies*, eds. George J. Brooke with Florentino García Martínez (Leiden: Brill, 1994), pp. 149–167.
Kant, Immanuel, *The Conflict of the Faculties*, translation and Introduction by Mary J. Gregor (Lincoln and London: University of Nebraska Press, 1798/1979).
Kapelrud, A. S., "*Neshek*," in *Theological Dictionary of the Old Testament*, G. Johannes Botterweck, Helmer Ringgren and Heinz-Josef Fabry, translated Douglas W. Stott (Grand Rapids, Mich.: Eerdmans, 1999), vol. X, pp. 61–65.
Katsh, Abraham I., *The Biblical Heritage of American Democracy* (Ktav Publications, 1977).
Kawashima, Robert S., "The Jubilee year and the return of cosmic purity," *Catholic Biblical Quarterly* 65 (2003), 370–389.
Kedar-Kopfstein, B., "*Qeren*," in *Theological Dictionary of the Old Testament*, eds. G. Johannes Botterweck, Helmer Ringgren and Heinz-Josef Fabry, translated David E. Green (Grand Rapids, Mich.: Eerdmans, 2004), vol. XIII, pp. 167–174.
Kennedy, L., *Ten Rillington Place* (London: Gollancz, 1961).
Kilgallen, John J., "To what are the Matthean exception-texts (5:32 and 19:9) an exception?," *Biblica* 61 (1980), 102–105.
Kingsolver, Barbara, "Foreword," in *The Essential Agrarian Reader: The Future Of Culture, Community, And The Land*, eds. Norman Wirzba and Barbara Kingsolver (USA: Counterpoint, 2003), pp. ix–xvii.
Kirby, Jill, *Broken Hearts: Family decline and the consequences for society* (London: Centre for Policy Studies, 2002).
Kitchen, Kenneth A., *On The Reliability of the Old Testament* (Grand Rapids: Eerdmans, 2003).
Kitchen, Kenneth A., "A preliminary look at Hurrian poetics," in *Studi Sul Vicino Oriente Antico*, ed. Simonetta Graziani (Naples: Istitute Universitario Orientale, 2000), pp. 555–561.
Kitchen, Kenneth A., *Ramesside Inscriptions: Translated and annotated translations. Volume III: Rameses II, his contemporaries* (Oxford: Blackwell, 2000).
Kitchen, Kenneth A., *Poetry of Ancient Egypt* (Paul Åströms Förlag: Jonsered, Sweden, 1999).
Kitchen, Kenneth A., "The patriarchal age: myth or history?," *Biblical Archaeology Review* 21 (1995), 48–57, 88–95.

Kitchen, Kenneth A., "Egypt, Ugarit, Qatna and covenant," in *Ugarit-Forschungen*, eds. Kurt Bergerhof, Manfried Dietrich and Oswald Loretz (Neukirchen-Vluyn: Neukirchener Verlag, 1979), pp. 453–464.

Klawans, Jonathan, *Purity, sacrifice, and the temple: Symbolism and supersessionism in the study of ancient Judaism* (Oxford: Oxford University Press, 2006).

Kleinhams, Martha-Marie, "Criminal justice approaches to paedophilic sex offenders," *Social and Legal Studies* 11 (2002), 233–255.

Klemm, David E., "Material grace: The paradox of property and possession," in *Having: Property and Possession in Religious and Social Life*, eds. William Schweiker and Charles Mathewes (Grand Rapids: Eerdmans, 2004).

Klingbeil, Gerald A., "The finger of God in the Old Testament," *Zeitschrift für die Alttestamentliche Wissenschaft* 112 (2000), 409–415.

Kohák, Erazim, "Perceiving the good," in *The Wilderness Condition: Essays on Environment and Civilization*, ed. Max Oelschlaeger (San Francisco: Sierra Club Books, 1992), pp. 173–187.

Köhler, Ludwig, *Hebrew Man* (London: SCM Press, 1956).

Kraeling, Emil G., *The Brooklyn Museum Aramaic Papyri: New Documents of the Fifth Century B.C. from the Jewish Colony at Elephantine* (New Haven: Yale University Press, 1953).

Krašovec, Joze, "Punishment and mercy in the primeval history", *Ephemerides Theologicae Lovanienses* 70 (1994), 5–33.

Kuehne, Dale, *Sex and the iWorld: Rethinking Relationship Beyond An Age of Individualism* (Grand Rapids: Baker Academic Press, 2009).

Labahn, A., "Antitheocractic tendencies in Chronicles," in *Yahwism After The Exile*, eds. Rainer Albertz and Bob Becking (Assen: Royal Van Gorcum, 2003), pp. 115–135.

Lear, Floyd Seyward, "*Crimen Laesae Maiestatis in the Lex Romana Wisigothorum*," *Speculum* 4 (1929), 73–87.

Lenchak, T. A., *"Choose Life!": A Rhetorical-Critical Investigation of Deuteronomy 28:69–30:20* (Rome: Pontifical Biblical Institute, 1993).

Leone, Massimo, "Divine dictation: Voice and writing in the giving of the law," *International Journal for the Semiotics of Law* 14 (2001), 161–177.

Leske, Adrian M., "Matthew 6:25-34: Human anxiety and the natural world," in *The Earth Story in the New Testament*, eds. Norman C. Habel and Vicky Balabanski, Earth Bible Series, 5 vols. (Sheffield: Sheffield Academic Press, 2002), vol. V, pp. 15–27.

Levenson, Jon D., "Creation and covenant," in *Old Testament Theology: Flowering and Future*, ed. Ben C. Ollenburger (Winona Lake: Eisenbrauns, 2004), pp. 409–423.

Levinson, Bernard M., *Legal Revision and Religious Renewal in Ancient Israel* (Cambridge: Cambridge University Press, 2008).

Levinson, Bernard M. "The first constitution: Rethinking the origins of rule of law and separation of powers in light of Deuteronomy," *Cardozo Law Review* 27 (2006), 1853–1888.

Lincoln, Andrew T., *Truth on Trial: The Lawsuit Motif in the Fourth Gospel* (Peabody, Mass.: Hendrickson, 2000).

Lincoln, Andrew T., "Trials, plots and the narrative of the fourth gospel," *Journal for the Study of the New Testament* 56 (1994), 3–30.

Lipiński, E., "The wife's right to divorce in the light of an ancient near eastern tradition," in *The Jewish Law Annual Volume 4*, ed. B. S. Jackson (Leiden: Brill, 1981), pp. 9–26.

Lloyd Jones, Gareth, "The Biblical Sabbath: An Oasis in Time," *Scripture Bulletin* 34 (2004), 14–23.
Longman III, Tremper, "Israelite genres in their Ancient Near Eastern Context," in *The Changing Face of Form Criticism for the Twenty-First Century*, eds. Marvin A. Sweeney and Ehud Ben Zvi (Grand Rapids: Eerdmans, 2003), pp. 177–195.
López, García, "Tôrâ," in *Theological Dictionary of the Old Testament*, eds. G. Johannes Botterweck, Helmer Ringgren and Heinz-Josef Fabry, translated David E. Green (Grand Rapids, Mich.: Eerdmans, 2007), vol. XV, pp. 609–644.
Lövestam, Evald, "Divorce and remarriage in the New Testament," in *The Jewish Law Annual*, ed. B. S. Jackson (Leiden: Brill, 1981), vol. IV, pp. 47–65.
Lucy, William, "Adjudication," in *The Oxford Handbook of Jurisprudence and Philosophy of Law*, eds. Jules Coleman and Scott Shapiro (Oxford: Oxford University Press, 2002), pp. 206–267.
Lukes, Stephen and Andrew Scull, eds. *Durkheim and the Law* (London: Blackwell, 1983).
McAfee, Gene, "Chosen people in a chosen land: Theology and ecology in the story of Israel's origins," in *The Earth Story in Genesis*, eds. Norman C. Habel and Shirley Wurst, Earth Bible Series, 5 vols. (Sheffield: Sheffield Academic Press, 2000), vol. II, 158–174.
McCarthy, D. J., *Treaty and Covenant* (Rome: Biblical Institute Press, 1978).
McClenney-Sadler, Madeline, A synopsis of key findings in *Re-covering the daughter's nakedness: A formal analysis of Israelite kinship terminology and the internal logic of Leviticus 18*, paper presented to Society of Biblical Literature Annual Meeting (2002), http://www.law2.byu.edu/Biblical_Law/papers/missingdaughter.pdf (accessed April 22, 2005).
Kelsey McColley, Diane, *A Gust for Paradise: Milton's Eden and the Visual Arts* (Chicago: University of Illinois Press, 1993).
McConville, J. Gordon, "Singular address in the Deuteronomic law and the politics of legal administration," *Journal for the Study of the Old Testament* 97 (2002), 19–36.
McKenzie, Donald A., "Judicial procedure at the town gate," *Vetus Testamentum* 14 (1964), 100–104.
Macdonald, Nathan, "Listening to Abraham—Listening to YHWH: Divine justice and mercy in Genesis 18:16–33," *Catholic Biblical Quarterly* 66 (2004), 25–43.
Macpherson, C. B., "Capitalism and changing concept of property," in *Feudalism, Capitalism and Beyond*, eds. Eugene Kamenka and R. S. Neale (Canberra: Australian National University Press, 1975), pp. 105–124.
Maier, Harry O., "There's a new world coming! Reading the apocalypse in the shadow of the Canadian Rockies," in *The Earth Story in the New Testament*, eds. Norman C. Habel and Vicky Balabanski, Earth Bible Series, 5 vols. (Sheffield: Sheffield Academic Press, 2002), vol. V, pp. 166–179.
Maine, Henry Sumner, *Ancient Law*, with introduction and notes by Sir Frederick Pollock (London: John Murray, 1930).
Malchow, Bruce, *Social Justice in the Hebrew Bible* (Minnesota: The Liturgical Press, 1996).
Malul, Meir, *Knowledge, Control and Sex: Studies in biblical thought, culture and worldview* (Tel Aviv-Jaffa: Archaeological Centre Publication, 2002).
Marböck, J., "*Nabal, nebala*," in *Theological Dictionary of the Old Testament*, eds. G. Johannes Botterweck, Helmer Ringgren and Heinz-Josef Fabry, translated David E. Green (Grand Rapids, Mich.: Eerdmans, 1998), vol. IX, pp. 157–171.

Marx, Karl, *Preface and Introduction to A Contribution to the Critique of Political Economy* (Peking: Foreign Languages Press, 1859/1976).
Matthews, Victor H., "Family relationships," in *Dictionary of the Old Testament: Pentateuch: A Compendium of Contemporary Biblical Scholarship*, eds. T. D. Alexander and D. W. Baker (Leicester: Apollos, 2003), pp. 291–299.
Matthews, Victor H., "Entrance ways and threshing floors: Legally significant sites in the Ancient Near East," *Fides et Historia* 19 (1987), 25–40.
Mauchline, John, *1 and 2 Samuel*, New Century Bible Commentary (London: Oliphants, 1971).
Mays, J. L., *Amos: A commentary* (London: SCM Press, 1969).
Mbuwayesango, Dora Rudo, "Can daughters be sons? The daughters of Zelophehad in patriarchal and imperial society," in *Relating to the Text: Interdisciplinary and Form-Critical Insights on the Bible*, eds. Timothy J. Sandoval and Carleen Mandolfo (London: Continuum, 2003), pp. 251–262.
Melnyk, Janet L. R., "When Israel was a child: Ancient Near Eastern Adoption Formulas and the Relationship between God and Israel," in *History and Interpretation*, eds. M. Patrick Graham et al., Journal for the Study of the Old Testament Supplement Series 173. (Sheffield: Sheffield Academic Press, 1993), pp. 245–259.
Meyers, Carol, *Discovering Eve: Ancient Israelite Women in Context* (Oxford: Oxford University Press, 1988).
Meyers, Carol L., "The roots of restriction: Women in early Israel," in *The Bible and Liberation*, ed. Norman K. Gottwald (Maryknoll: Orbis, 1983), pp. 289–306.
Meyers, Carol L., "Procreation, production and protection: Male-female balance in ancient Israel," *Journal of the American Academy of Religion* 51 (1983), 569–593.
Milgrom, Jacob, *Leviticus 23–27*, Anchor Bible Commentary (New York: Doubleday, 2001).
Milgrom, Jacob, *Leviticus 17–22*, Anchor Bible Commentary (New York: Doubleday, 2000).
Milgrom, Jacob, *Numbers* (Philadelphia: The Jewish Publication Society, 1990).
Millard, Alan R., "Recreating the tablets of the law," *Bible Review* (1994), 49–53.
Millard, Alan R., "The Bible B.C.: What can archaeology prove?," *Archaeology in the Biblical World* 1 (1991), 18–38.
Millennium Ecosystem Assessment, *Ecosystems and Human Well-being: Synthesis* (Island Press: Washington, DC, 2005), also available online at http://www.millenniumassessment.org/documents/document.356.aspx.pdf, accessed October 5, 2009.
Miller, James E., "Notes on Leviticus 18," *Zeitschrift für die Alttestamentliche Wissenschaft* 112 (2000), 401–403.
Mills, Paul, "Finance," in *Jubilee Manifesto*, eds. Michael Schluter and John Ashcroft (Leicester: InterVarsity Press/Jubilee Centre, 2005), pp. 196–215.
Mills, Paul, "The economy," in *Jubilee Manifesto*, eds. Michael Schluter and John Ashcroft (Leicester: InterVarsity Press/Jubilee Centre, 2005), pp. 216–233.
Mills, Paul, "The divine economy," *Cambridge Papers* 9 (2000), 1–4.
Moo, D. J., "Law," in *Dictionary of Jesus and the Gospels*, eds. Joel B. Green and Scot McKnight (Leicester: InterVarsity Press, 1992), pp. 450–461.
Morgan, Patricia, *Consequences: the failure of social re-engineering and the wider impact of family fragmentation*, paper presented at Jubilee Centre Sexual Offences Reform Conference, Lucy Cavendish College, University of Cambridge, December 15, 2005, pp. 46.

Mueller, James R., "The Temple Scroll and the Gospel Divorce Texts," *Revue du Qumran* 10 (1980), 247–56.
Mulder, Martin J. *1 Kings* (Peeters: Leuven, 1998).
Myers, Carol, "The family in early Israel," in *Families in Ancient Israel*, ed. Leo G. Perdue et al. (Westminster: John Knox Press, 1997), pp. 1–47.
Myers, Carol, "Procreation, production, and protection: Male-female balance in early Israel," *Journal of the American Academy of Religion* 51 (1983), 569–593.
Myers, Carol, "The roots of restriction: Women in early Israel," in *The Bible and Liberation*, ed. Norman K. Gottwald (Orbis: Maryknoll, 1983), pp. 289–306.
Neufeld, E., *Ancient Hebrew Marriage Laws* (London: Longmans, 1944).
Neusner, Jacob, *The Theology of the Halakhah*, Brill Reference Library of Judaism (Leiden: Brill, 2001).
Neusner, Jacob, *The Halakhah. An Encyclopaedia of the Law of Judaism. Volume I: Between Israel and God. Part A*, Brill Reference Library of Judaism (Leiden: Brill, 2000).
Newman, Thomas B., "The power of stories over statistics," *British Medical Journal* 327 (2003), 1424–427.
Newman, Louis E., "Covenant and contract: A framework for the analysis of Jewish ethics," *Journal of Law and Religion* 9 (1991), 89–112.
Newsom, Carol A., "Common ground: An ecological reading of Genesis 2–3," in *The Earth Story in Genesis*, eds. Norman C. Habel and Shirley Wurst (Sheffield: Sheffield Academic Press, 2000), pp. 60–72.
Niditch, Susan, *Oral World and Written Word: Orality and Literacy in Ancient Israel* (London: SPCK, 1997).
Niehaus, Jeffrey J., *God At Sinai: Covenant and Theophany in the Bible and Ancient Near East*, Studies in Old Testament Biblical Theology (Carlisle: Paternoster Press, 1995).
Noth, Martin, *Leviticus* (Norwich: SCM Press, 1977).
Noth, Martin, *The History of Israel*, third edition (New York: Harper & Row, 1960).
Novak, David, *Natural Law in Judaism* (Cambridge: Cambridge University Press, 1998).
Nozick, Robert, *Anarchy, State and Utopia* (London: Blackwell, 1974).
Ntreh, Abotchie, "The survival of Earth: An African reading of Psalm 104," in *The Earth Story in the Psalms and the Prophets*, ed. Norman C. Habel (Sheffield: Sheffield Academic Press, 2001), pp. 98–108.
O'Donovan, Oliver, "Where were you...?", in *The Care of Creation*, ed. R. J. Berry (Leicester: InterVarsity Press, 2000), pp. 90–93.
Oelschlaeger, Max, *Caring for Creation: An Ecumenical Approach to the Environmental Crisis* (New Haven: Yale University Press, 1994).
Office for National Statistics, *Statistical Bulletin: Marriages in England and Wales 2008* (London: Office for National Statistics, 11 February 2010).
Office for National Statistics, *Population Trends 136: Marriages and divorces during 2006 and adoptions in 2007: England and Wales* (London: Office for National Statistics, 2009).
Office for National Statistics, *Statistical Bulletin: Who is Having Babies? (2008)* (London: Office for National Statistics, 2009).
Office for National Statistics, *Population Trends 121: Report: 2003-based marital status and cohabitation projections for England and Wales* (London: Palgrave Macmillan, 2005).
Office for National Statistics, *Social Trends 31* (London: The Stationery Office, 2001).
Olley, John. W., "The wolf, the lamb, and a little child," in *The Earth Story in The Psalms and the Prophets*, ed. Norman C. Habel (Sheffield: Sheffield Academic Press, 2001), pp. 219–229.

Olley, John, "Mixed blessings for animals: The contrasts of Genesis 9," in *The Earth Story in Genesis*, eds. Norman C. Habel and Shirley Wurst (Sheffield: Sheffield Academic Press, 2000), pp. 130–139.

Oosthuizen, Martin J., "Deuteronomy 15:1–18 in Socio-Rhetorical Perspective," *Zeitschrift für Altorientalische und Biblische Rechtsgeschichte* 3 (1997), 64–91.

Otzen, Benedikt, "Beliyya'al," in *Theological Dictionary of the Old Testament*, eds. G. Johannes Botterweck and Helmer Ringgren, translated David E. Green (Grand Rapids, Mich.: Eerdmans, 1977), vol. 2, pp. 131–136.

Parris, J., *Scapegoat: The inside story of the trial of Derek Bentley* (London: Duckworth, 1991).

Parry, Robin, *Old Testament Story and Christian Ethics: The Rape of Dinah as a Case Study*, Paternoster Biblical Monographs (Milton Keynes: Wipf and Stock, 2004).

Patte, David, *The Gospel According to Matthew: A Structural Commentary on Matthew's Faith* (Philadelphia: Fortress Press, 1987).

Paul, Shalom, *Studies in the Book of the Covenant in the Light of Cuneiform and Biblical Law*, Supplements to *Vetus Testamentum* 17 (Leiden: Brill, 1970).

Pattenden, R., *English Criminal Appeals 1884–1994: Appeals against conviction and sentence in England and Wales* (Oxford: Clarendon Press, 1996).

Pennell, J. and G. Burford, *Family Group Decision Making: After the Conference; Progress in Resolving Violence and Promoting Well-Being; Outcome Report*, 2 vols. (St. Johns, Newfoundland: Memorial University of Newfoundland, School of Social Work, 1998).

Phillips, Anthony, *Essays in Biblical Law*, Journal for the Study of the Old Testament Supplement Series 344 (London: Continuum, 2002).

Phillips, Anthony, "*Nebalah*—a term for serious disorderly and unruly conduct," *Vetus Testamentum* 25 (1975), 237–242.

Piattelli, Daniela, "The marriage contract and bill of divorce in ancient Hebrew law," in *The Jewish Law Annual Volume 4*, ed. B. S. Jackson (Leiden: Brill, 1981), pp. 66–78.

Plant, Raymond, *Social Justice, Labour and the New Right*, Fabian Pamphlet 556 (London: Fabian Society, 1993).

Plaskow, Judith, *Standing Again at Sinai: Judaism from a feminist perspective* (San Francisco: Harper, 1991).

Popenoe, D., "American family decline, 1960–1990: A review and appraisal," *Journal of Marriage and the Family* 55 (1993), 527–541.

Porter, Jean, *Natural and Divine Law: Reclaiming the tradition for Christian ethics*. (Grand Rapids: Eerdmans, 1999).

Pottage, Alain, "The Measure of Land," *Modern Law Review* 57 (1994), 361–384.

Potter, H. D., "The new covenant in Jeremiah 31:31–34," *Vetus Testamentum* 33 (1983), 347–357.

Prance, Ghillean T., *The Earth Under Threat* (Leicester: Inter-Varsity Press, 1996).

Pressler, Carolyn, "Sexual violence and Deuteronomic Law," in *A Feminist Companion to Exodus to Deuteronomy*, ed. A. Brenner (Sheffield: Sheffield Academic Press, 1994), pp. 102–112.

Preuss, H. D., "*Damah*," in *Theological Dictionary of the Old Testament*, eds. G. Johannes Botterweck and Helmer Ringgren (Grand Rapids: Eerdmans 1978), vol. 3, pp. 250–260.

Pritchard, James B., *Ancient Near Eastern Texts Relating to the Old Testament* (Princeton: Princeton University Press, 1950).

Procacci, Giovanna, "Social economy and the government of poverty," in *The Foucault Effect: Studies in Governmentality*, eds. Graham Burchell, Colin Gordon and Peter Miller (Chicago: University of Chicago Press, 1991), pp. 151–168.

Qimron, Elisha, "Celibacy in the Dead Sea Scrolls and the Two Kinds of Sectarianism," in *The Madrid Qumran Congress Volume 1*, eds. Julio Trebolle Barrera and Luis Vegas Montaner (Leiden: Brill 1992), pp. 287–294.

Quesnell, Quentin, "Made themselves eunuchs for the kingdom of heaven" (Matthew 19:12), *Catholic Biblical Quarterly* 30 (1968), 335–358.

Rawls, John, *A Theory of Justice*, revised edition (Oxford: Oxford University Press, 1999).

Raz, Joseph, *The Morality of Freedom* (Oxford: Clarendon Press, 1990).

Regan, Tom, *Empty Cages: Facing the Challenge of Animal Rights* (Lanham: Rowman and Littlefield, 2004).

Tamarkin Reis, Pamela, "What Cain said: A note on Genesis 4:8," *Journal for the Study of the Old Testament* 27 (2002), 107–113.

Rendtorff, Rolf, *The Covenant Formula: An Exegetical and Theological Investigation*, translated by Margaret Kohl, Old Testament Studies (Edinburgh: T&T Clark 1998).

Riddell, James, Jeswald Salacuse and David Tabachnik, *The National Land Law of Zaire and Indigenous Tenure in Central Badandu, Zaire*, Land Tenure Center Paper 92 (University of Wisconsin-Madison: Land Tenure Centre, 1987).

Ringgren, Helmer, "Abad," in *Theological Dictionary of the Old Testament*, eds. G. Johannes Botterweck and Helmer Ringgren (Grand Rapids: Eerdmans, 1999), vol. X, pp. 376–390.

Robinson, Bernard P., "Jeremiah's new covenant: Jer. 31:31–34," *Scandinavian Journal of the Old Testament* 15 (2001), 181–204.

Rodríguez, Angel Manuel, "Sanctuary theology in the Book of Exodus," *Andrews University Seminary Studies* 24 (1986), 127–145.

Rogers, Robert Samuel, *Criminal Trials and Criminal Legislation Under Tiberius* (Connecticut: American Philological Association, 1935).

Rose, J., S. Panter and T. Wilkinson, *Innocents: How Justice Failed Stefan Kiszko and Lesley Molseed* (London: Forth Estate, 1998).

Rossing, Barbara R., "Alas for Earth! Lament and Resistance in Revelation 12," in *The Earth Story in the New Testament*, eds. Norman C. Habel and Vicky Balabanski, Earth Bible Series (Sheffield: Sheffield Academic Press, 2002), vol. V, pp. 180–192.

Rose, Nikolas and Mariana Valverde, "Governed by Law?," *Social and Legal Studies* 7 (1998), 541–551.

Roth, Martha T., *Law collections from Mesopotamia and Asia Minor*, second edition (Atlanta: Scholars Press, 1997).

Roth, Martha T., *Babylonian Marriage Agreements: 7th–3rd Centuries BC* (Neukirchen-Vluyn: Neukirchener Verlag, 1989).

Rothstein, David, "Gen. 24:14 and marital law in 4Q271 3: Exegetical aspects and implications," *Dead Sea Discoveries* 12 (2005), 189–204.

Rubenstein, Jeffrey L., "Nominalism and realism in Qumranic and Rabbinic Law: A reassessment," *Dead Sea Discoveries* 6 (1999), 157–183.

Ruzer, Serge, "The technique of composite citation in the Sermon on the Mount (Matt. 5:21–22, 33–37)," *Revue Biblique* 103 (1996), 65–75.

Sacks, Jonathan, *Radical Then, Radical Now: On Being Jewish* (London: Continuum, 2000).

Sanders, E. P., *Jewish Law from Jesus to the Mishnah* (London: SCM Press, 1990).

Sax, Joseph L., "Takings, private property and public rights," *Yale Law Journal* 181 (1971), 149–186.

Scharbert, J., "Qll," in *Theological Dictionary of the Old Testament*, eds. G. Johannes Botterweck, Helmer Ringgren and Heinz-Josef Fabry, translated David E. Green (Grand Rapids: Eerdmans, 2004), vol. XIII, pp. 37–44.
Schiffman, Lawrence H., "The Pharisees and their legal traditions according to the Dead Sea Scrolls," *Dead Sea Discoveries* 8 (2001), 262–277.
Schiffman, Lawrence H., "The prohibition of judicial corruption in the Dead Sea Scrolls, Philo, Josephus and Talmudic Law," in *Hesed Ve-Emet*, eds. Jodi Magness and Seymour Gitin (Atlanta: Scholars Press, 1998), pp. 155–178.
Schiffman, Lawrence H., "Laws pertaining to women in the Temple Scroll," in *The Dead Sea Scrolls: Forty Years of Research*, eds. Devorah Dimant and Uriel Rappaport (Leiden: Brill, 1992), pp. 210–228.
Schluter, Michael, "Family," in *Jubilee Manifesto*, eds. Michael Schluter and John Ashcroft (Leicester: InterVarsity Press/Jubilee Centre, 2005), pp. 154–174.
Schluter, Michael, "Welfare," in *Jubilee Manifesto*, eds. Michael Schluter and John Ashcroft (Leicester: InterVarsity Press/Jubilee Centre, 2005), pp. 175–195.
Schluter, Michael, "Roots," in *Christianity in a Changing World*, eds. Michael Schluter et al. (London: Marshall Pickering, 2000), pp. 81–91.
Schluter, Michael and Roy Clements, *Reactivating the Extended Family: From Biblical Norms to Public Policy in Britain*, Jubilee Centre Paper No. 1. (Cambridge: Jubilee Centre, 1986), also www.biblical-law.com.
Schramm, Brooks, "Exodus 19 and its Christian appropriation," in *Jews, Christians and the Theology of the Hebrew Scriptures*, eds. Alice Ogden Bellis and Joel S. Kaminsky (Atlanta: Society of Biblical Literature, 2000), pp. 326–351.
Schremer, Adiel, "Qumran polemic on marital law: CD 4:20-5:11 and its social background," in *The Damascus Document: A Centennial of Discovery*, eds. Joseph M. Baumgarten, Esther G. Chazon and Avital Pinnick (Leiden: Brill, 2000), pp. 147–160.
Sex Offences Review Group, *Setting the Boundaries: Reforming the law on sex offences*, 2 vols. (London: Home Office Communications Directorate, 2000), vol. I.
Sex Offences Review Group, *Setting the Boundaries: Supporting Evidence*, 2 vols. (London: Home Office Communications Directorate, 2000), vol. II.
Shead, Andrew G., "An Old Testament theology of the Sabbath year and jubilee," *Reformed Theological Review* 61 (2002), 19–33.
Sherman, Lawrence W., *Policing Domestic Violence: Experiments and Dilemmas* (The Free Press, 1992).
Sherwin-White, A. N., *Roman Society and Roman Law in the New Testament* (Oxford: Clarendon Press, 1963).
Simmonds, N. E., *Central Issues in Jurisprudence* (London: Sweet & Maxwell, 2008).
Simon, Uriel, "The poor man's ewe lamb: An example of a juridical parable," *Biblica* 48 (1967), 207–42.
Simpson, Bob, "Scrambling parenthood: English kinship and the prohibited degrees of affinity," *Anthropology Today* 22 (2006), 3–6.
Singer, Peter, "Heavy petting" (2001), http://www.utilitarian.net/singer/ accessed October 5, 2009.
Singer, Peter, "All animals are equal," in *Animal Rights and Human Obligations*, eds. Tom Regan and Peter Singer (New Jersey, 1989), pp. 148–162, http://www.utilitarian.net/singer/, accessed October 5, 2009.
Sivan, Gabriel, *The Bible and Civilization* (Jerusalem: Keter, 1973).
Ska, Jean-Louis, *Introduction to Reading the Pentateuch* (Winona Lake, In.: Eisenbrauns, 2006).

Smart, Carol, *The ties that bind: Law, marriage and the reproduction of patriarchal relations* (London : Routledge & Kegan Paul, 1984).
Smart, Catherine H. L., *King's College Chapel, Cambridge: The Great Windows* (London: Scala Publishers, 2005).
Social Justice Policy Group, *Breakthrough Britain: Ending the costs of social breakdown* (London: Centre for Social Justice, 2007).
Sperling, S. David, "The Law and the Prophet," in *Jews, Christians and the Theology of the Hebrew Scriptures*, eds. Alice Ogden Bellis and Joel S. Kaminsky (Atlanta: Society of Biblical Literature, 2000), pp. 123–136.
Spohn, William, *What Are They Saying About Scripture and Ethics?* (Paulist Press, 1996).
Sprinkle, Joe M., *Biblical Law and Its Relevance* (Lanham: University Press of America, 2006).
Stager, Lawrence E., "The Archaeology of the Family in Ancient Israel," *Bulletin of the American School of Oriental Research* 260 (1985), 1–36.
Stahl, Nanette, *Law and Liminality in the Bible*, Journal for the Study of the Old Testament Supplement Series 202 (Sheffield: Sheffield Academic Press, 1995).
Statistical Office of the European Communities, *Eurostat Yearbook* (Luxembourg: Office for Official Publications of the European Communities, 2001).
Stein, R. H., "Divorce," in *Dictionary of Jesus and the Gospels*, eds. Joel B. Green and Scot McKnight (Leicester: InterVarsity Press, 1992), pp. 192–199.
Steinmetz, Devora, "Vineyard, farm and garden: The drunkenness of Noah in the context of primeval history," *Journal of Biblical Literature* 113 (1994), 193–207.
Steyn, Mark, "Animal lovers," *The Spectator* August 11, 2001, 20–21.
Sterling, Joyce S. and Wilbert E. Moore, "Weber's analysis of legal rationalisation: A critique and constructive modification," *Sociological Forum* 2 (1987), 67–89.
Stone, Ken, *Sex, honour, and power in the Deuteronomistic history*, Journal for the Study of the Old Testament Supplement Series 234 (Sheffield: Sheffield Academic Press, 1996).
Sustainable Development Commission, *Progress: Sustainable Development Commission Critique* (London: Sustainable Development Commission, 2004).
Suzuki, D. and A. McConnell, *The Sacred Balance: Rediscovering our Place in Nature* (St. Leonards: Allen & Unwin, 1997).
Syrén, Roger, *The Forsaken First-Born: A Study of a Recurrent Motif in the Patriarchal Narratives*, Journal for the Study of the Old Testament Supplement Series 133 (Sheffield: Sheffield University Press, 1993).
Tellegen-Couperus, Olga, *A Short History of Roman Law* (London: Routledge, 1993).
Tigay, Jeffrey H., *Deuteronomy: The JPS Torah Commentary* (Philadelphia: The Jewish Publication Society, 1996).
Tigay, Jeffrey H., "Examination of the accused bride in 4Q159: Forensic medicine at Qumran," *Journal of the Ancient Near Eastern Society* 22 (1993), 129–134.
Tirosh-Samuelson, Hava, "Nature in the sources of Judaism," *Daedalus: Journal of the American Academy of Arts and Sciences*, 130 (2001), 99–124.
Trible, P. *Texts of Terror: Literary Feminist Readings of Biblical Narratives* (Minneapolis: Fortress Press, 1984).
Trible, P., *God and the Rhetoric of Sexuality* (Philadelphia: Fortress Press, 1978).
Twining, William L., *Globalisation and Legal Theory* (London: Butterworths, 2000).
Unger, Roberto Mangabeira, "The Critical Legal Studies Movement," *Harvard Legal Review* 96 (1983), 561–675.

United Nations Environment Programme, *Ecosystems and Biodiversity in Deep Waters and High Seas: Regional Seas Report and Studies No. 178* (New York: United Nations Environment Programme, 2006).

United Nations Development Programme, *Human Development Report 2004: Cultural liberty in today's diverse world* (New York: United Nations Development Programme, 2004).

United Nations Development Programme, *Human Development Report 1998: Consumption for Human Development* (Oxford: Oxford University Press, 1998).

Van Dam, Cornelis, *The Urim and Thummim: A Means of Revelation in Ancient Israel* (Winona Lake: Eisenbrauns, 1997).

Vanderkam, James C., "Sinai revisited," in *Biblical Interpretation at Qumran*, ed. Matthias Henze (Grand Rapids: Eerdmans, 2005), pp. 44–60.

Van Wolde, Ellen, "Does 'inna denote rape? A semantic analysis of a controversial word," *Vetus Testamentum* 52 (2005), 528–544.

Van Wolde, Ellen, "Love and hatred in a multiracial society: The Dinah and Shechem story in Genesis 34 in the context of Genesis 28-35," in *Reading from Right to Left*, eds. J. Cheryl Exum and H. G. M. Williamson, Journal for the Study of the Old Testament Supplement Series 373 (London: Continuum, 2003), pp. 435–449.

Van Wolde, Ellen, "In words and pictures: The sun in 2 Samuel 12:7-12," *Biblical Interpretation* 11 (2003), 259–278.

Van Wolde, Ellen, "The Dinah story: rape or worse?," *Old Testament Essays* 15 (2002), 225–239.

Van Wolde, Ellen, "The earth story as presented by the Tower of Babel narrative," in *The Earth Story in Genesis*, eds. Norman C. Habel and Shirley Wurst (Sheffield: Sheffield Academic Press, 2000), pp. 147–157.

Van Wolde, Ellen, "The story of Cain and Abel: A narrative study," *Journal for the Study of the Old Testament* 52 (1991), 25–41.

Vardaman, Jerry, "A new inscription which mentions Pilate as "Prefect"", *Journal of Biblical Literature* 81 (1962), 70–71.

Vermes, Geza, "Sectarian matrimonial halakah in the Damascus Rule," *Journal of Jewish Studies* 25 (1974), 197–202.

Vitousek, Peter M., Harold A. Mooney, Jane Lubchencho and Jerry M. Melillo, "Human domination of Earth's ecosystems," *Science* 277 (1997), 494–499.

Von Rad, Gerhard, *Old Testament Theology Volume II: The Theology of Israel's Prophetic Traditions*, translated D. M. G. Stalker (Edinburgh: Oliver and Boyd, 1970).

Von Rad, Gerhard, *Old Testament Theology Volume I: The Theology of Israel's Historical Traditions*, translated D.M.G. Stalker (Edinburgh: Oliver and Boyd, 1962).

Wagner, S., "*Kabash*," in *Theological Dictionary of the Old Testament*, eds. G. Johannes Botterweck, Helmer Ringgren and Heinz-Josef Fabry, translated David E. Green (Grand Rapids: Eerdmans, 1995), vol. VII, pp. 52–57.

Washington, H. C., "Lest he die in the battle and another man take her: Violence and the construction of gender in the laws of Deuteronomy 20-22," in *Gender and Law in the Hebrew Bible and the Ancient Near East*, eds. V. H. Matthews et al, Journal for the Study of the Old Testament Supplement Series 262 (Sheffield: Sheffield Academic Press, 1998), pp. 185–213.

Watts, James W., *Reading Law: The Rhetorical Shaping of the Pentateuch*, The Biblical Seminar 59 (Sheffield: Sheffield Academic Press, 1999).

Watts, James W., "Rhetorical strategy in the composition of the Pentateuch," *Journal for the Study of the Old Testament* 68 (1995), 3–22.

Webb, S. H., "Ecology vs. the peaceable kingdom," *Soundings* 79 (1996), 239–252.
Webster, Richard, *The Secret of Bryn Estyn: The making of a modern witch hunt* (Oxford: The Orwell Press, 2005).
Weinfeld, Moshe, *Normative and Sectarian Judaism in the Second Temple Period* (London: T&T Clark, 2005).
Weinfeld, Moshe, *Social Justice in Ancient Israel* (Jerusalem: Magnes Press, 1995).
Weinfeld, Moshe, *Deuteronomy and the Deuteronomic School* (Oxford: Clarendon Press, 1972).
Weisberg, Dvora E., "The Widow of Our Discontent: Levirate Marriage in the Bible and Ancient Israel," *Journal for the Study of the Old Testament* 28 (2004), 403– 429.
Welch, John W., *Law, magic, miracles and the trial of Jesus*, http://66.102.1.104/scholar?hl=en&lr=&q=cache:0LY2NCQ2as0J:www.law2.byu.edu/Biblical_Law/CurrentPapers/MagicSBL1205.pdf+john+welch+law+magic, accessed 5 May 5, 2007.
Wenham, Gordon, *Story As Torah*, Old Testament Studies (Edinburgh: T&T Clark, 2000).
Wenham, Gordon, *Genesis 16–50*, Word Biblical Commentary (Dallas: Waco, 1994).
Wenham, Gordon, "Sanctuary symbolism in the Garden of Eden story," *Proceedings of the World Council of Jewish Studies* 9 (1986), 19–25.
Wenham, Gordon J., *Leviticus*, New International Commentary on the Old Testament, (Grand Rapids: Eerdmans, 1979).
Wenham, Gordon J., "*Betulah:* A girl of marriageable age," *Vetus Testamentum* 22 (1972), 326–348.
Wenham, Gordon J. and William E. Heth, *Jesus and Divorce* (Carlisle: Paternoster Press, 2002).
Wesselius, J. W., "Joab's death and the central theme of the succession narrative (2 Samuel 9–1 Kings 2)," *Vetus Testamentum* 40 (1990), 336–351.
Westbrook, Raymond, "Biblical law," in *An Introduction to the History and Sources of Jewish Law*, eds. N. S. Hecht, B. S. Jackson, S. M. Passamaneck, D. Piattelli and A. M. Rabello (Oxford: Oxford University Press, 1996), pp. 1–17.
Westbrook, Raymond, "Social justice in the Ancient Near East," in *Social Justice in the Ancient World*, eds. K. D. Irani and Morris Silver (London: Greenwood Press, 1995), pp. 149–163.
Westbrook, Raymond, *Property and the Family in Biblical Law*, Journal for the Study of the Old Testament Supplement Series 113 (Sheffield: Sheffield Academic Press, 1991).
Westbrook, Raymond, "Adultery in Ancient Near Eastern Law," *Revue Biblique* 97 (1990), 542–580.
Westbrook, Raymond, *Studies in Biblical and Cuneiform Law* (Paris: Gabalda, 1988).
Westbrook, Raymond, "The prohibition of restoration of marriage in Deuteronomy 24:1–4," *Scripta Hierosolymitana* 31 (1986), 387–405.
Westbrook, Raymond, "Biblical and cuneiform law codes," *Revue Biblique* 92 (1985), 247–264.
Westermann, Claus, *Genesis 1–11*, translated John J. Scullion, Continental Commentary (Minneapolis: Fortress Press, 1994).
White, Leroy, "Turning reparation into reality," *Relational Justice Bulletin* 20 (2004), 6–8.
Whitelam, Keith W., *The Just King: Monarchical judicial authority in ancient Israel*, Journal for the Society of the Old Testament Supplement Series 12 (Sheffield: Journal for the Society of the Old Testament Press, 1979).

Whybray, Norman, "Slippery words IV: Wisdom," in *Wisdom: The Collected Articles of Norman Whybray*, eds. Katharine J. Dell and Margaret Barker (Aldershot: Ashgate, 2005), pp. 6–9.
Williams, F., *Rethinking Families* (London: Calouste Gulbenkian Foundation, 2004).
Williamson, Paul R., *Sealed With An Oath: Covenant in God's unfolding purpose*, New Studies in Biblical Theology (Downers Grove: Apollos/ InterVarsity Press, 2007).
Williamson, Paul R., *Abraham, Israel and the Nations: The patriarchal promise and its covenantal development in Genesis*, Journal for the Study of the Old Testament Supplement Series 315 (Sheffield: Sheffield Academic Press, 2000).
Wilson, Robert R., "Israel's judicial system in the preexilic period," *Jewish Quarterly Review* 74 (1983), 229–248.
Winter, P., "Sadoqite fragments IC 20, 21 and the exegesis of Genesis 1:27 in late Judaism," *Zeitschrift für die Alttestamentliche Wissenschaft* 68 (1956), 289–302.
Wirzba, Norman, *The Paradise of God: Renewing Religion in an Ecological Age* (New York: Oxford University Press, 2003).
Wittenberg, Gunther H., "The Vision of Land in Jeremiah 32," in *The Earth Story in the Psalms and the Prophets*, ed. Norman C. Habel, The Earth Bible, 5 vols. (Sheffield: Sheffield Academic Press, 2001), vol. 4, pp. 129–42.
Woffinden, B., *Miscarriages of Justice* (London: Hodder & Stoughton 1987).
World Wildlife Fund, *Living Planet Report 2006* (2006), http://assets.panda.org/downloads/living_planet_report.pdf; accessed October 5, 2009.
Wright, David P., "The compositional logic of the goring ox and negligence laws in the Covenant Collection (Ex. 21:28–36)," *Zeitschrift für Altorientalische und Biblische Rechtsgeschichte* 10 (2004), 93–142.
Wright, David P., "The Laws of Hammurabi as a source for the covenant collection (Exodus 20:23–23:19)," *MAARAV* 10 (2003), 11–87.
Wright, Tom, *Matthew for Everyone*, 2 vols. (London: SPCK, 2002), vol. I.
Wright, Tom, *Mark for Everyone* (London: SPCK, 2001).
Wright, N. T., *Jesus and the Victory of God* (London: SPCK, 1996).
Wright, N. T., *The New Testament and the People of God* (London: SPCK, 1993).
Wroe, Ann, *Pilate: The Biography of An Invented Man* (London: Vintage, 1999).
Wurst, Shirley, "Beloved, come back to me: Ground's theme song in Genesis 3?," in *The Earth Story in Genesis*, eds. Norman C. Habel and Shirley Wurst (Sheffield: Sheffield Academic Press, 2000), pp. 87–104.
Yaron, Reuven, "The Evolution of Biblical Law," *La formazione del dritto nel Vicino Oriente Antico* (1988), 76–108.
Yaron, Reuven, "Biblical law: Prolegomena," in *The Jewish Law Annual (Supplement Two): Jewish Law in Legal History and the Modern World*, ed. Bernard S. Jackson (Leiden: E.J. Brill, 1980), pp. 27–44.
Yaron, Reuven, "On divorce in Old Testament times," *Revue Internationale des Droits de L'Antiquité* 3 (1957), 117–128.
Zenger, Erich, *A God of Vengeance? Understanding the Psalms of Divine Wrath* (Westminster: John Knox Press, 1996).
Zeitlin, Irving M., "Max Weber's sociology of law," *University of Toronto Law Journal* 35 (1985), 183–214.
Zipor, Moshe A., "The cannibal women and their judgment before the helpless king (2 Kings 6:24ff)," *Abr-Nahrain* 35 (1998), 84–94.

INDEX OF BIBLICAL SOURCES

Citations may occur in either text or footnotes, and sometimes more than once on a particular page. Extended discussions are indicated in bold numbers.

Hebrew Bible

Genesis

1:1	70	1:28	51, 72, 78, 145, 153, 154, **155–156**, 157, 159, 162, 165, 167, 170, 171, 175, 184, 320, 467
1:1–2:3	70, 104, 162		
1:1–2:4	145, 151, 152, 153, 167, 181, 197	1:28–29	166
		1:28–30	167
1:1–2:25	145, 150, 179	1:29	51, 199, 233
1:1–23	151	1:30	156, 169
1:1–25	152, 154, 156, 157, 467	1:31	146, 152, 155, 166, 467
1:1–28	166	1	16, 17, 81, 155, 157, 164, 171, 413
1:1–25	159		
1:2	16, 73	1–2	78
1:2ff	71	1–3	162
1:3	51, 72, 152	1–9	85, 87
1:3–28	152	1–11	xxxiii, **16–17**, 17, 77, 82, 162, 274, 474
1:3–29	468		
1:4	155	2:2	71, 241
1:5–10	160	2:2–3	71, 151, 155, 172, 197
1:6	51	2:3	200
1:6–7	166	2:4	73
1:9	51, 166	2:4–25	157, 158
1:10	155, 156, 166	2:5	158, 159, 184
1:11	51	2:5–6	151
1:11–12	181	2:5–25	145, 151
1:11–13	237	2:7	158, 184
1:12	146, 467	2:7–8	158
1:14	51	2:8	184
1:20	51, 166	2:9–14	151
1:22	156	2:15	159
1:24	51, 166	2:15	159, 467
1:24–27	161	2:15–25	421
1:24–31	151	2:16–17	168, 169
1:26	152	2:17	162, 168
1:26	51, 145, 147, 151, 152, **153**, 154, 155, 156, 157, 159, 162, 184, 467, 476	2:19	158, 160, 161
		2:19–20	171
		2:20	160, 161
		2:22–24	319
1:26–27	79	2:23	161, 162, 319
1:26–29	151	2:23–25	151
1:27	86, 397, 398, 406	2:24	183, 320, 406
1:28	155	2	164, 171, 413
		2–3	81

Genesis (*cont.*)

3:1	163
3:1–13	162
3:6	163
3:7	164
3:7–13	163
3:8a	169
3:9–24	85
3:11	162
3:13	162
3:14	85
3:14–21	166
3:14–24	145, 162
3:15	163, 164
3:17	85
3:17–19	164
3:17–24	169
3:18	163
3:18–19	163
3:19	163, 166
3:21	164
3:23–24	164
3:24	164, 169
3	16, 171
4:1–2	166
4:1–16	17, 271, 273
4:1–16	275
4:2	166
4:3	166
4:3–5	272
4:4–5	275
4:6–7	272
4:7	274
4:7	272, 273, 282
4:8	273, 274, 275
4:8a	272
4:9	**77–78**, 273
4:9–16	85
4:10	78, 273, 275
4:10–11	275
4:11	85
4:12	274
4:14	274
4:15	275
4:16	275
4:17	275
4:23–24	17, 116, 280, 281, 320
4:24	244, 281
4	77, 162
6:1–4	17, 78
6:2	78
6:3	78
6:5	54
6:5–7	78
6:7–8	54
6:11	78, 165
6:11–13	145, 162, 165
6:12	54, 165, 170
6:13	165
6:17	166
6:17–18	35
6	55, 77, 166
7:2–9	81
7:7–9	397
7:9	171, 398
7:15	165
7:16	165
7:19–21	166
7:21–22	165
7	35, 54
8:1ff	167
8:11	167
8:21	54
8:21–22	70–71
9:1	167, 170
9:1–7	77, 79, 145, **167–168**, 171
9:1–17	35, 474
9:2	171
9:2–3	171
9:3	85, 170
9:3–4	168, 169, 170
9:3–5	168
9:4	79, 96, 170
9:5	86, 169, 170
9:5–6	85, **86–87**, 96, 167, 170, 264
9:6	86, 273
9:7	170
9:8–11	79
9:8–17	168
9:9–17	44
9:12–17	32
9:18–27	85
9:24–25	85
9	96
11	**16–17**, 162
11:29	323
12:1	239

INDEX OF BIBLICAL SOURCES 507

12:1–3	17, 41, 474	21:14	329
12:1–3	43	21:18	41
12:2	17, 43	21:27	32, 44
12:2–3	62, 225	23:3–20	305
12:3	17, 41, 474, 476	24:15	323
12	17	24:27	239
12–50	82	24	240, 323
12–25:18	17	25:27–34	191
12ff	474	26:1	38
13:10	74	26:2a	42
14	88	26:2–3	38
15:2–3	38	26:4a	38
15:5	38	26:4b	38
15:7	32	26:6–11	359
15:13	220	26:10	359
15:13–16	41	26:24	9, 42
15:16	459	26:27	338
15:18	180, 182	26:28	44
15:18–21	38	26:34–35	323
15	33, 38, 40, 41, 153, 179, 180, 476	26	38
16:6	322	27:41–45	38
17:2–14	38, 41	27:46–28:2	38
17:6	38	28:1–5	323
17:7	37	28:6–9	323
17:8	38, 180, 188	28:13	38
17:9	38, 43	28:14	38
17:9–14	41	28:13–15	38, 42
17:10–14	43	29:1–8	172
17:18–27	191	29:10–28	323
17:19	37	29:18–20	321
17:23	41	29:19–37:1	17
17:26	41	29:22	322
17	41, 43	29:24	322
18:2–8	74	29:27	321
18:16–33	74	29:27–30	320
18:17–19	87	29:29	322
18:18	103	29:30	321
18:19	88, 103, **138**	30:1	320
18:22	89	30:31	77
18:23	88	30:33	292, 296
18:23–32	88	31:20–21	289
18:25	88, 138	31:22–23	292
18:32	88	31:22–42	292
18	74, 85, 108	31:22ff	292
19:23–27	73	31:23	293
19:24–25	74	31:26	289
19:28	74	31:30	293
19	74, 75, 76	31:32	294, 305
20:12	323	31:37	293

Genesis (cont.)

31:44	44
31:44–52	46
31	292
34:2	330, 331
34:4	321, 331
34:5	332
34:6	331
34:7	330
34:8	333
34:8–10	324
34:9	324
34:11–12	333
34:12	330, 331
34:14	331
34:20–23	324
34:26	331
34:30–31	333
34:31	332
34	324, 327, 330, 332, 333, 344
35:2–4	324
35:6–7	324
35:9–12	324
35:22	191, 354
37:2–50:26	17
37:25	289
37:25–35	293
37:31–33	293
38	342
40:15	289
41:16	212
41:25	212
41:28	212
41:32	212
41:39	212
41	210
44:1–2	293
44:4–12	293
44:4–17	293
44:5	293
44:9	293
44:16	293, 294, 295, 305
44:16–17	295
44:17	294, 305
44	298, 305, 306
45:1–15	211
45:8	212
47:5–6	211
47:11	211
47:13–26	210
47:19	207, 237
47:19–21	233
47:23–25	210
47	208, 211, **212**, 233
49:3–4	191
49:4	354
49:5–7	333
49:28	318
50:10	372
50:15–21	211, 244
50:20	212

Exodus

1:8–22	43
1:11	237
1:11–14	221
1:13	224
1:14	224
2:11–15	269
2:12	269
2:14	120
2:16–21	269
2:23	269
2	120
2–4	120
3:7–8	180
3:8	181
3:10	212
4:21	223
4:22	437
5:1	26, 468
5:1–5	222
5:1–21	224
5:2	26
5:6–18	221
6:2	43
6:2–8	38, 43
6:4	220
6:5	38
6:6–7	62
6:6–7	38
6:7	36, 43
7–12	462
8:19	53
8:22–23	104
8:32	223

9:4	104	19:6	16, 41, 43, 49, 82, 114, 422, 432, 476
9:18–20	63		
9:26	104	19:7	50
10:22–23	104	19:9–23	47
11:7	104	19:10	49
12:29–32	224	19:13	201, 364
12–13	15	19:14	50
13:9	42	19:14–15	49
14:5–9	224	19:16	47
14:8	107	19:18	47, 49
16:6–7	237	19:20–21	50
16:16	237	19:21	49
16:16–20	237	19:25	50
16:18	237	19	43, 44, 46, 54, 55, 422
16:20	237	19–20	16
16:22	198	19–24	14, 48
16:23	71, 222	19–40	85, **89**
16:25–30	221	19–24	49
18:1	84, 122	19ff	168
18:10–12a	122	20:1	350
18:12b	122	20:1–5	64
18:13	120	20:1–17	14
18:13–15	110	20:2	15, 26, 32, 52
18:13–16	120	20:2–6	81
18:13–27	121, 123	20:2–17	xxxi, 53, 55
18:13–16	121	20:3–5	49, 54, 349
18:14	84	20:3–14	52, 349
18:15–16	120	20:4	10
18:17–26	122	20:7	49
18:18	121	20:8–11	71, 198
18:19	105, 121	20:8–11	221
18:20	18	20:12	349
18:21	123, 125	20:12–13	168
18:21–22	89, 123	20:13	273
18:22	121, 128	20:14	349, 367
18:24–26	89	20:17	11, 295
18:25	107, 119, 121, 473	20:18	49
18:26	117	20:18–19	49, 56, 133
18	84, 89, **120–121**, **123–124**, 128, 130, 133, 138	20:18–21	14
		20:18ff	6
19:1	45	20:19	54
19:1–24:2	47	20:19ff	20
19:1–25	14	20:22–23:33	14
19:3	50	20:23–23:19	6
19:3–6	5, 38, 43	20:26	339
19:4	32	20–31	54
19:4–6	38, 43	20–23	46
19:5	36, 38, 43, 114	21:1	108, 472
19:5–6	33, 52	21:1–2	15

Exodus (cont.)

21:1–7	23
21:1–22:16	xix, xxxiii, 5, 8, 198, 257, 268, 281, 285
21:2	**7–8**, 9, 230, 305
21:2–4	180, 304
21:2–6	23, 230
21:2–11	231
21:2–27	15, 22
21:6	117
21:7–11	334
21:10	320, 322
21:10–11	338, 419
21:11	338
21:12	255
21:12	256, 257, 258
21:12–14	254, **255–258**, 260, 261, 262, 266, **267–268**
21:13	256
21:13–14	256, 259, 265
21:13a	257, 258, 261
21:13b	257, 258
21:13b–14	258, 259
21:14	256, 257, 258, 262, 265, 266, 267, 268
21:16	257, 289, 290, 292
21:19	277
21:20	281, 282
21:20–21	281
21:21	118
21:22	278
21:22–25	5, 278
21:22a	261
21:22b	261
21:23	268
21:23–25	278, 279
21:24	253, 276, 282
21:24–25	275
21:24–25	5, **12**
21:26	276
21:27	276
21:28–29	170
21:28–30	270
21:28–35	21
21:29–30	268
21:30	282
21:31	281
21:32	170
21:35	2, 3, 4, 6, 26, 111
21:36	277
21:37	303
22:1	83, 228, 277, 290, **291–292**, 297, 299, 303, 304, 306, 308, 314
22:1–2	299
22:1–3	291
22:1–4	111, 288, 290, 291
22:1–5	116
22:1–4	299
22:2	13, 290, 299, 300, 301, 302
22:2–3	11, 12, 290, 300, **301–303**, 473
22:2–4	299
22:3	290, 291, 302, 306
22:4	289, 290, 291, 292, 294, 299, 303, 304
22:5	27, 290
22:7	77
22:8	295
22:15	402
22:15–16	402, 403
22:16	321
22:16–17	330, 331, **332–335**, 369, 370
22:17	333, 335
22:21	82
22:25	232
22:28	350, 435, 436, 443
22:29	83
22	334
23:1–8	108, 110, 472, 473
23:4–5	110, 282
23:8	25
23:9	14, 15, 82
23:10–11	198
23:12	152, 172, 198, 221
23:19	83
24:1–2	50
24:1–18	14
24:3	39, 53
24:3–8	43
24:4	46
24:4b–6	44
24:5–8	63
24:6–8	46
24:7	20, 44, 55
24:8	44
24:9	50
24:11	235

24:12	xxx, 50, 108, 472	34:29	50, 89
24:15–18	48	34:29–35	55
24:17	89	34:32	55
24	39	34	44, 53, 55
25:12	207	40:33–38	89, 168
28:3	111	85b	205
28:3–39	xxxiii		
28:36–38	199		
29:42b–46	37	**Leviticus**	
29:45	36	5:1	118
29:46	60	10:10–11	9
31:13	42	10:11	18, 108
31:18	51, 53, 55	11:45	37
32:1	54, 55	11	81
32:1–6	134	16:2ff	63, 169
32:2–4	54	16:15–16	168
32:4	44, 54, 90	16:34	244
32:7	50	17:10–14	97
32:7–8	54	17:14	168, 169
32:7–10	54	17:15ff	97
32:8	44	17–18	**97**
32:9	54	18:3	212
32:13	55	18:6–30	97
32:15	50	18:7	354
32:16	54, 468	18:8	354
32:19	44, 53, 54	18:8–20:11	356
32:26–27	54	18:9–20:17	356
32:27–28	55	18:13	400, 401
32:28	64	18:15–20:12	356
32	xxxiv, 34, 39, 44, 54, 55	18:16	325
32–34	54	18:17	21
33:3	54	18:17a–20:14	356
33:7–11	89	18:18	400
33:11	120	18:19–20:18	356
33:19	52, 468	18:20–20:10	356
34:1	53, 55	18:22	402
34:2	50	18:24–30	359
34:4	55	18:26	21
34:5ff	55	18	338, 354, 356, 384, 412
34:6–7	64, 110	19:1–37	396
34:10	39	19:2	396
34:10–27	39	19:09	200
34:11–16	323	19:9–10	234, 236
34:11–27	39	19:10	236
34:17	44	19:17	17, 18
34:17–26	44	19:17–18	27
34:21	172	19:18	27, 281, 282
34:27	55	19:19	396
34:28	xxxi	19:20	396

Leviticus (*cont.*)

19:27	200
19:34	28
19:37	396
19	396
20:	357, 361
20:2	356, 357, 358
20:2–5	349, 350, 384
20:2–6	349
20:2–27	349, 356, 358
20:3	350, 358, 359
20:3–6	356, **358**, **359**, **360**, 361, 379
20:4	350, 384
20:4–5	357
20:5	358, 359
20:5–21	349
20:6	350, 357, 358, 359
20:7–8	358
20:9	349, 350, 351, 352, 357, 361, 443
20:9–13	356
20:9–16	349, 356, 358, 361, 384
20:9–21	351, 379
20:10	352, 353, 357, 362, 363, 365, 409, 470
20:10–16	349, 361, 363, 364, 365, 366
20:10–21	349, 351, **352**, 353, 355, **361–362**, 366, 412
20:11	352, 353, 354, 357, 362, 363, 365
20:11–12	409
20:11–21	352, 354, 362
20:12	353, 357, 362, 363, 365
20:13	161, 353, 357, 362, 363, 365, 384
20:13–16	384
20:14	21, 353, 356, 357, 361, 362, 363, 365, **366**, 384, 409
20:15	160, 353, 357, 362, 363, 365
20:15–16	356, 384
20:16	353, 357, 362, 363–364, 365
20:17	353, 357, 360
20:17–18	356, 360
20:17–21	349, 356, 358, 360, 361
20:18	353, 357, 360
20:19	353, 356, 357, 360, 361
20:19–21	360
20:20	94, 353, 354, 356, 357
20:20–21	360
20:21	353, 354, 356, 357, 360
20:22	184, 367
20:22–26	358
20:23	359
20:24	384
20:26	367, 384
20:27	349, 357, 358
20	22, 263, 338, 347, **348–350**, 352, 354, **355–357**, 359, 364, 365, **366–367**, 375, 384, 385, 386, 409, 412, 474
21:7	340
21:9	366
21:14	340, 396
23:24	201
24:10–23	xxxiii, 19, 436
24:11	351, 436
24:13	132
24:13–23	22, 120
24:14	351
24:15	351
24:15–16	436
24:17	436
24:18	277, 280
24:19	280
24:20	277, 280
24:23	132, 280, 351
24	280
25:4	199
25:4–5	201
25:5	199, 200
25:6	201
25:6–7	199
25:8	201, 210
25:8–55	228
25:10	183, 204, 211, 246, 249
25:13	211
25:15–16	181
25:15–17	181
25:16	180
25:17	181
25:19	181
25:19–22	210
25:21	198
25:23	108, 157, 219, 238
25:23–24	180
25:25	183, 202
25:26–27	203

INDEX OF BIBLICAL SOURCES 513

25:28	202	6:5	200
25:29–30	180	6:22–27	16
25:35–38	232	9:6–14	19
25:36	233	10:10	45
25:36–38	232	10:11	45
25:37	182, 233	10:34	444
25:38	37, 234	11:16–30	123
25:39	229	11:26–28	123
25:39–40	229, 231	11:29	123
25:39–41	28, 228, 472	11	**123**
25:39–43	231	12:1–8	xxxi
25:39–46	231, 232, 241	12:8	212
25:40	180, 231	13:23	157
25:40–42	204	13:25ff	192
25:41	211	14:20–35	44
25:43	224	14	44, 134
25:44–45	231	15:32–36	xxxiii, 19
25:44–46	229, 231	15:35–36	132
25:45	229	16:32	272
25:46	229	20:29	372
25:47–49	229	21:14	19
25:47–54	229	21:33	262
25:47–55	2, 04	24–25	270
25:49	229, 318	27:1	183, 295
25:50	229	27:1–11	xxvi, xxxiii, 19, 23, 190, 192, 194, 469
25:54	229	27:1–11	195
25	xxv, xxvii, 183, 192, 202, **211–212**, 231, 244, 245, 247, 250, 475	27:3–4	xxxiii
		27:4	23, 192
26:12	36	27:5	295
26:14–45	76	27:5–11	109, 120
26:15	37	27:6	24
26:19–20	76	27:7	24, 192
26:41–43	206	27:7–11	194
26:44	37	27:8–11	109, 132, 195
26:45	37	33:51–54	119
26:46	xxx	33:54	183, 241, 248, 249
26	76	33	183, 185, 194, 203, 241
27:3	335	34	185
27	335	35:6–8	268
		35:9–29	xxvi
Numbers		35:9–34	266
		35:12	270
1:1	45	35:16	260, 262
3:38	169	35:16–18	261, 262
5:6–7	116	35:16–21	260, 261
5:11–31	295, 371	35:16–24	254, 260, 261, 262, 264
5:13	118	35:17	260, 261, 262
6:2–8	199	35:17–18	262

Numbers (cont.)

35:17–23	261, 474
35:18	260, 262
35:19	255
35:20	261, 274
35:20a	260
35:20b	260
35:21	260, 261
35:22	261
35:22–23	260, 261
35:22–28	265
35:22a	260
35:22b	260
35:23	260, 261
35:25	207
35:26–28	264
35:27	256
35:30	118
35:31–32	271
35:32	271
35:33	270
35:33–34	262, 271, 275
35:34	181
35	260, 262, **270–271**
36:1	24, 192
36:1–12	470
36:4a	193
36:4	192
36:5–6	24
36:5–7	193
36:7	119, 183, 473
36:9	119, 183, 473
36	24, 192, 193, 194, 195

Deuteronomy

1:1	44
1:5	18, 44
1:12	89
1:13	125
1:13	125, 130
1:15	107
1:15–17	125
1:16	113
1:16–17	105, 106
1:17	125
1:19–45	23
1:32–35	196
1:37	196
1	130
1ff	168
2:24–3:22	23
3:1–11	32
3:11	262
4:1	23, 196
4:6	16, 476
4:6–8	8, 83, 468, 470
4:8	4
4:26	46
4:32–33	48, 51
4:41–43	268
5:1ff	20
5:1–3	39
5:2–4	34, 44
5:2–5	23
5:2ff	67
5:6–21	xxxi
5:6–18	39
5:12–15	222
5:15	10, 221
5:16	172
5:16–17	168
5:18	273
5ff	39, 44
6:4–5	26
6:5	27
6:6–7	xxxiii
6:6–9	18
7:1–4	323
7:4	399
7:8	223
8:7	39
8:7–10	180
8:10	39
8:18	180
8–9	185
10:2	57
10:3	410
10:4	410
10:17	125
10:18	135
11:18	57
11:29	173
12:32	433
12:32–13:1	433
12:32–13:5	433
13:1	**433**
13:1–3	433

INDEX OF BIBLICAL SOURCES 515

13:5	434	17:8	109, 128
14:3–21	81	17:8–9	117, 118, 119
14:22–29	234, 469	17:8–13	108–109, 110
14:23	235	17:9	130
14:27	234	17:10–11	108, 472
14:28–29	234	17:11	xxxi, 109
14:29	220	17:17	320, 399
14	236	17:18	112
15:1	223	17:18–20	9, 110, 113
15:1–3	228	17:19–20	112
15:1–11	222, **224–227**	17	109
15:3	9, 223	18:15	435
15:4	224, 225	18:15–16	432
15:4–10	225	18:18–19	432
15:5	224	18:20	432
15:5–6	225	18:21–22	433
15:6	225	18:22	455
15:7	20, 222, 223, 224, 225	19:1–7	259
15:7–8	20, 28	19:1–13	266
15:7–9	224	19:3	268
15:7a	20	19:4–5	**258–259**
15:7b–8	20	19:4–10	265
15:8	222, 223, 225	19:4–13	254, 258, 260, 261, 262
15:9	223, 224, 225, **227–228**, 406	19:5–6	258, 264
15:9–10	473	19:5–7	258
15:10	224	19:6	255, 259
15:11	223, 224	19:6ff	260
15:12	230, 232	19:7	259, 260
15:12–15	16, 22, 23, 238	19:9	260
15:12–18	180, 230, 231, 232	19:9–10	**259**
15:17	232	19:11	**258–259**, 262, 274
15:18	230, 231	19:12	270
15	224, 227, 228, 243	19:15	118
16:13–15	234, 235	19:16–19	118
16:14–15	234	19:19	280
16:15	234	19:21	279
16:16	235	19	270
16:17	235	20:10–20	175, 189
16:18	113	20:13	175
16:18–19	25, 470	20:14	175
16:18–20	9, 118	20:19	174
16:19	25, 125	20:19–20	151, 173, 174, **175–176**
16:20	107, 113	21:1	289
16	236	21:10–14	372, 393
17:2	289	21:13	372
17:4	118	21:15–17	**13–14, 190–192**, 195
17:6	364	21:16	190
17:6	118	21:18–21	195, 196
17:6–7	371	21:19	117

Deuteronomy (cont.)

21:20	195–196	24:7	289
21:22–23	441	24:16	6
22:6–7	151	24:19	236
22:6–7	172	24:19–21	238
22:9	396	24:19–22	234, 236
22:9–11	396	24:22	238
22:11	372	25:5–10	116, 128, 183, 193, 290, 325, 354
22:13	371, 372	25:15–16	339
22:13–19	370	26:1–15	185
22:13–21	5, 368, 369, 370, **371–373**, 394	26:5	185
		26:5–9	187
22:13–27	367	26:5–10	186, 187
22:13–29	**368–370**	26:8–9	186
22:14	368, 372	26:10	187
22:15	369	26:11	187
22:17	370, 371, 394	26:12	238
22:18–19	370, 372	26:12–15	235
22:19	338	26:13	235
22:20–21	369, 370	26:14	235
22:21	117, 318, 373	26:17–18	36
22:22	289, 334, 354, 367, 368, 370, 371	26	186
		27:2–8	50
22:22–27	322	27:15–16	10
22:23–24	321, 370, 373, 374, 394	28:4–5	173
22:23–27	5, 371, 373	28:8	173
22:23–29	334	28:11–12	173
22:24	275, 374	28:15–68	34, 76
22:25	402	28:16–68	173
22:25–26	368, 374, 375	28:49	76
22:25–27	370, 374, 402	28:49–57	76
22:26	311, 374	28:53–57	136
22:27	275	28:58–68	76
22:28	334, 402	28:61	xxxi
22:28–29	330, **334–335**, 354, 370, 402, 403	28:63	196
		28:69–30:20	20
22:29	334	28	76, 173
23:13–14	339	29:1	33, 46
23:19–20	232	29:18–19	11
23:20	226	29:29	295
23:24	234, 236, 237	29–30	460
24:1	336, 337, 339, 405, 406, 407, 410	31:9–11	228
		31:10–13	20, 34, 50, 112
24:1–4	336, 337, 339, 409, **410–411**, 413, 415	31:26	46
		32:4	104
24:3	**337–338**	32:46–47	18
24:6	315	34:8	372

Joshua

1:7	xxxi
6	176
7:14–18	317
14–19	185, 249
15:18–19	322
17:14–18	183
20:1–9	266
20:7, 8	268
21:2	156, 184
23:2	32
23:9–10	32
24:5–12	32
24:22	46

Judges

1:6–7	280
7	176
9:4	48
9:46	48
11:37–40	320
14:1–5	321
14:18	327
15:2	337
19:27	117
19–21	325
21:18	325
21:20–23	325
21:20–237	327
21:21	325
21:22	325

Ruth

1–18	xxxiii
2:7	238
2:8–9	239
2:11	239
2:14	238
2:14	238
2:15	238
2:16	238
2:20	239
2:22	238, 239
2	240
4:1–12	117
4:11–12	240
4:13	322

1 Samuel

3–4	130
7:15–8:3	130
8:5	130, 131
8:5–6	131
8	294
10:25	131
12:1	294
12:3–5	294
14:24–26	130
14:41–42	133
14:45	134
16:13	191
17:7	262
18:17–29	324
18:25	321
18:27	321
20:8	32
22:16–18	134
31:13	372

2 Samuel

2:18–23	267
3:27	267
3:28–30	267
3:30	255
5:3	32
9:1	316
11:3	313
11:4	313
11:11	312
11:14–15	312
11:15	312
11:16	312
11:19–25	309
11:25	309
11	308
12:1	135
12:1–2	135
12:1–4	308
12:1–14	xxxiii
12:3	312, 314
12:4	312, 313
12:5	310, 315
12:6	310
12:7	310
12:7–14	308
12:9–10	311, 313

2 Samuel (*cont.*)

12:13	315
12:15–19	315
13:12	328, 347
13:13	328
13:13	328, 347
13:14	327
13:15	329
13:15–17	329
13:16	329
13:16–20	335
13:18	371
13:20	329
13:20–21	352
13:28–29	128, 315
13	**327–329**
14:1–20	128
14:1–24	xxxiii
14:2	128
14:6	275
14:7	271
14:8–11	271
14:20	111
14	271
15:2–4	134
15:13ff	134
16:20–22	375
16:21–22	354
16:23	313
18:14	315
23:34	313

1 Kings

1:12	267
1:21	267
1:49–53	267
1:50	265
1–2	xix
2:5	267
2:9	111
2:24–25	316
2:28–34	267
2:29–34	268
2:31–32	87, 267
2:32	87
2	316
3:4	90

3:9	90, 91
3:12	111
3:16–28	85, 90, 119, 160, 332
3:17–18	91
3:17–28	136
3:18	91
3:25	91
3:26	136
3:28	136
4:25	203
5:12	32
5:13–16	206
5:26	32
6:18	169
6:32	169
9:16	322
10:9	114
11:3–4	398
20:1–34	314
20:35–43	314
21:1–2	208
21:1–3	188
21:1–15	118
21:1–16	110, 119
21:7	131
21:8–10	110
21:10–13	118
21:11–13	189
21:17–21	135
21:21	189
21	xxxiii
22:10	117

2 Kings

6:24–7:2	135
6:26–27	107
6:27	136
6:29	136
6	136
7	136
17:13	xxxi
23	9

1 Chronicles

5:1	14
24:31	318

INDEX OF BIBLICAL SOURCES 519

2 Chronicles

2:17–18	206
5:10	46
17:9	112
19:5	109, 113
19:5–11	89
19:6	105, 126
19:7	113
19:8	109
19:10	112
19:10–11	117
19:11	105, 119, 130
19	109
36:21	205, 244, 246

Ezra

2:63	133
6:1–12	245
9–10	323
10:2	326
17:11–21	32

Nehemiah

7:65	133
9:6–8	17
9:8	37
9	37
13:23	326

Esther

7:8	156

Job

12:13	111
16:19	118
24:3	220
24:13–17	300, 301
24:14–16	13
24	13
29:11–14	117
29:21–22	117
29:25	117
38–39	151
39:5–8	170
39:9–12	170, 171
39:9–10	170
39	171

Psalms

2:1–2	447
5:2	107
7:1	265
7:11	276
7:14–16	276
8:3	53
10	137
17:8	266
19:1–4	78
19:7	24
19:7–8	113, 472
19:8	9, 24
19	xxxii, 70
24:3	49
24:4	49
24	49
28:5	155
29	71
72:4	106, 157
72:8	157
72	110, 157, 171
79:12	304
82:3	106
82	137, 469
91:1–4	266
103:6	135
104:3	444
104	151
110:1	443
119:45	447
119:130	70
119	xxxii, 70, 466
128:3	320
133:1	211
146:7–9	106, 135
147:19–20	82
147	70

Proverbs

1:7	125
1:8–9	xxxiii
1:15	88
1:33	98
2:6–8	111
2:16–17	319, 365, 407
3:1ff	87
3:3	57

Proverbs (cont.)

3:13	125
3:18	125
3:19	155, 160
6:27–29	226
6:29	290
6:29–35	300, 314
6:30	306
6:30–31	290, 304
6:32–35	290, 364
6:34–35	368
7:21	91
7:24–27	25, 470
8:22	70
8:22–31	21
8:22ff	xxxii
8:27	70
8:30	70
10:10	87
13:14	xxxii
14:4	151
16:29	165
17:23	125
22:22–23	135
24:23	25, 470
25:7–9	121
25:7–10	26, 473
25:9–10	111
25:11	21
26:27	73
28:21	25
29:4	125
29:14	315
30:21	340
30:23	340

Ecclesiastes

2:1	61

Isaiah

1:10	xxxi
1:23	134
2:2–3	83
2:3	xxxii
5:1–7	189
5:8	207
5:23	134
11:2	111
11:3	446
11:6–7	164
11:7	171
11:8	164
11:9	164
19:1	444
24:6	166
32:1–2	106
33:22	107
40–55	458
42:6–7	461
43:15	52
45:1	245
47:1–3	371
53:7	458
56:1	27
58:6–7	246
58:10	235
61:1–2	245, 247
61	**245–246**, 247, 475
65:25	171

Jeremiah

2:26	301
2:34	301
2:34–35	301
2:35	301
2	301
3:19	196
4:23	166
5:1	138
5:28–31	137
7:23	114
8:8–12	58
13:23	56
17:1	58
17:9–10	56
22:3	220
30–32	56
31:31	56
31:31–34	39, 56, 57, 58, 60, 63
31:31–33	39
31:31–34	39
31:32	57
31:33	36, 56, 61
31:34	59, 60
31	61, 63
32:37–39	62
32:38	36
32	62

INDEX OF BIBLICAL SOURCES 521

Lamentations

1:1	184

Ezekiel

8–11	460
13:9–16	397
13:10	397
16:8	319, 365
16:39	368
17	32
22:30	138
23:14–15	153
26:16–18	162
28:12–19	162
29	233
33:24–26	97
34:30	36
36:26–27	64
36:27	60
37:1–14	460
37:26	39
37:26–28	60
37:28	41, 60
37	39, 246
44:22	340

Daniel

7:2–7	443
7:13–14	443
7:17	443
7	443, 454, 459

Hosea

1:9	34
1:10	182
1–3	321, 365
2:2	336
2:16	xxxiii, 319
3:1	350
4:1	75
4:1–3	75, 166
4:6	9
4	76
4	**74–5**
11:1	437

Amos

1:3	80
1:6	80
1:9, 11	80
1:13	80
1–2	77
2:1	80
2:4	80
2:4–16	80
2:6–12	80
2:6–16	80
3:2	42
8:4–8	9
9:7	82

Micah

2:1–2	9, 188
2:2	183
3:11	134
4:4	189, 203
7:3	134

Zephaniah

1:3	166

Zechariah

7:9–10	108, 472
13:8	190

Malachi

2:14	32, 319, 365, 407

Apocryphal Books

1 Maccabees

2:6–8	436
2:66–68	437

2 Maccabees

8:4	436

New Testament

Matthew

3:2	414
3:12	414
4:17	414
5:1–7:29	273
5:13–16	165
5:14	461

522 INDEX OF BIBLICAL SOURCES

New Testament (cont.)

Matthew (cont.)

5:17	xxxii, 434
5:25–26	111
5:27–30	412
5:31	413
5:31–32	411, 412, 414, 415, 418
5:32	412, 413, 414
5:32a	413, 414
5:38–42	282
5:43–48	282
5	416, 422
5.27–28	355
6:12	243
6	243
7:19	414
7:21–23	433
7:28–29	434
12:1–14	435
12:8	243
12:10–13	468
12:48–50	98
15:19	355
17:24–27	437
18:21	475
18:21–22	243
18:21–35	282
18:22	282
18:32–35	244, 475
19:1–12	411, 414
19:2–3	415
19:3	415
19:3–9	420, 421
19:4–6	364, 420, 421
19:4–8	98
19:4–9	420, 421
19:7	415
19:8–9	113
19:9	415
19:10	420, 421
19:10–12	420
19:11	420
19:11–12	421
19:12	98, 420
19:16–22	420
19:23–24	420
19:25	420
19:26	420
21:13	442
22:35–40	27
25:29	414
25:31–33	161
26:5	441
26:57	440
26:57–68	439
26:59	440
26:61	445
26:63	442, 445
26:64	442, 445
26:65	445
26:65–66	446
26:67–68	446
27:1	439
27:2	449
27:4	447
27:11	454
27:11–14	449
27:12	454
27:12–14	454, 458
27:14	459
27:15–18	449
27:18	435
27:20–23	449
27:24	447, 449
27:26;	449
27:26	449, 451
27:27–31	455
27:62–66	441

Mark

2:5–7	436
2:23–28	435
3:6	430
6:17	409
7:1–23	435
7:8–13	435
7:9–13	410
7:14–15	410
10:1–12	409, 410
10:2	405, 415
10:3	405
10:4–9	405
10:5	405, 406
10:5–9	364, 408, 411, 416, 421
10:6–8	422
10:9	406, 407, 416
10:11–12	408
10:37	461
10:38–40	461

INDEX OF BIBLICAL SOURCES 523

10	410, 414	4:28–29	430
11:18	430, 438	4:28–30	247
12:12	430	4	475
12:13–17	437	6:34–35	243
12:17	437	7:20–23	434
14:30	446	7:22	434
14:53	439, 443	12:13–15	111
14:53–72	429	13:10–16	468
14:55	440	13:31	430
14:55–65	439	14:26	98
14:57–58	445	16:17	410
14:57–59	442	16:18	408
14:58	442	19:41–44	437
14:61	445	22:19–20	39
14:62	445	22:20	61
14:63–64	445	22:53	459
14:64	440	22:54	439
14:65	446	22:66	440
14:66–72	446	22:66–71	439
14:66	429	22:67	445
15:1a	439	22:67–69	445
15:1b	449	23:1	449, 454
15:2	454	23:2	437, 453
15:2–5	449	23:2–6	449
15:3	454	23:3	454
15:4–5	454	23:5	454
15:6–7	451	23:6–12	450
15:6–15	449	23:7–12	449
15:10	435	23:9	454
15:14	451	23:11	455
15:15	449, 451, 452	23:13–16	449
15:16–20	455	23:15	450
15:29	455	23:18–25	449
15:31	455	23:25	449
15:31–32	446	23:27–31	461
15:32	446	23:34	462
16:14	405	23:39	455
		23:41	457
Luke		23:42–43	462
		23:43	457
1:1–4	428	23:63–65	446
3:2	440	23:70	445
3:8	99	24:20	448
3:11	99		
3:14	61	**John**	
4:14	246		
4:14–21	246	1:19–27	438
4:23–27	247	2:19	437, 442
4:23–30	247	3:31–32	462
4:23ff	246	5:18	431, 436

John (*cont.*)

5:22	90, 161
7:1	430, 459
7:12	435
7:15	435
7:19	430
7:25	430
7:26	430
7:30	459
7:32	430
8:44	444
8:57–59	431
8:58	436
8:59	430
10:17–18	459
10:31–33	430
10:33	436
10:36	436
11:47–48	434, 439
11:49–52	447
11:49–53	438
11:49–54	431
11:50–52	460
11	434, 438
12:10	438
12:19	435
12:31–32	462
16:32	459
17:1	459
18:12–13	440
18:13	439
18:19	441, 445
18:19–24	439, 440
18:20–21	445
18:28–32	449
18:31	440
18:31–32	461
18:33	454
18:33–38	449
18:34–37	454
18:36	454
18:37	98
18:38	450
18:39–40	449
18:40	451
19:1	449
19:1–3	455
19:1–6	450
19:5	455
19:7	453
19:9	454
19:11	448
19:12	449, 452
19:16	449
19:19–22	447
19:21–22	450
19:41–20:17	165
20:30–31	428
21:25	428

Acts of the Apostles

3:22–23	435
4:25–28	448
7:54–59	441
10:42	124, 161
15:7–11	95
15:19–20	95
15:28–29	96
15:29	**96**
15	95, **96**, 97
17:31	161
25:15–16	458

Romans

1:18–32	98
2:12–16	98
2	98
3:25–26	462

1 Corinthians

7:3–4	409
7:10–11	408, 421
7:12–13	417
7:12–15	421
7:15	408, 417
7:17	421
15:45–49	161
15:52	201

2 Corinthians

3:3	60
3:7	64
3:7–9	64
3:18	64
5:10	276

Galatians

2:20	84
3:13	441

Ephesians

5:22–33	321

Colossians

1:15	161

1 Timothy

3:2	320
3:12	320
5:9	320

Hebrews

4:14	63
9:11–12	63
9:12	270
9:15	62
9:15–17	62
9:16	62
9	63
19:24	63

1 John

1:1	84

Revelation

2:7	171
19:15	90
21:9ff	321
22:1–2	171
22	165

GENERAL INDEX

A
Aaron, 222
Abel, 77–78, 85, 211, 253, 271–75
Abimelech, 44
Abner, 267
Abraham
   covenant with, 31, 37, 43–44, 82, 153, 180, 250
   descendants of, 323
   judgment and, 85, 87–89, 138
   promised land and, 185
   as prophet like Moses, 432
Absalom, 128, 134, 329
Acts of the Apostles, 95–97
Adam, 79, 160, 162, 319, 421
adjudication *See* judgment
Adoni-bezek (King), 279
Adonijah, 267
adultery
   Ancient Near Eastern law, 367
   consent and, 374–75
   forms of, 352–55, 353*t*, 367
   law of theft and, 308–316
   prosecution and penalty for, 368
   See also Jesus on marriage, divorce, adultery and remarriage; Qumran community and laws; sexual offences
Ahab (King), 110, 119, 131, 135, 136
   land dispute with Naboth, 188–89
   reign of, xxiii
Alfred the Great, xxvi
Allott, Philip, xxviii, 466, 475
Amnon, 128, 327–29
Amos, 79–80
Ancient Near East
   defined, xix
   divorce and remarriage in the, 336–38, 339, 340
   exercise of freedom in, 245
   judicial styles in the, 131
   legal sites in the, 117
   marriage ceremonies in the, 319
   punishment in, 275
   representations of deities and human rulers in the, 153
   scribal education in the, 112–13
   social justice in the, 113–14
   victory and rest motif in stories, 71
Ancient Near Eastern law
   adultery, 367
   biblical law vs., 2, 4–10, 29
   controversial or common cases in, 19
   covenant in, 31, 32, 33, 45–46, 47
   disinheritance, 195–96
   divine manifestation and, 48
   homicide, 278–79
   important ANE legal collections, 3*t*
   negotiation process, 47
   private legal arrangements, 4
   theft, 297, 299, 306, 315
   vassal treaties, 32
animals
   animal labor, 172
   bestiality, 353*t*, 357*t*, 362*t*, 363–64, 366, 385
   death of, 164
   extinction and endangered, 147
   naming the, 160–61
   predatory, 164
   relationship with humanity, 169–71
   Sabbath and, 172
   theft of, 290–292, 296, 299, 303–5
animal welfare, 148–149
Annas, 440
Apostolic Council of Jerusalem, 95–97
appeals, 109–110
Aquinas, Thomas, 93–94, 93*t*, 94
Aristotle, 93*t*
Ark of the Covenant, 1, 46, 47
Asahel, 267
Assyrian empire, end of, xxiii
Augustine of Hippo, 93*t*
Australia, 186
Avishur, Yitzhak, 48

B

B & L v. The United Kingdom (2009), 378nn 51, 381
Babylon, exile to, 56
banking *See* debt, banking and interest
Barabbas, 451, 460
Barth, Karl, 95
Barton, John, 77, 80, 83
Bathsheba, 267, 308, 310, 312–13, 315
Bell, Duran, 185
Benaiah, 87
berit See covenant(s)
Beveridge Committee Report, 225
Beveridge, William, 250
Bible
    covenant in the, 31, 32
    Hebrew vs. New Testament covenants, 35
    language of, xxix–xxx
    misreadings regarding the environment, 145–46
    naming in the, 160–62
biblical law
    Ancient Near Eastern law vs., 2, 4–10, 29
    Christianity and, xxv–xxvi, xxxv
    in common practice, xxxiv–xxxv
    complete structure of law, 194–95
    defined, xxxii–xxxiv, 465
    designed to promote wisdom, 19–20
    expression of wisdom, 21, 24–26
    didactic and incomplete nature of, 18–20
    dietary law, 79
    dynamism of, 22–24, 30
    English canon law and, xxvi
    English law (modern) and, xxix, xxxv
    God's involvement with humanity and, 14–16
    good for humanity and the world, 466–70
    history of transmission and interpretation, xxv
    importance of narrative, xxxiii–xxxiv, 14–16, 23, 40, 46, 64, 185, 209, 212, 228, 241
    influence of, xxv–xxvii
    Judaism and, xxxv
    lawyers and, xxxviii–xl
    literary/chiastic structure of, 15f, 21–22, 21t, 30
    modern law vs., 2, 11–14, 25, 29–30, 33–35, 215–18
    narrative reading of, 11–14, 267, 300, 337, 409, 416–419
    Noahide laws, 79
    overview, 477–78
    pragmatism and integrity, 472–73
    presupposition pool of, 1, 29
    relational character of, 26–29, 30
    relationship with Israel, 473–75
    requirement of wisdom, 28–29
    rhetorical nature of, 20–21, 30
    theology and, xiii, xv, xxviii, xxxiv, 5, 465–66, 477
    in the twenty-first century, xxvii–xxx
    United States law and, xxix
    Western culture and, xxxv
    wisdom and, 19, 21, 24–26, 30, 470–72
    See also Israel
Bilhah, 191
binary opposition,
    defined, 361
    examples of, 152, 163, 166, 174, 222–223, 231–232, 260, 358, 361–365
Blackstone, William, 93t, 302
blasphemy, 435–37, 442–44, 445t, 446
blood feud, 91, 255
blood taboos, 97
Boaz, 117, 238–39, 240
Bock, Darrell, 351
Bockmuehl, Markus, 75
British welfare system, 241
Brown, Gordon, 250
burning, as a form of punishment, 80, 356, 364–366

C

Caiaphas, 438, 440, 442, 443, 444, 447, 454, 460
Cain, 77–78, 81, 85, 211, 253, 271–75
calling and ethics, 97–100
Calvin, Jean, 404
Canaan, 187
cannibal mothers, 135–36
capital, 181, 188, 203, 213, 226–227, 250
capitalism, 250–51

capital offense *See* death penalty
Carmichael, Calum, 210, 211
Carr, David, 112, 113
Casperson, Lee W., 206
Catchpole, David R., 422
character, role of, 19, 58, 112–113, 118, 124, 127, 129, 138, 227, 470–471
children
  marriage and, 320–321
  false accusations in relation to, 451, 456–457, 458
Chiricigno, Gregory, 231
chosen people, 29, 153
Christianity, biblical law and, xxv–xxvi, xxxv, 404–5, 466
Cicero, Marcus Tullius, 93*t*
circumcision, 41–42
clans, 317–18
climate change, economics of, 149, 150
Clinton, William J., 372
Connolly, William, xxix
contract law, biblical covenant vs., 33–35
courts, central, 109–110, 110
courts, provincial, 108–110
Courts Services Agency, 140
covenant(s)
  Ancient near east, 32–34
  defined, 31, 32
  between God and Israel, 35–40
  Jewish vs. Christian, 35
  kinds of, 32
  modern vs. biblical, 33–35
covenant(s), biblical
  formula, 36–37, 36*t*, 38–39*t*, 40, 56
  new covenant (Hebrew Bible), 56–61
  new covenant (New Testament), 61–64
  with Noah, 35
  overview, 64
  transitional moments, 38–39*t*
  turning points in covenantal relations, 40–45
  types of covenant ceremonies, 40
  universal mode of, 35–36
  See also specific covenants
Covenant Code
  ANE laws and the, 5, 6–7
  defined, xix
creation narrative
  anthropocentric bias, 151
  continuity between the divine and, 69–73
  the Genesis mandate, 155–57
  God's relationship with creation, 153
  God's sovereignty over creation, 152
  humanity's vocation to care for the world, 152–155, 467
  humanity's creation, 157–59
  independent worth of creation, 146
  moral order and, 77
  naming the animals and Woman, 160–62
  postdiluvian re-creation, 167–71
  Sabbath and the, 245
  and the Ten Commandments, 51–52
  universal creation vs. humanity's creation, 150–52
  vertical hierarchy of the, 146–147
  See also Genesis
Criminal Justice Act 1967, 288
criminal justice Acts (England and Wales), 140
Criminal Justice and Immigration Act 2008, 302
criminal liability, individualization of, 6
criminal suspects and defendants, 458
Crown Prosecution Service, 140
crucifixion, 441, 461–62
Crüsemann, Frank, 9
curses, 76

D

Damascus Document, 393, 397, 399, 400–402
Daniel, 443
Das Kapital (Marx), 250
Daube, David, 77, 277, 278, 289, 290, 291
David (King)
  delivery of the *mohar* by, 321
  divine judgment upon, 135
  Joab story and, 267
  parable of Nathan, 308–316
  reign of, xxiii
  Ruth and, 242
  succession narrative, xix
  uprising against, 134–35
  wisdom and, 128
Davis, Ellen F., 146, 187, 200, 204
Day of Atonement, 211, 244

Dead Sea Scrolls, xxiv, 390–91
death penalty
　asylum and the, 266
　for false prophecy, 434
　for homicide, 264
　for kidnapping, 289
　modern law and biblical law regarding the, 375–76
　monarchy vs. local courts and the, 110, 189
　in Qumran law, 395
　revolts regarding the, 134
　for sexual offences/adultery, 25, 348, 353, 356, 357t, 364–65, 366, 370, 370t
　for theft, 289, 306
debt, banking and interest, 226–27, 232–34
debt slaves, 231–32, 305
Decalogue *See* Ten Commandments
Denning, Lord, xxv
Deuteronomy
　on debt slaves, 231–32
　dynamism of biblical law in, 22–23
　fruit trees and war, 173–76
　homicide in, 258–260, 259t, 265, 268, 270
　inheritance in, 190–93
　on kidnapping, 289–290
　on marriage, 333–36
　people and land in, 185–87
　on prophets, 433
　rhetorical nature of, 20
　social welfare in, 224–26
dietary laws, 79, 81, 97, 168–69
Dinah, 324, 330–33
disciples of Jesus, 165, 243, 244, 405, 408, 420, 422, 431, 435, 441, 461
disinheritance, 195–97
divine speech *See* speech, divine
divorce
　ANE law and custom regarding, 319, 336–38
　Christian church on, 404–5
　conflicting biblical texts regarding, 335
　language of, 329
　overview, 317, 345
　woman's property, 322
　remarriage, 338–40
　See also Jesus on marriage, divorce, adultery and remarriage; Qumran community and laws
Drop the Debt campaign, xxvii, 250, 475
due process, 118
Durkheim, Emile, 141
Dworkin, Ronald, xxxviii, 129, 194, 227

E
Ecological Debt Day, 148
economic capitalism, 148
The Economist, xxix
Eden, 85, 151, 162–65, 169, 364, 421
Egypt
　amnesty practices, 269
　contrast with Israel, 119, 203, 207–209, 212, 237
　ecosystem of, 187
　Egyptian tomb paintings, 238
　hoarding in, 237
　land economics in, 203, 207–9, 210–211
Eichler, B.L, 7, 13
Eleazar, Simeon ben, 61
Eleventh Commandment campaign, 31
Elijah, 135
　as "prophet like Moses," 432
Eliot, T.S., 133
England
　inheritance in, 190
　land title, 186
　marriage in, 341
　property rights and law in, 185, 200–201, 212–15, 217
　shoplifting in, 306–7
　See also Sexual Offences Act 2003; United Kingdom
English canon law, biblical law, and, xxvi
English law (medieval), 33–34
English law (modern)
　biblical law and, xxix, xxxv, 302
　consent in, 374, 375–76
　criminal justice, 139–40, 143
　environmental, 172
　homicide, 253–254, 262
　theft, 285, 286–88, 298
　vs. biblical covenant, 33

See also law, modern
English legal history, xxvi
environment *See* humanity and the environment
Ephraim, 191
Erasmus, 404
Esau, 191, 323
Eshnunna, 47
See also Laws of the Kingdom of Eshnunna
ethics and calling, 97–100
European Court of Human Rights, 378
European Court of Justice, 109
European Retail Theft Barometer 2006, 285, 287
European Union law, 109–110
Eve, 161, 162, 319, 421
Exodus
  common cases in, 19
  on debt slaves, 231
  dynamism of biblical law in, 22
  homicide in, 255–58, 256t, 257t, 268
  judgment in, 89–90
  literary/chiastic structure of, 15f, 21–22, 21t
  on marriage, 333–336
  on theft of animals, 290–92
the Exodus, 15–16, 62, 196
  Jethro's response to, 122
  jubilee and, 206–7
  justice and, 106–7
  Sabbath laws and, 222, 245
  social welfare laws and the, 241
  Ten Commandments and, 82
  time of, xxiii
"eye for an eye" rule, 11, 116, 275, 276–77, 282
See also vengeance
Ezekiel, 97

F
factory farming, 149
false prophecy/teachings
  all-Israel-outside-Qumran and, 397
  charges against Jesus, 425, 426, 431, 432–33, 434–35, 435t, 438, 446
  fall of Judah and, 58
family
  avenger of blood, 255
  defining modern, 342–43, 378–79
  dishonoring parents, 351–352
  economics, 207–9, 215, 218, 222, 224, 233–34, 237
  extended, 216, 229, 240, 317–18
  feuds, 127–28
  head of the, 318
  Jethro's legal system and the, 123
  jubilee laws and, 201–04, 229, 231
  kidnapping and, 289
  lack of family support, 220
  land and, 24, 119, 183, 207–09
  marriage within families, 323–324, 325
  sexual relations/offences and, 352–55, 357t, 358–360, 362–364, 362t, 378–79, 381
  social order founded on the, 141
  as witnesses and warriors, 293
  See also children; marriage
farming, factory, 149
Farrington, David P., 306
Feast of Booths, 234–35
financial crisis of 2007–9, 226–27
Finnis, John, 93t, 97
the Flood, 44, 54, 78, 165–67
forgiveness, 60, 243–244, 247, 282, 462
Foucault, Michel, 242
fruit trees, 173–176

G
Garden of Eden *See* Eden
Garland, David, 142
GDP (gross domestic product), 247
Genesis
  the Genesis mandate, 155–57
  judgment in, 162–67
  the rape of Dinah, 330–33
  vocation of Israel in, 16–17
  See also creation narrative
Gentile Christians
  Jewish lifestyle and, 72
  natural law and, 95–97
  relationships between Jews and, 79
gleanings law, 236–40
global financial crisis of 2007–9, 226–27
Global GDP, 247
global warming *See* climate change

God
  Cain and Abel narrative and, 274–75
  continuity between human acts of judgment and, 84–92
  continuity between the creation and, 69–73
  covenant with Abraham, 31, 37
  covenant with Israel, 31, 34, 35–40, 67
  finger of, 53
  humanity and, 14–16, 34, 55–56
  image of, 153
  intimacy with creation of man, 158–59
  involvement in lawmaking, 33
  judicial intervention of, 135
  land fertility and, 237, 239
  love of, 29
  marriage and, 319–20, 323
  with Moses as mediator, 48–50
  ownership of land, 179–182, 197, 199
  relationship with creation, 148–49, 150, 153
  relationship with Israel, 473–75
  role in human adjudication, 104–5, 105t
  role of theophany at Sinai, 47–48
  sexual offences and, 348, 350, 355, 356, 357t, 358, 359
  sovereignty over creation, 152
  theft and, 295
  as ultimate source of justice, 104, 111
  as ultimate source of wisdom, 111
  voice of, 133
  vs. Pharaoh, 223–24, 233–34
golden calf incident, 44, 54–55
Gomez (1992), 287–288
Gomorrah *See* Sodom and Gomorrah
Gospels
  as Passion narratives, 430
  on the trials of Jesus, 427–30
  See also specific Gospels
Grabbe, Lester L., 349
Gray, Kevin, 214
Gray, Susan Francis, 214
gross domestic product (GDP), 247
Grotius, Hugo, 93t
Guenther, Allen, 324

H
Ham, 85
Hammurabi (King), 33, 47
  See also Laws of King Hammurabi
Hamor, 324
Henry VIII, xxvi
hereditary blessing, 41
Herod (King), 450, 457
Heth, William E., 414
Hezekiah, 61
Hillel, 27
Hinks (2000), 287–88
Hittite Laws, xxiii, 3t
  animal theft, 303
  covenants, 33
  homicide, 278
  rule changes in, 19
  theft, 306
hoarding, 237
The Hollow Men (Eliot), 133
homicide
  asylum, 256, 256t, 257t, 258, 259, 259n 13, 259t, 260, 260t, 261, 261t, 263, 265–70, 275, 469
  avenger of blood, 87, 119, 254–55, 256, 258, 259, 260, 263, 264, 266, 268, 269, 271, 301
  Biblical law categories of, 263–64
  Cain and Abel narrative, 81, 271–275
  in Deuteronomy, 258–60, 259t, 265, 268, 270
  in Exodus, 255–58, 256t, 257t, 268
  humanity and divine justice and, 86–87
  law of theft and, 308–316
  modern law, 253–54, 264–65
  in Numbers, 260–63, 260t, 261t, 265, 270
  overview, 283
  pardons, 264, 265, 271
  ransom, 265, 268, 270–71
  rape and, 311
  vengeance and, 275–82
homosexual behavior
  as a 'form of adultery,' 353t
  death penalty and, 348
  equality and, 382–83
  incident of attempted gang rape, 73
  prohibition against, 161, 384
homosexual partnerships, 342
Hosea, unethical behavior and the created world, 74–76
Hugenberger, Gordon Paul, 319

humanity
    creation of, 157–62
    the Genesis mandate, 155–57
    God and, 14–16, 34, 55–56
    human acts of judgment and the
        divine, 84–92, 140
    human behavior and the created
        world, 73–76
    made in the image of God, 153
    punishment for sexual relations by, 356,
        357t, 358
    relationship with animals, 169–71
    relationship with creation, 148, 150–51
    speech acts, 160
    vocation of, 147–48, 152–55, 156–57,
        159, 475–77
humanity and the environment
    the Bible and, 145–46
    divine judgments and, 162–67
    ecojustice, 152–53
    environmental laws in Torah, 171–76
    environmental threat to the
        earth, 145–50
    interdependence of, 151
    moral nature of environmental
        crisis, 149–50
    mutuality between, 158
    overview, 145, 176
    Torah environmental laws, 171–76
    unethical behavior and the, 74–76
    war and trees, 173–76
Hussey (1924), 302
Hutton, Will, xxvii

I
infanticide, 91
inheritance and disinheritance, 183, 190–97
interest *See* debt, banking and interest
Isaac, 42, 44, 55, 323
Isaiah, 164, 171, 245–47
Ishmael, 191
Israel
    biblical law and God's relationship
        with, 473–75
    covenant with, 31
    exercise of freedom in, 245
    generosity and, 225
    God's relationship with, 26–27, 53
    Jesus and, 429

law and God, 53
resident aliens living in, 97
Second Temple period, 389–90
tribes of, 318
vocation of, 16–18, 30, 52, 82–83, 347,
    475–77
See also biblical law
Israel, State of, xxvi

J
Jackson, Bernard
    on asylum, 266
    on debt-slavery, 231
    on the covenant of circumcision, 41
    on agricultural damage, 27
    on false prophets, 433
    on the golden calf incident, 44
    on "life for life," 278
    on a narrative reading of Exodus, 12
    on the parable of Nathan, 311
    on the prophetic status of Jesus, 446
    on proportionality, 280
    on repetition at Sinai, 50
    on self-executing rules, 26
    on theft, 304, 305
    on trial of Jesus, 442
    on types of covenant ceremonies, 40
Jacob
    the Abrahamic covenant and, 42
    authority over Dinah, 330, 332–34
    inheritance and, 191
    Laban's daughters and, 289
    Laban's household idols and, 292–93,
        294, 305
    marriage of, 324
James, 95
Jehoram (King), 136
Jehoshaphat (King), xxiii, 84, 89, 105, 105t,
    109, 112–13
Jeremiah
    new covenant, 56–57
    trial of, 442
Jerusalem, fall of, 56
Jesus
    as high priest, 63
    as the New Adam, 161
    birth/death dates, xxiv
    crucifixion of, 441, 461–62
    disciples of, *See disciples of Jesus*

534 GENERAL INDEX

Jesus (cont.)
  on "eye for an eye" formula, 282
  judgment and, 90
  on judicial proceedings, 111
  on murder, 273
  new covenant and, 61–63
  on priority within biblical law, 27
  Sabbath and, 243–44, 246–47
  teachings of Jesus and biblical law, 23
  and Torah, 84, 434
  See also New Testament; trials of Jesus
Jesus on marriage, divorce, adultery and remarriage
  conflicting biblical texts regarding, 416–20
  use of the Eden narrative, 421
  Gospel According to Mark, 405–8
  Gospel According to Mattthew, 411–416
  marriage as vocation, 421–24
  overview, 423–24
  radical and traditional nature of, 409–410
  Torah and, 420–21
Jethro
  on God and human adjudicators, 105, 105t
  judicial system of, 89, 121–24, 125, 128
Jews, relationships between Gentiles and, 79
Jezebel (Queen), 110, 119, 131
Jezreel, 188
Joab, 87, 267
Job, 170
John the Baptist, 99, 433, 438
Joseph
  birth/death years, xxiii
  birthright of, 13–14, 191
  jubilee year and, 209–211, 212
  kidnapping of, 289
  Sabbath and, 245
  theft and, 293, 294, 295
Josephites, 192, 194, 195
Josephus, Flavius, 401, 438
Joshua, 183, 245
Joy on the Accession of Ramesses IV, 269
Jubilee 2000 campaign, xxvii, 250
jubilee year
  Day of Atonement, 211, 244
  as extension to weekly Sabbath, 197, 201

  family and personal fortunes and the, 201–5
  function of the jubilee laws, 211–12
  Isaiah on the, 246
  Joseph and the, 209–211, 212
  in the New Testament, 246–47
  observation of, 205–7
  social welfare and the, 228–32, 235–36, 248–49, 251
  vs. ancient Egypt's land tenure practices, 207–9
Judah, 295, 305
Judaism, biblical law and, xxxv
judges
  in biblical Israel, 121, 123, 130
  failure of, 134–35
  heads of households as, 123
  mediating divine decisions, 104–5
  role regarding oppressor and oppressed, 107
  selection, appointment, and retention, 124–25
Judges, Period of, xxiii
judgment
  Biblical adjudication vs. modern adjudication, 115–16, 115t
  discontinuity between divine and human acts of, 133–37
  divine and human interconnection regarding, 84–92
  divine judgment in the New Testament, 161
  in Genesis, 162–67
  homicide, 86–87
  in the New Testament, 462
  sacred adjudication, 104, 111, 119, 124, 127, 144
justice
  avoiding adjudication, 110–11
  biblical justice and the modern world, 139–44
  communal responsibility for, 108
  discernment process, 125–27
  divine justice and human adjudicators, 120–24, 462
  divinely-inspired, 111–14
  divinely-mandated social order and, 108
  ecojustice, 152–53

forms of adjudication in biblical
    Israel, 131–33
God as ultimate source of, 104
hard cases, 127–29
intergenerational justice, 216–217, 468
innovation in a divine justice
    system, 130–31
judging in a spiral, 137–39
local justice, 116–19, 140
miscarriage of justice, 431–32, 456–62
the oppressor and the oppressed, 106–7
overview, 103–4, 114–15, 144
prayer and, 137
provincial courts and, 108–10
range of authorities, 110
relational approaches to, 139–143
use of practical wisdom, 111

K
Kant, Immanuel, 93t
Kawashima, Robert S., 199
Keynes, John Maynard, 250
kidnapping, 288–90
Kings
    monarchical adjudication, 130–31
    monarchical evolution, 131
    monarchical privileges, 162–63
    role regarding oppressor and
        oppressed, 107
knowledge, of certain norms, 76–81
Kohák, Erazim, 146
kosher slaughtering laws, 170

L
Laban, 77, 289, 292–93, 294, 305
Lamech, 280
land and people
    biblical law and modern property
        law, 215–18
    divine ownership of land, 179–82,
        197, 199
    English law of property, 212–15
    inheritance and disinheritance, 183,
        190–97
    land title, 180–81, 186
    local justice and, 119
    narrative and, 185–90
    overview, 179, 218
    promised land and the Israelites, 182–85

property acquisition, 327
reform, 215, 217, 251
Sabbath, sabbatical year, 198–201, 212,
    216–17
Sabbath, weekly, 197–98, 211, 212
See also jubilee year
Land Registry Act (LRA) 2002, 213
land title, 186
Last Supper, 61–62
law, modern
    adjudication vs. biblical
        adjudication, 115–16, 115t
    biblical justice and, 139–144
    biblical law and modern property
        law, 215–18
    biblical law vs., 2, 11–14, 25, 29–30
    family, 317, 340–44
    hard cases, 129
    theft, 285, 286–288, 306–307
    See also contract law; English law
        (modern); *specific laws and legal topics*
*Lawrence v. Metropolitan Police
    Commissioner* (1972), 287
Law's Empire (Dworkin), xxxviii
Laws of King Hammurabi
    biblical law and, 5, 6, 7–8, 9
    burglary, 302
    in chronology, xxiii, 3t
    debt-slavery, 230
    divorce, 337
    literary context of the, 10
    narrative reading of the, 13
    theft, 306
Laws of King Lipit-Ishtar (of Isin), 3t
Laws of King Ur-Nammu (of Ur), xxiii,
    xxv, 3t
Laws of the kingdom of Eshnunna
    biblical law and, 4, 6, 7, 335
    in chronology, xxiii, 3t
    narrative reading of the, 13
Lawson, Mike, 451, 458
Lazarus, 434
Leah, 14
Legal Aid Board, 140
legal pluralism, xxx
legal positivism, xxviii, 68
Legal Text of Mose, 209
Lemech, 280, 281
Levitical massacre, 54

Leviticus
  chiastic structure of Levitcus 20, 358, 358t, 359t, 360t
  on debt slaves, 231–32
  Decalogue pattern in, 349–55, 349f, 353t
  sexual offences in, 348–49, 356–58, 357t, 361–64, 362t, 364–67, 365t
  on social welfare, 250
Lewis (1988), 298
lex talionis See vengeance
love, 29
Low Income Countries (LICs), 250
Luke (Gospel), trial before Herod in, 430
Luther, Martin, 404

M
Mabo ruling, 186
Maccabeean uprising, xxiv
Macmillan, Harold, 221
Macpherson, C.B., 203–204
Maimonides, xxiv, 79
male vs. female, 161–62
Malul, Meir, 42
manna, 237–38
Mari (city), 4, 47
Mari 372, 47
Mark (Gospel)
  Jesus vs. Peter in, 429–30
  on marriage, divorce, adultery and remarriage, 405–8
marriage
  betrothal period, 368–71, 370t, 373–74
  consent of the father for, 330, 332–33, 334–35, 335–36, 351, 369
  development of marriage in biblical law, 326–27
  endogamy vs. exogamy, 323–24
  extended family and, 240
  financial support of wives and daughters, 322
  forms of Israelite, 321–22, 324–25, 329–30
  heterosexual norm, 319–20, 342, 344, 362–63
  later development vs. biblical times, 326–27
  marriageable age, 369, 371
  modern vs. biblical, 340–44
  monogamy norm, 319–20
  New Testament on, 364
  overview, 317, 345
  paternity and, 371–73
  polygamy, 320, 342, 366, 384, 397–98, 410
  procreation and, 320–21
  regulated by custom, 319
  remarriage, 338–40
  by sexual intercourse/rape, 325, 327–29, 330–36
  virginity and, 368–71, 394–95
  See also family; Jesus on marriage, divorce, adultery and remarriage; Qumran community and laws
Martin, R v. (2001), 303
Marxism, 250–51
Marx, Karl, xxxvii
Masoretic Text, xix, 174
Matthew (Gospel)
  Jesus and the story of Israel, 429
  on marriage, divorce, adultery and remarriage, 411–16
McKellen, Sir Ian, 348
Menasseh, 191
mercy, 52, 64, 88, 244, 451, 468
Mesopotamia, 203, 229
Micaiah, as "prophet like Moses," 432
Middle Assyrian Laws, xxiii, 3t, 278, 335
Milgrom, Jacob, 206
Millennium Ecosystem Assessment, 146
Miqsat Ma'ase Ha-Torah, 395
miscarriage of justice, 431–32, 456–62
Mishnah, xxiv, 326, 336
Mishnah Kiddushin, 326–27
Mishpatim
  defined, xix
Moab, covenant at
  exile and restoration, 459–60
  framework of the, 46
  nature of the, 32
  Sinai covenant and the, 44–45
modern law *See* law, modern
monarchs *See* Kings
Morocco, 270
Morris (1984), 286
Morris, William, 250
mortality rates, 320
Mose, 209

GENERAL INDEX 537

Moses
  birth/death years, xxiii
  exile of, 269
  giving of the law and, 20
  God's command to Pharaoh, 26
  idolatry and, 433
  inheritance and, 196
  jubilee laws and, 212
  judicial appointees, 89, 107, 119, 124, 125
  judicial reforms, 89
  on justice, 113
  on King Og, 262
  as mediator/adjudicator, 9, 48–50, 55, 55–56, 120–24, 121*f*, 122*f*, 128, 133, 393–94
  Sabbath observation and, 221–22, 228
  on Sinaitic laws, 83
  teaching of biblical law, 18
  teachings in Deuteronomy, 23
  Ten Commandments and, 31, 53, 54
  See also Mount Sinai covenant; Ten Commandments
Mount Ebal, curse at, 173
Mount Gerizim, blessing at, 173
Mount Sinai covenant
  covenant with Abraham and the, 37, 43–44, 82
  divine and human judgment, 89–90
  exile and restoration, 459–60
  forms of revelation and the, 81–84
  golden calf incident, 54–55
  mediation and the, 48–50
  Moab covenant and the, 44–45
  nature of the, 32
  overview, 45–47
  promise to Abraham and the, 82
  role of theophany, 47–48
  vs. ANE covenants, 33
  vs. the new covenant, 57–61, 62–64, 63–64
  See also Moses; Ten Commandments
murder, procreation and, 167–68
Myers, Carol, 320

N
Nablus, 173
Naboth, 110, 118, 119, 188–89
naming in the Bible, 160–62
Naomi, 239

narrative stereotype, 13, 195, 222–223, 240
narrative typification, 154, 157, 172, 223, 239, 263, 349, 352, 363, 454
Nathan, 135, 267, 308–16
natural law
  biblical law and, 68–69
  continuity between different forms of revelation, 81–84
  continuity between divine and human acts of judgment, 84–92
  continuity between the divine and creation, 69–73
  continuity between the world and human behavior, 73–76
  defined, 67
  diversity and tension within, 92–95
  ethics and calling, 97–100
  Gentile Christians and, 95–97
  moral judgments and, 67–68
  overview, 100
  sense of obligation, 67–68
  universal knowledge of certain norms, 76–81
  vs. legal positivism, 68
Nebuchadnezzar II of Babylon, xxiii, xxiv
necrophilia, 21
Neshi, 209
Netherlands, 384
New Testament
  covenant formula in, 40
  divine character of human judgment in the, 90
  divine judgment in the, 161
  Hebrew Bible covenant vs. NT covenant, 35
  judgment in the, 462
  on marriage, 364
  new covenant, 61–64
  social welfare in the, 242–47
  Torah and the, 84
  universal norms in the, 98–99
  See also Jesus
Noah, 35, 44, 54, 85, 170
Noahide laws, 79, 95, 96, 97–98
Noth, Martin, 48
Novak, David, 78, 83
Numbers
  homicide in, 260–263, 260*t*, 261*t*, 265, 270
  inheritance in, 192–95

O

oceans, destructive practices regarding the, 147
Og (King), 262
outcasts, care for, 91
Owino (1996), 302

P

paradigm case,
  examples of, 97, 126–128, 233, 256, 259–262, 266, 308, 314, 334, 347, 352, 354, 356, 362, 401
Passion narratives *See* Gospels
Passover, 61–62
Passover privilege, 449t, 450–51
paternity, 371–73
Patriarchs, Period of, xxiii
Paul, 63–64, 98, 424
Pentateuch, xxxi
  narrative context of the, 14
  stopover at Sinai in the, 45
  vocation of Israel in the, 16–18
Peter, 95, 429
Pharaoh
  Abrahamic promise and, 43
  life under, 221–22, 222–24, 237
  God and, 15, 26, 53
  Joseph and, 210–11, 212
  land tenure practices, 207–9
  Moses and, 269
  plagues and, 104
  power of, 104
  pursuit of the Israelites, 107
  totalitarian rule of, 106
'Pharaonic economics,' 207–209, 215, 222, 224, 233–234, 237
Pharisees, 27, 401, 405–6, 410, 414–15, 418, 419, 420, 422, 424, 430, 434, 439
Pilate, Pontius, 439, 447–54, 457, 459
Plato, xxxvii
Pollock, Sir Frederick, xxvi
polygamy, 320, 342, 366, 384, 397–98, 410
poverty/poor persons
  adjudication and, 106n7
  debt slaves, 229, 231–32, 305
  generational poverty trap, 251
  gleaning law, 236–40
  land ownership and, 202, 207–9, 219–21
  low income countries, 250
  rich persons and, 134–35, 310–11, 312, 315–16
  sabbatical year, 198
procreation, murder and, 167–68
promised land, 23, 44, 107, 108, 119, 129, 133
  character of, 181–82
  cities of refuge, 268
  Israelites and the, 182–85
  mission to master the, 156–57
  narrative and, 185–90
property law *See* land and people
prostitutes, 332, 373
The Protests of the Eloquent Peasant, 315
Proverbs, wisdom and, 19, 25
  domestic context of, xxxiii, 19, 87
provincial courts, 108–110
punishment, 143
  in Biblical Israel, 118–19
Puritans, xxvi

Q

Qumran community and laws
  Dead Sea Scrolls and, 390–91
  divorce in, 397, 400
  marriage restrictions, 395–96, 400–402
  monarchical marriage provisions, 399–400
  monogamy norm in, 397–98
  Moses and, 393–94
  overview, 391–93, 403–4
  remarriage in, 397, 400
  sexual offences in, 402–3
  virginity, 394–95
  war captive brides, 393

R

Rachel, 14, 305
rain forests, 147, 173
rape, 73, 311, 325, 327–29, 330–36
Rashi (Solomon ben Isaac), xxiv, 174
Rawls, John, 248, 249
Rebekah, 239, 323
Reis, Pamela, 273
remarriage, 338–40, 404–5
  See also Jesus on marriage, divorce, adultery and remarriage; Qumran community and laws
Rendtorff, Rolf, 17, 36

'restonomics,' 197–198
retail crime, 285, 287, 306–7
retaliation *See* vengeance
Reuben, 191, 195
revelation, different forms of, 81–84
revenge *See* vengeance
Riggs v Palmer (1889), 129
righteousness, 27, 64, 79, 85, 87–88, 106, 114, 117, 138
Roman Catholic church, 404
Rose, Nikolas, 220
Rousseau, Jean-Jacques, 93t
Rowling, J.K., 248
rule of law, 11, 129
Ruth (book), 238–39
Ruth (person), 238, 239, 242
Rwanda, 141

S

Sabbath obligation/laws, 71–72, 151, 152
  animals and, 172
  God vs. Pharaoh, 222–24
  in Isaiah, 245–47
  jubilee years, 197
  in the New Testament, 243–45, 246–47
  'sabbath-plus,' 198–201
  'sabbath-squared,' 201, 241
  sabbatical year, 197, 198–201, 212, 216–17, 222–28, 243
  social welfare promoted by, 220–22
  'perpetual Sabbath,' 243
  weekly Sabbath, 197–98, 211, 212
Samaria, Fall of, xxiii
same-sex behavior *See* homosexual behavior
Samson, 327
Samuel, 294
Sanhedrin, 434, 438, 440, 441, 447, 449, 452, 453, 457
  See also trials of Jesus
Sargon II, 390
Saul (King), 131, 134, 321
  reign of, xxiii
Sax, Joseph L., 214
Scalia, Antonin, xxvi
Shechem (person), 324, 330–33
Second Temple period, 389–90, 424–25
  See also Jesus on marriage, divorce, adultery and remarriage; Qumran community and laws

self-executing rule, defined, xix, 26
  examples of, 26, 181, 291, 292, 306
semiotics, defined, xix
  examples of semiotic approach, 56, 57, 237, 262, 279
Sermon on the Mount, 111, 273, 411–12
the serpent, 163
Sex Offences Review Group, 376, 378
sexual intercourse
  marriage by, 325, 327–29
  metaphor for, 327
sexual offences
  biblical categories for, 349–55
  biblical law vs. modern law, 375–76, 377–78, 379, 381–82, 382–83, 384–85, 385–86
  consent and, 374–75, 375–76, 380–82
  death penalty for, 348, 353, 356, 357t, 364–65, 366, 370, 370t
  family and, 352–55, 357t, 358–60, 362–64, 362t, 381
  generational consequences, 352
  identity of sexual partners, 362–64, 362t
  Leviticus on well-ordered sexual relationships, 348–49
  in the New Testament, 364
  overview, 347–48, 366–67, 386–87
  punishment, 356–58, 358, 359, 359t, 364–67, 365t
  Qumran laws, 402–03
  society and, 358–60
  vs. normal sexual relations, 361–64, 362t
  See also Jesus on marriage, divorce, adultery and remarriage; Sexual Offences Act 2003; sexual relations
Sexual Offences Act 1956, 376
Sexual Offences Act 2003, 21, 374
  consent and, 380
  equality and the, 382–83
  family and, 378
  promoting the public good, 376–78, 385
  protection in the, 383–84
sexual relations
  forbidden, 97
  heterosexual monogamy, 78, 469
  illicit, 78
  prohibited, 21
  See also homosexual behavior; sexual offences

Shalmaneser V, 390
Shechem (place), 173
Shema, 26
shoplifting *See* retail crime
Sinai covenant *See* Mount Sinai covenant
Sinaitic laws, 81, 83
Singer, Peter, 385
slavery/slaves
   in the ANE, 7–8
   compensation for loss of a tooth or eye, 276–77
   in Exodus, 15
   jubilee year, 228–32
   sex with female slaves, 334
social justice, 240–42
social status, of victims, 21, 21t
social welfare
   biblical law and modern social welfare, 247–51
   gleanings law, 236–40
   God vs. Pharaoh, 222–24, 227–28, 233–34
   jubilee year, 228–32
   modern, 241–42
   national solidarity, 224–26
   overview, 219, 252
   in the prophetic literature and the New Testament, 242–47
   Sabbath laws and, 220–22, 235–36
   sabbatical year, 222–28, 243
   Sukkot celebrations, 234–35
   tithe laws, 234–35
   uses of capital, 226–28
   vs. social justice, 240–42
   vulnerable persons, 219–20
Sodom and Gomorrah, 73–74, 81, 87–89
Solomon (King), 87, 90–91, 132, 136, 267
   Joab story and, 267
   reign of, xxiii
Solomon ben Isaac (Rashi), xxiv
Solomon's Temple, 46
'Son of Man,' 442–443, 446, 459
South Korea, 217
speech
   Hebrew word for, 51
   powers of, 160
speech acts
   covenant with Isaac, 42

   defined, xix, 42n40
   humanity's, 160, 161–62
speech, divine
   Abraham and, 87–88
   chosen people and chosen species, 153
   the Genesis mandate, 155–56
   humanity and the environment, 145, 152, 157, 159
   judgment and, 166
   metamessages, 152
   Moses and, 50
   postdiluvian, 167, 168, 171
   universal creation, 152, 162, 171
spiritual jurisprudence, defined, xxix
Spohn, William, 81, 127
Stahl, Nanette, 167
Statute of Gloucester (1278), 264
Steinmetz, Devora, 85
Stephen, 440–41
Stern Review, 149, 150
stoning, as punishment, 350, 357t, 364, 365, 366, 394–395, 436, 441
succession narrative, defined, xix
Sukkot celebrations, 234–35
sustainable development, 147, 148

T
Tabernacle, 168, 268
Talmud, Babylonian, xxiv
Talmud, Jerusalem, xxiv
Tamar, 327–29, 373
Tekoa, woman of, 128, 309
the Temple, xxiii, xxiv, 437–38, 442, 445t, 446
Temple Scroll, 393, 394, 402
Ten Commandments
   adjudicatory process and God's words, 121
   constitutive of Israel's identity, 52
   covenant and the, 31, 32
   English law and the, xxvi
   the Exodus and the, 82
   finger of God and the, 53
   in Hosea, 75
   overview, 50–52
   pubic display of the, xxvi–xxvii, xxviiin12
   Sabbath obligation, 71–72

vision of the good for humanity and the world, 468
See also Mount Sinai covenant
Theft Act 1968, 286, 299
theft and burglary
  Ancient Near Eastern law, 297, 299
  God and, 295
  modern law, 285, 286–88, 298–99, 302–03
  negotiated penalties, 305–06
  at night, 299–303
  objective hot/lukewarm tests for theft, 290–98
  overview, 285, 316
  parable of Nathan, 308–16
  theft of animals, 290–92, 296, 299, 303–05
  theft of persons, 288–90
thematic repetition, defined, xix
  examples of, 43, 50, 62, 168, 172, 212, 269n 30, 275
theology
  ANE law and, 5–6
  biblical law and, xiii, xv, xxviii, xxxiv, 5, 465–66, 477
  of covenantal economics, 189
  environment and, 150
  Jewish vs. Christian, 35
  miscarriage of justice and, 427
  'Third Way,' the, 247–251
Thomas of Gresford, Lord, 380
Thummim, 133
tithe laws, 234–35
Torah
  defined, xiii
  environmental laws in, 171–76
  the Exodus and, 16
  horizon of the, xxx–xxxii
  human need for wisdom, 194–195
  internalization of, 113
  Moses and the Ten Commandments, 51
  Moses as mediator of, 9
  natural law and, 70–73
  new covenant and, 57–61, 63
  practical application of, 9
  reasons for obeying, 10
  translated to Greek, xxiv
Tractate Yevamot, 401

treaties, covenants and, 45–46
trees and war, 173–76
trials of Jesus
  charges against Jesus, 431–38, 441–47, 445t, 453–55
  Jewish authorities and Jesus, 430–31, 438–39
  Jewish proceedings, 439–41, 439t
  miscarriage of justice, 457–62
  mockery in the, 446, 446t, 455, 455tt
  nature of the Gospel records regarding the, 427–30, 447–48
  overview, 427, 463
  Roman proceedings, 447, 448–52, 449t, 454t
tribes, 317–18
Tyndale, William, 404

U
UK Children's Trust Fund, 251
UK Royal Commission on Criminal Justice, 458
United Kingdom, 142
  endowment for children at birth, 251
  financial crisis of 2007–09, 226–27
  marriage in, 341
  moral panics and extreme measures in the, 456
  national footprint, 148
  satanic abuse scares in, 457
  supermarket products in the, 148
  theft law, 307
  war metaphor regarding the environment, 150
  welfare system, 241
  See also England; Wales
United States, 142, 226, 384–85
  moral panics and extreme measures in the, 456
United States law
  biblical law and, xxix
  theft, 307
Uriah, 308, 309, 311–14
Urim, 133

V
Van Wolde, Ellen, 273
Varzy Papyrus, 296

vassal treaties, 32
vengeance, 275–82
Vermes, Geza, 397
victims, 142–43
　social status of, 21, 21t
virginity, 368–71, 394–95
vocation,
　of humanity, xl, 85, 140, 144, 145–148,
　　152–153, 155, 157–159, 162, 165,
　　167, 169, 171, 467, 476–477
　of Israel, 2, 16–18, 28, 30, 43, 52, 64, 82,
　　103, 108, 114, 185, 212, 218, 225,
　　247, 347, 384, 412, 422, 432, 442,
　　446, 460, 461, 463, 472, 475,
　　476–477
　of lawyers, xl, 477
　of marriage, 364, 421, 423–424

W
Wales, 140, 143, 213
　marriage in, 341
　shoplifting in, 306–07
　See also Sexual Offences Act 2003;
　　United Kingdom
war and trees, 173–76
'war captive woman,' 372, 392–393
war crimes, 79–81
Warner v. Metropolitan Police
　Commissioner (1968), 298
Weinfeld, Moshe, 113
welfare See social welfare
Wenham, Gordon J., 414
Westbrook, Raymond, 5, 281
Western culture, biblical law and, xxxv
Western legal philosophy, xxxvi–xxxviii
Wilbour Papyrus, 208–09

William of Ockham, 93–94
Wirzba, Norman, 153
wisdom
　and adjudication, 129
　competing interpretations of biblical
　　law and, 227
　for dispute resolution, 111
　divine adjudication and, 138, 139
　legal cases and, 128
　practical wisdom, 111, 115t
　pre-requisite of, 28–29
　promoted by Torah, 19–20
　Proverbs and, 19
　role of, 21
　Solomon and, 91
　triumph of Wisdom, 73
　Torah and, xxxii, 70
　Torah, an expression of, 21, 24–26
witnesses, 118
women
　economic independence and, 375
　financial support of, 322
　See also adultery; marriage
Woolf, Lord, xxxix, 143
Wright, David, 6
Wright, N.T., 428

Y
Yarim-Addu, 47

Z
Zabdai, Simon bar, 61
Zelophehad (daughters of), 23–24, 183,
　192–93, 194, 195
Zimri-Lim, 47
Zohar, 205

Lightning Source UK Ltd.
Milton Keynes UK
UKOW01n1827220317
297260UK00002B/7/P